HUMAN DEVELOPMENT 90/91

Eighteenth Edition

Editor

Larry Fenson
San Diego State University

Larry Fenson is a professor of psychology at San Diego State University. He received his Ph.D. in Child Psychology from the Institute of Child Behavior and Development at the University of Iowa in 1968. Dr. Fenson is a member of the MacArthur Foundation Research Network on Infancy and Early Childhood. His research focuses on early conceptual development, and he has authored articles on infant attention, symbolic play, concept development, and language acquisition.

Editor

Judith Fenson

Judith Fenson received a B.A. from Ohio University in 1963 and an M.A. from the University of New Mexico in 1965. She has contributed to a variety of research projects in medicine, psychology, and linguistics, and has authored various materials and study aids for students in psychology and child development.

Cover illustration by Mike Eagle

A Library of Information from the Public Press

The Dushkin Publishing Group, Inc.
Sluice Dock, Guilford, Connecticut 06437

The Annual Editions Series

Annual Editions is a series of over fifty volumes designed to provide the reader with convenient, low-cost access to a wide range of current, carefully selected articles from some of the most important magazines, newspapers, and journals published today. Annual Editions are updated on an annual basis through a continuous monitoring of over 200 periodical sources. All Annual Editions have a number of features designed to make them particularly useful, including topic guides, annotated tables of contents, unit overviews, and indexes. For the teacher using Annual Editions in the classroom, an Instructor's Resource Guide with test questions is available for each volume.

VOLUMES AVAILABLE

Africa
Aging
American Government
American History, Pre-Civil War
American History, Post-Civil War
Anthropology
Biology
Business and Management
Business Ethics
Canadian Politics
China
Comparative Politics
Computers in Education
Computers in Business
Computers in Society
Criminal Justice
Drugs, Society, and Behavior
Early Childhood Education
Economics
Educating Exceptional Children
Education
Educational Psychology
Environment
Geography
Global Issues
Health
Human Development

Human Resources
Human Sexuality
Latin America
Macroeconomics
Marketing
Marriage and Family
Middle East and the Islamic World
Money and Banking
Nutrition
Personal Growth and Behavior
Psychology
Public Administration
Social Problems
Sociology
Soviet Union and Eastern Europe
State and Local Government
Third World
Urban Society
Violence and Terrorism
Western Civilization,
  Pre-Reformation
Western Civilization,
  Post-Reformation
Western Europe
World History, Pre-Modern
World History, Modern
World Politics

Library of Congress Cataloging in Publication Data
Main entry under title: Annual Editions: Human development. 1990/91.
    1. Child study—Addresses, essays, lectures. 2. Socialization—Addresses, essays, lectures.
3. Old age—Addresses, essays, lectures. I. Fenson, Larry, comp.; Fenson, Judith, comp. II. Title:
Human development.
ISBN 0-87967-847-X   155'.05   72-91973
HQ768.A55

Eighteenth Edition

Manufactured by The Banta Company, Harrisonburg, Virginia 22801

Editors/ Advisory Board

To the Reader

In publishing ANNUAL EDITIONS we recognize the enormous role played by the magazines, newspapers, and journals of the *public press* in providing current, first-rate educational information in a broad spectrum of interest areas. Within the articles, the best scientists, practitioners, researchers, and commentators draw issues into new perspective as accepted theories and viewpoints are called into account by new events, recent discoveries change old facts, and fresh debate breaks out over important controversies.

Many of the articles resulting from this enormous editorial effort are appropriate for students, researchers, and professionals seeking accurate, current material to help bridge the gap between principles and theories and the real world. These articles, however, become more useful for study when those of lasting value are carefully *collected, organized, indexed,* and *reproduced* in a *low-cost format*, which provides easy and permanent access when the material is needed. That is the role played by *Annual Editions*. Under the direction of each volume's *Editor*, who is an expert in the subject area, and with the guidance of an *Advisory Board*, we seek each year to provide in each *ANNUAL EDITION* a current, well-balanced, carefully selected collection of the best of the public press for your study and enjoyment. We think you'll find this volume useful, and we hope you'll take a moment to let us know what you think.

Any history of the field of human development will reflect the contributions of the many individuals who helped craft the topical content of the discipline. For example, Binet launched the intelligence test movement, Freud focused attention on personality development, and Watson and Thorndike paved the way for the emergence of social learning theory. However, the philosophical principles that give definition to the field of human development have their direct ancestral roots in the evolutionary biology of Darwin, Wallace, and Spencer, and in the embryology of Preyer. Each of the two most influential developmental psychologists of the early twentieth century, James Mark Baldwin and G. Stanley Hall, was markedly influenced by questions about phylogeny (species' adaptation) and ontogeny (individual adaptation or fittingness). Baldwin's persuasive arguments challenged the assertion that changes in species precede changes in individual organisms. Instead, Baldwin argued, ontogeny not only precedes phylogeny but is the process that shapes phylogeny. Thus, as Robert Cairns points out, developmental psychology has always been concerned with the study of the forces that guide and direct development. Early theories stressed that development was the unfolding of already formed or predetermined characteristics. Many contemporary students of human development embrace the epigenetic principle which asserts that development is an emergent process of active, dynamic, reciprocal, and systemic change. This systems perspective forces one to think about the historical, social, cultural, interpersonal, and intrapersonal forces that shape the developmental process.

The study of human development involves all fields of inquiry comprising the social, natural, and life sciences and professions. The need for depth and breadth of knowledge creates a paradox: While students are being advised to acquire a broad-based education, each discipline is becoming more highly specialized. One way to combat specialization is to integrate the theories and findings from a variety of disciplines with those of the parent discipline. This, in effect, is the approach of *Annual Editions: Human Development 90/91*. This anthology includes articles that discuss the problems, issues, theories, and research findings from many fields of study. In most instances, the articles were written specifically to communicate information about recent scientific findings or controversial issues to the general public. As a result, the articles tend to blend the history of a topic with the latest available information. In many instances, the reader is challenged to consider the personal and social implications of the topic. The articles included in this anthology were selected by the editors with valued advice and recommendations from an advisory board consisting of faculty from community colleges, small liberal arts colleges, and large universities. Evaluations obtained from students, instructors, and advisory board members influenced the decision to retain or replace specific articles. Throughout the year we screen many articles for accuracy, interest value, writing style, and recency of information. Readers can have input into the next edition by completing and returning the article rating form in the back of the book.

Human Development 90/91 is organized into six major units. Unit 1 focuses on the origins of life, including genetic influences on development, and unit 2 focuses on development during infancy and early childhood. Unit 3 is divided into subsections addressing social, emotional, and cognitive development. Unit 4 addresses issues related to family, school, and cultural influences on development. Units 5 and 6 cover human development from adolescence to old age. In our experience, this organization provides great flexibility for those using the anthology with any standard textbook. The units can be assigned sequentially, or instructors can devise any number of arrangements of individual articles to fit their specific needs. In large lecture classes this anthology seems to work best as assigned reading to supplement the basic text. In smaller sections, articles can stimulate instructor-student discussions. Regardless of the instructional style used, we hope that our excitement for the study and teaching of human development is evident and catching as you read the articles in this eighteenth edition of *Human Development*.

Larry Fenson

Larry Fenson

Judith Fenson

Judith Fenson
Editors

Contents

Unit 1

Perspectives

Seven selections discuss genetic influences on development, focusing on reproductive technology, genetic influences, and exceptionality.

The concepts in bold italics are developed in the article. For further expansion please refer to the Topic Guide and the Index.

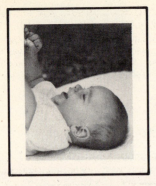

Unit 2

Development During Infancy and Early Childhood

Five selections discuss development of the brain and development of communication, emotions, and cognitive systems during the first years of life.

Unit 3

Development During Childhood

Eight selections examine human development during childhood, paying specific attention to social and emotional development and cognitive and language development.

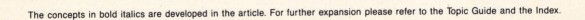

The concepts in bold italics are developed in the article. For further expansion please refer to the Topic Guide and the Index.

Unit 4

Family, School, and Cultural Influences on Development

Thirteen selections discuss the impact of home, school, and culture on child rearing and child development. The topics include parenting styles, family structure, stress, cultural influences, and education.

The concepts in bold italics are developed in the article. For further expansion please refer to the Topic Guide and the Index.

The concepts in bold italics are developed in the article. For further expansion please refer to the Topic Guide and the Index.

Unit 5

Development During Adolescence and Early Adulthood

Six selections examine some of the effects of social environment, sibling relationships, sex differences, and jealousy on human development during adolescence and early adulthood.

The concepts in bold italics are developed in the article. For further expansion please refer to the Topic Guide and the Index.

Unit 6

Development During Adulthood and Aging

Seven selections explore how family life-styles, loneliness, and depression relate to development during adulthood and consider how physical, cognitive, and social changes affect the aged.

The concepts in bold italics are developed in the article. For further expansion please refer to the Topic Guide and the Index.

Topic Guide

This topic guide suggests how the selections in this book relate to topics of traditional concern to human development students and professionals. It can be very useful in locating articles which relate to each other for reading and research. The guide is arranged alphabetically according to topic. Articles may, of course, treat topics that do not appear in the topic guide. In turn, entries in the topic guide do not necessarily constitute a comprehensive listing of all the contents of each selection.

TOPIC AREA	TREATED AS AN ISSUE IN:	TOPIC AREA	TREATED AS AN ISSUE IN:
Adolescence/ Adolescent Development	25. Alienation 35. Those Gangly Years 36. The Myth About Teen-Agers 37. Jealousy and Envy 39. Therapists Find Last Outpost	Creativity	6. Extraordinary People 7. Gifted by Nature 9. Where Pelicans Kiss Seals 18. Three Heads Are Better
Adulthood	27. Biology, Destiny, and All That 37. Jealousy and Envy 38. The Measure of Love 39. Therapists Find Last Outpost 43. The Prime of Our Lives	Day Care	10. "What Is Beautiful Is Good" 12. The Child-Care Dilemma
		Depression/ Despair	23. Children After Divorce
Aggression/ Violence	5. Men vs. Women 21. The Importance of Fathering 27. Biology, Destiny, and All That 30. Television and Behavior	Developmental Disabilities	1. Perfect People? 6. Extraordinary People 15. Resilient Children 20. Facts About Dyslexia 44. Aging
Aging	40. The Vintage Years 42. A Vital Long Life 44. Aging 46. The Myths of Menopause	Divorce	21. The Importance of Fathering 23. Children After Divorce 24. Children Under Stress
Alienation	25. Alienation 37. Jealousy and Envy	Education/ Educators	10. "What Is Beautiful Is Good" 17. Practical Piaget 18. Three Heads Are Better 19. How Kids Learn 20. Facts About Dyslexia 21. The Importance of Fathering 25. Alienation 28. Rumors of Inferiority 31. Master of Mastery 32. Moral Education 33. Why We Need to Understand Science
Attachment	15. Resilient Children 21. The Importance of Fathering 41. Family Ties		
Brain Organization/ Function	6. Extraordinary People 20. Facts About Dyslexia		
Cognitive Development	5. Men vs. Women 8. Ten Myths About Child Development 9. Where Pelicans Kiss Seals 11. Formal Education 17. Practical Piaget 18. Three Heads Are Better 19. How Kids Learn 20. Facts About Dyslexia 21. The Importance of Fathering 27. Biology, Destiny, and All That 28. Rumors of Inferiority 30. Television and Behavior 40. The Vintage Years	Emotional Development	7. Gifted by Nature 8. Ten Myths About Child Development 12. The Child-Care Dilemma 14. Building Confidence 20. Facts About Dyslexia 23. Children After Divorce 24. Children Under Stress 25. Alienation 27. Biology, Destiny, and All That 36. The Myth About Teen-Agers 37. Jealousy and Envy 38. The Measure of Love 39. Therapists Find Last Outpost 41. Family Ties
Competence	12. The Child-Care Dilemma 15. Resilient Children 26. The Child Yesterday		

TOPIC AREA	TREATED AS AN ISSUE IN:	TOPIC AREA	TREATED AS AN ISSUE IN:
Pregnancy	1. Perfect People? 2. The New Origins of Life	**Sex Differences/ Roles/Behavior/ Characteristics**	5. Men vs. Women 21. The Importance of Fathering 27. Biology, Destiny, and All That 35. Those Gangly Years
Prenatal Development	1. Perfect People?	**Social Skills/ Socialization**	21. The Importance of Fathering 28. Rumors of Inferiority 30. Television and Behavior 37. Jealousy and Envy 43. The Prime of Our Lives
Preschoolers	9. Where Pelicans Kiss Seals 11. Formal Education 12. The Child-Care Dilemma 23. Children After Divorce 26. The Child Yesterday		
Psychoanalytic	25. Alienation 26. The Child Yesterday	**Stress**	15. Resilient Children 23. Children After Divorce 24. Children Under Stress 25. Alienation
Puberty	35. Those Gangly Years 37. Jealousy and Envy		
Racism/Prejudice	10. "What Is Beautiful Is Good" 28. Rumors of Inferiority		
Self-Esteem/ Self-Control	14. Building Confidence 15. Resilient Children 27. Biology, Destiny, and All That 35. Those Gangly Years 37. Jealousy and Envy 41. Family Ties		

Perspectives

- Reproductive Technology (Articles 1-2)
- Genetic Influences (Articles 3-5)
- Exceptionality (Articles 6-7)

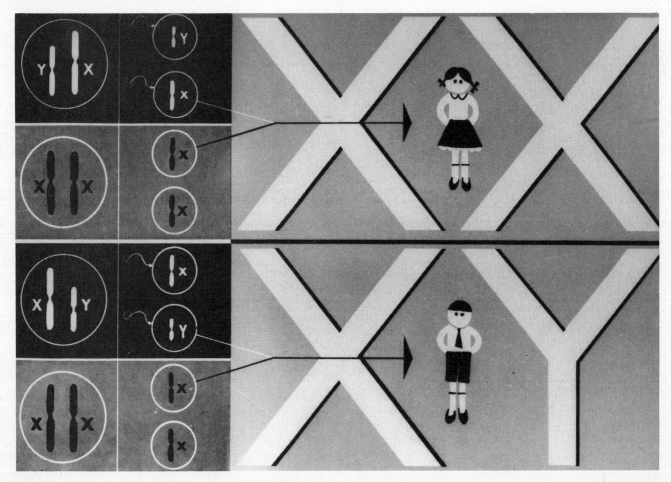

Advances in our knowledge of human development are increasingly becoming linked to progress in the fields of genetics, biochemistry, and medicine. Our two initial selections, reflecting this fact, deal with issues that are a product of medical and genetic advances. "Perfect People?" describes genetic screening and gene therapy—technology that would have seemed like science fiction to parents of the 1960s. For the prospective parent of the 1990s, however, reproductive technology is real, as are the related ethical, legal, and social issues that will not easily be resolved.

Some of these issues have been triggered by progress in "artificial" methods of achieving fertilization, as discussed in "The New Origins of Life." With this method, a sperm and ovum retain their dynamic characteristics; only the environment in which fertilization occurs or the technique for inserting the sperm into the womb changes. Opinions on this method range from viewing it as diabolic to seeing it as a "modern miracle."

Additional ethical problems have been generated by new ways of detecting anomalies prior to birth and by methods for sustaining life in highly premature infants. Thirty years ago, prematurity generally referred to infants born no more than two months prior to the expected date. Today infants born at less than seven months gestational age are brought to term with the assistance of biomedical technology. However, the quality of caregiving intervention received by prematurely born infants may not be equivalent to the quality of life-sustaining technology. But it is clear that, without modern technology, most premature infants weighing less than 1500 grams would die, regardless of the quality of caregiving they received.

The 1980s also witnessed a shift toward the nature end of the nature-nurture or heredity-environment continuum. The mounting evidence for the role of heredity on personality is reviewed in "How Genes Shape Personality." This swing toward hereditary influences has strengthened the case for sociobiology, a scientific frame of reference which posits that the behavior of human beings, and their body structure, are products of evolutionary factors. This article also explores some of the more radical and controversial ideas stemming from sociobiology; among them, the idea that sexism a product of centuries of male domination. Sexism and sex differences are explored in considerably more depth in "Men vs. Women," which concludes that, on many dimensions, women seem to have some advantages which begin at birth and continue throughout life. "The Gene Dream" describes a colossal new government-backed project which has as its target the mapping of the complete set of instructions for making a human being. This work promises to revolutionize the fields of medicine, biology, sociology, and psychology. Some scientists foresee the day when individuals can go to their doctors and obtain a computer readout of their complete genetic makeup, along with a diagnosis, prognosis, and suggested treatment.

Highly unusual patterns of development often offer unique insights into fundamental aspects of the growth process. The final component of the "Exceptionality" section contains two articles about two highly unusual types of exceptionality. The movie "Rain Man" has done much to publicize the "Savant Syndrome." This fascinating dysfunction is described in "Extraordinary People." All savants possess a remarkable memory, and their special abilities may vary from musical to artistic to remembering names and numbers. New technology for studying brain function may allow us to better understand this condition one day.

The final article, "Gifted by Nature," focuses on prodigies—individuals who possess phenomenal talent in fields such as mathematics and music at an extremely early age. Mozart, perhaps the most famous prodigy of all time, was composing symphonies at the age of eight. Studies of these gifted people have revealed that their success did not necessarily ensure them happiness.

Looking Ahead: Challenge Questions

Consider your current beliefs about abortion, genetic engineering, and socialized medicine. How do you think these views would be challenged if you learned that your baby-to-be was expected to be profoundly retarded?

If manipulation of genetic material can prevent the appearance of physical dysfunctions, might not similar manipulations be used to engineer intellectual abilities, personality traits, or socially desirable behaviors? What factors would constrain a society that attempted to actively and explicitly practice eugenics?

How does the study of exceptional individuals offer unusually high potential for revealing basic growth mechanisms? Are sufficient resources being devoted to this topic? Should the study of the gifted or the retarded be given higher priority? Why?

THE PROMISE AND THE PERIL OF GENETIC TESTING

PERFECT PEOPLE ?

Amy Virshup

SUSAN AND TOM MURPHY* HAVE GLIMPSED THE future. In the spring of 1984, when Susan was four months pregnant with their second child, they learned that their firstborn, sixteen-month-old Sarah*, had cystic fibrosis, an inherited, incurable disease that can mean a short, difficult life for its victims. Sarah would likely need constant medication and daily sessions of strenuous physical therapy. To make matters worse, no one could say whether the child Susan was carrying also had the disease.

Their doctor advised the Murphys to consider having an abortion. But they decided to have the baby, and after five tense months, their son was born—without the disease. Though both Tom and Susan wanted a large family, neither was willing to risk conceiving another child who might get CF.

Within two years, the Murphys changed their minds. By then, researchers abroad had found a way to home in on the gene that causes CF, and a prenatal test had become available in the United States for families who already had a child with the disease. A door had been opened for the Murphys, and they decided they could chance another pregnancy. Tom, Susan, and Sarah had preliminary analyses of their DNA—the body's basic genetic material—and Susan became pregnant in September 1986.

Just nine weeks into her pregnancy, she had chorionic villus sampling (CVS), a recently developed twenty-minute procedure similar to amniocentesis. The CVS material was sent to the lab, and the Murphys could only wait—and worry—for ten days. They'd never decided just what they would do if the news was bad, but abortion was a real option. The day before Thanksgiving, they got the news: Their unborn child did not have CF.

SUDDENLY, WITHOUT MUCH TIME TO PONDER THE MORAL and ethical implications, Americans are being thrust into the age of the tentative pregnancy. For many, the decision to have a child is made not at conception but when the lab sends back the test results. "The difference between having a baby twenty years ago and having a baby today," says ethics specialist Dr. John Fletcher of the National Institutes of Health, "is that twenty years ago, people were brought up to accept what random fate sent them. And if you were religious, you were trained to accept your child as a gift of God and make sacrifices. That's all changing."

Over the last decade, genetics has been revolutionized: Using remarkable new DNA technology, molecular biologists can now diagnose in the womb inherited diseases like CF, hemophilia, Huntington's chorea, and Duchenne muscular dystrophy. Genetics is advancing at unprecedented speed, and important breakthroughs are announced almost monthly.

Since each person's DNA is distinct, the potential uses of genetic testing seem limitless: It could settle paternity suits, take the place of dental records or fingerprints in forensic medicine, identify missing children, warn about a predisposition to diseases caused by workplace health hazards. By the mid-1990s, geneticists should be able to screen the general population for harmful genes and test—at birth—a person's likelihood of developing certain types of cancer, high blood pressure, and heart disease.

Besides the prenatal tests now commonly in use, doctors may have a blood test that screens fetal cells in a mother's bloodstream and determines the fetus's sex and whether it has any chromosomal disorders or inherited genetic diseases. Work toward the ultimate goal—gene therapy—has already begun.

But this technological wizardry has some vehement opponents. A French government committee made up of doctors and lawyers recently called for a three-year moratorium on prenatal genetic tests because of the fear that they would lead to "ethically reprehensible attempts to standardize human reproduction for reasons of health and convenience." This is similar to the objection that anti-abortionists have always raised and now extend to genetic testing. (The Vatican, in its recent "instruction" on birth technology, condemned any prenatal test that might lead to abortion.) These days, though, right-to-lifers are finding themselves with some odd allies—feminists, ethics specialists, and advocates for the handicapped who are unsettled by the implications of the new genetics. The tests, they argue, will winnow out fetuses so that only "acceptable products" will be born, thus devaluing the lives of the handicapped.

* Names marked with an asterisk have been changed.

From *New York*, July 27, 1987, pp. 26-34. Copyright © 1987 by News America Publishing, Inc.

WITHOUT MUCH DISCUSSION, AMERICANS ARE BEING THRUST INTO THE AGE OF THE TENTATIVE PREGNANCY.

Other critics fear that services for the handicapped will be cut back and that people will be saddled with new responsibilities rather than new opportunities—after all, never before have parents had such an ability to choose whether to accept a child with an inherited condition. In addition, they claim that the sophisticated tests will give employers and insurers the ability to discriminate on genetic grounds. (A 1982 study found that eighteen major American companies—Dow Chemical and du Pont among them—had done some sort of genetic testing.)

Strong as the opposition is, it's not likely that the genetic revolution will be stopped: Few people, given the chance to avoid the emotional, physical, and economic burdens of raising a handicapped child, are likely to refuse it. The widespread use of prenatal tests parallels the advance of feminism. As more and more women made careers, the tests took on added importance—especially since many working women are putting off childbirth until their mid-thirties, when chromosomal abnormalities are more common.

"I didn't feel I had a choice," says advertising executive Judith Liebman, who became pregnant for the second time at 40. "It wasn't 'Is CVS sophisticated enough that I want to take the risk?' The choice was 'Look, they're doing this test, they're recommending I take it because of my age, so I have to go with the medical profession and say that it's okay to take it.' "

As sociologist Barbara Katz Rothman writes in *The Tentative Pregnancy*, her study of genetic testing, "In gaining the choice to control the quality of our children, we may rapidly lose the choice not to control the quality, the choice of simply accepting them as they are."

"The Luddites had a point," says Rothman. "Not all technology is good technology, and not everything needs to be done faster and better."

Mount Sinai geneticist Fred Gilbert is tracking the CF gene. Like Gilbert, his lab is casual, low-key; the most spectacular thing about it is its slightly begrimed view. Notes are taped to shelves, a stack of papers and manila folders sits atop a file cabinet, and several odd-looking blue plastic boxes lined with paper towels are arrayed on the counter (they are used to separate pieces of DNA). Flipping through a looseleaf binder of test results, Gilbert, a burly man with a dark, full beard, talks about his patients like an old-fashioned family doctor—this father drinks, that mother is overburdened, another family's religious views have made it impossible for them to abort—but he knows most of them only from the reports of their genetic counselors and from their DNA, which is shipped to him from cities all over the country.

Two years ago, Gilbert began offering a biochemical enzyme test developed in Europe for cystic fibrosis; then, when DNA probes became available, in January 1986, he started running DNA diagnoses

THE DNA TEST

Scientists rarely know the location of a harmful gene among the 50,000 to 100,000 in human DNA, so they look instead for a genetic marker—a seemingly harmless variation in DNA that is inherited along with a disease gene. DNA looks like a twisted rope ladder, and its "rungs" are pairs of nucleic acids, which always join in the same way. In order to find a marker, a scientist must first extract DNA from an individual's cells. Then the DNA ladder is broken into two separate strands and cut into fragments by enzymes that are able to "read" the order of the nucleic acids.

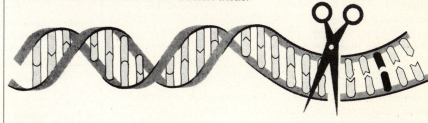

The cut-up DNA is separated and then exposed to a gene probe—a cloned piece of DNA that includes the variation being looked for. The probe is tagged with radioactivity.

If the probe bonds to a piece of DNA, then the genetic marker—and therefore a disease gene—is present.

Illustration by Anders Wenngren.

as well (both tests are about 95 percent accurate and are used to back each other up). Now Gilbert and his team extract DNA from the cells of families at risk for CF—his patients include a tenant farmer, an executive of a large firm, and several welfare families—expose it to gene probes that have been tagged with radioactivity, and then study photographs of the DNA, looking for the pattern that means the disease is present. Since CF is inherited recessively, there is a one-in-four chance in each pregnancy that the child might have the disease (AE p. 9).

This test can be used only by families who already have a child with the disease, but many people are betting on a CF screening test for the general population. After all, CF is the most common inherited disease in whites, striking about one child in 2,000. And now that scientists have moved in on the gene—in April, a British research team announced that it had found a marker that is even closer to it and may turn out to be the gene itself—development may be imminent. Since the test will be highly lucrative for its developer, there's a great incentive to come up with one; by one estimate, half the genetics labs in the country are looking for the CF gene. Gilbert, however, is not making money. Since the test he is using is still experimental, he is offering it at a minimal fee; for those who cannot afford it, the test is done free.

Even so, response to the test has been slow. The eight labs in the country offering DNA diagnosis have done about 400 tests, and Gilbert has completed just fifteen prenatal diagnoses using DNA. One problem is that some cystic-fibrosis specialists have been slow to tell their patients about the test. (The Murphys, for example, didn't learn about the test from their doctor; *they* had to tell *him* it was available.) The Cystic Fibrosis Foundation has also stayed away from the test, afraid of the association with abortion, and Gilbert gets no funds from it.

IN EVERY HUMAN CELL, THERE ARE 23 PAIRS OF CHROMO-somes that contain the 50,000 to 100,000 bits of genetic information called genes. The genes are made up of DNA (six feet of it in each cell), a long, two-stranded molecule. DNA, which looks like a tightly coiled rope ladder, is a compound made up of phosphate, sugar, and four nucleic acids: adenine (A), thymine (T), guanine (G), and cytosine (C). Each "rung" of the ladder (and there are 3 billion rungs in each person's DNA) is made up of a pair of nucleic acids, and they always join in the same way: Adenine connects only to thymine, guanine to cytosine. Only in the last few years have scientists been able to read the order of these nucleic acids.

Sequences of these four nucleic acids form genes. Genes, in turn, determine a person's physical characteristics, though no one knows the process that, for example, leads the genes for shape and form to generate the five fingers of the hand. A genetic disease often results from a "typo" in the order of the nucleic acids; like a misspelling in language, a typo in DNA can change the message of a gene. For example, the normal DNA code for glutamic acid is GAG, but in a person suffering from sickle-cell anemia, thymine replaces adenine (so the code reads GTG) and the blood is unable to absorb oxygen correctly. Surprisingly, though, only 10 percent of the base pairs actually form genes. The other 90 percent—mostly repetitive sequences—apparently have no meaning, and typos in that part of DNA seem to have no effect on health.

In the early seventies, researchers found a way to break the DNA ladder into two separate strands. When they exposed these strands of DNA to certain enzymes (substances that break up, or "cut," nucleic acids), they found that the enzymes could "read" DNA and make a cut at a specific sequence of bases. If just one base was changed—if, for example, adenine was substituted for thymine in the sequence GCAT, making it GCAA—the enzymes didn't cut. By looking at the size and number of DNA fragments created by a particular enzyme, researchers could tell when a typo existed.

Looking for the typo that causes a genetic disease like CF is like trying to find a person somewhere in the United States without knowing his name, the town he lives in, or even what part of the country he's in. But there are clues. For one thing, harmless variations in DNA are passed along with ones that cause diseases. Using enzymes, researchers were able to study the DNA from a family with a genetic disease and try to find typos (which they call RFLPs—restriction fragment-length polymorphisms) that traveled with the harmful gene. The RFLPs, then, are genetic flags or markers that let molecular biologists know that a disease gene is present.

Harvard's Dr. James Gusella was the first to have success: Studying a large family with Huntington's (a fatal disease that damages the central nervous system of its victims, usually when they reach mid-life), he cut family members' DNA and then exposed it to a dozen radioactively tagged genetic probes—each a cloned piece of DNA. One, called G8, was able to track the Huntington's gene in affected family members.

That connection showed up again when Gusella looked at other Huntington's families; he'd found a genetic marker for the disease. And, since G8 had been located on chromosome 4 (except for the X and Y sex chromosomes, pairs are numbered from 1 to 22), Gusella reasoned that the Huntington's gene was there as well. A genetic marker is only the first step, and Gusella

THE NEXT STAGE: GENE THERAPY

Prenatal diagnosis using DNA is still in its early stages, but scientists are already working on the ultimate genetic goal—gene therapy, which could render unnecessary the use of abortion after an inherited disease is diagnosed in the womb. Genetically engineered cures seem the stuff of science fiction; they conjure up Aldous Huxley's *Brave New World*, with its Betas, Gammas, and Alphas, all programmed to fit society's requirements. Though the advent of gene therapy is, as Dr. Richard Mulivor of the Coriell Institute puts it, "way down the line somewhere past Buck Rogers's time," it's likely to happen; a handful of researchers are already laying the groundwork for it. Ultimately, genetic cures would mean "correcting all the sperm and eggs as well, so you could never pass it on," says Mount Sinai's Dr. Robert Desnick. "I think that's a long, long way off. What geneticists are interested in doing today is providing therapy using DNA technology for those suffering from these diseases."

Potential gene therapists must do three things: put the new gene into the target cells, get the transplanted gene to replace the function of the harmful one, and show that the new gene doesn't harm the patient. Researchers are concentrating on diseases of the immune system—for example, adenosine deaminase deficiency (ADA, or "boy-in-the-bubble syndrome," whose victims are born without immune defenses)—because they involve white blood cells, which grow in bone marrow and are easily transplanted.

The most successful efforts have come from a team working under Dr. French Anderson of the National Institutes of Health. Collaborating with doctors at Memorial Sloan-Kettering, Anderson is removing bone marrow from monkeys, inserting the human gene for ADA into their bone-marrow cells, and then putting the cells back into the monkeys. Three weeks later, their blood is checked for traces of the human enzyme. So far, a Sloan-Kettering monkey known as Robert has been the star performer: His blood contained 0.5 percent of the human enzyme.

Gene cures won't be easy, though, and a different one will have to be developed for each inherited condition. Anderson's efforts are "good for a genetic disease of white cells," says Dr. Mulivor. "But the more dispersed the effect of the bad gene, meaning the number of tissues or organs involved, probably the less likelihood of gene therapy succeeding." —A.V.

is now trying to find the harmful gene itself. Other researchers are using similar technology to hunt the genes responsible for a host of inherited diseases.

Gusella's lab is just one of the thousands working on the frontiers of genetics. Molecular biology is one of the fastest-growing research specialties, as labs across the country join the search for harmful genes. The National Institutes of Health's yearly allocation for genetic research has increased by $73-million since 1984; in 1987, the NIH will spend an estimated $283 million.

Already, developments are flooding the scientific journals. Last October, Dr. Louis Kunkel of Boston Children's Hospital announced that he had discovered the gene responsible for Duchenne muscular dystrophy, a fatal disorder that strikes mostly boys, progressively destroying the muscles. Duchenne affects one in every 3,300 male children. A screening test for the general population is still several years away.

At Columbia University Medical School, Dr. Charles Cantor and Dr. Cassandra Smith are making the first attempt to map a human chromosome (No. 21); in mid-February, a group of researchers revealed that they had discovered a genetic marker for Alzheimer's disease; just a week later, researcher Janice Egeland announced that

CRITICS OF CVS FEAR THAT IT WILL ENCOURAGE MANY PARENTS TO SELECT THE SEX OF THEIR CHILD.

she'd found a genetic marker for manic depression among the Old Order Amish; a Swedish-American study of adoptees has linked alcoholism to heredity; and a blood test is in the works that will determine, at birth, a person's risk of developing atherosclerosis, a result of research that found a defective gene was a major cause of the disease for more than 2.3 million Americans.

"We're at the same point now in regard to genetic diseases that we were 50 years ago with infectious diseases," says Dr. Gerard McGarrity, president of the Coriell Institute for Medical Research in Camden, New Jersey. "In those days you had to worry about tuberculosis, polio, diphtheria, and everything else. I'm sure then that the concept of having a society virtually free of infectious diseases was mind-boggling. It's not beyond the realm of possibility to start thinking about a day when there's not going to be any genetic disease."

'TWENTY YEARS AGO, WHEN A WOMAN GAVE BIRTH to an impaired child, people would say, 'Oh, what a heartbreak that she has to live with that situation.' But you'd look for reasons for it," says writer Deborah Batterman, 37, who had amniocentesis during her pregnancy last year. "You'd say, 'I have to examine my life and see why this happened and what I can do to make the best of the situation.' That's the martyrdom indoctrination. We don't have to do that now. We're not raised to be martyrs."

Amniocentesis was the first step away from martyrdom. Introduced in the late sixties, it was the solution to a very specific problem: Women over 40 have an extremely high likelihood (one in 50) of having a child with Down syndrome, a condition caused by an extra copy of chromosome 21 in each cell and characterized by mental retardation, heart defects, and what people once called a "mongoloid" appearance. (A 25-year-old has a one-in-1,000 chance of having a child with Down.) As amnio became less risky, it was given to younger women. Today, it is routinely administered to women 35 and older; in this city, it's even used on women who are 32 or 33.

The test, done when a woman is about sixteen weeks pregnant, involves inserting a needle through the abdomen and drawing fluid from the amniotic sac surrounding the fetus. Fetal cells in the fluid are then grown and the chromosomes examined. Amnio is most often used to predict chromosomal abnormalities, like Down. It can also be used to look at DNA and to predict the sex of the child. Getting the results of an amnio takes about three weeks, which means that couples can't make a decision about abortion until the nineteenth week of pregnancy. A late abortion is so physically and emotionally harrowing that few genetic counselors believe amnio is used for frivolous reasons like sex selection.

Chorionic villus sampling can be done much earlier. The procedure has been used for just four years, and fewer than 30 medical centers around the country perform it. CVS is done at the ninth to eleventh week of pregnancy, and can take less than twenty minutes: While watching the position of the fetus on an ultrasound monitor, a doctor inserts a thin tube through the vagina and into the uterus, and then extracts a tiny piece of the placenta. Like amnio, CVS can be used to look at chromosomes and at DNA; it also predicts fetal sex. Often, the results are back in less than a week. Those who decide to abort can do so in the first trimester.

The test's critics fear that CVS will make it so easy to abort that couples will do so even if their child is diagnosed as having only a mildly disabling condition or a nonlethal disease, and they argue

that it will encourage parents to use prenatal diagnosis to choose the sex of their child.

If a blood test that can make the same predictions is developed, testing for gender seems even more likely, especially in cultures that have a strong bias in favor of males. If it seems improbable that couples would choose to abort because they're having a child of the "wrong" sex, consider that in just three months ProCare Industries sold 50,000 Gender Choice kits, which promised parents that they could pick the sex of their child by timing conception correctly. According to the FDA, the test is a fraud.

A third test, for alpha-fetoprotein (AFP), which is used to diagnose spina bifida (incomplete formation of the spinal column), a condition that causes birth defects ranging from severe retardation to mild physical disability, recently became the first prenatal screening technique mandated by law: Last April, California began requiring obstetricians to tell expectant mothers about it. The technique measures the level of a fetal protein in a mother's blood, and only those women with abnormal levels need a follow-up amnio. Unlike amnio or CVS, AFP is a blood test, and it's cheap—$50 (compared with about $1,000 for amnio and $1,200 for CVS). AFP screening is strongly recommended by the American College of Obstetricians and Gynecologists' legal committee, because the OB/GYNs believe that the test will help cut down on the growing number of "wrongful birth" malpractice suits.

'IN HER TINY SUBBASEMENT OFFICE AT NEW YORK HOSPITAL, genetic counselor Nancy Zellers, an energetic woman in her late thirties, sees fifteen couples each week. Her clients tend to be young, urban, and professional. Typical, she says, is "the banker who may be planning a very small family and she is going to live in an apartment in the city. And probably, because she established her career, she is getting started on children much later and she is going to have a limited family.

"Her concern is 'How is this going to fit into my life-style if it is not a normal child? How am I going to handle this? What's it going to do to my relationship?' Maybe both husband and wife have to work. What's it going to do to the family unit as a whole? I don't think they're unreasonable," says Zellers. "I think that they're anxious."

Susan Katz was. At 36, she is the New York editor-in-chief of Holt, Rinehart and Winston. Her dark hair is lightly streaked with gray, and her office is decorated with bright paintings signed by her seven-year-old daughter from her first marriage. Katz's husband, Howard Radin, owns a computer-software business.

During her first pregnancy, Susan had had a blood test for German measles but nothing else. "This time," she says, "I thought the chances of something being wrong—because I'm 36—are greater. My sense was that it was worth going through, and that people would have thought I was crazy not to have it."

Neither Katz nor Radin has a family history of genetic disease, so Susan had three tests: carrier screening for Tay-Sachs disease, which strikes one in every 2,500 Jews of Eastern and Central European ancestry and causes children to wither and die in their first years of life (both Katz and Radin are Jewish); amniocentesis, to look for Down syndrome; and the AFP test for spina bifida. All three were negative. Though they didn't talk about it much, both Susan and Howard think she would have had an abortion if a defect had turned up. "It's not even the time and the money as much as it breaks your heart," explains Susan. "I think part of the goal of raising a happy child is to create an independent adult, and I think of seriously impaired children as never reaching independent adulthood, and something about that is very sad to me."

"WOULD WE HAVE BEEN BETTER OFF WITHOUT WOODY GUTHRIE, WHO DIED OF HUNTINGTON'S?" ASKS AN ETHICIST.

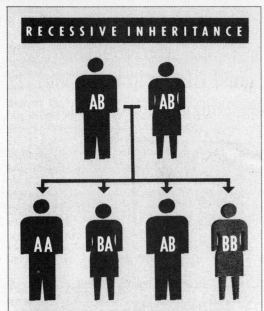

RECESSIVE INHERITANCE

Illustration by Anders Wenngren.

The healthy parents each have one normal gene and one defective, disease-causing one, so they are carriers. A child inherits one gene from each parent. Each child has a one-in-four chance of inheriting two normal genes and being healthy (far left), two chances in four of being a healthy carrier (inheriting one normal gene and one defective one; center), and one in four of inheriting two defective genes and having the disease (far right).

For many women, the decision to use a prenatal test is an automatic one—their friends have done it, their doctor recommends it, and they feel they'd be foolish not to—and among the white middle class, diagnosis in the womb is becoming routine. Deborah Batterman, for example, didn't think much about amnio. "I figured as long as I was going to have a baby at this stage, I might as well go through with it," she says. "Since you have choices today—abortion is available and you don't *have* to have a child—you may as well take advantage of all the options."

Though Batterman and her husband, Lew Dolin, never discussed what they would do if a defect turned up, she assumes that she would have had an abortion. "I guess we've all become a little bit cavalier about these decisions," she says. "It's available, it's easy, we don't have to think about the problems of bringing up a child with Down syndrome or something as terrible. So given those options, we just assume, Let's go for the healthy baby."

"I might be a good person and I love my family and all that, but I am not one of these people who would have been able to give a child I knew to be handicapped the right love and atten-

tion in this world," says Judith Liebman, who chose CVS during her second pregnancy (she had amnio during her first). "It'd be different if I didn't know. I am sure that there are women out there whose opinion is 'It is God's will.' Great! That is terrific. That is not my opinion. I can change it. And I don't think you get struck down for changing it. I think it's a true analysis of what you're ready to deal with."

SINCE GENETIC DISEASE IS RARE, PRENATAL TESTS ARE a reassurance for more than 98 percent of the couples who use them, a fact that genetic counselors emphasize when answering their critics. "I spend every Monday calling people and telling them that their results are normal," says Beth Fine, a genetic counselor at Chicago's Michael Reese Hospital and president of the National Society of Genetic Counselors. "And it's a pleasure.

"People always argue that these tests are a search-and-destroy mission, or encourage abortion," Fine continues, "but we have more pregnancies that result because of the availability of these tests. So there are many more people who can go ahead and get pregnant, as opposed to those who end up testing just to abort. It gives people an opportunity, and that's something you can't take away."

CVS may give that opportunity to even more couples. Melissa Gordon*, a doctor who lost a brother to hemophilia, wasn't sure if she could raise a son with the disease (hemophilia is passed from mothers to sons, and Gordon's child had a fifty-fifty chance of having the disease). When she wanted to become pregnant, none of the DNA probes for hemophilia were applicable to her case (they now are). Gordon consulted genetic counselor Fine and then decided to have CVS; if the child was male, she's decide whether to have an abortion.

"It was a very difficult decision, because we wouldn't know whether we were aborting a normal boy or not," says Gordon. "It would be impossible to go through a pregnancy that long [with amnio] and consider the possibility of an abortion that late. The other reason CVS was important was that if we decided not to abort, my plans to go back to work would have been very different." Happily, Gordon discovered at ten weeks that she was carrying a girl.

For people like Gordon, who have experienced the pain—physical and emotional—of inherited disease, the tests are especially reassuring. "We're allowing people to have healthy families," says genetic counselor Nancy Zellers. "I can't believe that if someone had a baby with Tay-Sachs and watched a child die before their eyes, anyone would expect them to take a risk of going through that again, if they really don't have to. Or can blame that family for having an early abortion rather than going through that again with another affected child. How much tragedy can people take?"

Neither CVS nor amnio can guarantee a healthy baby: Geneticists estimate that even *with* prenatal diagnosis, 2 to 4 percent of all children will be born with serious birth defects. Still, they allay the fears of prospective parents who feel incapable of caring for a child with a problem. "If we're talking about gross birth defects, terrible handicapping conditions, potentially fatal disease, a level of mental retardation that we don't think we can live with, I don't think there's anything wrong with people not wanting to have a child with serious problems," says Zellers. "We have to be willing to accept a certain amount of risk. It doesn't mean we're not sad, and burdened, and angry, and frustrated, and just devastated if a baby's born with something wrong with it. But a certain number of babies are going to be born with something wrong with them. And yet people are still having babies, right?"

EMILY PERL KINGSLEY CONSIDERS HERSELF A FEMI-nist; a member of NOW, she has belonged to the Abortion Rights Action League. At 47, Kingsley has won four Emmys as a writer for *Sesame Street,* and sometime in the next year, CBS will broadcast a film she wrote. But when she thinks about prenatal testing, Kingsley finds her feminism running up against her feelings about disability rights, her belief in a woman's right to choose to have an abortion colliding with her belief in the value of the lives of handicapped children. Her son, Jason, thirteen, has Down syndrome. "When you lose me," says Kingsley, "is when you say that the world would be better off without people like my son. I can't go along with that. The only drawback to Down is the pain that he will experience. I would do anything to save him that pain—short of killing him."

Though she was offered amniocentesis during her pregnancy, Kingsley passed on it (a decision she says she has never regretted). At 34, she was a year short of the cutoff date, and at the time, amnio was a risky procedure. Kingsley and her husband, Charles, were both on their second marriage, and both were sure they wanted the child. When Jason was born, their obstetrician suggested they might put him in an institution, tell their families he'd died, and try again. Instead, they took him home to Chappaqua and enrolled him in infant-stimulation classes designed to saturate Down children with information and activity.

Infant-stimulation classes were a new concept then, and the Kingsleys had no assurance that they'd be of any real help; today, Jason functions at a high level for a Down-syndrome child. Though he will probably never drive a car, live without some supervision, or go to Yale, Jason can read and write, manage in social situations, and follow complex directions. (He has also appeared on *Sesame Street* and other television shows.) "The idea that you ought to abort a child because he might turn out like my son is *crazy* to me," says Kingsley. "It's crazy."

For Kingsley and other disability-rights activists, their movement is a rerun of the civil-rights and feminist fights of the sixties and seventies, and their goals—acceptance by and access to the mainstream of society—are similar. "No one's entitled to tell us, 'No, you can't. Your kid isn't smart enough. Not smart enough to swim on this beach. Not smart enough to play with the kids in this group.' A lot of the things that they get away with saying to us—if they said, 'You can't get into this class because your skin is black . . .'"

This time around, though, they find themselves edging toward agreement with people who probably fought on the other side in those earlier battles—right-to-life activists and those on the political right who are opposed not only to prenatal testing but to all abortion. (Many disability-rights supporters don't object to abortion in general, only to abortion to prevent the birth of a handicapped child.)

Still, even within the movement, there's no consensus on prenatal testing. The disabled and their families, after all, are of no particular political persuasion, socioeconomic class, or religion. Instead, they are united by accidents of birth and chance. Though one woman who works with the mentally retarded claims that "the lives of the disabled are debased each time a disabled child is aborted," a large number of activists are unwilling to take a stand on prenatal diagnosis. Their concern, they say, is those who have already been born.

Most, like Carol Levine, an ethics specialist at the Hastings Center in Briarcliff Manor, feel that the severity of the disease must come into play—that a short life followed by a painful death might better be avoided, but that life in a wheelchair is not grounds for abortion. "There's a difference," says Levine, "between being able to test for a lethal disease like Tay-Sachs and a disease like cystic fibrosis that people are living with—not to great old age, but it's not incompatible with life and

even productive, happy life. So the choices that people will make are inevitably going to be colored by the differences in the conditions. I think it's pointed up even more in Huntington's disease, where people live to be 50. Would we have been better off without Woody Guthrie, who died of Huntington's? Well, I don't think anybody would say that. But is there a right answer? I don't think so."

Not everyone whose child would be affected by a disease chooses abortion: Of the fifteen pregnancies Fred Gilbert has studied with DNA probes, four have come up positive for CF, and half of those families kept the children. Parents who are told their child has Down syndrome can put him up for adoption; there are waiting lists of families happy to take Down babies. Even some Roman Catholic hospitals are now offering prenatal diagnosis (without abortion), on the theory that parents who know about their child's problems will be able to cope with them better. The numbers they see are dramatically lower than those at secular hospitals: At Creighton University Medical Center in Omaha, about 5 prenatal tests are done a month; New York Hospital, which is three times as large, does approximately 39 a *week*. And for some disabilities the abortion rate is high—91 percent of the women who get a positive diagnosis for Down syndrome terminate their pregnancies (many women who don't feel they could do it simply do not take the test).

"WE'RE ALL GENETIC MESSES," SAYS THE NA-tional Institutes of Health's John Fletcher. "There's no such thing as perfection, and there never will be." Yet each year, more people are searching for it. In Manhattan, about 50 percent of the women at risk for chromosomal abnormalities have prenatal diagnosis, while nationwide, the number of such women using the tests has more than doubled since 1977 (to about 20 percent). An Indiana hospital that did ten amnios in 1971 now does fifteen a *week*. In New York State, 40 percent of women 35 and over had some form of prenatal test in 1984, up from about 5 percent in 1977. As the tests become routine, the definition of abortable defects may become wider and, some people fear, parents may reject a potential child for what seem to be frivolous reasons. Ever more genetic hurdles might be set up, and in order to be born a fetus might have to clear them all.

"Anything that has an aspect of mental retardation is already quite unacceptable for most people," says Carol Levine. "I think that the limits of tolerability will be stretched very far. More and more things will be seen as disabilities, and smaller disabilities will be seen less tolerably than they are now. And a society that isn't tolerant of diversity is one that is bereft of imagination and creativity."

Prenatal diagnosis may also change our notion of parental responsibility. "To know that you're bringing forth a child who has to use a wheelchair. . . . With a few curb cuts, life in a wheelchair is not a tragedy," says Barbara Katz Rothman. "But then you're going to look at this particular kid who's going to say to you, 'I am in this wheelchair because you thought it was a good idea.' And there's going to be an element of truth in that. And that's an incredible responsibility to take on in a society that's not supportive of people in wheelchairs, people with mild retardation, people with any kind of problem. I think there's going to be a certain attitude: 'This isn't an act of God anymore that could happen to anybody; this is your selfish choice, lady.'"

But who can blame parents for wanting their children to be healthy? Though the treatments for diseases like CF and Duchenne muscular dystrophy have improved in recent years, there is still no cure for most of them, and victims may face frequent hospitalization and even early death. And though the lives of the disabled have improved immeasurably in the last

FOR MANY WOMEN WHO WORK, IT IS ALMOST IMPOSSIBLE TO VISUALIZE RAISING A SEVERELY HANDICAPPED CHILD.

decade, as federal regulations ensuring rights of the handicapped have been put into effect, discussions with the parents of handicapped children, and with those who work with them, reveal just how difficult life with a mentally or physically disabling condition can be. They speak of how hard it is to find a class for their child, of bus drivers who won't stop for people in wheelchairs, of New York's lack of simple amenities, like curb cuts, and, most important, of the cruel treatment their children receive, both from other youngsters and from adults.

"The burdens of raising a kid with Down syndrome have practically nothing to do with the child," says Emily Kingsley. "If anything, the child is easy. The burdens are the attitudes and prejudices you meet from people. Having to overcome their queasiness or whatever it is. People are afraid. 'My God, what if that happened to me?' Isn't it neater to keep these people in the closet and not have to think about them, not have to face them, not have to make ramps for them?"

FOR MANY WOMEN WHO WORK, IT IS ALMOST IMPOSSIBLE to visualize raising a severely handicapped child. "I think the real lives of women, especially women who work outside the home, mean that the juggling act implied in motherhood is already very, very tough," says Rayna Rapp, a New School anthropologist who has been studying prenatal diagnosis for the last three years. "And compared with most Western societies, we have fewer social services, fewer maternity benefits, less day care. All of those very large-scale factors go into an assessment at the time of a life crisis. You're not thinking in general about what it means to be the mother of *a* child; you're thinking rather specifically about how your life will change to become the parent of a disabled child, right now and here. And I'm not arguing that if the services were perfect everybody would go ahead and have a disabled baby. But I think some people might have a very different sense of it if the climate around disability and disability services was transformed."

Rapp, 41, is a quick, small woman with shaggy brown hair. She began her anthropological study of prenatal diagnosis after going through the experience herself. Pregnant for the first time at 36, Rapp saw amnio as part of the trade-off she had to make because she had devoted 10 years of her life to her academic and political concerns. As it turned out, she was one of the unlucky 2 percent: The fetus was diagnosed as having Down.

"When Nancy [her genetic counselor] called me twelve days after the tap," Rapp wrote in a *Ms.* article about her amnio, "I began to scream as soon as I recognized her voice.... The image of myself, alone, screaming into a white plastic telephone is indelible." Rapp and her husband, Mike Hooper, decided to have an abortion.

"It was a decision made so that my husband and I could have a certain kind of relationship to a child and to each other and to our adult lives," says Rapp. "It had a lot to do with a sense of responsibility, starting out life as older parents. That was the choice, to have delayed childbearing to do the other things we had done in life. And that meant we had to confront something that was very, very upsetting. But in some senses, I wouldn't have wished away the last ten years of my life in order not to have faced the decision.

"Paradoxically," says Rapp, "there's less choice for people who are better educated to understand prenatal diagnosis. The more you know about this technology, the more likely you are to feel its necessity. But unless the conditions under which Americans view, deal with, and respond to a range of disabling conditions are also put up for discussion about choice—until that larger picture changes—I think it's real hard for many, many people to imagine making a choice other than abortion for something like Down."

IN FACT, AS SCREENING TESTS FOR INHERITED DISEASES like CF, Huntington's, and the muscular dystrophies become available in the next decade, it's likely that many couples—especially urban, middle-class ones—will consider them a normal part of pregnancy. And as prenatal diagnosis is done earlier in pregnancy, the likelihood that prospective parents will decide to have an abortion for one of those conditions will probably also increase. That attitude is deeply disturbing to opponents of the tests, including Dr. Brian Scully, a Catholic infectious-diseases specialist who works with CF patients at Columbia-Presbyterian Medical Center. Scully, who grew up in Ireland, is opposed to genetic testing—for any condition—that leads to abortion. "The idea that I'm only going to have a child if it's going to be a perfect child, that I'll only accept a baby if it's an acceptable baby—I don't sympathize with that at all," says Scully. "I don't want children to have cystic fibrosis. But to say that if you have cystic fibrosis I'm not going to have you, I think that's wrong."

In 1985, Scully denounced the tests in a letter to *The Lancet,* a widely read British medical journal. In return, he got a note from a London biochemist who, in Scully's words, "rationalized that it was just that they were helping nature. A proportion of babies are lost because of defects naturally—I forget what that proportion is—but he felt that they were just supporting nature, and weeding out the undesirable, imperfect children. And he felt that was fine. I would say, Why not wait until they're born, and you can get everybody."

Like other decisions forced on us by advancing technology, the choice involved in genetic testing can exceed one's moral grasp. And while Scully raises an important argument, the pro-choice position is just as cogent: Can parents who have seen one child suffer with a disease be forced to risk having another? Should people be told they must have a child—even one they don't feel capable of caring for? And, in the case of a disease like Tay-Sachs, does anyone benefit from the child's being born? Parents must make all those decisions for themselves—not lightly, but with awareness of the real moral weight of the final choice. And there's no right answer, a fact that Susan Murphy acutely understands. "I don't think that you should judge people by the decisions they make, whether it's to terminate or not to terminate a pregnancy," she says. "Because you don't know what hell they went through."

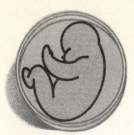

The age of the test-tube baby is fast developing. Already science has produced an array of artificial methods for creating life, offering solutions to the growing problem of infertility. In these stories, TIME explores the startling techniques, from laboratory conception to surrogate mothers, and examines the complex legal and ethical issues they raise.

The New Origins of Life

How the science of conception brings hope to childless couples

A group of women sit quietly chatting, their heads bowed over needlepoint and knitting, in the gracious parlor at Bourn Hall. The mansion's carved stone mantelpieces, rich wood paneling and crystal chandeliers give it an air of grandeur, a reflection of the days when it was the seat of the Earl De La Warr. In the well-kept gardens behind the house, Indian women in brilliant saris float on the arms of their husbands. The verdant meadows of Cambridgeshire lie serenely in the distance. To the casual observer, this stately home could be an elegant British country hotel. For the women and their husbands, however, it is a last resort.

Each has come to the Bourn Hall clinic to make a final stand against a cruel and unyielding enemy: infertility. They have come from around the globe to be treated by the world-renowned team of Obstetrician Patrick Steptoe and Reproductive Physiologist Robert Edwards, the men responsible for the birth of the world's first test-tube baby, Louise Brown, in 1978. Many of the patients have spent more than a decade trying to conceive a child, undergoing tests and surgery and taking fertility drugs. Most have waited more than a year just to be admitted to the clinic. Some have mortgaged their homes, sold their cars or borrowed from relatives to scrape together the $3,510 fee for foreign visitors to be treated at Bourn Hall (British citizens pay $2,340). All are brimming over with hope that their prayers will be answered by in-vitro fertilization (IVF), the mating of egg and sperm in a laboratory dish. "They depend on Mr. Steptoe utterly," observes the husband of one patient. "Knowing him is like dying and being a friend of St. Peter's."

In the six years that have passed since the birth of Louise Brown, some 700 test-tube babies have been born as a result of the work done at Bourn Hall and the approximately 200 other IVF clinics that have sprung up around the world. By year's end there will be about 1,000 such infants. Among their number are 56 pairs of test-tube twins, eight sets of triplets and two sets of quads.

New variations on the original technique are multiplying almost as fast as the test-tube population. Already it is possible for Reproductive Endocrinologist Martin Quigley of the Cleveland Clinic to speak of "old-fashioned IVF" (in which a woman's eggs are removed, fertilized with her husband's sperm and then placed in her uterus). "The modern way," he notes, "mixes and matches donors and recipients." Thus a woman's egg may be fertilized with a donor's sperm, or a donor's egg may be fertilized with the husband's sperm, or, in yet another scenario, the husband and wife contribute their sperm and egg, but the resulting embryo is carried by a third party who is, in a sense, donating the use of her womb. "The possibilities are limited only by your imagination," observes Clifford Grobstein, professor of biological science and public policy at the University of California, San Diego. Says John Noonan, professor of law at the University of California, Berkeley: "We really are plunging into the Brave New World."

Though the new technologies have raised all sorts of politically explosive ethical questions, the demand for them is rapidly growing. Reason: infertility, which now affects one in six American couples, is on the rise. According to a study by the National Center for Health Statistics, the incidence of infertility among married women aged 20 to 24, normally the most fertile age group, jumped 177% between 1965 and 1982. At the same time, the increasing use of abortion to end unwanted pregnancies and the growing social acceptance of single motherhood have drastically reduced the availability of children for adoption. At

Catholic Charities, for instance, couples must now wait seven years for a child. As a result, more and more couples are turning to IVF. Predicts Clifford Stratton, director of an in-vitro lab in Reno: "In five years, there will be a successful IVF clinic in every U.S. city."

It is a long, hard road that leads a couple to the in-vitro fertilization clinic, and the journey has been known to rock the soundest marriages. "If you want to illustrate your story on infertility, take a picture of a couple and tear it in half," says Cleveland Businessman James Popela, 36, speaking from bitter experience. "It is not just the pain and indignity of the medical tests and treatment," observes Betty Orlandino, who counsels infertile couples in Oak Park, Ill. "Infertility rips at the core of the couple's relationship; it affects sexuality, self-image and self-esteem. It stalls careers, devastates savings and damages associations with friends and family."

For women, the most common reason for infertility is a blockage or abnormality of the fallopian tubes. These thin, flexible structures, which convey the egg from the ovaries to the uterus, are where fertilization normally occurs. If they are blocked or damaged or frozen in place by scar tissue, the egg will be unable to complete its journey. To examine the tubes, a doctor uses X rays or a telescope-like instrument called a laparoscope, which is inserted directly into the pelvic area through a small, abdominal incision. Delicate microsurgery, and, more recently, laser surgery, sometimes can repair the damage successfully. According to Beverly Freeman, executive director of Resolve, a national infertility-counseling organization, microsurgery can restore fertility in 70% of women with minor scarring around their tubes. But for those whose tubes are completely blocked, the chance of success ranges from 20% to zero. These women are the usual candidates for in-vitro fertilization.

Much has been learned about the technique since the pioneering days of Steptoe and Edwards. When the two Englishmen first started out, they assumed that the entire process must be carried out at breakneck speed: harvesting the egg the minute it is ripe and immediately adding the sperm. This was quite a challenge, given that the collaborators spent most of their time 155 miles apart, with Edwards teaching physiology at Cambridge and Steptoe practicing obstetrics in the northwestern mill town of Oldham. Sometimes, when one of Steptoe's patients was about to ovulate, the doctor would have to summon his partner by phone. Edwards would then jump into his car and charge down the old country roads to Oldham. Once there, the two would remove the egg and mate it with sperm without wasting a moment; by the time Lesley Brown became their patient, they could perform the procedure in two minutes flat. They believed that speed was the important factor in the conception of Louise Brown.

As it happens, they were wrong. Says Gynecologist Howard Jones, who, together with his wife, Endocrinologist Georgeanna Seegar Jones, founded the first American in-vitro program at Norfolk in 1978: "It turns out that if you get the sperm to the egg quickly, most often you inhibit the process." According to Jones, the pioneers of IVF made so many wrong assumptions that "the birth of Louise Brown now seems like a fortunate coincidence."

Essential to in-vitro fertilization, of course, is retrieval of the one egg normally produced in the ovaries each month. Today in-vitro clinics help nature along by administering such drugs as Clomid and Pergonal, which can result in the development of more than one egg at a time. By using hormonal stimulants, Howard Jones "harvests" an average of 5.8 eggs per patient; it is possible to obtain as many as 17. "I felt like a pumpkin ready to burst," recalls Loretto Leyland, 33, of Melbourne, who produced eleven eggs at an Australian clinic, one of which became her daughter Zoe.

According to Quigley, the chances for pregnancy are best when the eggs are retrieved during the three- to four-hour period when they are fully mature. At Bourn Hall, women remain on the premises, waiting for that moment to occur. Each morning, Steptoe, now 71 and walking with a cane, arrives on the ward to check their charts. The husband of one patient describes the scene: "Looking at a woman like an astonished owl, he'll say, 'Your estrogen is rising nicely.' The diffidence is his means of defense against desperate women. They think he can get them pregnant just by looking at them."

When blood tests and ultrasound monitoring indicate that the ova are ripe, the eggs are extracted in a delicate operation performed under general anesthesia.

The surgeons first insert a laparoscope, which is about ⅓ in. in diameter, so that they can see the target: the small, bluish pocket, or follicle, inside the ovary, where each egg is produced. Then, a long, hollow needle is inserted through a second incision, and the eggs and the surrounding fluid are gently suctioned up. Some clinics are beginning to use ultrasound imaging instead of a laparoscope to guide the needle into the follicles. This procedure can be done in a doctor's office under local anesthesia; it is less expensive than laparoscopy but may be less reliable.

Once extracted, the follicular fluid is rushed to an adjoining laboratory and examined under a microscope to confirm that it contains an egg (the ovum measures only four-thousandths of an inch across). The ova are carefully washed, placed in petri dishes containing a solution of nutrients and then deposited in an incubator for four to eight hours. The husband, meanwhile, has produced a sperm sample. It is hardly a romantic moment, recalls Cleveland Businessman Popela, who made four trips to Cambridgeshire with his wife, each time without success. "You have to take the jar and walk past a group of people as you go into the designated room, where there's an old brass bed and a couple of *Playboy* magazines. They all know what you're doing and they're watching the clock, because there are several people behind you waiting their turn."

The sperm is prepared in a solution and then added to the dishes where the eggs are waiting. The transcendent moment of union, when a new life begins, occurs some time during the next 24 hours, in the twilight of an incubator set at body heat. If all goes well, several of the eggs will be fertilized and start to divide. When the embryo is at least two to eight cells in size, it is placed in the woman's uterus. During this procedure, which requires no anesthetic, Steptoe likes to have the husband present talking to his wife. "The skill of the person doing the replacement is very important," he says. "The womb doesn't like things being put into it. It contracts and tries to push things out. We try to do it with as little disturbance as possible."

The tension of the next two weeks, as the couple awaits the results of pregnancy tests, is agonizing. "Women have been known to break out in hives," reports Linda Bailey, nurse-coordinator at the IVF program at North Carolina Memorial Hospital in Chapel Hill. Success rates vary from clinic to clinic; some centers open and close without a single success. But even the best clinics offer little more than a 20% chance of pregnancy. Since tiny factors like water quality seem to affect results, both physicians and patients tend to become almost superstitious about what else might sway the odds. Said one doctor: "If someone

told us that painting the ceiling pink would make a difference, we would do it."

In recent years, IVF practitioners have discovered a more reliable way of improving results: transferring more than one embryo at a time. At the Jones' clinic, which has one of the world's highest success rates, there is a 20% chance of pregnancy if one embryo is inserted, a 28% chance if two are used and a 38% chance with three. However, transferring more than one embryo also increases the likelihood of multiple births.

For couples who have struggled for years to have a child, the phrase "you are pregnant" is magical. "We thought we would never hear those words," sighs Risa Green, 35, of Framingham, Mass., now the mother of a month-old boy. But even if the news is good, the tension continues. One-third of IVF pregnancies spontaneously miscarry in the first three months, a perplexing problem that is currently under investigation. Says one veteran of Steptoe's program: "Every week you call for test results to see if the embryo is still there. Then you wait to see if your period comes." The return of menstruation is like a death in the family; often it is mourned by the entire clinic.

Many couples have a strong compulsion to try again immediately after in vitro fails. Popela of Cleveland compares it to a gambling addiction: "Each time you get more desperate, each time you say, 'Just one more time.'" In fact, the odds do improve with each successive try, as doctors learn more about the individual patient. But the stakes are high: in the U.S., each attempt costs between $3,000 and $5,000, not including travel costs and time away from work. Lynn Kellert, 31, and her husband Mitchell, 34, of New York City, who tried seven times at Norfolk before finally achieving pregnancy, figure the total cost was $80,000. Thus far, few insurance companies have been willing to foot the bill, arguing that IVF is still experimental. But, observes Grobstein of UCSD, "it's going to be increasingly difficult for them to maintain that position."

Second and third attempts will become easier and less costly with the wider use of cryopreservation, a process in which unused embryos are frozen in liquid nitrogen. The embryos can be thawed and then transferred to the woman's uterus, eliminating the need to repeat egg retrieval and fertilization. Some 30% to 50% of embryos do not survive the deep freeze. Those that do may actually have a better chance of successful implantation than do newly fertilized embryos. This is because the recipient has not been given hormones to stimulate ovulation, a treatment that may actually interfere with implantation.

Opinion is sharply divided as to how

age affects the results of IVF. Although most clinics once rejected women over age 35, many now accept them. While one faction maintains that older women have a greater tendency to miscarry, Quigley, for one, insists that "age should not affect the success rate." Curiously, the Joneses in Norfolk have achieved their best results with women age 35 to 40. This year one of their patients, Barbara Brooks of Springfield, Va., had a test-tube son at age 41; she can hardly wait to try again.

Doctors are also beginning to use IVF as a solution to male infertility. Ordinarily, about 30 million sperm must be produced to give one a chance of penetrating and fertilizing the egg. In the laboratory, the chances for fertilization are good with only 50,000 sperm. "In vitro may be one of the most effective ways of treating men with a low sperm count or low sperm motility, problems that affect as many as 10 million American men," says Andrologist Wylie Hembree of Columbia-Presbyterian Medical Center in New York City.

While most clinics originally restricted IVF to couples who produced normal sperm and eggs, this too is changing. Today, when the husband cannot supply adequate sperm, most clinics are willing to use sperm from a donor, usually obtained from one of the nation's more than 20 sperm banks. An even more radical departure is the use of donor eggs, pioneered two years ago by Dr. Alan Trounson and Dr. Carl Wood of Melbourne's Monash University. The method can be used to bring about pregnancy in women who lack functioning ovaries. It is also being sought by women who are known carriers of genetic diseases. The donated eggs may come from a woman in the Monash IVF program who has produced more ova than she can use. Alternately, they could come from a relative or acquaintance of the recipient, providing that she is willing to go through the elaborate egg-retrieval process.

At Harbor Hospital in Torrance, Calif., which is affiliated with the UCLA School of Medicine, a team headed by Obstetrician John Buster has devised a variant method of egg donation. Instead of fertilizing the ova in a dish, doctors simply inseminate the donor with the husband's sperm. About five days later, the fertilized egg is washed out of the donor's uterus in a painless procedure called lavage. It is then placed in the recipient's womb. The process, which has to date produced two children, "has an advantage over IVF," says Buster, "because it is nonsurgical and can be easily repeated until it works." But the technique also has its perils. If lavage fails to flush out the embryo, the donor faces an unwanted pregnancy.

The most controversial of the new methods of reproduction does not depend on advanced fertilization techniques. A growing number of couples are hiring surrogate mothers to bear their children. Surrogates are being used in cases where the husband is fertile, but his wife is unable to sustain pregnancy, perhaps because of illness or because she had had a hysterectomy. Usually, the hired woman is simply artificially inseminated with the husband's sperm. However, if the wife is capable of producing a normal egg but not capable of carrying the child, the surrogate can be implanted with an embryo conceived by the couple. This technique has been attempted several times, so far without success.

The medical profession in general is apprehensive about the use of paid surrogates. "It is difficult to differentiate between payment for a child and payment for carrying the child," observes Dr. Ervin Nichols, director of practice activity for the American College of Obstetrics and Gynecology. The college has issued strict guidelines to doctors, urging them to screen carefully would-be surrogates and the couples who hire them for their medical and psychological fitness. "I would hate to say there is no place for surrogate motherhood," says Nichols, "but it should be kept to an absolute minimum."

In contrast, in-vitro fertilization has become a standard part of medical practice. The risks to the mother, even after repeated attempts at egg retrieval, are "minimal," points out Nichols. Nor has the much feared risk of birth defects materialized. Even frozen-embryo babies seem to suffer no increased risk of abnormalities. However, as Steptoe points out, "we need more research before we know for sure."

The need for research is almost an obsession among IVF doctors. They are eager to understand why so many of their patients miscarry; they long to discover ways of examining eggs to determine which ones are most likely to be fertilized, and they want to develop methods of testing an embryo to be certain that it is normal and viable. "Right now, all we know how to do is look at them under the microscope," says a frustrated Gary Hodgen, scientific director at the Norfolk clinic.

Many scientists see research with embryos as a way of finding answers to many problems in medicine. For instance, by learning more about the reproductive process, biologists may uncover better methods of contraception. Cancer research may also benefit, because tumor cells have many characteristics in common with embryonic tissues. Some doctors believe that these tissues, with their tremendous capacity for growth and differentiation, may ultimately prove useful in understanding and treating diseases such as childhood diabetes. Also in the future lies the possibility of identifying and then correcting genetic defects in embryos. Gene therapy, Hodgen says enthusiastically, "is the biggest idea since Pasteur learned to immunize an entire generation against disease." It is, however, at least a decade away.

American scientists have no trouble dreaming up these and other possibilities, but, for the moment, dreaming is all they can do. Because of the political sensitivity of experiments with human embryos, federal grant money, which fuels 85% of biomedical research in the U.S., has been denied to scientists in this field. So controversial is the issue that four successive Secretaries of Health and Human Services (formerly Health, Education and Welfare) have refused to deal with it. This summer, Norfolk's Hodgen resigned as chief of pregnancy research at the National Institutes of Health. He explained his frustration at a congressional hearing: "No mentor of young physicians and scientists beginning their academic careers in reproductive medicine can deny the central importance of IVF–embryo transfer research." In Hodgen's view the curb on research funds is also a breach of government responsibility toward "generations of unborn" and toward infertile couples who still desperately want help.

In an obstetrics waiting room at Norfolk's in-vitro clinic, a woman sits crying. Thirty-year-old Michel Jones and her husband Richard, 33, a welder at the Norfolk Navy yard, have been through the program four times, without success. Now their insurance company is refusing to pay for another attempt, and says Richard indignantly, "they even want their money back for the first three times." On a bulletin board in the room is a sign giving the schedule for blood tests, ultrasound and other medical exams. Beside it hangs a small picture of a soaring bird and the message: *You never fail until you stop trying.* Michel Jones is not about to quit. Says she: "You have a dream to come here and get pregnant. It is the chance of a lifetime. I won't give up."

—*By Claudia Wallis. Reported by Mary Cronin/London, Patricia Delaney/Washington and Ruth Mehrtens Galvin/Norfolk*

THE GENE DREAM

Scientists are mapping our complete genetic code, a venture that will revolutionize medicine—and ethics.

Natalie Angier

Natalie Angier, *a New York City–based science writer, is the author of* Natural Obsessions: The Search for the Oncogene.

At first glance, the Petersons* of Utah seem like a dream family, the kind you see only on television. They're devout, traditional and very, very loving. Bob Peterson works at a hospital near home to support the family while he finishes up a master's program in electrical engineering. Diane, who studied home economics at Brigham Young University, is a full-time wife and mother. And her time is certainly full: The Petersons have five sons and two daughters, ranging in age from two to 13. (As Mormons, the parents don't practice birth control.)

The children are towheaded, saucer-eyed and subject to infectious fits of laughter. During the summer months, the backyard pool is as cheerily deafening as the local Y.

---

*Not their real name.

Says Diane, "Our kids really like just spending time together."

Yet for all the intimacy and joy, the Petersons' story is threaded with tragedy. One of the daughters has cerebral palsy, a nerve- and muscle-cell disorder. The malady isn't fatal, but the girl walks with great difficulty, and she's slightly retarded. Three of the other children suffer from cystic fibrosis, a devastating genetic disease in which the lungs become clogged with mucus, the pancreas fails, malnutrition sets in, and breathing becomes ever more labored. Thus far, their children's symptoms have been relatively mild, but Bob and Diane know the awful truth: Although a person with cystic fibrosis may live to be 20 or even 30, the disease is inevitably fatal.

"Right now, the kids don't act sick," says Bob. "They go on thinking, 'I have a normal life.'" But, he admits softly, "We know it won't last forever. If they do get bad, then we won't have a choice. We'll have to put them in a hospital."

The Petersons realize their children's ailments aren't likely to be cured in the immediate future, but they're battling back the best way possible. Bob, Diane, and their seven children, as well as the three surviving grandparents, have all donated blood samples to biologist Ray White and his team at the University of Utah in Salt Lake City. Scientists are combing through the DNA in the blood, checking for the distinctive chemical patterns present only in cystic fibrosis patients.

Their work is part of a vast biomedical venture recently launched by the government to understand all the genes that either cause us harm or keep us healthy. It's medicine's grandest dream: By comprehending the genome—the complete set of genetic information that makes us who we are—in minute detail, scientists hope to answer the most enigmatic puzzles of human nature. The effort is so immense in its scale and goals that some have called it biology's equivalent of the Apollo moonshot, or the atom bomb's Manhattan project.

In fact, it's the most ambitious scientific project ever undertaken; it will cost a whopping $3 billion and take at least 15 years to complete. By the

 From *American Health*, March 1989, pp. 103-106, 108. Copyright © by American Health Partners and the author.

HUMAN GENE MAPS

The latest maps for chromosomes one through six show the location of genes associated with hereditary disorders.

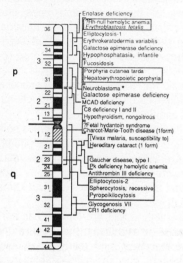

Enolase deficiency
[?Rh-null hemolytic anemia
Erythroblastosis fetalis]
Elliptocytosis-1
Erythrokeratodermia variabilis
Galactose epimerase deficiency
Hypophosphatasia, infantile
Fucosidosis
[Porphyria cutanea tarda
Hepatoerythropoietic porphyria]
Neuroblastoma *
Galactose epimerase deficiency
MCAD deficiency
C8 deficiency I and II
Hypothyroidism, nongoitrous
?Fetal hydantoin syndrome
Charcot-Marie-Tooth disease (1form)
[Vivax malaria, susceptibility to]
[Hereditary cataract (1 form)]
Gaucher disease, type I
Pk deficiency hemolytic anemia
Antithrombin III deficiency
Elliptocytosis-2
Spherocytosis, recessive
Pyropoikilocytosis
Glycogenosis VII
CR1 deficiency

Factor V deficiency

1

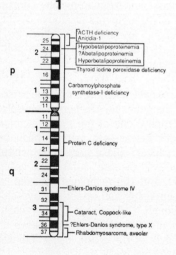

[ACTH deficiency
Aniridia-1]
[Hypobetalipoproteinemia
?Abetalipoproteinemia
Hyperbetalipoproteinemia]
Thyroid iodine peroxidase deficiency
Carbamoylphosphate
synthetase-I deficiency

Protein C deficiency

Ehlers-Danlos syndrome IV

Cataract, Coppock-like

?Ehlers-Danlos syndrome, type X
Rhabdomyosarcoma, aveolar

2

☐ Allelic disorders (due to different mutations in the same gene)
[ ] Nondisease
* Cancers
■ Malformation syndrome
{ } Specific infections with a single-gene basis for susceptibility
italics Maternofetal incompatibility

Adapted from gene maps provided by Dr. Victor A. McKusick

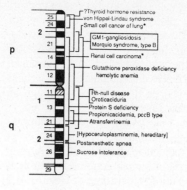

?Thyroid hormone resistance
von Hippel-Lindau syndrome
Small cell cancer of lung*
[GM1-gangliosidosis
Morquio syndrome, type B]
Renal cell carcinoma*
Glutathione peroxidase deficiency
hemolytic anemia
Rh-null disease
Oroticaciduria
Protein S deficiency
Propionicacidemia, pccB type
Atransferrinemia
[Hypoceruloplasminemia, hereditary]
Postanesthetic apnea
Sucrose intolerance

3

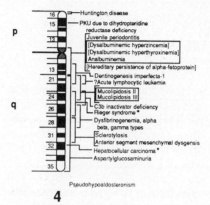

Huntington disease
PKU due to dihydropteridine
reductase deficiency
Juvenile periodontitis
[Dysalbuminemic hyperzincemia]
[Dysalbuminemic hyperthyroxinemia]
Analbuminemia
[Hereditary persistence of alpha-fetoprotein]
Dentinogenesis imperfecta-1
?Acute lymphocytic leukemia
[Mucolipidosis II
Mucolipidosis III]
C3b inactivator deficiency
Rieger syndrome *
Dysfibrinogenemia, alpha
beta, gamma types
Sclerotylosis
Anterior segment mesenchymal dysgenesis
Hepatocellular carcinoma *
Aspartylglucosaminuria

Pseudohypoaldosteronism

4

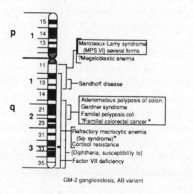

[Maroteaux-Lamy syndrome
(MPS VI) several forms]
?Megaloblastic anemia
Sandhoff disease
[Adenomatous polyposis of colon:
Gardner syndrome
Familial polyposis coli
?Familial colorectal cancer *]
Refractory macrocytic anemia
(5q- syndrome)*
Cortisol resistance
[Diphtheria, susceptibility to]
Factor VII deficiency

GM-2 gangliosidosis, AB variant

5

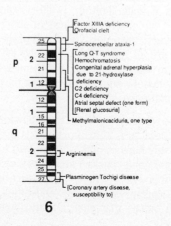

Factor XIIIA deficiency
Orofacial cleft
Spinocerebellar ataxia-1
Long Q-T syndrome
Hemochromatosis
Congenital adrenal hyperplasia
due to 21-hydroxylase
deficiency
C2 deficiency
C4 deficiency
Atrial septal defect (one form)
[Renal glucosuria]
Methylmalonicaciduria, one type

Argininemia

Plasminogen Tochigi disease
{Coronary artery disease,
susceptibility to}

6

time researchers are through, they will have deciphered the complete genome. They'll have drawn up a detailed genetic "map," with the size, position and role of all 100,000 human genes clearly marked. And they'll have figured out each gene's particular sequence of chemical components, called nucleotides.

Though there are only four types of nucleotides, represented by the letters A, T, C and G, spelling out all the combinations that make up our total genetic heritage will fill the equivalent of one million pages of text. "What we'll have," says Dr. Leroy Hood, a biologist at the California Institute of Technology in Pasadena, "is a fabulous 500-volume 'encyclopedia' of how to construct a human being." Nobel laureate Walter Gilbert goes so far as to describe the human genome as "the Holy Grail of biology."

Some scientists, however, think their colleagues are chasing a will-o'-the-wisp. Current genetic engineering techniques, say critics, are too embryonic to attempt anything as massive as sequencing the entire genome. Dr. Robert Weinberg of the Whitehead Institute in Cambridge, MA, calls the whole project "misguided" and doubts that scientists will gain major insights even if they can sequence it.

Still, researchers involved in the Human Genome Initiative insist the knowledge will revolutionize the fields of medicine, biology, health, psychology and sociology, and offer a bounty of applications. Using advanced recombinant DNA techniques, scientists will pluck out the genes that cause the 4,000 known hereditary diseases, including childhood brain cancer, familial colon cancer, manic depression, Huntington's disease—the neurological disorder that killed folk singer Woody Guthrie—and neurofibromatosis, or Elephant Man's disease. Beyond analyzing rare inherited disorders, researchers will glean fresh insights into the more common and complicated human plagues, such as heart disease, hypertension, Alzheimer's, schizophrenia, and lung and breast cancer. Those studies will enable scientists to develop new drugs to combat human disease.

But the Genome Initiative is not restricted to the study of sickness. As biologists decode the complete "text" of our genetic legacy, they'll be asking some profound questions: Are there genes for happiness, anger, the capacity to fall in love? Why are some people able to gorge themselves and still stay slim, while others have trouble losing weight no matter how hard they diet? What genetic advantages turn certain individuals into math prodigies, or Olympic athletes? "The information will be fundamental to us *forever*," says Hood, "because that's what we are."

The most imaginative scientists foresee a day when a physician will be able to send a patient's DNA to a lab for scanning to detect any genetic mutations that might jeopardize the patient's health. Nobel laureate Paul Berg, a biochemistry professor at Stanford, paints a scenario in which we'll each have a genome "credit card" with all our genetic liabilities listed on it. We'll go to a doctor and insert the card into a machine. Instantly reading the medical record, the computer will help the doctor to put together a diagnosis, prognosis and treatment course. Says Caltech's Hood, "It's going to be a brave new world."

Coping with that new world will demand some bravery of our own. Once our genetic heritage has been analyzed in painstaking detail, we'll have to make hard choices about who is entitled to that information, and how the knowledge should be used (see "Genetic Secrets: Who Should Know?"). This technology is proceeding at an incredible rate, and we have to be sure that it doesn't lead to discrimination in jobs, health insurance or even basic rights, says Dr. Jonathan Beckwith, a geneticist at Harvard Medical School. "We don't want a rerun of eugenics, where certain people were assumed to be genetically inferior, or born criminals."

For better or worse, politicians are convinced that the knowledge is worth seeking. This year, Congress has earmarked almost $50 million for genome studies and, if current trends continue, by 1992 the government should be spending about $200 million annually. Opponents worry the price tag could leave other worthy biomedical projects in the lurch.

Even at that level of funding, the genome project could be beyond the resources of any single country. That's why research teams from Europe, Asia, North America and New Zealand have joined to form the Human Genome Organization. Among other goals, the newly created consortium plans to distribute money for worthwhile projects worldwide. Meanwhile, the Paris-based Center for the Study of Human Polymorphism distributes cell samples to researchers and shares their findings through an international data bank.

In this country, Nobel laureate James Watson, the co-discoverer of the molecular structure of DNA, is in charge of human genome research at the National Institutes of Health. And Dr. Charles Cantor, a highly respected geneticist from New York's Columbia University, has accepted the top spot at the Department of Energy's Human Genome Center.

THE GENETIC HAYSTACK

The Genome Initiative is sure to affect everybody. Doctors estimate that each of us carries an average of four to five severe genetic defects in our DNA. The majority of those mutations are silent: They don't affect you. However, if you were to marry someone who carries the same defect, you could have a child who inherits both bad genes and is stricken with the disease.

Most genetic flaws are so rare that your chances of encountering another silent carrier are slim—let alone marrying and conceiving a child with such a person. But some defects are widespread. For example, five out of 100 people harbor the mutant cystic fibrosis gene; seven out of 100 blacks carry the trait for sickle cell anemia. Bob and Diane Peterson are both cystic fibrosis carriers—but they didn't realize their predicament until they gave birth to afflicted children.

For all the improvements of the last 10 years, prenatal diagnosis techniques remain limited. Doctors can screen fetuses for evidence of about 220 genetic disorders, but most of the tests are so time-consuming and expensive they won't be done unless family history suggests the child may have a disease.

One reason it's difficult to screen for birth defects is that most genes are devilishly hard to find. The 50,000 to 100,000 genes packed into every cell of your body are arrayed on 23 pairs of tiny, sausage-shaped chromosomes, which means that each chromosome holds a higgledy-piggledy collection of up to 4,400 genes. Scientists cannot look under a microscope to see the individual genes for cystic fibrosis, Down's syndrome or any other birth defect; instead, they must do elaborate chemical operations to distinguish one human gene from another. So daunting is the task of identifying individual genes that scientists have determined the chromosomal "address" of only about 2% of all human genes. "It's like finding a needle in a haystack," says Utah's Ray White.

Scientists must first chop up the 23 pairs of human chromosomes into identifiable pieces of genetic material and then study each fragment separately. To make the cuts, they use restriction enzymes—chemicals that break the bonds between particular sequences of nucleotides, the chemical components of genes.

Normally, restriction enzymes snip genetic material at predictable points, as precisely as a good seamstress cuts a swatch of fabric. But scientists have found that the enzymes also cut some fragments at unexpected places, yielding snippets that are longer than normal. It turns out that these variations are inherited, and many have been linked to certain genetic abnormalities. The fragments even serve as reference points for map-making efforts. The DNA segments produced by this technique are nicknamed "riff-lips," for restriction fragment length polymorphisms (RFLPs).

In the past three years, DNA sleuths have used the technique to isolate the genes for Duchenne muscular dystrophy, one of the most common genetic diseases; a grizzly childhood eye cancer; and a hereditary white-blood-cell disease commonly called CGD. But the technique remains labor-intensive and in some ways old-fashioned. Armies of graduate students and postdoctoral fellows do the bulk of the work, using tedious, error-prone methods.

Scientists everywhere are racing to build superfast computers to sort through chromosome samples and analyze RFLP patterns. Until they're devised, researchers are learning to make do. At White's lab, for instance, researchers have jerry-rigged a device that automatically dispenses exceedingly small samples of DNA into rows of test tubes. "It can do in two days what used to take a researcher two weeks," says a technician.

THE HAPGOODS BECOME IMMORTAL

Despite all the technology, the genome project remains deeply human—even folksy. That's because the people donating their blood and genes are from ordinary families who happen to have something extraordinary to offer. They're families like the Petersons, whose DNA may contain clues to cystic fibrosis.

Or they're families like the Hapgoods, whose greatest claim to fame may be their ability to live long and multiply. Brenda and Sam Hapgood,* a Mormon couple in their early 50s, are plump and boisterous, and love to be surrounded by people. That may explain why, although they have five girls, four boys, three sons-in-law, two daughters-in-law and five grandchildren, they wouldn't mind having a few more kids around. Says Brenda, "I almost wish I hadn't stopped at nine!"

The Hapgoods are one of 40 Utah families helping White construct a so-called linkage map of human DNA. He's trying to find chemical markers in the genome that are "linked" with certain genes. The markers will serve as bright signposts, dividing the snarl of genes into identifiable neighborhoods—just as road signs allow a traveler to pin down his location. Finding those markers is a crucial first step toward identifying the genes themselves, and for providing researchers with a decent chart of the terrain.

That's where the Hapgoods come in. To detect those tiny patches in the DNA that stand out from the background of surrounding genetic material, White must be able to compare the genomes of many related people over several generations. Mormon families are large, and they don't tend to move around much, so it's easy for White to get blood samples from many generations of a given family.

"The researchers told us there are lots of big families around," says Brenda. "What made us special was that all the grandparents were still with us."

In 1984, Brenda, Sam, their parents and nine children all donated blood to White's researchers. Lab technicians then used a special process to keep the blood cells alive and dividing forever—

ensuring an infinite supply of Hapgood DNA for study. "Our linkage families are becoming more and more important as we go to the next stage of mapping," says Mark Leppert, one of White's colleagues. "Hundreds of researchers from all over will be using the information from their DNA."

"We're going to go down in medical history!" Brenda says excitedly. "But you know what I'm really worried about?" one son-in-law teases her. "They might decide to clone you!"

Another reason the Hapgoods were chosen for the linkage study is because, in contrast to the Petersons, they didn't seem to have any major hereditary diseases. White wanted his general-purpose map to be a chart of normal human DNA. Ironically, however, two years after the Hapgoods first donated blood, one of the daughters gave birth to a son with a serious genetic defect known as Menkes' disease, a copper deficiency.

The child is two years old but looks like a deformed six-month-old. He has 100 or more seizures a day. Half his brain and most of his immune system have been destroyed. Cradled in his mother Carol's arms, he moans steadily and sadly. "This is as big as he'll get," says Carol. "He'll only live to be four at the very most."

Carol and Brenda hope that the genome project will someday bring relief for Menkes victims. "We originally volunteered for the study to help the scientists out, to help their research," says Brenda. "But now we see that it could be important for people like us."

THE BIG PAYOFF

"You don't need to have the whole project done before you start learning something," says Dr. Daniel Nathans, a Nobel laureate and professor of molecular biology and genetics at Johns Hopkins University in Baltimore. "There are things to be learned every step of the way." The first spin-offs are likely to be new tests for hereditary diseases. Within one to three years, biologists hope to have cheap and accurate probes to detect illnesses known to be caused by defects in a single gene, such as susceptibility to certain kinds of cancers.

Another inherited ailment that could quickly yield to genome research is manic depression, which is also thought to be caused by an error in any

one of several genes. The psychiatric disorder afflicts 1% of the population—2.5 million people in the U.S. alone—yet it's often difficult to diagnose. With the gene isolated, experts will be better able to distinguish between the disease and other mood disorders, explains Dr. Helen Donis-Keller, a professor of genetics at Washington University in St. Louis.

Of even greater relevance to the public, the Genome Initiative will give investigators their first handle on widespread disorders such as cancer, high blood pressure and heart disease. Researchers are reasonably certain that multiple DNA mutations share much of the blame for these adult plagues, but as yet they don't know which genes are involved. Only when biologists have an itemized map of the genome will they be able to detect complex DNA patterns that signal trouble in many genes simultaneously.

As the quest proceeds, surprises are sure to follow. "There are probably hundreds or thousands of important hormones yet to be isolated," says Dr. David Kingsbury, a molecular biologist at George Washington University. Among them, he believes, are novel proteins that help nerve cells grow, or *stop* growing. Such hormones could be made into new cancer drugs that target tumors while leaving the rest of the body unscathed.

"I have an intuitive feeling that this is going to open up all sorts of things we couldn't have anticipated," says Donis-Keller. "Even mundane things like obesity and baldness—imagine the implications of having new therapies for them!"

The human genome also holds keys to personality and the emotions. Department of Energy gene chief Charles Cantor says it's estimated that half of our 100,000 genes are believed to be active only in brain cells, indicating that much of our DNA evolved to orchestrate the subtle dance of thought, feeling, memory and desire. "There are genes that are very important in determining our personality, how we think, how we act, what we feel," says Cantor. "I'd like to know how these genes work." Donis-Keller is also curious. "Is panic disorder inherited? Is autism?" she wonders. "These are controversial questions we can start to clarify."

Like the first Apollo rocket, the Hu-

GENETIC SECRETS: WHO SHOULD KNOW

For all the enthusiasm surrounding the Human Genome Initiative, a few thoughtful observers have sounded a note of caution. The more we find out about our inborn quirks and predispositions, they warn, the greater is our responsibility not to abuse that information.

"What kinds of knowledge will be generated, and who will have access to that knowledge?" asks Dr. Thomas Murray, director of the Center for Biomedical Ethics at Case Western Reserve School of Medicine in Cleveland. There are broad issues society must confront:

■ Insurance Repercussions. Insurance companies may charge a significantly higher premium—or deny coverage—to anyone with a genetic susceptibility to a serious illness. Insurers might even require pregnant women to undergo a prenatal genetic workup and threaten to drop coverage if problems are spotted. This could influence some women to opt for abortion.

Some ethicists worry that society will also begin to make harsh value judgments about the genetic fitness of a fetus.

■ Genetic Discrimination. Employers might exploit genome information to discriminate against employees—not only with markers for heart disease or cancer, but depression, hyperexcitability, paranoia or any other personality trait deemed undesirable.

■ To Know or Not to Know. Would you really want to know you have an inborn risk for an incurable disease? Dr. Nancy Wexler, a psychologist at Columbia University College of Physicians and Surgeons, helped develop a genetic marker test for Huntington's disease, one of the most insidious of central nervous system afflictions. But Wexler, who has a 50/50 chance she inherited the disease from her mother, is wary about taking the test herself. Sometimes, she says, "ignorance can be bliss."

man Genome Initiative has cleared the launch pad in a noisy flame of promise. Its crew is international, and so too will be the fruits of exploration. When the human genome is sequenced from tip to tail, the DNA of many people is likely to be represented—perhaps that of the Hapgoods and the Petersons, perhaps that of a Venezuelan peasant family. "It's going to be a genetic composite," predicts Yale professor of genetics Frank Ruddle. "The Indians will work on their genomes, the Russians on theirs, the Europeans on theirs. We'll pool the data and have one great patchwork quilt.

"I get a lot of pleasure out of thinking of this as a world project. No one single person will be immortalized by the research. But it will immortalize us all."

HOW GENES SHAPE PERSONALITY

Scientists have speculated for generations that people are the products of their genes, but proof was lacking. Now that has changed. Solid evidence demonstrates that our very character is molded by heredity. If so, how much did Baby M's future hinge on which family got her? It's a new and disturbing twist in the nature-nurture debate.

■ Baby M's legal fate, at least for now, was decided in a New Jersey courtroom last week. But the judge's decision to award the 1-year-old girl to William and Elizabeth Stern, the biological father and his wife, rather than to the infant's surrogate mother, Mary Beth Whitehead, may be largely incidental to the kind of person Baby M will become. To a growing number of scientists, the baby who will now be known as Melissa Stern has already been irreversibly stamped by her genes.

A century after Charles Darwin voiced his philosophy of survival of the fittest, 60 years after the Tennessee "monkey trial" and the eugenics movement, 30 years after the unraveling of the human genetic code and a decade after the advent of a controversial theory of heredity called sociobiology, scientists are turning up impressive evidence that heredity has a greater influence on one's personality and behavior than either one's upbringing or the most crushing social pressure. The debate over what has been called "nature vs. nurture" seems to be taking a decisive turn.

New results from studies of identical twins—plus a host of findings in behavioral and animal research—are leading many scientists to conclude that genes not only control such physical characteristics as eye color and height but also profoundly influence human behavior and personality. "The pendulum is definitely swinging toward the side of the biologists and away from the environmentalists," says psychiatrist Herbert Leiderman of the Center for Advanced Study in the Behavioral Sciences at Stanford University.

Questions and dilemmas

That judgment raises vexing questions and troubling dilemmas. Are we who we are—rich or poor, smart or stupid, outgoing or retiring, aggressive or timid, law-abiding or criminal—because of genetic traits passed down through the ages? If genetic variations explain why children score differently on cognitive tests, for example, educators might well conclude that schools can do little to improve the performance of slow learners. Can heredity be overridden through social programs and the way we rear our children? If judicial officials accept that criminals tend to be born, not made, the result could be a throw-away-the-keys mentality that precludes rehabilitation.

A darker fear is running through the debate—that genetic determinism could be misused to "prove" that some races are inferior, that male dominance over women is natural and that social progress is impossible because of the relentless pull of the genes. "You can no longer simply assume equality when you are able to easily demonstrate subtle differences between people at the genetic level," warns microbiologist David Baltimore, a Nobel laureate at the Massachusetts Institute of Technology.

Much of the key investigative work on the role of genes in human behavior is done at the Minnesota Center for Twin and Adoption Research. Some researchers call it a "human ark"; hundreds of sets of twins have paraded through its doors since 1979 to be minutely scrutinized and tested. The center released its latest bombshell late in 1986. After exhaustively testing 348 sets of twins, including 44 pairs of identical twins raised separately, the institute's researchers concluded that how people think and act—their very personality—is determined more by the DNA in their cells than by society's influences. As detailed in the chart on page 23, such attributes as respect for authority, a vivid imagination and a propensity to talk to strangers were found to be largely preordained at conception. "The evidence is so compelling that it is hard to understand how people could *not* believe in the strong influence of genetics on behavior," says psychologist David Lykken of the Minnesota project.

Other studies have shown that genes seem to help explain alcoholism, depression and obesity—even sexual roles and preferences, and such phobias as fear of snakes and of strangers. The research bolsters what parents have always sensed: Even within a single family, each child, right from birth, is different. While parents may have the impression with their first child that they are the prime molders of his or her fate, the arrival of a second baby makes it clear that babies arrive with built-in likes and dislikes. "Every parent of one child is an environmentalist, and every parent of more than one becomes a geneticist," quips David Rowe, a University of Oklahoma psychologist who has studied how parents mold a child's character and ability.

A budding science

The claim that genes undergird human society is made most ardently by the young science of sociobiology. Drawing on biology, anthropology, law, psychology and economics, sociobiologists take the view that genes and environment act as parts of a single system, sometimes in concert and sometimes quite separately. In this view, the human mind, rather than being a tabula rasa to be filled in from birth by family and society, is "hard wired" before birth with a predisposed personality. This predisposition can be enhanced or suppressed, but not eliminated, by child rearing and other nurturing experiences. Sociobiologists believe that such traits as aggression, criminal tendencies and intellectual ability may be biologically inevitable.

Take criminal behavior. Research by psychologist Sarnoff Mednick at the University of Southern California shows that criminal tendencies follow striking hereditary patterns. Mednick traced the lives of 14,000 adopted children, looking for criminal echoes between the generations. To a remarkable degree, children whose biological parents were convicts were much more likely to become criminals themselves. Mednick and Harvard criminologist James Q. Wilson carefully point out that child rearing and other social factors certainly help determine who becomes a criminal—but they conclude that it is factors with a strong hereditary component, such as personality, physique and intelligence, that make some individuals likely criminals.

When Mednick announced his controversial findings, he was advised by several of his colleagues to burn them. "Some people had built their careers on the assumption that heredity was not a key player in human behavior," he says. "They just could not separate scientific fact from political dogma."

Mednick is confident that the small percentage of youngsters with genetic traits likely to predispose them to criminal behavior could be screened out and given special attention. "Aside from the obvious benefits to society," he says, "we would be diverting these children from criminal activities that lead to very unhappy lives." But Mednick's modest proposal is unlikely to get a tryout in the United States. The most recent effort to fund such research was explicitly rejected by Congress as racially motivated.

"Culture on a leash"

Sociobiology came to public view in 1975, when Harvard zoologist Edward O. Wilson published *Sociobiology: The New Synthesis,* which embodied an inflammatory philosophy he later summarized in a now notorious phrase: "Genes hold the culture on a leash." Although Wilson repeatedly explained that he doesn't mean that particular kinds of people are genetically superior to others, he was doused at a scientific meeting in 1978 with a bucket of water by protesters who denounced him as a "racist" and "Nazi."

In fact, Wilson and his colleagues have built their case carefully. They draw heavily on the many similarities between the ways people act and the unthinking behavior of lower animals. Hundreds of species from insects to primates display strikingly human courtship rituals, territorial claims and aggressiveness. Mallard ducks, for example, are known to commit what human beings would call rape. Chimpanzees form groups that conduct warlike raids and even genocide on neighboring tribes. Ant colonies have a social hierarchy that includes slaves. Mountain bluebirds engage in adultery. Dolphins often try to save injured dolphins from drowning. Lizards, seagulls and dogs as well as other species exhibit homosexual behavior. And throughout the animal kingdom, males usually are aggressors.

For the sociobiologists, that seems only logical. "All of us alive today are the result of 4 billion years of evolution," says biologist Robert Trivers of the University of California at Santa Cruz. "We have a set of genes that got here through a process we now understand as natural selection. These inter-

act with the environment to mold our behavior."

Love—or selfishness?

Couched in blandly academic language, the logic sounds unassailable. But sociobiologists like to ask, for example, whether a mother who dies to save her children—running back into a burning house, perhaps—is propelled, at the most fundamental level of biology, less by love than by genetic selfishness. Or whether prospective parents who undergo prenatal tests to detect such disorders as Tay-Sachs disease, sickle-cell anemia and Down's syndrome are simply practicing eugenics in modern dress by trying to weed out less-than-perfect human beings. And the way they get into trouble with their skeptical colleagues is by answering both questions: Probably.

How could "selfish genes" send a courageous mother to her death? The explanation, proposed by British anthropologist Richard Dawkins in 1976, is that self-sacrificing, altruistic behavior is simply a gene's built-in way of insuring its continued existence. Dawkins calls human beings "survival machines—robot vehicles that are blindly programed to preserve the selfish molecules known as genes."

Giving up your life to benefit others would scarcely seem to help propagate your genes. Sociobiologists point out, however, that while a mother who dies in rescuing her two children from a fire has sacrificed one copy of her genetic message, she has saved two copies—two offspring, each carrying all her genes. It's not so strange, then, that individual members of species from insects to Homo sapiens often risk their lives for their fellows. Bees die to save the hive. A bird will often give a warning cry to a flock of an approaching predator, even though it means that the sentinel almost certainly will die.

The selfish gene is one of the most divisive issues in the nature-nurture debate. Critics say that Dawkins's "my species right or wrong" tenet is simplistic. "Genes do not plan and scheme," says Harvard biologist Stephen Jay Gould. "They do not act as witting agents of their own preservation." Instead, Gould and others argue, people learn new ways to behave in response to changing situations and pass those successful behaviors on to their kin, perhaps counterbalancing messages passed through the chromosomes. If a selfish gene exists, they insist, social norms may overwhelm it.

When sociobiologists contend that their work is merely the latest chapter in the Darwinian revolution, they provoke a visceral reaction in many quar-

Extroverts are born, not made

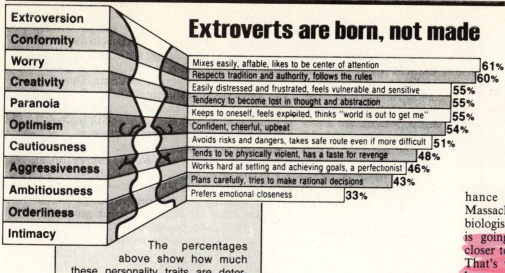

Extroversion	
Conformity	
Worry	
Creativity	
Paranoia	
Optimism	
Cautiousness	
Aggressiveness	
Ambitiousness	
Orderliness	
Intimacy	

Mixes easily, affable, likes to be center of attention	61%
Respects tradition and authority, follows the rules	60%
Easily distressed and frustrated, feels vulnerable and sensitive	55%
Tendency to become lost in thought and abstraction	55%
Keeps to oneself, feels exploited, thinks "world is out to get me"	55%
Confident, cheerful, upbeat	54%
Avoids risks and dangers, takes safe route even if more difficult	51%
Tends to be physically violent, has a taste for revenge	48%
Works hard at setting and achieving goals, a perfectionist	46%
Plans carefully, tries to make rational decisions	43%
Prefers emotional closeness	33%

The percentages above show how much these personality traits are determined by heredity rather than culture. The figures are based on new findings from the Minnesota Center for Twin and Adoption Research. Investigators there gave a lengthy test called the Multidimensional Personality Questionnaire to hundreds of identical twins and compared the results with those from the population at large, using standard computer programs that analyze statistical variation. For the 11 traits listed, researchers are confident they can make very close estimates of how much genes influence behavior in the general population—but what the percentages will be in one individual is impossible to say.

ters. "One of the more certain ways of insuring a lively and often acrimonious debate is to whisper the word 'sociobiology' in a crowd of academics," says Brandeis University anthropologist D. Neil Gomberg, who follows sociobiology at a discreet distance.

Unable to hold back the swelling tide of evidence for the importance of genes, supporters of the nurture side of the equation have tried to fight back with words. They cite the work of Ivan Pavlov, the famed Soviet psychologist whose salivating dogs inspired his description of the conditioned response, and B. F. Skinner, the Harvard psychologist renowned for his experiments with conditioning of rats and pigeons. Both behaviorists believed that individuals are programed totally by learned responses to the environment.

To call attention to what they see as the dangers of subscribing to genetic destiny, the nurturists lob political grenades. Those who believe in the prima-

cy of genes, observes Harvard biologist Ruth Hubbard, "portray people as biologically adapted to live in competitive, hierarchical societies in which men dominate women and a small, privileged group of men dominates everyone else." That "simplistic and dangerous" philosophy, says Christopher Jencks, a professor at Northwestern University at Evanston, Ill., ignores that crime, poverty and alienation have social causes, too.

Finally, the nurturists raise the specter that the principles of sociobiology are likely to be used irresponsibly by would-be social engineers. The eugenics movement of the 1920s, for instance, promised to improve the human species through selective breeding—but found a home instead in the horrific death-camp "medical experiments" of Josef Mengele in Germany. Critics of sociobiology hear an ominous echo in recent advances in genetic engineering that can select and en-

hance certain characteristics. Says Massachusetts Institute of Technology biologist Ethan Signer: "This research is going to bring us one more step closer to genetic engineering of people. That's where they figure out how to have us produce children with ideal characteristics. Last time around, the ideal children had blond hair, blue eyes and Aryan genes."

The Shockley case

Such worries aren't just hypothetical. Just three years ago, William Shockley, a Nobel Prize-winning physicist who argues that blacks are genetically inferior in intelligence to whites, took the stand in a $1 million libel suit against the *Atlanta Constitution* to discourse on "dysgenics"—his theory that intelligence is declining because of overbreeding among the "genetically disadvantaged," a category in which he includes most blacks. People of childbearing age whose IQ's measure below 100, whose incomes are too low to be taxed and who agree to be sterilized, Shockley proposed, should be paid $1,000 for each IQ point below 100. A column in the newspaper had compared his views to Nazi efforts to wipe out Jews and produce a superhuman race. The jury agreed that Shockley had indeed been libeled but awarded him a token $1 because he'd used the trial as a forum to draw attention to his views.

Singapore, on the other hand, has bought the Shockley doctrine. In this bustling Westernized country, people with less than a university education are rewarded for agreeing to be sterilized after the birth of their first or second child, and parents with degrees are being given incentives to have large numbers of children. Prime Minister Lee Kuan Yew promotes the policy by saying that gradual genetic deterioration will cause Singapore's national "levels of competence" to drop. "Our economy will falter, the administration will suffer and the society will decline," says Lee.

Could Shockley and Lee be right? Do different social classes have distinct genetic traits? Do "upper" classes gradually accumulate a superior gene pool? David Lebedoff, a Minneapolis attorney and author of the 1981 book *The New Elite,* answers yes to these last two questions. He puts the case for what he terms "biological stratification" bluntly: "People still marry within their social and economic class, but membership in such classes has come to depend more on measurable intelligence and less on circumstances of birth. People of high IQ marry other people of high IQ."

The ingredients that go into intelligence, however, go beyond genes. Intrigued because black youngsters seemed to score lower on standard IQ tests than their white counterparts, psychologist Sandra Scarr of the University of Virginia studied a group of black children raised by white, middle-class families. These children's IQ scores averaged 20 points higher than those of the other black children, large-ly because their home environments were superior. "IQ is a combination of heredity and educational environment," asserts Scarr. "A lot of agony has been fostered because the idea got out that intelligence was inborn and unchangeable."

Technology has given this flawed idea an updated twist. The Repository for Germinal Choice, a sperm bank in California, lures prospective mothers with the genes of Nobel Prize winners and other men of high achievement, some no longer living. So far, 39 children have been born with deep-frozen sperm from the repository—but it's too soon to tell whether genetic firepower has produced superior brainpower.

Given that no investigator has demonstrated that any one human being is 100 percent genetically preordained, the nature-nurture equation should be brought into perspective. "A lot of people have the simple-minded notion that a gene turns on and magically blossoms into a behavior," declares Gerald McClearn, a psychologist and twins researcher at Pennsylvania State University. "A gene can produce a nudge in one direction or another, but it does not directly control behavior. It doesn't take away a person's free will." Even E. O. Wilson, the most radical sociobiologist, doesn't believe that behavior goose-steps to the cadence of the genes. "Admitting that we are all influenced in different ways by our genetic coding doesn't reduce our freedom to do what we want to do," he says. The latest research clearly tips the scales toward the nature side—and that's all it does. Researchers agree that people are creatures both of their genetic coding and of their cultural and environmental experience. All scientists are doing is learning the proportions of the recipe.

Stanley N. Wellborn

MEN VS. WOMEN

Biology may not be destiny, but these days researchers are finding some significant differences between the sexes–and, in many ways, women are coming out ahead

 There was a time, not so long ago, when all the answers seemed clear. Everyone *knew* which was the weaker sex: Analyzed in terms of political power and bodily brawn, wasn't it obvious? Turn-of-the-century scientists produced learned tracts solemnly warning against an excess of exercise or education for girls: Too much activity—or thinking—would divert needed blood from their reproductive systems. Pseudoscientists meticulously measured human brains and found women's wanting (along with those of blacks and Irishmen). And when the new science of intelligence testing turned up repeated and systematic superiority among girls, researchers kept tinkering with the tests until they produced the "right" results.

We've come a long way since those bad old days. We have also moved beyond a backlash of 1970s feminist scholarship, which insisted with equal ideological fervor that apart from the obvious dimorphism of human beings, there were *no* real differences between the sexes—that seeming disparities in mental abilities, emotional makeup, attitudes and even many physical skills were merely the product of centuries of male domination and male-dominated interpretation.

Lately, in bits and pieces that are still the subject of lively debate, science has been learning more about the fine points of how men and women differ—more about their physiology, their psychology, the interplay between the two and the subtle ways society influences both. Among the questions these studies may help answer:

■ Are more women doomed to die of heart attacks as they rise to positions of power in the work world? Or are they peculiarly protected from the stresses that beleaguer modern men?

■ Is there something to be learned from female longevity that might help improve and prolong the lives of men?

■ Are boys always going to be better at math than girls? And why is it that there have been relatively few women of acknowledged artistic genius?

■ Are men, by nature, better suited than women to lead and manage other people? Or is it possible that society would be better off with women's ways in the board rooms, female fingers near the nuclear buttons?

The old answers, once so sure, just won't do any more. In *The Myth of Two Minds,* her provocative 1987 book analyzing findings on sex differences, Beryl Lieff Benderly put the argument succinctly: "Who had the stronger shoulders, who might unpredictably become pregnant, clearly meant a great deal when work and warfare ran on muscle power and conception lay as far beyond human control as the weather. But now, when every American fingertip commands horsepower by the thousands, when the neighborhood drugstore and clinic offer freedom from fertility, those two great physical differences weigh very lightly indeed in the social balance."

While scientists still have a long way to go, research in a dozen disciplines—from neurology, endocrinology and sports medicine to psychology, anthropology and sociology—is beginning to point in the same direction: There are differences between the sexes beyond their reproductive functions, the pitch of their voices, the curves of elbows and knees, the fecundity of hair follicles. Many of these differences suggest that women are at least as well equipped as men for life in the modern world—and that in some ways they are, in fact, the stronger sex.

DIVERGING PATHS
Differences appear as early as six weeks after conception

FETUS At first, the embryo has all the equipment to become either sex. The only clue to its destiny is buried deep in the genetic code, in the 23rd chromosome pair. In the sixth week of development, if the embryo has inherited a Y chromosome from its father, a gene signals the start of male development. In both sexes, hormones begin to prepare the brain for the changes of puberty a dozen years away.

INFANT At birth, the skeletons of girls are slightly more mature than those of boys. Some studies have suggested that newborn girls are slightly more responsive to touch and that infant boys spend more time awake. There is also evidence that boy infants respond somewhat earlier to visual stimuli, girls to sounds and smells.

TODDLER Boys gain and pass girls in skeletal maturity by the end of the first year. At the age of 2, boys begin to show signs of greater aggressiveness. At 3, a slight, early female edge in verbal ability disappears—but by 10 or 11, it is back. Boys begin to show superiority in spatial skills at the age of 8 or so, and at 10 or 11, they start outperforming girls in math.

ADOLESCENT Girls begin to fall behind in body strength. In both male and female, reproductive organs develop rapidly. Both spurt in height; when it is over, the average male will be 10 percent taller than the female. Meanwhile, the female superiority in verbal skills increases. So does the male edge in spatial skills and math.

ADULT The mature woman carries twice as much body fat as a man. And the man carries 1½ times as much muscle and bone. Because of the female hormone estrogen, which works to keep women's bodies in peak childbearing condition, women have some built-in health advantages—including more-pliable blood vessels and the ability to process fat more efficiently—and safely—than men.

OLD AGE After menopause, estrogen production drops off, and women lose some of the protection the hormone formerly provided. Even so, the advantages of her fertile decades persist for at least 15 years: Only slowly, for example, do the blood vessels become more rigid. The male can continue spermatogenesis into the late 80s and early 90s.

BODY

The distinctions are more than just skin-deep

If God created man first, He or She apparently took advantage of hindsight when it came to woman. Except for the moment of conception (when 13 to 15 males are conceived for every 10 females), the distaff side simply has a better chance at survival. Spontaneous abortions of boys outnumber those of girls. More males than females die during infancy, youth and adulthood. In every country in the world where childbirth itself no longer poses mortal danger to women, the life expectancy of females exceeds that of males. And in the United States, the gap is growing. A baby girl born today can look forward to nearly 79 years—seven more than a baby boy.

Why? Some of the answers seem to lie deep in the genes. Others doubtless float in the hormones that carry messages from organ to organ, even, some researchers believe, "imprinting" each human brain with patterns that can affect the ways it responds to injury and disease. The research suggests that females start out with some distinct biological advantages. Among them:

■ **THE GENETIC CODE.** Genesis was wrong: Women came first—embryologically speaking, at least. Genetically, the female is the basic pattern of the species; maleness is superimposed on that. And this peculiarity of nature has the side effect of making males more vulnerable to a number of inherited disorders.

The reason lies in the way our genes determine who's a male and who's a female. A normal embryo inherits 23 chromosomes from the mother and 23 from the father. One of these chromosome pairs, the 23rd, determines what sex the baby will be. From the mother, the embryo always receives an X chromosome. From the father, it receives either an X, creating a female, or a Y, creating a male.

The Y chromosome carries little more than the genetic signal that, in the sixth week of development, first defeminizes the embryo, then starts the masculinization process. In a female, the X chromosome supplied by the father duplicates much of the genetic information supplied by the mother. Thus, if there are potentially deadly genetic anomalies on one of the female's X chromosomes, the other may cancel their effects. But the male embryo has no such protection: What's written on his sole X chromosome rules the day. Among the X-linked troubles he is more likely to inherit: Colorblindness, hemophilia, leukemia and dyslexia.

■ **THE ESTROGEN FACTOR.** The main task of the female sex hormones, or estrogens, is to keep the female body prepared to carry and care for offspring. But as it turns out, what's good for female reproduction is also good for the arteries. One effect of estrogens, for example, is to keep blood vessels pliable in order to accommodate extra blood volume during pregnancy. That also reduces the risk of atherosclerosis. And because a developing fetus needs lots of carbohydrates but is unable to use much fat, the mother's body must be able to break down the extra fat left behind after the fetus's demands are met. Estrogen makes this happen by stimulating the liver to produce high-density lipoproteins (HDL), which allow the body to make more efficient use of fat—and help to keep arteries cleared of cholesterol.

The male hormone testosterone, by contrast, causes men to have a far higher concentration of *low*-density lipoprotein. "LDL forms and fixes in large amounts to the lining of the blood vessels," explains endocrinologist Estelle Ramey. "They become narrower and more fragile." That didn't matter 2 million years ago, when men were far more physically active: Exercise lowers the LDL count.

Long after menopause, when estrogen production drops dramatically, women maintain the cardiovascular advantages built up during their childbearing years. The Framingham study, a 24-year examination of the health of almost 6,000 men and women between the ages of 30 and 59, found approximately twice the incidence of coronary heart disease in men as in women, even in the upper age

REMARKABLE DIFFERENCES

Between 130 and 150 males are conceived for every 100 females. About 105 boys are born for every 100 girls. But by the time they reach the age of 20, there are only about 98 males per 100 females. And among those 65 and older, just 68 men survive for every 100 women.

Females have a better sense of smell than males from birth onward. They are also more sensitive to loud sounds. But males are more sensitive to bright light—and can detect more subtle differences in light.

It is physiologically more difficult for women than for men to maintain a desirable weight and still meet their nutritional needs.

Women on average spend 40 percent more days sick in bed than do men.

Sexual perversions—foot fetishes, for instance—are an almost exclusively male phenomenon.

Boys get more than 90 percent of all perfect scores of 800 on the math section of the Scholastic Aptitude Test. And the gap between SAT math scores for boys and girls is greatest—about 60 points higher for males—among students who are in the top 10 percent of their class.

Infant girls show a strong, early response to human faces—at a time when infant boys are just as likely to smile and coo at inanimate objects and blinking lights.

Boys are far more likely than girls to be left-handed, nearsighted and dyslexic (more than 3 to 1). Males under 40 are also more likely than females to suffer from allergies and hiccups.

ILLUSTRATIONS BY SCOTT SAWYER FOR USN&WR

range. And in an analysis of the health patterns of 122,000 U.S. nurses, Graham Colditz, assistant professor at Harvard Medical School, has found that women who use estrogen supplements after menopause cut their risk of heart attacks by a third.

So—would men live longer if they took doses of estrogens? So far, the answer is a resounding no. In experiments where men received estrogen supplements, "they dropped like flies," says Elaine Eaker, an epidemiologist at the National Institutes of Health—from heart attacks. Eaker speculates that men don't have the proper receptor sites for estrogen.

But there may be hope for greater longevity in highly experimental work on macrophages, cells that form part of the immune system. Macrophages, Ramey explains, "gobble up" unmetabolized glucose that randomly affixes itself to DNA—and would eventually cause damage. As people age, the macrophage system slows, and the damage gets worse. "Macrophage activity in females, because of estrogen, is much higher," says Ramey. It's the hope of researchers that they can find a way to increase and prolong that activity in both sexes.

■ **THE STRESS SYNDROME.** "Women," Ramey declares flatly, "respond better to stress." Although the evidence on how stress hurts the human body is still equivocal, there are two main hypotheses. The first is mechanical: Elevation of heart rate and blood pressure due to stress promotes damage to the inner lining of the artery wall, laying the groundwork for heart disease. The second is chemical: Increased production of stress hormones promotes arterial damage.

Ramey is one scientist who is convinced that stress does damage. And she puts the blame squarely on testosterone—and the fact that while the world has changed substantially, men's bodies have not. In the world where primitive man evolved, "testosterone is the perfect hormone." In effect, it orders neuroreceptors in the brain to drop everything else and react as quickly as possible to a release of stress hormones. This greater reaction to stress may be damaging in the long run, but the short-term benefits were much more important in an age when "the life expectancy was about 23," says Ramey. Today, when the average man is less likely to be threatened by a saber-toothed tiger than by a corporate barracuda, his stress reaction is exactly the same—and just as damaging to long-term health.

Perhaps because testosterone isn't egging them on, women seem to respond to stressful situations more slowly, and with less of a surge of blood pressure and stress hormones. Some researchers suspect that psychosocial factors also play a big role.

Dr. Kathleen Light, a specialist in behavioral medicine at the University of North Carolina, thinks women may have a different perception of just what situations are threatening. Women show much less stress than men, for instance, when asked to solve an arithmetic problem. But Light's preliminary data in a study of public speaking show that women experience about the same surge in blood pressure as men. "Women may respond more selectively than men," she suggests. "We think this reflects learned experience."

But Karen Matthews is not so sure. Postmenopausal women, she observes, show higher heart rates and produce more stress hormones than women who are still menstruating. This leads her back to the reproductive hormones. One possible conclusion: Estrogens may be better adapted than testosterone for the flight-or-fight situations of modern life.

■ **THE BRAIN PLAN.** Men's and women's brains really are different. Over the last decade, researchers have discovered that in women, functions such as language ability appear to be more evenly divided between the left and right halves of the brain; in men, they are much more localized in the left half. After strokes or injuries to the left hemisphere, women are three times less likely than men to suffer language deficits.

What accounts for these differences in brain organization? One clue: The central section of the corpus callosum, a nerve cable connecting the left and right halves of the brain, seems to be thicker in women than in men, perhaps allowing more right-brain-left-brain communication.

Many researchers think that sex hormones produced early in fetal development—as well as after birth—literally "sex" the brain. In young animals, says neuroendocrinologist Bruce McEwen of New York's Rockefeller University, "the brain cells respond to testosterone by becoming larger and developing different kinds of connections."

These changes add up to big behavioral differences. Inject a female rat pup with testicular hormones, for instance, and it will mount other females just like a male. And it's not just a matter of mating. Male rat pups deprived of testicular hormones perform more poorly on maze tests than normal males; young females injected with testicular hormones do better. Many researchers are convinced that hormones have similar effects on human brains. Males produce testosterone from the third to the sixth month of gestation. Another burst is released just after birth, and then one final spurt at the onset of puberty—roughly coinciding with the time boys begin to surpass girls in math. What's more, males with an abnormality that makes their cells insensitive to testosterone's effects have cognitive profiles identical to girls: Their verbal IQ is higher than in normal males and their "performance" IQ (correlated with mechanical ability) is inferior to that of normal males.

Such findings are highly controversial. Feminist scholars, in particular, fear that they will give new life to the notion that biology is destiny—and that females just aren't the equal of men at certain tasks. But biodeterminists tend to ignore a critical difference between humans and other animals: The hugely complex human brain is not simply the sum of its synapses. There are other factors at play.

MIND

Different ways of thinking, from math to morals

Declare that women are more sensitive to the color red, and you get a few raised eyebrows. Argue that females are—by nature—not as good as males at mathematics, and you'll get outrage. Not surprisingly, intellectual ability is the arena in which sex differences are most hotly disputed. The stakes are high: Research findings can influence funding and policy decisions in everything from education to employment.

Most of the controversy over sex differences has focused on the longstanding male edge on tests of math aptitude. And it was further fueled in 1980, when Johns Hopkins University researchers Camilla Benbow and Julian Stanley reported on a study of 10,200 gifted junior-high students who took the Scholastic Aptitude Test between 1972 and 1979. Their conclusion: Boys were far more likely than girls to be mathematically talented. The researchers went on to speculate that there may be 13 male math geniuses for every female with such talent—and that the sex differences in math are the result of biological factors, perhaps exposure to the male sex hormone testosterone.

The Johns Hopkins studies were savagely attacked from the moment they were released. For one thing, the SAT's regularly have shown wider differences in male-female scores than other math tests. And the population that Benbow and Stanley studied is by definition exceptional: Its performance does not necessarily mean anything about boys and girls in general.

MATTERS OF LIFE AND DEATH

About 60 percent of the gap in mortality rates between the sexes is the result of increased social risks for men—smoking, drinking and fatal accidents; some demographers expect women will lose some of that advantage soon, as the rise of female smoking during the 1950s begins to show up in the statistics. The other 40 percent seems rooted in biology. Women are sick more often than men and more likely to suffer from chronic conditions. But men are more likely to suffer from killers like heart disease. The bottom line: The risk of death is higher for males of all ages—and for every leading cause of death.

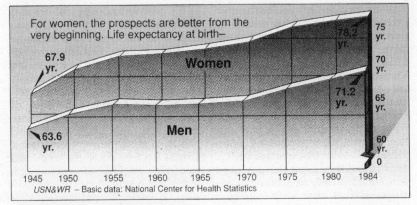

For women, the prospects are better from the very beginning. Life expectancy at birth—

67.9 yr. ... 78.2 yr. ... 75 yr. ... 70 yr. ... Women ... 71.2 yr. ... 65 yr. ... 63.6 yr. ... Men ... 60 yr. ... 0

1945 1950 1955 1960 1965 1970 1975 1980 1984

USN&WR – Basic data: National Center for Health Statistics

WOMEN
Chronic conditions that afflict women between the ages of 45 and 64 more often than they appear in men of the same age group. The percentages indicate the higher prevalence of each disorder among women, as compared with its rate among men

Nonfatal	
Thyroid diseases	551%
Bladder infection, disorders	382%
Anemias	378%
Bunions	335%
Spastic colon	305%
Frequent constipation	253%
Varicose veins	233%
Migraine headaches	175%
Diverticulitis of intestines	152%
Chronic enteritis and colitis	111%
Sciatica	85%
Trouble with corns, calluses	82%
Neuralgia and neuritis	79%
Gallstones	64%
Arthritis	59%
Dermatitis	59%
Gastritis and duodenitis	54%
Heart rhythm disorders	43%
Diseases of retina	32%

Fatal	
Asthma	41%
High blood pressure*	8%

MEN
Chronic conditions that afflict men between the ages of 45 and 64 more often than they appear in women of the same age group. Percentages indicate the higher prevalence of each disorder among men, as compared with its rate among women

Nonfatal	
Visual impairments	49%
Hearing impairments	46%
Paralysis, complete or partial	25%
Tinnitus	21%
Hernia of abdominal cavity	18%
Intervertebral disk disorders	14%
Hemorrhoids	5%

Fatal	
Emphysema	59%
Atherosclerosis	54%
Ischemic heart disease	51%
Cerebrovascular disease	32%
Liver disease including cirrhosis	23%
Other selected heart diseases	3%
Ulcer of stomach, duodenum	3%

* A risk factor for fatal circulatory diseases. Women's higher prevalence rates are thought to reflect earlier diagnosis and control, compared with men. For younger, premenopausal women, high blood pressure is less common than among men, and more men die from the disease because of damage done to their blood vessels at the younger age, when they do contract it in higher proportions.
USN&WR—Basic data: Lois Verbrugge of University of Michigan and unpublished data from the National Health Interview Surveys, 1983-85

ILLUSTRATION BY DALE GLASGOW AND CHART BY SARAH SHAW—USN&WR

But many other tests have consistently turned up a male superiority in math as well. And the explanation of the results offered by critics—that boys traditionally have been *expected* to do better at math, so they got more encouragement from parents and teachers—doesn't quite wash, either. Girls get better average *grades* in math at every level.

Lately, some researchers have found hints that testosterone plays a role in enhancing math aptitude: Girls who have received abnormal doses of it in the womb seem to do better than average on the tests.

Whatever the explanation, however, the gap is narrowing. According to psychologist Janet Hyde of the University of Wisconsin, a preliminary analysis of dozens of studies of sex differences suggests that the gap has been cut in half in the past seven years.

But on another cognitive front—visual-spatial ability—males still hold an undisputed edge. The male advantage begins to show up around the age of 8, and it persists into old age.

Some simple explanations are tempting: A few researchers have even suggested that a single, sex-linked gene is responsible for the male edge in analyzing and mentally manipulating three-dimensional objects. Like hemophilia, such a sex-linked trait could be carried by both men and women but would become active in a woman only rarely—when both of her X chromosomes carried the gene. Men, who have only one

X chromosome, would by contrast need only a single copy of the gene to acquire the ability.

But there are no rigorous data to support the idea: No gene has been identified, nor has anyone been able to trace the inheritance of an enhanced spatial ability from mothers to sons—as has been done extensively in the case of hemophilia. Moreover, most researchers are skeptical that such a complex ability as spatial reasoning could possibly rest in a single gene.

Many researchers are thus beginning to suspect that the male superiority is the product of a combination of factors—genetic, hormonal and cultural—with roots deep in humanity's hunting-gathering past.

Nature vs. nurture

Separating out those various factors is a daunting task. One promising approach is to study sex differences as they develop, rather than merely focusing on aptitude-test scores. Among the recent findings:
■ Females are more attracted to people and males to objects.

Numerous studies show that girl infants between 5 and 6 months detect differences in photographs of human

faces, while males of the same age do not. In addition, writes psychologist Diane McGuinness, studies on very young infants show that "females smile and vocalize only to faces, whereas males are just as likely to smile and vocalize to inanimate objects and blinking lights." McGuinness concludes that there probably is a biological predisposition in females to caretaking behavior that is later reinforced by observing adults.
■ Boys have a shorter attention span.

McGuinness has conducted a series of studies of sex differences in preschool children. Her results are intriguing: In a given 20-minute interval, boys did an average of 4.5 different activities, while girls concentrated on 2.5. Girls started and finished more projects than the boys. Boys were more distractible, interrupting their play to look at something else almost four times as often as girls—and they also spent more time in general watching other kids. Why the difference? "Maybe boys are just more visually oriented, and they learn by watching," McGuinness suggests.
■ Boys and girls differ in their approach to moral problems.

The pioneering work in the study of moral development was carried out 20 years ago by Harvard psychologist Law-

Are males better at math? Try it yourself

Tests of cognitive ability have long shown a male edge in mathematics and visual-spatial skills and a female advantage in work needing verbal aptitude

Mathematical

A kindergarten class wants to buy a $77 tropical tree for the school. If the teacher agrees to pay twice as much as the class and the administration promises to pay four times as much as the class, how much should the teacher pay?

(A) $11.00   (C) $22.00
(B) $15.40   (D) $25.70
                (E) $38.50

Answer: C

If x, y and z are three positive whole numbers and x > y > z, then, of the following, which is closest to the product xyz?

(A) (x-1)yz   (C) xy(z-1)
(B) x(y-1)z   (D) x(y+1)z
                  (E) xy(z+1)

Answer: A

Boys and girls do about equally well at arithmetic-problem solving. But when it comes to higher mathematics, boys have long shown a distinct advantage on average—even over girls who have taken comparable courses.

Spatial-visual

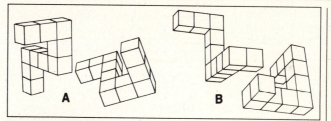

Can these pairs of three-dimensional objects be superimposed by rotation?

Answers: A yes; B yes

Males consistently outscore females in spatial-visual-abilities tests. At a young age, they are better on mazes; later, they show particular talent on exercises requiring mental manipulation of three-dimensional "objects" like those in the drawing above. The average 12-year-old boy knows that the water level remains horizontal in both glasses, but about half of college women get the answer wrong.

Verbal

Five girls are sitting side by side on a bench. Jane is in the middle, and Betty sits next to her on the right. Alice is beside Betty, and Dale is beside Ellen, who sits next to Jane. Who are sitting on the ends?

Answer: Dale and Alice

Assume that these glasses are half filled with water. Draw a line to indicate the top of the waterline in each.

Mark the "word" that *best* fills the blank:

A gelish lob relled perfully.

I grolled the _____ meglessly.

(A) gelish (B) lob (C) relled (D) perfully

Answer: B

During early adolescence, girls begin to outperform boys on tests of verbal ability, including questions designed to measure their understanding of logical relationships. The female edge persists into adulthood.

Sources: *Bias in Mental Testing*, by Arthur R. Jensen (the Free Press); *The Psychology of Sex Differences*, by Eleanor Emmons Maccoby and Carol Nagy Jacklin (Stanford University Press); *Sex Differences in Cognitive Abilities*, by Diane F. Halpern (Lawrence Erlbaum Associates); College Entrance Examination Board

rence Kohlberg. But as one of his former students, Carol Gilligan, notes, Kohlberg's research seemed to assume that "females simply do not exist": He studied 44 boys over 20 years, but no girls.

Gilligan has retraced some of Kohlberg's steps, including girls this time, and found some highly interesting differences between the sexes. One example: Gilligan posed one of the "moral dilemmas" Kohlberg used in his studies to a boy and a girl, both 11 years old. The dilemma involves the case of "Heinz," who faces the choice of stealing a drug his wife needs to stay alive but which he cannot afford, or obeying the law and letting her die. Jake, the boy, thought Heinz should steal the drug because a life is worth more than property. Amy, the girl, argued that the problem was more complicated: "I think there might be other ways besides stealing it, like if he could borrow the money or make a loan or something. If he stole the drug, he might save his wife then, but if he did, he might have to go to jail, and then his wife might get sicker again and he couldn't get more of the drug."

In Gilligan's analysis, Amy sees the moral problem in terms of "a narrative of relationships that extend over time." Jake, by contrast, sees a "math problem."

Even a few years ago, research on sex differences still met enormous resistance from feminists and others who believed that merely posing the question was unscientific at best, politically inspired at worst. Diane McGuinness recalls the rejection she received once from a scientific journal when she submitted a paper on cognitive processes in males and females. One of the scientific referees who reviewed the paper wrote: "The author *purports* to find sex differences. Who cares!"

That attitude is beginning to change. "As time passes, people are less frightened and less rigid," says Grace Baruch, associate director of the Center for Research on Women at Wellesley College. Scholars are finding that a focus on "female" psychology and behavior can add much to a body of knowledge built almost exclusively upon studies of males. And new statistical techniques have also made the investigation of sex differences more reliable.

The new wave of results has even made converts of researchers who were skeptical that sex differences existed. "I've had to revise my view considerably," confesses Purdue University social psychologist Alice Eagly. Still, she adds, "the public needs to be warned that knowing a person's sex doesn't allow you to predict much of anything about him or her." The overlap between men and women is still much greater than their average differences. There are males who

are every bit as adept at verbal skills as even the best females—and women who are better at math than most men.

ATTITUDE

In politics and management, the "gender gap" is real

There is one difference between the sexes on which virtually every expert and study agree: Men are more aggressive than women. It shows up in 2-year-olds. It continues through school days and persists into adulthood. It is even constant across cultures. And there is little doubt that it is rooted in biology—in the male sex hormone testosterone.

If there's a feminine trait that's the counterpart of male aggressiveness, it's what social scientists awkwardly refer

to as "nurturance." Feminists have argued that the nurturing nature of women is not biological in origin, but rather has been drummed into women by a society that wanted to keep them in the home. But the signs that it is at least partly inborn are too numerous to ignore. Just as tiny infant girls respond more readily to human faces, female toddlers learn much faster than males how to pick up nonverbal cues from others. And grown women are far more adept than men at interpreting facial expressions: A recent study by University of Pennsylvania brain researcher Ruben Gur showed that they easily read emotions such as anger, sadness and fear. The only such emotion men could pick up was disgust.

What difference do such differences make in the real world? Among other things, women appear to be somewhat less competitive—or at least competitive in different ways—than men. At the Harvard Law School, for instance, female students enter with credentials just as outstanding as those of their male peers. But they don't qualify for the prestigious *Law Review* in proportionate

---

A DIFFERENCE OF OPINION

Percentage-point margins by which women adopt these positions more than men. (Negative numbers indicate men agree more than women.)

	1964-71	1972-76	1977-83	1984-88
Oppose–				
Use of force	12.2%	8.3%	8.4%	9.0%
Strong defense	7.2%	5.7%	5.9%	1.1%
Support–				
Spending on social programs	3.2%	2.2%	4.1%	3.6%
Government regulation	3.0%	4.9%	7.2%	-1.1%
Traditional values	-0.9%	2.2%	3.6%	5.4%
Women's rights	-3.6%	-2.1%	-2.3%	-3.7%

USN&WR–Basic data: Study by Robert Y. Shapiro and Harpreet Mahajan and Roper Center for Public Opinion Research at Univ. of Connecticut

Gender gap in action

Share of men and women surveyed who would vote for–

■ Bush   ▦ Dukakis

Women: 34% / 58%   Men: 40% / 50%

USN&WR–Basic data: Gallup Poll on July 22-24, 1988, of 1,001 registered voters

Share of men and women surveyed who feel the following descriptions apply to Bush or Dukakis–

Strong leader
Women: 43% / 57%   Men: 50% / 52%

Cares about people
Women: 51% / 70%   Men: 50% / 68%

Has a vision for the future
Women: 59% / 72%   Men: 63% / 66%

USN&WR–Basic data: Washington Post-ABC News Poll May 19-25, 1988, of 1,172 registered voters

CHART BY SARAH SHAW—USN&WR

numbers, a fact some school officials attribute to women's discomfort in the incredibly competitive atmosphere.

Students of management styles have found fewer differences than they expected between men and women who reach leadership positions, perhaps because many successful women deliberately imitate masculine ways. But an analysis by Purdue social psychologist Alice Eagly of 166 studies of leadership style did find one consistent difference: Men tend to be more "autocratic"—making decisions on their own—while women tend to consult colleagues and subordinates more often.

Studies of behavior in small groups turn up even more differences. Men will typically dominate the discussion, says University of Toronto psychologist Kenneth Dion, spending more time talking and less time listening.

Political fallout

The aggression-nurturance gulf even shows up in politics. The "gender gap" in polling is real and enduring: Men are far more prone to support a strong defense and tough law-and-order measures such as capital punishment, for instance, while women are more likely to approve of higher spending to solve domestic social problems such as poverty and inequality. Interestingly, there is virtually no gender gap on "women's issues," such as abortion and day care; in fact, men support them slightly *more* than women.

That fact might serve as a lesson in this year's election campaign. Alarmed at George Bush's low marks among women, his strategists have aimed their candidate directly at the "women's issues." It may be the wrong tactic. A close look at recent polls suggests that it's not the specifics of his programs, but a far bigger problem—his weak image in terms of strength, compassion and vision—that bothers women voters about Bush. And there's a political footnote to the differences between the sexes in the Democratic camp. Veteran strategist Kirk O'Donnell, a top adviser to Michael Dukakis, says flatly that his is one of the best campaign organizations he has ever observed—with a remarkable lack of intramural squabbling, which O'Donnell attributes squarely to the unusually high number of women in senior positions.

Applied to the female of the species, the word "different" has, for centuries, been read to mean "inferior." At last, that is beginning to change. And in the end, of course, it's not a question of better or worse. The obvious point—long lost in a miasma of ideology—is that each sex brings strengths and weaknesses that may check and balance the other; each is half of the human whole.

by Merrill McLoughlin with Tracy L. Shryer, Erica E. Goode and Kathleen McAuliffe

Extraordinary People

Understanding the remarkable abilities of the "idiot savant" could help us unlock deep secrets about our own minds.

Darold Treffert, M.D.

Darold Treffert, M.D., a psychiatrist, has been director of several Wisconsin psychiatric hospitals, and has studied savants for the last twenty-six years. He lectures frequently on the subject throughout the country.

LESLIE HAS NEVER HAD any formal musical training. Yet upon hearing Tchaikovsky's Piano Concerto no. 1 for the first time when he was a teenager, he played it back on the piano flawlessly and without hesitation. He can do the same with any other piece of music, no matter how long or complex. Yet he cannot hold a utensil to eat and can only repeat in monotone that which is spoken to him. Leslie is blind, is severely mentally handicapped, and has cerebral palsy.

George and his identical twin brother, Charles, can rattle off all the years in which your birthday fell on a Thursday. They can also tell you, within a span of forty thousand years backward or forward, the day of the week on which any date you choose fell, or will fall. In their spare time George and Charles swap twenty-digit prime numbers for amusement. Yet they cannot add simple figures or even tell you what a formula is, let alone write one out.

Kenneth is thirty-eight years old but has a mental age of eleven. His entire conversational vocabulary consists of fifty-eight words. Yet he can give the population of every city and town in the United States that has a population of over five thousand; the names, number of rooms, and locations of two thousand leading hotels in America; the distance from each city and town to the largest city in its state; statistics concerning three thousand mountains and rivers; and the dates and essential facts of over two thousand leading inventions and discoveries.

All of these people are examples of the fascinating phenomenon called the *idiot savant,* a term coined by J. Langdon Down of London some one hundred years ago, when the word *idiot* did not have the negative, comical implication it now carries. At that time, *idiot* was an accepted medical and psychological term referring to a specific level of intellectual functioning—an IQ level of less than twenty-five. The word *savant* was derived from a French word meaning "to know" or "man of learning." The observation that persons with severe mental handicap displayed advanced levels of learning, albeit in very narrow ranges, led to the once descriptive, still colorful juxtaposition of the two words.

Understandably, some people object to the term *idiot savant* because the word *idiot* now gives the condition a connotation that is neither deserved nor fair. Therefore, the terms *savant* and *Savant Syndrome* will be used hereafter in referring to these remarkable people and the astonishing phenomenon they represent.

Savant syndrome is a condition in which persons with major mental illness or major intellectual handicap have spectacular islands of ability and brilliance that stand in stark, startling contrast to their handicaps. In some savants—those I call *talented savants*—the skills are remarkable simply in contrast to the handicap, but in other, more rare savants—those I call *prodigious*—the abilities and skills would be remarkable even if seen in normal people.

Until now, the scientific articles and media presentations describing the several hundred savants discovered during this past century have been isolated, anecdotal accounts of single individuals and their extraordinary stories. But there is much more to Savant Syndrome than interesting stories. Among these remarkable people, diverse as they may at first appear, is a commonality that deserves study, for in the future it may provide a key to better understanding not only how *they*—handicapped but with uncommon talent—function, but also how *we*—without handicap but with common talent—function as well. Of particular promise is what Savant Syndrome might tell us about memory (and thus conditions such as Alzheimer's disease), the nature of creativity, and the elusive relationship between memory and emotion.

At present, the significance of Savant Syndrome lies in our inability to explain it. The savants stand as a clear reminder of our ignorance about ourselves, for no model of brain function—particularly memory—could be complete unless it included and accounted for this remarkable condition.

When confronted by Savant Syndrome, so many questions leap up: How can extremely handicapped persons possess these islands of genius? What do they have in common? Why, with all the skills in the human repertoire, do the skills of the savant always fall in such narrow ranges and include such rare talents as calendar calculating?

Why is phenomenal memory seen in all the savants, no matter what exceptional individual skills they exhibit? Is the savant's memory qualitatively different from normal memory? Is their genius a direct result of their deficiencies, or do the two factors coexist coincidentally?

What can we learn about this spectacular dysfunction of mind and memory that might provide clues to normal mind and memory? Might the existence of these geniuses among us suggest that some such genius lies within each of us, waiting to be tapped?

The time has come to take the savants out of the "Gee Whiz" category and learn what we can about them, and from them—not just about memory and brain function, but about human potential as well.

I MET MY FIRST SAVANT on July 1, 1959. I was twenty-six years old and had just completed a residency in psychiatry at University Hospital in Madison, Wisconsin.

My first professional assignment was to develop and direct a thirty-bed Children's Unit at Winnebago State Hospital near Oshkosh, Wisconsin. As I walked onto the unit that first day, I noticed David. He stood there with a device he had fashioned out of cardboard and pencils that held a rolled-up paper scroll on which perhaps a hundred names were neatly written. As David turned the pencil on which the scroll had been wound, each name came into view, one at a time, through an opening in the cardboard that had been placed over the scroll. The device looked just like the window on the front of a bus where the destinations are listed and changed as the bus

route changes. And that's just what it was. The names on David's homemade scroll were the names of streets—Capitol Drive, State Street, Lincoln Avenue. David had memorized the bus system of Milwaukee. If you gave him the number of a bus and the time of day, he could tell you at which corner the bus was then stopping.

David was a very disturbed boy. His violent temper and his severe behavioral problems necessitated continuous hospitalization. His overall functioning was at a very low level—except for this one peculiar area of exceptional ability. He would have made a great cab dispatcher.

There were other savants on this unit. Billy could make free throws. Could he ever make free throws! He was like a baseball pitching machine, except he used a basketball. He always stood in exactly the same place at the free-throw line, with his feet in exactly the same position and his body in the same stance. For every shot his arm motions were identical, as were the arcs of the ball. He never missed. He showed no emotion, no overcorrection or undercorrection. There was nothing to correct. He was a basketball robot. Unfortunately, he had the same robot-like approach to everything. His mutism and his inability to communicate were evidence of his profound emotional and behavioral disturbance, which required his hospitalization on a long-term basis.

Then there was Tony. Unlike Billy, Tony did use language and, in fact, was a voracious reader. But he, too, had a serious behavioral condition that caused him to make vicious attacks against himself, and sometimes toward others. Tony knew history. He delighted each day in approaching visitors or staff—including new young doctors like me—asking them the significance of that particular date in history. Usually he elicited no answer, or just a few wild guesses, and so Tony would begin spouting off a long list of events that occurred throughout history on that day, much like the radio announcer on the morning show that I listened to on my way to work. Except that the announcer read his information

from an almanac. Tony, it seemed, was an almanac.

There were other cases on the unit similar to those of David, Billy, and Tony. I was struck by the islands of intelligence, even genius, that existed in what otherwise was a sea of severe handicap and disability. I soon became fascinated by this paradox of ability and disability, and began my research studying its appearance in patients with Early Infantile Autism, a form of childhood schizophrenia marked by withdrawal. My work eventually put me in touch with researchers throughout the world who were working in related fields. But it also left me with some lingering questions regarding Savant Syndrome—questions that remained unanswered for years.

AFTER TWO YEARS developments in my career forced me to put aside my work with Savant Syndrome until 1979, when I left Winnebago to begin a private practice and run a 150-bed community mental health center in the nearby community of Fond du Lac. Though I had mentally filed away the data on the autistic children I had seen fifteen years earlier on the Children's Unit—and on the savant skills present in some of them—the phenomenon continued to intrigue me.

I didn't see many autistic children in my Fond du Lac practice. What I did see, though, were a number of adult patients on whom I was conducting sodium amytal (truth serum) interviews as a means of enhancing their recall of buried memories and hidden traumas. In those interviews, patients remembered—in extraordinarily minute detail—a whole variety of experiences they thought they had forgotten. It was a demonstration of memory powers that, like Savant Syndrome, seemed to redefine human potential.

In some instances an entire journey down a particular street on a particular night would be recalled with exquisite attention to particulars—changing traffic lights, street signs, and passing cars. Both the patients and I were often startled by the voluminous amount of material that was in storage but unavailable in an everyday waking state. It was as if some

Some researchers have suggested that such extraordinary talents might be acquired from a shared field of knowledge similar to psychologist Carl Jung's "collective unconscious."

sort of tape recorder were running all the time, recording all of our experiences. The memories were there. What was missing was access and recall.

Simultaneously, reports were cropping up in scientific literature about neurosurgical studies of brain mapping, especially concerning the use of tiny electrical probes to determine epileptogenic foci—the seizure trigger—in the exposed cortex of patients who suffered certain kinds of seizures. The brain itself has no pain fibers within it; the pain fibers are in the surrounding capsule of the brain, the dura mater. Once the dura is numbed with a local anesthetic, the patient can remain awake while the surgeon uses a tiny electrical probe to find the site where certain kinds of seizures are triggered. This site then can be surgically removed and some seizure disorders corrected. In the random search for these foci, the probe hits a variety of spots on the cortex, and when it does, memories flood the patient's consciousness.

These memories, long forgotten by our conscious minds, are the kind of "random" recollections we often experience in our dreams: the fifth birthday party, including all the guests present; a day in class twenty years earlier; a walk on a particular path on a particular day, complete with the accompanying aromas and sound. If we were to remember such dream memories upon awakening, we would dismiss them, wondering, Where did that come from? But we know their origin in these instances: The probe had activated a circuit or pathway not ordinarily available to us.

I filed away these accounts, too, along with my observations of the savants I had known, as I continued to be busy with many other things.

Then, in June 1980, I met Leslie Lemke.

THE DEPARTMENT of social services had invited May Lemke and her remarkable foster son, Leslie—then twenty-eight—to give a concert honoring the foster parents of the county. I did not attend, but a short time afterward, in the wake of the publicity that followed, I became intrigued and decided to visit Leslie and his foster parents at their small cottage on Lake Pewaukee.

When I arrived, Leslie was sitting in a chair in his music room, a converted porch. He sat motionless and silent, but he seemed contented and at ease. He echoed my name when May told him who I was. Then he sat motionless and mute once again. May could hardly wait for him to play for me. She was so proud. Despite his blindness he walked unaided,

feeling his way, from the chair to the piano.

Then he played. I don't recall what the song was, but I do recall what I felt—astonishment, fascination, and inspiration. I still have the same reaction, many years and many tunes later, whenever I see and hear Leslie play. Here was someone with a triple handicap—blindness, retardation, and cerebral palsy—playing, for his audience of three, a concert worthy of an audience of a thousand. Though he had had no formal training, piece after piece poured forth: hymns, concertos, arias, popular songs, and imitations of singers. Some pieces he sang; some he just played. Some of the lyrics were in English, some in German, and some in Greek.

Leslie is the most remarkable savant I have ever met, read about, or studied. He was born prematurely in Milwaukee on January 31, 1952, and his mother immediately gave him up for adoption. He spent the first months of his life at Milwaukee County Children's Home. There it was noticed that the baby did not open his eyes, which were swollen and hard and had cloudy corneas. The doctors diagnosed his condition as retrolental fibroplasia, a disorder often seen in premature infants in which the retina proliferates wildly and sometimes, as in this case, blocks drainage in the eye, creating childhood glaucoma or a condition called *buphthalmos*. When Leslie was four months old, his left eye had to be removed. Six weeks later his right eye also was removed because of the glaucoma and because his doctors feared that the eye would burst. That was the source of Leslie's blindness.

Soon thereafter, at age six months, this frail and pathetic baby was given to the care of a remarkable woman. May Lemke was then fifty-two. She had been a nurse/governess and had developed a reputation for the extraordinary skill and love she showed in caring for children, handicapped or well. May received a call from the Social Services Department of Milwaukee County and, without a moment's hesitation, took on the role of foster mother, tutor, therapist, mentor, model, cheerleader, and inspiration to this blind, palsied, and intellectually handicapped little boy.

When Leslie was seven years old, May bought him a piano. She would play and sing for her foster son, running his fingers up and down the keyboard so he could identify the notes. By age eight Leslie could play the piano as well as a number of other instruments, including bongo drums, ukulele, concertina, xylo-

phone, and accordion. By nine Leslie had learned to play the chord organ. Medical notes indicate that, at age ten, Leslie still was not conversant, with the exception of repetition and imitation. He required help in dressing himself. He could not feed himself anything that required the use of utensils.

One evening, when Leslie was about fourteen, he watched a movie on television called *Sincerely Yours*, starring Dorothy Malone and Basil Rathbone. May and her husband, Joe, watched it, too, but then went to bed. At about three o'clock in the morning, May awoke, thinking that Joe had left the television on. She went to the living room to check. There sat Leslie. He had crawled over to the piano and was playing Tchaikovsky's Piano Concerto no. 1—the theme song to *Sincerely Yours*—vigorously and flawlessly. Leslie had heard it one time. That was sufficient. He played it through from beginning to end.

To this day, if you ask Leslie to play that piece, you get not only the song, but the entire television introduction, mimicked exactly as he heard it in true echolalic fashion: "Tonight's movie is *Sincerely Yours*, starring Dorothy Malone and Basil Rathbone. As he falls in love with the beautiful black-haired woman . . . [In the background are heard the beautiful strains of Tchaikovsky's Piano Concerto no. 1.] And now, *The Sunday Night Movie* is proud to present . . ." Usually, there is no stopping Leslie once he begins. He's like a jukebox: You put in your quarter and you hear the whole song. Until recently, the *Sincerely Yours* recitation and lengthy piece were virtually unstoppable. (That was a real hazard during Leslie's live television appearances, where time was so very limited.) Leslie now can be persuaded to stop, or at least to bring the piece to an end more quickly, with a gentle tap on the shoulder from Mary Parker, May's daughter, who acts as Leslie's guardian and caretaker now that May is frail.

Leslie was twenty-two years old when, in 1974, he gave his first public concert, at the Waukesha County Fair, a few miles from his home. He played and sang his hymns and did his Louis Armstrong and Tiny Tim imitations. He was a smash hit. He was "incredible," the newspaper said. As would happen at all of his concerts to follow, the audience members at the Waukesha County Fair shook their heads in astonishment and wiped tears from their eyes as he closed the concert with "Everything Is Beautiful."

Leslie recently completed a tour that included twenty-six cities in Japan. His repertoire now features thousands of pieces and is continually expanding. He is gradually becoming more polished in his presentations, more spontaneous in his conversations, and more sociable in his interaction. He appears to love what he is doing, is remarkably good at it, and seems to enjoy the appreciation and applause of his audiences, whether large or small, prestigious or ordinary, young or old. He has not yet reached his limits.

My personal familiarity with Leslie and his remarkable family made me a popular interview subject whenever the media turned to the topic of savants. These exposures put me in touch with a wide variety of researchers and scientists around the world who shared an interest in this condition. They in turn brought many new cases to my attention, cases I never would have known about were it not for this sudden attention to and curiosity about the puzzling paradox of being backward and brilliant at the same time.

THE OVERRIDING QUESTION for any researcher in this field is all too obvious: How do they do it? How does someone like Leslie Lemke, a person of clear deficiency, achieve such greatness in one limited area? I have found that there are about as many theories attempting to answer this question as there have been investigators. Many of the theories stem from the study of a single case, so-called "undemocratic" research that often provides useful information but also is rather idiosyncratic and limited. Among the recent research, I have found no single finding or theory that could explain all savants. But several theories could explain aspects of the syndrome and are worth exploring.

Eidetic imagery. Some researchers link Savant Syndrome to this fairly rare phenomenon in which a person continues to "see" an object as an afterimage for as long as forty seconds after it has been taken away. The retained image is intensely vivid and absolutely accurate. The term also is used by some to describe what popularly is known as photographic memory (whereby the afterimage can be recalled later and viewed as if it were a photograph). While some studies have found a higher number of "eidekers" among savants than among non-savants, other studies have not documented this difference. At any rate, eidetic imagery is not uniformly present in all savants and thus could not serve as a universal explanation for the condition.

Heredity. Could the savant be the product of two coincidentally inherited genes—one for retardation and the other for special abilities? While some investigators have found higher incidences of special skills in the families of savants, others have not. Thus, like eidetic imagery, heredity cannot serve as the sole explanation.

Sensory deprivation. Other researchers have postulated that Savant Syndrome may be a consequence of social isolation or biologically impaired sensory input. While social isolation does apply to some savants—those in deprived institutional settings, for example—many others come from stimulating environments where they received a great deal of personal attention. There are similar problems with the theory that the syndrome results from some biological form of sensory deprivation such as blindness or deafness. While some sensorily deprived individuals do develop savant skills, most do not.

Impaired ability to think abstractly. Under this theory, organic brain damage reduces the savant's ability to think abstractly, and the savant compensates by developing and refining concrete abilities as well as a vivid memory. While this is an accurate characterization of many savants, it is only a description—not an explanation—of the syndrome.

Compensation for defects and reinforcement from praise. There is no doubt that the praise that savants receive for their unusual skills can compensate for feelings of inferiority and aid in their development of relationships. Yet these same dynamics are factors for many developmentally disabled people, and only a few achieve the performance level of the savant. There must be specific and unique factors that separate the savant from the rest of the mentally handicapped.

Right brain/left brain localization and other organic factors. While not an absolute rule, the left brain hemisphere generally is responsible for skills that require intellect, cognition and logic, such as reading and speaking. The right hemisphere deals with abilities that are more intuitive and nonverbal, such as painting, sculpting, and playing music. In general, skills most often seen in savants are those associated with right hemisphere function, and those lacking tend to be left-hemisphere-related. Could Savant Syndrome result from damage to the left hemisphere of the brain?

One case lending impetus to this last theory involves a normal nine-year-old boy who suffered a gunshot wound very precisely confined to the left side of the brain, leaving him deaf, mute, and paralyzed on the right side. Following that injury, the boy developed a savant-like ability to troubleshoot and repair mechanical devices, presumably resulting from increased function in his undamaged right hemisphere.

Unfortunately, there has been very little research to confirm left brain damage in savants. It is interesting to note, however, that in two of the three reported cases where CAT scans (detailed x-rays of the brain) were performed on savants, there was clear evidence of such left brain damage. The other reported CAT scan—on a very high-functioning autistic savant with mathematical skills—showed an undamaged left brain.

No doubt some savants do have left brain damage as we generally think of it—trauma or injury before, during, or after birth. Yet, in the case of the identical twins George and Charles, both of whom had identical calculating skills, it seems most unlikely that both of them would have incurred such an injury in exactly the same area of the brain to give them their identical abilities. Their case argues for genetic or behavioral factors as well—or perhaps for some other process affecting the left brain.

FURTHER INSIGHT into the damaged-left-brain theory is provided by the 1987 findings of Harvard neurologists Norman Geschwind and Albert Galaburda, who studied right brain/left brain development and cerebral dominance. The doctors note that, from conception onward, the left brain is larger than the right and that it completes its growth and development later than the right brain in utero, leaving it vulnerable for a longer period of time to a variety of prenatal influences and injury. One such influence is the male sex hormone testosterone, which in the male fetus reaches levels that have been shown to impair neural cell development in some instances. This testosterone effect could therefore produce the type of left brain "damage" postulated for the savant.

Such damage—coming before birth at a time when the brain is still developing—would result in right brain cells being recruited for what would ordinarily be left brain circuits. A "pathology of superiority" of the right brain would then develop, along with a preponderance of right-brain-type skills—the kind of skills seen in the savant.

According to Geschwind and Galaburda, testosterone-caused damage would account as well for the correspondingly high male-to-female ratios seen in savants and in other "left brain" disorders such as dyslexia, delayed speech, autism, stuttering, and hyperactivity. It correlates as well with the higher incidence of left-handedness in males.

Further implications can be drawn from the fact that a striking number of savants were born prematurely. The phenomenon of massive brain cell death in humans just before birth is well established and commonly accepted. There are many more brain cells in the fetus than can possibly make connections, and those unconnected neural cells are simply discarded late in the pregnancy.

Geschwind and Galaburda point out that when left brain injury occurs early in pregnancy—as postulated by the testosterone theory—there is still a large reservoir of spare right brain neurons available to accommodate a neuronal shift to the right hemisphere. Indeed, the right brain actually becomes enlarged compared to the left. Could the savant's premature birth prevent the normal brain-cell die-off and provide a large reservoir of right brain cells that, when recruited, produce the extraordinary right brain skills seen in the savant?

Another body of research that could be of importance in understanding the savant is the work of Mortimer Mishkin, M.D., and others at the National Institute of Mental Health. Mishkin outlined two types of memory, each with its own distinct pathways: cognitive or associative memory, in which facts or stimuli first are consciously recognized, then sorted, stored, and later recalled; and habit memory, more a system of conditioned reflexes, such as that used when driving a complex daily route to work while thinking about other things. It is the latter that more accurately characterizes savant memory—the "memory without consciousness" described over and over again in savant literature. Mishkin points to data suggesting two different neurological pathways, or circuits, for these two different kinds of memory. In the savant, it appears that habit memory pathways compensate for damaged cognitive memory circuits.

Clearly, the one quality or trait that all savants have in common, irrespective of their particular skills, is phenomenal memory. It is memory of a specific type: literal, vivid, reflex-like, unconscious, devoid of emotion, tremendously deep but impressively narrow. This is in dramatic contrast to memory in the rest of us, which tends to be much more conscious, highly associative, more abstract,

less literal and precise, emotion-laden, and tremendously wide-ranging in subject matter but conspicuously limited in depth. Savants' unique memory function and circuitry distinguishes them from non-savants and points to the most fruitful area of further study.

Indeed, recent findings from new x-ray studies of the brain and autopsy data suggest that, in addition to the savant's left hemisphere damage, there is corresponding damage in lower brain areas, including those that control memory circuitry. This could explain the characteristic appearance in the savant of both right brain skills and an over developed reliance on habit memory.

Combining the various theories and new research, then, the talented savant emerges as an individual whose left-brain function has been disrupted as a result of some brain injury— perhaps sex-linked— occurring before, during, or after birth that leads to a compensatory increase in right brain function. The left brain damage is coupled with lower brain damage as well, causing a reliance on habit memory circuitry. These two factors somehow combine to produce the savant's characteristic cluster of abilities. Constant repetition and practice then refine these circuits, resulting in conspicuous talent within an exceedingly narrow range.

This scenario would account for the talented savants—those whose skills are remarkable simply in contrast to their obvious mental handicaps. However, in order to explain the prodigious savants, we must take into account some inherited factors as well. The prodigious savant's access to the vast rules of mathematics, art, or music could not be learned by practice alone. Some researchers have suggested that such extraordinary talents might be acquired from a shared field of knowledge similar to psychologist Carl Jung's "collective unconscious," or that these skills could reflect knowledge gained in so-called "past lives." These are explanations that no one can confirm or refute, but they are nevertheless explanations held by some.

Clearly, in both varieties of savant, intense concentration, practice, compensatory drives, and reinforcement play major roles in developing and polishing the skills made possible by this idiosyncratic brain function. But there is another factor as well: the deep care and concern that families or other caregivers have for the savants—not just for what they can do but for who they are; not just for what is missing but for all that remains. By radiating so much love,

encouragement, and praise, they serve to reinforce and motivate in ways that are truly touching and inspirational.

UNTIL RECENTLY, almost all of the technical advances in the study of the brain have allowed us to better and more precisely view brain *structure*: Are all the parts there? Now, for the first time, new technology, such as the positron emission tomography (PET) scan and similar devices, allows researchers to better study brain *function*, the actual way the brain works. Such new technology for studying the brain, coupled with new knowledge about the brain, has far-reaching implications for understanding savants—and thus ourselves.

For starters, the savant's "memory without consciousness"—Leslie's exact mimicry of an overheard German song or a random conversation, for example—can be studied in detail. Surely this distinct memory—so deep but so narrow, so vast but so emotionless—arises from circuitry far different from our ordinary memory, which is shallow and limited but far more flexible, associative, and creative.

By allowing us to better understand memory circuitry, savants may help us counteract the disruption of memory pathways by conditions such as Alzheimer's disease. Such brain repair might take any one of several forms: pharmacologic (with memory-enhancing drugs), neurologic (with brain cells recruited from unaffected areas and rerouted over new pathways), electrical (with brain-pacing devices such as those now used to treat certain types of epilepsy and to pace the electrical system of the heart), or neurosurgical (with brain grafts and neuronal transplants such as those now used in the treatment of Parkinson's disease).

Almost everything we have learned about health we have learned from the study of disease. Thus, from the research on Alzheimer's disease may come applications for expanding and enhancing normal memory. Each of us has tremendous numbers of memories—literally a lifetime's worth—stored in an organ to which we have relatively poor access. In our dreams, under hypnosis, or in sodium amytal interviews, some of this stored data cascades forth. And, as mentioned earlier, when neurosurgeons touch the cortex of a patient's brain with a tiny electrical probe, it also triggers thousands of memories of which the patient is unaware.

It seems "lost" memories have not disappeared; they have simply been misfiled, making them difficult to find. Normal memory enhancement, whether pharmocologic, electrical, or by some other method, promises to someday allow us to tap that tremendous reservoir of data we all possess but cannot now access.

The link between memory and creativity is another area in which studying savants may lead us to better understand ourselves. Their tremendous skills aside, savants almost exclusively echo and mimic—there is little or no creativity involved in what they do. Adding improvisation to existing music—as striking as that is—is still not the same as creating a new musical idea. Alonzo Clemons, a sculpting savant, can recreate fantastically what he sees but cannot do free-form sculpting. This is not to detract from such remarkable skills. It is simply to say that they differ from the creative process, and that difference warrants further study.

Savants, as a group, also demonstrate an unusual emotional flatness. Again, this trade-off is a mixed blessing. While they may miss some of the peaks of normal human emotion, they seem to be spared the valleys. While they may not shout at a ball game or weep at a movie, they also seem to be free of performance jitters or bouts of deep despair or cynicism. They may never feel ecstasy, but neither will they feel despondency. With further study, this emotional detachment may provide clues to the normal interplay of memory and emotion.

Indeed, we can learn a great deal about human potential from the jarring contradiction—the magnificent coexistence of deficiency and superiority—that is Savant Syndrome. We can learn that handicap need not necessarily blur hope and that stereotyping and labeling serve only to obscure—in a pernicious manner—an individual's strengths. We can learn the difference between paucity of emotion and purity of emotion. From the families, teachers, and therapists of the savant, we can learn that in dealing with people who have problems—even severe ones—it is not enough to care *for* those people: We must care *about* them as well. We can learn that there is a difference between sharing the spirit and shaping the spirit. We can learn how to work with a differently shaped soul—to understand, to actualize, and to appreciate it—while still respecting its uniqueness.

In short, a complete understanding of human experience requires that we include and account for Savant Syndrome. Until then, we will be able only to marvel at people such as Leslie Lemke, Alonzo Clemons, or the calendar calculator named George who can compute twenty-digit prime numbers but cannot add two plus two. "It's fantastic I can do that," he says.

For now, it truly is.

Gifted by nature, prodigies are still mysteries to Man

Extraordinarily talented children have been astonishing audiences for centuries, but scientists don't know what makes them tick

By Roderick MacLeish

Novelist, critic and journalist Roderick MacLeish is a commentator on National Public Radio. He lives in Washington, D.C., when he is not traveling abroad.

In the summer of 1764, London turned itself inside out to celebrate the 26th birthday of George III. The streets were crowded with visitors, jugglers, puppet shows and pickpockets. The warm June nights glittered with the plumage of the gentry at balls and levees. At the Great Room in Spring Garden, two sensational Austrian children were on display. Their father had advertised them in the newspapers as "Prodigies of Nature." The little boy, Wolfgang, was eight and his sister, Marianne, was 12. Their mature, effortless skill at the organ and harpsichord amazed everybody who heard them. They could play any music presented to them at first reading.

By then, Wolfgang Amadeus Mozart was already an established child celebrity. He had performed, and charmed, in half the great cities of Europe. The Holy Roman Emperor, Francis I, had proclaimed him "a little magician." He had composed chamber music of extraordinary technical virtuosity and he was about to write his first three symphonies. When Mozart died shortly before his 36th birthday, he left two legacies. Ultimately, the world recognized him as one of the finest composers who ever lived. And he will be remembered forever as history's most famous child prodigy.

"The little world of childhood with its familiar surroundings," wrote the distinguished Swiss psychologist Carl Gustav Jung, "is a model of the greater world." But it is as true today as it was in Mozart's time that prodigies may not fit into either world. They are blessed by phenomenal gifts denied to everybody else they know. They tend to display those gifts in fields where few others excel—in mathematics, music and chess, less frequently in literature and art. They enjoy, many of them, the sublime satisfaction of extraordinary achievement, the thrill of public adulation and the material wealth such success can engender.

Even so, there are afflictions as well as rewards for the prodigiously talented. Some prodigies pay for their genius with a tormenting sense of their own uniqueness. Some become targets of bewildering hostilities. Some burn out early at the peak of their powers while others self-destruct before ever fulfilling their early promise. As adults, even the most successful prodigies sometimes question the value of their lives and accomplishments. "I have a longing which grows stronger as I get older," confesses the acclaimed American concert pianist Eugene Istomin, "to be mediocre."

One of the leading practitioners in the relatively new field of prodigy research is psychologist David Henry Feldman of Tufts University in Medford, Massachusetts. Feldman divides prodigies into at least two groups. Omnibus prodigies, he says, are those who excel in two or more fields of endeavor, whereas single-purpose prodigies, like Mozart, have one supreme gift. Single-purpose prodigies far outnumber their more versatile counterparts.

Perhaps the best-known example of a single-purpose prodigy in the 20th century is the American violinist Yehudi Menuhin. Born in New York in 1916, he began lessons at five and made his debut with the San Francisco Symphony Orchestra when he was seven. Critics were astounded by his technical virtuosity and uncanny understanding of the great works he performed.

Still active today, he remains one of the world's most revered musicians.

Children of uncommon talent have been amazing their audiences for ages. One of the musical world's most conspicuous youngsters was the pianist and composer Felix Mendelssohn. Born in Hamburg 175 years ago, he had composed a fair amount of music by the time he was 11. When he was 16, he had already written 13 string symphonies and some of his most imaginative chamber music. His fourth opera was produced in Berlin when he was all of 18.

John Stuart Mill, the prominent 19th-century British philosopher, is another of history's celebrated child prodigies. He was force-fed an education by his father, the historian and economist James Mill. John Stuart read Greek at three and became his sister's tutor when he was eight. He had worked his way through elementary geometry and algebra, and a vast body of literature and history, by the time he was 12.

Born in 1881, Daisy Ashford was the child of British Roman Catholic parents. At four, she produced a comic masterpiece about a Jesuit priest that featured a fictional Pope's visit to London. Her famous novel, *The Young Visiters*, was written when she was nine. It is a funny, utterly enchanting portrayal of genteel life in the Victorian era from a child's point of view. *The Young Visiters* sold hundreds of thousands of copies over many decades and is still in print. Daisy stopped writing as she entered her teens. She died at 90 in 1972.

Unhappily for many prodigies, success has not always been accompanied by equal measures of happiness. When he was 20, John Stuart Mill suffered a shattering mental crisis. Overwhelmed by despair, he began to question the struggle for erudition which had occupied his life. "The end had ceased to charm. . . ." he wrote years later. "I seemed to have nothing left to live for." Other well-known prodigies experienced similar setbacks.

A number of history's most famous prodigies had something else in common: they did not live exceptionally long lives. Raphael produced masterpieces as a teenager and died on his 37th birthday. Composer Franz Schubert died when he was 31. Scientist Blaise Pascal died before he was 40. It is almost as if nature, in compensation, endowed these and other prodigies with a capacity for immense productivity.

Dr. Rima Laibow, a child psychiatrist in Dobbs Ferry, New York, has observed firsthand the problems that bedevil contemporary prodigies. They live, she says, under the burden of their isolation and, to make matters worse, the role of a destructive force is often unwittingly thrust upon them. "They create immense competitiveness in their families," Laibow emphasizes. "The kid's smarter than his well-educated father. The resentment spills out. . . . It's very difficult to have one child performing phenomenally while everybody else is poking along the way most people do."

Educating prodigies can be a serious problem, too. In school with children their own age, they become bored, frustrated and may simply switch off learning altogether. If sent to a university where his intellect can be accommodated, a ten-year-old genius can't fit in. Emotionally, he's still ten.

The parents of normal children often feel threatened by child prodigies. Laibow tells about a three-year-old who was sitting in a playground sandbox drawing the schematic design of a car he was inventing. The mother of one of his playmates came over and erased his intricate markings in the sand. "Children shouldn't be allowed to do those things," the woman said. "It just confuses them." The little boy had in fact been deeply engrossed in what was, to him, fun. "It wiped him out," Laibow says.

There is another baffling phenomenon: the child prodigy as fantasy-inspirer. Sidney is nine. He is a classic omnibus prodigy. At birth he registered the neurological reactions of a three-month-old baby. At four, he could write and read nine languages. He has the potential talents of a virtuoso violinist. When he was 22 months old, Sidney began studying Hebrew with a private tutor. "She was wonderful with him," his mother recalls. "She sat on the floor with him, taught him, cuddled him and played with him. Then one day I walked in and heard her telling Sidney he was the Messiah." Sidney finished his instruction in Hebrew with somebody else.

Many children, as they enter adolescence, begin to turn away from their families and toward their fellow teenagers for affection, support and a sense of belonging. This can be a particularly rough time in the lives of child prodigies. They know they're different. Other adolescents know or sense it, too. The prodigy may simply bury his genius to win social acceptablity. Or he may plod on, brilliant and alone. "The suffering," says David Feldman of Tufts, "can be severe."

Mac Randall is poised at the edge of that adolescent minefield. At 11, he is a slender, self-possessed boy with the vocabulary of a grown man, a subtle sense of humor and a Christopher Robin haircut. He taught himself how to operate an electric typewriter when he was three. At four he began to write horror stories and fantasies. To fuel his writing, Mac worked his way through studies of the solar system, dinosaurs, the lives of composers and the history of comic strips. He also read parts of Shakespeare, Henrik Ibsen and Edmond Rostand. His own literary output is less remarkable for structure than it is for depth and maturity of content. His ideas range across philosophy and religion to startling memoirs.

Mac is the only child of a second marriage. When he was little, his family lived in the country surrounded by animals. "If you want to get right down to it," Mac says, "I was raised by two dogs, some cows and horses."

His mother, Janice, a former schoolteacher, began to get concerned about him when he was four. "He was just learning so much," she recalls. "He really did have to come to an understanding of where he had to limit his emotional responses. One day I found him in tears listening to a recording of *Romeo and Juliet*, and that was sort of *it*. He knew that he simply couldn't allow himself to go on that way." As for being hyperstimulated, Mac agrees. "I used to be," he says. "But I've calmed down a lot now."

When Mac was six, his parents moved to the city so that he could have friends and get the special schooling they felt his gifts demanded. He is guarded about the whole subject of prodigious children, as if he senses the problems that may lie ahead of him. "I never tell anybody that I'm a prodigy," he says, "but they eventually find out. When you do it that way and don't go around saying, 'Hey, I'm a genius,' they sort of like you a lot more."

Lately, Mac's creative drive has begun to focus on other things besides literature. Since he was two, he has been fascinated by music. He began with the classics, on which he holds firm opinions. "I still have a fondness for Bach," he says. "I enjoy Beethoven's Seventh. I don't like the Pastoral Symphony." With the death of John Lennon in 1980, Mac became absorbed in rock music and recently finished writing the music and libretto of a rock opera.

Like most adolescents, Mac is no stranger to apprehension. The difference is that he can articulate his with considerable candor. "I'm afraid of not having any friends. I used to be not a very social person but I knew a lot of people who were, so I took on their characteristics. Now I'm a much more open person." An interviewer asked him recently if his precocity has presented him with any serious problems. The grin faded. Mac looked at the questioner for a moment. "Not yet," he said cryptically.

Jaime Laredo, the Bolivian-born violinist, was brought to the United States by his family to find teachers who could cope with his extraordinary talent. Laredo says he knew that he was slightly special as a little kid. "But I don't remember ever being teased or anything like that," he says. Unlike Laredo, pianist Eugene Istomin, 58, felt alienated as a child. The son of Russian immigrants, he was raised in a musical home and, as he recalls with some irony, was once "put in a school for little geniuses." He speaks of creating "masks of regularity" for himself to deal with the world. "I had," Istomin says, "no connection with other children except through sports." Consequently, he played street games, boxed and became a rabid baseball fan, which he still is.

Another rough time for many prodigies occurs with the advent of the so-called "mid-life crisis," which usually occurs in the teenage years. "The mind starts asking you questions," says Jean-Bernard Pommier, the French concert pianist and conductor. "Who are you? What do you know? What is the difference between you and other people? If you aren't prepared to answer these questions, you can be lost."

By "lost" Pommier is referring to what students of the prodigy phenomenon call "burnout." It is, simply, a sudden end to a brilliant young person's interest in learning, in performing, in *being* brilliant.

Norbert Wiener and William James Sidis were turn-of-the-century child prodigies who both were educated in Cambridge, Massachusetts. Wiener graduated from Tufts at 14, won his doctorate from Harvard before he was 20 and went on to become one of the great mathematicians of his time. He was a pioneer in the field of cybernetics, a science which forms part of the basis of computer technology. Sidis entered Harvard when he was 11. He amazed his teachers with a lecture on mathematics. Newspapers and magazines wrote articles about him. Then Sidis graduated and dropped out of sight. He drifted from job to job and ended up living alone. His major interest seemed to be collecting streetcar transfers from all over the world. He died at the age of 46 in 1944. Sidis burned out. Wiener did not. What was the critical difference between the two child prodigies? Nobody really knows.

Notwithstanding centuries of fascination with child prodigies, there has been little serious study of them until recently. Work is under way now at several major universities, and some interesting common denominators have been identified.

The vast majority of prodigious youngsters are boys. They tend to be the first-born children of middle-class families. Often, their parents are beyond the usual child-bearing age; many prodigies apparently are born by Caesarean section. There is a high incidence among child prodigies of parents who seem to be trying to realize their own ambitions through their amazing offspring. And, curiously enough, prodigies tend to have a bizarre and, occasionally, a downright off-color sense of humor.

Even now, prodigies defy definition

Despite the recent upsurge in research, there is still no universally accepted definition of the child prodigy. Webster's dictionary says a prodigy is "a highly gifted or academically talented child." That's pretty vague, and David Feldman of Tufts prefers a somewhat more specific description because of all the variables in the lives and traits of superbright children. "A child prodigy," he says, "is a person who performs at or near the level of a professional at a very early age."

The conventional yardstick of intellectual ability is a standard IQ test. Many educators consider anyone who scores above 150 or so on such tests to be a "genius." But Harvard University psychologist Howard Gardner believes IQ tests probably fail to identify many brilliant and talented youngsters because they focus on only two skills, language and mathematics. In his provocative new book, *Frames of Mind: The Theory of Multiple Intelligences*, Gardner asserts that the human mind is not a single entity but a constellation of seven specific intelligences, each controlled by different parts of the brain. These intelligences include musical ability, bodily talent, spatial perception and personal sensitivity as well as linguistic and mathematical skills. They develop according to their own timetables and they operate independently, but they can function cooperatively, as well. One or more intelligences can outshine the rest, Gardner says, and musical talent is usually the first intelligence to emerge—conceivably because musical ability does not seem to require as much experience in the real world as other skills.

Gardner's theory of multiple intelligences appears to offer a possible avenue to understanding the prodigy phenomenon. But how is the seed planted in the first place, and what is the scenario for its full flowering? Initially, Gardner speculates, a youngster's potential for a particular kind of brilliance is transmitted by the parents, who may not have any special gifts themselves but who do have talent in one or both family backgrounds. The child's extraordinary ability is usually revealed at an early age by a crystallizing event—a moment of revelation which signals to youngster and parent alike that the talent is there.

"Just having the gene is not enough," Gardner maintains. "The potential has to be triggered by something in the environment, and it must be nourished."

David Feldman concurs with Gardner's emphasis on the importance of nurture as well as nature. In fact, Feldman is the originator of the "coincidence" theory of child prodigies, which holds that, for genius to occur, "all of the things that go into it must coincide at exactly the right time, in exactly the right place under exactly the right conditions. There has to be a cultural preparation and an appreciative audience."

Feldman's coincidence theory goes a long toward explaining certain conspicuous historical explosions of genius—the outburst of great literature during the Elizabethan era, for example, and the torrent of immortal music that flowed out of Vienna in the 18th and 19th centuries. Currently, Feldman says, about 50 percent of the chess prodigies in the United States live in San Francisco, Los Angeles and New York. Their homes are in population centers where there are chess clubs—where interest in the game runs high. Seven-year-old chess whizzes in these three cities can test themselves against other gifted or experienced players. They have been born in a period of history which believes in encouraging chess prodigies.

"Imagine Einstein being born in the same place—but 5,000 years ago," Feldman says. "He would have been walking around wondering why there was air,

but he might not have made it to his 12th year."

There is some evidence that the nation's population of gifted children—and, possibly, prodigies—is growing. James T. Webb, professor and assistant dean at Wright State University in Dayton, Ohio, reports that staff members at the institution who test large numbers of children have detected a startling proportion in the 170- to 180-IQ range. "Something strange is happening out there," he says.

Superbaby diet: tapioca, Bach and math

One strange thing that is happening out there is the appearance of the so-called "superbaby movement." Ambitious mothers and fathers are flashing vocabulary cards at their toddlers as they eat their tapioca, and feeding them a diet of mathematics and Johann Sebastian Bach to boot. Glenn Doman, a Pennsylvanian with a background in physiotherapy, is considered the reigning prophet of the superbaby movement. He has proclaimed that "our individual genetic potential is that of Leonardo, Shakespeare, Mozart, Michelangelo. . . ."

Many child development specialists are worried about the effects of trying to pressure kids into prodigiousness. Pediatricians are seeing children with backlash symptoms: headaches, tummy-aches, hair-tearing, anxiety and depression. This kind of pressure, says child psychiatrist Rima Laibow, "makes for trouble."

Another, even stranger development is the Repository for Germinal Choice, a sperm bank in Escondido, California, which accepts deposits solely from donors who are outstanding intellectual achievers, including Nobel Prize winners. Not long ago, an unmarried Los Angeles psychologist, Afton Blake, selected as the father of her child a computer scientist, who was identified by the repository only as Number 28. At four months, the child, a boy named Doron, had the motor skills of an infant twice his age and now, at one and a half years, he evinces special interest in music.

Implicit in developments like the repository and the superbaby movement is the notion that children are mere commodities. This view disgusts many of the researchers and psychologists who are studying phenomenal young human beings—primarily because these children are natural, if unusual, members of the human family. Above all, scholars of the child prodigy phenomenon are filled with wonder at the mystery which confronts them daily. Recently David Feldman was asked to speculate on why a Mozart or a John Stuart Mill suddenly appears in the endless river of mortal generations. Do prodigies get that way because of environment, genes or God?

The young psychologist thought for a moment. Then he shrugged. "Perhaps all of the above," he said.

Development During Infancy and Early Childhood

No period in human development has received more attention during the past quarter century than infancy. Part of the explosion in infant research focuses on the study of the basic abilities of the infant. Can newborn infants imitate facial expressions? Can they discriminate one sound from another? What can be said about memory processes during infancy? It has become evident that infants are far from the passive, unknowing beings they were once thought to be. Rather, they are increasingly regarded as being responsive to environmental stimulation, are viewed as equipped with organized behavior patterns, and are capable of mental operations right from the start. The many skills of the newborn multiply dramatically over the first several years of life, transforming the physically helpless infant into a child who, by age three or even earlier, is capable of thinking, communicating, and skillfully solving problems. Knowledge of the readiness to learn that is now so evident in infants and toddlers has brought with it questions about the best ways to nurture early intellectual and social development. One point of view, supported by many parents eager to give their young children a head start toward academic success, places emphasis on a relatively limited band of school-related skills. In "Formal Education and Early Childhood Education: An Essential Difference," David Elkind argues that this view is a dangerously narrow one which fails to recognize the importance of everyday experience in creating meaningful learning opportunities for the young child. Elkind's view is supported by the voices of many other early childhood experts who caution that structured learning experiences bring with them the risk of placing too much pressure on the child; they argue that such pressures can, in turn, stunt creativity and turn learning into drudgery rather than a spontaneous process of dis-covery. This issue and nine others are addressed by Julius Segal in his article "Ten Myths About Child Development."

Often we focus on the intellectual development of the child to the near exclusion of the more whimsical and creative aspects of the growing process. In a refreshing change of pace, Ellen Winner describes the charming features of children's artistic development in "Where Pelicans Kiss Seals."

"The Child-Care Dilemma" considers a critical problem in the United States: the lack of quality supplemental child-care facilities for children. Fifty percent of working mothers, and about 9 million children, are involved. Such figures point out the magnitude of the problem and the urgent need for effective solutions. In addition, we have relatively little information about how day care influences child development. In the article "What Is Beautiful Is Good," evidence is presented which suggests that something as basic as a child's physical appearance can shape the attributes adults assign to the child.

Looking Ahead: Challenge Questions

Discuss the pros and cons of beginning as early as possible to teach young children skills such as reading and math. Explain your arguments.

What effect does work have on the development of attachment relationships between mother and infant, or on the effectiveness of discipline in school-age children? Does society have a responsibility to provide supplementary care for children of working mothers? Does industry have this responsibility?

Should we pay more attention to the child's artistic endeavors? Why or why not?

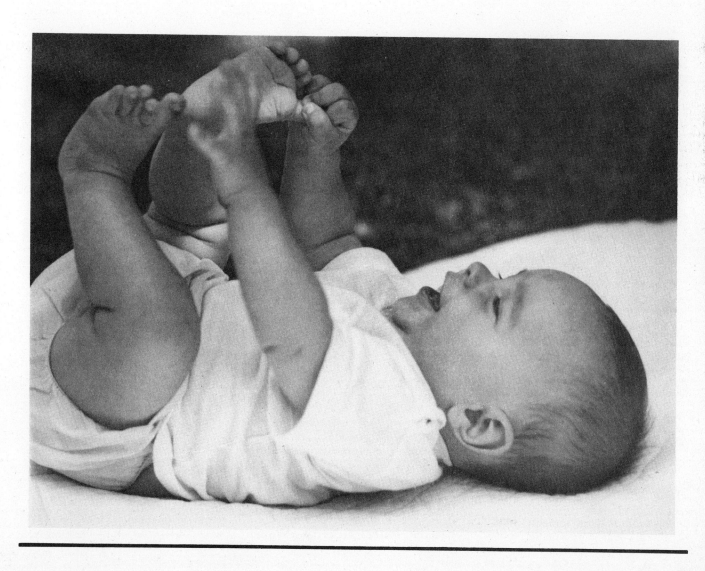

10 Myths About Child Development

Modern research helps us sort out fact from fiction when it comes to theories about raising our children.

Mastering motor skills early is *not* a sign of superior intelligence.

Julius Segal

Julius Segal, Ph.D., a contributing editor of *Parents* Magazine, is a psychologist, author, and lecturer whose latest book is *Winning Life's Toughest Battles* (Ballantine).

"The 'evil eye' can bring harm to children admired by strangers."

"The fatter the child, the healthier."

"Spare the rod, and spoil the child." When I was a youngster, those were among the erroneous beliefs voiced by adults on my block. If you are like most parents, you, too, probably have theories about what makes kids tick—what determines the shape of a child's personality and behavior. Some of these notions have been passed along to you by your parents, others picked up from friends, still others culled from convincing TV talk-show guests.

In previous generations little scientific information was available by which parents could assess the validity of such theories. Today, however, child-development researchers have accumulated a rich store of knowledge to help us understand how and why children unfold as they do.

Based on today's scientific evidence, it appears that many of the ideas parents have about child development are rooted in myth rather than reality. Over the past few years I have kept a record of such unfounded notions as they were expressed to me by mothers and fathers during lectures and workshops around the country. Here are ten of them, all dealing with the child's early years.

1 You can tell in infancy how bright a child is likely to be later on.

Many parents continue to believe, as mine did, that the pace and quality of a baby's early achievements—reaching, sitting, crawling, babbling—are sure indications of that child's later capacities.

To examine this notion, researchers have conducted studies in which the same children were tested over long periods—in some cases from the first weeks of life to adulthood. As babies, the children were given so-called infant IQ tests, tapping such sensory and motor skills as the ability to recognize their mother, turn the pages of a book, or imitate words. Their scores were correlated with the results of later IQ tests, which tap mainly problem-solving, reasoning, and verbal skills.

The correlations have turned out to be negligible. Except, of course, in cases of extreme retardation, scores on even the most reputable tests of infant intelligence bear virtually no relationship to the scores that children achieve on standard IQ tests later on. Clearly the child's proficiency in mastering early sensory and motor tasks tells us little, if anything, about later intellectual ability.

Thus, for example, early agility in building blocks or skill in imitating an adult stirring with a spoon (two items in the widely used Bayley Scale of Infant Development) provides scant indication of the child's "smarts" later on, when schooling begins in earnest, and virtually no indication of how the child will function intellectually in the later years of childhood. Most researchers agree that regardless of the hype surrounding recently developed tests, the world of the infant and the world of the nine-year-old, say, are just too different to allow us to make either the triumphant ("a bud-ding Einstein") or dismal ("a slow learner") projections many parents make about their little ones.

2 The more stimulation a baby gets, the better.

There is no doubt that babies are more receptive to stimulation from the outside world than either psychologists or parents had ever imagined in the past. Thus it is for good reason that mothers and fathers have been encouraged to begin right from the start to exercise the baby's senses—for example, placing bright, intriguing objects around the room and over the crib, playing music, reading, talking. The notion that a stimulating environment can have a positive effect on the intellectual capacities of babies—perhaps by actually influencing the brain's rate of growth—is no myth.

But it *is* a myth to assume that the larger the amount of early stimulation you provide, the more beneficial it will be. The truth is that babies can be *over*stimulated—which is what many parents, intent on beginning to groom their progeny for college in the cradle, end up doing. Indeed, bombarding newborns with heavier doses of new sensations than they are physiologically prepared for can sometimes inhibit progress. Psychologists Paul H. Mussen, Ph.D., John J. Conger, Ph.D., and Jerome Kagan, Ph.D., cite an example in their textbook, *Essentials of Child Development and Personality* (Harper & Row): "It is possible that the three-week-old baby, biologically too immature to reach for the brightly-colored mobile, may become more upset by the presence of the mobile than if nothing were present."

Observant parents have probably noticed that too much stimulation can be very disconcerting for the baby who is still not up to dealing with the pressure of all that input. Some simply become agitated or cry. Others try to push away the irritating stimulus—the intrusive rattle, toy, talking face, or finger. Still others withdraw, turning inward to avoid the relentless assault on their senses, and some simply tune out altogether and wisely drop off to sleep. Given such clues, parents are wise to curb the "enrichment activity." What the baby seems to be saying is "Enough already! My nervous system isn't quite ready for all that stuff."

3 If a baby cries every time Mother leaves her, it is an early sign of emotional insecurity.

If this were so, virtually every child would have to be regarded as emotionally insecure. Experiments throughout the world have shown that at a certain point in their early development, all babies become agitated, cry, and show an increased heart rate typical of a state of anxiety when separated from their mother or other steady caretaker. Starting at about eight months for some children—but usually peaking at about twelve to fifteen months for most—the experience is almost sure to bring distress and tears, and then the impact begins to weaken. The pattern applies equally in every region in which children have been studied, including American cities, isolated villages in the Guatemalan highlands, towns in Israel, and remote areas of the Kalahari Desert, in Africa.

Babies reared at home by their mother and those who spend much of their early life at a day-care center are equally likely to show separation anxiety. There are individual differences among kids, of course, in how soon the experience begins and how long it lasts, but overall it appears to be a universal phenomenon of early childhood—regardless of other aspects of the child's personality or of the nature of child-rearing practices.

4 You'll spoil the baby if you respond to his demands too quickly.

University of Virginia psychologist Mary D. Salter Ainsworth, Ph.D., and her associates carefully analyzed mother-infant interactions as they actually took place in the home. Some mothers responded to their babies as soon as they fussed or cried. Others did not, out of the belief that in doing so they would be overindulging the child and thus hampering normal development.

The results of this and related studies show that in the first year or so of life, children—still dependent and needy—are not "spoiled" by parents who are responsive and attentive. Babies tend to become more compliant—and more independent as well—when their signals of distress are responded to without delay. It is babies whose calls for help are answered slowly or ignored altogether who tend to make a habit of crying and whining and who are more hesitant about beginning to explore the world on their own.

5 "Bonding" between parent and infant must take place immediately after the baby's birth.

The idea of a now-or-never time for skin-close contact between mother or father and newborn arose from research with animals. Scientists have shown that there is indeed a period shortly after birth when infant sheep, chickens, geese, swans, and other animals are genetically programmed to latch on to the first moving object they see—their mother—and to follow it around. The process is called imprinting because the image of Mother becomes so indelibly imprinted in the "mind" of the infant animal that it cannot be erased. Moreover, when this imprinting process is disrupted, the system of signals that guides the mother-infant relationship becomes disorganized—and so does the newborn's behavior.

It is a gigantic leap, however, from chicks to children. A similarly critical period has never been reliably demonstrated for human infants, who form attachments to their caretakers much more gradually. Instead of being a static, one-time event, bonding is a process, a dynamic and continuous one. Thus a reciprocal, loving attachment is still realizable even when early contact is delayed—as it is for many mothers and their prematurely born infants, or when illness of either the newborn or mother intervenes. Moreover, secure bonds can and often do develop between children and their adoptive parents, coming together months or even years after the children's birth.

The bottom line is clear: There is no brief, miraculous period of early parent-child interaction that will define the child's future. Opportunities to build the kind of emotional intimacy that helps children thrive are available well beyond the opening hours and days of parenthood.

6 Special talents surface early or not at all.

Many kids who are born with unique aptitudes do not find the opportunities to discover them—let alone express them—until their childhood has passed. Robert Albert, Ph.D., at Pitzer College, in Claremont, California, has studied the developmental patterns of exceptionally gifted youngsters. He concludes that it is only in early adolescence that many kids recognize their skills and begin to build their identity around them. "During the early years," says Albert, "sometimes as a result of crystallizing experiences in the high school science lab or the theater workshop, a talented scientist or performer emerges, and a dazzling career takes shape."

We know today that it is simply not possible to view a child's inherent nature and life experiences as independent forces. In order to become a football star, for example, a child would have to inherit a combination of such traits as agility, speed, and endurance. But without exposure to the sport and opportunity to practice, even the best-endowed child would not become truly outstanding at this activity.

Consider the case of jazz musician Louis Armstrong, a true genius who helped propel a new musical art form. He was actually a neglected and abandoned child. It was only years later, while Armstrong was living in the New Orleans Colored Waifs Home for Boys, that someone taught him to play an instrument and his profound talent was ignited.

There are instances, of course, in which enormous endowment and exposure come together early. Mozart was clearly born with a remarkable genius for musical creation—and his magnificent products began to emerge at age five as a result of his father's steady instruction and because a harpsichord quickly became the center of his life. But no deadline exists for such a happy merger between innate talent and the opportunity to express it.

7 An only child is likely to have problems relating to other people.

Influenced by this widespread myth, many parents of single children expect them to become maladjusted loners with a self-centered approach to life. However, as University of Wisconsin psychologist Diane E. Papalia, Ph.D., and Sally Wendkos

Olds document in their textbook, *Human Development* (McGraw-Hill), research does not bear out this negative view—a fact that should be of special interest to that 10 percent of American couples opting to have only one child.

Instead, Papalia and Olds point out that only children are inclined in their early years to be bright, successful, self-confident, resourceful, and popular with their peers. Moreover, they are "just as likely to grow up to be successful in jobs, marriages, and parenthood experiences."

Studies do show that only children tend to be somewhat less eager for social intimacy. For example, they become involved with fewer organizations, have fewer friends, and generally lead a less intense social life than kids who grow up with siblings. On the other hand, they are likely to become the leaders of the organizations they do join, and they generate close friendships. Most important, their lives are marked by no less contentment than those of youngsters raised with siblings.

8 Children who suffer early neglect and deprivation will not realize their normal potential.

Many couples, seeking to adopt a child who has already endured traumatic beginnings, are unduly troubled by this belief. While there is little doubt that prolonged early stress and privation can hamper development, the ill effects are more often reversible than either parents or professionals have assumed. Under the proper conditions for growth, initial handicapping circumstances can be overcome. Indeed, Lewis P. Lipsitt, Ph.D., professor of psychology and medical science and director of the Brown University Child Study Center, in Providence, observes that such circumstances may spark the quest to succeed. "In some cases," says Lipsitt, "early adversity may serve as a launching pad for self-realization and achievement."

University of London child psychiatrist Michael Rutter, M.D., points out that even severely deprived children, not rescued from their appalling situations until the age of six or seven, are capable of achieving normal intellectual functions. One study, for example, showed an increase of about 30 IQ points among

Many of the ideas parents have about child development are based on myth rather than reality. Successful child rearing requires a balance of love, discipline, and guidance.

orphaned kids who'd been moved from a poor institution to a better one at age six. "It is quite clear," writes Rutter in *Maternal Deprivation Revisited* (Penguin Books), "that major environmental improvements in middle-class childhood can lead to substantial increases in IQ."

The same pattern applies when early impairments are due to physical rather than psychological causes. A group of Hawaiian children who suffered birth trauma—including potentially dangerous periods of anoxia, or lack of oxygen—were

studied over a span of eighteen years. Their initial impairments were linked to later problems in development only when combined with persistently poor environmental circumstances such as chronic poverty, family instability, or illness of the mother. Those children who were raised in an intact family and with nurturing, stimulating parents showed few, if any, negative effects of the complications endured at birth—unless, of course, they had suffered severe damage to the central nervous system.

The data strike an optimistic note.

Although a highly unfavorable environment can produce damage, young kids often prove to be resilient and malleable—capable of changing when circumstances change. Under the proper conditions, early deficits can be erased and the potential for a productive life fulfilled.

9 Spare the rod, and spoil the child.

Probably no child-rearing fiction has been as convincingly disproved as this one—yet it is still devoutly believed by countless parents, who inflict physical pain in the name of discipline as a cornerstone of their child-rearing techniques.

The myth that corporal punishment pays dividends undoubtedly carries higher stakes for our kids than any other discussed in this article. Research has convincingly demonstrated that using the "rod" creates children who are not more obedient but who are instead simply more angry and aggressive than other kids. Parents who routinely slap or strike their children are actually handing them a model of violence to imitate—and many do indeed grow to be abusive, some even murderously so.

Physical punishment may initially appear effective. For example, a three-year-old "strapped" for scratching up Mom's new coffee table is not likely to go near that table for a while, but ultimately the child-victim learns mainly how important it is not to get caught—and to even the score. In the long run, corporal punishment is surely not a proficient technique for inducing children to adhere to parental standards. As they grow, children will tend to follow the guidance of those who inspire affection and admiration, not fear or contempt.

10 Parental conflicts don't affect children who don't yet talk.

Most parents are aware that it is disturbing to children of school age when Mother and Father carry on arguments in their presence. We know from youngsters' responses to parental quarrels how sensitive they are to the tensions that sometimes descend like a cloud on the household—and to hearing expressions of suspicion, anger, or contempt. For good reason, therefore, we try to avoid exposing our quarrels to the kids in the household.

But it has been assumed by most parents that the same care need not necessarily be taken in the case of infants and toddlers, who, to quote one neighbor, "are too young to know and understand." That assumption, it now turns out, does not hold up. In studies conducted both in the natural environment of the home and in research laboratories, it is clear that even very young children can be acutely sensitive to arguments and other displays of interpersonal static in their environment.

At the National Institute of Mental Health, in Bethesda, Maryland, psychologists Carolyn Zahn-Waxler, Ph.D., and Mark Cummings, Ph.D., have found that in homes where conflict is high, children as young as eighteen months to two years become sufficiently upset to actually make efforts to break up their parents' battles. Moreover, they have shown that when two-year-olds at play become aware of arguments around them—even between strangers—they get rattled and begin acting more aggressively toward their peers. The evidence is compelling: Even before they can tell us about it, many children are remarkably well "tuned in" to the quality of the interpersonal relationships in their environment.

Where Pelicans Kiss Seals

IN THE SURPRISING WORLD OF CHILDREN'S ART, DELIGHTFUL IMAGES AND ORIGINAL RULES ARE CREATED TO REPRESENT THE WORLD.

ELLEN WINNER

Ellen Winner is a psychologist at Boston College and at Project Zero of Harvard University.

The story of how children learn to draw seems at first glance to be a simple one: At a very early age they begin by scribbling with any available marker on any available surface. At first the children's drawings are simple, clumsy and unrealistic; gradually they become more technically skilled and realistic.

But the development of drawing is not quite so simple and straightforward. In fact, the story turns out to be quite complex. Watch a 2-year-old scribbling. The child moves the marker vigorously across the page, leaving a tangled web of circular and zig zag lines. It looks as if the marks themselves are an accident—the unintended result of the child's arm movements. But if you replace the child's marker with one that leaves no trace, the child will stop scribbling, as psychologist James Gibson and Patricia Yonas, then a graduate student, showed in 1968. Even though very young children enjoy moving their arms vigorously, they are also interested in making marks on a surface.

If we do not watch a scribble in the making, but only see the final product, it may look like a meaningless tangle of lines. And this is how scribbles have traditionally been viewed—as nonsymbolic designs. But 1- and 2-year-olds are rapidly mastering the concept that words, objects and gestures stand for things. So why shouldn't they also grasp that marks on a page can stand

for things? Some of the more recent studies of children as they scribble suggest that these early scrawls are actually experiments in representa-

TO A 2-YEAR-OLD, SCRIBBLES AREN'T JUST SCRIBBLES, THEY'RE A PLANE FLYING ACROSS THE SKY.

tion—although not purely pictorial representation.

Psychologist Dennie Wolf, preschool teacher Carolee Fucigna and psychologist Howard Gardner of Project Zero at Harvard University studied how the drawing of nine children developed from age 1 to 7. The researchers took detailed notes on the process of scribbling, and their investigations show us that children have surprising representational abilities long before they spontaneously produce a recognizable form.

At first the representation is almost entirely gestural, not pictorial. Wolf observed a 1½-year-old who took the marker and hopped it around on the page, leaving a mark with each imprint and explaining as she drew, "Rabbit goes hop-hop" (Figure 1). This child was symbolizing the rabbit's motion, not its size, shape or color. The meaning was carried primarily by the marker itself, which stood for the rab-

bit, and by the process of marking. Someone who saw only the dots left on the page would not see a rabbit. Nonetheless, in the process of marking, the child was representing a rabbit's movement. Moreover, the dots themselves stood for the rabbit's footprints. Here in the child's earliest scribbles we already see glimmerings of the idea that marks on a page can stand for things in the world.

Two-year-olds rarely spontaneously create recognizable forms in their scribbles, but they have the latent ability to do so. When Wolf or Fucigna dictated to 2-year-olds a list of features (head, tummy, arms, legs), these children plotted the features systematically on the page, placing them in correct relative positions (Figure 2). But they lacked the notion that a line stands for the edge of an object and had no way to represent parts of features, since each feature was either a point or a patch. The children clearly understood, however, that marks on a surface can be used to stand for features "out there," off the page, and that they can be used to show the relative spatial locations of features.

Typically at age 3, but sometimes as early as age 2, children's spontaneous scribbles become explicitly pictorial. They often begin by making gestural scribbles but then, noticing that they have drawn a recognizable shape, label and further elaborate it. For example, one 3½-year-old studied by Wolf, Gardner and Fucigna looked at his scribble and called it "a pelican kissing a seal." He then went on to add eyes and freckles so that the drawing would look even more like a pelican and a seal (Figure 3). Another child, on the eve of his second birthday, made some seemingly unreadable marks, looked at his picture and said with confidence, "Chicken pie and noodies" (his word for noodles). Clearly he saw the similarity between the lines on the page and noodles on a plate.

Sometimes children between 2 and 3 will use both gestural and pictorial modes at different times. A 2-year-old studied by art educator John Matthews of Goldsmiths College in London drew a cross-like shape, then looked at it and called it "an airplane." One month later, this same child moved his brush all around in a rotating motion while announcing, "This is an airplane." The label was the same, but the processes and products were different. In the first case, the drawing was an airplane because it looked like one. In the second case, it was an airplane because the marker moved like one, leaving a record of the airplane's path.

With pictorially based representations, the child begins to draw enclosed shapes such as circular forms and discovers that a line can be used to represent an object's edge. This major milestone marks the child's invention of a basic rule of graphic symbolization. This invention cannot be attributed to closer observation of nature, since objects don't have lines around them. Nor can it be attributed to the influence of seeing line drawings. As shown by psychologist John Kennedy at the University of Toronto, congenitally blind children and adults, when asked to make drawings (using special equipment), also use lines to stand for an object's boundaries.

Sometime around 3 to 4 years of age, children create their first image of a human—the universal "tadpole"—consisting of a circle and two lines for legs. Figure 4 shows a typical tadpole, with a circle standing for either the head alone, or, more probably, head and trunk fused; it has two legs but no arms. It was drawn by a 3-year-old; by 4, children begin to distinguish the head from the trunk and often add arms to their figures.

The tadpole is indisputably a purely graphic (rather than gestural) representation of a human. But why would children universally invent such an odd image to stand for a person? Many people believe that children draw humans in this queer fashion because this is the best they can do; the tadpole is simply a failed attempt at realistic representation. According to some investigators, including psychol-

Figure 1: While hopping a marker around the page, a 1½-year-old said, "Rabbit goes hop, hop, hop" and made these marks.

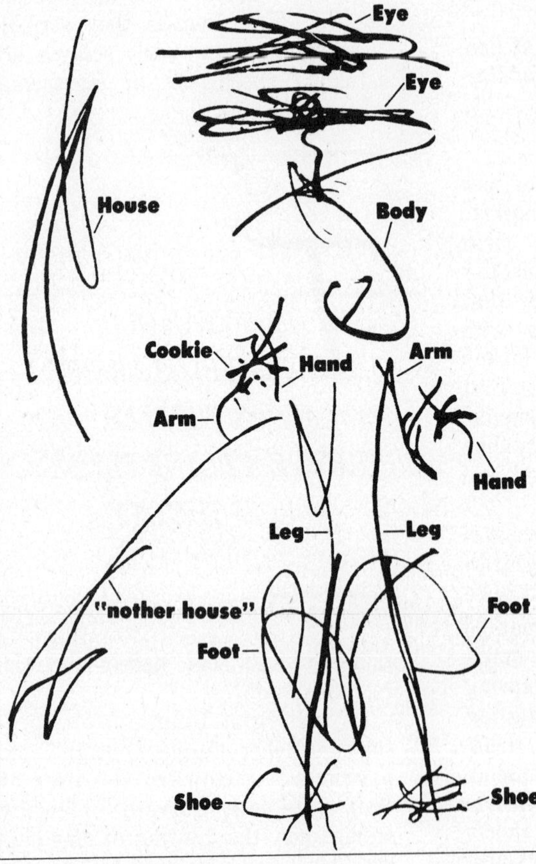

Figure 2: When someone dictates a list of body parts, even 2-year-olds can show them in their correct positions.

ogist Jean Piaget, children's drawings are intended to be realistic, but children draw what they know rather than what they see. Hence, the tadpole, with its odd omissions of trunk and arms, must indicate children's lack of knowledge about the parts of the human body and how they are organized.

Psychologist Norman Freeman of the University of Bristol has a different way of accounting for the typical omissions. He notes that children draw a person from top to bottom, in sequence. We know from verbal-memory tasks that people are subject to "primacy" and "recency" effects—that is,

after hearing a sequence of words, they recall best the words they heard first and last and tend to forget those that came in between. The child, Freeman argues, is showing such effects in drawing, recalling the head (drawn first) and legs (drawn last) and forgetting the parts in the middle. As Freeman sees it, tadpoles result from deficient recall, not deficient concepts.

But other research suggests that we should look on the tadpole more positively. Psychologist Claire Golomb of the University of Massachusetts in Boston suggests that children know more about the human body than

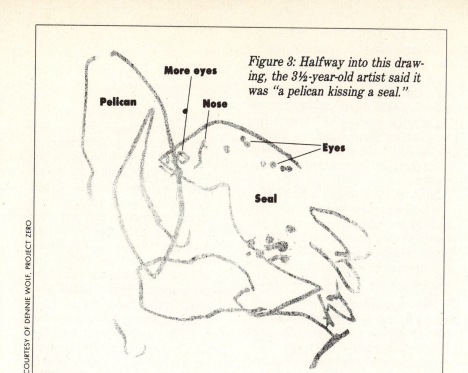

Figure 3: Halfway into this drawing, the 3½-year-old artist said it was "a pelican kissing a seal."

More eyes

Pelican

Nose

Eyes

Seal

COURTESY OF DENNIE WOLF, PROJECT ZERO

about how to draw it, and their body-part omissions are not due to forgetting. She found that when 3-year-olds were asked to name body parts, they almost always mentioned arms, although they typically omitted them from their tadpoles. She also discovered that such children were less likely to create tadpoles when they made Play-Doh people or when they were given a two-dimensional assemble-the-parts task. Even on a drawing task, when Golomb gave children a drawing

*W*HY DO 3-YEAR-OLDS FIRST DRAW A PERSON AS AN ODD ARMLESS 'TADPOLE'— A CIRCLE WITH TWO LINES?

of a head with features to complete, 3- and 4-year-olds (who ordinarily drew tadpoles) typically differentiated a head and a trunk. Finally, if children were asked to draw someone playing ball—a task implicitly requiring that

they draw arms—they were likely to include them (Figure 5).

One 3-year-old drew a tadpole but described it in full detail as she drew it, naming parts that were not there, such as feet, cheeks and chin. Clearly, this child was not trying to show all of these parts, because she made no special marks for them. Instead, her simple figure stood for an entire human in all its complexity.

Although adults make drawings that are far more complex, they, too, do not (and cannot) draw all that they see. Young children are more selective than adults, no doubt because drawing is difficult for them, but also because they have not yet been fired up by the peculiarly Western pictorial ideal of realism.

Psychologist Rudolf Arnheim, formerly of the University of Michigan, argues that children try to create the simplest form that can still be "read" as a human. Because they have a limited repertoire of forms, they reduce them to simple geometric shapes. In the case of the tadpole, they usually reduce the human body to a circle and two straight lines.

Adult artists often deliberately select a limited repertoire of forms and, like children, reduce natural forms to a few simple geometric shapes. They recognize that realism is but one ideal among many and may choose not to be realistic. Young children, however,

seem to draw simple geometric shapes in part because realism does not spark their interest. Once they do catch the desire for realism, Golomb says, that desire begins to overcome their natural tendency to simplicity, leading them toward more complex, graphically differentiated drawing.

By late childhood or early adolescence, children in our culture begin to master linear perspective, the Western system for creating the illusion of three-dimensional depth on a two-dimensional surface, invented and perfected during the Renaissance.

Many people believe that the ability to use perspective is taught, either explicitly in art class or tacitly through exposure to pictures showing such perspective. But something far more creative on the part of children may be happening, says psychologist John Willats, formerly of the North East London Polytechnic.

Willats seated groups of children of different ages in front of a table with objects on it and asked them to draw what they saw (Figure 6a). The children, 108 in all, who were from 5 to 17 years old, used six different systems of perspective; these, Willats found, formed a developmental sequence:

The 5- and 6-year-olds were entirely unable to represent depth. They simply drew a rectangular box for the tabletop and let the objects float above it (stage 1: Figure 6b). Seven- and 8-year-olds drew the tabletop as a straight line or thin surface and placed the objects on that line (stage 2: Figure 6c). Again, their pictures contained no recognizable strategy for representing depth.

At about age 9, children made their first readable attempts to depict the third dimension. They drew the tabletop as a rectangle and placed the objects inside or on top of the rectangle (stage 3: Figure 6d). These children had invented a system for representing depth: To depict near objects, draw them on the bottom of the page; to depict far objects, draw them on the top of the page. In other words, transform near or far in the world into down or up on paper. No one teaches a child to draw this way. Moreover, no child actually sees a tabletop as a rectangle (unless looking at it from a bird's-eye view). Hence, this strategy is a genuine invention.

Younger adolescents drew the table-

Picasso: I used to draw like Raphael, but it has taken me a whole lifetime to learn to draw like children.

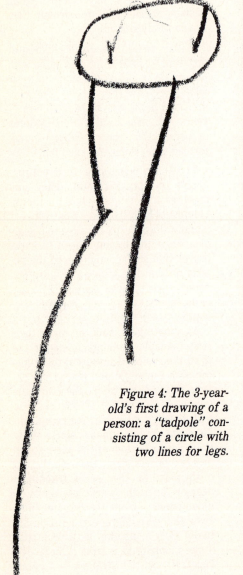

Figure 4: The 3-year-old's first drawing of a person: a "tadpole" consisting of a circle with two lines for legs.

top as a parallelogram rather than as a rectangle (stage 4: Figure 6e). As in the previous stage, they incorrectly drew the lines parallel, not converging, but they now correctly used oblique lines to represent edges receding in space. Again, such a system for representing depth is neither taught nor based on visual experience, since using parallel lines is not optically correct.

In the last two stages, older adolescents drew in perspective, making the lines of the tabletop converge. Some made the lines converge only slightly (naïve perspective—stage 5: Figure 6f); others achieved geometrically correct perspective (stage 6: Figure 6g).

This sequence cannot be explained simply by a growing desire and ability to draw objects as they really appear, because as children develop, their drawings actually get less realistic before they get more realistic. A tabletop, viewed from eye level, might be seen as an edge (stage 2), or from a bird's-eye view it might be seen as a rectangle (stage 3). But no one ever sees a tabletop as a parallelogram (stage 4) or with incorrectly converging edges (stage 5).

Willats believes this sequence does not result from copying pictures in perspective. After all, he argues, in our culture drawings with perspective rarely depict a rectangular surface as either a rectangle (stage 3) or a parallelogram (stage 4).

But I believe these two stages may indeed be attempts to copy the perspective seen in pictures. A tabletop drawn in perspective shows its surface (and stage 3 is an advance over stage 2 because it shows the surface), and its lines are at nonright angles (and stage 4 is an advance over stage 3 because the angles are oblique). But if children are trying to copy perspective drawings, they are doing it at their own developmental level. For example, in stage-4 drawings, children reduce what should be a trapezoid to a simpler, more regular parallelogram.

One way to test the effect of exposure to pictorial perspective is to ask children to copy such pictures. Freeman did just this, finding that although children could not copy the model's perspective system accurately, they could adopt a system more advanced than the one they used spontaneously. Freeman showed children

Some children show more drawing ability than others and produce elaborate, realistic drawings at an early age. When others are still drawing tadpoles, these children are drawing human figures with differentiated body parts in correct proportion and are even putting depth cues into their drawings. People often assume that these advanced artists are brighter than those who lag behind and produce primitive, undifferentiated, unrealistic drawings.

Indeed, psychologists have developed intelligence tests based, in part, on the assumption that drawing level reflects cognitive level, IQ or both. For instance, as part of the Stanford-Binet Intelligence Scale, children are asked to copy shapes, and the Goodenough-Harris Draw-a-Man test uses drawing as a measure of IQ, with more parts and details yielding higher scores.

But studies of both normal and abnormal people show that drawing ability is independent of ability in other areas. The most dramatic evidence comes from studies of idiot savants who, despite severe retardation, autism or both, draw at an astonishingly sophisticated level.

The best-known case, studied by psychologist Lorna Selfe, formerly of the University of Nottingham, is that of Nadia, an autistic child who, as early as age 3½, drew in an optically realistic style reminiscent of Leonardo da Vinci. In addition to her studies of Nadia, Selfe compared retarded autistic children who were gifted in drawing with normal children of the same mental age. She found that the retarded children were better able to depict proportion, depth and the overlap of objects in space.

In a similar vein, psychologists Neil O'Connor and Beate Hermelin of the Medical Research Council Developmental Psychology Project in London studied five young-adult idiot savants who had special drawing ability but very low verbal and performance IQ scores and com-

ARE SMARTER CHILDREN BETTER ARTISTS?

Top: Nadia, 5½, extremely autistic and artistic, made the drawing (left) that resembles a Leonardo da Vinci sketch (right). Below: An early elementary school child drew in perspective, revealing unusual ability.

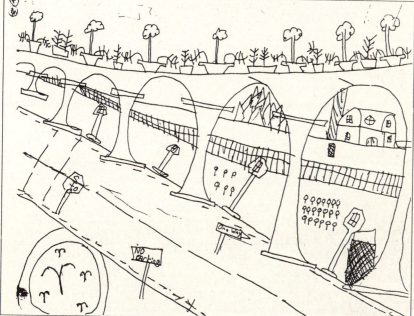

providing details or in their levels of motor control and coordination.

If gifted artists—both retarded and nonretarded—aren't necessarily more intelligent, what skills enable them to draw better than other people? To address this question, O'Connor and Hermelin used a battery of other tests, all of which assessed visual memory. When retarded artists were compared with retarded nonartists, the artists outperformed the nonartists on all tests.

Visual-memory skill, independent of IQ, also seems to help normal children to excel at drawing. Recently, Hermelin and O'Connor compared artistically gifted normal children with nongifted children matched in IQ. They found that the artists had superior memory for two-dimensional designs and were more skilled at identifying incomplete pictures.

With psychologist Elizabeth Rosenblatt at Harvard's Project Zero, I recently completed a study along the same lines. We compared preadolescent children, selected by their art teachers as gifted in drawing, with other children selected as average in drawing ability. We showed the youngsters pairs of pictures and asked them to indicate their preferences. Later we showed them the paired pictures again, but one member of each pair had been slightly altered (in line quality, color, form, composition or content). We asked the children to identify which member of each pair had been changed and to say what was different about it.

The artistically gifted students performed significantly better than the nonartists on both aspects of this task, even though, when they first saw the pictures, they did not know that they would be asked later to recall them. Apparently, children with drawing talent simply cannot forget the patterns they see around them, just as musicians often report being unable to get melodies out of their minds.

pared them with other equally mentally retarded people who had no special drawing ability. They gave these two groups a battery of tests, including the Draw-a-Man test. On this test the retarded artists performed at a much higher level than the equally retarded nonartists; their performance was also much higher than their IQ scores would have predicted. The retarded artists particularly excelled in their ability to depict body proportion, rather than in depicting specific features,

ages 5 to 8 a drawing of a table in oblique perspective (stage 4) and asked them to copy it. About half of the children produced stage-3 drawings. What is significant is that, in their attempts at imitation, half of these children—who were at the age when they would be expected to make stage-1 or stage-2 drawings—actually drew at stage 3.

Thus, children do not acquire perspective by directly copying pictures drawn in perspective. But exposure to such pictures does stimulate them to try a perspective system at least one step more advanced than they might otherwise use.

Children as well as adults are in conflict when drawing in perspective because this way of drawing does not match what we know about objects. For example, a table drawn in perspective does not show the top surface as a rectangle, yet we know the tabletop is rectangular. Although we would like to show things as we see them, we also want to show them as we know they are. Perhaps this is why, as shown by psychologist Margaret Hagen and Harry Elliot, then a graduate student at Boston University, adults prefer drawings with stage-4 perspective to those with stage-6 perspective; stage-6 drawings make objects look too distorted.

Knowing that a good pictorial likeness is not necessarily an exact copy of a scene as it actually appears, artists often deliberately break the rules of perspective. For example, to correct for the size distortion called for by the rules of perspective, they may draw a distant mountain larger than it would appear in a photograph. Perhaps for similar reasons, children may not at first draw objects with optical realism; they are interested in showing things in the most informative way rather than showing exactly how things look.

Do children improve further as they get older? If realism is the standard, the answer is clearly yes. For example, their figures become more complex, and they can represent depth through linear perspective. But I believe, on esthetic grounds, that children's drawings actually get worse with age.

Figure 5: A young child, asked to draw people playing ball, includes arms.

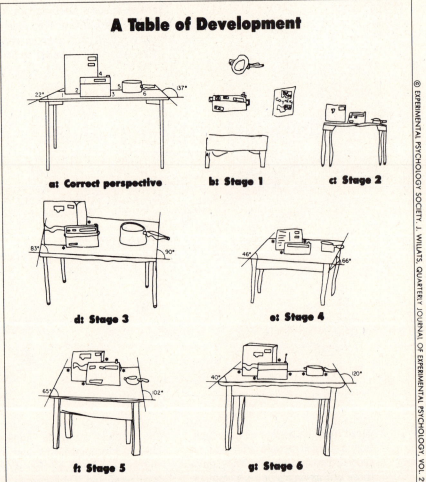

Figure 6: As children develop, they become better at representing depth. The first table (a), drawn in correct perspective, shows what the children were trying to copy.

© EXPERIMENTAL PSYCHOLOGY SOCIETY. J. WILLATS, QUARTERLY JOURNAL OF EXPERIMENTAL PSYCHOLOGY, VOL. 299, 1977. P. 162.

9. Where Pelicans Kiss Seals

Figures 7 and 8: This 6-year-old's drawing (top) is free, fanciful and inventive. An 11-year-old's drawing (bottom) is neater and more realistic but also less inventive.

Because preschool children are unconcerned with realism, their drawings are free, fanciful and inventive. Suns may be green, cars may float in the sky and complex, irregular forms in nature are reduced to a few regular geometric shapes. They produce simple, strong pictures that evoke the abstractions found in folk, "primitive" and contemporary art (Figure 7).

The older child's drawing may be more realistic, neat and precise, but, in my opinion, it is also less imaginative and less striking (Figure 8). Suns are now appropriately yellow and placed carefully in the corner of the picture, and cars now rest firmly on the ground.

This development is inextricably tied up with acquiring the technical skills essential for adult artistic activity. Nonetheless, once such skills are mastered, artists often turn back to young children's drawings for inspiration and may work hard to do consciously and deliberately what they once did effortlessly and because they had no choice. "I used to draw like Raphael," Picasso is quoted as saying, "but it has taken me a whole lifetime to learn to draw like children."

"What Is Beautiful Is Good": The Importance of Physical Attractiveness in Infancy and Childhood

Linda A. Jackson

Ph.D. University of Rochester
Associate Professor, Department of Psychology
Michigan State University

Hiram E. Fitzgerald

Ph.D. University of Denver
Professor, Department of Psychology
Michigan State University

"She's so ugly!" "He's got a big nose!" "She's too fat!" Most parent have heard one or more of these comments from their children and can probably recall making similar comments themselves, both as children and as adults. Yet the typical response from parents overhearing such comments from their children goes something like "That's not nice. It's not what a person looks like but what's inside the person that matters." Good advice! But do children take it? Do adults take it? Decades of research in social psychology on the effects of physical appearance on the perception and treatment of others suggests that this advice goes largely unheeded. In fact, children and adults do "judge the book by its cover" and the tendency to do so has implications not only for the immediate interaction but also for the self concepts of those who are responded to on the basis of their appearance.

Research on people's reactions to attractive and unattractive infants, children, and adults has revealed one striking similarity. Across all of these age groups attractive individuals are reacted to more favorably than unattractive individuals, an observation commonly referred to as the "what is beautiful is good" stereotype. Like it or not, the benefits of beauty are evident at birth. For example, in one study nurses gave better prognosis for the intellectual development of attractive premature infants than unattractive premies. By three months of age it is clear that "all babies do not look alike." There are beautiful babies and beauty counts.

What is beauty in infancy? Research indicates that several clearly distinctive physical characteristics are associated with "cuteness" in infants. Most are facial characteristics. Short and narrow facial features, large eyes and pupils, and a large forehead make an infant appear "cute." Female infants reach a "cuteness peak" at nine months of age while male infants reach their "cuteness peak" at eleven months. This difference in peak cuteness is presumed to reflect the more rapid physical development of female infants compared to male infants. If asked to guess the sex of an infant, adults are more likely to guess "female" if the infant is cute, although they rate infants identified as female as less cute. These findings suggest that more stringent standards of physical attractiveness for females than for males exist as early as infancy. Other factors which influence the cuteness ratings of infants are facial expression and birth order. Smiling infants are rated as cuter than crying infants. First born infants are rated as cuter than later born infants, apparently because first borns tend to be better dressed and groomed than later borns. Not surprisingly, parents rate their infants as cuter than strangers rate them, suggesting that there is some truth to the statement that "beauty is in the eye of the beholder."

Given the evidence that infants do not "all look alike," at least in terms of their cuteness, do differences in their appearance have an effect on adult reactions to them? The answer is an unequivocal "yes." The initial adult response to an unfamiliar infant, the smile, occurs regardless of the infant's cuteness. However, the subsequent response to an unfamiliar infant, the prolonged gaze, is affected by the infant's cuteness. Cuter infants are looked at longer than less cute infants, at least in situations where the adult has a choice about what to look at. Psychologists have speculated that the greater time spent looking at cute infants may result in more care-giving behaviors directed toward them than toward their less cute age mates. For example, in day care situations where caregivers must continually make choices about how to divide their attention among equally familiar infants, being cute may reap benefits. Day care centers with high turnover, in which infants are unfamiliar to caregivers, may be even more susceptible to the effects of an infant's cuteness on the amount of attention and caregiving provided to him or her.

Results of the research on the effects of infants' cuteness on their parents' reactions to them lead to similar conclusions. Mothers of infants who were rated as cute by strangers maintain more eye contact, more ventral holding contact (tummy to tummy), and kiss their infants more than mothers of infants rated as less cute by strangers. Differences in behavior related to the infants' cuteness have also been observed in fathers. Greater stimulation, as evidenced by touching, kissing and moving, is provided by fathers of cute infants than by fathers of less cute infants. Fathers' ratings of their infants' cuteness at three months of age were related to their caregiving behaviors toward their infants, and to ratings of their relationship with their infants. These relations were not obtained for mothers. Taken as a whole, the research suggests that the benefits of beauty begin in infancy and include the responses of parents as well as strangers. However, it is important to keep in mind that parents rate their infants as cuter than strangers rate them, the "eye of the beholder" effect.

Turning from the effects of attractiveness in infancy to its effects in early childhood, it would be heartening to find that appearance factors become less important as there is more and more of the "person within" to respond to. Such is not the case, however. In keeping with the "what is beautiful is good" stereotype, ratings of unfamiliar children by both adults and agemates indicate that attractive children are perceived as more intelligent, popular, and desirable as friends than unattractive children. These differences are evident among raters as young as three years old. Even teachers are not immune to the effects of a child's attractiveness. In one study teachers were asked to rate an unfamiliar child who had committed a transgression. A photograph of the child attached to the description of the transgression indicated that the child was either attractive or unattractive. Teachers rated the transgression as more serious, rated the child as more antisocial, recommended more severe punishment,

and believed the child was more likely to transgress again when the child was unattractive than when she or he was attractive. Other research supports the conclusion that attractive children have an advantage over unattractive children in first encounters with peers and with adults. These findings have important implications since first encounters often set the stage for the development of friendships and expectations for future behavior.

But what about the attractiveness of familiar children? Commonsense suggests that with greater familiarity there should be less of a tendency to behave toward others in stereotypic ways. While there is some evidence to support this commonsense assumption, there is also evidence to support the equally commonsense assumption that being good looking is an asset even among friends. Attractive classmates are viewed as more popular and as having more socially desirable characteristics than unattractive classmates as early as preschool. However, the benefits of beauty among acquaintances appear to be limited to girls. In fact, the research suggests that attractiveness may be a liability for school-aged boys. In several studies children have rated their attractive male classmates as more incompetent, antisocial, and disliked than their unattractive male classmates. Teachers rated attractive unfamiliar boys as more uncontrolled, impulsive, and unpredictable compared to unattractive boys. The basis for this differential response to attractive boys and girls has yet to be understood. It may be that the strong association between attractiveness and "female" or "femininity" is responsible for the negative effects of boys' attractiveness on other's perceptions of them, but additional research is needed to test the validity of this explanation.

Given the above evidence that physical attractiveness influences perceptions of children, does it also influence behavior toward them? Research suggests that there are differences in the treatment of attractive and unattractive children, although the evidence is not as strong as the evidence for differences in perceptions. In one study in which undergraduate women were asked to role play a child's parent, unattractive children were punished more severely than attractive children. In another study, small but significant relations were found between the actual grades of elementary school children and their physical attractiveness. A third study showed that the attractiveness of seventh graders influenced the amount of time teachers spent interacting with them. Attractive seventh graders were interacted with more than unattractive seventh graders, although a similar relation was not obtained for younger children. It has also been observed that teachers' referrals for remedial help are more likely for attractive children than for unattractive children.

Thus, the bulk of research indicates that attractive

Facts About Physical Attractiveness in Infancy and Early Childhood

1. There are distinctive physical characteristics related to ratings of physical attractiveness in infancy. Short and narrow facial features, big eyes and pupils, and a large forehead make an infant "cute."

2. An infant's "cuteness" is related to the amount of time parents and strangers spend looking at the infant. This difference in visual attention has implications for the amount of caregiving behaviors received by attractive and unattractive infants.

3. The "what is beautiful is good" stereotype is evident in children as young as three years. Attractive age mates are believed to be more intelligent, sociable, and desirable as friends than unattractive age mates.

4. The behavior of teachers is influenced by the child's physical attractiveness. Transgressions by unattractive children are viewed as more serious and as deserving of more severe punishment than the same transgressions of attractive children. Teachers believe that unattractive children who transgress are more antisocial and more likely to transgress again than attractive children.

5. Physical attractiveness may be a liability for school-aged boys, in contrast to its ubiquitous benefits for girls of all ages. Attractive boys are viewed by their peers as more antisocial, and dislikable than unattractive boys. Teachers view attractive boys as more impulsive, uncontrollable, and unpredictable compared to unattractive boys.

6. Small but significant relations have been found between children's attractiveness and their school grades and performance on standardized tests of achievement.

7. Variability in ratings of attractiveness within cultures, differences in what constitutes attractiveness between cultures, and cultural differences in the importance of physical attractiveness must be taken into account in understanding the implications of physical attractiveness.

---

and unattractive infants and young children are perceived differently, and behaved toward differently by children, parents, and other adults. It would therefore be surprising if attractive and unattractive children did not themselves differ in some important ways. Both commonsense psychology and a wealth of research on the self-fulfilling prophecy suggests that what we are is, at least in part, a reflection of how other people see us. There is some evidence of behavior differences between attractive and unattractive children. Relations between attractiveness and scores on standardized achievement tests have been found. Attractive children score higher than unattractive children and this difference increases with age. On the other hand, no relations between attractiveness and IQ scores has been found. Studies of preschoolers indicate that attractive children spend less time in solitary play than average attractiveness or unattractive children. When playing with same-sex age mates, attractive 5-year-olds are less aggressive, less active, and show a slight preference for feminine toys compared to unattractive 5-year-olds. Although the evidence is not overwhelming in its quantity, it nevertheless points to some important differences in the behavior of attractive and unattractive children, differences which have implications for the development of the self concept and adult adjustment.

Exactly what are the implications of the research on the effects of physical attractiveness in infancy and early childhood for parents of today's young children?

Does this research imply that parents should do their utmost to make their children physically attractive so that they may reap the benefits of beauty? Or should parents simply resign themselves to the empirical proof of the fact that books are sometimes judged by their covers? We believe that neither of these extremes is implied by the research on physical attractiveness and young children for a number of reasons. First, much of this research has compared attractive children to unattractive children when, in fact, most children fall somewhere in between. Those few studies which have included average unattractiveness groups often, but not always, find no differences between average and very attractive children. Thus, children of average attractiveness appear to be just as well off as very attractive children, in terms of other's perceptions of them and other's behavior toward them.

Secondly, physical attractiveness, like other physical attributes, is not a particularly stable characteristic over the span of childhood physical development. While the "ugly duckling turned swan" is an extreme example of the instability of physical appearance, most parents are well aware of how much their childrens' appearance changes from year to year. Taken together with the evidence that beauty is, to some extent, in the eye of the beholder, the effects of appearance on the reactions of others are likely to be quite variable over the course of childhood development.

Third, the effects of others' reactions to the child based on the childs' physical appearance are likely to be swamped by the effects of reactions based on other, more enduring and more important characteristics. For example, teachers' reactions to a child depend more on such characteristics as his or her personality, social skills, and academic performance than on his or her physical appearance. This is not to deny the importance of the effects of physical attractiveness demonstrated in the research. But these effects need to be put in a proper perspective.

Finally, it is important to point out that while there is some consensus about what constitutes physical attractiveness in infancy and early childhood, there is also considerable variability within cultures, and even greater variability between cultures in ratings of attractiveness. Cultures also differ in the emphasis they place on physical appearance compared to other characteristics. Since much of the research demonstrating the "what is beautiful is good" stereotype has been conducted in the United States, the generalizability of the results to other cultures remains an open question.

Formal Education and Early Childhood Education: An Essential Difference

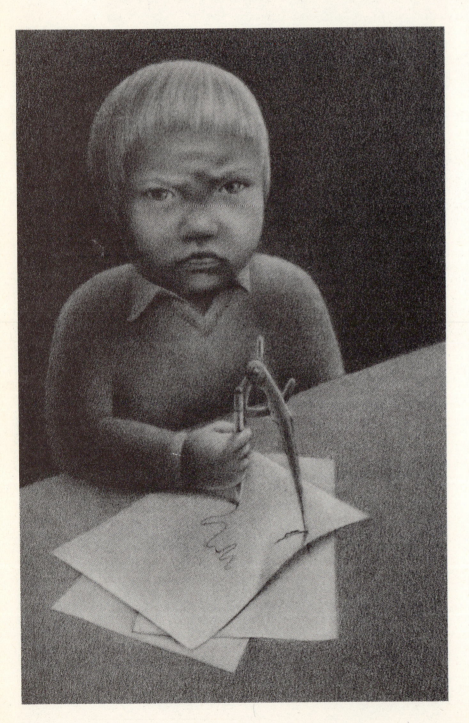

Educational programs devised for school-age children are being applied to the education of younger children, as well. Why is the special character of learning in early childhood being ignored by people who should know better?

David Elkind

DAVID ELKIND is a professor of child study and resident scholar at the Lincoln Filene Center for Citizenship and Public Affairs, Tufts University, Medford, Mass. He is the author of The Hurried Child *(Reading, Mass.: Addison-Wesley, 1981) and* The Miseducation of Children: Superkids at Risk *(New York: A.A. Knopf, 1986). ©1986, David Elkind.*

YOUNG CHILDREN do not learn in the same ways as older children and adults. Because the world of things, people, and language is so new to infants and young children, they learn best through direct encounters with their world rather than through formal education involving the inculcation of symbolic rules. The fact of this difference is rooted in the observations of such giants of child study as Froebel, Montessori, and Piaget, and it is consistently supported by the findings of research in child development.[1] This fact was also recognized by the ancients, who described the child of 6 or 7 as having attained the "age of reason."

Given the well-established fact that young children learn differently, the conclusion that educators must draw is a straightforward one: the education of young children must be in keeping with their unique modes of learning. If we

From *Phi Delta Kappan*, May 1986, pp. 631-636. © 1986, Phi Delta Kappan, Inc.

accept this conclusion, what is happening in the U.S. today is truly astonishing. In a society that prides itself on its openness to research and on its respect for "expert" opinion, parents, educators, administrators, and legislators are blatantly ignoring the facts, the research, and the consensus of experts about how young children learn and how best to teach them.

All across the country, educational programs devised for school-age children are being applied to the education of young children, as well. In such states as New York, Connecticut, and Illinois, administrators are advocating that children enter formal schooling at age 4. The length of many kindergarten programs has been extended to a full day, and nursery school programs have become prekindergartens. Moreover, many of these kindergartens have introduced curricula (including workbooks and papers) once reserved for first-graders. And a number of writers, in books addressed to parents, advocate the teaching of reading and math to infants and very young children.[2]

This transformation of thinking regarding early childhood education raises at least three questions that I will attempt to answer here. First, why is this happening? As we have seen, both theory and research consistently agree that young children learn differently from older children and adults. And no one really questions the principle that education should be adapted to the learning abilities of the students to be instructed. Why is the special character of learning in early childhood being ignored by so many people who should know better?

The second question depends on the first. Even if young children are being taught in the manner of older children, what harm is there in that? After all, it could be that we have merely been coddling young children by not introducing them to a rigorous academic program at an early age. Doesn't the new research on infants and young children substantiate their eagerness to learn and the importance of the early years for intensive instruction? We will see below that this is not quite the case.

The third question follows from the first two. If it can be demonstrated that early, formal instruction does more harm than good, what can we do about it? After all, that is the direction, however mistaken, in which U.S. society as a whole is heading. Formal instructional programs for infants and young children are expanding not only in academic

areas but also in sports, the arts, and computer science. To oppose these trends is to ignore the social consensus and to run counter to the culture at large. We live in a democratic society in which the majority rules, so what can a minority do even if it wants to?

WHY BEGIN SO SOON?

In America, educational practice is determined by economic, political, and social considerations much more than it is by what we know about what constitutes good pedagogy for children. Until the 1960s, however, early childhood education was an exception to this general rule. Early childhood education programs were, for the most part, privately run and well adapted to the developmental needs of the children they served. Even kindergartens in public schools had a special status and were generally free of the social pressures that influenced the rest of elementary and secondary education.

All of that changed in the 1960s, however, when early childhood education was abruptly shoved into the economic, political, and social spotlight. At that moment, early childhood education lost its innocence and its special status. Like elementary and secondary education, early childhood education became a ground on which to fight social battles that had little or nothing to do with what was good pedagogy for children. The formal symbol of this mainstreaming of early childhood education came with the passage by Congress of the Head Start legislation in 1964. For the first time, early childhood programs were being funded by the federal government.

What brought about this change during the Sixties? In many ways early childhood education was the scapegoat of the social movements of that turbulent decade. Elementary and secondary education were already under attack on two different fronts. First, such events as the launching of Sputnik I in 1957, the demise of progressive education, and the publication of such books as *Why Johnny Can't Read* focused the spotlight of criticism on American education. One explanation (actually, a rationalization) for the problems that such close scrutiny revealed was that children were poorly prepared for school and that early childhood education should be more academically rigorous so that children could move more rapidly once they entered school.

The second front on which education was trying to fight a rear-guard action

was in the arena of the civil rights movement. One of the main issues taken up by this movement was the unequal schooling of minorities. Schools for black children, for example, were obviously inferior in quality to those for white children. Again, one explanation (rationalization) was that black children were poorly prepared for school. It wasn't the schools, the argument ran, but the preparation that led to the lower achievement levels of black children. The Head Start legislation was one response to this claim.

One major consequence of this institutionalization of early childhood education was the introduction of a new conception of infants and young children. Educational practice is not alone in being determined by the social, economic, and political tenor of the times. The conception of the child changes with the times as well. For example, a dominant conception of the child in the 19th century — dictated by the religious orthodoxy of the time — was the notion of the "sinful child." Educating the sinful child necessarily involved "breaking the will" by whatever harsh means were needed to do so.

The advent of Freudian psychology in the early 20th century, along with the continuing secularization and urbanization of American society, gradually replaced the concept of the sinful child with the concept of the "sensual child." Freud's depiction of infantile sexuality and his theories regarding the central role of sexuality in the formation of neuroses focused attention on the development of a "healthy personality."[3] Progressive education had as one of its aims the open, spontaneous expression of feelings and emotions (judged to be healthy) rather than their suppression or repression (judged to be unhealthy). During the reign of the sensual child, there was less concern with the child's intellectual development, which, in an emotionally healthy child, was presumed to take care of itself.

The intellectual importance given early childhood education by the civil rights movement and the education reform movement of the 1960s was inconsistent with the concept of the sensual child. A new concept of infants and young children was, therefore, required. This new concept had to be in keeping with the new significance attached to academic education during the early years. What emerged was the concept of the "competent infant." Unwittingly, perhaps, social scientists of the time, caught up in the emotion of the social movements, fostered this conception through unwarranted reinterpretations of established facts about the cognitive development of young children.

Jerome Bruner, for example, though he was not trained in child development or in education, became a guru of the education reform movement of the day.[4] His totally unsubstantiated claim that "you can teach any child any subject matter at any age in an intellectually honest way" became a touchstone of the new conception of the "competent infant." In the same way, Benjamin Bloom's ambiguous statement that a young child attains half of his or her intellectual ability by the age of 4 (based on well-known correlations between I.Q. scores attained by the same subjects at different ages) was another foundation for the conception of the "competent infant."[5] Finally, James McV. Hunt's idea of the malleability of I.Q. (an idea that had always been accepted by reputable psychometricians) was presented as a new idea that was in opposition to the mental testing establishment's supposed advocacy of a fixed I.Q.[6]

Thus the conception of the competent infant and young child was dictated by social and political forces rather than by any new data or findings about the modes of learning of young children. Whatever psychological theory or educational research that was brought to bear to reinforce this conception had been carefully selected and interpreted to support the notion of early childhood competence. Contrary evidence was ignored. The facts were made to fit the hypothesis rather than the hypothesis being changed to accommodate the facts. In short, our conception of the child at any point in history has been much more dependent on social, political, and economic considerations than on the established facts and theories of child development.

The concept of the competent infant was also congruent with the changing lifestyles of American middle-class families. During the reign of the sensual child, middle-class values dictated that mothers stay at home and rear their children, lend support to their husbands, and run the home. Home economics became a major department for women in most colleges and universities of the time and reflected these values. Within that set of middle-class values, the concept of a sensual infant who was in need of a mother's ministrations fit quite comfortably.

In the past two decades, however,

The conception of the competent infant and young child was dictated by social and political forces rather than by any new data or findings.

thanks partly to the women's movement and partly to the shift in U.S. society from an industrial to a postindustrial economy, the middle-class value system has changed dramatically. The women's movement accentuated women's need for choice in the matter of whether to stay home or to pursue a career. At the same time, a postindustrial economy can make use of more women in the workforce than an industrial economy. In the past, factory work required the large muscles of men, but, with the miniaturization of modern technology, the small motor skills and dexterity of women are in greater demand. Likewise, now that our economy is becoming primarily a service economy, the social skills of women are also much in demand.

Another change in the circumstances of the middle class has contributed to the growing number of middle-class women in the workforce. As divorce has become socially acceptable, divorce rates have soared, and it is now expected that more than half of all marriages will end in divorce. In more than 90% of these cases, it is the mother who retains custody of the children. And because alimony and child support are rarely enough to live on, divorced mothers swell the ranks of working women.

One result of these changes in lifestyle and values has been that middle-class women are entering the workforce in ever-increasing numbers. More than 50% of U.S. women are now employed outside the home, and it is estimated that by the year 2000 between 80% and 90% of women will be in the workforce. One consequence of this social movement is that increasing numbers of infants and young children are being cared for outside the home. Current estimates place the number of children under the age of 6 who are receiving one or another form of out-of-home care at six million.

The conception of the competent infant is clearly more in keeping with these contemporary family styles than is the conception of the sensual infant. A competent infant can cope with the separation from parents at an early age. He or she is able to adjust with minimal difficulty to baby sitters, day-care centers, full-day nursery schools, and so on. If some parents feel residual pangs of guilt about leaving their young offspring in out-of-home care, they can place their youngster in a high-pressure academic program. If the child were not in such a program, the parents tell themselves, he or she would fall behind peers and would not be able to compete academically when it is time to enter kindergarten. From this perspective, high-pressure academic preschool programs are for the young child's "own good."

The social dynamics behind the pressure to place young children in educational programs appropriate for school-age children now become painfully clear. The truth is that the many changes in our society have not been accompanied by adequate provisions for the out-of-home care of all the young children who require it. Consequently, parents are putting pressure on elected officials to provide more early childhood care. This has been the primary motivation for full-day kindergartens, starting school at age 4, and so on. Although the avowed reasons for these proposals are to be found in "new" research showing the need for early childhood education, the "new" data consist of nothing more than the "old" (and always dubious) data from the 1960s. The real reason for these programs is that elected officials are feeling pressure from voters to offer out-of-home care for young children.

There is another motive for introducing formal instruction in early childhood programs. This comes from our intuitive psychology regarding technology and human behavior. Much intuitive psychology derives from emotions and feelings rather than from reason and balanced judgment. Nonetheless, such intuitions seem so obviously correct that one thinks it foolish even to question them. (The so-called "gambler's fallacy" is a case in point: the gambler believes that the number of previous losses increases his or her probability of winning, while, in fact, there is no relationship between the two.)

The intuition regarding human behavior and technology is equally fallacious. The intuition is that human potentials are altered by technology. With respect to children, this intuition is often expressed by saying that, thanks to such innovations as television and computers, children today are brighter and more sophisticated than children in the past. This intuition has reinforced and supported the conception of the competent infant and has been used to rationalize the formal instruction of preschool children.

Technology, however, neither changes human potential nor accelerates human development. Technology extends and amplifies our human potentials, but it does not alter them. The telephone extends our hearing; television extends our vision; computers extend our memories. But neither our capacity for hearing, nor our capacity for seeing, nor our capacity for remembering have been changed by the technology. Modern weaponry may have amplified our ability to express our aggression, but it has neither heightened nor lessened our tendency to be aggressive. There is simply no truth in the intuitive belief that technology alters human potential.

Exactly the same holds true with respect to children. Computers have not improved children's intellectual capacities; they have only amplified the limitations of young children's thinking. Consider "turtle geometry," an application of the computer language Logo, created by Seymour Papert for use with preschool and school-age children.[7] Children learn to write programs that move the cursor in different directions to draw figures on a video screen. The sequence of directions then becomes an elementary program for drawing the figure. One instruction, however, gives young children a great deal of trouble. This is the instruction to rotate the cursor in different directions without moving it. Young children do not easily understand that you can change direction while standing still, and they have difficulty grasping this command. Thus the use of the technology only amplifies the limitations of young children's thinking.

Television provides another example. Programs such as "Sesame Street" and "The Electric Company" were supposed to make learning to read easier for young children. However, the rapid presentation of material on these programs is much too fast for the information-processing abilities of young children. It could be that these programs, geared to the information-processing speeds of adults and older children, have amplified the attentional limitations of young children, with negative consequences for their reading abilities.

We miseducate children whenever we put them at risk for no purpose. Formal instruction puts excessive demands on young children.

These programs have been on the air for almost 20 years, and during that time "attentional deficits" have become the leading form of learning disability. Yet most people continue to believe that these programs have improved children's reading abilities. Such intuitive belief that children today are brighter and more sophisticated than previous generations tops off the list of commonly accepted reasons for the formal instruction of young children.

THE HARM OF EARLY INSTRUCTION

What harm is there in exposing young children to formal instruction involving the inculcation of symbolic rules? The harm comes from what I have called "miseducation."[8] We miseducate children whenever we put them at risk for no purpose. The risks of miseducating young children are both short- and long-term. The short-term risks derive from the stress, with all its attendant symptoms, that formal instruction places on children; the long-term risks are of at least three kinds: motivational, intellectual, and social. In each case, the potential psychological risks of early intervention far outweigh any potential educational gain.

Short-term risks. Stress is a demand for adaptation. In this broad sense, of course, stress is coincident with life itself. In a narrower, clinical sense, however, stress refers to any excessive demand for adaptation. What is excessive, in turn, depends on both the individual and the demands made.

Elsewhere I have suggested that each individual has two sources of energy with which to cope with stress.[9] One of these is what I call "clock energy." This

is the energy that we use up in pursuing the tasks of daily living, and it is replenished by food and rest. By contrast, what I call "calendar energy" is the energy involved in growth and development that is given us in a more or less fixed quantity and that determines our total life span.

The early symptoms of stress are those associated with clock energy: fatigue, loss of appetite, and decreased efficiency. When the excessive demands continue without adequate time for replenishment, an individual must draw on his or her calendar energy. When this happens, such psychosomatic stress symptoms as headaches and stomachaches that can injure the organism and shorten the life span begin to appear. In young children exposed to formal instruction, both types of stress symptoms are frequently seen.

The reason for this is not difficult to understand. Formal instruction puts excessive demands on young children. A concrete example may help make this point. The learning of young children is "permeable" in the sense that they do not learn in the narrow categories defined by adults, such as reading, math, science, and so on. At the level at which young children learn, there are no sharp boundaries. When young children make soup, for example, they learn the names of vegetables (language), how to measure ingredients (math), the effects of heat on the hardness and softness of the vegetables (science), and the cross-sectional shapes of the vegetables (geometry). It would be nonsense, however, to single out any one of these learnings as a separate lesson in any of the subjects listed in parentheses.

The focus on a specific learning task, as demanded by formal instruction, is thus at variance with the natural mode of learning of the young child. From the viewpoint of formal instruction, the multiple learning potential of the young child is seen as evidence of distractability or the currently more fashionable phrase, attentional deficit. The pressure to focus on one avenue of learning, such as letter or word identification, is very stressful for young children. Pediatricians around the country report an increase in stress-related symptoms in young children.[10] A pediatrician I met at a meeting of the National Academy of Pediatrics told me that he is treating a 4-year-old who has peptic ulcers.

To be sure, formal instruction is but one of the many demands made on a young child in a formal program of education. The child is also separated from his or her parents, a second stress; is in a new and unfamiliar place with strange children and adults, a third stress; and is required to learn new rules of conduct, still another stress. Although the demands of formal instruction may not be sufficient in themselves to overstrain the young child's reservoir of clock energy, the combination of stresses associated with formal schooling can be sufficient to produce symptoms.

By contrast, young children in a sound program of early childhood education have the support of activities nicely suited to their learning styles. This eliminates the stresses occasioned by the curriculum and the stilted teacher/student interactions inherent in formal instruction.

Long-term effects. One long-term danger of early instruction is the potential harm it can do to the child's motivation to learn. In addition to being permeable, the spontaneous learning of young children is self-directed. Children learn their native language not because anyone "teaches" them that language in a formal way but because they have both the need and the capacity to learn language. They use the language models and verbal interactions provided by their environment to acquire this most complicated skill. Young children have their own set of learning priorities.

Certainly some things need to be taught to very young children. For example, they need to learn what might be called the "healthy" fears: for example, not to touch fire, not to insert fingers in electrical sockets, and not to cross streets without looking both ways. Such learning is not self-directed, but it is necessary for survival. On the intellectual plane, however, children's natural curiosity about the world around them is a strong directive for learning the basic categories and concepts of the physical world. Sound early childhood education encourages children's self-directed learning by providing an environment that is rich in materials to explore, manipulate, and talk about.

When adults intrude in this self-directed learning and insist on their own learning priorities, such as reading or math, they interfere with the self-directed impulse. Children can learn something from this instruction, but it may be something other than what the adults intended. A child may learn to become dependent on adult direction and not to trust his or her own initiative. Erik Erikson has described early childhood as the period when the balance is struck between the sense of initiative

and the sense of guilt.[11] *And this balance has consequences for a lifetime.*

A child whose self-directed learning is encouraged will develop a sense of initiative that will far outweigh a sense of guilt about getting things started. On the other hand, a child whose self-directed learning is interfered with, who is forced to follow adult learning priorities, may acquire a strong sense of guilt about *any* self-initiated activities. One risk of early formal instruction, then, is that it may encourage a sense of guilt at the expense of a sense of initiative.

Let me recount an anecdote to make this risk concrete. Several years ago I met a renowned psychiatrist who told me the following story. In the 1930s, psychologist Myrtle McGraw carried out what has become a classic study of the contributions of nature and nurture to motor development.[12] McGraw's study involved twin boys, Johnny and Jimmy. In her study, McGraw trained one of the twins, Johnny, in a variety of motor tasks, such as riding a tricycle and climbing. Jimmy was not trained. Johnny soon surpassed Jimmy in the skills in which he had been trained. On the other hand, after the training was discontinued, Jimmy quickly caught up with his brother, so that, by the end of the year in which the training was initiated, there was no difference in the motor skills of the twins. In motor learning, maturation appeared to be at least as important as training.

What the psychiatrist told me, however, was that he had seen the twins several years after the investigation had been completed. When he examined the boys, he found a striking difference in their personalities and, particularly, in their approach to learning. Johnny, the twin who had been trained, was diffident and insecure. He seemed always to be looking for adult direction and approval of his activities. Jimmy, the untrained twin, was quite the opposite. Self-confident and self-assured, he undertook activities on his own without looking to adults for guidance and direction. Though this example is anecdotal, it does illustrate the potential risk of too much adult intervention in the self-directed learning of young children.

Early formal instruction also puts the child at intellectual risk. Jean Piaget emphasized the importance of what he called "reflective abstraction" for the mental ability of the child.[13] A child who is engaging in self-directed learning can reflectively abstract from those activities. That reflective abstraction encourages the growth of new mental

abilities. Piaget cited the example of a child who is rearranging 10 pebbles. First, the child makes them into a square, then into a circle, and next into a triangle. What the child discovers, as a result of that activity, is that no matter how he or she arranges the pebbles they still remain 10 in number. In effect, the child has learned the difference between perception and reason. Perceptually, it appears as if there are more pebbles in one configuration than in another. Reason tells the child that they are the same.

When adults intrude on a child's learning, they also interfere with the process of reflective abstraction. Formal instruction presents the child with some content to be learned. Flash cards present the child with a visual configuration that the child must first discriminate and then memorize. Teaching young children phonics is another example of presenting the child with an association that he or she must learn without much active intervention or exploration. Rote learning and memorization, the stuff of much formal education, provide little opportunity for reflective abstraction. Such reflective abstraction, however, is essential for the full realization of a child's cognitive abilities.

Introducing formal instruction too early also puts the child at social risk. One aspect of formal instruction — thankfully absent in sound early childhood education — is the introduction of the notions of "correct" and "incorrect." These notions not only orient the child's thinking but also introduce social comparison. One child gets an answer right, and another gets it wrong. Therefore, one child is smarter, somehow better than the other. Such social comparisons are harmful enough among school-age children, but they are truly damaging among preschoolers.

This damage can occur because the focus on right and wrong turns the child away from self-directed and self-reinforcing sources of self-esteem. Instead, it directs children to look primarily to adults for approval and to social comparison for self-appraisal. This works against the formation of self-esteem that a child attains from successfully completing a self-initiated and self-directed task. From the point of view of socialization, the danger of early instruction is that it can make children too dependent on others for their sense of self-worth. Sound early childhood education encourages children to feel good about themselves as a consequence of their own achievements.

To be sure, the foregoing descriptions

of damage to motivation, intellectual growth, and self-esteem are potential risks that are not always realized in every child who is miseducated. But why put a child at risk in the first place? There is really no evidence that early formal instruction has any lasting or permanent benefits for children. By contrast, the risks to the child's motivation, intellectual growth, and self-esteem could well do serious damage to the child's emerging personality. It is reasonable to conclude that the early instruction of young children derives more from the needs and priorities of adults than from what we know of good pedagogy for young children.

WHAT CAN WE DO?

The miseducation of young children, so prevalent in the United States today, ignores the well-founded and noncontroversial differences between early childhood education and formal education. As educators, our first task is to reassert this difference and insist on its importance. We have to reeducate parents, administrators, and legislators regarding what is sound education for young children. And we must make it clear that it is not out-of-home care for young children that is potentially harmful — only the wrong kind of out-of-home care. Sound early childhood education is an extension of the home, not of the school.

As a profession, we have no choice but to go public. Those who are making money from the miseducation of young children are the ones about whom parents hear and read the most. We need to write for popular magazines, speak out on television forums, and encourage newspaper articles about the difference between good early childhood education and miseducation. We are in a war for the well-being of our children, and in this war the media are our most powerful weapon. It is a war we can never absolutely win, no matter how hard we fight. But, unless we fight as hard as we can, it is a war we will certainly lose.

---

1. Sheldon H. White, "Some General Outlines of the Matrix of Developmental Changes Between 5 and 7 Years," *Bulletin of the Orton Society*, vol. 20, 1970, pp. 41-57.
2. See, for example, Glen Doman, *Teach Your Baby to Read* (London: Jonathan Cape, 1965); Peggy Eastman and John L. Barr, *Your Child Is Smarter Than You Think* (New York: Morrow, 1985); and Sidney Ledson, *Teach Your Child to Read in 60 Days* (Toronto: Publishing Company, Ltd., 1975).
3. Sigmund Freud, "Infantile Sexuality," in A. A. Brill, ed., *The Basic Writings of Sigmund Freud* (New York: Random House, 1938).
4. Jerome Bruner, *The Process of Education* (Cambridge, Mass.: Harvard University Press, 1960).
5. Benjamin S. Bloom, *Stability and Change in Human Characteristics* (New York: Wiley, 1964).
6. James McV. Hunt, *Intelligence and Experience* (New York: Ronald Press, 1961).
7. Seymour Papert, *Mindstorms* (New York: Basic Books, 1980).
8. David Elkind, *The Miseducation of Children: Superkids at Risk* (New York: A.A. Knopf, 1986).
9. David Elkind, *All Grown Up and No Place to Go: Teenagers in Crisis* (Reading, Mass.: Addison-Wesley, 1984).
10. T. Berry Brazelton, quoted in E.J. Kahn, "Stressed for Success," *Boston Magazine*, December 1985, pp. 178-82, 255-57.
11. Erik H. Erikson, *Childhood and Society* (New York: Norton, 1950).
12. Myrtle B. McGraw, *A Study of Johnny and Jimmy* (New York: Appleton-Century-Crofts, 1935).
13. Jean Piaget, *The Psychology of Intelligence* (London: Routledge & Kegan Paul, 1950).

The Child-Care Dilemma

Millions of U.S. families face a wrenching question: Who's minding the kids?

The smell of wet paint wafts through the house on a tree-lined street on Chicago's North Side. Marena Mc-Pherson, 37, chose a peach tint for the nursery: a gender-neutral color. But the paint had a will of its own and dried a blushing shade of pink. Ah well, no time to worry about that. With the baby due in less than a month, there are too many other concerns. Like choosing a name, furnishing the baby's room, reading up on infant care and attending childbirth classes. Above all, McPherson must tackle the overriding problem that now confronts most expectant American mothers: Who will care for this precious baby when she returns to work?

An attorney who helps run a Chicago social-service agency, McPherson has accumulated two months of paid sick leave and vacation time. She plans to spend an additional four months working part time, but then she must return to her usual full schedule. So for several months she has been exhaustively researching the local child-care scene. The choices, she has learned, are disappointingly few. Only two day-care centers in Chicago accept infants; both are expensive, and neither appeals. "With 20 or 30 babies, it's probably all they can do to get each child's needs met," says McPherson. She would prefer having a baby-sitter come to her home. "That way there's a sense of security and family." But she worries about the cost and reliability: "People will quit, go away for the summer, get sick." In an ideal world, she says, she would choose someone who reflects her own values and does not spend the day watching soaps. "I suspect I will have to settle for things not being perfect."

That anxiety has become a standard rite of passage for American parents. Beaver's family, with Ward Cleaver off to work in his suit and June in her apron in the kitchen, is a vanishing breed. Less than a fifth of American families now fit that model, down from a third 15 years ago. Today more than 60% of mothers with children under 14 are in the labor force. Even more striking: about half of American women are making the same painful decision as McPherson and returning to work before their child's first birthday. Most do so because they have to: seven out of ten working mothers say they need their salaries to make ends meet.

With both Mom and Dad away at the office or store or factory, the child-care crunch has become the most wrenching personal problem facing millions of American families. In 1986, 9 million preschoolers spent their days in the hands of someone other than their mother. Millions of older children participate in programs providing after-school supervision. As American women continue to pour into the work force, the trend will accelerate. "We are in the midst of an explosion," says Elinor Guggenheimer, president of the Manhattan-based Child Care Action Campaign. In ten years, she predicts, the number of children under six who will need daytime supervision will grow more than 50%. Says Jay Belsky, a professor of human development at Pennsylvania State University: "We are as much a society dependent on female labor, and thus in need of a child-care system, as we are a society dependent on the automobile, and thus in need of roads."

At the moment, though, the American child-care system—to the extent that there is one—is riddled with potholes. Throughout the country, working parents are faced with a triple quandary: day care is hard to find, difficult to afford and often of distressingly poor quality. Waiting lists at good facilities are so long that parents apply for a spot months before their children are born. Or even earlier. The Empire State center in Farmingdale, N.Y., received an application from a woman attorney a week after she became engaged to marry. Apparently she hoped to time her pregnancy for an anticipated opening. The Jeanne Simon center in Burlington, Vt., has a folder of applications labeled "preconception."

Finding an acceptable day-care arrangement is just the beginning of the struggle. Parents must then maneuver to maintain it. Michele Theriot of Santa Monica, Calif., a 37-year-old theatrical producer, has been scrambling ever since her daughter Zoe was born 2½ years ago. In that short period she has employed a Danish au pair, who quit after eight months; a French girl, who stayed 2½ months; and an Iranian, who lasted a week. "If you get a good person, it's great," says Theriot, "but they have a tendency to move on." Last September, Theriot decided to switch Zoe into a "family-care" arrangement, in which she spends seven hours a day in the home of another mother. Theriot toured a dozen such facilities before selecting one. "I can't even tell you what I found out there," she bristles. In one home the "kids were all lined up in front of the TV like a bunch of zombies." At another she was appalled by the filth. "I sat my girl down on the cleanest spot I could find and started interviewing the care giver. And you know what she did?" asks the incredulous mother. "She began throwing empty yogurt cups at my child's head. As though that was playful!"

Theriot is none too sure that the center she finally chose is much better. Zoe's diapers aren't always changed, instructions about giving medicine are sometimes ignored, and worse, "she's started having nightmares." En route to day care on a recent day, Zoe cried out, "No school! No school!" and became distraught. It is time, Theriot concludes, to start the child-care search again.

Fretting about the effects of day care on children has become a national preoccupation. What troubles lie ahead for a generation reared by strangers? What kind of adults will they become? "It is scaring everybody that a whole generation of children is being raised in a way that has never happened before," says Edward Zigler, professor of psychology at Yale and an authority on child care. At least one major survey of current research, by Penn State's Belsky, suggests that extensive day care in the first year of life raises the risk of emotional problems, a conclusion that has mortified already guilty working parents. With high-quality supervision costing upwards of $100 a week, many families are placing their children in the hands of untrained, overworked personnel. "In some places, that means one woman taking care of nine babies," says Zigler. "Nobody doing that can give them the stimulation they need. We encounter some real horror stories out there, with babies being tied into cribs."

The U.S. is the only Western industrialized nation that does not guarantee a working mother the right to a leave of absence after she has a child. Although the Supreme Court ruled last January that states may require businesses to provide maternity leaves with job security, only 40% of working women receive such protection through their companies. Even for these, the leaves are generally brief and unpaid. This forces many women to return to work sooner than they would like and creates a huge demand for infant care, the most expensive and difficult child-care service to supply. The premature separation takes a personal toll as well, observes Harvard Pediatrician T. Berry Brazelton, heir apparent to Benjamin Spock as the country's preeminent guru on child rearing. "Many parents return to the workplace grieving."

New York City Police Officer Janis Curtin resumed her assignment in south Queens just eight weeks after the birth of Peter. The screaming sirens and shrill threats of street thugs were just background noise to a relentless refrain in her head: "Who can I trust to care for my child?" She tried everything, from leaving Peter at the homes of other mothers to handing him over to her police-officer husband at the stationhouse door when they worked alternating shifts. With their schedules in constant flux, there were snags every step of the way. Curtin was more fortunate than most workers: police-department policy allows a year of unpaid "hardship" leave for child care. She decided to invoke that provision.

The absence of national policies to help working mothers reflects traditional American attitudes: old-fashioned motherhood has stood right up there with the flag and apple pie in the pantheon of American ideals. To some people day-care centers, particularly government-sponsored ones, threaten family values; they seem a step on the slippery slope toward an Orwellian socialist nightmare. But such abstract concerns have largely receded as the very concrete need for child care is confronted by people from all walks of life.

Child care is fast emerging as a political issue. At least three Democratic presidential candidates have been emphasizing the need for better facilities and calling for

federal action. Former Arizona Governor Bruce Babbitt has proposed that the U.S. Government establish a voucher system to help low-income parents pay for day care. Delaware Senator Joseph Biden favors federal child-care subsidies for the working poor and tax incentives to encourage businesses to provide day care. If elected, he vows, he will set up a center for White House employees as an example to other employers. Massachusetts Governor Michael Dukakis, who has established the country's most comprehensive state-supported day-care system, would like to see the Federal Government fund similar programs throughout the U.S.

Last week the issue surfaced on Capitol Hill. In the House, Republican Nancy Johnson of Connecticut and Democrat Cardiss Collins of Illinois introduced legislation to establish a national clearinghouse for information on child-care services. A Senate subcommittee began hearings focused on the shortage of good-quality, affordable day care. Says Chairman Christopher Dodd of Connecticut: "It's about time we did something on this critical problem."

Without much federal help, the poorest mothers are caught in a vise. Working is the only way out of poverty, but it means putting children into day care, which is unaffordable. "The typical cost of full-time care is about $3,000 a year for one child, or one-third of the poverty-level income for a family of three," says Helen Blank of the Children's Defense Fund in Washington. As a result, many poor mothers leave their young children alone for long periods or entrust them to siblings only slightly older. Others simply give up on working.

Rosalind Dove, 29, of Los Angeles, is giving it her best shot. A single mother of four, she worked for five years as a custodian in a public high school, bringing home $1,000 in a good month. "I was paying $400 a month for child care," she recalls. "We didn't buy anything." When that failed, she began bringing her children to work with her, hiding them in an empty home-economics classroom while she mopped floors and hauled huge barrels of trash for eight hours a day. "I'd sneak them in after the teacher left and check on them every 30 minutes or so." She finally quit last February and slipped onto the welfare rolls. She applied for state child-care assistance, only to learn there were 3,000 others on the waiting list. Frustrated, she returned to work this month. "Don't ask me how I'm going to manage," she says.

Child care has always been an issue for the working poor. Traditionally, they have relied on neighbors or extended family and, in the worst of times, have left their children to wander in the streets or tied to the bedpost. In the mid-19th century the number of wastrels in the streets was so alarming that charity-minded society ladies established day nurseries in cities around the country. A few were sponsored by employers. Gradually, local

regulatory boards began to discourage infant care, restrict nursery hours and place emphasis on a kindergarten or Montessori-style instructional approach. The nurseries became nursery schools, no longer suited to the needs of working mothers. During World War II, when women were mobilized to join wartime industry, day nurseries returned, with federal and local government sponsorship. Most of the centers vanished in the postwar years, and the Donna Reed era of the idealized nuclear family began.

Two historic forces brought an end to that era, sweeping women out of the home and into the workplace and creating a new demand for child care. First came the feminist movement of the '60s, which encouraged housewives to seek fulfillment in a career. Then economic recessions and inflation struck in the 1970s. Between 1973 and 1983, the median income for young families fell by more than 16%. Suddenly the middle-class dream of a house, a car and three square meals for the kids carried a dual-income price tag. "What was once a problem only of poor families has now become a part of daily life and a basic concern of typical American families," says Sheila B. Kamerman, a professor of social policy and planning at Columbia University and co-author of *Child Care: Facing the Hard Choices.* Some women are angry that the feminist movement failed to foresee the conflict that would arise between work and family life. "Safe, licensed child care should have been as prominent a feminist rallying cry as safe, legal abortions," observes Joan Walsh, a legislative consultant and essayist in Sacramento.

In the early 1970s, there was a flurry of congressional activity to provide child-care funds for the working poor and regulate standards. But under pressure from conservative groups, Richard Nixon vetoed a comprehensive child-development program in 1971, refusing, he said, to put the Government's "vast moral authority" on the side of "communal" approaches to child rearing. The Reagan Administration has further reduced the federal role in child care. In inflation-adjusted dollars, funding for direct day-care subsidies for low- and middle-income families has dropped by 28%.

California, Minnesota, Massachusetts, New York and Connecticut are among the few states that have devoted considerable resources to improving child-care programs. Most states have done virtually nothing. Thirty-three have lowered their standards and reduced enforcement for licensed day-care centers. As of last year, 23 states were providing fewer children with day care than in 1981.

Nor have American businesses stepped in to fill the void. "They acknowledge that child care is an important need, but they don't see it as their problem," says Kamerman. Of the nation's 6 million employers, only about 3,000 provide some sort of child-care assistance. That is up from about 100 in 1978, but most merely provide advice or referrals. Only about 150 employers provide on-site or near-site day-care centers. "Today's corporate personnel policies remain stuck in a 1950s time warp," charges David Blankenhorn, director of the Manhattan-based Institute for American Values. "They are rooted in the quaint assumption that employees have 'someone at home' to attend to family matters."

There are basically three kinds of day care in the U.S. For children under five, the most common arrangement is "family" or "home-based" care, in which toddlers are minded in the homes of other mothers. According to a Census Bureau report called *Who's Minding the Kids,* 37% of preschool children of working mothers spend their days in such facilities. An additional 23% are in organized day-care centers or preschools. The third type of arrangement, which prevails for older children and for 31% of those under five, is supervision in the child's own home by a nanny, sitter, relative or friend.

Home-based groups are popular primarily because they are affordable, sometimes costing as little as $40 a week. The quality depends on the dedication of the individual mothers, many of whom are busy not only with their paid charges but with their own children as well. Darlene Daniels, 31, a single mother of three in Chicago, has been through four such sitters in six months. Two proved too expensive and careless for Daniels, who was earning $7 an hour as a janitor; another robbed her. "For most people, it's not their own kids, and they're just looking at the dollar sign," she complains.

Only eight states have training requirements for home-based centers. Regulations governing the ratio of attendants to tots vary widely. In Maryland there must be one adult for every two children under age two. But in Georgia each adult is allowed to care for up to ten children under age two and, in Idaho, twelve.

A private nanny or au pair usually assures a child more individual attention. Professional couples, who must work long hours or travel, often find that such live-in arrangements are the only practical solution, though the cost can exceed $300 a week. However, most live-in sitters in the U.S., unlike the licensed nannies of Britain, have no formal training. Many speak English poorly, and agencies frequently do a cursory job of screening them. A Dallas mother who asked an attorney friend to run a check on her newly hired nanny was told the woman was wanted for writing bad checks. "People need a license to cut your hair but not to care for your child," observes Elaine Claar Campbell, a Chicago investment banker. She and her lawyer-husband Ray, armed with five

pages of questions, spent three months interviewing more than 50 people, before settling on Clara Hawkes, 47, an artist from Santa Fe whose own daughter is a National Merit Scholar. "You don't want to gamble with your child," says Ray.

Au pairs, usually European girls between 18 and 25, are less expensive, receiving an average of $100 a week plus room and board. Most stay only a year, and few have legal working papers. The immigration law that took effect this month will make the employers of such workers liable for fines up to $10,000, though the Immigration and Naturalization Service does not plan an aggressive crackdown on domestic help.

Concerns about legality have led more families to hire American au pairs—frequently teenage girls from the Midwest and often Mormons. "We Mormons come from big families, so we have experience with kids," explains Karen Howell, 19, a Californian who is spending a year with a Washington, D.C., family. "We don't drink, and we know the meaning of hard work." Two agencies—the Experiment in International Living and the American Institute for Foreign Study—have Government permission to bring in 3,100 European au pairs a year on cultural-exchange visas. Although the programs are more expensive than traditional au pair arrangements, host families are assured that their helpers are legal.

The professional day-care center is the fastest-growing option for working parents. There are an estimated 60,000 around the country, about half nonprofit and half operated as businesses. Costs vary widely, from $40 a week to as much as $120. In the best centers, children are cared for by dedicated professionals. At the nonprofit Empire State center in Farmingdale, N.Y., teachers make up lesson plans even for infants. Empire, which receives partial funding from New York State, keeps parents closely informed of their child's development. "If a child takes a first step, develops in the least, that parent is called," says Director Ana Fontana.

Not all day-care centers are so conscientious. Day-care staffers rank in the lowest 10% of U.S. wage earners, a fact that contributes to an average turnover rate of 36% a year. Says Caroline Zinsser of the Center for Public Advocacy Research in Manhattan: "It says something about our society's values that we pay animal caretakers more than people who care for our children." Gilda Ongkeko is delighted with the quality of the Hill an' Dale Family Learning Center in Santa Monica, Calif., attended by Jason, 4. In her job as owner of a preschool-supply company, she has come to appreciate how unusual it is. "I've been to over 1,000 child-care centers," she says, "and I'd say that 90% of them should be shut down. It's pathetic."

Experts worry that a two-tier system is emerging, with quality care available to the affluent, and everyone else settling for less. "We are at about the same place with child care as we were when we started universal education," says Zigler of Yale. "Then some kids were getting Latin and Greek and being prepared for Harvard, Yale and Princeton. Other kids were lucky if they could learn to write their own name."

In 1827 Massachusetts led the way to universal education by becoming the first state to require towns with 500 or more families to build high schools. Now it is showing the way to universal child care. Aided by a booming economy, the state has worked out a program with employers, school boards, unions and nonprofit groups to encourage the expansion and improvement of child-care facilities. Small companies and groups can receive low-interest loans from the state to build day-care facilities. Funds are earmarked for creating centers in public housing projects. School systems can get financial aid for after-school programs. A statewide referral network serves both individual parents and corporations looking for child care.

Emilia Davis, 38, of Boston's working-class Roslindale section, is the beneficiary of another of the state's far-reaching programs. After years of dependence on welfare to support herself and her five children, Davis, who is separated from her husband, is now going to college with the ultimate hope of finding a job. The state's E.T. (employment and training) program provides her with vouchers for day care in the public housing complex where she lives. "Child care is an absolute precondition if one is serious about trying to help people lift themselves out of poverty," insists Governor Dukakis. Though the state will spend an estimated $27 million on day care under the E.T. program this year—and a total of $101 million on all child-care related services—it claims to have saved $121 million in welfare costs last year alone. Next month the state will begin a pilot program that will pay 20% to 40% of child-care costs for 150 working-class families.

San Francisco has adopted another innovative approach. It requires developers of major new commercial office and hotel space to include an on-site child-care center or pay $1 per sq. ft. of space to the city's child-care fund. The state of California is spending $319 million this year on child-care subsidies for 100,000 children. It also funds a network of 72 resource and referral agencies.

Because such state programs are the exception, a number of political leaders and lobbying groups are calling for federal intervention. This summer a coalition of 64 groups—including the National Education Association, the American Federation of Teachers and the Child Welfare League of America—will propose a comprehensive national child-care bill, which will probably call for increased support to help low- and moderate-income families pay for child care. Legislation has already been introduced in both houses of Congress to create a national parental-leave policy.

In an era of towering federal deficits, much of the future initiative will have to come from the private sector. By the year 2000, women will make up half the work force. Says Labor Secretary Bill Brock: "We still act as though workers have no families. Labor and management haven't faced that adequately, or at all."

A few companies are in the forefront. Merck & Co., a large pharmaceutical concern based in Rahway, N.J., invested $100,000 seven years ago to establish a day-care center in a church less than two miles from its headquarters. Parents pay $550 a month for infants and $385 for toddlers. Many spend lunch hours with their children. "I can be there in four minutes," says Steven Klimczak, a Merck corporate-finance executive whose three-year-old daughter attends the center. "It's very reliable, and that's important in terms of getting your job done."

Elsewhere in the country, companies have banded together to share the costs of providing day-care services to employees. A space in Rich's department store in downtown Atlanta serves the children of not only its own employees but also of workers at the Federal Reserve Bank of Atlanta, the First National Bank of Atlanta, Georgia-Pacific and the Atlanta *Journal* and *Constitution* newspapers.

Businesses that have made the investment in child care say it pays off handsomely by reducing turnover and absenteeism. A large survey has shown that parents lose on average eight days a year from work because of child-care problems and nearly 40% consider quitting. Studies at Merck suggest that the company also saves on sick leave due to stress-related illness. "We have got an awful lot of comments from managers about lessened stress and less unexpected leave time," says Spokesman Art Strohmer. At Stride Rite Corp., a 16-year-old, on-site day-care center in Boston and a newer one at the Cambridge headquarters have engendered unusual company loyalty and low turnover. "People want to work here, and child care seems to be a catalyst," says Stride Rite Chairman Arnold Hiatt. "To me it is as natural as having a clean-air policy or a medical benefit."

The generation of workers graduating from college today may find themselves in a better position. They belong to the "baby-bust" generation, and their small numbers, says Harvard Economist David Bloom, will force employers to be creative in searching for labor. Child-care arrangements, he says, will be the "fringe benefits of the 1990s." The economics of the situation, if nothing else, will provoke a change in the attitude of business, just as the politics of the situation is changing the attitude of government. In order to attract the necessary women—and men—employers are going to have to help them find ways to cope more easily with their duties as parents.

—By Claudia Wallis.
Reported by Jon D. Hull/Los Angeles, Melissa Ludtke/Boston and Elizabeth Taylor/Chicago

Development During Childhood

- Social and Emotional Development (Articles 13-16)
- Cognitive and Language Development (Articles 17-20)

Most of the changes that occur during the transition to childhood—as well as those that occur during childhood itself—involve social, cognitive, and language development. The articles in this section touch upon contemporary themes pertaining to each of these developmental domains.

In the last 60 years, there has been a shift in the traits parents would like to see their children develop. Parents in the 1920s wanted their children to show obedience to authority and conformity, while today, parents want their children to show tolerance for others and to demonstrate initiative.

Two selections offer recommendations to parents regarding personality development. Bruce Baldwin tells us in "Building Confidence" that many parents use academic achievement as a measure of their child's motivation. However, the way parents respond to their children can facilitate or destroy the development of positive motivation. Baldwin suggests that parents can help create a healthy atmosphere for achievement motivation by implementing his "Confidence Builder's Checklist."

In a classic study, Thomas, Chess, and Birch identified three basic types of temperament: easy, difficult, and slow-to-warm-up children. Most children display difficult behavior on occasion, as is pointed out in "Dealing With Difficult Young Children." A child's temperament has a great influence on how individuals react to him or her and this, in turn, can affect the child's personality development. Anne Soderman recommends strategies for parents and teachers to help deal with difficult behaviors.

All life transitions create some degree of stress. Although some children react to stress by striking out against its perceived source, and others respond to it by withdrawing and attempting to isolate themselves, some children seem to take stress-producing situations in stride. These "invulnerable" or "resilient" children, as pointed out in "Resilient Children," have developmental histories that may include extreme poverty or chronic family stress. Most people would consider both factors to be potentially damaging to the development of personal and social competence skills. Yet these resilient children do not become victims; instead, they develop effective interpersonal skills. Without question, studies of these children will contribute important knowledge to our understanding of personality development and child-rearing practices.

The articles in the "Cognitive and Language Development" subsection focus on developmental changes in cognitive processing, challenges to IQ definitions of intelligence, the way children learn, and issues related to reading and language acquisition. During the past two decades, the study of cognitive development was dominated by Piaget's theory. This theory is reviewed in "Practical Piaget: Helping Children Understand." Equally important, however, are the examples provided by the author as to how Piaget's theory can be translated into practice. Although the theory provides a rich description of what a child can and cannot do during a particular stage of development, it is less adequate for explaining how a child acquires various cognitive skills. Thus, many developmentalists have turned to information-processing models in an effort to integrate cognitive psychology with cognitive developmental theory. Information-processing research has directed attention to individual differences in skill acquisition, challenging traditional concepts of intelligence; this is addressed in "Three Heads Are Better Than One."

Young children learn best when they can touch, explore, and move about. Knowing what is best and actually implementing these findings into the classroom are two different matters. In the "Back to Basics" movement of the 1980s, homework, drills, and discipline have been emphasized. However, children at the age of six are not physically ready to sit for sustained periods; they think concretely rather than abstractly. The article "How Kids Learn" points out that young children should be taught by different methods than those used for older children, and illustrates teaching methods especially suitable for younger pupils.

Children who have difficulty learning to read for no apparent reason are termed dyslexic. Though the exact cause is not known, some possible causes are discussed in "Facts About Dyslexia"; treatment and prognosis are also considered.

Looking Ahead: Challenge Questions

Children who are described as resilient are an enigma. How would you explain such strength of personality in the face of so many potentially disruptive influences in their

Unit 3

lives? What coping mechanisms seem to provide resilient children with such strength of character?

The ability to solve problems ranks high among lay definitions of intelligence. Yet problem-solving ability is not exactly the same as the intelligence measured by IQ tests. Which do you believe is the better measure of intelligence? The fact that all human beings are not equally intelligent, any more than they are not equally tall, suggests biological variation in the distribution of intelligence. What characteristics of an individual do you think of when you refer to someone as being intelligent? How does dyslexia mask intelligence?

It is said that socialization is a two-way street. How does this apply to child temperament?

THE GREAT PARENTAL VALUE SHIFT

■

FROM
OBEDIENCE
TO
INDEPENDENCE

**Parents used to raise their children to be
dutiful. Today they're raising
them to be self-
reliant.**

Anne Remley

Anne Remley is a writer in Ann Arbor, Michigan.

Which trait would you, as a parent, prefer your child to develop: tolerance for others or obedience to authority? Chances are you'd choose the former, unless you were a parent 60 years ago.

The traits U.S. parents want to see in their children have changed dramatically during this century. In the 1920s, parents emphasized obedience, conformity and respect for home and church. Today, parents are more likely to want their youngsters to think for themselves, accept responsibility, show initiative and be tolerant of opposing views. This virtual revolution in values, charted by University of Michigan sociologist Duane Alwin, has far-reaching implications for parent-child relationships, not to mention the country.

Alwin found graphic evidence of parents' changing goals in the famous "Middletown" research, started in 1924 by sociologists Helen and Robert Lynd and replicated 54 years later by sociologists Theodore Caplow, of the University of Virginia, and Howard Bahr and Bruce Chadwick of Brigham Young University.

In the 1920s, the Lynds asked 141 mothers in "Middletown" (later revealed to be Muncie, Indiana) which traits they most emphasized in rearing their children. The women reviewed a list of qualities ranging from "patriotism" to "social mindedness" (see chart). The three top choices were "loyalty to the church," "strict obedience" and "good manners," showing a strong preference for traits linked to conformity.

Fifty-four years later, a new generation of Muncie mothers had virtually opposite child-rearing goals. Traits linked to autonomy, such as "independence" and "tolerance," which received low rating from mothers in 1924, were among these mothers' top choices, while loyalty to the church, strict obedience and good manners were selected by fewer than a fourth. This metamorphosis is not unique to "Middletown." Surveys done by the National Opinion Research Center (NORC) at the University of Chicago between 1964 and 1986 reveal a similar shift nationwide. Qualities associated with autonomy and independence, such as having good sense and sound judgment, have been increasingly selected as desirable traits for children. Meanwhile, traits linked to conformity, such as obedience to parents, cleanliness and acting as a boy/girl should, have dwindled in popularity. This growing preference for autonomy has swept across class lines, including both white- and blue-collar families.

There are various reasons for this move towards greater individualism, according to Alwin. "It's an increasingly complex world," he says. "Parents want their kids to succeed in it, to survive in it. They know that good jobs require being able to think for yourself."

Another key reason for this shift, he says, is the increased education of parents today. "The farther you go in school, the more you are encouraged to think for yourself and the more likely you are to see that as a positive value for your children."

The rising number of working mothers and single parents has also made self-reliance among children desirable. Pressed for time and energy, these parents often encourage their youngsters to take more responsibility for themselves, tackling homework on their own, transporting themselves back and forth to school or minding younger siblings.

Changes in the religious scene have also affected the shift in parental values. For example, Detroit-area Roman Catholics — despite a doctrine promoting obedience to church authority — have increasingly said they want independent-minded offspring, according to surveys conducted by the University of Michigan's Institute for Social Research during the past 25 years.

Alwin, who analyzed the surveys, found that Catholic parents' values changed as their income, job status and schooling increased and as ethnic Catholics entered the American mainstream. The far-reaching debate over church authority launched in the '60s by the Second Vatican Council helped encourage this shift as well.

This major shift in parental values is not restricted to the United States. Every year since 1951, West German opinion pollsters have asked a large sample of adults what qualities should be stressed in rearing children. In 1951, "self reliance and free will" were selected by 28 percent of the German respondents, while "obedience and following rules" were close behind, at 25 percent. But by 1983, self-reliance had jumped to 49 percent, while obedience had dropped to just 9 percent in the German surveys. Studies in Italy, England and Japan suggest a similar trend.

The emphasis on youthful autonomy can raise some perplexing dilemmas for parents. Tasha LeBow-Wolfe, a mother from Michigan, says, "I've treated Alexis as if she had a mind of her own ever

The Traits Parents Value

▦ Percent in 1924
☐ Percent in 1978

Social Mindedness	Strict Obedience	Loyalty to Church	Tolerance	Patriotism	Good Manners	Independence
13 / 26	45 / 17	50 / 22	6 / 47	21 / 5	31 / 23	25 / 76

In 1924 a group of mothers from "Middletown" (Muncie, Indiana) chose three traits they wanted their children to develop, revealing a strong leaning toward conformity. The preferences of mothers 54 years later, in contrast, emphasized autonomy. The numbers above represent the percentage of mothers who listed the trait as one of their three choices.

since she was a baby. When she was 6 months old and sitting in her crib, I used to ask her what she wanted to do next, what she wanted to eat or to wear. But now that she's 4, sometimes I really want her to mind me. The other day I told her, 'Alexis, you're going to do this right now because I say so!' She looked up at me astounded—as if to say, 'What's going on here? You're changing the rules on me!'"

Sociologist Alwin cites similar experiences in rearing his own three daughters. "For years, my wife and I have urged our kids to think for themselves. Now, when we want them to do something, we have to appeal to their self-interest, their sense of fairness and logic. I probably use the word 'obey' once every six months. But sometimes it's frustrating when you want them to go along with you."

Parents may be beginning to temper their idealism with a measure of pragmatic necessity, according to a 1986 NORC survey of U.S. adults. It found that obedience is regaining favor with the youngest group of adults—those in their late teens and early 20s. When asked which traits best prepare a child for life, these young adults did give top priority to autonomy, but they also emphasized obedience.

Despite this minor boost for conformity, the trend toward independence is not likely to fade. Society has been gradually shifting toward a more open and tolerant view of children for a long time.

In past centuries, children in Western cultures were prized primarily as farm workers and laborers whose meager earnings helped their families survive. By the 1600s affluent and educated parents in England and the American colonies began to adopt a more child-centered, affectionate and permissive stance, thinking in terms of nurturing youngsters' developing skills and talents. In the late 1800s, this view began to spread across class lines. Working and living conditions improved, education increased and children began to be seen as "economically worthless but emotionally priceless," in the words of Columbia University sociologist Viviana Zelizer.

These days, U.S. classrooms increasingly reflect an autonomous approach. "The public schools are listening to parents' goals for children to have more independence and learn how to put their knowledge to use," says psychologist David Weikart, director of the High/Scope Educational Research Foundation in Michigan. Weikart says the trend is toward "independent problem-solving, where the child sees himself as an effective actor, who says, 'I can do

something about this, I'm capable, I can take the initiative.'"

Weikart is working with Massachusetts Sen. Edward Kennedy's staff on legislation governing a curriculum for the proposed Smart Start program, a blend of early childhood education and day care that would affect thousands of 4-year-olds in this country. Weikart advocates a preschool approach that encourages children to think independently, to solve their own problems and to share their plans and progress with others. "We know it works," he says.

In studying ways to help disadvantaged students, Weikart found that preschool programs emphasizing independent thinking yielded lasting benefits. At age 15, their graduates reported better family relationships, more jobs and extracurricular activities and far less delinquency and drug use than students whose preschool program had stressed obedience and conformity. The independent-minded students had "a sense of control over what was going on" in their lives, says Weikart.

But some people fear that Americans' enchantment with autonomy may go too far. Parents may be inadvertently creating a generation of aggressive, competitive, cutthroat adults. "We value independence and training kids to be self-reliant," points out Harvard University psychiatrist Alvin Poussaint, "but people can get too much individuality." Carried to excess, individualism can lead to isolation and alienation, Poussaint warns.

Alwin argues that the trend toward autonomy does not mean that parents and teachers are rearing self-centered youngsters who care only for their own wishes. Parents are also emphasizing values such as "tolerance," "helping others" and "working hard" that will balance out increased autonomy, he says.

Poussaint believes that "*inter*dependence is more appropriate now. We need approaches that bring people together." He wants schools and parents to emphasize cooperation and other techniques that youngsters will need if they are to live and work with others in a spirit of mutual support. A healthy measure of connectedness among people is crucially important, he says. Indeed, it may be essential if society is to survive.

Building Confidence

Discover Your Child's Natural Motivation

Dr. Bruce A. Baldwin

Dr. Bruce A. Baldwin is a practicing psychologist who heads Direction Dynamics, a consulting service specializing in promoting professional development and quality of life in achieving men and women. He responds each year to many requests for seminars on topics of interest to professional organizations and businesses. This article has been adapted from a chapter of Baldwin's new book on parenting, Beyond the Cornucopia Kids: How to Raise Healthy Achieving Children. *For busy achievers, he has also written* It's All in Your Head: Lifestyle Management Strategies for Busy People. *Both are available in bookstores or from Direction Dynamics in Wilmington, North Carolina.*

Tim is in the fifth grade. So far, he's been a rather poor student. Testing has revealed no learning disabilities, but Tim isn't achieving to his potential. He just doesn't seem to care about his homework. He'd rather spend his time making forts with his friends or just tinkering in the garage.

Annette lives just a few doors away. She's a very bright student and loves school. Always willing to tackle new projects, she's a rising star. When not at school, she reads and does extra projects. Her teachers are as proud of her accomplishments as her parents are. As dedicated as she is, she is expected to go far by all who know her.

Now for the compelling question: "Which of these two students is motivated and which is not?" If you answered that Annette has lots of motivation and Tim has virtually none, you would be very wrong. Actually, both of these young people are highly motivated. The difference lies in where their energies are focused. Tim likes to tinker and work outdoors, while Annette likes to study and learn within a classroom environment. The contrast between these two young people also debunks the myth of the "unmotivated" person. As an adult or as a child, there is no such thing.

While everyone is motivated, their directions for personal motivation vary greatly. What parents are most concerned about in an "unmotivated" child is that the child is not "achieving to potential" in school. They realize how important learning is to future success. They fear that their child, whose energies are focused primarily on nonacademic endeavors, will never "make it." Sometimes such parental fears are well founded. Sometimes they are not. Close examination of the emotional reasons for achieving is required to tell the difference.

It may be that both Tim and Annette have healthy achievement motivation. But for the sake of argument, let's look at some other possibilities. Tim, for example, may not be academically oriented because of past experiences that have been turned into emotionally painful failures as the result of his parents' responses. Thus, his nonacademic inclinations may be motivated by the fear of more failures. On the other hand, Annette may be driven to high accomplishments because she has learned that this is the only way she can get any kind of positive response from her parents. For her, success has become heavily linked to self-esteem, so she can't stop achieving.

In these typical situations, appearances are deceptive. Depending on prior experiences, the academic motivations of Tim and Annette could be healthy or unhealthy. The point is that parents' understanding of their children is absolutely essential to developing healthy achievement motivation. In order to gain a clear perspective on the maturation of their children, parents must overcome at least three emotional barriers that tend to distort their perceptions. These barriers are:

Parental frustration with the child's irresponsibility. A familiar lament of parents heard everywhere: "We try so hard, but no matter what we do to teach our kids sound values and responsible behavior, it just doesn't seem to take." The fact is that children will learn values if they are reinforced consistently and modeled well by their parents. Far too often, parents let their frustration and anger determine their responses to their children, and those responses are often emotionally destructive. Parents must be calm, cool and consistently positive in responding to their children's endeavors.

Fears about the child's ultimate ability to "make it." Parental frustration, without an understanding of the childhood learning process, can give way to deep fears about a child's future. "I don't want my son to fail," or "I want my daughter to have all that I have and more." These fears often lead parents to begin pressuring children at an early age to achieve. Such responses, however, may cause some children to rebel and resist learning. A vicious cycle often ensues in which the parents push harder and harder, provoking a child to resist all the more stubbornly.

Parental fantasies about what a child should become as an adult. Virtually every parent has a fantasy about what a child can be and should be. But if parents' fantasies are allowed to become expectations, the child can be lost in the parents' grand vision. A child's directions become what the parent wants them to be, and in the process, a child's interests, aptitudes and aspirations may be completely ignored. A far healthier strategy is for parents to encourage their child to develop career directions and personal potentials without imposing their own.

The dynamics of healthy achievement motivation are not difficult to understand. The hard part for overburdened parents is to change their negative responses to healthy ones.

The first step is to begin to see each of your children as unique. The second is to

3. CHILDHOOD: Social and Emotional Development

move beyond your own frustrations, fears and fantasies that can distort your responses. These shifts will help you to gain a better perspective on the developmental process that will eventually lead to emotional maturity, personal responsibility and ultimately, to success. Then, to keep your momentum for change going, here are some additional ideas about how to respond in ways that will encourage the development of healthy achievement motivation in your children.

The Confidence Builder's Checklist

Volumes have been written on the specifics of creating healthy achievement motivation in children. A consistent core of suggestions, however, appears time and again. It is a mistake to think that it costs money to build achievement motivation in children. It doesn't. What it does cost is some thinking through, some understanding and some change in the way you communicate with your children. Essentially, the values communicated by parents' responses to their children either encourage the development of positive motivation or destroy it.

Let's face it—creating confidence is never easy; its source lies in positive achievement experiences. While all children will not become high achievers as adults, with help all children *can* develop their personal potential in this area. Here is the Confidence Builder's Checklist to help you get started.

Understand that learning takes place in many different contexts besides schoolwork. It occurs in free and unstructured play, through trial and error in accomplishing personally meaningful tasks, through relating to peers, and in projects that are self-initiated and carried to completion. Although there are no grades for these activities, you should realize their importance to the total development of your children and make time for them.

Make a clear distinction between "helping out" and "taking over" when your children have a project. You should make helpful suggestions and get involved with what your children are doing, but not too much. Be wary of getting conned into taking over and doing everything for your children. Instead, try to let your child set the tone and make his own mistakes without any "I told you so" recriminations.

Treat failure as an inevitable and necessary part of success. This positive value should always be evident in your parental responses. Avoid name-calling for goofing up or making a mistake. Instead, try to help your child analyze what went wrong and thereby develop strategies to overcome the problem. Never forget to keep an upbeat "work smarter, not harder" attitude.

There should be no question that you value quality over quantity. Children often become overinvolved in outside activities these days. Keep a watchful eye on your children, and place reasonable limits on their extracurricular involvements. Mandate some time for your children to relax—it will help them gain deeper benefits from the activities that remain.

Reinforce personal commitment and perseverance in spite of obstacles. In other words, one of your achievement values should be that you finish what you start, or at least take it to a reasonable end point. Don't permit your child to quit an activity or a project just because the going gets rough. This teaches the child to confront obstacles, not avoid them.

Help your child set attainable goals. Often, children who are left to their own devices set unrealistic goals for themselves. Some of their objectives may be impossible, while other mistakes may result from overestimating their capabilities. Your input can help to place personal effort and project practicality in perspective.

Recognize that cooperation is often more important than competition. You already know that very competitive parents sometimes teach their own "win at all costs" orientation to their children. Parents should know better. The adversarial relationships that are born of competitiveness often interfere with developing positive attitudes toward teamwork, cooperative efforts and getting along well with others. Emphasize cooperation and working well with people instead.

Reinforce adequate advance preparation for meeting any personal challenge. "Anything worth doing is worth doing well" is the value behind preparation. Get your children to think through what they will need to carry out a realistic plan; then help them get ready. Discourage children from thoughtlessly rushing into a challenging situation which may result in needless mistakes or even danger.

Unconditional positive acceptance should always be present when you are involved with your children. Your children should know from experience that you love them no matter what, that your acceptance of them is *not* contingent on their being the best or always successful. If given that awareness, children are emotionally freed to do their best because they're not afraid to fail.

Help your child to keep achievements in healthy perspective. In other words, when your child comes out number one or successfully meets a challenge, it should be understood that this does not mean he or she is better than anyone else. Success means that, in this instance, your child was simply more dedicated or more

skilled, or tried harder. Avoid creating "good, better, best" hierarchies.

The positive feedback you give should be behaviorally specific. Far too much of the time, criticism is quite detailed, but positive feedback is given in very general terms. To be useful, positive feedback must be behaviorally specific. And the result will be that your children will consistently receive from you usable information about what they did right.

"Personal best" is the frame of reference in which your child evaluates accomplishments. Avoid the trap of the perfectionist who always finds something wrong. Instead, encourage your child to reach for his or her personal best and to recognize differences in personalities and capabilities. No matter what mistakes are made, always try to find something right about what a child has accomplished.

In whatever your child does, reinforce personal responsibility for actions taken. Don't permit your child to blame circumstances or other people for his or her failures. In all ways, mandate good sportsmanship—and that means accepting failures gracefully. Only naive parents encourage scapegoating instead of a careful examination of personal performance to spot needed areas of improvement.

Talk to your children about their work, but do it in casual and optimistic ways. You can not only make achieving a creative challenge, but you also spark enthusiasm by the way you talk about it. Tell interesting stories about yourself and help your children to conceptualize ideas and strategies through your dialogue. As a result, they will be encouraged to ask questions and communicate with you.

Become a "resource development specialist" for your children. If your children don't know something, help them to find the answer without doing it for them. You may suggest specific books, people to call and talk to, or even particular places where they can watch how something is done. Encourage this kind of resourcefulness and outreach by your children, and take pride in seeing how quickly they learn to do it themselves.

Attention to detail should be encouraged as part of all achievement endeavors. Equipment should be inspected, homework checked and the finer points of an activity examined. Children are notorious for global perception, but they can gain an edge by attending to details. Most won't learn this skill unless it is taught to them. It is one of several important base line skills that ensure quality work. It also helps to prevent mistakes of omission.

In broader perspective, healthy achievement motivation is a personal asset that enhances every part of life. Wise parents recognize the importance of achievement motivation in more than just career terms. It is a value system that becomes a primary means for personal expression and gaining emotional fulfillment. As it develops in children, healthy motivation brings with it four confidence qualities that make day-to-day living easier for a lifetime:

Change is not threatening. If a healthy achiever has an inner sense of control, there is no perception of self as a victim of circumstance, of other people, or of the vicissitudes of life. This person is capable not only of "going with the flow," but also of determining the direction of the flow most of the time.

Challenge is not feared. The healthy achiever does not fear carefully considered risks because failure is not personally threatening. In fact, failure is seen as an opportunity to learn. As a result, healthy achievers see opportunities for personal growth in both their failures and their successes. It's a win-win situation.

There is no need for defensiveness. The healthy achiever is aware of and accepts his own personal strengths and weaknesses, and personal growth is directed toward further developing strengths and removing weaknesses or vulnerabilities. One result of this orientation is that healthy achievers, secure within, have no need to be defensive. Positive feedback and helpful advice are gracefully accepted.

Self-esteem is internally based. The healthy achiever is not emotionally driven to win always, to be number one, or to have the most of everything in order to feel good about himself. Because self-esteem and positive acceptance are based within, that person feels less personal vulnerability when he or she encounters a failure. This quality permits achievement to be an expression of self rather than a way to allay deep insecurity.

The "I can make things happen!" attitude is a powerful quality that enables a person to make choices no matter how adverse the circumstances. As such, healthy achievement motivation is an index of deep personal strength, adaptive coping and emotional hardiness.

Someone has said that luck is where opportunity and preparation meet. Because the healthy achiever is well prepared, opportunities are found even in adversity. As a wit once commented: "When opportunity knocks, most people complain about the noise." That's characteristic of those who are insecure about meeting challenges. But it doesn't *have* to happen that way. It all depends on your perspective. The healthy achiever opens the door.

Resilient Children

Emmy E. Werner

Emmy E. Werner, *Ph.D., is Professor of Human Development and Research Child Psychologist, University of California at Davis, Davis, California.*

Research has identified numerous risk factors that increase the probability of developmental problems in infants and young children. Among them are biological risks, such as pre- and perinatal complications, congenital defects, and low birth weight; as well as intense stress in the caregiving environment, such as chronic poverty, family discord, or parental mental illness (Honig 1984).

In a 1979 review of the literature of children's responses to such stress and risks, British child psychiatrist Michael Rutter wrote:

> There is a regrettable tendency to focus gloomily on the ills of mankind and on all that can and does go wrong.... The potential for prevention surely lies in increasing our knowledge and understanding of the reasons why some children are *not* damaged by deprivation.... (p. 49)

For even in the most terrible homes, and beset with physical handicaps, some children appear to develop stable, healthy personalities and to display a remarkable degree of resilience, i.e., the ability to recover from or adjust easily to misfortune or sustained life stress. Such children have recently become the focus of attention of a few researchers who have asked *What is right with these children?* and, by implication, *How can we help others to become less vulnerable in the face of life's adversities?*

The search for protective factors

As in any detective story, a number of overlapping sets of observations have begun to yield clues to the roots of resiliency in children. Significant findings have come from the few longitudinal studies which have followed the same groups of children from infancy or the preschool years through adolescence (Block and Block 1980; Block 1981; Murphy and Moriarty 1976; Werner and Smith 1982). Some researchers have studied the lives of minority children who did well in school in spite of chronic poverty and discrimination (Clark 1983; Gandara 1982; Garmezy 1981; 1983; Kellam et al. 1975; Shipman 1976). A few psychiatrists and psychologists have focused their attention on the resilient offspring of psychotic patients (Anthony 1974; Bleuler 1978; Garmezy 1974; Kauffman et al. 1979; Watt et al. 1984; Werner and Smith 1982) and on the coping patterns of children of divorce (Wallerstein and Kelly 1980). Others have uncovered hidden sources of strength and gentleness among the uprooted children of contemporary wars in El Salvador, Ireland, Israel, Lebanon, and Southeast Asia (Ayala-Canales 1984; Fraser 1974; Heskin 1980; Rosenblatt 1983). Perhaps some of the most moving testimonials to the resiliency of children are the life stories of the child survivors of the Holocaust (Moskovitz 1983).

All of these children have demonstrated unusual psychological strengths despite a history of severe and/or prolonged psychological stress. Their personal competencies and some unexpected sources of support in their caregiving environment either compensated for, challenged, or protected them against the adverse effects of stressful life events (Garmezy, Masten, and Tellegren 1984). Some researchers have called these children *invulnerable* (Anthony 1974); others consider them to be *stress resistant* (Garmezy and Tellegren 1984); still others refer to them as *superkids* (Kauffman et al. 1979). In our own longitudinal study on the Hawaiian island of Kauai, we have found them to be *vulnerable, but invincible* (Werner and Smith 1982).

These were children like Michael for whom the odds, on paper, did not seem very promising. The son of teen-age parents, Michael was born prematurely and spent his first three weeks of life in the hospital, separated from his mother. Immediately after his birth, his father was sent with the Army to Southeast Asia for almost two years. By the time Michael was eight, he had three younger siblings and his parents were divorced. His mother left the area and had no further contact with the children.

And there was Mary, born to an overweight, nervous, and erratic mother who had experienced several miscarriages, and a father who was an unskilled farm laborer with only four years of education. Between Mary's fifth and tenth birthdays, her mother had several hospitalizations for repeated bouts with mental illness, after having inflicted both physical and emotional abuse on her daughter.

Yet both Michael and Mary, by age 18, were individuals with high self-esteem and sound values, caring for others and liked by their peers, successful in school, and looking forward to their adult futures.

We have learned that such resilient children have four central characteristics in common:

- an active, evocative approach toward solving life's problems, enabling them to negotiate successfully an abundance of emotionally hazardous experiences;
- a tendency to perceive their experiences constructively, even if they caused pain or suffering;
- the ability, from infancy on, to gain other people's positive attention;
- a strong ability to use faith in order to maintain a positive vision of a meaningful life (O'Connell-Higgins 1983).

Protective factors within the child

Resilient children like Mary and Michael tend to have temperamental characteristics that elicit positive responses from family members as well as strangers (Garmezy 1983; Rutter 1978). They both suffered from birth complications and grew up in homes marred by poverty, family discord, or parental mental illness, but even as babies they were described as active, affectionate, cuddly, good natured, and easy to deal with. These same children already met the world on their own terms by the time they were toddlers (Werner and Smith 1982).

Resilient children tend to have temperamental characteristics that elicit positive responses from family members as well as strangers.

Several investigators have noted *both* a pronounced autonomy and a strong social orientation in resilient preschool children (Block 1981; Murphy and Moriarty 1976). They tend to play vigorously, seek out novel experiences, lack fear, and are quite self-reliant. But they are able to ask for help from adults or peers when they need it.

Sociability coupled with a remarkable sense of independence are characteristics also found among the resilient school-age children of psychotic parents. Anthony (1974) describes his meeting with a nine-year-old girl, whose father was an alcoholic and abused her and whose mother was chronically depressed. The girl suffered from a congenital dislocation of the hip which had produced a permanent limp, yet he was struck by her friendliness and the way she approached him in a comfortable, trustful way.

The same researcher tells of another nine-year-old, the son of a schizophrenic father and an emotionally disturbed mother, who found a refuge from his parents' outbursts in a basement room he had stocked with books, records, and food. There the boy had created an oasis of normalcy in a chaotic household.

Resilient children often find a refuge and a source of self-esteem in hobbies and creative interests. Kauffman et al. (1979) describes the pasttimes of two children who were the offspring of a schizophrenic mother and a depressed father:

> When David (age 8) comes home from school, he and his best friend often go up to the attic to play. This area ... is filled with model towns, railroads, airports and castles.... He knows the detailed history of most of his models, particularly the airplanes.... David's older sister, now 15, is extraordinarily well-read. Her other interests include swimming, her boyfriend, computers and space exploration. She is currently working on a computer program to predict planetary orbits. (pp. 138, 139)

The resilient children on the island of Kauai, whom we studied for nearly two decades, were not unusually talented, but they displayed a healthy androgyny in their interests and engaged in hobbies that were not narrowly sex-typed. Such activities, whether it was fishing, swimming, horseback riding, or hula dancing, gave them a reason to feel proud. Their hobbies, and their lively sense of humor, became a solace when things fell apart in their lives (Masten 1982; Werner and Smith 1982).

In middle childhood and adolescence, resilient children are often engaged in acts of "required helpfulness" (Garmezy, in press). On Kauai, many adolescents took care of their younger siblings. Some managed the household when a parent was ill or hospitalized; others worked part-time after school to support their family. Such acts of caring have also been noted by Anthony (1974) and Bleuler (1978) in their studies of the resilient offspring of psychotic parents, and by Ayala-Canales (1984) and Moskovitz (1983) among the resilient orphans of wars and concentration camps.

Protective factors within the family

Despite chronic poverty, family discord, or parental mental illness, most resilient children have had the opportunity to establish a close bond with at least one caregiver from whom they received lots of attention during the first year of life. The stress-resistant children in the Kauai Longitudinal Study as well as the resilient offspring of psychotic parents studied by Anthony (1974) had enough good nuturing to establish a basic sense of trust.

Some of this nuturing came from substitute caregivers within the family, such as older siblings, grandparents, aunts, and uncles. Such alternate caregivers play an important role as positive models of identification in the lives of resilient children, whether they are reared in poverty (Kellam et al. 1975), or in a family where a parent is mentally ill (Kauffman et al. 1979), or coping with the aftermath of divorce (Wallerstein and Kelly 1980).

Resilient children seem to be especially adept at actively recruiting surrogate parents. The latter can come from the ranks of babysitters, nannies, or student roomers (Kauffman et al. 1979); they can be parents of friends (Werner and Smith 1982), or even a housemother in an orphanage (Ayala-Canales 1984; Moskovitz 1983).

The example of a mother who is gainfully and steadily employed appears to be an especially powerful model of identification for resilient girls reared in poverty, whether they are Black (Clark 1983), Chicana (Gandara 1982), or Asian-American (Werner and Smith 1982). Maternal employment and the need for sibling caregiving seems to contribute to the pronounced autonomy and sense of responsibility noted among these girls, especially in households where the father is permanently absent.

Structure and rules in the household

and assigned chores enabled many resilient children to cope well in spite of poverty and discrimination, whether they lived on the rural island of Kauai, or in the inner cities of the American Midwest, or in a London borough (Clark 1983; Garmezy 1983; Rutter 1979).

Resilient children also seem to have been imbued by their families with a sense of coherence (Antonovsky 1979). They manage to believe that life makes sense, that they have some control over their fate, and that God helps those who help themselves (Murphy and Moriarty 1976). This sense of meaning persists among resilient children, even if they are uprooted by wars or scattered as refugees to the four corners of the earth. It enables them to love despite hate, and to maintain the ability to behave compassionately toward other people (Ayala-Canales 1984; Moskovitz 1983).

Protective factors outside the family

Resilient children find a great deal of emotional support outside of their immediate family. They tend to be well-liked by their classmates and have at least one, and usually several, close friends and confidants (Garmezy 1983; Kauffman et al. 1979; Wallerstein and Kelly 1980; Werner and Smith 1982). In addition, they tend to rely on informal networks of neighbors, peers, and elders for counsel and advice in times of crisis and life transitions.

Resilient children are apt to like school and to do well in school, not exclusively in academics, but also in sports, drama, or music. Even if they are not unusually talented, they put whatever abilities they have to good use. Often they make school a home away from home, a refuge from a disordered household. A favorite teacher can become an important model of identification for a resilient child whose own home is beset by family conflict or dissolution (Wallerstein and Kelly 1980).

In their studies of London schools, Rutter and his colleagues (1979) found that good experiences in the classroom could mitigate the effects of considerable stress at home. Among the qualities that characterized the more successful schools were the setting of appropriately high standards, effective feedback by the teacher to the students with ample use of praise, the setting of good models of behavior by teachers,

and giving students positions of trust and responsibility. Children who attended such schools developed few if any emotional or behavioral problems despite considerable deprivation and discord at home (Pines 1984).

Early childhood programs and a favorite teacher can act as an important buffer against adversity in the lives of resilient young children. Moskovitz (1983), in her follow-up study in adulthood of the childhood survivors of concentration camps, noted the pervasive influence of such a warm, caring teacher.

Participation in extracurricular activities or clubs can be another important informal source of support for resilient children. Many youngsters on Kauai were poor by material standards, but they participated in activities that allowed them to be part of a cooperative enterprise, whether being cheerleader for the home team or raising an animal in the 4-H Club. Some resilient older youth were members of the Big Brothers and Big Sisters Associations which enabled them to help other children less fortunate than themselves. For still others emotional support came from a church group, a youth leader in the YMCA or YWCA, or from a favorite minister, priest, or rabbi.

The shifting balance between vulnerability and resiliency

For some children some stress appears to have a steeling rather than a scarring effect (Anthony 1974). But we need to keep in mind that there is a shifting balance between stressful life events which heighten children's vulnerability and the protective factors in their lives which enhance their resiliency. This balance can change with each stage of the life cycle and also with the sex of the child. Most studies in the United States and in Europe, for example, have shown that boys appear to be more vulnerable than girls when exposed to chronic and intense family discord in childhood, but this trend appears to be reversed by the end of adolescence.

As long as the balance between stressful life events and protective factors is manageable for children they can cope. But when the stressful life events outweigh the protective factors, even the most resilient child can develop problems. Those who care for children, whether their own or others, can help

restore this balance, either by *decreasing* the child's exposure to intense or chronic life stresses, or by *increasing* the number of protective factors, i.e., competencies and sources of support.

Implications

What then are some of the implications of the still tentative findings from studies of resilient children? Most of all, they provide a more hopeful perspective than can be derived from reading the extensive literature on problem children which predominates in clinical psychology, child psychiatry, special education, and social work. Research on resilient children provides us with a focus on the self-righting tendencies that appear to move some children toward normal development under all but the most persistent adverse circumstances.

Those of us who care for young children, who work with or on behalf of them, can help tilt the balance from vulnerability to resiliency if we

- accept children's temperamental idiosyncracies and allow them some experiences that challenge, but do not overwhelm, their coping abilities;
- convey to children a sense of responsibility and caring, and, in turn, reward them for helpfulness and cooperation;
- encourage a child to develop a special interest, hobby, or activity that can serve as a source of gratification and self-esteem;
- model, by example, a conviction that life makes sense despite the inevitable adversities that each of us encounters;
- encourage children to reach out beyond their nuclear family to a beloved relative or friend.

Research on resilient children has taught us a lot about the special importance of surrogate parents in the lives of children exposed to chronic or intense distress. A comprehensive assessment of the impact on siblings, grandparents, foster parents, nannies, and babysitters on the development of high risk children is elaborated upon in Werner (1984).

Outside the family circle there are other powerful role models that give emotional support to a vulnerable child. The three most frequently encountered in studies of resilient children are: a favorite teacher, a good neighbor, or a member of the clergy.

There is a special need to strengthen

such informal support for those children and their families in our communities which appear most vulnerable because they lack—temporarily or permanently—some of the essential social bonds that appear to buffer stress: working mothers of young children with no provisions for stable child care; single, divorced, or teen-age parents; hospitalized and handicapped children in need of special care who are separated from their families for extended periods of time; and migrant or refugee children without permanent roots in a community.

Two other findings from the studies of resilient children have implications for the well-being of all children and for those who care for them.

(1) At some point in their young lives, resilient children were required to carry out a socially desirable task to prevent others in their family, neighborhood, or community from experiencing distress or discomfort. Such acts of *required helpfulness* led to enduring and positive changes in the young helpers.

(2) The central component in the lives of the resilient children that contributed to their effective coping appeared to be a feeling of confidence or faith that things *will work out* as well as can be reasonably expected, and that the odds *can* be surmounted.

The stories of resilient children teach us that such a faith can develop and be sustained, even under adverse circumstances, if children encounter people who give meaning to their lives and a reason for commitment and caring. Each of us can impart this gift to a child—in the classroom, on the playground, in the neighborhood, in the family—*if we care enough.*

Bibliography

Anthony, E. J. "The Syndrome of the Psychologically Invulnerable Child." In *The Child in His Family 3: Children at Psychiatric Risk,* ed. E. J. Anthony and C. Koupernik. New York: Wiley, 1974.

Antonovsky, A. *Health, Stress and Coping: New Perspectives on Mental and Physical Well-being.* San Francisco: Jossey-Bass, 1979.

Ayala-Canales, C. E. "The Impact of El Salvador's Civil War on Orphan and Refugee Children." M.S. Thesis in Child Development, University of California at Davis, 1984.

Bleuler, M. *The Schizophrenic Disorders: Long-term Patient and Family Studies.* New Haven: Yale University Press, 1978.

Block, J. H. and Block, J. "The Role of Ego-Control and Ego-Resiliency in the Organization of Behavior." In *The Minnesota Symposia on Child Psychology 13: Development of Cognition, Affect and Social Relations,* ed. W. A. Collins. Hillsdale, N.J.: Erlbaum, 1980.

Block, J. "Growing Up Vulnerable and Growing Up Resistant: Preschool Personality, Pre-Adolescent Personality and Intervening Family Stresses." In *Adolescence and Stress,* ed. C. D. Moore. Washington, D.C.: U.S. Government Printing Office, 1981.

Clark, R. M. *Family Life and School Achievement: Why Poor Black Children Succeed or Fail.* Chicago: University of Chicago Press, 1983.

Fraser, M. *Children in Conflict.* Harmondsworth, England: Penguin Books, 1974.

Gandara, P. "Passing Through the Eye of the Needle: High Achieving Chicanas." *Hispanic Journal of Behavioral Sciences* 4, no. 2 (1982): 167–180.

Garmezy, N. "The Study of Competence in Children at Risk for Severe Psychopathology." In *The Child in His Family 3: Children at Psychiatric Risk,* ed. E. J. Anthony and C. Koupernik. New York: Wiley, 1974.

Garmezy, N. "Children Under Stress: Perspectives on Antecedents and Correlates of Vulnerability and Resistance to Psychopathology." In *Further Explorations in Personality,* ed. A. I. Rabin, J. Aronoff, A. M. Barclay, and R. A. Zucker. New York: Wiley, 1981.

Garmezy, N. "Stressors of Childhood." In *Stress, Coping and Development,* ed. N. Garmezy and M. Rutter. New York: McGraw-Hill, 1983.

Garmezy, N. "Stress Resistant Children: The Search for Protective Factors." In *Aspects of Current Child Psychiatry Research,* ed. J. E. Stevenson. *Journal of Child Psychology and Psychiatry,* Book Supplement 4. Oxford, England: Pergamon, in press.

Garmezy, N.; Masten, A. S.; and Tellegren, A. "The Study of Stress and Competence in Children: Building Blocks for Developmental Psychopathology." *Child Development* 55, no. 1 (1984): 97–111.

Garmezy, N. and Tellegren, A. "Studies of Stress-Resistant Children: Methods, Variables and Preliminary Findings." In *Advances in Applied Developmental Psychology,* ed. F. Morrison, C. Lord, and D. Keating. New York: Academic Press, 1984.

Heskin, K. *Northern Ireland: A Psychological Analysis.* New York: Columbia University Press, 1980.

Honig, A. "Research in Review: Risk Factors in Infants and Young Children." *Young Children* 38, no. 4 (May 1984): 60–73.

Kauffman, C.; Grunebaum, H.; Cohler, B.; and Gamer, E. "Superkids: Competent Children of Psychotic Mothers." *American Journal of Psychiatry* 136, no. 11 (1979): 1398–1402.

Kellam, S. G.; Branch, J. D.; Agrawal; K. C.; and Ensminger, M. E. *Mental Health and Going to School.* Chicago: University of Chicago Press, 1975.

Masten, A. "Humor and Creative Thinking in Stress-Resistant Children." Unpublished Ph.D. dissertation, University of Minnesota, 1982.

Moskovitz, S. *Love Despite Hate: Child Survivors of the Holocaust and Their Adult Lives.* New York: Schocken Books, 1983.

Murphy, L. and Moriarty, A. *Vulnerability, Coping and Growth from Infancy to Adolescence.* New Haven: Yale University Press, 1976.

O'Connell-Higgins, R. "Psychological Resilience and the Capacity for Intimacy." Qualifying paper, Harvard Graduate School of Education, 1983.

Pines, M. "PT Conversation: Michael Rutter: Resilient Children." *Psychology Today* 18, no. 3 (March 1984): 60, 62, 64–65.

Rosenblatt, R. *Children of War.* Garden City, N.Y.: Anchor Press, 1983.

Rutter, M. "Early Sources of Security and Competence." In *Human Growth and Development,* ed. J. Bruner and A. Garton. New York: Oxford University Press, 1978.

Rutter, M. "Protective Factors in Children's Responses to Stress and Disadvantage." In *Primary Prevention of Psychopathology 3: Social Competence in Children,* ed. M. W. Kent and J. E. Rolf. Hanover, N.H.: University Press of New England, 1979.

Rutter, M.; Maughan, B.; Mortimore, P.; and Ouston, J; with Smith, A. *Fifteen Thousand Hours: Secondary Schools and Their Effects on Children.* Cambridge, Mass.: Harvard University Press, 1979.

Shipman, V. C. *Notable Early Characteristics of High and Low Achieving Low SES Children.* Princeton, N.J.: Educational Testing Service, 1976.

Wallerstein, J. S. and Kelly, J. B. *Surviving the Breakup: How Children and Parents Cope with Divorce.* New York: Basic Books, 1980.

Watt, N. S.; Anthony, E. J.; Wynne, L. C.; and Rolf, J. E., eds. *Children at Risk for Schizophrenia: A Longitudinal Perspective.* London and New York: Cambridge University Press, 1984.

Werner, E. E. *Child Care: Kith, Kin and Hired Hands.* Baltimore: University Park Press, 1984.

Werner, E. E. and Smith, R. S. *Vulnerable, but Invincible: A Longitudinal Study of Resilient Children and Youth.* New York: McGraw-Hill, 1982.

This is one of a regular series of Research in Review columns. The column in this issue was edited by Elizabeth H. Brady, M.A., Professor and Chair, Department of Educational Psychology, California State University, Northridge, Northridge, California.

Dealing with Difficult Young Children

Strategies for Teachers and Parents

Anne K. Soderman

Anne K. Soderman, Ph.D., is Assistant Professor in the Department of Family and Child Ecology, Michigan State University, East Lansing, Michigan.

Young children's personality development remains one of the most intriguing and widely debated issues for both parents and teachers. This article will review what we know about individual temperament and recommend ways to understand and build upon children's strengths.

Individual Temperament

Generations of parents and child development professionals have recognized that children exhibit individual personality traits. As early as 1924, Gesell wrote that

The personality of the child grows like an organic structure. . . . Original nature . . . provides certain tendencies or materials, but the final patterns of personality are the result of education and experience. (p. 3)

Much of the research on temperament has been conducted only in the past two decades. Thomas, Chess, and Birch (1968) collected parent interviews and observed 136 children in natural settings from infancy to preadolescence. They identified nine characteristics of temperament that they clustered into three basic types.

• *Easy* children were moderately low in intensity, adaptable, approachable, predictable with body functions, and positive in mood (40 percent of the sample).

• *Difficult* children were often negative in mood, adapted slowly to change, had unpredictable biological functions, and frequently exhibited intense reactions (10 percent of the sample).

• *Slow-to-warm-up* children took longer to adapt than the easy children and demonstrated low activity and intensity levels (15 percent of the sample). Children who did not appear to fit in any of these categories comprised the remaining 35 percent of the group.

A flurry of responses followed, many of which either challenged or extended this pioneering work. For example, Bates (1980) criticized the research methodology of asking parents to assess their own children. He held that difficult temperament in children is an adult social perception with only a "modest empirical foundation."

Early infant behaviors (such as susceptibility to emotional stimulation; strength and speed of response; and quality, fluctuation, and intensity of mood) were

---

Children's temperament affects how others react to them and influences their personality development.

---

examined closely for indications that they might predict later personality traits (Goldsmith and Gottesman 1981; Als 1981; Dunn and Kendrick 1980). Plomin (1982) praised the Thomas, Chess, and Birch study because it balanced the tendency throughout the 1950s and 1960s to blame children's behavioral problems on their mothers.

In a rebuttal supporting the validity of their earlier findings, Thomas, Chess, and Korn (1982) argued that their within-the-child definition of difficult temperament was not only valid but also practical in looking at later behavioral difficulty in children. They noted that

the concept of difficult temperament as a within-the-infant characteristic in no way implies a fixed immutable trait . . . but can be modified or altered by post-

natal genetic or maturational influences, situational context, or the effect of the child-environmental interactional process. (p. 15)

Meanwhile Brazelton (1978) observed that an infant's personality may be a determining factor in whether adults react to the child positively or negatively. In an effort to identify infants likely to encounter difficulties in relationships because of their temperament, Brazelton and his colleagues created the Neonatal Behavioral Assessment Scale (NBAS) (1973). This scale elicits and measures whether infants can calm themselves, whether they can shut out disturbing stimuli, their need for stimulation, their level of sociability, and the organization and predictability of their behavior. Although the instrument does not necessarily predict later development, it does offer reliable information about newborn behavior that may cause potential bonding problems (Gander and Gardiner 1981).

Another tool for assessing temperaments in infants and preschool children is a questionnaire designed by Carey and McDevitt (1978). It is based on the nine characteristics identified by Thomas and Chess (1977). According to Powell (1981), principal uses of the questionnaire are to serve as a basis for a general discussion of a child's temperament so that the child's needs can be met better, and to help with clinical problems "of which infant temperament can be a part" (p. 111).

In summary, we know that
• very early in life infants have identifiable personalities
• some traits of children's personalities produce behaviors that are perceived by others as ranging from easy to difficult
• young children's behaviors are con-

tinually being modified or intensified depending upon adults' responses

Influences on Behavior

The child's own traits and behaviors, environmental influences, and adults' perceptions and reactions all affect long term personality development. Thomas, Chess, and Korn (1982) remind us that

To debate whether a child's characteristics or parental perceptions or other environmental influences are more important is antithetical to the view which sees them *all* as all-important in a constantly evolving sequence of interaction and mutual influence. (p. 15)

When children are difficult, less confident adults will doubt themselves, feel guilty, and be anxious about the child's future and their relationship. Unless the difficult behaviors (or perceptions of difficult behaviors) can be satisfactorily modified, a sense of helplessness often begins to influence all interactions with the child. Dreams of being a competent parent or teacher may yield to the harsh reality that the child is unhappy, out of control, and not developing to full potential. Initial pride over the child's assertiveness may turn to disapproval and even rejection. Burned out adults are often the result. Such adult responses, in turn, have a marked effect on whether additional stress will be put upon the child.

Does labeling children *difficult* have a harmful effect in itself? Such identification may damage children if parents and teachers do not approach the child's behavior in a positive way that will build on the child's strengths (Rothbart 1981).

While this concern about the effect of labeling is a valid issue, there is no question that some children *are* more pleasant and sociable than others. Elkind (1981) has pointed out that children are members of a hurried society. Children who cannot adapt to tight schedules, rigorous learning programs, and a fast pace, or who become easily frustrated when stressed, will most likely have difficulty functioning well.

Knowing what to look for in children's behavior, and how to interpret it, can help us find ways to help children cope.

Temperamental Characteristics

Regardless of the cause of the behavioral difficulty, the practical implications for difficult children appear very early. Children are active agents in their own socialization, and their temperament affects how others react to them and influences their further personality development. Several temperamental characteristics, and adult perceptions or misperceptions of them, all influence children's personality. Important questions to keep in mind when considering each of these traits are:

• Is the behavior developmentally appropriate for the child's age? Does the behavior exceed what might reasonably be expected when the child's experiences are taken into account?

• Does the child consistently exhibit one or more of these difficult behaviors?

• How much does the adult's behavior style contrast with that of the child?

Unless we know what to expect of children at each age, it is easy to label a child difficult when in reality the child is exhibiting normal behaviors which may vary from day to day and are related to the child's experiences. Likewise, if the adult's personality or energy level is very different from the child's, it is easy to misperceive the meaning of the child's behaviors. The behaviors described here represent extremes along a continuum. Readers are cautioned to carefully consider each of the questions above when reviewing these possible indicators of behavioral difficulty.

Activity Level

This trait refers to the proportion of a child's motor activity and inactivity. Are quiet and active behaviors balanced? A difficult child may be viewed as excessively active, always on the go, unable to sit still, or always touching something. At the other extreme, a child may be seen as too passive, with no spirit or motivation, who just sits. Young children are generally full of healthy energy!

Rythmicity

The child's internal biological time-clock is the key to rythmicity. Are sleep, hunger, eating, and elimination patterns predictable or unpredictable? Does a toddler or preschool child have difficulty settling down easily for scheduled rest or sleep, only to fall asleep at other times? Children who have a healthy sense of independence can often frustrate adults who are eager to maintain a tight schedule!

Approach/Withdrawal

A child's *initial* responses to new objects, people, or foods may indicate that the child is approachable or withdrawn. Children who are too approachable may seem to have no fear or may be willing to accept any suggestion regardless of its appropriateness. Repeated crying, clinging, or avoiding almost all new experiences may indicate that the child is too withdrawn.

This trait affects children's decision making patterns; their ability to prevent overstimulation; and their need to escape uncomfortable, difficult, or unpleasant situations. It can be particularly problematic for adults and children who function differently from each other, or who have a contrasting base of experiences.

Adaptability

Adaptability is an indication that the child responds positively to change. Some children will find it difficult to accept a change in routine, a new sibling, or other important events, even when given time to adjust. Others may hold grudges, or be considered stubborn or resistant. Refusal to care for themselves, or to advance in skill level of an activity, may indicate that the child has a great deal of difficulty adapting. Early school adjustment may be particularly problematic.

Adults should give children every reasonable chance to assess the situation, figure out what should be done, and then experience the consequences of their decisions.

Intensity of Reaction

Energy level and response to stimuli are related to impulse control. Situations which call for an emotional response are especially indicative of the child's ability to cope. Some children may act without thinking, react quickly with anger, grieve too long after a loss, or become too excited when happy. These children are most often described as aggressive. At the other extreme are children who have a bland exterior—they hide their emotions or exhibit little intensity in emotional situations.

Responsiveness Threshold

The level of stimulation necessary to evoke a response may also indicate difficult behaviors. Some children are extremely sensitive to or overstimulated by noise, touch, smell, temperature, light, color, or similar factors, while others will respond slowly or not at all to the same stimuli. Experience can play a large part in a child's responsiveness threshold. A child living on a busy city street may not hear a blaring siren, while such a sound in more isolated areas may rightly cause a frightened reaction.

Mood

This trait deals with a balance between behaviors that are joyful, friendly, and satisfied with those that are not positive. Some children will express a range of moods, while others will react similarly to nearly every situation. They may complain, whine, cry frequently, or fuss. Bad days are frequent, and adults may go out of their way to avoid conflict. Parents and teachers may feel guilty because the child rarely looks happy or joyful.

Attention Span and Resistance

How much time does the child spend pursuing an activity, especially one with obstacles? Can the child return to the activity if interrupted? Some children seem scattered, cannot attend to any task, and move rapidly without any true involvement. Others may be obsessed with one specific activity, such as completing puzzles or playing with a single toy. Age of the child and appropriateness of the activities are important factors here.

Distractibility

Closely related to attention span and resistance is the child's vulnerability to interference when pursuing any activity. Some children may become so completely absorbed that they forget to use the bathroom, or may resist distraction even from a prohibited activity. Others will be unable to shut out typical distractions such as noise. In infancy and toddlerhood distractibility may be an asset when children need to be distracted! In older children, however, distractibility may interfere with the child's ability to attend to responsibilities.

Strategies for Parents and Teachers

You probably recognize some of these difficult behaviors in nearly every child you know! Many of these behaviors can be difficult for an adult to deal with at the moment, but may not indicate that the child has any long term personality problem. A pattern of these behaviors may indicate more serious difficulties, however, and consultation with a specialist is recommended for those children. The recommendations here will focus on ways adults can help children cope with occasional difficulties.

The way in which parents and teachers deal with young children's difficult behavior can have a lasting effect on the children's emerging personality. May (1981) discusses the fragile balance between power and powerlessness in altering interpersonal relationships. Adults can intensify children's difficulties and increase stress if they respond inappropriately. Examples of inappropriate responses would be for the adult to

• ignore difficult behaviors
• coerce children to comply with adult

expectations
• shame or compare children to others
• label children with derogatory words
• inflict verbal or physical punishment

Positive change requires that the adult keep children's self-esteem intact while helping them become knowledgeably involved in the process of modifying their own behavior. Adults can help children cope with their own behaviors by using a variety of strategies.

Respect the Child

Individual differences exist as a result of both heredity and the environment. Children's difficult behaviors do not necessarily indicate that the child is intentionally being difficult, is stubborn, or that the adult is inadequate. Instead, the adult can respect the child by closely assessing the situation and working out a plan to help the child cope.

Evaluate Behavior Objectively

Our own temperamental style and personality play a critical role when we evaluate any child's positive or negative qualities. How do our behavior and expectations affect the child? As adults, we may need to change our behaviors before we can effectively work with a difficult child.

Structure the Environment

A close look at the environment may reveal the causes of some difficult behaviors. Are children asked to sit quietly for longer periods than they can legitimately manage? Are noise levels too high or is lighting too harsh? Changing the pace of the day to balance vigorous and calm times, providing a place for quiet activities, or rearranging traffic patterns, for example, may establish a climate for more appropriate behaviors.

Set Effective Limits

Unless children know the limits, and those limits are reasonable, difficult behaviors are likely to follow. Review the rules you have set to make sure they are appropriate, and then discuss them with the children. Natural and logical consequences should result when children do not observe the limits, such as loss of the privilege to use an item.

Often a subtle cue from the adult is all that is needed to remind children before their behavior becomes unacceptable.

Use Positive Interactions

Once we understand how the child interacts with others, we can help children modify their behaviors. With very young children who may be egocentric, for example, adults can state how the child's behavior affects the feelings of

others. Rather than expecting an immediate change, you may want to identify steps for making progress.

Be Patient

Helping children to modify their behavior, or modifying your own, is a long range goal. During the process, there must be opportunity to correct behaviors in a nonthreatening atmosphere. Instead of redirecting children too quickly or making decisions for them, adults should give children every reasonable chance to assess the situation, figure out what should be done, and then experience the consequences of their decisions.

Work with Colleagues and Parents

Most teachers and parents are doing the best job they know how to do. If, however, we see negative interaction styles between other adults and a difficult child, we need to approach those adults as partners in trying to help the child cope more effectively. We can note areas of interaction that are difficult for us and stress the normal variations that may be found in young children. It is important for us to understand that a child's behavior, while it may be irritating, can be quite innocent. Our reactions to that behavior, therefore, can sow feelings of inferiority and insecurity or, on the other hand, competence and strong self-esteem.

Once we go beyond feeling guilty or trying to blame someone about a child's behavior, we can work more cooperatively with others.

Conclusions

Many of the recommendations here are common sense techniques that apply to all human relationships—it is the consistent and intentional use of these strategies that makes a difference in children's personality development. Our attitudes toward children, adults, and ourselves play a key role in ensuring successful collaborative efforts to help children become more effective in their relationships.

Bibliography

Als, H. "Assessing Infant Individuality." In *Infants at Risk: Assessment and Intervention,* eds. C. C. Brown and T. B. Brazelton. Boston: Johnson & Johnson, 1981.

Bates, J. E. "The Concept of Difficult Temperament," *Merrill-Palmer Quarterly* 26, no. 4 (October 1980): 299–319.

Brazelton, T. B. "Introduction," In *Organization and Stability of Newborn Behavior: A Commentary on the Brazelton Neonatal Behavior Assessment Scale,* ed. A. Sameroff. *Monographs of the Society* for *Research in Child Development* 43, no. 5–6 (1978): 1–13.

Buss, A. H. and Plomin, R. A. *A Temperamental Theory of Personality*. New York: Wiley, 1975.

Carey, W. B. and McDevitt, S. C. "Revision of the Infants' Temperament Questionnaire," *Pediatrics* 61, no. 5 (May 1978): 735–739.

Dunn, J. and Kendrick, C. "Studying Temperament and Parent-Child Interaction: Comparison of Interview and Direct Observation." *Developmental Medicine and Child Neurology* 22, no. 4 (August 1980): 484–496.

Escalona, S. K. *The Roots of Individuality: Normal Patterns of Development in Infancy,* Chicago: Aldine, 1958.

Elkind, D. *The Hurried Child*. Reading, Mass.: Addison-Wesley, 1981.

Freedman, D. G. "Infancy, Biology, and Culture," In *Developmental Psychobiology: The Significance of Infancy*, ed. L. P. Lipsitt. Hillsdale, N.J.: Erlbaum, 1976.

Gander, M. J. and Gardiner, H. W. *Child and Adolescent Development*. Boston: Little, Brown, 1981.

Gardner, H. G. *Developmental Psychology*. Boston: Little, Brown, 1981.

Gesell, A. "The Development of Personality: Molding Your Child's Character." *The Delineator* (April 1924).

Goldsmith, H. H. and Gottesman, I. I. "Origins of Variation in Behavioral Style: A Longitudinal Study of Temperament in Twins." *Child Development* 52, no. 1 (March 1981): 91–103.

May, R. *Power and Innocence: A Search for the Sources of Violence*. New York: Dell, 1981.

McDevitt, S. C. and Carey, W. B. "The Measurements of Temperaments in 3–7 Year-old Children." *Journal of Child Psychology and Psychiatry* 19, no. 3 (July 1978): 245–253.

Plomin, R. "The Difficult Concept of Temperament: A Response to Thomas, Chess, and Korn." *Merrill-Palmer Quarterly* 28, no. 1 (January 1982): 25–33.

Powell, M. *Assessment and Management of Developmental Changes and Problems in Children*. St. Louis: Mosby, 1981.

Rothbart, M. K. "Measurement of Temperament in Infancy." *Child Development* 52, no. 2 (June 1981): 569–678.

Sheldon, W. H. *The Varieties of Human Physique*. New York: Harper & Row, 1940.

Sugarman, G. I. and Stone, M. N. *Your Hyperactive Child*. Chicago: Henry Regnery Co., 1974.

Thomas, A. and Chess, S. *Temperament and Development*. New York: New York University Press, 1968.

Thomas, A.; Chess, S.; and Birch, H. G. *Temperament and Behavior Disorders in Children*. New York: New York University Press, 1968.

Thomas, A.; Chess, S.; and Korn, S. J. "The Reality of Difficult Temperament." *Merrill-Palmer Quarterly* 28, no. 1 (January 1982): 1–20.

Torgersen, A. M. and Kringlen, E. "Genetic Aspects of Temperamental Differences in Infants." *Journal of American Academy of Child Psychiatry* 17, no. 3 (Summer 1978): 433–444.

Practical Piaget: Helping Children Understand

Sharon L. Pontious

SHARON L. PONTIOUS, RN, PhD, is an assistant professor at the University of Texas at El Paso, College of Nursing. She was a doctoral student at New Mexico State University, Las Cruces, N.M., when she wrote this article.

Three-year-old Jennifer asks her mother over and over for a cookie while her mother is busy cooking. In frustration, her mother finally says, "Hold your horses, Jennifer!" Bewildered, Jennifer goes to her room, picks up three toy horses and holds them. Five minutes later, Jennifer goes back to the kitchen still holding the horses and meekly asks, "Mommy, now can I have a cookie?"

A child's thought process and understanding are not just a miniature version of adult thought and comprehension. Nursing care of children is incomplete, unhelpful, and even detrimental for the child when nurses use adult language to explain or teach. Inappropriate language may be used because adults overestimate the child's level of understanding(1).

According to Jean Piaget, the way the child perceives the world, thinks, reasons, and uses language is qualitatively different in each of the following age groups: sensorimotor (birth to 2 years), preoperational (2 to 7 years), concrete operations or school-age (7 to 12 years), and

formal operations, or adolescence through adulthood (12 years on)(2). While it is true that children between five to eight years demonstrate certain characteristics of both preoperational and concrete thinking stages, I have found children up to age seven consistently understand words used for preoperational children. However, they do not understand many of the words appropriate for children in the concrete stage, especially when they are sick.

According to Piaget, children up to age two learn about the world by using their senses—seeing, hearing, touching, smelling, and tasting. Thought and reasoning are just emerging, and language is primarily imitation of what is heard. For this reason, verbal explanations are virtually meaningless.

Preoperational child. The child from 2 to 7 years sees the world strictly from his own viewpoint. Unable to even imagine there is another way of seeing things, he refuses to accept anyone else's view.

In this phase, the child perceives the gross outward appearance

of objects, but is capable of seeing only one aspect of that object at a time. For example, if a nurse tells this age child, "Take a red pill," he will be confused because he can focus on either "red" or "pill," but not both. At this stage, thinking is literal, concrete, and in the present(3). Thus, drinking a medicine to take away a headache makes no sense because the medicine goes into the stomach, not the head.

The preoperational child thinks in absolutes; things are either good or bad, right or wrong, white or black, hurt or don't hurt. He reasons transductively: going to the hospital is punishment for something he did.

He also is animistic: all objects have life and intention. For example, Jami, a 4-year-old, says the moon follows him wherever he goes because it is his best friend. The combination of transductive reasoning, animism, and focusing on only one aspect of an object leads a child of this age to say, "The needle (on the syringe) makes people well." He does not understand that there is medicine in the syringe and that it is pushed into the body through the needle(4). In addition, the 2- to 7-year-old judges people by the consequence to himself. Thus, the nurse who gives him a shot is bad because she hurt him.

Since a child of this age believes everyone sees things the way he does and knows what he's thinking, language is used only to mimic adult conversation. Many of the words he uses, he does not yet truly understand.

Concrete operational child. This child views the world more objectively and realistically, since he's capable of understanding others' viewpoints and, later in this stage, of combining them with his own. The 7- to 12-year-old's thinking, although still concrete, now includes the past and some future as well as the present. These children are more flexible and able to see some things as relative. For example, a shot hurts a little or a lot. They are aware of reversibility; objects are the same, even if their form changes: an ice cube is water.

The school-age child can classify objects or experiences by using multiple characteristics—size, color, shape, and mass—in order to conceptualize a whole from parts. Piaget has determined that school-age children learn conservation (aspects of objects remain constant when form changes) in the following sequence: first, size in terms of substance and length, then weight, then volume; then they learn time in terms of past, present, and future, then time independent of perceptual data, such as meals, TV programs, light, or darkness; then one hour is one hour, whether it seems to go quickly or slowly(3,5).

The school-age child's ability to reason is the beginning of deductive logic. He solves problems by trial and error(3). Animism is now only used for natural phenomena beyond his manipulation. For example, an 8-year-old said, "The sun comes up to give people warmth and light."

The 7- to 12-year-old judges actions by their logical effect. He can separate the intent from the behavior and outcome. This child now will say, "The shot hurt, but it will make me feel better."

Words to the school-age child,

according to Piaget, represent reality—objects or concepts. Language is used to communicate his thoughts to others and to learn viewpoints other than his own. However, he does not thoroughly comprehend words that have multiple meanings or those which stand for things he has not yet experienced.

Applying the Theory

I find that it is best when working with children to use easily understood words that have one meaning, do not instill fear or anxiety, and are not too sophisticated for the child. Some words to avoid:

cut (implies pain to preoperational child);

incision (instills fear of bodily harm or mutilation to school-age child or adolescent);

fix (implies to a 2- to 7-year-old that he is broken like a stepped-on toy);

organs (causes confusion between functional parts of body and musical instruments);

take (implies to a 2- to 7-year old removal of something, such as TPR, blood pressure);

test (is not understood by 2-to 7-year-old, denotes pass or fail to school-age child;

dye (implies "die" to both preoperational and concrete operational children).

These words are not helpful because they increase the child's anxiety and decrease the child's understanding and/or confidence.

A nurse, preparing six-year-old Bobby for heart surgery, said, "The doctor is going to fix your heart, so you will feel better." Immediately, Bobby became very upset, crying and screaming, "Don't let him fix me." Bobby's anxiety and fear were increased because his father frequently had tried to fix his toys, but usually Bobby had to throw them away because his dad couldn't fix them. Bobby feared the doctor would be unable to "fix" him, and he, too, would be thrown away. A better explanation for a school-age child would be to say, "The doctor is going to help you so you can run and play with your friends and you won't get as tired as you do now."

Remember, the 2-to 7-year-old doesn't know anything exists inside

of him. He is concerned primarily with the consequence of the action (surgery) to him.

Instead of saying "take" your temperature or blood pressure, say, "I'm going to see how warm you are" to a preoperational child, or, "I'm going to measure how much heat your body's making" to a school-age child. Measurement of components of blood or urine can be described in like fashion.

Whereas most words with multiple meanings are confusing, especially to the preoperational child and young school-age child, truthfulness is equally important for all ages. Honesty is especially important to older school-age children because they can easily see through "white lies." For example, a seven-year-old became very fearful of an upcoming meatotomy when the nurse said, "This shot will not hurt." A painful injection followed, and then she said, "I'm going to take you for a little ride now." She should have said, "It's time to go to the operating room now." From that time on, this same child refused to let that nurse come near him.

Four-year-old Tami began crying uncontrollably immediately after she vomited. When she finally quieted down, she said, "All my stuffing came out!" She had previously seen her torn Raggedy Ann's stuffing come out. Once the problem was realized, it was explained to Tami that throwing up was OK. Her tummy was like a balloon filled with water and when it was squeezed, the water came out, but the water could be replaced. It was then explained that the tummy holds food and water, and when it feels sick, it pushes out the food and water. Tami then looked in the mirror and, as if relieved, came back smiling and saying, "All of my other stuffing is still there!"

One day, five-year-old Mona came running up to a nurse pointing to her chest and saying, "This is bumping, I can feel it. I'm sick!" Although Mona had just listened to her heart with a stethoscope, she didn't understand that the heart was under her chest skin, nor could she associate it with what she had just heard. Thus, when you try to tell a 2- to 7-year-old child about a part of him he can't see, it is necessary to use things he can see, touch, hear, and relate to concretely.

Manuel, a six-and-one-half-year-old, had a bladder infection but refused to take his medicine. To explain why he needed the medicine, he was told to pretend he could unzip the skin from his head to his toes. Pointing to his bladder, the nurse told him he would see a thing like the water-filled plastic bag that he was holding.

This bladder keeps his urine inside of it until it gets full and he urinates. But his bladder was hurting because tiny things called germs had gotten inside it. The germs made his bladder hurt. Other tiny, white things called blood cells, like the white flecks in the water in the plastic bag he held, were trying to kill the other tiny bad germs.

Manuel shook the plastic bag up and said, "Just like the good army men try to kill the bad people?" The nurse answered, "Yes!" He was then told the medicine he drank was helping the white blood cells kill the germs. Three hours later, I overheard Manuel asking the staff, "Is it time to take my medicine now?"

I find that for school-age children lifelike pictures or drawings, three-dimensional models, or the visible man doll with clear plastic skin and realistic veins, arteries, and body parts shown in proper perspective inside the body make what is inside more real. Then I relate the function of these parts to the problem or treatment a specific child is having. For example, nine-year-old Danny was frightened of IVs. He would scream whenever anyone even touched the IV. He did not know what the IV was for, where it went in his body, and thought the doctors were punishing him by taking one needle out and inserting another one. Danny was also sure the IV was going to kill him by sucking out all his blood, because he remembered seeing blood back up into the tubing.

A nurse showed him with a visible man doll that blood ran all over the body, inside little tubes. Danny asked, "Just like water in little rivers?" The nurse answered, "Yes," and using straws, she inserted an IV needle inside a straw

explaining, "This way water and sugar are added to blood."

She explained further that the water would give each of his body parts a drink to keep them from being thirsty. The sugar would give his body energy even faster than if it went into his stomach first, so the IV was a short cut. He was then reassured that the doctors and nurses did not want to hurt or punish him, but that since his stomach needed a rest (previously explained), the IV was the only way to give him water and energy.

Danny was also given an appropriate way to cope with pain. He was told he could cry when the needle was put into his vein, because it hurts, but to hold that arm still so nursing staff didn't have to stick him again. Danny proceeded to start IVs on all of his dolls. The next time Danny needed the IV

changed, he kept his arm still and told the doctors why he needed it.

To explain what a simple fracture of a leg or arm is to the 2- to 7-year-old child, I use a tissue wrapped around a tongue blade. I tell the child, "Let's pretend this tongue blade is your bone and the tissue is your skin. Now let's break the bone just like you did when you fell." Then, in front of the child, the tongue blade is broken. "OK, does this look as if it is broken?" The child says, "No." Then I hand the tissue to the child, and say, "Unwrap it and see if the tongue blade is broken." The child is surprised to find a broken tongue blade. "OK, wrap up the broken bone and let's see how it looks now." This should be repeated until the child shows understanding by asking something like, "Is this why my leg doesn't *look* broken, too?" At this point, for

Characteristics of Children's Thinking

	Preoperational (2- to 7-year old)	Concrete (7- to 12-year old)
Perception:	views world in terms of self	views world he can manipulate or experience objectively
	refuses others' viewpoints	combines own with others' viewpoints
Thought:	classifies by one characteristic	classifies by multiple dimensions of object
	literal concrete	concrete present and past, some future
	present tense absolute	begins relativism reversibility conservation of length and substance, size, weight, volume, time
Reasoning:	transductive	begins deductive logic (trial and error problem solving)
	animism	animism only of some natural phenomenon
	judges action by consequence to self	judges action by logical effect separates cause and intent from outcome
Language:	words represent one aspect or use of object; vague and global concepts	comprehends common meaning talks to communicate thoughts and to understand others' viewpoints

school-age children, it is appropriate to show them their x-rays, pointing out where the bone is broken and then explaining how new bone grows.

The same technique can be used to explain casts and traction. For example, a nursing student made a bed and traction apparatus so a doll could be placed in traction by an eight-year-old. Bobbins were used for pulleys, dimes for weights, and heavy thread for the rope. The student explained the purpose and how each part of the apparatus worked.

Both age groups of children should be encouraged to apply casts to a doll to help them understand what a cast is made of, know that it is still their leg or arm under the cast, and to help alleviate fears of how the cast is put on.

Research has shown that effective explanation of cast application and removal must include a description of the procedure, as well as a description of what the child will see, hear, feel, and in what position he will be placed[5]. Just before the child's cast is to be removed, have the doll's cast removed in the proper way so that the child sees lots of dust, feels vibrations and possible warmth on his arm or leg, and hears loud noises from the cast cutter.

The nurse can use the way a child perceives the world and his reasoning ability to encourage eating or drinking. Knowing that things appear to be larger to the 2- to 7-year-old child when they seem to take up more space, the nurse can make the same amount of food appear to be less. For example, on a small plate, push vegetables close together in a small pile, place only six to eight pieces of meat close together, and give a whole piece of bread instead of halves or quarters.

Do not try to encourage the preoperational child to eat by saying, "You can eat all of your food just like Tommy." This age child can't classify, so Tommy is not like him at all, and, furthermore, he won't care what Tommy did, since his only concern is for himself. Instead, you might try using animism. For example, tell a five-year-old to give his hungry tummy some beef, or suggest that the peas really want to live in his tummy and he can "help them go home" by putting them in his mouth.

A 2-to 7-year-old can be encouraged to drink by giving him a short, but large-diameter, glass and filling it a third to half full. You can also tape a picture on the bottom of a clear glass because he will want to drink it empty to see the surprise. Other useful techniques are to mark lines on the cup and give him a star for each line he drinks down to or give him a funny-shaped glass or straw for drinking.

These ideas will not work with a school-age child. With the 7- to 12 year-old, you can concretely explain that in order to get strong like his favorite hero, he is going to have to give his body energy. Food is what makes his body grow and run, just as gasoline makes the car run. When his body runs out of food or the car runs out of gas, both slow down and then stop.

Children from 7 to 12 can be enticed to eat foods that appear fun to eat. For example, cut a piece of meat in a circle shape; use one large olive for each eye, a strip of crunchy carrot or bacon for the mouth, and a dot of ketchup or mustard for the nose. For breakfast serve a "Mickey Mouse" face made from three pan-cakes, strawberries, and bacon. For lunch, serve a spaceship made from a hot dog, cheese, and potato chips. These ideas are also good for younger children.

Encourage the school-age child to participate in planning his meals by giving him two or more choices of each food group. Be sure all of the choices you offer are available. Do not serve either age group mixed food, such as casseroles or stews. The reason for this is that typically children from four to nine years believe that food sits in their stomach as it appears on their plates.

Be sure to encourage all children (any age) to first eat or drink what they need most. Children live for now, not the future, so as soon as they are full, no amount of persuasion will make them eat or drink more. However, serving small amounts of attractive, nourishing food six to eight times per day may meet the child's needs better, since he will be hungry each time.

Nurses can provide helpful total nursing care to children if they apply Piaget's theory of cognitive development in designing their explanations and teaching plans for children. Words used must be appropriate, simple, nonambiguous, and truthful.

References

1. Smith, E. C. Are you really communicating? Am.J.Nurs. 77:1966-1968, Dec. 1977.
2. Richmond, P. G. An Introduction to Piaget. New York, Basic Books, 1971.
3. Maier, H. W. Three Theories of Child Development: The Contributions of Erik H. Erikson, Jean Piaget, and Robert R. Sears and their Applications. rev. ed. New York, Harper & Row 1978.
4. Steward, M., and Regalbuto, G. Do doctors know what children know? Am.J.Orthopsychiatry 45: 146-149, Jan. 1975.
5. Piaget, Jean, and Inhelder, Barbel. Psychology of the Child. New York, Basic Books, 1969.

PROFILE

ROBERT J. STERNBERG

Three Heads are Better than One

*THE TRIARCHIC THEORY SAYS WE
ARE GOVERNED BY THREE ASPECTS OF INTELLIGENCE
AND SUGGESTS WAYS OF MAXIMIZING STRENGTHS
AND MINIMIZING WEAKNESSES.*

ROBERT J. TROTTER

*Robert J. Trotter is a senior editor at
Psychology Today.*

I really stunk on IQ tests. I was just terrible," recalls Robert J. Sternberg. "In elementary school I had severe test anxiety. I'd hear other people starting to turn the page, and I'd still be on the second item. I'd utterly freeze."

Poor performances on IQ tests piqued Sternberg's interest, and from rather inauspicious beginnings he proceeded to build a career on the study of intelligence and intelligence testing. Sternberg, IBM Professor of Psychology and Education at Yale University, did his undergraduate work at Yale and then got his Ph.D. from Stanford University in 1975. Since then he has written hundreds of articles and several books on intelligence, received nu-

merous fellowships and awards for his research and proposed a three-part theory of intelligence. He is now developing an intelligence test based on that theory.

Running through Sternberg's work is a core of common-sense practicality not always seen in studies of subjects as intangible as intelligence. This practical bent, which stems from his early attempts to understand his own trouble with IQ tests, is also seen in his current efforts to devise ways of teaching people to better understand and increase their intellectual skills.

Sternberg got over his test anxiety in sixth grade after doing so poorly on an IQ test that he was sent to retake it with the fifth-graders. "When you are in elementary school," he explains,

"one year makes a big difference. It's one thing to take a test with sixth-graders, but if you're taking it with a bunch of babies, you don't have to worry." He did well on the test, and by seventh grade he was designing and administering his own test of mental abilities as part of a science project. In 10th grade he studied how distractions affect people taking mental-ability tests.

After graduating from high school, he worked summers as a research assistant, first at the Psychological Corporation in New York, then at the Educational Testing Service in Princeton, New Jersey. These jobs gave him hands-on experience with testing organizations, but he began to suspect that the intelligence field was not going anywhere. Most of the tests being used were pretty old, he says, and there seemed to be little good research going on.

This idea was reinforced when Sternberg took a graduate course at Stanford from Lee. J. Cronbach, a leader in the field of tests and measurements. Intelligence research is dead, Cronbach said; the psychometric approach—IQ testing—has run its course and people are waiting for something new. This left Sternberg at a loss. He knew he wanted to study in-

what was going on, but that was just a delusion on my part." Psychology comes out of everyday experiences, Sternberg says. And his own experiences—teaching and working with graduate students at Yale—gave him the idea that there was much more to intelligence than what his componential theory was describing. He brings this idea to life with stories of three idealized graduate students—Alice, Barbara and Celia.

Alice, he says, is someone who looked very smart according to con-

analytically, but they just don't have good ideas of their own.

Sternberg thinks he knows why people with high GRE scores don't always do well in graduate school. From elementary school to college, he explains, students are continuously reinforced for high test-smarts. The first year of graduate school is similar—lots of multiple-choice tests and papers that demand critical thinking. Then around the second year there is a transition, with more emphasis on creative, or synthetic, thinking and having good ideas. "That's a different skill," Sternberg says. "It's not that test taking and critical thinking all of a sudden become unimportant, it's just that other things become more important."

When people who have always done well on tests get to this transition point, instead of being continually reinforced, they are only intermittently reinforced. And that is the kind of reinforcement most likely to sustain a particular type of behavior. "Instead of helping people try to improve their performance in other areas, intermittent reinforcement encourages them to overcapitalize on test-smarts, and they try to use that kind of intelligence in situations in which it is not relevant.

"The irony is that people like Alice may have other abilities, but they never look for them," he says. "It's like psychologists who come up with a theory that's interesting and then try to expand it to everything under the sun. They just can't see its limitations. It's the same with mental abilities. Some are good in certain situations but not in others."

The second student, Barbara, had a very different kind of record. Her undergraduate grades were not great, and her GRE scores were really low by Yale standards. She did, however, have absolutely superlative letters of recommendation that said Barbara was extremely creative, had really good ideas and did exceptional research. Sternberg thought Barbara would continue to do creative work and wanted to accept her. When he was outvoted, he hired her as a research associate. "Academic smarts," Sternberg says, "are easy to find, but creativity is a rare and precious commodity."

Sternberg's prediction was correct. In addition to working full time as a

PSYCHOLOGY COMES OUT OF EVERYDAY EXPERIENCES; WORKING WITH GRADUATE STUDENTS SUGGESTED THAT HIS THEORY OF INTELLIGENCE WAS INCOMPLETE.

telligence, but he didn't know how to go about it.

About this time, an educational publishing firm (Barron's) asked Sternberg to write a book on how to prepare for the Miller Analogies Test. Since Sternberg had invented a scheme for classifying the items on the test when he worked for the Psychological Corporation, which publishes the test, he was an obvious choice to write the book. Being an impecunious graduate student, he jumped at the chance, but he had an ulterior motive. He wanted to study intelligence and thought that because analogies are a major part of most IQ tests, working on the book might help. This work eventually led to his dissertation and a book based on it.

At this stage, Sternberg was analyzing the cognitive, or mental, processes people use to solve IQ test items, such as analogies, syllogisms and series. His research gave a good account of what people did in their heads, he says, and also seemed to account for individual differences in IQ test performance. Sternberg extended this work in the 1970s and in 1980 published a paper setting forth what he called his "componential" theory of human intelligence.

"I really thought I had the whole bag here," he says. "I thought I knew

ventional theories of intelligence. She had almost a 4.0 average as an undergraduate, scored extremely high on the Graduate Record Exam (GRE) and was supported by excellent letters of recommendation. She had everything that smart graduate students are supposed to have and was admitted to Yale as a top pick.

"There was no doubt that this was Miss Real Smarto," Sternberg says, and she performed just the way the tests predicted she would. She did extremely well on multiple-choice tests and was great in class, especially at critiquing other people's work and analyzing arguments. "She was just fantastic," Sternberg says. "She was one of our top two students the first year, but it didn't stay that way. She wasn't even in the top half by the time she finished. It just didn't work out. So that made me suspicious, and I wanted to know what went wrong."

The GRE and other tests had accurately predicted Alice's performance for the first year or so but then got progressively less predictive. And what became clear, Sternberg says, is that although the tests did measure her critical thinking ability, they did not measure her ability to come up with good ideas. This is not unusual, he says. A lot of people are very good

research associate she took graduate classes, and her work and ideas proved to be just as good as the letters said they would be. When the transition came, she was ready to go. "Some of the most important work I've done was in collaboration with her," Sternberg says.

Barbaresque talent, Sternberg emphasizes, is not limited to psychology graduate school. "I think the same principle applies to everything. Take business. You can get an MBA based on your academic smarts because graduate programs consist mostly of taking tests and analyzing cases. But when you actually go into business, you have to have creative ideas for products and for marketing. Some MBA's don't make the transition and never do well because they overcapitalize on academic smarts. And it's the same no matter what you do. If you're in writing, you have to have good ideas for stories. If you're in art, you have to have good ideas for artwork. If you're in law.... That's where Barbaresque talent comes in."

The third student was Celia. Her grades, letters of recommendation and GRE scores were good but not great. She was accepted into the program and the first year, Sternberg says, she did all right but not great. Surprisingly, however, she turned out to be the easiest student to place in a good job. And this surprised him. Celia lacked Alice's super analytic ability and Barbara's super synthetic, or creative, ability, yet she could get a good job while others were having trouble.

Celia, it turns out, had learned how to play the game. She made sure she did the kind of work that is valued in psychology. She submitted her papers to the right journals. In other words, Sternberg says, "she was a street-smart psychologist, very street-smart. And that, again, is something that doesn't show up on IQ tests."

Sternberg points out that Alice, Barbara and Celia are not extreme cases. "Extremes are rare," he says, "but not good. You don't want someone who is incredibly analytically brilliant but never has a good idea or who is a total social boor." Like all of us, Alice, Barbara and Celia each had all three of the intellectual abilities he described, but each was especially good in one aspect.

After considering the special quali-

ties of people such as Alice, Barbara and Celia, Sternberg concluded that his componential theory explained only one aspect of intelligence. It could account for Alice, but it was too narrow to explain Barbara and Celia. In an attempt to find out why, Sternberg began to look at prior theories of intelligence and found that they tried to do one of three things:

Some looked at the relation of intelligence to the internal world of the individual, what goes on inside people's heads when they think intelligently. "That's what IQ tests measure, that's what information processing tasks measure, that's the componential theory. It's what I had been doing," Sternberg says. "I'd take an IQ test problem and analyze the mental processes involved in solving it, but it's still the same damned problem. It's sort of like we never got away from the IQ test as a standard. It's not that I thought the componential work was wrong. It told me a lot about what made Alice smart, but there had to be more."

Other theories looked at the relation of intelligence to experience, with experience mediating between what's inside—the internal, mental world—and what's outside—the external world. These theories say you have to look at how experience affects a person's intelligence and how intelligence affects a person's experiences. In other words, more-intelligent people create different experiences. "And that," says Sternberg, "is where Barbara fits in. She is someone who has a certain way of coping with novelty that goes beyond the ordinary. She can see old problems in new ways, or she'll take a new problem and see how some old thing she knows applies to it."

A third kind of theory looks at intelligence in relation to the individual's external world. In other words, what makes people smart in their everyday context? How does the environment interact with being smart? And what you see, as with Celia, is that there are a lot of people who don't do particularly well on tests but who are just extremely practically intelligent. "Take Lee Iacocca," Sternberg says. "Maybe he doesn't have an IQ of 160 (or maybe he does, I don't know), but he is extremely effective. And there are plenty of people who are that way. And there are plenty of people going

ACADEMIC SMARTS ARE EASY TO FIND, BUT CREATIVITY IS RARE AND PRECIOUS.

around with high IQ's who don't do a damned thing. This Celiaesque kind of smartness—how you make it in the real world—is not reflected in IQ tests. So I decided to have a look at all three kinds of intelligence."

He did, and the result was the triarchic theory. A triarchy is government by three persons, and in his 1985 book, *Beyond IQ*, Sternberg suggests that we are all governed by three aspects of intelligence: componential, experiential and contextual. In the book, each aspect of intelligence is described in a subtheory. Though based in part on older theories, Sternberg's work differs from those theories in a number of ways. His componential subtheory, which describes Alice, for example, is closest to the views of cognitive psychologists and psychometricians. But Sternberg thinks that the other theories put too much emphasis on measuring speed and accuracy of performance components at the expense of what he calls "metacomponents," or executive processes.

"For example," he explains, "the really interesting part of solving analogies or syllogisms is deciding what to do in the first place. But that isn't isolated by looking at performance components, so I realized you need to look at metacomponents—how you plan it, how you monitor what you are doing, how you evaluate it after you are done. [See "Stalking the IQ Quark," *Psychology Today*, September 1979.]

"A big thing in psychometric theory," he continues, "is mental speed. Almost every group test is timed, so if you're not fast you're in trouble. But I came to the conclusion that we were really misguided on that. Almost ev-

THE TRIARCHIC THEORY

Componential

Alice had high test scores and was a whiz at test-taking and analytical thinking. Her type of intelligence exemplifies the componential subtheory, which explains the mental components involved in analytical thinking.

Experiential

Barbara didn't have the best test scores, but she was a superbly creative thinker who could combine disparate experiences in insightful ways. She is an example of the experiential subtheory.

Contextual

Celia was street-smart. She learned how to play the game and how to manipulate the environment. Her test scores weren't tops, but she could come out on top in almost any context. She is Sternberg's example of contextual intelligence.

ILLUSTRATIONS BY JEAN TUTTLE

A BIG THING IN IQ TESTING IS SPEED, BUT ALMOST EVERYONE REGRETS SOME DECISION THAT WAS MADE TOO FAST.

seemed to know what insight is."

Sternberg and Davidson analyzed how several major scientific insights came about and concluded that insight is really three things: selective encoding, selective combination and selective comparison. As an example of selective encoding they cite Sir Alexander Fleming's discovery of penicillin. One of Fleming's experiments was spoiled when mold contaminated and killed the bacteria he was studying. Sternberg says most people would have said, "I screwed up, I've got to throw this out and start over." But Fleming didn't. He realized that the mold that killed the bacteria was more important than the bacteria. This selective encoding insight—the ability to focus on the really critical information—led to the discovery of a substance in the mold that Fleming called "penicillin." "And this is not just something that famous scientists do," Sternberg explains. "Detectives have to decide what are the relevant clues, lawyers have to decide which facts have legal consequences and so on."

The second kind of insight is selective combination, which is putting the facts together to get the big picture, as in Charles Darwin's formulation of the theory of natural selection. The facts he needed to form the theory were already there; other people had them too. But Darwin saw how to put them together. Similarly, doctors have to put the symptoms together to figure out what the disease is. Lawyers have to put the facts together to figure out how to make the case. "My triarchic theory is another example of selective combination. It doesn't have that much in it that's different from what other people have said," Stern-

eryone regrets some decision that was made too fast. Think of the guy who walks around with President Reagan carrying the black box. You don't want this guy to be real fast at pushing the button. So, instead of just testing speed, you want to measure a person's knowing when to be fast and when to be slow—time allocation—it's a metacomponent. And that's what the componential subtheory emphasizes."

The experiential subtheory, which describes Barbaresque talent, emphasizes insight. Sternberg and graduate student Janet E. Davidson, as part of a study of intellectual giftedness, concluded that what gifted people had in common was insight. "If you look at Hemingway in literature, Darwin in science or Rousseau in political theory, you see that they all seemed to be unusually insightful people," Sternberg explains. "But when we looked at the research, we found that nobody

berg admits. "It's just putting it together that's a little different."

A third kind of insight is selective comparison. It's relating the old to the new analogically, says Sternberg. It involves being able to see an old thing in a new way or being able to see a new thing in an old way. An example is the discovery of the molecular structure of benzene by German chemist August Kekule, who had been struggling to find the structure for some time. Then one night he had a dream in which a snake was dancing around and biting its own tail. Kekule woke up and realized that he had solved the puzzle of benzene's structure. In essence, Sternberg explains, Kekule could see the relation between two very disparate elements—the circular image of the dancing snake and the hexagonal structure of the benzene molecule.

Sternberg and Davidson tested their theory of insight on fourth-, fifth- and sixth-graders who had been identified through IQ and creativity tests as either gifted or not so gifted. They used problems that require the three different kinds of insights. A selective-encoding problem, for example, is the old one about four brown socks and five blue socks in a drawer. How many do you have to pull out to make sure you'll having a matching pair? It's a selective-encoding problem because the solution depends on selecting and using the relevant information. (The information about the 4-to-5 ratio is irrelevant.)

As expected, the gifted children were better able to solve all three types of problems. The less gifted children, for example, tended to get hung up on the irrelevant ratio information in the socks problem, while the gifted children ignored it. When the researchers gave the less gifted children the information needed to solve the problems (by underlining what was relevant, for example), their performance improved significantly. Giving the gifted children this information had no such effect, Sternberg explains, because they tended to have the insights spontaneously.

Sternberg and Davidson also found that insight skills can be taught. In a five-week training program for both gifted and less gifted children, they greatly improved children's scores on insight problems, compared with children who had not received the training. Moreover, says Sternberg, the gains were durable and transferable. The skills were still there when the children were tested a year later and were being applied to kinds of insight problems that had never appeared in the training program.

Sternberg's contextual subtheory emphasizes adaptation. Almost everyone agrees that intelligence is the ability to adapt to the environment, but that doesn't seem to be what IQ tests measure, Sternberg says. So he and Richard K. Wagner, then a graduate student, now at Florida State University, tried to come up with a test of adaptive ability. They studied people in two occupations: academic psychologists, "because we think that's a really important job," and business executives, "because everyone else thinks that's an important job." They began by asking prominent, successful people what one needs to be practically intelligent in their fields. The psychologists and executives agreed on three things:

First, IQ isn't very important for success in these jobs. "And that makes sense because you already have a restricted range. You're talking about people with IQ's of 110 to 150. That's not to say that IQ doesn't count for anything," Sternberg says. "If you were talking about a range from 40 to 150, IQ might make a difference, but we're not. So IQ isn't that important with regard to practical intelligence."

They also agreed that graduate school isn't that important either. "This," says Sternberg, "was a little offensive. After all, here I was teaching and doing the study with one of my own graduate students, and these people were saying graduate training wasn't that helpful." But Sternberg remembered that graduate school had not fully prepared him for his first year on the job as an academic. "I really needed to know how to write a grant proposal; at Yale, if you can't get grants you're in trouble. You have to scrounge for paper clips, you can't get students to work with you, you can't get any research done. Five years later you get fired because you haven't done anything. Now, no one ever says you are being hired to write grants, but if you don't get them you're dead meat around here." Sternberg, who has had more than $5 million in grants in the past 10 years, says he'd be five years behind where he is now without great graduate students.

"What you need to know to be practically intelligent, to get on in an environment," Sternberg says, is tacit knowledge, the third area of agreement. "It's implied or indicated but not always expressed, or taught." Sternberg and Wagner constructed a test of such knowledge and gave it to senior and junior business executives and to senior and junior psychology professors. The results suggest that tacit knowledge is a result of learning from experience. It is not related to IQ but is related to success in the real world. Psychologists who scored high on the test, compared with those who had done poorly, had published more research, presented more papers at conventions and tended to be at the better universities. Business executives who scored high had better salaries, more merit raises and better performance ratings than those who scored low.

The tacit-knowledge test is a measure of how well people adapt to their environment, but practical knowledge also means knowing when not to adapt. "Suppose you join a computer software firm because you really want to work on educational software," Sternberg says, "but they put you in the firm's industrial espionage section and ask you to spy on Apple Computer. There are times when you have to select another environment, when you have to say 'It's time to quit. I don't want to adapt, I'm leaving.'"

There are, however, times when you can't quit and must stay put. In such

THERE ARE PLENTY OF PEOPLE GOING AROUND WITH HIGH IQ'S WHO DON'T DO A DAMNED THING.

situations, you can try to change the environment. That, says Sternberg, is the final aspect of contextual, or practical, intelligence—shaping the environment to suit your needs.

One way to do this is by capitalizing on your intellectual strengths and compensating for your weaknesses. "I don't think I'm at the top of the heap analytically," Sternberg explains. "I'm good, not the greatest, but I think I know what I'm good at and I try to make the most of it. And there are some things I stink at and I either try to make them unimportant or I find other people to do them. That's part of how I shape my environment. And that's what I think practical intelligence is about—capitalizing on your strengths and minimizing your weaknesses. It's sort of mental self-management.

"So basically what I've said is there are different ways to be smart, but ultimately what you want to do is take the components (Alice intelligence), apply them to your experience (Barbara) and use them to adapt to, select and shape your environment (Celia). That is the triarchic theory of intelligence."

What can you do with a new theory of intelligence? Sternberg, who seems to have a three-part answer for every question (and whose triangular theory

*I*T'S REALLY IMPORTANT TO ME THAT MY WORK HAS AN EFFECT THAT GOES BEYOND THE PSYCHOLOGY JOURNALS, TO BRING INTELLIGENCE INTO THE REAL WORLD AND THE REAL WORLD INTO INTELLIGENCE.

of love will be the subject of a future *Psychology Today* article), says, "I view the situation as a triangle." The most important leg of the triangle, he says, is theory and research. "But it's not enough for me to spend my life coming up with theories," he says. "So I've gone in two further directions, the other two legs of the triangle—testing and training."

He is developing, with the Psychological Corporation, now in San Antonio, Texas, the Sternberg Multidimensional Abilities Test. It is based strictly on the triarchic theory and will measure intelligence in a much broader way than traditional IQ tests do. "Rather than giving you a number that's etched in stone," he says, "this test will be used as a basis for diag-

nosing your intellectual strengths and weaknesses."

Once you understand the kind of intelligence you have, the third leg of the triangle—the training of intellectual skills—comes into play. One of Sternberg's most recent books, *Intelligence Applied*, is a training program based on the theory. It is designed to help people capitalize on their strengths and improve where they are weak. "I'm very committed to all three aspects," Sternberg says. "It's really important to me that my work has an effect that goes beyond the psychology journals. I really think it's important to bring intelligence into the real world and the real world into intelligence."

How Kids Learn

Ages 5 through 8 are wonder years. That's when children begin learning to study, to reason, to cooperate. We can put them in desks and drill them all day. Or we can keep them moving, touching, exploring. The experts favor a hands-on approach, but changing the way schools teach isn't easy. The stakes are high and parents can help.

BARBARA KANTROWITZ & PAT WINGERT

With Howard Manly in Atlanta and bureau reports

It's time for number games in Janet Gill's kindergarten class at the Greenbrook School in South Brunswick, N.J. With hardly any prodding from their teacher, 23 five- and six-year-olds pull out geometric puzzles, playing cards and counting equipment from the shelves lining the room. At one round table, a group of youngsters fits together brightly colored wooden shapes. One little girl forms a hexagon out of triangles. The others, obviously impressed, gather round to count up how many parts are needed to make the whole.

After about half an hour, the children get ready for story time. They pack up their counting equipment and settle in a circle around Gill. She holds up a giant book about a zany character called Mrs. Wishy-washy who insists on giving farm animals a bath. The children recite the whimsical lines along with Gill, obviously enjoying one of their favorite tales. (The hallway is lined with drawings depicting the children's own interpretation of the book; they've taken a few literary liberties, like substituting unicorns and dinosaurs for cows and pigs.) After the first reading, Gill asks for volunteers to act out the various parts in the book. Lots of hands shoot up. Gill picks out four children and

they play their parts enthusiastically. There isn't a bored face in the room.

This isn't reading, writing and arithmetic the way most people remember it. Like a growing number of public- and private-school educators, the principals and teachers in South Brunswick believe that children between the ages of 5 and 8 have to be taught differently from older children. They recognize that young children learn best through active, hands-on teaching methods like games and dramatic play. They know that children in this age group develop at varying rates and schools have to allow for these differences. They also believe that youngsters' social growth is as essential as their academic achievement. Says Joan Warren, a teacher consultant in South Brunswick: "Our programs are designed to fit the child instead of making the child fit the school."

Educators call this kind of teaching "developmentally appropriate practice"—a curriculum based on what scientists know about how young children learn. These ideas have been slowly emerging through research conducted over the last century, particularly in the past 30 years. Some of the tenets have appeared

The Lives and Times of Children

Each youngster proceeds at his own pace, but the learning curve of a child is fairly predictable. Their drive to learn is awesome, and careful adults can nourish it. The biggest mistake is pushing a child too hard, too soon.

● Infants and Toddlers

They're born to learn. The first important lesson is trust, and they learn that from their relationships with their parents or other caring adults. Later, babies will begin to explore the world around them and experiment with independence. As they mature, infants slowly develop gross motor (sitting, crawling, walking) and fine motor (picking up tiny objects) skills. Generally, they remain egocentric and are unable to share or wait their turn. New skills are perfected through repetition, such as the babbling that leads to speaking.

■ 18 months to 3 years

Usually toilet training becomes the prime learning activity. Children tend to concentrate on language development and large-muscle control through activities like climbing on jungle gyms. Attention spans lengthen enough to listen to uncomplicated stories and carry on conversations. Vocabulary expands to about 200 words. They enjoy playing with one other child, or a small group, for short periods, and learn that others have feelings too. They continue to look to parents for encouragement and protection, while beginning to accept limits on their behavior.

▲ 3-year-olds

Generally, they're interested in doing things for themselves and trying to keep up with older children. Their ability to quietly listen to stories and music remains limited. They begin telling stories and jokes. Physical growth slows, but large-muscle development continues as children run, jump and ride tricycles. They begin to deal with cause and effect; it's time to plant seeds and watch them grow.

● 4-year-olds

They develop better small motor skills, such as cutting with scissors, painting, working with puzzles and building things.
They can master colors, sizes and shapes. They should be read to and should be encouraged to watch others write; let them scribble on paper but try to keep them away from walls.

■ 5-year-olds

They begin to understand counting as a one-to-one correlation. Improved memories make it easier for them to recognize meaningful words, and with sharper fine motor skills, some children will be able to write their own names.

▲ Both 4s and 5s

Both groups learn best by interacting with people and concrete objects and by trying to solve real problems. They can learn from stories and books, but only in ways that relate to their own experience. Socially, these children are increasingly interested in activities outside their immediate family. They can play in groups for longer periods, learning lessons in cooperation and negotiation. Physically, large-muscle development continues, and skills such as balancing emerge.

● 6-year-olds

Interest in their peers continues to increase, and they become acutely aware of comparisons between themselves and others. It's a taste of adolescence: does the group accept them? Speech is usually well developed, and children are able to joke and tease. They have a strong sense of true and false and are eager for clear rules and definitions. However, they have a difficult time differentiating between minor and major infractions. Generally, children this age are more mature mentally than physically and unable to sit still for long periods. They learn better by firsthand experiences. Learning by doing also encourages children's "disposition" to use the knowledge and skills they're acquiring.

■ 7- to 8-year-olds

During this period, children begin developing the ability to think about and solve problems in their heads, but some will continue to rely on fingers and toes to help them find the right answer. Not until they're 11 are most kids capable of thinking purely symbolically; they still use real objects to give the symbols—such as numbers—meaning. At this stage they listen better and engage in give and take. Generally, physical growth continues to slow, while athletic abilities improve—children are able to hit a softball, skip rope or balance on a beam. Sitting for long periods is still more tiring than running and jumping.

under other names—progressivism in the 1920s, open education in the 1970s. But they've never been the norm. Now, educators say that may be about to change. "The entire early-childhood profession has amassed itself in unison behind these principles," says Yale education professor Sharon Lynn Kagan. In the last few years, many of the major education organizations in the country—including the National Association for the Education of Young Children and the National Association of State Boards of Education—have endorsed remarkably similar plans for revamping kindergarten through third grade.

Bolstered by opinions from the experts, individual states are beginning to take action. Both California and New York have appointed task forces to recommend changes for the earliest grades. And scores of individual school districts like South Brunswick, figuring that young minds are a terrible thing to waste, are pushing ahead on their own.

The evidence gathered from research in child development is so compelling that even groups like the Council for Basic Education, for years a major supporter of the traditional format, have revised their thinking. "The idea of putting small children in front of workbooks and asking them to sit at their desks all day is a nightmare vision," says Patte Barth, associate editor of Basic Education, the council's newsletter.

At this point, there's no way of knowing how soon change will come or how widespread it will be. However, there's a growing recognition of the importance of the early grades. For the past few years, most of the public's attention has focused on older children, especially teenagers. "That's a Band-Aid kind of approach," says Anne Dillman, a member of the New Jersey State Board of Education. "When the product doesn't come out right, you try and fix it at the end. But we really have to start at the beginning." Demographics have contributed to the sense of urgency. The baby boomlet has replaced the baby-bust generation of the 1970s. More kids in elementary school means more parents asking if there's a better way to teach. And researchers say there is a better way. "We've made remarkable breakthroughs in understanding the development of children, the development of learning and the climate that enhances that," says Ernest Boyer of The Carnegie Foundation for the Advancement of Teaching. But, he adds, too often, "what we know in theory and what we're doing in the classroom are very different."

The early grades pose special challenges because that's when children's attitudes toward school and learning are shaped, says Tufts University psychologist David Elkind. As youngsters move from home or preschool into the larger, more competitive world of elementary school, they begin to make judgments about their own abilities. If they feel inadequate, they may give up. Intellectually, they're also in transition, moving from the intensely physical exploration habits of infancy and toddlerhood to more abstract reasoning. Children are born wanting to learn. A baby can spend hours studying his hands; a toddler is fascinated by watching sand pour through a sieve. What looks like play to an adult is actually the work of childhood, developing an understanding of the world. Studies show that the most effective way to teach young kids is to capitalize on their natural inclination to learn through play.

But in the 1980s, many schools have tried to do just the opposite, pressure instead of challenge. The "back to basics" movement meant that teaching methods intended for high school students were imposed on first graders. The lesson of the day was more: more homework, more tests, more discipline. Children should be behind their desks, not roaming around the room. Teachers should be at the head of the classrooms, drilling knowledge into their charges. Much of this was a reaction against the trend toward open education in the '70s. Based on the British system, it allowed children to develop at their own pace within a highly structured classroom. But too many teachers and principals who tried open education thought that it meant simply tearing down classroom walls and letting children do whatever they wanted. The results were often disastrous. "Because it was done wrong, there was a backlash against it," says Sue Bredekamp of the National Association for the Education of Young Children.

At the same time, parents, too, were demanding more from their elementary schools. By the mid-1980s, the majority of 3- and 4-year-olds were attending some form of pre-school. And their parents expected these classroom veterans to be reading by the second semester of kindergarten. But the truth is that many 5-year-olds aren't ready for reading—or most of the other academic tasks that come easily to older children—no matter how many years of school they've completed. "We're confusing the numbers of years children have been in school with brain development," says Martha Denckla, a professor of neurology and pediatrics at Johns Hopkins University. "Just because a child goes to day care at age 3 doesn't mean the human brain mutates into an older brain. A 5-year-old's brain is still a 5-year-old's brain."

As part of the return to basics, parents and districts demanded hard evidence that their children were learning. And some communities took extreme measures. In 1985 Georgia became the first state to require 6-year-olds to pass a standardized test before entering first grade. More than two dozen other states proposed similar legislation. In the beginning Georgia's move was hailed as a "pioneering" effort to get kids off to a good start. Instead, concedes state school superintendent Werner Rogers, "We got off on the wrong foot." Five-year-olds who used to spend their days finger-painting or singing were hunched over ditto sheets, preparing for the big exam. "We would have to spend a month just teaching kids how to take the test," says Beth Hunnings, a kindergarten teacher in suburban Atlanta. This year Georgia altered the tests in favor of a more flexible evaluation; other states have changed their minds as well.

The intense, early pressure has taken an early toll. Kindergartners are struggling with homework. First graders are taking spelling tests before they even understand how to read. Second graders feel like failures. "During this critical period," says David Elkind in his book "Miseducation," "the child's bud-

In Japan, First Grade Isn't a Boot Camp

Japanese students have the highest math and science test scores in the world. More than 90 percent graduate from high school. Illiteracy is virtually nonexistent in Japan. Most Americans attribute this success to a rigid system that sets youngsters on a lock-step march from cradle to college. In fact, the early years of Japanese schooling are anything but a boot camp; the atmosphere is warm and nurturing. From kindergarten through third grade, the goal is not only academic but also social—teaching kids to be part of a group so they can be good citizens as well as good students. "Getting along with others is not just a means for keeping the peace in the classroom but something which is a valued end in itself," says American researcher Merry White, author of "The Japanese Educational Challenge."

Lessons in living and working together grow naturally out of the Japanese culture. Starting in kindergarten, youngsters learn to work in teams, with brighter students often helping slower ones. All children are told they can succeed if they persist and work hard. Japanese teachers are expected to be extremely patient with young children. They go over lessons step by step and repeat instructions as often as necessary. "The key is not to scold [children] for small mistakes," says Yukio Ueda, principal of Mita Elementary School in Tokyo. Instead, he says, teachers concentrate on praising and encouraging their young charges.

As a result, the classrooms are relaxed and cheerful, even when they're filled with rows of desks. On one recent afternoon a class of second graders at Ueda's school was working on an art project. Their assignment was to build a roof with poles made of rolled-up newspapers. The children worked in small groups, occasionally asking their teacher for help. The room was filled with the sound of eager youngsters chatting about how to get the job done. In another second-grade class, the subject was math. Maniko Inoue, the teacher, suggested a number game to practice multiplication. After a few minutes of playing it, one boy stood up and proposed changing the rules just a bit to make it more fun. Inoue listened carefully and then asked if the other students agreed. They cheered, "Yes, yes," and the game continued according to the new rules.

Academics are far from neglected in the early grades. The Education Ministry sets curriculum standards and goals for each school year. For example, third graders by the end of the year are supposed to be able to read and write 508 characters (out of some 2,000 considered essential to basic literacy). Teachers have time for play and lessons: Japanese children attend school for 240 days, compared with about 180 in the United States.

Mothers' role: Not all the teaching goes on in the classroom. Parents, especially mothers, play a key role in education. Although most kindergartens do not teach writing or numbers in any systematic way, more than 80 percent of Japanese children learn to read or write to some extent before they enter school. "It is as if mothers had their own built-in curriculum," says Shigefumi Nagano, a director of the National Institute for Educational Research. "The first game they teach is to count numbers up to 10."

For all their success in the early grades, the Japanese are worried they're not doing well enough. After a recent national curriculum review, officials were alarmed by what Education Minister Takeo Nishioka described as excessive "bullying and misconduct" among children—the result, according to some Japanese, of too much emphasis on material values. So three years from now, first and second graders will no longer be studying social studies and science. Instead, children will spend more time learning how to be good citizens. That's "back to basics"—Japanese style.

BARBARA KANTROWITZ *with* HIDEKO TAKAYAMA *in Tokyo*

ding sense of competence is frequently under attack, not only from inappropriate instructional practices . . . but also from the hundred and one feelings of hurt, frustration and rejection that mark a child's entrance into the world of schooling, competition and peer-group involvement." Adults under similar stress can rationalize setbacks or put them in perspective based on previous experiences; young children have none of these defenses. Schools that demand too much too soon are setting kids off on the road to failure.

It doesn't have to be this way. Most experts on child development and early-childhood education believe that young children learn much more readily if the teaching methods meet their special needs:

Differences in thinking: The most important ingredient of the nontraditional approach is hands-on learning. Research begun by Swiss psychologist Jean Piaget indicates that somewhere between the ages of 6 and 9, children begin to think abstractly instead of concretely. Younger children learn much more by touching and seeing and smelling and tasting than by just listening. In other words, 6-year-olds can easily understand addition and subtraction if they have actual objects to count instead of a series of numbers written on a blackboard. Lectures don't help. Kids learn to reason and communicate by engaging in conversation. Yet most teachers still talk at, not with, their pupils.

Physical activity: When they get to be 10 or 11, children can sit still for sustained periods. But until they are physically ready for long periods of inactivity, they need to be active in the classroom. "A young child has to make a conscious effort to sit still," says Denckla. "A large chunk of children can't do it for very long. It's a very energy-consuming activity for them." Small children actually get more tired if they have to sit still and listen to a teacher talk than if they're allowed to move around in the classroom. The frontal lobe, the part of the brain that applies the brakes to children's natural energy and curiosity, is still immature in 6- to 9-year-olds, Denckla says. As the lobe develops, so does what Denckla describes as "boredom tolerance." Simply put, learning by doing is much less boring to young children.

Language development: In this age group, experts say language development should not be broken down into isolated skills—reading, writing and speaking. Children first learn to reason and to express themselves by talking. They can dictate stories to a teacher before they actually read or write. Later, their first attempts at composition do not need to be letter perfect; the important thing is that they learn to communicate ideas. But in many classrooms, grammar and spelling have become more important than content. While mastering the technical aspects of writing is essential as a child gets older, educators warn against emphasizing form over content in the early grades. Books should also be interesting to kids—not just words strung together solely for the purpose of pedagogy. Psychologist Katherine Nelson of the City University of New York says that her extensive laboratory and observational work indicates that kids can learn language—speaking, writing or reading—only if it is presented in a way that makes sense to them. But many teachers still use texts that are so boring they'd put anybody to sleep.

Socialization: A youngster's social development has a profound effect on his academic progress. Kids who have trouble getting along with their classmates can end up behind academically as well and have a higher incidence of dropping out. In the early grades especially, experts say youngsters should be encouraged to work in groups rather than individually so that teachers can spot children who may be having problems making friends. "When children work on a project," says University of Illinois education professor Lillian Katz, "they learn to work together, to disagree, to speculate, to take turns and de-escalate tensions. These skills can't be learned through lecture. We all know people who have wonderful technical skills but don't have any social skills. Relationships should be the first 'R'."

Feelings of competence and self-esteem: At this age, children are also learning to judge themselves in relation to others. For most children, school marks the first time that their goals are not set by an internal clock but by the outside world. Just as the 1-year-old struggles to walk, 6-year-olds are struggling to meet adult expectations. Young kids don't know how to distinguish between effort and ability, says Tynette Hills, coordinator of early-childhood education for the state of New Jersey. If they try hard to do something and fail, they may conclude that they will never be able to accomplish a particular task. The effects of obvious methods of comparison, such as posting grades, can be serious. Says Hills: "A child who has had his confidence really damaged needs a rescue operation."

Rates of growth: Between the ages of 5 and 9, there's a wide range of development for children of normal intelligence. "What's appropriate for one child may not be appropriate for another," says Dr. Perry Dyke, a member of the California State Board of Education. "We've got to have the teachers and the staff reach children at whatever level they may be at . . . That takes very sophisticated teaching." A child's pace is almost impossible to predict beforehand. Some kids learn to read on their own by kindergarten; others are still struggling to decode words two or three years later. But by the beginning of the fourth grade, children with very different histories often read on the same level. Sometimes, there's a sudden "spurt" of learning, much like a growth spurt, and a child who has been behind all year will catch up in just a few weeks. Ernest Boyer and others think that multigrade classrooms, where two or three grades are mixed, are a good solution to this problem—and a way to avoid the "tracking" that can hurt a child's self-esteem. In an ungraded classroom, for example, an older child who is having problems in a particular area can practice by tutoring younger kids.

Putting these principles into practice has never been easy. Forty years ago Milwaukee abolished report cards and started sending home ungraded evaluations for kindergarten through third grade. "If anything was developmentally appropriate, those ungraded classes were," says Millie Hoffman, a curriculum specialist with the Milwaukee schools. When the back-to-basics movement geared up nationally in the early 1980s, the city bowed to pressure. Parents started demanding letter grades on report cards. A traditional, direct-teaching approach was introduced into the school system after some students began getting low scores on standardized tests. The school board ordered basal readers with controlled vocabularies and contrived stories. Milwaukee kindergarten teachers were so up-

A Primer for Parents

When visiting a school, trust your eyes. What you see is what your child is going to get.

⬤ Teachers should talk to small groups of children or individual youngsters; they shouldn't just lecture.

◼ Children should be working on projects, active experiments and play; they shouldn't be at their desks all day filling in workbooks.

▲ Children should be dictating and writing their own stories or reading real books.

⬤ The classroom layout should have reading and art areas and space for children to work in groups.

◼ Children should create freehand artwork, not just color or paste together adult drawings.

▲ Most importantly, watch the children's faces. Are they intellectually engaged, eager and happy? If they look bored or scared, they probably are.

set by these changes that they convinced the board that their students didn't need most of the standardized tests and the workbooks that go along with the readers.

Some schools have been able to keep the progressive format. Olive School in Arlington Heights, Ill., has had a nontraditional curriculum for 22 years. "We've been able to do it because parents are involved, the teachers really care and the children do well," says principal Mary Stitt. "We feel confident that we know what's best for kids." Teachers say they spend a lot of time educating parents about the teaching methods. "Parents always think school should be the way it was for them," says first-grade teacher Cathy Sauer. "As if everything else can change and progress but education is supposed to stay the same. I find that parents want their children to like school, to get along with other children and to be good thinkers. When they see that happening, they become convinced."

Parental involvement is especially important when schools switch from a traditional to a new format. Four years ago, Anne Norford, principal of the Brownsville Elementary School in Albemarle County, Va., began to convert her school. Parents volunteer regularly and that helps. But the transition has not been completely smooth. Several teachers refused to switch over to the more active format. Most of them have since left the school, Norford says. There's no question that some teachers have trouble implementing the developmentally appropriate approach. "Our teachers are not all trained for it," says Yale's Kagan. "It takes a lot of savvy and skill." A successful child-centered classroom seems to function effortlessly as youngsters move from activity to activity. But there's a lot of planning behind it—and that's the responsibility of the individual teacher. "One of the biggest problems," says Norford, "is trying to come up with a program that every teacher can do—not just the cadre of single people who are willing to work 90 hours a week." Teachers also have to participate actively in classroom activities and give up the automatic mantle of authority that comes from standing at the blackboard.

Teachers do better when they're involved in the planning and decision making. When the South Brunswick, N.J., schools decided in the early 1980s to change to a new format, the district spent several years studying a variety of curricula. Teachers participated in that research. A laboratory school was set up in the summer so that teachers could test materials. "We had the support of the teachers because teachers were part of the process," says teacher consultant Joan Warren.

One residue of the back-to-basics movement is the demand for accountability. Children who are taught in nontraditional classrooms can score slightly lower on commonly used standardized tests. That's because most current tests are geared to the old ways. Children are usually quizzed on specific skills, such as vocabulary or addition, not on the concepts behind those skills. "The standardized tests usually call for one-word answers," says Carolyn Topping, principal of Mesa Elementary School in Boulder, Colo. "There may be three words in a row, two of which are misspelled and the child is asked to circle the correctly spelled word. But the tests never ask, 'Does the child know how to write a paragraph?'"

Even if the tests were revised to reflect different kinds of knowledge, there are serious questions about the reliability of tests on young children. The results can vary widely, depending on many factors—a child's mood, his ability to manipulate a pencil (a difficult skill for many kids), his reaction to the person administering the test. "I'm appalled at all the testing we're doing of small children," says Vanderbilt University professor Chester Finn, a former assistant secretary of education under the Reagan administration. He favors regular informal reviews and teacher evaluations to make sure a student understands an idea before moving on to the next level of difficulty.

Tests are the simplest method of judging the effectiveness of a classroom—if not always the most accurate. But there are other ways to tell if children are learning. If youngsters are excited by what they are doing, they're probably laughing and talking to one another and to their teacher. That communication is part of the learning process. "People think that school has to be either free play or all worksheets," says Illinois professor Katz. "The truth is that neither is enough. There has to be a balance between spontaneous play and teacher-directed work." And, she adds, "you have to have the other component. Your class has to have intellectual life."

Katz, author of "Engaging Children's Minds," describes two different elementary-school classes she visited recently. In one, children spent the entire morning making identical pictures of traffic lights. There was no attempt to relate the pictures to anything else the class was doing. In the other class, youngsters were investigating a school bus. They wrote to the district and asked if they could have a bus parked in their lot for a few days. They studied it, figured out what all the parts were for and talked about traffic rules. Then, in the classroom, they built their own bus out of cardboard. They had fun, but they also practiced writing, problem solving, even a little arithmetic. Says Katz: "When the class had their parents' night, the teacher was ready with reports on how each child was doing. But all the parents wanted to see was the bus because their children had been coming home and talking about it for weeks." That's the kind of education kids deserve. Anything less should get an "F."

Facts About Dyslexia

Developmental dyslexia is a specific learning disability characterized by difficulty in learning to read. Some dyslexics also may have difficulty in learning to write, to spell and, sometimes, to speak or to work with numbers. The exact cause of dyslexia is not known, but we do know that it affects children who are academically capable, physically and emotionally healthy and who come from good home environments. In fact, many children with dyslexia have the advantages of excellent schools, high mental ability and parents who are well-educated and value learning.

Children are subject to a broad range of reading problems, many of which have an identifiable cause. However, a small group of children have difficulty in learning to read for no apparent reason. These children are called dyslexic. It is estimated that as many as 15 percent of American students may be classified as dyslexic.

Defining Dyslexia

Over the years, the term dyslexia has been given a variety of definitions, and for this reason, many teachers have resisted using the term at all. Instead, they have used such terms as "reading disability" or "learning disability" to describe conditions more correctly designated as dyslexia. Although there is no universally recognized definition of dyslexia, the one presented by the World Federation of Neurology has won broad respect: "A disorder manifested by difficulty in learning to read despite conventional instruction, adequate intelligence and sociocultural opportunity."

Symptoms

Children with dyslexia are not all alike. The only trait they share is that they read at levels significantly lower than is typical for children of their age and intelligence. This reading lag usually is described in terms of grade level. For example, a 4th-grader who is reading at a second grade level is said to be two years behind in reading.

Referring to grade level as a measure of reading is convenient, but it can be misleading. A student who has a 2-year lag when he is in fourth grade has a much more serious problem than a 10th-grader with a 2-year lag. The 4th-grader has learned few of the reading skills that have been taught in the early grades, while the 10th-grader, by this measure, has mastered eight years, or 80 percent, of the skills needed to be a successful reader.

Samuel T. Orton, a neurologist who became interested in the problems of learning to read in the 1920s, was one of the first scientific investigators of dyslexia. In his work with students in Iowa and New York, he found that dyslexics commonly have one or more of the following problems:

• difficulty in learning and remembering printed words;
• letter reversal (b for d, p for q) and number reversals (6 for 9) and changed order of letters in words (tar for rat, quite for quiet) or numbers (12 for 21);
• leaving out or inserting words while reading;
• confusing vowel sounds or substituting one consonant for another;
• persistent spelling errors;
• difficulty in writing.

Orton noted that many dyslexics are lefthanded or ambidextrous and that they often have trouble telling left from right. Other symptoms he observed include delayed or inadequate speech; trouble with picking the right word to fit the meaning desired when speaking; problems with direction (up and down) and time (before and after, yesterday and tomorrow); and clumsiness, awkwardness in using hands, and illegible handwriting. Orton also found that more boys than girls show these symptoms and that dyslexia often runs in families. Fortunately, most dyslexics have only a few of these problems, but the presence of even one is sufficient to create unique educational needs.

Possible Causes

Most experts agree that a number of factors probably work in combination to produce the disorder. Possible causes of dyslexia may be grouped under three broad categories: educational, psychological and biological.

Reprinted from *Children Today*, November/December 1985, pp. 23-27. *Children Today,* published by the office of Human Development Services, U.S. Department of Health and Human Services.

Educational Causes

Teaching Methods. Some experts believe that dyslexia is caused by the methods used to teach reading. In particular, they blame the whole-word (look-say) method that teaches children to recognize words as units rather than by sounding out letters. They think that the phonetic method, which teaches children the names of letters and their sounds first, provides a better foundation for reading. They claim that the child who learns to read by the phonetic method will be able to learn new words easily and to recognize words in print that are unfamiliar as well as to spell words in written form after hearing them pronounced. Other reading authorities believe that combining the whole-word and the phonetic approaches is the most effective way to teach reading. Using this method, children memorize many words as units, but they also learn to apply phonetic rules to new words.

Whatever method they support, experts who think that instructional practices may cause dyslexia agree that strengthening the beginning reading programs in all schools would significantly decrease the number and the severity of reading problems among school children.

Nature of the English Language. Many common English words do not follow phonetic principles, and learning to read and spell these words can be difficult, especially for the dyslexic. Words such as cough, was, where and laugh are typical of those words that must be memorized since they cannot be sounded out. While such words undoubtedly contribute to reading problems, they constitute only a small percent of words in English and so cannot be considered a primary cause of dyslexia.

Intelligence Tests. The commonly accepted definition of dyslexia as a reading disability affecting children of normal intelligence is based on the assumption that we can measure intelligence with a fair degree of accuracy. Intelligence test results, usually referred to as IQ scores, must be interpreted carefully. IQ scores may be affected by factors other than intelligence. Those IQ tests which require the child to read or write extensively pose special problems for the dyslexic. Scores from such tests may reflect poor language skills rather than actual intelligence. Even those IQ tests that are individually administered and demand little or no reading and writing may fail to give a fair measure of intelligence; dyslexics often develop negative attitudes toward all testing situations. In addition, conditions such as noise, fatigue or events immediately preceding the testing session may adversely affect test results. With such a range of possible influences on IQ scores, we must regard these scores as, at best, an estimate of the range of the child's scholastic aptitude and, at worst, a meaningless number that can unjustly label the student.

Psychological Causes

Some researchers attribute dyslexia to psychological or emotional disturbances resulting from inconsistent discipline, absence of a parent, frequent change of schools, poor relationships with teachers or other causes. Obviously, a child who is unhappy, angry or disappointed with his or her relations with parents or other children may have trouble learning. Sometimes such a child is labelled lazy or stupid by parents and friends—even by teachers and doctors. Emotional problems may result from rather than cause reading problems. Although emotional stress may not produce dyslexia, stress can aggravate any learning problem. Any effective method of treatment must deal with the emotional effects of dyslexia.

Biological Causes

A number of investigators believe that dyslexia results from alterations in the function of specific parts of the brain. They claim that certain brain areas in dyslexic children develop more slowly than is the case for normal children, and that dyslexia results from a simple lag in brain maturation. Others consider the high rate of lefthandedness in dyslexics as an indication of differences in brain function. This theory may have some validity. Another theory is that dyslexia is caused by disorders in the structure of the brain. Few researchers accepted this theory until very recently, when brains of dyslexics began to be subjected to post-mortem examination. These examinations have revealed characteristic disorders of brain development. It now seems likely that structural disorders may account for a significant number of cases of severe dyslexia.

Genetics probably play a role as well. Some studies have found that 50 percent or more of affected children come from families with histories of dyslexia or related disorders. The fact that more boys than girls are affected could mean that nongenetic biological factors as well as environmental/sociological factors could contribute to the problem.

Treatment

Educators and psychologists generally agree that the remedial focus should be on the specific learning problems of dyslexic children. Therefore, the usual treatment approach is to modify teaching methods and the educational environment. Just as no two children with dyslexia are exactly alike, the teaching methods used are likewise varied.

Children suspected of being dyslexic should be tested by trained educational specialists or psychologists. By using a variety of tests, the examiners are able to identify the types of mistakes the child commonly makes. The examiner is then able to diagnose the problem and, if the child is dyslexic, make specific recommendations for treatment such as tutoring, summer school, speech therapy or placement in special classes. The examiner may also recommend specific remedial approaches. Since no method is equally effective for all children, remediation should be individually designed for each child. The child's educational strengths and weaknesses, estimated scholastic aptitude (IQ), behavior patterns and learning style, along with the suspected causes of the dyslexia, should all be considered when developing a treatment plan. The plan should spell out those skills the child is expected to master in a specific time period, and it should describe the methods and materials that will be used to help the child achieve those goals.

Treatment programs for dyslexic children fall into three general categories: developmental, corrective and remedial. Some programs combine elements from more than one category.

The *developmental* approach is sometimes described as a "more of the same" approach: Teachers use the methods that have been previously used believing that these methods are sound, but that the child needs extra time and attention. Small-group or tutorial sessions in which the teacher can work on reading with each child allow for individual attention. Some researchers and educators believe, however, that this method is not effective for many children.

The *corrective* reading approach also uses small groups in tutorial sessions, but it emphasizes the child's assets and interests. Those who use this method hope to encourage children to rely on their own special abilities to overcome their difficulties.

The third approach, called *remedial*, was developed primarily to deal with shortcomings of the first two methods. Proponents of this method try to resolve the specific educational and psychological problems that interfere with learning. The instructor recognizes a child's assets but directs teaching mainly at the child's deficiencies. Remedial teachers consider it essential to determine the skills that are the most difficult and then to apply individualized techniques in a structured, sequential way to remedy deficits in those skills. Material is organized logically and reflects the nature of the English language. Many educators advocate a multisensory approach, involving all the child's senses

to reinforce learning: listening to the way a letter or word sounds; seeing the way a letter or word looks; and feeling the movement of hand or mouth muscles in producing a spoken or written letter, word or sound.

Prognosis

For dyslexic children, the prognosis is mixed. The disability affects such a range of children and presents such a diversity of symptoms and such degrees of severity that predictions are hard to make.

Parents of dyslexic children may be told such things as "the child will read when he is ready" or "she'll soon outgrow it." Comments like these fail to recognize the seriousness of the problem. Recent research shows that dyslexia does not go away, that it is not outgrown and that extra doses of traditional teaching have little impact.

Fortunately, educators are becoming more aware of the complexities of dyslexia, placing greater emphasis on choosing the most appropriate teaching method for each child. Teachers are more willing to provide remedial teaching over longer periods of time, whereas prior practice often has been to cut off services if observable changes fail to occur in a limited time. Some dyslexics improve quickly, others make steady but very slow progress, and still others are highly resistant to instruction. Many have persistent spelling problems. Some acquire a basic reading skill but cannot read fluently.

A child's ability to conquer dyslexia depends on many things. An appropriate remedial program is critical. However, environmental and social conditions can undermine any treatment program. The child's relationships with family, peers and teachers have a major effect on the outcome of instruction. In a supportive atmosphere, a child's chance of success is enhanced. Attitudes such as "expectancy," the degree to which a teacher expects a child to learn, are important. Children who sense that they are not expected to succeed seldom do. Since slight progress in reading ability can make an enormous difference in academic success and vocational pursuits,

children need to know that they are expected to progress.

The earlier dyslexia is diagnosed and treatment started, the greater the chance that the child will acquire adequate language skills. Untreated problems are compounded by the time a child reaches the upper grades, making successful treatment more difficult. Older students may be less motivated because of repeated failure, adding another obstacle to the course of treatment. The time at which remediation is given also affects a dyslexic's chances. Often, remedial programs are offered only in the early grades even though they may be needed through high school and college. Remedial programs should be available as long as the student makes gains and is motivated to learn. Adults can make significant progress, too, although there are fewer programs for older students.

A dyslexic child's personality and motivation may influence the severity of the condition. Because success in reading is so vital to a child, dyslexia can affect his or her emotional adjustment. Repeated failure takes it toll. The child with dyslexia may react to repeated failure with anger, guilt, depression, resignation and even total loss of hope and ambition; he or she may require counseling to overcome these emotional consequences of dyslexia. With help a dyslexic child can make gains but the assistance must be timely and thorough, dealing with everything that affects progress. For the child whose dyslexia is identified early, with supportive family and friends, with a strong self-image, and with a proper remedial program of sufficient length, the prognosis is good.

NICHD Research Support

The National Institute of Child Health and Human Development (NICHD) supports many studies designed to determine how most children learn to read and what may interfere with or prevent some children from acquiring this important skill. Some investigators are attempting to develop language tests that can predict which 5- or 6-year-old children have the necessary skills to learn to read and those who are at risk for reading failure. If these investigators are successful it is likely that many cases of dyslexia can be prevented. Other scientists are attempting to identify children at risk for dyslexia through the use of modern neurological examination procedures, including electroencephalography and PET scans (Positron Emission Tomography, an imaging technique that measures brain activity).

Some scientists supported by the NICHD are studying the children from families that have a higher than normal incidence of dyslexia and related language disorders to determine a possible genetic cause of the reading disorder. Other investigators are concentrating their research efforts on the development of specific descriptions of various subtypes of dyslexia with the hope that more appropriate therapies can then be planned.

Although a number of important advances have been made through research, many unanswered questions remain about this developmental disorder of childhood. Our ultimate goal is the complete prevention of dyslexia as well as other specific learning disabilities. Intermediate to that goal is the early identification of all children who are at risk for dyslexia so that prompt and appropriate procedures can be administered which will preclude the manifestation of dyslexic symptoms, or minimize their effects on the child's intellectual, academic, psychological or social development.

Although impressive evidence exists concerning the specific behaviors and neurological characteristics of dyslexia, continued research is essential. Such medical and educational research, along with sound diagnostic techniques and individually-designed educational programs, can open the doors through which the dyslexic may enter into full participation in our literate society.

This article was written by staff members of the Orton Dyslexia Society and the National Institute of Child Health and Human Development (NICHD), NIH.

For Further Information on Dyslexia

American Academy of Pediatrics
P.O. Box 927
141 Northwest Point Rd.
Elk Grove Village, IL 60007
(800) 433-9016 or (312) 228-5005

American Speech-Language-Hearing Association (ASHA)
10801 Rockville Pike
Rockville, MD 20852
(301) 897-5700

Association for Children and Adults with Learning Disabilities (ACLD)
4156 Library Rd.
Pittsburgh, PA 15234
(412) 341-1515

Council for Exceptional Children (CEC)
1920 Association Dr.
Reston, VA 22091
(703) 620-3660

National Institute of Child Health and Human Development (NICHD)
Office of Research Reporting
Bldg. 31, Rm. 2A32
9000 Rockville Pike
Bethesda, MD 20205
(301) 496-5133

Orton Dyslexia Society
724 York Rd.
Baltimore, MD 21204
(301) 296-0232

Family, School, and Cultural Influences on Development

In the early 1900s, behaviorists held that children should be reared strictly, in order to correctly shape their behavior. Post–World War II advice leaned toward permissive forms of child-rearing. Today, child-rearing advice seems to have struck a middle road between the strict and permissive approaches. Parents are encouraged to provide their children with ample love, to cuddle their infants, to use reason as the major disciplinary technique, and to encourage verbal interaction—all in an environment where rules are clearly spelled out and enforced. Suggestion, persuasion, and explanation have become the preferred techniques of rule enforcement, rather than spanking or withdrawal of love.

Perhaps our modern-day opinions on child-rearing merely reflect the ebb and flow of advice over the ages. On the other hand, contemporary child-rearing advice may reflect a growing awareness of effective child-rearing based upon knowledge gained from the scientific study of human development, and a growing aversion to the excessive violence, aggression, and alienation in contemporary American society. Weighted against this breath of optimism are daily reports of sexual and physical abuse and extreme neglect of children, sexism, racism, and countless instances of family stress that contribute to teenage pregnancy, suicide, and delinquency.

The two articles in the first section focus on issues that affect large numbers of parents. In "Positive Parenting," Bruce Baldwin describes what he calls "Cornucopia Kids"—kids who want it all, right now, without working for it. Many parents, with the best of intentions, overindulge their children and produce kids who learn they can get something for nothing. These children often grow into adults who can't function in the "real world." Guidelines are suggested to help parents provide an environment in which their children can develop sound values.

Although it is easy to bemoan the decline of the nuclear family, the fact of its decline remains. Increasing numbers of American women have sole responsibility for child care and child support; that is, most single-parent families are father-absent families. In "The Importance of Fathering," Alice Honig reviews evidence suggesting that both father absence and father presence have important consequences for sex-role development, social adjustment, and cognitive achievement.

As we enter the last decade of the 20th century, families are perhaps subject to more sources of psychological stress than at any time in the recent past. The marked increase in single-parent families, the decline of intergenerational families, and the increase in teenage mothers have added to the problems of parenting. These factors and others have strained the support services available for families in our society. Families that are stressed, either because of external or internal conditions, may turn to expedient child rearing techniques even when they are aware of "expert" opinion. One such expediency is the use of physical punishment in order to "discipline" children. However, physical punishment is an ineffective form of discipline that teaches lack of self-control and promotes the use of aggression in order to control someone else's behavior.

Divorce is one of the more common major sources of stress. Regardless of who wins custody, children do not have an easy time adjusting to the separation of their parents. Suggestions for helping children to cope often require a level of parental cooperation that may be unrealistic. Additional sources of stress are discussed in "Children Under Stress." Many young children are being pushed too hard and too fast academically; poor children suffer from peer pressures and are more likely to be abused and neglected; children experiment with drugs and alcohol at an earlier age. The long-term effects of stress in children are not yet known but represent an understandable concern. In spite of forces threatening to tear families apart, however, the influence of the family on the life of an individual remains strong and pervasive.

As David Elkind points out in "The Child Yesterday, Today, and Tomorrow," until the 1960s, middle class children growing up in intact homes served as the basic model for discussion about child development. The picture has changed dramatically, with cultural variations now commanding an ever-increasing share of the attention of both researchers and practitioners. The selections in this section profile some of the many influences of culture on development. "Television and Behavior" considers the ways in which television influences children's lives and values. Among the many influences of TV are the roles projected for men and women and for ethnic minorities. Two other articles address sexual and ethnic issues. In "Rumors of Inferiority," differences in performance between blacks and whites are linked to blacks' self-doubt, feelings of inferiority, and fear of intellectual abilities—by-products of a longstanding process of discrimination. "Black Children, Black Speech" identifies black English as a separate dialect. In "Biology, Destiny, and All That," Paul Chance reviews evidence for sex differences, and concludes that many differences between the sexes are differences in how characteristics are expressed rather than absolute differences.

School expands a child's social network beyond the neighborhood peer group and often presents new social adjustment problems. In "Alienation and the Four Worlds of Childhood," Urie Bronfenbrenner draws attention to the

increase in disorganized families and environment, which contribute to alienation from family, friends, school, and work.

The family is the first major socialization force to which the child is exposed. However, as early as infancy, children become involved with the second major force in socialization—the schools. Infants attend day care, preschoolers attend nursery school, and older children attend public or private elementary schools. School often represents children's first exposure to extended separation from the home and to significant caregivers other than parents. Most children experience little difficulty adapting to school, but for others the adjustment is more problematic. The articles in the final subsection highlight several issues in education: "An Emerging Synthesis in Moral Education" explores the role of the school in moral education, while "Master of Mastery" deals with the need for innovation in educational strategies. In "Why We Need to Understand Science," Carl Sagan argues that an appreciation of science is essential so that citizens can make informed decisions about policy matters pertaining to science and technology.

Looking Ahead: Challenge Questions

Do you agree with the premise that sex role attitudes about marriage, parenting, and family relationships are fragile and correlate poorly with actual behavior? If not, what kind of evidence would you require in order to be convinced?

Do you think that most divorces provide an atmosphere in which parents can set aside their conflicts and animosities sufficiently to act in the best interests of their children?

It is relatively easy to blame teen pregnancy and teen substance abuse on the disorganization of the American family. It is far more difficult to suggest effective solutions to the problems. What changes do you believe should be instituted in American society to resolve such problems as divorce, child abuse, teen pregnancy, racism, sexism, and substance abuse?

How do you define what is moral? Is your definition based on how children use moral reasoning or on how they behave? Do you believe that moral education is the responsibility of the school, or of the family? What criteria will you use to establish guidelines for the discipline of your children?

Most of the concern about influences of TV has focused on the promotion of violence and the creation of negative ethnic and sexual stereotypes. What are some other areas of concern? Are there any significant benefits of TV to children?

The Importance of Fathering

Alice Sterling Honig

Alice Sterling Honig is Associate Professor, Department of Child and Family Studies, at Syracuse University, Syracuse, New York.

Margaret Mead once observed that fathers are a "biological necessity but a social accident." Little appreciation of the direct role and importance of fathering was expressed scarcely a quarter of a century ago by the pioneer advocate of infant attachment (to mother), John Bowlby:

In the young child's eyes, father plays second fiddle and his value increases only as the child's vulnerability to deprivation decreases. Nevertheless, as the illegitimate child knows, fathers have their uses even in infancy. Not only do they provide for their wives to enable them to devote themselves to the care of the infant and toddler, but, by providing love and companionship, they support her emotionally and help her maintain that harmonious contented mood in the aura of which the infant thrives (1958, p. 363).

Hand-in-hand with this belief in the minimal direct influence of fathers went societal views that gave approval to those fathers who were at their desks by 7:30 a.m. and who often did not return home from business until well past the bedtime of small children. Thus, society's "theory" of what constitutes a good father focused one-dimensionally on the role of provider and excluded the role of nurturer and socializer of the young.

Research has indeed sometimes tended to confirm the peripheral nature of the fathering role. Knox & Gilman (1974) questioned 102 first-time fathers regarding their preparation for, and adaptation to, fatherhood. Most fathers had had little preparation for their role. They participated minimally in the day-to-day care of the new baby. In another study of middle-class families in Boston, 43 percent of the fathers had never changed a diaper. Rebelsky & Hanks (1971) reported that new fathers spent 37 seconds per day in one-to-one verbal interaction with baby. Finally, to complete this picture of father as "second-class" parent, 40 percent of American children surveyed preferred television to their fathers (Dodson, 1979)!

Father Absence

More than six million children live in fatherless families. Much research on fathering has concentrated on the effects of father absence. The main question seems to be "How, and how much, are children harmed by growing up in a fatherless home?" Reviews of research and bibliographic searches suggest that psychosexual and emo-

tional maladaptive functioning occurs more often in conjunction with father absence than presence (Herzog & Sudia, 1973; Honig, 1977; Lynn, 1974). Father absence has been found to be negatively related to sex role development, moral development, cognitive competence and to social adjustment.

The impact of father absence has to be assessed in terms of total family functioning under conditions of that absence. Much of the research seems to imply that when a father is missing, only that variable alone is affecting the child's development. Yet, family climate and clusters of family attributes concomitant with father absence may be far more important for a child's development than the actual number of parents present in the home. For example, in a supportive neighborhood or in a three-generation household, grandfather or older relatives may be available as masculine and fathering role models for young children.

Another aspect that is critical in reviewing the findings on fatherless children has to do with the mother's expressed attitudes toward the child and toward the absent father. A mother who derogates the absent father and/or the child will very likely cause profound self-doubt in a son and distrust of males in a daughter.

Thus, out of the father-absence stud-

From *Dimensions*, October 1980, pp. 33-38, 63. Reprinted by permission of the author and Dimensions, the Journal of the Southern Association of Children Under Six, Little Rock, Arkansas.

ies comes a fairly consistent picture. Fathering is important.

Research on Effects of Fathers Present

Recent societal changes have triggered an upsurge of interest in fatherhood. Twenty-five years ago, only 1.5 million mothers worked, compared to 14 million today. More than one-third of all mothers of children under six work outside the home. Almost 1,400,000 children live in single-parent families headed by fathers (Mendes, 1976). A re-examaination of father roles and the importance of fathering seems then to flow from a rapid increase in working wives and mothers; increasing flexibility in divorce custody arrangements; and increasing pressure on fathers to shoulder some of the child-rearing responsibilities traditionally "relegated" to mothers.

Interviews with college-educated young men and women turned up almost unanimous agreement among these young people that the decision to parent in their lives was closely tied to an egalitarian expectation of fathers' role in sharing the care of the infant and in assuming an important role in child-rearing (Honig, 1980).

Fathers and Infants

A wide variety of recent studies focuses on fathering in the infancy period — that period formerly left to maternal ministrations. Father-infant research of the past few years has consistently shown that fathers can be quite competent. They are sensitive to infant cues and responsive to the signals of newborns. Fathers are quite as likely, if given the chance through sympathetic and facilitative hospital birthing procedures, to bond lovingly with their babies.

When low-income fathers who had not participated in the birth experience were observed in the days after delivery, they proved just as nurturant and stimulating with their infants as the mothers — if the fathers were observed alone with their babies (Parke & Sawin, 1980). The moral may be that father needs time alone with baby to build a love relationship. Mothers have traditionally always had such time together. An intimate father-infant relationship may require the same "twosome" quality that love relationships usually need to grow and deepen.

Infants 12-21 months, brought up by both parents, did not register any preference for either parent, when separation protest, vocalizing and smiles were the measures used (Kotelchuck, 1972; Lamb, 1976). In the former study,

Babies with fathering get more variety in life.

those few infants who did not relate well to father (that is, spend at least 15 seconds near him on his arrival), came from families with the lowest amount of father caregiving. Thus, it looks as if baby attachment to fathers follows a general rule that you get what you give. Fathers who spend loving attentive time with infants will have infants who attach well to them and under ordinary conditions prefer paternal company equally. Data indicate, however, that when distressed, infants may still turn to mother as primary comforter.

Strong differences are reported in the ways in which fathers interact with infants compared to mothers. "When they have the chance, fathers are more visually attentive and playful (talking to the baby, imitating the baby) but they are less active in feeding and caretaking activities such as wiping the child's face or changing diapers" (Parke & Sawin, 1980, p. 204).

Lamb reports that "when both parents are present, fathers are more salient persons than mothers. They are more likely to engage in unusual and more enjoyable types of play, and hence, appear to maintain the infant's attention more than the mothers do" (1976, p. 324). In short, "fathers seem to be more fun for babies! Fathers play different kinds of games with infants, more vigorous games" (Honig, 1979a, p. 247).

Split-screen motion picture work by Daniel Stern and by T. Berry Brazelton at Harvard Medical School reveals distinctive patterns of interaction of father and mother with baby. Mothers and infants play more reciprocal vocalization games. Baby limb movements tend to be smooth and more rounded with mothers. Fathers use more bursts of a tapping kind of touch. Babies show more angular and abrupt body movements to father's touch. What turns out, delightfully, is that the contributions of maternal and paternal touch and vocal reciprocity patterns from earliest infancy differ.

Babies with fathering get more variety in life. There is the priceless redundancy that paternal loving, extra stimulation and sensitivity to signals afford for advancing development. There is also the variation on human interaction themes and variation in gender and style that help a child grow up learning more perceptively to deal with differing patterns of adult interaction, expectancies and styles.

When their fathers have also tended to their needs, babies cope better with strangers. Babies seem to learn more skills to put them at ease socially in strange situations. Father-infant interactions may add social resilience to an infant's social repertoire. The fact that fathers, albeit limited to after-work interaction time, are salient figures in interaction with infants is well illustrated in Friendlander, et al.'s analysis of infants' natural language environments in the home (1972). Systematic analysis of tape-recorded utterances of fathers to infants revealed that one infant, raised primarily by an English-speaking mother, but talked to regularly and prompted abundantly by father in Spanish daily, was able to demonstrate good understanding of many Spanish words at one year of age.

Quality of father's interaction time, as so well predicted by Eriksonian theory for mothers, seems to count strongly for the positive special influence that fathers can have not only as attachment figures but as boosters of infant language learning.

Fathers and the Development of Intellective Achievements

Ainsworth's pioneer work in attachment has delineated the ways in which baby's secure attachment to mother by one year is related to the organization of socio-emotional behavior up to at least five years and to early achievement of developmental milestones (1979). Sroufe and his colleagues (1979) have demonstrated that securely attached infants are better problem solvers and tool users when challenged with somewhat difficult tasks as toddlers and preschoolers.

Just how involved are fathers in teaching their children, and how important is fathering for the development of child intellectual competence?

Social class and sex of child have been found as significant confounding variables in studies that attempt to assess father impact on cognitive achievement. Deal & Montgomery (1971) observed the techniques used by fathers, from professional and non-professional families, to teach their five-year-old sons two sorting tasks. Professional fathers verbalized more, used more complete sentences and more verbal rewards than non-professional fathers.

An interview study with black fathers from three social classes revealed that middle-class black fathers' scores in the domains of "provision of developmental stimulation" and "qual-

4. FAMILY, SCHOOL, AND CULTURAL INFLUENCES: Parenting

. . . Paternal nurturance has been found to be positively related to high child achievement.

ity of the language environment" were significantly higher than scores for fathers in the upper-lower or lower-lower social class groups. And the amount of enriching home stimulation was significantly highest for middle-class fathers of daughters (Honig & Main, 1980).

Paternal verbal and cognitive interactions seem to differ as a function of child sex. The research results are often confusing. McAdoo (1979) found that middle- and working-class black fathers interacted more with sons than with daughters. There was a significant positive relationship between fathers' warmth and nurturance and amount of interaction with child. Epstein & Radin (1975) observed social class differences related to cognitive achievement among male children. Among middle-class boys, there was a positive relationship between paternal nurturance and child's Binet I.Q. Among lower-class boys, paternal restrictiveness had a negative impact on the child's cognitive explorations.

The researchers speculate that "it may be that in the working class, where sex role stereotypes are strongest, intellectual and academically-oriented activities are viewed as feminine and hence not appropriate for boys" (p. 838). They report that fathers seem to interfere with daughters' task motivation by restrictiveness and by offering mixed messages that they will both meet and ignore daughters' explicit needs.

Lamb & Frodi (1980) have speculated that, in effect, when a warm father encourages femininity in a daughter and yet believes, traditionally, that femininity and achievement are incompatible, a girl may have grave doubts or conflict about the appropriateness of achievement for women. Alternatively, fathers may not be as strong role models as mothers for girls' intellective development. Research provides too little and conflicting evidence to decide this point. Crandall and colleagues (1964), for example, found that daughters who demonstrated excellence in reading and arithmetic had mothers who often praised and rewarded their intellectual efforts and seldom criticized them. Yet, in Bing's (1963) study, father's strictness was related to verbal achievements of daughters even more than sons'.

More often than not, paternal nurtur-

ance has been found to be positively related to high child achievement. High-achieving college students reported that their fathers were more accepting and somewhat less controlling than fathers described by low-achievers (Cross & Allen, 1969). When parents are too anxiously intrusive in trying to foster intellectual achievement, their efforts may have unfortunate effects.

Teahan (1963) administered a questionnaire to low-achieving college freshmen (who had previously done well in school) and their parents. These sons had fathers who felt that children should make only minor decisions, that they should always believe their parents, that they should be under their parents' complete control and that it was wicked to disobey parents. The picture emerged of a clash between a domineering, punitive, overprotective father — and his underachieving son.

It is possible that the relationship among the variables of paternal nurturance, high academic expectations, sex-role attitudes, quality of cognitive facilitation, and marital congruence with spouse may interact in subtle and complex ways to foster a child's intellectual competence.

Rapidly changing beliefs about the roles of fathers may increase the confusion among research findings as to paternal influence on achievement. Talcott Parsons' theory (Parsons & Bales, 1955), for example, that fathers were "instrumental" and mothers "expressive" with children may be outdated by evolving new beliefs. Parsons hypothesized that father comes to be seen by the child as representative of the outside world. Father is the significant major parent to make strong demands that expand a child's horizons for achievement. Such a simplified role dichotomy is no longer acceptable in the value system of many families.

But there is some research support for this conceptualization. Cox, in a 1962 dissertation with gifted fourth to sixth graders, found that their fathers and mothers showed a predominant pattern of affection, setting firm limits and positive relationships. Fathers, especially, set high expectations for their gifted high-achieving children.

A summary of the main thrust of the research so far would counsel that a father who wishes to have positive

academic influence should have high academic expectations, be a helpful teacher, remain nurturant, but respond with flexibility, perceptivity and sensitivity over time to a child's changing needs for assuming autonomous responsibility for the child's own learning career and social life.

Fathers and Sex Role Development

Research indicates that fathers are more focused on sex role differences. They influence sex stereotyping more than mothers. Fathers have preference for male offspring. By one year, fathers prefer boy babies. Fathers talk more to sons than to daughters.

The father's character and the extent to which he has made a success of his personal life, plus his easy affection with his son and his loving relationship with the mother, have been suggested as the foundation for a son's ready acceptance of being male and, in turn, confident acceptance of the role of husband and father in adulthood (Green, 1976).

A father who is violent, contemptuous toward women and overbearing may impair his daughter's ability to grow up "feminine." She may grow up without a basic sexual understanding that men and women can be equally accepting of and tender with each other. Young girls who have grown up with a good relationship with an admiring, nurturant father have been found to relate easily and well in college relationships with young men (Johnson, 1963).

Two-thirds of the world's 800 million illiterates are females. Dominant males in many third-world societies devalue the potential for intellectual development of their daughters and wives. Yet, even in the United States, subtle, intellectual devaluating of daughters occurs at many levels. Research on conversational management techniques reveals that fathers interrupt their children more than mothers do, and daughters are interrupted more than sons. Fathers engage in simultaneous speech more with daughters than with sons. Boys and girls get different messages about their status and role in society. Girls are more interruptible than their brothers — which suggests in a not-so-subtle way that they are less important (Greif, 1980).

Such prejudices run deep. Perhaps

Fathers are important for adequate sex role development of daughters as well as sons.

only as this nation commits itself to teaching parenting skills and family life courses at all educational levels will prospective parents begin to become aware of the impelling and compelling influences they can have on the growth of emotionally healthy and self-actualized daughters and sons in the future.

Fathers are important for adequate sex role development of daughters as well as sons. Daughters' conceptualizations of the worth of fathers may be persistently distorted by being raised in households bereft of a father. Girls then may in some way expect that only women are strong and can take care of families and men are weak and cannot be expected to do so.

What does such sex role learning presage for tomorrow's families? Green has summarized the important role that fathers play in a daughter's sex role development: "A young girl learns how to be a female from her similarly shaped mother. But she will learn how to be a girl who likes men, or does not trust or feel affection for men by the way she responds to her father" (p. 165).

Recent studies on androgynous roles for both mothers and fathers are beginning to reveal some of the fathering patterns that may emerge as new beliefs about masculinity and the fathering role become more widespread. Fathers classified as androgynous by the Bem Sex Role Inventory have been found to be more involved in day-to-day care, activities and play with their children than those classified as masculine. Fathers classified as masculine, married to women classified as androgynous or masculine provided the next highest level of involvement with children. The least involved were masculine fathers married to feminine women (Russell, 1978).

Fathering and Prosocial Child Behaviors

School vandalism, rising delinquency at younger ages and crime in the streets have all helped to spur interest in the area of prosocial behaviors such as empathy, altruism, generosity and helpfulness. Most of the research has focused on female parents, models and teachers. In a study that inquired about fathering patterns, Rutherford & Mussen (1968) played a game with nursery school boys who then had an opportunity to share some of their winnings with friends. The most generous boys, by action and by teacher rating, much more frequently described their fathers as nurturant and warm parents and as models of generosity, sympathy and compassion.

Hoffman (1975) used sociometric questionnaries to assess fifth-grade pupils' reputations for altruism and consideration of others. Children nominated the three same-sexed classmates who were most likely to "stick up for a kid that the other kids are making fun of or calling names" and "to care about how other kids feel and try not to hurt their feelings." Parents of the children were then asked to rank 18 life values. The fathers of those boys rated as most helpful and considerate (and the mothers of similar girls) ranked altruism high in their own hierarchy of values.

Yarrow & Scott (1972) found a child's consideration of others, as assessed by classmates' nominations, to be related to maternal and not paternal affection among middle-class children. However, lower-class boys' (but not girls') consideration for others was significantly related to father and mother affection.

Middle-class six- and eight-year-old boys were found to be more generous when high paternal affection and high maternal child-centeredness were present (as measured by parental Q Sorts). These relationships did not hold for girls (Feshbach, 1973). The level of altruism modeled by fathers appears to be a factor in the development of sons' prosocial behaviors. In a review of studies of the development of prosocial behaviors in children, Mussen & Eisenberg-Berg (1977) conclude that "nurturance is most effective in strengthening predispositions toward prosocial behavior when it is part of a pattern of child-rearing that prominently features the modeling of prosocial acts" (p. 92).

The converse has been found also. Where fathers are relatively unaffectionate and controlling, authoritarian and rejecting, and not likely to trust their sons, boys have been found high in aggression (Feshbach, 1973; Stevens & Mathews, 1978).

Fathering in Alternate Life Styles

Just beginning to receive the research attention they so critically deserve are stepfathers, divorced fathers with custody, divorced fathers with only visitation rights, and single unwed fathers*. In 1974, slightly over six million children were living with a stepparent. Rallings (1976) has summarized some of the sociological findings on the extent of stepparenting and the adjustment problems faced by stepfathers in particular, and Pannor, et al. (1971) have focused on studies of unwed fathers.

Hetherington, Cox & Cox (1976) have documented the extent of the disruption on children's lives where father is the non-custodial parent. Divorced parents are less consistent with children; they are less likely to use reasoning and explanation. There is a steady decline in nurturance expressed by divorced fathers toward their children. Two years after divorce, negative affect and distressful symptoms were diminished in girls. Yet boys from divorced families were still more hostile and less happy than boys from nuclear families.

When the father was emotionally mature, then frequency of father's contact with the child was associated with more positive mother-child interactions. When the father was poorly adjusted or there was disagreement and inconsistent attitudes toward the child, or there was ill will between the former spouses, then frequent visitation was associated with poor mother-child functioning and disruptions in the children's behavior.

Wallerstein and Kelly (1980) followed children of divorced families for five years. Boys particularly reported depressed and difficult feelings when there was not consistent attentive relationship maintained with the father. One-third of this middle-class sample of children were still considerably disturbed in functioning after five years.

The intimate relationship of fathers and children seems to be particularly crucial for positive adjustment of sons after divorce. Yet, parental conflict and immaturity can vitiate positive effects of frequent contact. Clearly more urgent is sensitivity to children's needs by both parents after divorce. The effect of divorce per se on children

---

*All of the articles in the Special Issue of the October 1979 *Family Coordinator* (Volume 28) are addressed to "Men's Roles in the Family."

When nourished by father love and intimate responsive care, babies become well attached to their fathers.

is not as critical as parental conflict and immaturity.

Gasser & Taylor (1976) inquired into the role adjustments faced by single-parent fathers. The middle-class fathers interviewed assumed major responsibility for all child-care activities, sought outside supports, and curtailed club meetings and educational attainments. These fathers felt that they were able to cope with the responsibilities of home management although they may have formerly assumed little responsibility while married. Single fathering no more seems to guarantee unhappiness than does nuclear family living (Katz, 1979). The ways in which stresses and burdens are handled seems to be more indicative of whether a family functions fairly happily than whether one or two parents are present.

Father Involvement: Intervention Programs

Although the overwhelming number of programmatic efforts to enhance parenting skills in the past decade has focused on mothers, some programs have been involved with fathers as part of a family focus of intervention. Middle-class mothers and fathers of babies under 12 months were trained to increase their social competence with infants (Dickie & Carnahan, 1979). Post-training home observations showed that training affected trained fathers the most. They were superior to trained mothers and to control mothers and fathers in anticipating infants' needs, responding more appropriately to the infants' cues and providing more frequent verbal and non-verbal contingent responses. Infants sought interaction least with untrained fathers and most with trained fathers. An extra benefit accrued to the marital partners: trained mothers and fathers thought their spouses were more competent than did untrained mothers and fathers.

An experimental program in Chicago with a small number of low-income families in an urban housing project found that fathers could be more actively involved in their children's educational experiences when male workers tailored the home visitation program specially for the fathers. Tuck (1969) has described this model for working with black fathers.

The Importance of Fathering

The importance of fathering has become more and more evident as research in this area proliferates. Some comments are appropriately representative of major findings to date and some as suggestions for needed research.

Men who traditionally have rejected expression of tender feelings or a range of emotional responsiveness as unmanly may need to rethink "what is masculinity" in light of the needs of infants for fathers and the delights of intimacy with infants for fathers. As Lamb elegantly expresses this: "It is important not to confuse conformity to traditional sex role prescriptions with the security of gender identity or with mental health." Provided an individual's gender identity is secure, a wide range of gender roles can be assumed (1979, p. 942).

The myth that only mothers can nurture an infant seems just that — a myth. Fathers are just as upset by squalling babies as are mothers. Fathers can be as attentive to infant cues as mothers. When nourished by father love and intimate responsive care, babies become well attached to their fathers.

Paternal nurturance may be related in complex ways to cognitive achievement in children. The family serves as a nurturing matrix that allows a child's natural curiosity and exploration to flourish into developmental learnings. A child filled with anxiety or despair that he or she is neither cared for nor cared about cannot focus well on learning tasks whether a father is absent or present. Future research should focus on the complex interweave of factors in family and community that facilitate intellectual engagement and achievement, rather than on putative effects of father absence or presence conceived of as a single variable of an heuristically critical nature.

Process rather than status variables have proved more relevant to child intellective attainments (Honig, 1979b). Indeed, in a father-present family where book-learning is considered sissyish, it is not difficult to predict that despite father presence, neither cognitive strivings nor academic excellence may be a goal of father or son.

Because the effects of fathering may

be related to marital harmony, economic stress and a host of social and cultural variables, future emphasis in fathering research needs to enquire into the covariation of factors that affect father influence on child development. For example, Park & Sawin's (1977) studies demonstrated that both mother and father show more interest when they are together with the newborn. They count toes, check ears, and smile at the infant more.

Clarke-Stewart (1979) found, in a small sample-size but provocative study, that as mothers rear a contented, interesting baby, fathers, after the first year, are lured by such an attractive infant into increased interactions. Triadic effects of fathers and mothers and infants need to be examined. Pederson's (1975) finding that father's warmth and affection helps support the mother and make her more effective with the baby is relevant. Research must be sensitive both to direct and to indirect effects of fathering.

The relation of fathers to the development of altruism, empathy and the gentler arts of positive relations with others deserves far more research effort. If a parent preaches "love thy neighbor" but father models proudly his "he-man" imperviousness and insensitivity to the feelings and rights of others, particularly wife and children, then present research suggests that children will practice what they live rather than what they are told.

As divorce statistics increase, more and more ways to help children weather parental storms and uncouplings must be found. Divorce findings reveal that the role of a well-adjusted father who can communicate without strong rancor with his ex-spouse can do much through intimate, consistent contact with children, post-divorce, to help heal the distress and anger that divorce entails for children. Otherwise, what "frees" the parents may engender possible long-lasting grief and academic difficulty, particularly for sons.

Single parents may have a harder job rearing children well because of the extra stresses that may ensue when there is lack of a supporting other person. Yet, single fathers may have a very high motivation to parent. Strong positive motivation has been known to overcome "handicaps" far more severe than those involved in single fathering.

Despite the many studies which sug-

. . . Fathering may still be a profound and deeply satisfying experience in human intimacy and engagement.

gest that diapering and child care in early infancy are not the occupation of choice for many fathers (and some mothers too), fathering may still be a profound and deeply satisfying experience in human intimacy and engagement. It may be well to remember the impressive findings from the long-term study of Terman's gifted children. When gifted boys were reinterviewed decades later at age 62, they agreed that the greatest source of satisfaction in their lives was their families.

Sears (1977) has commented that in spite of autonomy and great average success in their occupations, these men placed greater importance on having achieved satisfaction in their family life than in their work. Furthermore, these men believed that they had found such satisfaction. May it be so for fathers of the future. Such a deep conviction and satisfaction would augur well for the children of tomorrow.

Fathering education is not yet politically an "in" issue for society. Yet, a man needs to learn fathering the way he would learn to play ball or set up a business or cook a gourmet meal — early and with lots of practice, patience and encouragement. Communities must become alert to the ways schools and service organizations can provide opportunities for boys to learn about and to nurture younger children responsively and responsibly.

REFERENCES

Ainsworth, M.D.S. Attachment: Retrospect and prospect. Presidential address presented at the Biennial Meeting of the Society for Research in Child Development, San Francisco, March, 1979.

Bing, E. Effect of childrearing practices on development of differential cognitive abilities. *Child Development*, 1963, *34*, 631-648.

Bowlby, J. The nature of the child's tie to his mother. *International Journal of Psychoanalysis*, 1958, *39*, 350-373.

Clarke-Stewart, A. The father's impact on mother and child. Paper presented at the Biennial Meeting of the Society for Research in Child Development, New Orleans, March, 1979.

Crandall, V. J., Dewey, R., Katkovsky, W. & Preston, A. Parents' attitudes and behaviors and grade-school children's academic achievements. *Journal of Genetic Psychology*, 1964, *104*, 53-66.

Cross, H. J. & Allen, J. Relationship between memories of parental behavior and academic achievement motivation. Proceedings of the 77th Annual Convention, American Psycho-

logical Association, Washington, D.C., September, 1969, 285-286.

Deal, T. N. & Montgomery, L. L. Techniques fathers use in teaching their young sons. Paper presented at the Meeting of the Society for Research in Child Development, Minneapolis, April 1971.

Dickie, J. R. & Carnahan, S. Training in social competence: The effect on mothers, fathers and infants. Paper presented at the Biennial Meeting of the Society for Research in Child Development, San Francisco, March, 1979.

Dodson, F. How to make your man a great father. *Harper's Bazaar*, April, 1979, p. 155, 194.

Epstein, A. S. & Radin, N. Motivational components related to father behavior and cognitive functioning in preschoolers. *Child Development*, 975, *46*, (No. 4), 831-839.

Feshback, N. The relationship of child rearing factors to children's aggression, empathy, and related positive and negative social behaviors. Paper presented at the NATO Conference on the Determinants and Origins of Aggressive Behavior, Monte Carlo, Monaco, July, 1973.

Friedlander, B. Z., Jacobs, A. C., Davis, V. B. & Wetstone, H. S. Time-sampling analysis of infants' natural language environments in the home. *Child Development*, 1972, *43*, 730-740.

Gasser, R. D. & Taylor, C. M. Role adjustment of single parent fathers with dependent children. Family Coordinator, 1976, *25*, (No. 4), 397-402.

Green, M. *Fathering*. New York: McGraw-Hill, 1976.

Greif, E. Sex differences in parent-child conversations, ERIC, ED 174 337, 1980.

Herzog, E. & Sudia, C. Children in fatherless families. In B. M. Caldwell & H.N. Ricciuti, (Eds.) *Review of Child Development Research Vol. 3*, Chicago: University of Chicago Press, 1973.

Hetherington, E. M., Cox, M. & Cox, R. Divorced fathers. *Family Coordinator*, 1976, *25*, 417-428.

Hoffman, M. L. Altruistic behavior and the parent-child relationship. *Journal of Personality and Social Psychology*, 1975, *31*, 937-943.

Honig, A. S. *Fathering: A bibliography*. Urbana, Illinois: ERIC (Document Reproduction Service No. 142293: (Cat No. 164) 1977.

Honig, A. S. A review of recent infancy research. *The American Montessori Society Bulletin*, 1979, *17* (No. 3 & 4) (a)

Honig, A. S. *Parent involvement in early childhood education*. 2nd Edition. Washington, D.C.: National Association for the Education of Young Children, 1979. (b)

Honig, A. S. Choices: To parent or not to parent. Paper presented at the 6th Annual Symposium on Sex Education, Toulouse, France, July, 1980.

Honig, A. S. & Main, G. Black fathering in three social class groups. Manuscript submitted for publication, 1980.

Johnson, M. M. Sex role learning in the nuclear family. *Child Development*, 1963, *34*, 319-333.

Katz, A. J. Lone fathers: Perspectives and implications for family policy. *The Family Coordinator*, 1979, *28*, 521-528.

Knox, I. D. & Gilman, R. C. The first year of fatherhood. Paper presented at the National Council on Family Relations, Missouri, 1974.

Kotelchuck, M. *The nature of the child's tie to his father*. Unpublished doctoral dissertation, Harvard University, 1972.

Lamb, M. E. The role of the father: An overview. In M. E. Lamb (Ed.) *The role of the father in child development*, New York: Wiley, 1976.

Lamb, M. E. Paternal influences and the father's role: A personal perspective. *American Psychologist*, 1979, *34*, 938-943.

Lamb, M. E. & Frodi, A. M. The role of the father in child development. In R. R. Abidin (Ed.) *Parent education and intervention handbook*. Springfield, Illinois: Charles C. Thomas, 1980.

Lynn, D. B. *The father: His role in child development*. Belmont, California: Brooks Cole, 1974.

McAdoo, J. L. Father-child interaction patterns and self esteem in black preschool children. *Young Children*, 1979, *34*, 46-53.

Mendes, H. A. Single fatherhood. *Social Work*, 1976, *21*, (No. 4), 308-312.

Mussen, P. & Eisenberg-Berg, N. *Roots of caring, sharing, and helping*. San Francisco: W. H. Freeman, 1977.

Pannor, R., Evans, B. W. & Massarik, F. *The unmarried father*. New York: Springer Publishing Co., 1971.

Parke, R. D. & Sawin, D. D. Fathering: It's a major role. *Psychology Today*, 1977, *11*, 108-113.

Parke, R. D. & Sawin, D. B. Fathering: It's a major role. H. E. Fitzgerald (Ed.) *Human Development 80/81*. Guilford, Connecticut: Dushkin, 1980.

Parsons, T. & Bales, R. F. *Family, socialization and interaction process*. Glencoe, Illinois: Free Press, 1955.

Pederson, F. A. Mother, father, and infant as an interactive system. Paper presented at the Symposium Fathers and Infants at the meetings of the American Psychological Association, Chicago, August, 1975.

Rallings, E. M. The special role of stepfather. *Family Coordinator*, 1976, *25*, 445-450.

Rebelsky, F. & Hanks, C. Fathers verbal interactions with infants in the first three months of life. *Child Development*, 1971, *42*, 63-68.

Russell, G. The father role and its relation to masculinity, femininity, and androgyny. *Child Development*, 1978, *49*, 1174-1181.

Rutherford, E. & Mussen, P. Generosity in nursery school boys. *Child Development*, 1968, *39*, 755-765.

Sears, R. R. Sources of life satisfactions of the Terman gifted men. *American Psychologist*, 1977, *32*, 119-128.

Sroufe, L. A. The coherence of individual development: Daily care, attachment, and subsequent developmental issues. *American Psychologist*, 1979, *34*, 834-341.

Stevens, J. H., Jr. & Mathews, M. (Eds.) *Mother/child, father/child relationships*. Washington, D. C.: National Association for the Education of Young Children, 1978.

Teahan, J. E. Parental attitudes and college success. *Journal of Educational Psychology*, 1963, *54*, 104-109.

Tuck, S. A model for working with black fathers. Paper presented at the Annual Meeting of the American Orthopsychiatric Association, San Francisco, 1969.

Wallerstein, J. S. & Kelly, J. B. Divorce counseling: A community service for families in the midst of divorce. In R. R. Abidin (Ed.) *Parent education and intervention handbook*. Springfield, Illinois: Charles C. Thomas, 1980.

Yarrow, M. R. & Scott, R. M. Imitation of nurturant and non-nurturant models. Journal of Personality and Social Psychology, 1972, *23*, 259-270.

Positive Parenting

How to Avoid Raising Cornucopia Kids

Dr. Bruce A. Baldwin

Dr. Bruce A. Baldwin is a practicing psychologist who heads Direction Dynamics, a consulting service specializing in promoting professional development and quality of life in achieving men and women. He responds each year to many requests for seminars on topics of interest to professional organizations and businesses. This article has been adapted from Baldwin's new book on parenting, Beyond the Cornucopia Kids: How to Raise Healthy Achieving Children! *For busy achievers, he has written* It's All in Your Head: Lifestyle Management Strategies for Busy People! *Both are available in bookstores or from Direction Dynamics in Wilmington, North Carolina.*

A recent advertisement promoting one company's top-of-the-line product had a catchy headline: "'I have the simplest of tastes. . . . I am always satisfied with the best'—Oscar Wilde." This same headline unfortunately hits home with all too many frustrated parents these days. From coast to coast, in cities and hamlets, parents are deeply troubled about their children.

Their concern is focused on their children's expectations. Children today want it all—right now—and they don't particularly want to work for it. Parents are expected to keep their offspring up with the latest fashions and every fad item, and to provide lavish supplies of spending money. All unearned, of course.

From an objective point of view, these children of good families remain immature. Parents complain that they don't seem to be motivated to do anything but have a good time. More often than not, they are rude and self-centered. And even after they leave home, someone else is still expected to provide it all and to foot the bills. These are the Cornucopia Kids. They are becoming more common with each passing year.

Cornucopia Kids simply don't deal well with the "real world" because they've never been exposed to it. They are children who learn through years of direct experience in the home that the good life will always be available for the asking, without personal accountability or achievement motivation. These indulged children have lived their lives in an artificial environment created by naive and compliant parents. Life is always easy. They've never had to struggle; nor are they expected to give back in return for what they've been given. The real world, when at last they confront it, finds them unprepared and overwhelmed.

In other words, these are children who are indulged materially from an early age. They get their way with parents through persuasion or manipulation, and they escape the consequences of their actions. Their parents help out by taking over and doing their work for them. Lucky children? Far from it. These kids have everything—*except what they really need.* What they need is a sound value system and associated achievement-oriented skills that will enable them to confront the real world and succeed there. Only parents can provide these necessities.

While there is no question that Cornucopia Kids are on the increase these days, it is ironic that the parents who raise them usually do so with the best of intentions. These parents work hard. They are achievers, and through dedication and sacrifice they've attained financial success. Then, without thinking about what they are doing, they begin indiscriminately to share their largess with their children—and it's mighty easy to do.

These days there is more in the stores, and the kids want it all. There is more discretionary income in two-career families. Credit is easy and instantaneous. Sophisticated advertising links products with status and personal adequacy. Having what is necessary to be part of the "in crowd" is reinforced by the child's peers. The result is tremendous pressure on parents to give and to give in. Some parents simply buy this material-oriented lifestyle outright. Many others rationalize what they are doing because everyone else seems to be doing the same thing. Still others, busy and overwhelmed with responsibility, are simply worn down and just give up trying to do what is right for their kids.

It takes much more character to be a good parent now than it did several decades ago. Back in the late '40s and '50s, most middle-class parents made enough to get by. Income was allocated to necessities and there was not much left over. Back then, if the kids wanted something extra, there was only one way to get it, and that was to work for it. For some people these days all that has changed. The central issue facing parents now is different and more difficult: "If we have it to give and the kids know that we have it to give, are we strong enough to say no?"

It's well known that struggle builds confidence and confidence builds character. The life-styles of indulged children today make for a most difficult transition when they leave home and are on their own. On the other hand, it is entirely possible for parents to provide a home environment in which children learn healthy values that will help them to grow into adulthood as emotionally mature and responsible achievers. Further, parents need not apologize for their successes, but an important distinction must be clearly understood. Just because parents have made it economically, it does not follow that children must be indulged.

To help parents see through the superficiality of many of the negative values permeating our society and being adopted wholesale via the immaturity of children, there are several myths, each of which has to do with material indulgence, that must be directly confronted and resolved.

A child who has everything is advantaged and therefore more likely to succeed. Experience shows that quite the opposite often happens. A child who gets everything for nothing learns to expect everything for nothing. As an adult, this expectation may continue unabated, and that young adult may find no base of experience from which to deal effectively with the problems, sacrifices, struggles, setbacks and hard work required in the real world. They become marginal workers who continue to rely on their parents to provide them with the life-style to which they have become accustomed.

Having everything helps a child feel loved and secure. Hogwash and horsefeathers! In no way does indulging a child contribute to his or her self-esteem and personal security. When given everything, children never learn to deal effectively with the real world and its expectations. What is learned is dependence on others, particularly parents. As a result, personal confidence never develops. Loving a child entails providing a sound set of values and effective life skills. Love does not include giving in to everything a child wants. Indulged children feel helpless, hopeless, depressed and insecure when everything isn't being provided for them.

The child who is given everything is protected from the emotional pain and frustration of exclusion by peers. Children often complain vociferously about having to do chores, or about not having the absolute best of everything, or about being forced to endure what is perceived to be unfair parental discipline. This is especially true when their peers seem to have everything, without household responsibilities, and always seem to escape the consequences of their actions. From the immature perspective of a child, it is a totally unfair situation. From a developmental perspective, however, it's a wise parent who helps a child learn accountability and responsibility through positive experiences at home *regardless of what that child's peers do.* That child will then be able to fit into the real world and deal positively with its frustrations.

This is not to imply that our purpose is to deprive the youngsters of the good things in life, or of the joys and freedom of childhood. The goal is to provide children with sound values and solid skills throughout their developmental years so that they will be self-sufficient when the time comes to leave the family. Teaching these behaviors requires persistence, patience and knowledge on the part of parents, all applied consistently and positively through the growing years.

These adaptive responses are learned very slowly during the course of development. And they are learned with difficulty by children, who are all born completely impulsive, essentially self-centered and absolutely pleasure-oriented. But this

seemingly insurmountable task is being done every day by wise parents who understand the big picture. "Parents must give their children what they need, not what they want" is one of the fundamentals of raising healthy achieving children these days. Here are some ideas to help you put that guideline into practice in your home.

The Benefits of Struggle

Learning to strive toward personal goals in healthy ways is an invaluable life skill; yet many parents do not really understand the positive psychological benefits of struggle. They perceive it only in terms of personal pain and deprivation. Certainly, most children resist working for what is wanted, and as a result, many parents unwittingly short-circuit their children's healthy striving through indiscriminate giving and giving in. Thus, immense potential for learning remains untapped.

Successfully meeting challenges is certainly not an easy lesson to learn during childhood. As an adult, however, these same skills are even more difficult, sometimes impossible, to acquire when there is no foundation of healthy childhood striving. Parents must, despite their material success in life, create a challenging environment for their children. The payoffs for setting goals, working hard to reach them and overcoming obstacles along the way are deep and lasting. Here is a baker's dozen of these payoffs just for starters.

Developing a clear perception of reality. A common childhood fantasy is one about growing up, quickly becoming rich and famous, and then living happily ever after. In a young child such a fantasy is fine. However, if during the course of development a child is not exposed to the realities of setting and achieving personal goals, then such fantasies may persist into adulthood. These adults become "dreamers" who have great ideas about what they're going to do but never seem to get around to doing it. This is a common pattern in adult Cornucopia Kids. Their dreams remain dreams because they don't know how to make them come true.

Defining personal limits and strengths. It is through confrontation with adversity that self-awareness develops. During the course of healthy striving to meet challenges, a process of self-evaluation takes place naturally. Supportive feedback from parents and significant others who see the broader perspective further helps a child to define positive and negative responses. Once weaknesses and strengths are clearly conceptualized, a child is in a position to maximize positive traits and find ways to strengthen weaknesses. Cornucopia Kids don't bene-

fit from such experiences because they have never had to put themselves on the line. With their parents' help, these "soft" kids are sheltered and pampered instead.

Accepting failure as a part of learning. Henry Ford believed that "failure is the opportunity to begin again more intelligently." Children who are sheltered and indulged typically don't confront failure or learn to deal with it. Rather, they are rescued from the consequences of their actions or parents fix problems and otherwise make life so easy that no challenges or chances for experiencing failure are encountered. Such children, as adults, cannot deal with setbacks because they have no experience doing so. They are more likely to give up when the going gets difficult or try to find someone to "take over" for them as they did in childhood.

Learning to delay gratification. Young children expect immediate gratification. So do Cornucopia Kids, even as adults. They want it all right now. In children, this expectation is natural, but in Cornucopia Kids it is a significant defect. Learning to delay gratification—to wait for a payoff until later—is a lesson in perseverance. It's "hanging in there" until setbacks, obstacles or problems are overcome. Cornucopia Kids don't have to learn perseverance—they just get parents to gratify them "right now" instead.

Developing the capacity for self-discipline. Self-discipline always involves a choice. People consciously choose to do either what is right, what is easy or what is pleasurable. Self-discipline is the capacity to impose internal limits on one's own behavior rather than relying on external sources (parents, teachers, other authorities) to set behavioral boundaries. Cornucopia Kids, whose every whim is satisfied, are usually quite impulsive and are consistently allowed to escape taking responsibility for their actions. As a result, these immature persons never learn to anticipate the possible consequences of their actions or to set their own internal limits. One consequence of this is that they are often in trouble—but that's okay; their parents will bail them out.

Attaining long-term goals becomes possible. Parents often complain that today's kids seem to want everything *right now.* This is especially true of indulged children who are given everything *right now.* These disadvantaged children rarely have to struggle, sacrifice or deny themselves short-term rewards to get what they want. Yet success today requires just that ability. Learning to work for long-term goals requires self-sacrifice, and healthy achievers have practiced that skill all along at home. Cornucopia Kids haven't often had to do so.

Understanding the effort-reward relationship. An important asset in adult life is to have learned that there is a direct relationship between effort and reward. Studying harder for an exam brings a better grade. Doing those extras on the job brings a merit raise or even a promotion. But if a child is given everything merely because it is asked for, or practices manipulation to get it, this important effort-reward relationship has no chance to develop. In its stead grows the false perception that everything in life comes easily. For Cornucopia Kids that may be true at home, but the rest of the world doesn't work that way.

Building a reservoir of confidence. Many people naively believe that confidence comes through emotional support from others and "go get 'em" pep talks. While outside support is certainly helpful, the crucial element in personal confidence is a base of personal experience from which to confront challenges and succeed despite adversity. Those who constantly need massive infusions of external support have *not* developed a foundation of success experiences.

Experiencing the internal rewards of accomplishment. A feeling of pride and the satisfaction of accomplishment can only be experienced when effort has been expended toward attaining a personal goal. "It was hard but I've done it, and it makes me feel good" is emotionally reinforcing and accompanies any tangible rewards that may accrue from one's efforts.

Creating appreciation for personal property. A child who earns the money to buy a bicycle not only experiences pride in that accomplishment but also tends to take very good care of the bike. Why? Because the personal effort involved in obtaining it is attached to its value. A common characteristic of Cornucopia Kids is that they have lots of possessions but don't bother to take care of them. Abuse and neglect usually extend to the property of parents, siblings and friends. In their eyes, property can always be replaced by parents with little effort. With that certainty, why should a child take care of anything?

Gaining practice in making appropriate choices. Parents are fond of saying to their children, "You can't have your cake and eat it, too." From the Cornucopia Kids' point of view, the response is simple: "Wanna bet?" To the extent that they are consistently indulged, Cornucopia Kids *can* have it both ways. They can misbehave and escape the consequences. With parental help, they can enjoy rewards without effort. Kids who have it all continue to expect it all, even as adults. But healthy achievers set priorities and make healthy choices because that's what they have been taught to do all along at home.

Developing a sense of personal control. As a child successfully meets challenges and attains personal goals, he or she develops an internalized sense of control. "I know how to make good things happen" is part of the psychological makeup of a healthy achiever. It is this kind of child who, later as an adult, can meet the world on its own tough terms and succeed. By contrast, those who are materially indulged and allowed to escape the consequences of their behavior remain childlike and insecure. They must

Raising a well-balanced child requires a sensitivity to what is too much in the form of material things. Today's children are too often spoiled at an early age, and as a consequence have unrealistic expectations of what they are due in later life.

depend on others to "make good things happen." Those others are most often parents, and the process becomes increasingly expensive and exasperating as the years pass.

Nourishing healthy self-esteem. Self-direction, propelled by an awareness of internal control, is linked to a sense of personal adequacy and healthy self-esteem. Self-sufficiency is a major ingredient in feeling good about yourself. Cornucopia Kids are not self-sufficient and they know it. As a result, they are insecure, often frightened and emotionally dependent young men and women. "Take care of me" becomes the refrain in their relationship with their parents. With these characteristics it's practically impossible for them to feel good about themselves.

The Consequences of Neglect

Creating a challenging home environment where children can learn healthy life values is possible *regardless of income level*. It's the parents' knowledge (or the lack of it) that makes the difference. For example, it is not uncommon to find parents with modest incomes creating Cornucopia Kids when they cannot really afford it. Just as frequently, those who are extremely well off can be found raising healthy achieving children. The important question is whether parents allow negative material values and the demands of their children to subvert positive parenting.

Interestingly, parents who give too much and give in to their children often admit that they feel something is wrong with what they are doing. But, they argue, no one else seems to be doing what their intuition tells them is right. Up and down the street, neighbors strive to keep up with one another. Colleagues at work boast of how they give and give to their children. In some areas, it's almost a contest among status-minded adults to see who can give their children more and bigger and better. On the home front, the kids know exactly how to apply pressure, and our materialistic culture reinforces the "need" to acquire a continually renewed supply of expensive possessions to keep abreast of the latest fashions and fads.

It takes a strong parent with character and clear values to see through all of this pressure and do what is best—not what is easiest. To their credit, more parents are doing just that. These savvy parents, achievers themselves, are beginning to recognize the serious problems that result from giving too much materially and not giving enough of what children really need: healthy values and adaptive life skills. Conversely, the problems that accrue from an indulgent parental style can easily last a lifetime.

It is not to the benefit of parents, children or society to raise Cornucopia Kids. Yet many parents manage to do just that, without seeing the long-range effects of their day-to-day actions.

For parents who are still wavering in their commitment to do what is right, not what is easy, here's a bit of wisdom to keep in mind: Every person is born with an equal opportunity to become unequal. In a democracy, basic constitutional rights are given to each person, but there the guarantees end, and individuals must use their skills and expertise either to make their way in the world or to fail. Cornucopia Kids, pampered and indulged early in life, just don't have an equal chance.

CHILDREN AFTER DIVORCE

WOUNDS THAT DON'T HEAL

Judith S. Wallerstein

Judith S. Wallerstein is a psychologist and author of "Second Chances: Men, Women & Children a Decade After Divorce," to be published in February by Ticknor & Fields. This article, adapted from the book, was written with the book's co-author, Sandra Blakeslee, who is a regular contributor to The New York Times.

As recently as the 1970's, when the American divorce rate began to soar, divorce was thought to be a brief crisis that soon resolved itself. Young children might have difficulty falling asleep and older children might have trouble at school. Men and women might become depressed or frenetic, throwing themselves into sexual affairs or immersing themselves in work.

But after a year or two, it was expected, most would get their lives back on track, at least outwardly. Parents and children would get on with new routines, new friends and new schools, taking full opportunity of the second chances that divorce brings in its wake.

These views, I have come to realize, were wishful thinking. In 1971, working with a small group of colleagues and with funding from San Francisco's Zellerback Family Fund, I began a study of the effects of divorce on middle-class people who continue to function despite the stress of a marriage breakup.

That is, we chose families in which, despite the failing marriage, the children were doing well at school and the parents were not in clinical treatment for psychiatric disorders. Half of the families attended church or synagogue. Most of the parents were college educated. This was, in other words, divorce under the best circumstances.

Our study, which would become the first ever made over an extended period of time, eventually tracked 60 families, most of them white, with a total of 131 children, for 10, and in some cases 15, years after divorce. We found that although some divorces work well—some adults are happier in the long run, and some children do better than they would have been expected to in an unhappy intact family—more often than not divorce is a wrenching, long-lasting experience for at least one of the former partners. Perhaps most important, we found that for virtually all the children, it exerts powerful and wholly unanticipated effects.

Our study began with modest aspirations. With a colleague, Joan Berlin Kelly—who headed a community mental-health program in the San Francisco area—I planned to examine the short-term effects of divorce on these middle-class families.

We spent many hours with each member of each of our 60 families—hearing their first-hand reports from the battleground of divorce. At the core of our research was the case study, which has been the main source of the fundamental insights of clinical psychology and of psychoanalysis. Many important changes, especially in the long run, would be neither directly observable nor easily measured. They would become accessible only through case studies: by examining the way each of these people processed, responded to and integrated the events and relationships that divorce brings in its wake.

We planned to interview families at the time of decisive separation and filing for divorce, and again 12 to 18 months later, expecting to chart recoveries among men and women and to look at how the children were mastering troubling family events.

We were stunned when, at the second series of visits, we found family after family still in crisis, their wounds wide open. Turmoil and distress had not noticeably subsided. Many adults were angry, and felt humiliated and rejected, and most had not gotten their lives back together. An unexpectedly large number of children were on a downward course. Their symptoms were worse than they had been immediately after the divorce. Our findings were absolutely contradictory to our expectations.

Dismayed, we asked the Zellerbach Fund to support a follow-up study in the fifth year after divorce. To our surprise, interviewing 56 of the 60 families in our original study, we found that although half the men and two-thirds of the women (even many of those suffering economically) said they were more content with their lives, only 34 percent of the children were clearly doing well.

Another 37 percent were depressed, could not concentrate in school, had trouble making friends and suffered a wide range of other behavior problems. While able to function on a daily basis, these children were not recovering, as everyone thought they would. Indeed most of them were on a downward course. This is a powerful statistic, considering that these were children who were functioning well five years before. It would be hard to find any other group of children—except, perhaps, the victims of a natural disaster—who suffered such a rate of sudden serious psychological problems.

The remaining children showed a mixed picture of good achievement in some areas and faltering achievement in others; it was hard to know which way they would eventually tilt.

The psychological condition of these children and adolescents, we found, was related in large part to the overall quality of life in the post-divorce family, to what the adults had been able to build in place of the failed marriage. Children tended to do well if their mothers and fathers, whether or not they remarried, resumed their parenting roles, managed to put their differences aside, and allowed the children a continuing relationship with both parents. Only a handful of kids had all these advantages.

We went back to these families again in 1980 and 1981 to conduct a 10-year follow-up. Many of those we had first interviewed as children were now adults. Overall, 45 percent were doing well; they had emerged as competent, compassionate and courageous people. But 41 percent were doing poorly; they were entering adulthood as worried, underachieving, self-deprecating and sometimes angry young men and women. The rest were strikingly uneven in how they adjusted to the world; it is too soon to say how they will turn out.

At around this time, I founded the Center for the Family in Transition, in Marin County, near San Francisco, which provides counseling to people who are separating, divorcing or remarrying. Over the years, my colleagues and I have seen more than 2,000 families—an experience that has amplified my concern about divorce. Through our work at the center and in the study, we have come to see divorce not as a single circumscribed event but as a continuum of changing family relationships—as a process that begins during the failing marriage and extends over many years. Things are not getting better, and divorce is not getting easier. It's too soon to call our conclusions definitive, but they point to an urgent need to learn more.

It was only at the 10-year point that two of our most unexpected findings became apparent. The first of these is something we call the sleeper effect.

A divorce-prone society is producing its first generation of young adults, men and women so anxious about attachment and love that their ability to create enduring families is imperiled.

The first youngster in our study to be interviewed at the 10-year mark was one who had always been a favorite of mine. As I waited for her to arrive for this interview, I remembered her innocence at age 16, when we had last met. It was she who alerted us to the fact that many young women experience a delayed effect of divorce.

As she entered my office, she greeted me warmly. With a flourishing sweep of one arm, she said, "You called me at just the right time. I just turned 21!" Then she startled me by turning immediately serious. She was in pain, she said.

She was the one child in our study who we all thought was a prime candidate for full recovery. She had denied some of her feelings at the time of divorce, I felt, but she had much going for her, including high intelligence, many friends, supportive parents, plenty of money.

As she told her story, I found myself drawn into unexpected intricacies of her life. Her trouble began, typically, in her late teens. After graduating from high school with honors, she was admitted to a respected university and did very well her freshman year. Then she fell apart. As she told it, "I met my first true love."

The young man, her age, so captivated her that she decided it was time to have a fully committed love affair. But on her way to spend summer vacation with him, her courage failed. "I went to New York instead. I hitchhiked across the country. I didn't know what I was looking for. I thought I was just passing time. I didn't stop and ponder. I just kept going, recklessly, all the time waiting for some word from my parents. I guess I was testing them. But no one—not my dad, not my mom—ever asked me what I was doing there on the road alone."

She also revealed that her weight dropped to 94 pounds from 128 and that she had not menstruated for a year and a half.

"I began to get angry," she said. "I'm angry at my parents for not facing up to the emotions, to the feelings in their lives, and for not helping me face up to the feelings in mine. I have a hard time forgiving them."

I asked if I should have pushed her to express her anger earlier.

She smiled patiently and said, "I don't think so. That was exactly the point. All those years I denied feelings. I thought I could live without love, without sorrow, without anger, without pain. That's how I coped with the unhappiness in my parents' marriage. Only when I met my boyfriend did I become aware of how much feeling I was sitting on all those years. I'm afraid I'll lose him."

It was no coincidence that her acute depression and anorexia occurred just as she was on her way to consummate her first love affair, as she was entering the kind of relationship in which her parents failed. For the first time, she confronted the fears, anxieties, guilt and concerns that she had suppressed over the years.

Sometimes with the sleeper effect the fear is of betrayal rather than commitment. I was shocked when another young woman—at the age of 24, sophisticated, warm and friendly—told me she worried if her boyfriend was even 30 minutes late, wondering who he was with and if he was having an affair with another woman. This fear of betrayal occurs at a frequency that far exceeds what one might expect from a group of people randomly selected from the population. They suffer minute to minute, even though their partners may be faithful.

In these two girls we saw a pattern that we documented in 66 percent of the young women in our study between the ages of 19 and 23; half of them were seriously derailed by it. The sleeper effect occurs at a time when these young women are making decisions with long-term implications for their lives. Faced with issues of commitment, love and sex in an adult context, they are aware that the game is serious. If they tie in with the wrong man, have children too soon, or choose harmful life-styles, the effects can be tragic. Overcome by fears and anxieties, they begin to make connections between these feelings and their parents' divorce:

"I'm so afraid I'll marry someone like my dad."

"How can you believe in commitment when anyone can change his mind anytime?"

"I am in awe of people who stay together."

We can no longer say—as most experts have held in recent years—that girls are generally less troubled by the divorce experience than boys. Our study strongly indicates, for the first time, that girls experience serious effects of divorce at the time they are entering young adulthood. Perhaps the risk for girls and boys is equalized over the long term.

When a marriage breaks down, men and women alike often experience a diminished capacity to parent. They may give less time, provide less discipline and be less sensitive to their children, since they are themselves caught up in the maelstrom of divorce and its aftermath. Many researchers and clinicians find that parents are temporarily unable to separate their children's needs from their own.

In a second major unexpected finding of our 10-year study, we found that fully a quarter of the mothers and a fifth of the fathers had not gotten their lives back on track a decade after divorce. The diminished parenting continued, permanently disrupting the child-rearing functions of the family. These parents were chronically disorganized and, unable to meet the challenges of being a parent, often leaned heavily on their children. The child's role became one of warding off the serious depression that threatened the parents' psychological functioning. The divorce itself may not be solely to blame but, rather, may aggravate emotional difficulties that had been masked in the marriage. Some studies have found that emotionally disturbed parents within a marriage produce similar kinds of problems in children.

These new roles played by the children of divorce are complex and unfamiliar. They are not simple role reversals, as some have claimed, because the child's role becomes one of holding the parent together psychologically. It is more than a caretaking role. This phenomenon merits our careful attention, for it affected 15 percent of the children in our study, which means many youngsters in our society. I propose that we identify as a distinct psychological syndrome the "overburdened child," in the hope that people will begin to recognize the problems and take steps to help these children, just as they help battered and abused children.

One of our subjects, in whom we saw this syndrome, was a sweet 5-year-old girl who clearly felt that she was her father's favorite. Indeed, she was the only person in the family he never hit. Preoccupied with being good and helping to calm both parents, she opposed the divorce because she knew it would take her father away from her. As it turned out, she also lost her mother who, soon after the divorce, turned to liquor and sex, a combination that left little time for mothering.

A year after the divorce, at the age of 6, she was getting herself dressed, making her own meals and putting herself to bed. A teacher noticed the dark circles under her eyes, and asked why she looked so tired. "We have a new baby at home," the girl explained. The teacher, worried, visited the house and discovered there was no baby. The girl's story was designed to explain her fatigue but also enabled her to fantasize endlessly about a caring loving mother.

Shortly after this episode, her father moved to another state. He wrote to her once or twice a year, and when we saw her at the five-year follow-up she pulled out a packet of letters from him. She explained how worried she was that he might get into trouble, as if she were the parent and he the child who had left home.

"I always knew he was O.K. if he drew pictures on the letters," she said. "The last two really worried me because he stopped drawing."

Now 15, she has taken care of her mother for the past 10 years. "I felt it was my responsibility to make sure that Mom was O.K.," she says. "I stayed home with her instead of playing or going to school. When she got mad, I'd let her take it out on me."

I asked what her mother would do when she was angry.

"She'd hit me or scream. It scared me more when she screamed. I'd rather be hit. She always seemed so much bigger when she screamed. Once Mom got drunk and passed out on the street. I called my brothers, but they hung up. So I did it. I've done a lot of things I've never told anyone. There were many times she was so upset I was sure she would take her own life. Sometimes I held both her hands and talked to her for hours I was so afraid."

In truth, few children can rescue a troubled parent. Many become angry at being trapped by the parents' demands, at being robbed of their separate identity and denied their childhood. And they are saddened, sometimes beyond repair, at seeing so few of their own needs gratified.

Since this is a newly identified condition that is just being described, we cannot know its true incidence. I suspect that the number of overburdened children runs much higher than the 15 percent we saw in our study, and that we will begin to see rising reports in the next few years—just as the reported incidence of child abuse has risen since it was first identified as a syndrome in 1962.

The sleeper effect and the overburdened-child syndrome were but two of many findings in our study. Perhaps most important, overall, was our finding that divorce has a lasting psychological effect on many children, one that, in fact, may turn out to be permanent.

Children of divorce have vivid memories about their parents' separation. The details are etched firmly in their minds, more so than those of any other experiences in their lives. They refer to themselves as children of divorce, as if they share an experience that sets them apart from all others. Although many have come to agree that their parents were wise to part company, they nevertheless feel that they suffered from their parents' mistakes. In many instances, conditions in the post-divorce family were more stressful and less supportive to the child than conditions in the failing marriage.

If the finding that 66 percent of the 19- to 23-year-old young women experienced the sleeper effect was most unexpected, others were no less dramatic. Boys, too, were found to suffer unforeseen long-lasting effects. Forty percent of the 19- to 23-year-old young men in our study, 10 years after divorce, still had no set goals, a limited education and a sense of having little control over their lives.

In comparing the post-divorce lives of former husbands and wives, we saw that 50 percent of the women and 30 percent of the men were still intensely angry at their former spouses a decade after divorce. For women over 40 at divorce, life was lonely throughout the decade; not one in our study remarried or sustained a loving relationship. Half the men over 40 had the same problem.

In the decade after divorce, three in five children felt rejected by one of their parents, usually the father—whether or not it was true. The frequency and duration of visiting made no difference. Children longed for their fathers, and the need increased during adolescence. Thirty-four percent of the youngsters went to live with their fathers during adolescence for at least a year. Half returned to the mother's home disappointed with what they had found. Only one in seven saw both mother and father happily remarried after 10 years. One in two saw their mother or their father undergo a second divorce. One in four suffered a severe and enduring drop in the family's standard of living and went on to observe a lasting discrepancy between their parents' standards of living.

We found that the children who were best adjusted 10 years later were those who showed the most distress at the time of the divorce—the youngest. In general, pre-schoolers are the most frightened and show the most dramatic symptoms when marriages break up. Many are afraid that they will be abandoned by both parents and they have trouble sleeping or staying by themselves. It is therefore surprising to find that the same children 10 years later seem better adjusted than their older siblings. Now in early and mid-adolescence, they were rated better on a wide range of psychological dimensions than the older children. Sixty-eight percent were doing well, compared with less than 40 percent of older children. But whether having been young at the time of divorce will continue to protect them as they enter young adulthood is an open question.

Our study shows that adolescence is a period of particularly grave risk for children in divorced families. Through rigorous analysis, statistical and otherwise, we were able to see clearly that we weren't dealing simply with the routine angst of young people going through transition but rather that, for most of them, divorce was the single most important cause of enduring pain and anomie in their lives. The young people told us time and again how much they needed a family structure, how much they wanted to be protected, and how much they yearned for clear guidelines for moral behavior. An alarming number of teenagers felt abandoned, physically and emotionally.

For children, divorce occurs during the formative years. What they see and experience becomes a part of their inner world, influencing their own relationships 10 and 15 years later, especially when they have witnessed violence between the parents. It is then, as these young men and women face the developmental task of establishing love and intimacy, that they most feel the lack of a template for a loving relationship between a man and a woman. It is here that their anxiety threatens their ability to create new, enduring families of their own.

As these anxieties peak in the children of divorce throughout our society, the full legacy of the rising divorce rate is beginning to hit home. The new families being formed today by these children as they reach adulthood appear particularly vulnerable.

Because our study was such an early inquiry, we did not set out to compare children of divorce with children from intact families. Lacking fundamental knowledge about life after the breakup of a marriage, we could not know on what basis to build a comparison or control group. Was the central issue one of economics, age, sex, a happy intact marriage—or would any intact marriage do? We began, therefore, with a question— What is the nature of the divorce experience?—and in answering it we would generate hypotheses that could be tested in subsequent studies.

This has indeed been the case. Numerous studies have been conducted in different regions of the country, using control groups, that have further explored and validated our findings as they have emerged over the years. For example, one national study of 699 elementary school children carefully compared children six years after their parents' divorce with children from intact families. It found—as we did—that elementary-age boys from divorced families show marked discrepancies in peer relationships, school achievement and social adjustment. Girls in this group, as expected, were hardly distinguishable based on the experience of divorce, but, as we later found out, this would not always hold up. Moreover, our findings are supported by a litany of modern-day statistics. Although one in three children are from divorced families, they account for an inordinately high proportion of children in mental-health treatment, in special-education classes, or referred by teachers to school psychologists. Children of divorce make up an estimated 60 percent of child patients in clinical treatment and 80 percent—in some cases, 100 percent—of adolescents in inpatient mental hospital settings. While no one would claim that a cause and effect relationship has been established in all of these cases, no one would deny that the role of divorce is so persuasively suggested that it is time to sound the alarm.

All studies have limitations in what they can accomplish. Longitudinal studies, designed to establish the impact of a major event or series of events on the course of a subsequent life, must always allow for the influence of many interrelated factors. They must deal with chance and the uncontrolled factors that so often modify the sequences being followed. This is particularly true of children, whose lives are influenced by developmental changes, only some of which are predictable, and by the problem of individual differences, about which we know so little.

Our sample, besides being quite small, was also drawn from a particular population slice—predominately white, middle class and relatively privileged suburbanites.

Despite these limitations, our data have generated working hypotheses about the effects of divorce that can now be tested with more precise methods, including appropriate control groups. Future research should be aimed at testing, correcting or modifying our initial findings, with larger and more diverse segments of the population. For example, we found that children—especially boys and young men—continued to need their fathers after divorce and suffered feelings of rejection even when they were visited regularly. I would like to see a study comparing boys and girls in sole and joint custody, spanning different developmental stages, to see if greater access to both parents counteracts these feelings of rejection. Or, does joint custody lead to a different sense of rejection—of feeling peripheral in both homes?

It is time to take a long, hard look at divorce in America. Divorce is not an event that stands alone in childrens' or adults' experience. It is a continuum that begins in the unhappy marriage and extends through the separation, divorce and any remarriages and second divorces. Divorce is not necessarily the sole culprit. It may be no more than one of the many experiences that occur in this broad continuum.

Profound changes in the family can only mean profound changes in society as a whole. All children in today's world feel less protected. They sense that the institution of the family is weaker than it has ever been before. Even those children raised in happy, intact families worry that their families may come undone. The task for society in its true and proper perspective is to strengthen the family—all families.

A biblical phrase I have not thought of for many years has recently kept running through my head: "Watchman, what of the night?" We are not I'm afraid, doing very well on our watch—at least for our children. We are allowing them to bear the psychological, economic and moral brunt of divorce.

And they recognize the burdens. When one 6-year-old boy came to our center shortly after his parents' divorce, he would not answer questions; he played games instead. First he hunted all over the playroom for the sturdy Swedish-designed dolls that we use in therapy. When he found a good number of them, he stood the baby dolls firmly on their feet and placed the miniature tables, chairs, beds and, eventually, all the playhouse furniture on top of them. He looked at me, satisfied. The babies were supporting a great deal. Then, wordlessly, he placed all the mother and father dolls in precarious positions on the steep roof of the doll house. As a father doll slid off the roof, the boy caught him and, looking up at me, said, "He might die." Soon, all the mother and father dolls began sliding off the roof. He caught them gently, one by one.

"The babies are holding up the world," he said.

Although our overall findings are troubling and serious, we should not point the finger of blame at divorce per se. Indeed, divorce is often the only rational solution to a bad marriage. When people ask whether they should stay married for the sake of the children, I have to say, "Of course not." All our evidence shows that children exposed to open conflict, where parents terrorize or strike one another, turn out less well-adjusted than do children from divorced families. And although we lack systematic studies comparing children in divorced families with those in unhappy intact families, I am convinced that it is not useful to provide children with a model of adult behavior that avoids problem-solving and that stresses martyrdom, violence or apathy. A divorce undertaken thoughtfully and realistically can teach children how to confront serious life problems with compassion, wisdom and appropriate action.

Our findings do not support those who would turn back the clock. As family issues are flung to the center of our political arena, nostalgic voices from the right argue for a return to a time when divorce was more difficult to obtain. But they do not offer solutions to the wretchedness and humiliation within many marriages.

Still we need to understand that divorce has consequences—we need to go into the experience with our eyes open. We need to know that many children will suffer for many years. As a society, we need to take steps to preserve for the children as much as possible of the social, economic and emotional security that existed while their parents' marriage was intact.

Like it or not, we are witnessing family changes which are an integral part of the wider changes in our society. We are on a wholly new course, one that gives us unprecedented opportunities for creating better relationships and stronger families—but one that also brings unprecedented dangers for society, especially for our children.

Broken homes: 3 in 5 born today will live with a single parent by age 18.

Child care: 2 of 4 children age 13 and under live with parents who both work.

Drugs: 1 child in 6 has tried marijuana and 1 in 3 alcohol before 9th grade.

Sex: The share of girls under 15 who have had sex has tripled in 2 decades.

Suicide: The rate for youths under 15 has tripled since 1960.

CHILDREN UNDER STRESS

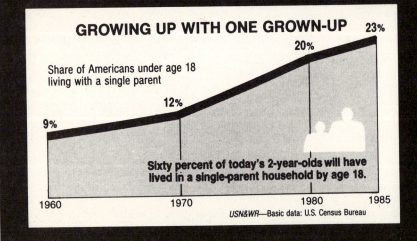

GROWING UP WITH ONE GROWN-UP

Share of Americans under age 18 living with a single parent

9% 12% 20% 23%

Sixty percent of today's 2-year-olds will have lived in a single-parent household by age 18.

1960   1970   1980   1985

USN&WR—Basic data: U.S. Census Bureau

■ Whatever happened to childhood?

Gone are the worries about dying from the flu, toiling in sweatshops or 5-mile treks to the country school. But for the children of the '80s, a host of psychological pressures have superseded the physical stresses previous generations had to bear.

What the late child psychologist Selma Fraiberg called "the magic years" don't seem so magical any more. Whether they come from cities, suburbs or farms, stable families or broken homes, kids today must cope with a world in which both parents work, sex and drugs cloud even the grade-school yard and violence is only as far away as the living-room television screen.

"The age of protection for children has ended," says Dr. Lawrence Brain, director of child and adolescent services at the Psychiatric Institute of Washington, D.C. "Today's children are increasingly thrust into independence and self-reliance before they have the skills and ability to cope." Laments Ann Gannon, 47, a Bethesda, Md., mother of 13 children, ages 2 to 23: "We're not letting them stop and smell the roses. We don't play sports for fun any more. Children today are constantly being pushed."

Most of the 48 million Americans under age 14 aren't candidates for therapy. But mental-health professionals and child experts are alarmed by the rising proportion of troubled children. "There is a growing awareness and growing incidence of psychological stress on children," says David Elkind, child psychologist and author of *The Hurried Child: Growing Up Too Fast Too Soon.*

The polls seem to bear Elkind out. According to a recent survey by Louis Harris & Associates, 3 out of 4 adults said they believed that the problems facing today's children are more severe than those they faced as children. Fewer than half believed that the nation's children are basically happy. One in 8 said their child had mental or emotional problems, and 1 in 20 admitted their child has had drug problems.

High cost of child rearing

"Today, preadolescence is more stressful than it used to be," says pediatrician and best-selling author T. Berry Brazelton. In his practice, Brazelton reports, there is a greater incidence of such psychosomatic ailments as wheezing, dizziness, chest pains and stomach problems among patients ages 10 to 12 than there was 10 years ago. In fact, up to 35 percent of American kids suffer stress-related health problems at some point, from pulling out one's hair to headaches, says psychologist Nicholas Zill, executive director of Child Trends, a research group in Washington, D.C.

The stress on children begins at home. The "typical" American family—with dad at work, mom baking cakes and kids engaging only in innocent mischief—is mainly the stuff of television reruns. Families of the '80s bear little resemblance to the Cleaver clan. Today, only 1 in 5 families with children is composed of a father as breadwinner, mother at home and children under 18, compared with 41 percent 10 years ago, according to the Bureau of Labor Statistics. Spurred largely by economic pressures, women with young children have joined men in 9-to-5 jobs in record numbers over the last decade.

Each family member is going a separate way, as if "he is a corporation in a different business, and the family residence functions like the holding company," suggests Carl Thoresen, professor of education and psychology at Stanford University. "It's as if nobody's home any more."

It's no wonder families need the extra income. The average cost of raising a child born in 1984 to age 18 jumped to $140,927, according to a report by the Conference Board, a business-research group. Thirty years ago, it cost a third as much. The annual bill for one year of child rearing consumed 29 percent of the median family's budget in 1984, compared with an estimated 11 percent in 1966. "I used to think I would be able to stay home with my children," says Gale Whitfield, a Chicago nurse. But Whitfield and her husband David, a lab technician and part-time real-estate agent, found that their combined income of $55,000 last year was barely enough to support the eight children they share from their current and previous marriages.

Fewer children per family

The Whitfields are an unusually large family, by any norms. But parents today are having fewer children per family, which can have the effect of stepping up the pressure on each child. Twenty years ago, 31 percent of all families with children had only one child under 18; now, 42 percent have only one child under 18. And far fewer families—6 percent vs. 20 percent two decades ago—have four or more children. "I've never seen such a high level of caring [from parents]," says Susie Bond, a nursery-school teacher in suburban Washington, D.C. "But, you can lose perspective on what's good for your kid. Kids don't have time to play, to do nothing."

Some of the current stresses are self-inflicted by a generation of status-conscious parents. "There are cults about strollers," says Marian Blum, educational director of the Child Study Cen-

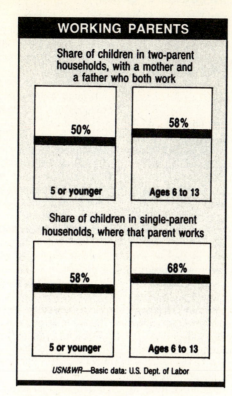

WORKING PARENTS

Share of children in two-parent households, with a mother and a father who both work

50%	58%
5 or younger	Ages 6 to 13

Share of children in single-parent households, where that parent works

58%	68%
5 or younger	Ages 6 to 13

USN&WR—Basic data: U.S. Dept. of Labor

ter at Wellesley College. "You've got to have the right stroller or you're not a good parent. You've got to dress the kid in certain clothes or you're not a good parent. If your kid doesn't go to a certain school, you're not a good parent."

Indeed, most of the pressures on kids stem from America's new lifestyles. Take day care, for example. At least 7 million children nationwide are cared for in family day-care homes or in child-care centers. Baby-sitting a child in someone else's home for a fee accounts for about three fourths of all child care outside the home. The quality of family day care can vary greatly: Seventy-five to 90 percent of family day-care facilities are unlicensed or unregistered, says Representative George Miller (D-Calif.), chairman of the Select Committee on Children, Youth and Families.

Generally, the consensus is that sending children under age 3 to day care is more stressful for the kids than staying at home with a parent or a familiar baby-sitter. While research studies indicate that good-quality day care is not harmful to the very young, the stress of separation from the parents plus the pressures of a competitive program can exacerbate tensions, says Tufts University's Elkind. Warns Dr. Arnold Samuels, a child expert at Chicago's Institute for Psychoanalysis: "The child must comply with the environment; the program doesn't always respond to the child."

With more mothers and fathers pushing papers than strollers, toddlers barely out of diapers are being shipped to

preschool. Half of the children under age 6 who live with both parents have working mothers and fathers, compared with 28 percent in 1970. Last year, 39 percent of all 3-and-4-year-olds were enrolled in preschool; 11 percent in 1965. "It seems that kids are enrolled in nursery school as soon as the mother gets pregnant," notes Dr. Judy Howard, a pediatrician at the University of California at Los Angeles.

The kindergarten hustle

In New York City, Mayor Edward Koch has pledged that by 1989 every 4-year-old will be eligible for enrollment in a publicly funded, voluntary prekindergarten program, making New York one of the first major cities to open classes to children that young. "This isn't a prekindergarten boot camp," insists Marian Schwarz, Koch's coordinator of youth services. Twenty-odd other states have plans for similar programs, and some educators are worried about how these programs will be implemented. "What used to be the second-grade curriculum is now in first grade, and the first-grade curriculum is being brought into kindergarten," says Polly Greenberg, publications director of the National Association for the Education of Young Children. Many kids, she argues, are being pushed too hard academically, too fast.

Partly because more families have both parents in the work force, all-day (6-hour) kindergarten programs are increasing. More than a third of all kindergarten children go a full day, compared with a fifth in 1973. In Stamford, Conn., for instance, all 11 elementary schools have offered full-day kindergarten since 1980. Moreover, many nursery schools offer "extended day" programs for families where both parents work outside the home.

But sending children to kindergarten before they are ready can harm them, according to some studies. Research by James Uphoff, an Ohio education professor, and June Gilmore, an Ohio psychologist, found that children who were enrolled in kindergarten below the age of 5 years and 3 months or in first grade before 6 years and 3 months don't do as well in subsequent schooling as those who began school later.

Uphoff's study of 278 pupils in the Hebron, Nebr., Elementary School suggests that parents should think twice before they push kids to start earlier than their classmates. "Summer children"—those born during the summer months and younger than most of their classmates—accounted for 75 percent of the school's academic failures.

The evidence is by no means one-sided. Even prekindergarten programs can have major benefits—as long as

For many kids, the community net is gone

Growing up poor

The numbers tell a sorry story: 7 million white children and 4 million black children under age 15 in the U.S. live below the poverty line. One out of five children in America is poor, with children nearly twice as likely to be poor today as adults or the elderly. "We have become the first nation in history," laments Senator Daniel Patrick Moynihan (D-N.Y.), "where the children are the poorest segment of the population."

While divorce and separation are no longer unusual in higher-income families, half of all poor children grow up in households headed by women, and a quarter of poor black children live in homes where Mom has never married. "My mother *is* my father," says Reggie Minnis, an eighth grader at Chicago's Albert Einstein Elementary, a South Side school where 90 percent of the students are from single-parent families. Children in such homes often "become the boss of the family because a parent is always away," notes guidance counselor Annie Stephens of Houston's E. O. Smith Middle School. "When they try to become the boss of the school, they wreak havoc among the other kids."

In the 1950s, malnutrition, ill health and poverty were far more common among children, yet most poor children lived in rural communiites that provided leadership that today is often missing. Marian Wright Edelman, head of the Washington, D.C.-based Children's Defense Fund, recalls her childhood in Bennettsville, S.C., as a time when "the churches, schools and your family all reinforced the message that you could make it, even if you were poor. We all expected to go to college and didn't have time to get into trouble." Poor children today, particularly in the inner city, are more isolated from others who have climbed out of the slums. "That community net, the role models—the doctor, the police officer and the minister," she says, "are not there now."

Peer pressure fills the vacuum of authority created by absent fathers and other missing role models, often with destructive results. Many poor children come to feel as though they've done something wrong if they refrain from sex, drugs, or joining a gang. "My buddies were delighted that I did well in school,"

says James Comer, a professor at Yale University's Child Study Center who grew up in East Chicago. "Poor kids today, particularly black ones, are considered turncoats or sellouts if they do well."

More abuse, more neglect

Though today's poor kids differ in some ways from their predecessors, they share the experience of scraping by—and the stress that comes with it. Compared with the children of middle or upper-income families, poor children are seven to eight times more likely to experience child abuse and neglect, and two to three times more likely to grow up in families headed by parents who describe their health as only fair or poor. Preschool children in mother-only families are also estimated to use mental-health facilites four times more often than children from two-parent families.

Not by bread alone

Social scientists are increasingly concerned about a link between being poor as a child and experiencing handicaps later in life—such as giving birth out of wedlock, becoming dependent on welfare, and dropping out of school. "There was 'nothing broke' in poor people who grew up in earlier years except that many had been subjected to terrible racism," says Charles Murray of the Manhattan Institute for Policy Research. "When they got the chance, they took it; it's a lot tougher now to help kids who don't know how to go to work or deal with a supervisor by the time they're 20."

Some critics say too much emphasis has been given to government aid to poor children, while too little has been paid to providing guidance. Education Under Secretary Gary Bauer, who heads an administration task force on families, argues that "parents and teachers have mistakenly tried to be morally neutral to the nth degree in recent years. What we learned out of the antipoverty efforts of the 1960s is that children, just like man, cannot live by bread alone."

Others stress that the civil-rights movement and such anti-poverty programs as Head Start opened doors to many poor children. Maintains Robert Coles, Harvard psychiatrist and author of the five-volume study *Children of Crisis*, "There is more hope and expectation among poor children today than there was 30 years ago." At the same time, he notes, government efforts to reach out to the excluded are considerably more circumscribed today than they were during the 1960s and 1970s. Says Coles: "The time where society tells poor kids 'come and join in' is fading."

they emphasize play, not academic skills. Findings from a 20-year study by the High/Scope Educational Research Foundation show that children who attend preschool are less likely to require special educational services, are more likely to graduate from high school and get better-paying jobs and are less likely to receive welfare in adulthood.

There's little doubt that harried parents beget harried children. "Children have a greater concern about time than is normal," says Principal Rudolph White of Carderock Springs Elementary School in Bethesda, Md. One result of all the hurrying is that "the child's sense of achievement is compressed." Unlike previous generations, children's daily routines are likely to be dictated by Mom and Dad's workload. "Their schedules for meals, bedtime and baths are not predictable the way kids' schedules used

to be," says Blum. Even so-called quality time—the special time parents devote to their children—cannot compensate for a lack of quantity time, argues Deborah Fallows, author of *A Mother's Work*. "It's hard to program quality-time moments. They just happen."

Quality-time squeeze

A recent study by the University of Michigan Institute for Social Research found that working mothers spend an average of 11 minutes daily of quality time (defined as exclusive playing or teaching) with their kids during weekdays and about 30 minutes per day on the weekends. Fathers spend about 8 minutes of quality time with their kids on weekdays and 14 minutes on weekends. Nonworking mothers spend 13 minutes per day of quality time with their children.

It's far from clear that children with

working mothers are being disadvantaged. A recent Kent State University study of 573 elementary-school students in 38 states found that, on average, children of working mothers scored higher on IQ and reading tests, had better communication skills, were absent fewer days and were more self-reliant than children of nonworking mothers. But not all children of working mothers fared equally well. Children did better if their mothers worked part time rather than full time, were married rather than divorced and worked at high-status jobs.

Even the most self-reliant children face a dangerous world. Everything from the milk carton at breakfast—plastered with pictures of missing children—to the evening news can be a chilling reminder of this fact. There's extra stress on kids who feel there are situations where they have to take care of themselves. Says Blum of Wellesley: "What children need to know is that the grown-ups in their world—parents, baby-sitters, neighbors—are there to take care of them and keep them safe." For Marie La Vere, 14, of Marine City, Mich., the fright is real. "I'm scared," she says. "You hear about kids getting killed all the time. You hear about people disappearing."

A stack of research points to the conclusion that TV is one of the culprits. "Violence on television does lead to aggressive behavior by children and teenagers who watch the programs. Children who watch a lot of violence on television come to accept violence as normal behavior," says a 1982 report by the National Institute of Mental Health. Others argue that just because "heavy viewers" may be more violent or don't read as well or get lower scores on IQ tests—all of which are the case—doesn't mean that TV causes those problems.

TV as baby-sitter

What isn't disputed is that in many homes, TV has become an easy substitute for family interaction. According to the A. C. Nielsen Company, children watch an average of 4 hours a day, and some estimates go as high as 6 hours. "TV saps the energy out of family life," says child expert Marie Winn, author of *The Plug-In Drug*. For America's estimated 7 million latchkey kids under age 14—who are alone until their parents return from work—TV can be the only friendly voice in an otherwise empty home. TV also may be partly responsible for raising false expectations. "The people on TV are so well off economically that many kids don't understand why they can't buy clothes and live like that," says Aletha Huston, codirector of the University of Kansas Center for Research on the Influence of Television on Children. "There's this notion that everybody should be happy all the time [on TV]," adds Jo Ann Allen, professor of social work at the University of Michigan. "People can't be happy all the time."

For some, the strains of growing up in the '80s prove too much. Mimicking adult behavior, more children experiment with alcohol and other drugs at an earlier age than ever before. "It's not uncommon to find kids initiating alcohol or marijuana use at ages 9 or 10," says Catherine Bell, chief of the National Institute of Drug Abuse (NIDA) prevention branch. The blend of peer pressure and curiosity can unleash self-destructive habits. "When children like themselves, they do positive things like eat healthy foods and won't take drugs or alcohol," says Dr. Lee Salk, professor of psychology, psychiatry and pediatrics at Cornell University Medical School. Although there are signs that drug use by older teens has leveled off—except for cocaine—more of their younger siblings are experimenting with drugs, NIDA estimates. "They tell you if you do it [smoke marijuana], it will make you feel good," says Adam Royder, 10, a Houston fifth grader.

Sex has become an issue for more kids at an earlier age, too. "Your parents tell you, 'Don't have sex until you're married.' But people do on television," says Michigan ninth grader La Vere. Nearly a quarter of 15-to-19-year-old girls had sexual intercourse before age 16. In 1984, the rate of illegitimate births among teenage girls was almost double that in 1970.

Along with grown-up problems like drug abuse, suicide and depression are becoming kid stuff. America's overall suicide rate peaked in 1977 and has decreased for all groups except kids under 15. Last year, about 300 children under age 15 committed suicide, double the number in 1980. Dr. Brain of the Psychiatric Institute of Washington says that, in reviewing a two-year period of admissions, 80 percent of children age 5 through 13 were clinically depressed, had attempted suicide or were experiencing suicidal thoughts. Among the cases were an 8-year-old who deliberately ran in front of a car, a 9-year-old who tried to hang himself and a 12-year-old who took a drug overdose.

Three years ago, Judie Smith, director of educational services at the Dallas Suicide and Crisis Center, encountered her youngest suicide attempt: A 5-year-old boy, whose 8-year-old brother dialed the hot line. The parents were contacted before the boy carried out his threat.

More cases of depression among children are being reported. While some experts say that indicates better diagnosis, not a higher incidence of troubles, a number of studies suggest that at least 5 percent of all children suffer significant episodes of depression. The rate of serious depression for children age 6 to 12 is about 2 percent, and for adolescents the rate may go as high as 15 percent, says Andres Pumariega, director of child and adolescent psychiatry at the University of Texas. "Only in the last decade did we acknowledge that kids could be depressed," Smith says.

The stresses felt by children with families go double for children of broken homes. In the last 15 years, 15.6 million marriages ended in divorce, disrupting the lives of 16.3 million children under age 18. The number of preschoolers living with a single divorced parent soared 111 percent in the last 15 years. Half of new marriages this year will fail, predict government statisticians. "I have one friend whose parents are so angry at each other she says she doesn't ever want to get married," says an 11-year-old private-school student in San Francisco. "So many kids in my class have divorced parents."

Divorce's legacy

Not surprisingly, children of divorce show more signs of stress than others. According to a 10-year study by Judith Wallerstein, executive director of the Center for The Family in Transition near San Francisco, who has looked at the impact of divorce on 130 middle-class children, 37 percent of them were more emotionally troubled five years after the divorce than they were initially. Fear of divorce affects their love lives later, Wallerstein says. The subjects in her study "enter relationships with a high level of anxiety and have more trouble with marriage—they want a stable relationship more and are more worried about it [than children of nondivorced parents]."

The remarriage of a divorced parent often adds to, rather than subtracts from, a child's stress, by shattering his or her last hopes for a reconciliation and rearranging family loyalties. An estimated 1,300 stepfamilies are formed every day, points out the Stepfamily Association of America. "The hardest thing is getting along with my new stepmother's daughter," says a 12-year-old Atlanta girl who lives with her father, his new wife, and a 6-year-old stepsister. "I can talk to my dad about it sometimes, but mostly he's busy." The mere thought of parents' remarrying upsets many kids. "I'd come home from dates and find one of my daughters camped out in a sleeping bag beside my bed," says Mary Wudtke, a Chicago insurance executive who divorced seven years ago when her girls were 10 and 12.

In single-parent homes, children are often expected to stand in for the absent adult by doing household chores and caring for younger siblings. Although most middleclass kids under age 14 live in two-parent families, the percentage of these children living in female-headed middleclass families increased from 9 percent to 13 percent in the last decade. "Some of these children lead two lives. They're grown-ups at home and they come to school to be children," says elementary-school counselor Ynolia Bell Trammell of John Codwell Elementary School in Houston. One of her students, for instance, 11-year-old Joseph Jackson, often dozed in class. His teacher finally discovered the reason: Joseph's mother works until midnight, and he baby-sits for his 1-year-old brother. "Sometimes, he wakes up early in the morning, and I have to, too," Joseph says.

Dr. Benjamin Spock on bringing up today's children

Don't push your kids too hard

Q Dr. Spock, why are today's children under stress?

Partly because we've given up so many of the comforts and sources of security of the past, such as the extended family and the small, tightly knit community and the comfort and guidance that people used to get from religion.

Q How do working mothers affect kids?

It is stressful to children to have to cope with groups, with strangers, with people outside the family. That has emotional effects, and, if the deprivation of security is at all marked, it will have intellectual effects, too.

We know now that if there's good day care it can substitute pretty well for parental care. But, though we're the richest country the world has ever known, we have nowhere near the amount of subsidized day care we need. We're harming our children emotionally and intellectually to the degree that they're in substandard day care.

Q Are children raised in single-parent homes more stressed than other kids?

It's not that a single parent can't raise a child well but that it's harder to raise a child in most cases with one parent than it is with two parents. The parents can comfort and consult and back up each other.

Q Do parents harm kids by pushing them to achieve?

Our emphasis on fierce competition and getting ahead minimizes the importance of cooperation, helpfulness, kindness, lovingness. These latter qualities are the things that we need much more than competitiveness. I'm bothered, for instance, at the way we coach young children in athletics and, even more ludicrous, the interest we focus on superkids. It hasn't gone very far, but there are parents who, when they hear that other children are learning to read at the age of 2, think, "My God, we should be providing reading instruction, too," without ever asking the most significant question: "Does it make the child a better reader or is there any other advantage to learning to read at 2 rather than waiting until age 6?" It imposes strains on children. It teaches them that winning is the important thing. We've gone much too far in stressing winning.

I was in Japan lecturing a few years ago, and they told me that the rate of suicide among elementary schoolchildren is shockingly high and that Japanese elementary schoolchildren commit suicide because they are afraid that they aren't getting grades high enough to satisfy their parents. We haven't gotten that far in the United States, but we're certainly headed that way.

Q What child-rearing advice is best suited to the 1980s?

We can at least bring up children with a strong feeling that they're in the world not just for their own fulfillment—although I think fulfillment is fine—but also to be useful and to help others. Children should be brought up with a strong feeling that there are lots of problems in the neighborhood, the nation and the world, and that they're growing up to help solve those problems.

That emphasis on helpfulness should begin at a very early age with things as simple as letting them help set the table. Never say, "It's easier for me to do it myself." You should encourage children to be helpful, and not by scolding them or forcing them but by supporting them or complimenting when they're helpful.

Q Are there specific things to avoid?

Absolutely no violence on television. Don't give war toys. These are poisonous to children. This whole Rambo spirit is a distressing thing, especially in the most violent country in the world.

Q Is watching television harmful to kids?

A lot of what they see brutalizes sexuality. In simpler societies, you don't see people smashing each other in the face or killing each other. The average American child on reaching the age of 18 has watched 18,000 murders on TV. Yet we know that every time a child or an adult watches brutality, it desensitizes and brutalizes them to a slight degree. We have by far the highest crime rates in the world in such areas as murders within the family, rape, wife abuse, child abuse. And yet we're turning out more children this way, with this horrible profusion of violence that children watch on TV. It's a terrible thing.

Q Do the new stresses on kids make them better equipped to deal with adult stresses?

No. Human beings do make some adjustment to stresses, but that doesn't mean that they're doing better by being brought up with stresses. It's going to make them more tense, more harsh, more intensely competitive and more greedy. I don't think people can live by that. It is a spiritual malnutrition, just like a lack of vitamins or a lack of calories.

Q What kind of parents will today's children make?

If they're brought up with tension and harshness, then they'll do the same with their children. Everybody acquires his attitude and behavior toward his children by how he was treated in his own childhood. What was done to you in childhood, you are given permission to do. To put it more positively, parental standards are what make for a better society, and poor parental standards are what makes for a deteriorating society.

Q Is it harder to be a parent today?

Yes. When I started pediatric practice in '33, parents worried about polio and pneumonia and ear abscesses. Now they have to worry about drugs and teenage pregnancy and nuclear annihilation.

Time bombs or strong characters?

The long-term effects of stress on tomorrow's adults are yet to be determined, but there are some disturbing clues. Because studies show that children tend to repeat parental patterns with their own children—child abuse is a prime example—a self-perpetuating cycle of destructive behavior may already be in motion. "We're going to be delivering time bombs of potential destruction into society," warns Dr. Salk. Adds Lois Lane, a clinical social worker in Marin County, Calif. "What worries me a lot is that these stressed, disturbed kids aren't going to be a whole lot better before they have kids of their own. So you've got the problem of sick parents and sicker kids. It will be a generational crisis."

Other research, which emphasizes children's amazing ability to snap back from adversity, offers a more hopeful prognosis. Says Jerome Kagan, a developmental psychologist at Harvard and the leading proponent of the resiliency theory: "Ninety percent of the kids experiencing stress today will learn to cope with it. A child is remarkably plastic." Some studies bolster the view that kids who are victimized can overcome early

traumas. After World War II, for instance, orphans from Balkan countries who had roamed homeless and eaten out of garbage cans were later adopted by middle-class families in America and fared well. Similar reports exist for orphans of the Korean War.

The advice most experts offer parents for minimizing stress on children is really just common sense: Communicate. Respect the child's individuality instead of making comparisons with others. Set a good example, and don't push them.

A small number of parents who can afford to are even re-evaluating whether the stresses of two-income families are worth it. A case in point: Carol Orsborn and her husband Dan, who have two children and run a public-relations agency in San Francisco, recently scaled back their work hours and living standards, including moving to a smaller house, to do this. "If we didn't have it all, we felt guilty. If we did, we felt exhausted," says Carol Orsborn, the author of *Enough Is Enough: Exploding the Myth of Having It All.*

There are other signs that a backlash against pushing kids too fast may be building. A few states, such as New

Hampshire and Oklahoma, promote "developmental screening" tests designed to place kids in appropriately paced classes or signal parents to hold their children back a year. New Hampshire has two decades of experience in creating "readiness classes" that use an informal, play-oriented approach for 6-year-olds who don't score well on developmental tests. At L. J. Campbell School in Atlanta, educators have broken down the kindergarten curriculum into steps for kids to reach at their own pace. Soon, first, second and third grades will be subdivided into academic steps that allow slower kids more time to catch up without being stigmatized.

Small ripples perhaps, but taken together, they reflect second thoughts about the cult of the superkid. Still, the social changes that have pushed the fast-forward button on childhood are irreversible. The age of innocence is shorter than it has ever been before.

by Beth Brophy with Maureen Walsh of the Economic Unit, Art Levine, Andrea Gabor, Betsy Bauer, Lisa Moore and bureau reports

ALIENATION

AND THE FOUR WORLDS OF CHILDHOOD

The forces that produce youthful alienation are growing in strength and scope, says Mr. Bronfenbrenner. And the best way to counteract alienation is through the creation of connections or links throughout our culture. The schools can build such links.

Urie Bronfenbrenner

Urie Bronfenbrenner is Jacob Gould Shurman Professor of Human Development and Family Studies and of Psychology at Cornell University, Ithaca, N.Y.

To be alienated is to lack a sense of belonging, to feel cut off from family, friends, school, or work—the four worlds of childhood.

At some point in the process of growing up, many of us have probably felt cut off from one or another of these worlds, but usually not for long and not for more than one world at a time. If things weren't going well in school, we usually still had family, friends, or some activity to turn to. But if, over an extended period, a young person feels unwanted or insecure in several of these worlds simultaneously or if the worlds are at war with one another, trouble may lie ahead.

What makes a young person feel that he or she doesn't belong? Individual differences in personality can certainly be one cause, but, especially in recent years, scientists who study human behavior and development have identified an equal (if not even more powerful) factor: the circumstances in which a young person lives.

Many readers may feel that they recognize the families depicted in the vignettes that are to follow. This is so because they reflect the way we tend to look at families today: namely, that we see parents as being good or not-so-good without fully taking into account the circumstances in their lives.

Take Charles and Philip, for example. Both are seventh-graders who live in a middle-class suburb of a large U.S. city. In many ways their surroundings seem similar; yet, in terms of the risk of alienation, they live in rather different worlds. See if you can spot the important differences.

CHARLES

The oldest of three children, Charles is amiable, outgoing, and responsible. Both of his parents have full-time jobs outside the home. They've been able to arrange their working hours, however, so that at least one of them is at home when the children return from school. If for some reason they can't be home, they have an arrangement with a neighbor, an elderly woman who lives alone. They can phone her and ask her to look after the children until they arrive. The children have grown so fond of this woman that she is like another grandparent—a nice situation for them, since their real grandparents live far away.

Homework time is one of the most important parts of the day for Charles and his younger brother and sister. Charles's parents help the children with their homework if they need it, but most of the time they just make sure that the children have a period of peace and quiet—without TV—in which to do their work. The children are allowed to watch television one hour each

night—but only after they have completed their homework. Since Charles is doing well in school, homework isn't much of an issue, however.

Sometimes Charles helps his mother or father prepare dinner, a job that everyone in the family shares and enjoys. Those family members who don't cook on a given evening are responsible for cleaning up.

Charles also shares his butterfly collection with his family. He started the collection when he first began learning about butterflies during a fourth-grade science project. The whole family enjoys picnicking and hunting butterflies together, and Charles occasionally asks his father to help him mount and catalogue his trophies.

Charles is a bit of a loner. He's not a very good athlete, and this makes him somewhat self-conscious. But he does have one very close friend, a boy in his class who lives just down the block. The two boys have been good friends for years.

Charles is a good-looking, warm, happy young man. Now that he's beginning to be interested in girls, he's gratified to find that the interest is returned.

PHILIP

Philip is 12 and lives with his mother, father, and 6-year-old brother. Both of his parents work in the city, commuting more than an hour each way. Pandemonium strikes every weekday morning as

 From *Phi Delta Kappan*, February 1986, pp. 430-436. Reprinted by permission of the author and Phi Delta Kappan.

the entire family prepares to leave for school and work.

Philip is on his own from the time school is dismissed until just before dinner, when his parents return after stopping to pick up his little brother at a nearby day-care home. At one time, Philip took care of his little brother after school, but he resented having to do so. That arrangement ended one day when Philip took his brother out to play and the little boy wandered off and got lost. Philip didn't even notice for several hours that his brother was missing. He felt guilty at first about not having done a better job. But not having to mind his brother freed him to hang out with his friends or to watch television, his two major after-school activities.

The pace of their life is so demanding that Philip's parents spend their weekends just trying to relax. Their favorite weekend schedule calls for watching a ball game on television and then having a cookout in the back yard. Philip's mother resigned herself long ago to a messy house; pizza, TV dinners, or fast foods are all she can manage in the way of meals on most nights. Philip's father has made it clear that she can do whatever she wants in managing the house, as long as she doesn't try to involve him in the effort. After a hard day's work, he's too tired to be interested in housekeeping.

Philip knows that getting a good education is important; his parents have stressed that. But he just can't seem to concentrate in school. He'd much rather fool around with his friends. The thing that he and his friends like to do best is to ride the bus downtown and go to a movie, where they can show off, make noise, and make one another laugh.

Sometimes they smoke a little marijuana during the movie. One young man in Philip's social group was arrested once for having marijuana in his jacket pocket. He was trying to sell it on the street so that he could buy food. Philip thinks his friend was stupid to get caught. If you're smart, he believes, you don't let that happen. He's glad that his parents never found out about the incident.

Once, he brought two of his friends home during the weekend. His parents told him later that they didn't like the kind of people he was hanging around with. Now Philip goes out of his way to keep his friends and his parents apart.

THE FAMILY UNDER PRESSURE

In many ways the worlds of both

Institutions that play important roles in human development are rapidly being eroded, mainly through benign neglect.

teenagers are similar, even typical. Both live in families that have been significantly affected by one of the most important developments in American family life in the postwar years: the employment of both parents outside the home. Their mothers share this status with 64% of all married women in the U.S. who have school-age children. Fifty percent of mothers of preschool children and 46% of mothers with infants under the age of 3 work outside the home. For single-parent families, the rates are even higher: 53% of all mothers in single-parent households who have infants under age 3 work outside the home, as do 69% of all single mothers who have school-age children.[1]

These statistics have profound implications for families — sometimes for better, sometimes for worse. The determining factor is how well a given family can cope with the "havoc in the home" that two jobs can create. For, unlike most other industrialized nations, the U.S. has yet to introduce the kinds of policies and practices that make work life and family life compatible.

It is all too easy for family life in the U.S. to become hectic and stressful, as both parents try to coordinate the disparate demands of family and jobs in a world in which everyone has to be transported at least twice a day in a variety of directions. Under these circumstances, meal preparation, child care, shopping, and cleaning — the most basic tasks in a family — become major challenges. Dealing with these challenges may sometimes take precedence over the family's equally important child-rearing, educational, and nurturing roles.

But that is not the main danger. What

threatens the well-being of children and young people the most is that the external havoc can become internal, first for parents and then for their children. And that is exactly the sequence in which the psychological havoc of families under stress usually moves.

Recent studies indicate that conditions at work constitute one of the major sources of stress for American families.[2] Stress at work carries over to the home, where it affects first the relationship of parents to each other. Marital conflict then disturbs the parent/child relationship. Indeed, as long as tensions at work do not impair the relationship between the parents, the children are not likely to be affected. In other words, the influence of parental employment on children is indirect, operating through its effect on the parents.

That this influence is indirect does not make it any less potent, however. Once the parent/child relationship is seriously disturbed, children begin to feel insecure — and a door to the world of alienation has been opened. That door can open to children at any age, from preschool to high school and beyond.

My reference to the world of school is not accidental, for it is in that world that the next step toward alienation is likely to be taken. Children who feel rootless or caught in conflict at home find it difficult to pay attention in school. Once they begin to miss out on learning, they feel lost in the classroom, and they begin to seek acceptance elsewhere. Like Philip, they often find acceptance in a group of peers with similar histories who, having no welcoming place to go and nothing challenging to do, look for excitement on the streets.

OTHER INFLUENCES

In contemporary American society the growth of two-wage-earner families is not the only — or even the most serious — social change requiring accommodation through public policy and practice in order to avoid the risks of alienation. Other social changes include lengthy trips to and from work; the loss of the extended family, the close neighborhood, and other support systems previously available to families; and the omnipresent threat of television and other media to the family's traditional role as the primary transmitter of culture and values. Along with most families today, the families of Charles and Philip are experiencing the unraveling and disintegration of social institutions that in the past were central to the health and well-being of children and their parents.

Notice that both Charles and Philip come from two-parent, middle-class families. This is still the norm in the U.S. Thus neither family has to contend with two changes now taking place in U.S. society that have profound implications for the future of American families and the well-being of the next generation. The first of these changes is the increasing number of single-parent families. Although the divorce rate in the U.S. has been leveling off of late, this decrease has been more than compensated for by a rise in the number of unwed mothers, especially teenagers. Studies of the children brought up in single-parent families indicate that they are at greater risk of alienation than their counterparts from two-parent families. However, their vulnerability appears to have its roots not in the single-parent family structure as such, but in the treatment of single parents by U.S. society.[3]

In this nation, single parenthood is almost synonymous with poverty. And the growing gap between poor families and the rest of us is today the most powerful and destructive force producing alienation in the lives of millions of young people in America. In recent years, we have witnessed what the U.S. Census Bureau calls "the largest decline in family income in the post-World War II period." According to the latest Census, 25% of all children under age 6 now live in families whose incomes place them below the poverty line.

COUNTERING THE RISKS

Despite the similar stresses on their families, the risks of alienation for Charles and Philip are not the same. Clearly, Charles's parents have made a deliberate effort to create a variety of arrangements and practices that work against alienation. They have probably not done so as part of a deliberate program of "alienation prevention" — parents don't usually think in those terms. They're just being good parents. They spend time with their children and take an active interest in what their children are thinking, doing, and learning. They control their television set instead of letting it control them. They've found support systems to back them up when they're not available.

Without being aware of it, Charles's parents are employing a principle that the great Russian educator Makarenko employed in his extraordinarily success-ful programs for the reform of wayward adolescents in the 1920s: "The maximum of support with the maximum of challenge."[4] Families that produce effective, competent children often follow this principle, whether they're aware of it or not. They neither maintain strict control nor allow their children total freedom. They're always opening doors — and then giving their children a gentle but firm shove to encourage them to move on and grow. This combination of support and challenge is essential, if children are to avoid alienation and develop into capable young adults.

From a longitudinal study of youthful alienation and delinquency that is now considered a classic, Finnish psychologist Lea Pulkkinen arrived at a conclusion strikingly similar to Makarenko's. She found "guidance" — a combination of love and direction — to be a critical predictor of healthy development in youngsters.[5]

No such pattern is apparent in Philip's family. Unlike Charles's parents, Philip's parents neither recognize nor respond to the challenges they face. They have dispensed with the simple amenities of family self-discipline in favor of whatever is easiest. They may not be indifferent to their children, but the demands of their jobs leave them with little energy to be actively involved in their children's lives. (Note that Charles's parents have work schedules that are flexible enough to allow one of them to be at home most afternoons. In this regard, Philip's family is much more the norm, however. One of the most constructive steps that employers could take to strengthen families would be to enact clear policies making such flexibility possible.)

But perhaps the clearest danger signal in Philip's life is his dependence on his peer group. Pulkkinen found heavy reliance on peers to be one of the strongest predictors of problem behavior in adolescence and young adulthood. From a developmental viewpoint, adolescence is a time of challenge — a period in which young people seek activities that will serve as outlets for their energy, imagination, and longings. If healthy and constructive challenges are not available to them, they will find their challenges in such peer-group-related behaviors as poor school performance, aggressiveness or social withdrawal (sometimes both), school absenteeism or dropping out, smoking, drinking, early and promiscuous sexual activity, teenage parenthood, drugs, and juvenile delinquency.

This pattern has now been identified in a number of modern industrial societies, including the U.S., England, West Germany, Finland, and Australia. The pattern is both predictable from the circumstances of a child's early family life and predictive of life experiences still to come, e.g., difficulties in establishing relationships with the opposite sex, marital discord, divorce, economic failure, criminality.

If the roots of alienation are to be found in disorganized families living in disorganized environments, its bitter fruits are to be seen in these patterns of disrupted development. This is not a harvest that our nation can easily afford. Is it a price that other modern societies are paying, as well?

A CROSS-NATIONAL PERSPECTIVE

The available answers to that question will not make Americans feel better about what is occurring in the U.S. In our society, the forces that produce youthful alienation are growing in strength and scope. Families, schools, and other institutions that play important roles in human development are rapidly being eroded, *mainly through benign neglect*. Unlike the citizens of other modern nations, we Americans have simply not been willing to make the necessary effort to forestall the alienation of our young people.

As part of a new experiment in higher education at Cornell University, I have been teaching a multidisciplinary course for the past few years titled "Human Development in Post-Industrial Societies." One of the things we have done in that course is to gather comparative data from several nations, including France, Canada, Japan, Australia, Germany, England, and the U.S. One student summarized our findings succinctly: "With respect to families, schools, children, and youth, such countries as France, Japan, Canada, and Australia have more in common with each other than the United States has with any of them." For example:

• The U.S. has by far the highest rate of teenage pregnancy of any industrialized nation — twice the rate of its nearest competitor, England.

• The U.S. divorce rate is the highest in the world — nearly double that of its nearest competitor, Sweden.

• The U.S. is the only industrialized society in which nearly one-fourth of all infants and preschool children live in families whose incomes fall below the poverty line. These children lack such basics as adequate health care.

• The U.S. has fewer support systems for individuals in all age groups, including adolescence. The U.S. also has the highest incidence of alcohol and drug abuse among adolescents of any country in the world.[6]

All these problems are part of the unraveling of the social fabric that has been going on since World War II. These problems are not unique to the U.S., but in many cases they are more pronounced here than elsewhere.

WHAT COMMUNITIES CAN DO

The more we learn about alienation and its effects in contemporary post-industrial societies, the stronger are the imperatives to counteract it. If the essence of alienation is disconnectedness, then the best way to counteract alienation is through the creation of connections or links.

For the well-being of children and adolescents, the most important links must be those between the home, the peer group, and the school. A recent study in West Germany effectively demonstrated how important this basic triangle can be. The study examined student achievement and social behavior in 20 schools. For all the schools, the researchers developed measures of the links between the home, the peer group, and the school. Controlling for social class and other variables, the researchers found that they were able to predict children's behavior from the number of such links they found. Students who had no links were alienated. They were not doing well in school, and they exhibited a variety of behavioral problems. By contrast, students who had such links were doing well and were growing up to be responsible citizens.[7]

In addition to creating links within the basic triangle of home, peer group, and school, we need to consider two other structures in today's society that affect the lives of young people: the world of work (for both parents and children) and the community, which provides an overarching context for all the other worlds of childhood.

Philip's family is one example of how the world of work can contribute to alienation. The U.S. lags far behind other industrialized nations in providing child-care services and other benefits designed to promote the well-being of children and their families. Among the most needed benefits are maternity and paternity leaves, flex-time, job-sharing

> Caring is surely an essential aspect of education in a free society; yet we have almost completely neglected it.

arrangements, and personal leaves for parents when their children are ill. These benefits are a matter of course in many of the nations with which the U.S. is generally compared.

In contemporary American society, however, the parents' world of work is not the only world that both policy and practice ought to be accommodating. There is also the children's world of work. According to the most recent figures available, 50% of all high school students now work part-time — sometimes as much as 40 to 50 hours per week. This fact poses a major problem for the schools. Under such circumstances, how can teachers assign homework with any expectation that it will be completed?

The problem is further complicated by the kind of work that most young people are doing. For many years, a number of social scientists — myself included — advocated more work opportunities for adolescents. We argued that such experiences would provide valuable contact with adult models and thereby further the development of responsibility and general maturity. However, from their studies of U.S. high school students who are employed, Ellen Greenberger and Lawrence Steinberg conclude that most of the jobs held by these youngsters are highly routinized and afford little opportunity for contact with adults. The largest employers of teenagers in the U.S. are fast-food restaurants. Greenberger and Steinberg argue that, instead of providing maturing experiences, such settings give adolescents even greater exposure to the values and lifestyles of their peer group. And the adolescent peer group tends to emphasize immediate gratification and consumerism.[8]

Finally, in order to counteract the

mounting forces of alienation in U.S. society, we must establish a working alliance between the private sector and the public one (at both the local level and the national level) to forge links between the major institutions in U.S. society and to re-create a sense of community. Examples from other countries abound:

• Switzerland has a law that no institution for the care of the elderly can be established unless it is adjacent to and shares facilities with a day-care center, a school, or some other kind of institution serving children.

• In many public places throughout Australia, the Department of Social Security has displayed a poster that states, in 16 languages: "If you need an interpreter, call this number." The department maintains a network of interpreters who are available 16 hours a day, seven days a week. They can help callers get in touch with a doctor, an ambulance, a fire brigade, or the police; they can also help callers with practical or personal problems.

• In the USSR, factories, offices, and places of business customarily "adopt" groups of children, e.g., a day-care center, a class of schoolchildren, or a children's ward in a hospital. The employees visit the children, take them on outings, and invite them to visit their place of work.

We Americans can offer a few good examples of alliances between the public and private sectors, as well. For example, in Flint, Michigan, some years ago, Mildred Smith developed a community program to improve school performance among low-income minority pupils. About a thousand children were involved. The program required no change in the regular school curriculum; its principal focus was on building links between home and school. This was accomplished in a variety of ways.

• A core group of low-income parents went from door to door, telling their neighbors that the school needed their help.

• Parents were asked to keep younger children out of the way so that the older children could complete their homework.

• Schoolchildren were given tags to wear at home that said, "May I read to you?"

• Students in the high school business program typed and duplicated teaching materials, thus freeing teachers to work directly with the children.

• Working parents visited school classrooms to talk about their jobs and about how their own schooling now helped them in their work.

WHAT SCHOOLS CAN DO

As the program in Flint demonstrates, the school is in the best position of all U.S. institutions to initiate and strengthen links that support children and adolescents. This is so for several reasons. First, one of the major — but often unrecognized — responsibilities of the school is to enable young people to move from the secluded and supportive environment of the home into responsible and productive citizenship. Yet, as the studies we conducted at Cornell revealed, most other modern nations are ahead of the U.S. in this area.

In these other nations, schools are not merely — or even primarily — places where the basics are taught. Both in purpose and in practice, they function instead as settings in which young people learn "citizenship": what it means to be a member of the society, how to behave toward others, what one's responsibilities are to the community and to the nation.

I do not mean to imply that such learnings do not occur in American schools. But when they occur, it is mostly by accident and not because of thoughtful planning and careful effort. What form might such an effort take? I will present here some ideas that are too new to have stood the test of time but that may be worth trying.

Creating an American classroom. This is a simple idea. Teachers could encourage their students to learn about schools (and, especially, about individual classrooms) in such modern industrialized societies as France, Japan, Canada, West Germany, the Soviet Union, and Australia. The children could acquire such information in a variety of ways: from reading, from films, from the firsthand reports of children and adults who have attended school abroad, from exchanging letters and materials with students and their teachers in other countries. Through such exposure, American students would become aware of how attending school in other countries is both similar to and different from attending school in the U.S.

But the main learning experience would come from asking students to consider what kinds of things *should* be happening — or not happening — in American classrooms, given our na-

tion's values and ideals. For example, how should children relate to one another and to their teachers, if they are doing things in an *American* way? If a student's idea seems to make sense, the American tradition of pragmatism makes the next step obvious: try the idea to see if it works.

The curriculum for caring. This effort also has roots in our values as a nation. Its goal is to make caring an essential part of the school curriculum. However, students would not simply learn about caring; they would actually engage in it. Children would be asked to spend time with and to care for younger children, the elderly, the sick, and the lonely. Caring institutions, such as daycare centers, could be located adjacent to or even within the schools. But it would be important for young caregivers to learn about the environment in which their charges live and the other people with whom their charges interact each day. For example, older children who took responsibility for younger ones would become acquainted with the younger children's parents and living arrangements by escorting them home from school.

Just as many schools now train superb drum corps, they could also train "caring corps" — groups of young men and women who would be on call to handle a variety of emergencies. If a parent fell suddenly ill, these students could come into the home to care for the children, prepare meals, run errands, and serve as an effective source of support for their fellow human beings. Caring is surely an essential aspect of education in a free society; yet we have almost completely neglected it.

Mentors for the young. A mentor is someone with a skill that he or she wishes to teach to a younger person. To be a true mentor, the older person must be willing to take the time and to make the commitment that such teaching requires.

We don't make much use of mentors in U.S. society, and we don't give much recognition or encouragement to individuals who play this important role. As a result, many U.S. children have few significant and committed adults in their lives. Most often, their mentors are their own parents, perhaps a teacher or two, a coach, or — more rarely — a relative, a neighbor, or an older classmate. However, in a diverse society such as ours, with its strong tradition of volunteerism, potential mentors

abound. The schools need to seek them out and match them with young people who will respond positively to their particular knowledge and skills.

The school is the institution best suited to take the initiative in this task, because the school is the only place in which all children gather every day. It is also the only institution that has the right (and the responsibility) to turn to the community for help in an activity that represents the noblest kind of education: the building of character in the young.

There is yet another reason why schools should take a leading role in rebuilding links among the four worlds of childhood: schools have the most to gain. In the recent reports bemoaning the state of American education, a recurring theme has been the anomie and chaos that pervade many U.S. schools, to the detriment of effective teaching and learning. Clearly, we are in danger of allowing our schools to become academies of alienation.

In taking the initiative to rebuild links among the four worlds of childhood, U.S. schools will be taking necessary action to combat the destructive forces of alienation — first, within their own walls, and thereafter, in the life experience and future development of new generations of Americans.

1. Urie Bronfenbrenner, "New Worlds for Families," paper presented at the Boston Children's Museum, 4 May 1984.
2. Urie Bronfenbrenner, "The Ecology of the Family as a Context for Human Development," *Developmental Psychology,* in press.
3. Mavis Heatherington, "Children of Divorce," in R. Henderson, ed., *Parent-Child Interaction* (New York: Academic Press, 1981).
4. A.S. Makarenko, *The Collective Family: A Handbook for Russian Parents* (New York: Doubleday, 1967).
5. Lea Pulkkinen, "Self-Control and Continuity from Childhood to Adolescence," in Paul Baltes and Orville G. Brim, eds., *Life-Span Development and Behavior,* Vol. 4 (New York: Academic Press, 1982), pp. 64-102.
6. S.B. Kamerman, *Parenting in an Unresponsive Society* (New York: Free Press, 1980); S.B. Kamerman and A.J. Kahn, *Social Services in International Perspective* (Washington, D.C.: U.S. Department of Health, Education, and Welfare, n.d.); and Lloyd Johnston, Jerald Bachman, and Patrick O'Malley, *Use of Licit and Illicit Drugs by America's High School Students — 1975-84* (Washington, D.C.: U.S. Government Printing Office, 1985).
7. Kurt Aurin, personal communication, 1985.
8. Ellen Greenberger and Lawrence Steinberg, *The Work of Growing Up* (New York: Basic Books, forthcoming).

The Child Yesterday, Today, and Tomorrow

David Elkind

The child is a gift of nature, the image of the child is man's creation. It is the image of the child, rather than nature's gift, that determines educational practice in any historical epoch. And the image of the child, man's creation, is as often wrong as it is correct. Wrong images are more powerful and more easily grasped than true ones. In the present as in the past, our task as educators of young children is not simply to be true to nature's gift, but also to fight against the false images that, in any age, threaten the healthy education of young children.

Images of the past

The image of the child in antiquity was that of young citizen who had to be educated by the laws and culture of society. The children of Babylon went to school at age 6 and even poor children learned to read and write except that their books were bricks and their writing tools

This article is, with a few minor changes, the address Dr. Elkind gave at NAEYC's November 1986 Annual Conference at the Opening General Session, Washington Hilton Hotel. **David Elkind** *is NAEYC's President.*

a reed and damp clay. Children in ancient Greece played with go-carts and dolls, and at the age of 7 boys went to school. In ancient Rome, women had a more equal place and both boys and girls went to school where the discipline was strict and where they learned to write with a stylus and wax tablet.

During the Middle Ages, children fared less well and the prevailing image of the child was that of chattel, or piece of property consistent with the ideology of serfdom. The medieval castle was no place for a child, built as it was for defense rather than for comfort. The children of serfs worked and lived with the animals. Discipline was strict and punishment harsh. In England, there was a brief, golden era for children during the reign of Good Queen Bess. And during this era, the faithful nanny begins to appear in folklore and literature.

Toward the end of the 17th Century, the struggle between Cavaliers and Puritans was reflected in their quite dissimilar images of children. The Cavaliers held a mixed image of the child as part nuisance, part plaything. In contrast, the Puritans constructed an image of the child as one tainted with original sin. "Your child," wrote James Janeway, "is never too young to go to hell."

In this country the images of children changed with our rapidly changing society. In colonial times children were seen as financial assets who could help work the farm or be apprenticed out of the home at an early age. The children of slaves were an extreme example of this, but they were not the only children who labored from dawn to dark. With the industrial revolution, children, especially the children of immigrants and the poor, came to be seen as cheap factory workers until the cruelty of child labor was made public. The ensuing social reform movement transformed the image of the child from one of cheap factory labor to one of apprentice to factory work. Instead of being sent to the factory, children were sent to school to prepare them to work in factories. School bells, like factory whistles, signaled the beginning and the end of the school day. And children, like their parents, carried lunch pails to be opened at the noon whistle.

As we see, there have been many different images of children, some of which were more beneficial to child health, welfare, and education than others. And there have always been those who, at any given point in history, have been critical of the image of the child current at that time. Often this criticism took the form of an attack on parents and upon parenting, but in fact it was an attack upon the then "accepted" image of the child. A review of these attacks upon the images of the child that were raised in earlier times is instructive. It tells us that the image of the child at any point in history never goes unchallenged and that the challengers in the past, as today, often come from the ranks of early childhood educators.

The criticism of prevailing images of the child has a long history. For his ideal Republic, Plato wanted children to be raised by professional child caretakers, and St. Augustine proclaimed, "Give me other mothers and I will give you other worlds." Rousseau's opening statement in *Emile* to the effect that everything is good as it comes from the hand of the Maker and deteriorates in the hands of man, is an indictment of the image of the child as a young savage who had to be socialized.

Pestalozzi and Froebel did not criticize parents directly, but did believe that parents needed to be given a truer image of the child that would result in more healthy childrearing practices. Parent education was an important component of early childhood education practiced by Pestalozzi and Froebel. Pestalozzi's book, *How Gertrude Teaches Her Children,* which is subtitled *An Attempt To Help Mothers Teach Their Own Children,* reflects this emphasis upon training parents. The same theme was repeated in Froebel's *The Education of Man* and in his *Songs for Mothers and Nursery Songs.*

Their successor Maria Montessori never criticized parents either, but she had less faith in parent education than her predecessors. Like Plato she wanted children reared by professionals, not by parents. For her, childrearing was too important a task to be left to untrained parents whose image of the child gave too little credit to their budding intellecual powers.

In the past, the prevailing image of the child that dictated childrearing and education was determined by a complex of social, economic, and cultural factors that may have had little or nothing to do with the natural child. And since early times, there have been critics

of the prevailing conception of the child. These critics fought to replace the false image of the child with a truer one that would provide for a healthier, happier, and more productive child life.

Images of the present

Historically, predominant images of the child were derived from the prevailing political, social, or religious ethos. What is remarkable about modern images of the child is that they are, or are said to be, scientific in origin. Unfortunately, their scientific origin has not rendered them any more valid than those that had social, political, or religious derivations. In some ways, the scientific origin of some of the contemporary images of the child makes them even more difficult to combat than previous images. I want now to usurp the role of critic and review and comment upon three modern images of the child that have contributed to what I call miseducation, namely putting children at risk for no purpose.

The sensual child

The advent of Freudian psychology gave rise to the image of the sensual child. In this view, the child was "polymorphous perverse" in the sense of having the whole gamut of sexual instincts and proclivities that were once reserved to adults. In Freudian terms, children whose sexual instincts were unduly repressed were destined to become neurotic. The childrearing and educational implications of this image of the sensual child were straightforward. Children had to be allowed to express themselves, and play was the natural medium of self-expression. With adequate self-expression at home and at school, children would develop healthy personalities and their intelligence would take care of itself.

Like so many images of the child, this idea contains a partial truth. Freud made it clear that a certain amount of repression was healthy,

indeed necessary, for people to live in a society. It was *excessive* repression, not repression, that produced neuroses. But that point was sometimes lost on those who fought for expression at all costs.

The malleable child

Another image of the child that has dominated contemporary thought has come from the anthropologists who were concerned with the conflict between generations. The leading writers of this genre were Kingsley Davis, Ruth Benedict, and Margaret Mead. Although they differed in detail, they were all making the same point, namely, when it comes to adapting to social change, children are plastic and adaptable whereas adults are rigid and unadaptable. Children, they argued, are better suited to social change than are adults.

Davis, for example, argued that adults are locked into the orientation they received as children and this makes it difficult, if not impossible, for them to appreciate the changed circumstances of their offspring, hence the generational conflict. Benedict said that adults are independent and children are dependent, and that it was the adult's inability to deal with the child's growing independence that was the cause of the generational conflict. And Margaret Mead argued that in a rapidly changing culture, children, who are free of ingrained habits of thought, are much better able to adapt to new and changing technologies than adults.

This image of child malleability in contrast to adult rigidity is sometimes misinterpreted. Anthropologists are talking about change in the overall society, *not* about changes within the immediate family. When a family moves, the children have more trouble with the change than adults. And, while divorce may be hard on adults, it is certainly much harder on children. Children thrive on consistency, stability, and security, while it is adults

Courtesy U.S. Department of Labor

about programs to inform young children about the threats of nuclear war. Presumably, children have to be exposed to this idea at an early age so they will be better prepared for a nuclear holocaust when it comes. Even if one accepts this shaky premise, it has to be recognized that the concept of nuclear war is completely foreign to young children, who do not even have a conception of biological death, much less of millions of people and the power of nuclear weapons to destroy them. Recent suggestions that young children be taught about AIDS also stem from this wrongheaded image of child malleability.

To be sure, children are fresh learners to the extent that they are not handicapped by previous ideas and concepts. But this does not mean that they are ready to learn everything and anything—far from it. Their openness to learning is limited and we need to recognize these limitations. There is a time and a place for everything and early childhood education is not the time nor the place to teach children computer programming, the threat of nuclear war, or for that matter, the dangers of AIDS.

The competent infant

Perhaps the most pervasive and most pernicious contemporary image of the child is one that has been promoted by psychologists writing in the 60s. Responding to the Civil Rights Movement, to the War on Poverty, and to the inadequacies of the educational system, many writers gave voice to a vision of childhood that would undo these wrongs and undo them at an early age. All these wrongs, it was said, could be righted if we only got to children early enough. The result was a new image of infants and young children as having much more capacity to learn academic skills than children, regardless of background, actually have. It is true that all young children have intellectual abilities and that their thinking should be encouraged but

who seek new experience and adventure. Children adapt less easily to change within the family than adults do, but the reverse image fostered by a misapplication of social scientists' ideas about change in society persists and contributes to miseducation.

The introduction of computers into early childhood education, and the teaching of programming to young children, is a direct offshoot of this malleability conception. It is simply a fact of technological development that as technology develops it requires more, rather than less, intellectual maturity. A child can use a shovel but not a power shovel; a child can use a hand saw or hand drill, but not a power saw or power drill; a child can ride a horse, but cannot drive an automobile and certainly cannot fly an airplane. The more advanced the technology, the more advanced the intelligence required to use it. Modern warfare is another example. Modern weapons require college

graduates if they are to be used properly. The modern army has no place for a Sergeant York trained with a hunting rifle. And even when a technology is easy to use, such as television, it can still be dangerous to young children.

Yet the idea that children should be programming and running computers persists despite the fact that the complexity and technological sophistication of computers is far beyond what a young child can really comprehend and master. To be used by young children, computers have to be converted into teaching machines presenting programmed learning. And programmed learning is simply boring. Exposing young children to computers in this way runs the risk that they will get turned off to computers before they have a chance to see what they can really do. It is a good example of miseducation, of putting children at risk for no purpose.

In the same way, I am often asked

within the context of their psychological stage of development. This 60s image of the child as consumer of skills has come to haunt us in the 80s.

In his book *The Process of Education,* Jerome Bruner voiced his now famous hypothesis that you can "teach any child, any subject matter at any age in an intellectually responsible way." Bruner was really speaking to curriculum writers and probably did not fully appreciate the extent to which his hypothesis would be accepted, not as a hypothesis, but rather as a fact by the public at large. And it has also become the motto of entrepreneurs hawking flash cards to parents with the proclamation that you can teach a young child "anything."

But is it true? It is only true if you either redefine the child or redefine the subject matter. The curriculum writers of the 60s, academicians such as Max Beberman at the University of Illinois or Robert Karplus at Berkeley knew their subject matter but not young children. The curricula they designed in effect redefined the competence of children without recourse to children's actual abilities or limitations. For example, variable base arithmetic was said to be easier for children to learn than base ten arithmetic. But even parents had trouble with variable base arithmetic! It was also claimed that children would learn math better if it were introduced as a language. Instead of answering what is the sum of 2 + 2, children were asked to "Make this sentence true."

The error here came from confusing what is simple to an expert in a subject with what is simple for the novice. Simplicity is the end result of learning a skill or a discipline, not its starting point. Reading is simple once you know how, but is far from simple when you first start out. Understanding multiple base arithmetic may be simple once you know base ten, but not if you don't. Understanding the relation of lan-

guage to mathematics is simple if you have a firm grasp of language and mathematics, but not if you don't. We have to always be aware of the danger of assuming that the end point for us as adults should be the starting point for children.

The other side of Bruner's hypothesis requires redefining the subject matter. When an infant who responds to flash cards is said to be "reading" or doing "math," these subject matters have been drastically redefined. Suppose, for example, that I tell you that I can balance 100 pounds on my finger. You would not believe me. But suppose I take out a 3 × 5 card and write *100 pounds* on it. Now I put the card on my finger, and voilà, I am holding 100 pounds on my finger. Claiming to teach infants to read and do math is the same; it is a sleight-of-hand trick accomplished by redefining what is usually meant by reading and by math.

Yet people are taken in by this trickery and really believe that they are teaching their children these subjects. And this trickery has another negative fallout effect. Redefining the subject matter makes it much easier to acquire. Parents then believe that their child who is "reading" flash cards at age 2 is a budding genius. But they will be disappointed in the end. Unfortunately, making a task easier does not make children brighter.

Another contribution to the image of the competent infant came from educational psychologist Benjamin Bloom who argued from statistical summaries of IQ data that 4-year-olds had attained half of their intellectual ability and that it was incumbent upon us to impose formal learning on young children because otherwise we might lose out on this period of phenomenal mental growth. This idea that you must teach as much as possible to young children because their minds are growing so rapidly has become part of the contemporary folk wisdom and is deeply ingrained in

our contemporary image of the child.

But is it true? Bloom was talking about mental test data, not about mental growth. Because infants and young children are not good test takers, their intelligence test performance is not a good index of their later test performance. By the age of 4, however, the child is sufficiently verbal and has sufficient ability to concentrate attention, and her or his test performance is a better index of true ability. From the test score a child attains at the age of 4 you can predict with some 50% accuracy what that child's test score will be at age 17. And that is all that a child attaining half of her or his mental ability at age 4 means.

It does not mean that at age 4 the child has half of all the knowledge, skills, and values she or he will ever have. It does not mean that if a child attains an IQ of 100 at age 4 she or he will attain an IQ score of 200 at age 17. It does not mean that a child at age 4 is a better learner than she or he will be at age 17. Even if we grant that mental growth is rapid during the early years of life, it does not follow as dawn follows the night, that this calls for formal, teacher-directed learning. During periods of rapid mental growth, children seek out the stimuli to nourish themselves mentally. We serve them best by providing an environment rich in materials to observe, explore, manipulate, talk, write, and think about. You do not prune during the growing season.

Still a third writer who has contributed to the contemporary image of the competent infants is J. McV. Hunt. In his book *Intelligence and Experience* he surveyed a great deal of evidence and concluded that intelligence was malleable and not fixed, the view he attributed to professionals of the time. But no reputable psychologist ever claimed that intelligence was fixed. In 1954, in a chapter of the *Handbook of Child Psychology,* Florence Goodenough made it clear that all

petence and abilities. This thesis fit in neatly with the other ideas about infant competence and gave it a historical dimension.

More recent historians of childhood, like Pollack, have shown Aries was wrong. Even in the times Aries was writing, diaries of parents show quite clearly that adults appreciated that children were different from adults and had to be treated differently. Sir Francis Bacon, writing in the 16th Century, even talked about the value of "allowances" and the negative effects of not giving a child a sufficient allowance, and suggested that "The proof is best when men keep their authority towards their children, but not their purse."

These four ideas, then, that a child can be taught any subject at any age, that children have half their intellectual ability at age 4 when mental growth is more rapid, that the IQ is malleable, and that childhood is an invention, all emerged in the 1960s to form a new image of child competence. Although this new image may have corrected a previous image that played down child competence, it went to the other extreme. Ideas meant to improve the conditions of low-income children have been taken over by middle-class parents and have become the rationale for much of the miseducation of young children today.

As in the past, we have not only to assert the values of child-centered early childhood education, but we must also struggle to reveal the concepts of early childhood malleability and competence for what they are, namely distortions of how young children really grow and learn.

Images of the future

Given the brief history I have just outlined, it seems reasonable to predict that the false images of children today will be replaced by equally false images tomorrow. I have no crystal ball, only a belief that history is prologue and that the

the evidence supported the view that the environmental factors accounted for between 20 and 40% of an individual's IQ.

Up until the 60s, however, psychologists were mainly concerned with middle-class children who, presumably, had maximized their environmental potential. It was only when attention was turned to low-income children who had less than optimal environmental input that the significance of environmental input became a matter of concern. Consider the following analogy. Suppose you place a group of undernourished children on a full calorie, well-balanced diet. Surely such children will make significant gains in both height and weight, but similar gains will not be made by children who are already on a full calorie, well-balanced diet. The potential benefits of an improved program are always relative to the quality of the previous environment.

This idea of intellectual malleability has become common cur-

rency among parents who are being told that with the proper program of stimulation they can have a "brighter child" or that they can raise their child's IQ. Yet there is no evidence that children growing up in an environment where they are talked to, played with, and read to, and which is rich in things to look at, listen to, and explore, will derive additional benefit from prescribed exercises and symbolic materials. If anything, most middle-class children today are over- rather than understimulated.

The last contributor to the image of the competent child is not a psychologist but a historian. In his book *Centuries of Childhood,* Phillip Aries argues that childhood is a social invention and that there was no such conception in the Middle Ages when children were depicted and treated much as adults. The implication is that for the last couple of hundred years we have been coddling children and infantalizing them and ignoring their true com-

image of the child at any point in history always fills the predominant parent needs and defenses of that developmental epoch. We have to ask then what the needs of future parents will be and how these will be reflected in a new image of the child.

Our society is already a service and information society with more than 70% of our population in these occupations. I believe that we will eventually get high quality child care for all those youngsters who need it and that those who care for infants and young children will have positions of respect and will be paid well. We may even have parent professionals to care for and rear other people's children. This will not happen immediately and without a great deal of hard work and pain, but I do believe we will get there.

What then? What new image will emerge when the image of the malleable competent child has run its course? What sort of image of the child will be most in keeping with the needs of tomorrow's parents? If present trends continue, it appears that parents will spend less time than ever parenting. Once parents no longer feel guilty or uncomfortable about this, the need for the image of child intellectual competence will diminish. In its place will emerge a new image of child social sophistication and self-sufficiency. In an information and service society these are the requisite skills. We already see hints of this in the current emphasis upon social cognition. Psychologists are eager to point out that Piaget was wrong and that infants and young children are much more socially skilled than we gave them credit for being.

And while it may be true that children are more socially proficient and self-sufficient than we may have recognized, they will not be as socially proficient as the image of social sophistication will have us believe. And the cycle will once again repeat itself, the next generation of early childhood educators will have to challenge the new image of the child as, to use the computer term that may well become the catchword of this new image, *an expert system* with respect to social interaction. The next generation will once again have to reassert the values of sound early childhood education.

Our task as early childhood educators then is never ending. Each generation presents a new challenge and a new battle. And it is a battle that we can never really win, because each new generation is prone to the same mistakes. Yet if we do not fight it is a battle we can most assuredly lose. For those of us in early childhood education it is a battle well worth fighting and, even if we fall before our time, we can take comfort in the knowledge that there will always be others, sufficiently committed to the well-being of young children, to carry on the fight.

Bibliography

Aries, P. (1962). *Centuries of childhood.* New York: Knopf.

Benedict, R. (1938). Continuities and discontinuities in cultural conditioning. *Psychiatry, 1,* 161–167.

Bloom, B. (1964). *Stability and change in human behavior.* New York: Wiley.

Bruner, J. (1962). *The process of education.* Cambridge, MA: Harvard University Press.

Davis, K. (1940). The sociology of parent-youth conflict. *American Sociological Review, 5,* 523–525.

Freud, S. (1905). *Three essays on sexuality.* New York: Basic.

Hunt, J. McV. (1961). *Intelligence and experience.* New York: Ronald.

Mead, M. (1970). *Culture and commitment.* New York: Natural History Press/Doubleday.

Pollack, L. (1983). *Forgotten children.* Cambridge: Cambridge University Press.

BIOLOGY, DESTINY, AND ALL THAT

Grabbing hold of a tar baby
of research findings, our writer
tries to pull apart truth from myth
in ideas about the differences
between the sexes.

Paul Chance

Paul Chance is a psychologist, writer, and contributing editor of *Psychology Today*.

In the 1880s, scholars warned against the hazards of educating women. Some experts of the day believed that too much schooling could endanger a woman's health, interfere with her reproductive ability, and cause her brain to deteriorate. In the 1980s we laugh at such absurd ideas, but have we (men and women alike) really given up the ancient idea that a woman is fundamentally an inferior sort of man? It seems not.

It's hard to find evidence these days of gross discrimination against women as a company policy. Successful lawsuits have made that sort of prejudice expensive. Yet evidence of more subtle forms of bias abound. The sociologist Beth Ghiloni conducted a study while she was a student at the University of California, Santa Cruz, that shows that some corporations are meeting the demands of affirmative action by putting women into public relations posts. Public relations is important but distant from the activities that generate revenue, so PR assignments effectively keep women out of jobs that include any real corporate power. Thus, women increasingly complain of facing a "glass ceiling" through which they can see, but cannot reach, high level corporate positions.

It seems likely that such discrimination reflects some very old ideas about what men and women are like. Men, the stereotype has it, are aggressive and self-confident. They think analytically, and are cool under fire. They enjoy jobs that offer responsibility and challenge. They are, in other words, ideally suited for important,

high-level positions. Put them on the track that may one day lead to corporate vice president.

Women, the thinking goes, are passive and filled with self-doubt. They think intuitively, and are inclined to become emotionally distraught under pressure. They therefore enjoy jobs that involve working with people. Give them the lower-rung jobs in the personnel department, or send them to public affairs.

Figuring out how truth and myth intertwine in these stereotypes is difficult. The research literature on sex differences is a tar baby made of numbers, case studies, and anecdotal impressions. To paraphrase one researcher, "If you like ambiguity, you're gonna love sex-difference research." Nevertheless, let us be brave and take the stereotypes apart piece by piece.

Aggression

On this there is no argument: Everyone agrees that men are more aggressive than women. In a classic review of the literature, the psychologists Eleanor Maccoby of Stanford University and Carol Jacklin of the University of Southern California found that boys are more aggressive than girls both physically and verbally, and the difference begins to show up by the age of 3. Boys are more inclined to rough-and-tumble play; girls have tea parties and play with dolls.

The difference in aggressiveness is most clearly seen in criminal activity. There are far more delinquent boys than girls, and prisons are built primarily to contain men. The most aggressive crimes, such as murder and assault, are especially dominated by men.

It seems hardly likely that male aggressiveness, as it is documented by the research, would win favor among personnel directors and corporate headhunters. Yet aggressiveness is considered not only a virtue but an essential trait for many jobs. Vice President George Bush learned the value of aggressiveness when he managed to put aside his wimp image by verbally attacking the CBS news anchorman Dan Rather on national television. The assumption seems to be that the same underlying trait that makes for murderers, rapists, and strong-arm bandits also, in more moderate degree or under proper guidance, makes people more competitive and motivated to achieve great things.

But the research suggests that women may be just as aggressive in this more civilized sense as men. For instance, most studies of competitiveness find no differences between the sexes, according to the psychologists Veronica Nieva and Barbara Gutek, co-authors of *Women and Work*. And many studies of achievement motivation suggest that women are just as eager to get things done as men.

Self-confidence

Men are supposed to be self-confident, women full of self-doubt. Again there is some evidence for the stereotype, but it isn't particularly complimentary to males. Various studies show that males overestimate their abilities, while females underestimate theirs. Researchers have found, for instance, that given the option of choosing tasks varying in difficulty, boys erred by choosing those that were too difficult for them, while girls tended to select tasks that were too easy.

Other research shows that women are not only less confident of their ability to do a job, when they succeed at it they don't give themselves credit. Ask them why they did well and they'll tell you it was an easy task or that they got lucky. Ask men the same thing and they'll tell you they did well because of their ability and hard work.

It is perhaps this difference in self-confidence that makes women better risks for auto insurance, and it may have something to do with the fact that almost from the day they can walk, males are more likely to be involved in pedestrian accidents.

Rational Thinking

A great many studies have found that men do better than women on tests of mathematical reasoning. Julian Stanley, a psychologist at Johns Hopkins University, has been using the mathematics portion of the Scholastic Aptitude Test to identify mathematically gifted youths. He and his colleagues have consistently found that a majority of the high scoring students are boys. Stanley reports that "mathematically gifted boys outnumber gifted girls by a ratio of about 13 to 1." Moreover, the very best scores almost inevitably come from boys.

But while some findings show that men are

"It's unlikely that male aggressiveness, as documented by research, would win favor among personnel directors."

better at mathematical reasoning, there is no evidence that they are more analytical or logical in general. In fact, the superiority of men at mathematical problem solving seems not to reflect superior analytical thinking but a special talent men have for visualizing objects in space. Women are every bit the match of men at other kinds of problems such as drawing logical conclusions from written text. Indeed, girls have an advantage over boys in verbal skills until at least adolescence.

As for the idea that women are more intuitive, forget it. Numerous studies have shown that women are better at reading body language, and it is probably this skill (born, perhaps, of the need to avoid enraging the more aggressive sex) that gives rise to the myth of women's intuition. In reality, women and men think alike.

Emotionality

In Victorian England, to judge by the novels of the day, a woman was no woman at all if she didn't feel faint or burst into tears at least once a week. The idea that women are more emotional than men, that they feel things more deeply and react accordingly, persists. Is it true?

No. Carol Tavris and Carole Wade, psychologists and co-authors of *The Longest War: Sex Differences in Perspective*, write that the sexes are equally likely to feel anxious in new situations, to get angry when insulted, to be hurt when a loved one leaves them, and to feel embarrassed when they make mistakes in public.

The sexes are equally emotional, but there are important differences in how willing men and women are to express emotions, which emotions they choose to express, and the ways in which they express them. If you ask men and women in an emotional situation what they are feeling, women are likely to admit that they are affected, while men are likely to deny it. Yet studies show that when you look at the psychological correlates of emotion—heartbeat, blood pressure, and the like—you find that those strong silent men are churning inside every bit as much as the women.

Men are particularly eager to conceal feelings such as fear, sorrow, and loneliness, according to Tavris and Wade. Men often bottle these "feminine" feelings even with those they hold most dear.

Another difference comes in how emotions are expressed. Women behave differently depending upon what they feel. They may cry if sad, curse if angry, pout if their pride is hurt. Men tend to respond to such situations in a more or less uniform way. Whether they have been jilted, frightened, or snubbed, they become aggressive. (Men, you will recall, are very good at aggression.) As for the notion that keeping one's head is characteristic of men, well, don't get sore fellows, but it ain't necessarily so.

Men's math superiority reflects a special talent for visualizing objects in space.

Job Interests

If you ask men and women what they like about their work, you will get different answers. In 1957, Frederick Herzberg published a study of what made work enjoyable to employees. Men, he concluded, enjoyed work that offered responsibility and challenge. For women, on the other hand, the environment was the thing. They wanted an attractive work area, and some pleasant people to talk to while they did whatever needed to be done. Give your secretary an office with some nice wallpaper, put a flower on her desk once in a while, and she'll be happy.

Experts now agree, however, that such differences probably reflect differences in the jobs held by the people studied. You may get such findings, suggest *Women and Work* co-authors Nieva and Gutek, if you compare female file clerks and male engineers—but not if you compare female and male engineers. In a study of workers in various jobs, Daphne Bugental, a psychologist at the University of California, Santa Barbara, and the late Richard Centers found no consistent differences in the way men and women ranked "intrinsic" job characteristics such as responsibility and challenge and "extrinsic" characteristics such as pleasant surroundings and friendly co-workers. In other words, the dif-ferences in what men and women find interesting about work reflect differences in the kinds of work men and women characteristically do. People in relatively high level jobs enjoy the responsibility and challenge it offers; people in low level jobs that offer little responsibility and challenge look elsewhere for satisfaction.

Where Do the Differences Come From?

So, what differences separate the boys from the girls? Men are reported to be more aggressive than women in a combative sense, but they are not necessarily more competitive. Men are more confident, perhaps recklessly so, and women may be too cautious. Men are not more likely to be cool under fire, but they are more likely to become aggressive regardless of what upsets them. Men are not more analytic in their thinking, nor women more intuitive, but men are better at solving mathematical problems, probably because they are better at spatial relationships. Finally, women are less interested in the responsibility and challenge of work, but only because they usually have jobs that offer little responsibility and challenge.

While this seems to be the gist of the matter, it leaves open the question of whether the differences are due to biology or to environment. Are

THE DEVELOPMENT OF THE "WEAKER SEX"
(AND THE DEMORALIZATION OF THE DUDE).

VASSAR GRADUATE.—"These are the dumb-bells I used last term in our gymnasium; won't one of you gentleman just put them up? It's awfully easy."

"All-male groups may be better at brainstorming, while all-female groups may be better at finding a solution."

men more aggressive because they are born that way or because of lessons that begin in the cradle? Are women less confident than men because different hormones course through their blood, or because for years people have told them that they can't expect much from themselves?

The research on the nature-nurture question is a candy store in which people of varying biases can quickly find something to their liking. Beryl Lieff Benderly, an anthropologist and journalist, critiqued the physiological research for her new book, *The Myth of Two Minds*. The title tells the story. She even challenges the notion that men are stronger than women. "The plain fact is that we have no idea whether men are 'naturally' stronger than women," she writes. Short of conducting an experiment along the lines of *Lord of the Flies*, we are unlikely to unravel the influences of nature and nurture to everyone's satisfaction. Nevertheless, research does offer hints about the ways that biology and environment affect stereotypical behavior. Take the case of aggression. There are any number of studies linking aggression to biological factors. Testosterone, a hormone found in much higher levels in men than in women, has been found in even larger quantities in criminally aggressive males. Castration, which decreases the level of testosterone, has been used for centuries to produce docile men and animals. And girls who have had prenatal exposure to high levels of testosterone are more tomboyish than other girls.

Yet biology is not quite destiny. In her famous *Six Cultures* study, the anthropologist Beatrice Whiting and her colleagues at Harvard University found that in each of the societies studied, boys were more aggressive than girls. But the researchers also found such wide cultural differences that the girls in a highly aggressive society were often more aggressive than the boys in another, less aggressive society.

The same mix of forces applies wherever we look. Biology may bend the twig in one direction, but the environment may bend it in another. But whether biology or environment ultimately wins the hearts and minds of researchers is less important than how the differences, wherever they come from, affect behavior in the workplace. If someone explodes in anger (or breaks down in tears) in the midst of delicate contract negotiations, it matters little to the stockholders whether the lost business can, in the end, be blamed on testosterone or bad toilet training. The more important question is, what are the implications of sex difference research for business?

What Difference Do the Differences Make?

The research on sex differences suggest three points that people in business can usefully consider. First, the differences between the sexes are small. Researchers look for "statistically significant" differences. But statistically significant differences are not necessarily practically significant. There is a great deal of overlap between the sexes on most characteristics and especially on the characteristics we have been considering. Men are, on average, better at solving mathematical problems, but there are many women who are far above the average man in this area. Women are, on average, less confident than men. But there are many men who doubt themselves far more than the average woman. A study of aggressiveness is illustrative. The psychologist D. Anthony Butterfield and the management expert Gary N. Powell had college students rate the ideal U.S. President on various characteristics, including aggressiveness. Then they had them rate people who were running for President and Vice President at the time: Ronald Reagan, Walter Mondale, George Bush, and Geraldine Ferraro. Researchers found that the ideal president was, among other things, aggressive. They also found that Geraldine Ferraro was judged more aggressive than the male candidates. The point is that it is impossible to predict individual qualities from group differences.

Indeed, Carol Jacklin suggests that differences in averages may give a quite distorted view of both sexes. She notes that while, on average, boys play more aggressively than girls, her research shows that the difference is due to a small number of very aggressive boys. Most of the boys are, in fact, very much like the girls. "I'd be willing to bet," Jacklin says, "that much of the difference in aggressiveness between men and women is due to a small number of extremely aggressive men—many of whom are in prison—and that the remaining men are no more aggressive than most women."

Second, different doesn't necessarily mean inferior. It is quite possible that feminine traits (in men or women) are assets in certain situations, while masculine traits may be advantageous in other situations. The psychologist Carol Gilligan, author of *In a Different Voice*, says that women are more comfortable with human relationships than men are, and this may sometimes give them an edge. For instance, Roderick Gilkey and Leonard Greenhalgh, psychologists at Dartmouth University, had business students simulate negotiations over the purchase of a used car and television advertising time. The women appeared better suited to the task than the men. They were more flexible, more willing to compromise, and less deceptive. "Women can usually come to an agreement on friendly terms," says Greenhalgh. "They're better at avoiding impasses."

In another study, the psychologist Wendy Wood of Texas A&M University asked college students to work on problems in groups of three.

"Biology
may bend the
twig in one
direction, but
the environment
may bend it in
another."

Some groups consisted only of men, others of women. The groups tried to solve problems such as identifying the features to consider in buying a house. The men, it turns out, came up with more ideas, while the women zeroed in on one good idea and developed it. Wood concluded that all-male groups might be better for brainstorming, while all-female groups might be better for finding the best solution to a problem.

Third, sometimes people lack the characteristics needed for a job until they are in the job. Jobs that offer responsibility and challenge, for example, tend to create a desire for more responsibility and challenge. While there are research studies to support this statement, an anecdote from the sociologist Rosabeth Moss Kanter is more telling. Linda, a secretary for 17 years in a large corporation, had no interest in being anything but a secretary, and when she was offered a promotion through an affirmative action program, she hesitated. Her boss persuaded her to take the job and she became a successful manager and loved the additional responsibility and challenge. She even set her sights on a vice president position. As a secretary, Linda would no doubt have scored near the female stereotype. But when she became a manager, she became more like the stereotypical male.

Kanter told that story a dozen years ago, but we are still struggling to learn its lesson. A discrimination case against Sears, Roebuck and Company recently made news. The Equal Employment Opportunity Commission (EEOC) argued that Sears discriminated against women because nearly all of the employees in the company who sell on commission are men. Sears presented evidence that women expressed little interest in commission-sales work, preferring the less risky jobs in salaried sales. In the original decision favoring Sears, the U.S. District Court had found that "noncommission saleswomen were generally happier with their present jobs at Sears, and were much less likely than their male counterparts to be interested in other positions, such as commission sales. . . ." But in the U.S. Court of Appeals, Appellate Judge Cudahy, who dissented in part from the majority, wrote that this reasoning is "of a piece with the proposition that women are by nature happier cooking, doing the laundry, and chauffeuring the children to softball games than arguing appeals or selling stocks."

The point is not that employees must be made to accept more responsible positions for their own good, even if it is against their will. The point is that business should abandon the stereotypes that lock men and women into different, and often unequal, kinds of work. If it finally does, it will discover the necessity—and value—of finding ways of enticing men and women into jobs for which, according to the stereotypes, they are not suited. If business doesn't do that, it may discover that differences between men and women really do separate the sexes.

The hidden obstacles to black success.

RUMORS OF INFERIORITY

Jeff Howard and Ray Hammond

Jeff Howard is a social psychologist; Ray Hammond is a physician and ordained minister.

TODAY'S black Americans are the beneficiaries of great historical achievements. Our ancestors managed to survive the brutality of slavery and the long history of oppression that followed emancipation. Early in this century they began dismantling the legal structure of segregation that had kept us out of the institutions of American society. In the 1960s they launched the civil rights movement, one of the most effective mass movements for social justice in history. Not all of the battles have been won, but there is no denying the magnitude of our predecessors' achievement.

Nevertheless, black Americans today face deteriorating conditions in sharp contrast to other American groups. The black poverty rate is triple that of whites, and the unemployment rate is double. Black infant mortality not only is double that of whites, but may be rising for the first time in a decade. We have reached the point where more than half of the black children born in this country are born out of wedlock—most to teenage parents. Blacks account for more than 40 percent of the inmates in federal and state prisons, and in 1982 the probability of being murdered was six times greater for blacks than for whites. The officially acknowledged high school dropout rate in many metropolitan areas is more than 30 percent. Some knowledgeable observers say it is over 50 percent in several major cities. These problems

not only reflect the current depressed state of black America, but also impose obstacles to future advancement.

The racism, discrimination, and oppression that black people have suffered and continue to suffer are clearly at the root of many of today's problems. Nevertheless, our analysis takes off from a forward-looking, and we believe optimistic, note: we are convinced that black people today, because of the gains in education, economic status, and political leverage that we have won as a result of the civil rights movement, are in a position to substantially improve the conditions of our communities using the resources already at our disposal. Our thesis is simple: the progress of any group is affected not only by public policy and by the racial attitudes of society as a whole, but by that group's capacity to exploit its own strengths. Our concern is about factors that prevent black Americans from using those strengths.

It's important to distinguish between the specific circumstances a group faces and its capacity to marshal its own resources to change those circumstances. Solving the problems of black communities requires a focus on the factors that hinder black people from more effectively managing their own circumstances. What are some of these factors?

Intellectual Development. Intellectual development is the primary focus of this article because it is the key to success in American society. Black people traditionally have understood this. Previous generations decided that segregation had to go because it relegated blacks to the backwater of American society, effectively denying us the opportunities, exposure, and competition that form the basis of intellectual development. Black intellectual development was one of the major benefits expected from newly won access to American institutions. That development, in turn, was expected to be a foundation for future advancement.

YET NOW, three decades after *Brown v. Board of Education*, there is pervasive evidence of real problems in the intellectual performance of many black people. From astronomical high school dropout rates among the poor to substandard academic and professional performance among those most privileged, there is a disturbing consistency in reports of lagging development. While some black people perform at the highest levels in every field of endeavor, the percentages who do so are small. Deficiencies in the process of intellectual development are one effect of the long-term suppression of a people; they are also, we believe, one of the chief causes of continued social and economic underdevelopment. Intellectual underdevelopment is one of the most pernicious effects of racism, because it limits the people's ability to solve problems over which they are capable of exercising substantial control.

Black Americans are understandably sensitive about discussions of the data on our performance, since this kind of information has been used too often to justify attacks on affirmative action and other government efforts to improve the position of blacks and other minorities. Nevertheless, the importance of this issue demands that black people and all others interested in social justice overcome our sensitivities, analyze the problem, and search for solutions.

The Performance Gap. Measuring intellectual performance requires making a comparison. The comparison may be with the performance of others in the same situation, or with some established standard of excellence, or both. It is typically measured by grades, job performance ratings, and scores on standardized and professional tests. In recent years a flood of articles, scholarly papers, and books have documented an intellectual performance gap between blacks and the population as a whole.
• In 1982 the College Board, for the first time in its history, published data on the performance of various groups on the Scholastic Aptitude Test (SAT). The difference between the combined median scores of blacks and whites on the verbal and math portions of the SAT was slightly more than 200 points. Differences in family income don't explain the gap. Even at incomes over $50,000, there remained a 120-point difference. These differences persisted in the next two years.
• In 1983 the NCAA proposed a requirement that all college athletic recruits have a high school grade-point average of at least 2.0 (out of a maximum of 4.0) and a minimum combined SAT score of 700. This rule, intended to prevent the exploitation of young athletes, was strongly opposed by black college presidents and civil rights leaders. They were painfully aware that in recent years less than half of all black students have achieved a combined score of 700 on the SAT.
• Asian-Americans consistently produce a median SAT

score 140 to 150 points higher than blacks with the same family income.
• The pass rate for black police officers on New York City's sergeant's exam is 1.6 percent. For Hispanics, it's 4.4 percent. For whites, it's 10.6 percent. These are the results *after* $500,000 was spent, by court order, to produce a test that was job-related and nondiscriminatory. No one, even those alleging discrimination, could explain how the revised test was biased.
• Florida gives a test to all candidates for teaching positions. The pass rate for whites is more than 80 percent. For blacks, it's 35 percent to 40 percent.

This is just a sampling. All these reports demonstrate a real difference between the performance of blacks and other groups. Many of the results cannot be easily explained by socioeconomic differences or minority status per se.

WHAT IS the explanation? Clear thinking about this is inhibited by the tendency to equate performance with ability. Acknowledging the performance gap is, in many minds, tantamount to inferring that blacks are intellectually inferior. But inferior performance and inferior ability are not the same thing. Rather, the performance gap is largely a behavioral problem. It is the result of a remediable tendency to avoid intellectual engagement and competition. Avoidance is rooted in the fears and self-doubt engendered by a major legacy of American racism: the strong negative stereotypes about black intellectual capabilities. Avoidance of intellectual competition is manifested most obviously in the attitudes of many black youths toward academic work, but it is not limited to children. It affects the intellectual performance of black people of all ages and feeds public doubts about black intellectual ability.

I. INTELLECTUAL DEVELOPMENT

The performance gap damages the self-confidence of many black people. Black students and professional people cannot help but be bothered by poor showings in competitive academic and professional situations. Black leaders too often have tried to explain away these problems by blaming racism or cultural bias in the tests themselves. These factors haven't disappeared. But for many middle-class black Americans who have had access to educational and economic opportunities for nearly 20 years, the traditional protestations of cultural deprivation and educational disadvantage ring hollow. Given the cultural and educational advantages that many black people now enjoy, the claim that all blacks should be exempt from the performance standards applied to others is interpreted as a tacit admission of inferiority. This admission adds further weight to the questions, in our own minds and in the minds of others, about black intelligence.

The traditional explanations—laziness or inferiority on the one hand; racism, discrimination, and biased tests on the other—are inaccurate and unhelpful. What is required is an explanation that accounts for the subtle influences people exert over the behavior and self-confidence of other people.

Developing an explanation that might serve as a basis for corrective action is important. The record of the last 20 years suggests that waiting for grand initiatives from the outside to save the black community is futile. Blacks will have to rely on our own ingenuity and resources. We need local and national political leaders. We need skilled administrators and creative business executives. We need a broad base of well-educated volunteers and successful people in all fields as role models for black youths. In short, we need a large number of sophisticated, intellectually developed people who are confident of their ability to operate on an equal level with anyone. Chronic mediocre intellectual performance is deeply troubling because it suggests that we are not developing enough such people.

The Competitive Process. Intellectual development is not a fixed asset that you either have or don't have. Nor is it based on magic. It is a process of expanding mental strength and reach. The development process is demanding. It requires time, discipline, and intense effort. It almost always involves competition as well. Successful groups place high value on intellectual performance. They encourage the drive to excel and use competition to sharpen skills and stimulate development in each succeeding generation. The developed people that result from this competitive process become the pool from which leadership of all kinds is drawn. Competition, in other words, is an essential spur to development.

Competition is clearly not the whole story. Cooperation and solitary study are valuable, too. But of the various keys to intellectual development, competition seems to fare worst in the estimation of many blacks. Black young people, in particular, seem to place a strong negative value on intellectual competition.

Black people have proved to be very competitive at some activities, particularly sports and entertainment. It is our sense, however, that many blacks consider intellectual competition to be inappropriate. It appears to inspire little interest or respect among many youthful peer groups. Often, in fact, it is labeled "grade grubbing," and gives way to sports and social activity as a basis for peer acceptance. The intellectual performance gap is one result of this retreat from competition.

II. THE PSYCHOLOGY OF PERFORMANCE

Rumors of Inferiority. The need to avoid intellectual competition is a psychological reaction to an image of black intellectual inferiority that has been projected by the larger society, and to a less than conscious process of internalization of that image by black people over the generations.

The rumor of black intellectual inferiority has been around for a long time. It has been based on grounds as diverse as twisted biblical citations, dubious philosophical arguments, and unscientific measurements of skull capacity. The latest emergence of this old theme has been in the controversy over race and IQ. For 15 years newsmagazines and television talk shows have enthusiastically taken up the topic of black intellectual endowment. We have watched authors and critics debate the proposition that blacks are genetically inferior to whites in intellectual capability.

Genetic explanations have a chilling finality. The ignorant can be educated, the lazy can be motivated, but what can be done for the individual thought to have been born without the basic equipment necessary to compete or develop? Of course the allegation of genetic inferiority has been hotly disputed. But the debate has touched the consciousness of most Americans. We are convinced that this spectacle has negatively affected the way both blacks and whites think about the intellectual capabilities of black people. It also has affected the way blacks behave in intellectually competitive situations. The general expectation of black intellectual inferiority, and the fear this expectation generates, cause many black people to avoid intellectual competition.

OUR HYPOTHESIS, in short, is this. (1) Black performance problems are caused in large part by a tendency to avoid intellectual competition. (2) This tendency is a psychological phenomenon that arises when the larger society projects an image of black intellectual inferiority and when that image is internalized by black people. (3) Imputing intellectual inferiority to genetic causes, especially in the face of data confirming poorer performance, intensifies the fears and doubts that surround this issue.

Clearly the image of inferiority continues to be projected. The internalization of this image by black people is harder to prove empirically. But there is abundant evidence in the expressed attitudes of many black youths toward intellectual competition; in the inability of most black communities to inspire the same commitment to intellectual excellence that is routinely accorded athletics and entertainment; and in the fact of the performance gap itself—especially when that gap persists among the children of economically and educationally privileged households.

Expectancies and Performance. The problem of black intellectual performance is rooted in human sensitivity to a particular kind of social interaction known as "expectancy communications." These are expressions of belief—verbal or nonverbal—from one person to another about the kind of performance to be expected. "Mary, you're one of the best workers we have, so I know that you won't have any trouble with this assignment." Or, "Joe, since everyone else is busy with other work, do as much as you can on this. When you run into trouble, call Mary." The first is a positive expectancy; the second, a negative expectancy.

Years of research have clearly demonstrated the powerful impact of expectancies on performance. The expectations of teachers for their students have a large effect on academic achievement. Psychological studies under a variety of circumstances demonstrate that communicated expectations induce people to believe that they will do well or poorly at a task, and that such beliefs very often trigger responses that result in performance consistent with the expectation. There is also evidence that "reference group expectancies"—directed at an entire category of people rather than a particular individual—have a similar impact on the performance of members of the group.

EXPECTANCIES do not always work. If they come from a questionable source or if they predict an outcome that is too inconsistent with previous experience, they won't have much effect. Only credible expectancies—those that come from a source considered reliable and that address a belief or doubt the performer is sensitive to—will have a self-fulfilling impact.

The widespread expectation of black intellectual inferiority—communicated constantly through the projection of stereotyped images, verbal and nonverbal exchanges in daily interaction, and the incessant debate about genetics and intelligence—represents a credible reference-group expectancy. The message of the race/IQ controversy is: "We have scientific evidence that blacks, because of genetic inadequacies, can't be expected to do well at tasks that require great intelligence." As an explanation for past black intellectual performance, the notion of genetic inferiority is absolutely incorrect. As an expectancy communication exerting control over our present intellectual strivings, it has been powerfully effective. These expectancies raise fear and self-doubt in the minds of many blacks, especially when they are young and vulnerable. This has resulted in avoidance of intellectual activity and chronic underperformance by many of our most talented people. Let us explore this process in more detail.

The Expectancy/Performance Model. The powerful effect of expectancies on performance has been proved, but the way the process works is less well understood. Expectancies affect behavior, we think, in two ways. They affect performance behavior: the capacity to marshal the sharpness and intensity required for competitive success. And they influence cognition: the mental processes by which people make sense of everyday life.

Behavior. As anyone who has experienced an "off day" knows, effort is variable; it is subject to biological cycles, emotional states, motivation. Most important for our discussion, it depends on levels of confidence going into a task. Credible expectancies influence performance behavior. They affect the intensity of effort, the level of concentration or distractibility, and the willingness to take reasonable risks—a key factor in the development of self-confidence and new skills.

Cognition. Expectations also influence the way people think about or explain their performance outcomes. These explanations are called "attributions." Research in social psychology has demonstrated that the causes to which people attribute their successes and failures have an important impact on subsequent performance.

All of us encounter failure. But a failure we have been led to expect affects us differently from an unexpected failure. When people who are confident of doing well at a task are confronted with unexpected failure, they tend to attribute the failure to inadequate effort. The likely response to another encounter with the same or a similar task is to work harder. People who come into a task expecting to fail, on the other hand, attribute their failure to lack of ability. Once you admit to yourself, in effect, that "I don't have what it takes," you are not likely to approach that task again with great vigor.

Indeed, those who attribute their failures to inadequate effort are likely to conclude that more effort will produce a better outcome. This triggers an adaptive response to failure. In contrast, those who have been led to expect failure will attribute their failures to lack of ability, and will find it difficult to rationalize the investment of greater effort. They will often hesitate to continue "banging my head against the wall." They often, in fact, feel depressed when they attempt to work, since each attempt represents a confrontation with their own feared inadequacy.

THIS COMBINED EFFECT on behavior and cognition is what makes expectancy so powerful. The negative expectancy first tends to generate failure through its impact on behavior, and then induces the individual to blame the failure on lack of ability, rather than the actual (and correctable) problem of inadequate effort. This misattribution in turn becomes the basis for a new negative expectancy. By this process the individual, in effect, internalizes the low estimation originally held by others. This internalized negative expectancy powerfully affects future competitive behavior and future results.

The process we describe is not limited to black people. It goes on all the time, with individuals from all groups. It helps to explain the superiority of some groups at some areas of endeavor, and the mediocrity of those same groups in other areas. What makes black people unique is that they are singled out for the stigma of genetic intellectual inferiority.

The expectation of intellectual inferiority accompanies a black person into each new intellectual situation. Since each of us enters these tests under the cloud of predicted failure, and since each failure reinforces doubts about our capabilities, all intellectual competition raises the specter of having to admit a lack of intellectual capacity. But this particular expectancy goes beyond simply predicting and inducing failure. The expectancy message explicitly ascribes the expected failure to genes, and amounts to an open suggestion to black people to understand any failure in intellectual activity as confirmation of genetic inferiority. Each engagement in intellectual competition carries the weight of a test of one's own genetic endowment and that of black people as a whole. Facing such a terrible prospect, many black people recoil from any situation where the rumor of inferiority might be proved true.

For many black students this avoidance manifests itself in a concentration on athletics and socializing, at the expense of more challenging (and anxiety-provoking) academic work. For black professionals, it may involve a tendency to shy away from competitive situations or projects, or an inability to muster the intensity—or commit the time—necessary to excel. This sort of thinking and behavior certainly does not characterize all black people in competitive settings. But it is characteristic of enough to be a serious problem. When it happens, it should be understood as a less than conscious reaction to the psychological burden of the terrible rumor.

The Intellectual Inferiority Game. There always have been constraints on the intellectual exposure and development of black people in the United States, from laws prohibiting the education of blacks during slavery to the Jim Crow laws and "separate but equal" educational arrangements that persisted until very recently. In dismantling these legal barriers to development, the civil rights movement fundamentally transformed the possibilities for black people. Now, to realize those possibilities, we must address the mental barriers to competition and performance.

The doctrine of intellectual inferiority acts on many black Americans the way that a "con" or a "hustle" like three-card monte acts on its victim. It is a subtle psychological input that interacts with characteristics of the human cognitive apparatus—in this case, the extreme sensitivity to expectancies—to generate self-defeating behavior and thought processes. It has reduced the intellectual performance of millions of black people.

Intellectual inferiority, like segregation, is a destructive idea whose time has passed. Like segregation, it must be removed as an influence in our lives. Among its other negative effects, fear of the terrible rumor has restricted discussion by all parties, and has limited our capacity to understand and improve our situation. But the intellectual inferiority game withers in the light of discussion and analysis. We must begin now to talk about intellectual performance, work through our expectations and fears of intellectual inferiority, consciously define more adaptive attitudes toward intellectual development, and build our confidence in the capabilities of all people.

THE expectancy/performance process works both ways. Credible positive expectancies can generate self-confidence and result in success. An important part of the solution to black performance problems is converting the negative expectancies that work against black development into positive expectancies that nurture it. We must overcome our fears, encourage competition, and support the kind of performance that will dispel the notion of black intellectual inferiority.

III. The Commitment to Development

In our work with black high school and college students and with black professionals, we have shown that education in the psychology of performance can produce strong performance improvement very quickly. Black America needs a nationwide effort, now, to ensure that all black people—but especially black youths— are free to express their intellectual gifts. That effort should be built on three basic elements:

• Deliberate control of expectancy communications. We must begin with the way we talk to one another: the messages we give and the expectations we set. This includes the verbal and nonverbal messages we communicate in day-to-day social intercourse, as well as the expectancies communicated through the educational process and media images.

• Definition of an "intellectual work ethic." Black communities must develop strong positive attitudes toward intellectual competition. We must teach our people, young and mature, the efficacy of intense, committed effort in the arena of intellectual activity and the techniques to develop discipline in study and work habits.

• Influencing thought processes. Teachers, parents, and other authority figures must encourage young blacks to attribute their intellectual successes to ability (thereby boosting confidence) and their failures to lack of effort. Failures must no longer destroy black children's confidence in their intelligence or in the efficacy of hard work. Failures should be seen instead as feedback indicating the need for more intense effort or for a different approach to the task.

The task that confronts us is no less challenging than the task that faced those Americans who dismantled segregation. To realize the possibilities presented by their achievement, we must silence, once and for all, the rumors of inferiority.

Who's Responsible? Expectations of black inferiority are communicated, consciously or unconsciously, by many whites, including teachers, managers, and those responsible for the often demeaning representations of blacks in the media. These expectations have sad consequences for many blacks, and those whose actions lead to such consequences may be held accountable for them. If the people who shape policy in the United States, from the White House to the local elementary school, do not address the problems of performance and development of blacks and other minorities, all Americans will face the consequences: instability, disharmony, and a national loss of the potential productivity of more than a quarter of the population.

However, when economic necessity and the demands of social justice compel us toward social change, those who have the most to gain from change—or the most to lose from its absence—should be responsible for pointing the way.

It is time that blacks recognize our own responsibility. When we react to the rumor of inferiority by avoiding intellectual engagement, and when we allow our children to do so, black people forfeit the opportunity for intellectual development that could extinguish the debate about our capacities, and set the stage for group progress. Blacks must hold ourselves accountable for the resulting waste of talent—and valuable time. Black people have everything to gain—in stature, self-esteem, and problem-solving capability—from a more aggressive and confident approach to intellectual competition. We must assume responsibility for our own performance and development.

BLACK CHILDREN, BLACK SPEECH

Black English is not just 'sloppy talk,' but a dialect with structure and form

Dorothy Z. Seymour

Dorothy Z. Seymour is an editorial specialist in linguistics for an educational publisher.

"Cmon, man, les git goin'!" called the boy to his companion. "Dat bell ringin'. It say, 'Git in rat now!' " He dashed into the school yard.

"Aw, f'get you," replied the other. "Whe' Richuh? Whe' da' muvvah? He be goin' to schoo'."

"He in de' now, man!" was the answer as they went through the door.

In the classroom they made for their desks and opened their books. The name of the story they tried to read was "Come." It went:

> Come, Bill, come.
> Come with me.
> Come and see this.
> See what is here.

The first boy poked the second. "Wha' da' wor'?"

"Da' wor' *is*, you dope."

"*Is*? Ain't no wor' *is*. You jivin' me? Wha' da' wor' mean?"

"Ah dunno. Jus' *is*."

To a speaker of Standard English, this exchange is only vaguely comprehensible. But it's normal speech for thousands of American children. In addition it demonstrates one of our biggest educational problems: children whose speech style is so different from the writing style of their books that they have difficulty learning to read. These children speak Black English, a dialect characteristic of many inner-city Negroes. Their books are, of course, written in Standard English. To complicate matters, the speech they use is also socially stigmatized. Middle-class whites and Negroes alike scorn it as low-class poor people's talk.

Teachers sometimes make the situation worse with their attitudes toward Black English. Typically, they view the children's speech as "bad English" characterized by "lazy pronunciation," "poor grammar," and "short, jagged words." One result of this attitude is poor mental health on the part of the pupils. A child is quick to grasp the feeling that while school speech is "good," his own speech is "bad," and that by extension he himself is somehow inadequate and without value. Some children react to this feeling by withdrawing; they stop talking entirely. Others develop the attitude of "F'get you, honky." In either case, the psychological results are devastating and lead straight to the dropout route.

It is hard for most teachers and middle-class Negro parents to accept the idea that Black English is not just "sloppy talk" but a dialect with a form and structure of its own. Even some eminent black educators think of it as "bad English grammar" with "slurred consonants" (Professor Nick Aaron Ford of Morgan State College in Baltimore) and "ghettoese" (Dr. Kenneth B. Clark, the prominent educational psychologist).

Parents of Negro school children generally agree. Two researchers at Columbia University report that the adults they worked with in Harlem almost unanimously preferred that their children be taught Standard English in school.

But there is another point of view, one held in common by black militants and some white liberals. They urge that middle-class Negroes stop thinking of the inner-city dialect as something to be ashamed of and repudiated. Black author Claude Brown, for example, pushes this view.

Some modern linguists take a similar stance. They begin with the premise that no dialect is intrinsically "bad" or "good," and that a nonstandard speech style is not defective speech but different speech. More important, they have been able to show that Black English is far from being a careless way of speaking the Standard; instead, it is rather a rigidly-constructed set

From *Commonweal*, November 19, 1987. Copyright © 1987 by Commonweal Foundation.

of speech patterns, with the same sort of specialization in sounds, structure, and vocabulary as any other dialect.

The Sounds of Black English

Middle-class listeners who hear black inner-city speakers say "dis" and "tin" for "this" and "thin" assume that the black speakers are just being careless. Not at all; these differences are characteristic aspects of the dialect. The original cause of such substitutions is generally a carryover from one's original language or that of his immigrant parents. The interference from that carryover probably caused the substitution of /d/ for the voiced *th* sound in *this*, and /t/ for the unvoiced *th* sound in *thin*. (Linguists represent language sounds by putting letters within slashes or brackets.) Most speakers of English don't realize that the two *th* sounds of English are lacking in many other languages and are difficult for most foreigners trying to learn English. Germans who study English, for example, are surprised and confused about these sounds because the only Germans who use them are the ones who lisp. These two sounds are almost nonexistent in the West African languages which most black immigrants brought with them to America.

Similar substitutions used in Black English are /f/, a sound similar to the unvoiced *th*, in medial word-position, as in *birfday* for *birthday*, and in final word-position, as in *roof* for *Ruth* as well as /v/ for the voiced *th* in medial position, as in *bruvver* for *brother*. These sound substitutions are also typical of Gullah, the language of black speakers in the Carolina Sea Islands. Some of them are also heard in Caribbean Creole.

Another characteristic of the sounds of Black English is the lack of /l/ at the end of words, sometimes replaced by the sound /w/. This makes a word like *tool* sound like *too*. If /l/ occurs in the middle of a Standard English word, in Black English it may be omitted entirely: "I can hep you." This difference is probably caused by the instability and sometimes interchangeability of /l/ and /r/ in West African languages.

One difference that is startling to middle-class speakers is the fact that Black English words appear to leave off some consonant sounds at the end of words. Like Italian, Japanese and West African words, they are more likely to end in vowel sounds. Standard English *boot* is pronounced *boo* in Black English. *What* is *wha*. *Sure* is *sho*. *Your* is *yo*. This kind of difference can make for confusion in the classroom. Dr. Kenneth Goodman, a psycholinguist, tells of a black child whose white teacher asked him to use *so* in a sentence—not "sew a dress" but "the other *so*." The sentence the child used was "I got a *so* on my leg."

A related feature of Black English is the tendency in many cases not to use sequences of more than one final consonant sound. For example, *just* is pro-

nounced *jus'*, *past* is *pass*, *mend* sounds like *men* and *hold* like *hole*. *Six* and *box* are pronounced *sick* and *bock*. Why should this be? Perhaps because West African languages, like Japanese, have almost no clusters of consonants in their speech. The Japanese, when importing a foreign word, handle a similar problem by inserting vowel sounds between every consonant, making *baseball* sound like *besuboru*. West Africans probably made a simpler change, merely cutting a series of two consonant sounds down to one. Speakers of Gullah, one linguist found, have made the same kind of adaptation of Standard English.

Teachers of black children seldom understand the reason for these differences in final sounds. They are apt to think that careless speech is the cause. Actually, black speakers aren't "leaving off" any sounds; how can you leave off something you never had in the first place?

Differences in vowel sounds are also characteristic of the nonstandard language. Dr. Goodman reports that a black child asked his teacher how to spell rat. "R-a-t," she replied. But the boy responded "No ma'am, I don't mean rat mouse, I mean rat now." In Black English, *right* sounds like *rat*. A likely reason is that in West African languages, there are very few vowel sounds of the type heard in the word *right*. This type is common in English. It is called a glided or dipthongized vowel sound. A glided vowel sound is actually a close combination of two vowels; in the word *right* the two parts of the sound "eye" are actually "ah-ee." West African languages have no such long, two-part, changing vowel sounds; their vowels are generally shorter and more stable. This may be why in Black English, *time* sounds like *Tom*, *oil* like *all*, and *my* like *ma*.

Language Structure

Black English differs from Standard English not only in its sounds but also in its structure. The way the words are put together does not always fit the description in English grammar books. The method of expressing time, or tense, for example, differs in significant ways.

The verb *to be* is an important one in Standard English. It's used as an auxiliary verb to indicate different tenses. But Black English speakers use it quite differently. Sometimes an inner-city Negro says "He coming"; other times he says "He be coming." These two sentences mean different things. To understand why, let's look at the tense of West African languages; they correspond with those of Black English.

Many West African languages have a tense which is called the habitual. This tense is used to express action which is always occurring and it is formed with a verb that is translated as *be*. "He be coming" means something like "He's always coming," "He usually comes," or "He's been coming."

In Standard English there is no regular grammatical construction for such a tense. Black English speakers, in order to form the habitual tense in English, use the word *be* as an auxiliary: *He be doing it. My Momma be working. He be running.* The habitual tense is not the same as the present tense, which is constructed in Black English without any form of the verb *to be*: *He do it. My Momma working. He running.* (This means the action is occurring right now.)

There are other tense differences between Black English and Standard English. For example, the non-standard speech does not use changes in grammar to indicate the past tense. A white person will ask, "What did your brother say?" and the black person will answer, "He say he coming." (The verb *say* is not changed to *said*.) "How did you get here?" "I walk." This style of talking about the past is paralleled in the Yoruba, Fante, Hausa, and Ewe languages of West Africa.

Expression of plurality is another difference. The way a black child will talk of "them boy" or "two dog" makes some white listeners think Negroes don't know how to turn a singular word into plural word. As a matter of fact, it isn't necessary to use an *s* to express plurality. In Chinese and Japanese, singular and plural are not generally distinguished by such inflections; plurality is conveyed in other ways. For example, in Chinese it's correct to say "There are three book on the table." This sentence already has two signals of the plural, *three* and *are*; why require a third? This same logic is the basis of plurals in most West African languages, where nouns are often identical in the plural and the singular. For example, in Ibo, one correctly says *those man*, and in both Ewe and Yoruba one says *they house*. American speakers of Gullah retain this style; it is correct in Gullah to say *five dog*.

Gender is another aspect of language structure where differences can be found. Speakers of Standard English are often confused to find that the nonstandard vernacular often uses just one gender of pronoun, the masculine, and refers to women as well as men as *he* or *him*. "He a nice girl," even "Him a nice girl" are common. This usage probably stems from West African origins, too, as does the use of multiple negatives, such as "Nobody don't know it."

Vocabulary is the third aspect of a person's native speech that could affect his learning of a new language. The strikingly different vocabulary often used in Negro Non-standard English is probably the most obvious aspect of it to a casual white observer. But its vocabulary differences don't obscure its meaning the way different sounds and different structure often do.

Recently there has been much interest in the African origins of words like *goober* (peanut), *cooter* (turtle), and *tote* (carry), as well as others that are less certainly African, such as *to dig* (possibly from the Wolof *degan*, "to understand"). Such expressions seem colorful rather than low-class to many whites; they become assimilated faster than their black originators do. English professors now use *dig* in their scholarly articles, and current advertising has enthusiastically adopted *rap*.

Is it really possible for old differences in sound, structure, and vocabulary to persist from the West African languages of slave days into present-day inner city Black English? Easily. Nothing else really explains such regularity of language habits, most of which persist among black people in various parts of the Western Hemisphere. For a long time scholars believed that certain speech forms used by Negroes were merely leftovers from archaic English preserved in the speech of early English settlers in America and copied by their slaves. But this theory has been greatly weakened, largely as the result of the work of a black linguist, Dr. Lorenzo Dow Turner of the University of Chicago. Dr. Turner studied the speech of Gullah Negroes in the Sea Islands off the Carolina coast and found so many traces of West African languages that he thoroughly discredited the archaic-English theory.

When anyone learns a new language, it's usual to try speaking the new language with the sounds and structure of the old. If a person's first language does not happen to have a particular sound needed in the language he is learning, he will tend to substitute a similar or related sound from his native language and use it to speak the new one. When Frenchman Charles Boyer said "Zees ees my heart," and when Latin American Carmen Miranda sang "Souse American way," they were simply using sounds of their native languages in trying to pronounce sounds of English. West Africans must have done the same thing when they first attempted English words. The tendency to retain the structure of the native language is a strong one, too. That's why a German learning English is likely to put his verb at the end: "May I a glass beer have?" The vocabulary of one's original language may also furnish some holdovers. Jewish immigrants did not stop using the word *bagel* when they came to America; nor did Germans stop saying *sauerkraut*.

Social and geographical isolation reinforces the tendencies to retain old language habits. When one group is considered inferior, the other group avoids it. For many years it was illegal to give any sort of instruction to Negroes, and for slaves to try to speak like their masters would have been unthinkable. Conflict of value systems doubtless retards changes, too. As Frantz Fanon observed in *Black Skin, White Masks*, those who take on white speech habits are suspect in the ghetto, because others believe they are trying to "act white." Dr. Kenneth Johnson, a black linguist, put it this way: "As long as disadvantaged black children live in segregated communities and most of their relationships are confined to those within their own subculture, they will not replace their functional nonstandard dialect with the nonfunctional standard dialect."

Linguists have made it clear that language systems that are different are not necessarily deficient. A judgment of deficiency can be made only in comparison with another language system. Let's turn the tables on Standard English for a moment and look at it from the West African point of view. From this angle, Standard English: (1) is lacking in certain language sounds, (2) has a couple of unnecessary language sounds for which others may serve as good substitutes, (3) doubles and drawls some of its vowel sounds in sequences that are unusual and difficult to imitate, (5) lacks a method of forming an important tense, (6) requires an unnecessary number of ways to indicate tense, plurality and gender, and (7) doesn't mark negatives sufficiently for the result to be a good strong negative statement.

Now whose language is deficient?

How would the adoption of this point of view help us? Say we accepted the evidence that Black English is not just a sloppy Standard but an organized language style which probably has developed many of its features on the basis of its West African heritage. What would we gain?

The psychological climate of the classroom might improve if teachers understood why many black students speak as they do. But we still have not reached a solution of the main problem. Does the discovery that Black English has pattern and structure mean that it should not be tampered with? Should children who speak Black English be excused from learning the Standard in school? Should they perhaps be given books in Black English to learn from?

Any such accommodation would surely result in a hardening of the new separatism being urged by some black militants. It would probably be applauded by such people as Roy Innis, Director of C.O.R.E., who is currently recommending dual autonomous education systems for white and black. And it might facilitate learning to read, since some experiments have indicated that materials written in Black English syntax aid problem readers from the inner city.

But determined resistance to the introduction of such printed materials into schools can be expected. To those who view inner-city speech as bad English, the appearance in print of sentences like "My mama, he work" can be as shocking and repellent as a four-letter word. Middle-class Negro parents would probably mobilize against the move. Any strategem that does not take into account such practicalities of the matter is probably doomed to failure. And besides, where would such a permissive policy on language get these children in the larger society, and in the long run? If they want to enter an integrated America they must be able to deal with it on its own terms. Even Professor Toni Cade of Rutgers, who doesn't want "ghetto accents" tampered with, advocates mastery of Standard English because, as she puts it, "if you want to get ahead in this country, you must master the language of the ruling class." This has always been true, wherever there has been a minority group.

The problem then appears to be one of giving these children the ability to speak (and read) Standard English without denigrating the vernacular and those who use it, or even affecting the ability to use it. The only way to do this is to officially espouse bi-dialectism. The result would be the ability to use either dialect equally well—as Dr. Martin Luther King did—depending on the time, place, and circumstances. Pupils would have to learn enough about Standard English to use it when necessary, and teachers would have to learn enough about the inner-city dialect to understand and accept it for what it is—not just a "careless" version of Standard English but a different form of English that's appropriate in certain times and places.

Can we accomplish this? If we can't, the result will be continued alienation of a large section of the population, continued dropout trouble with consequent loss of earning power and economic contribution to the nation, but most of all, loss of faith in America as a place where a minority people can at times continue to use those habits that remind them of their link with each other and with their past.

Television and Behavior

Research Conclusions of the

1982 NIMH Report and Their Policy Implications

Eli A. Rubinstein
University of North Carolina

ABSTRACT: Research on television and behavior in the 1970s has recently been reviewed and evaluated in a two-volume report from the National Institute of Mental Health. The general conclusion is that television is an important influence on child development in ways well beyond earlier findings that focused on violence and aggression. Despite these findings, no industry change seems forthcoming and none is likely until some continuing process is developed for translating knowledge into action.

In early 1980, the National Institute of Mental Health (NIMH) initiated an examination and assessment of the relevant scientific literature that had accumulated in the decade since the 1972 Surgeon General's Report on Television and Social Behavior. With the aid of an outside group of advisors, the NIMH commissioned 24 comprehensive review papers on major areas of active research in the field. The emphasis was on entertainment television. Not included, therefore, was research on news programming or on political socialization. The review papers were prepared by scientists known to be expert in the topics they reviewed. In early 1982, this 10-year update was published in two volumes. A smaller summary volume presented an overview for the general public. The 24 technical reports were included in a second volume.

If any single statement epitomizes what was found it might be the following:

Television can no longer be considered as a casual part of daily life, as an electronic toy. Research findings have long since destroyed the illusion that television is merely innocuous entertainment. While the learning it provides is mainly incidental rather than direct and formal, it is a significant part of the total acculturation process. (NIMH, 1982, Vol. 1, p. 87)

That conclusion best summarizes what almost 20 years of research and more than 3,000 scientific studies have found. Getting to that generalization from the specific documentation has not been an easy task. Nor has this scientific consensus been without some strident criticism, mainly from television industry spokespersons.

Even accepting that consensus, a much more difficult task remains largely to be accomplished: determining how to use the scientific findings for the betterment of television and its viewers. I will return to that issue at the end of this article.

What are the major research findings that document the conclusion that television is now a significant influence on child development? The 10-year update of the 1972 Report to the Surgeon General divides the research output of the past decade into five major categories: cognitive and affective aspects of television; violence and aggression; social beliefs and social behavior; television and social relations; and television and health. In addition, the update looks at the role of television in American society.

The research activity in each of these areas varies considerably. As might be expected, much emphasis has continued on the issue of violence and aggression. This is partially due to the stimulus from the original 1972 report, which was devoted almost entirely to this topic. In contrast to that earlier focus, research has now moved much beyond the violence theme and has begun to look at the broad panorama of possible interactions between the viewer and what is seen on the television screen. Indeed, perhaps the most significant development is just this shift from the relatively narrow confines of violence on television to the large perspective. A look at the variety of evidence is in order.

Violence and Aggression

The most widely publicized conclusion of the 1982 NIMH report was on televised violence. The press and the network news all had stories in early May 1982 which highlighted the finding that violence on television does lead to aggressive behavior by children.

Simultaneous with the media coverage of this aspect of the report, the television networks issued statements calling the report "inaccurate," without specifying what those inaccuracies were. Nor have

From *American Psychologist*, July 1983, pp. 820-825. Copyright © 1983 by the American Psychological Association, Inc.
Reprinted by permission.

the network officials subsequently identified those presumed flaws.[1]

Granted that the data are complex and that no single study unequivocally documents the connection between televised violence and later aggressive behavior, the convergence of evidence from many studies is overwhelming and was so interpreted in the NIMH report.

In the simplest terms, only three possibilities exist in this equation. (1) Television has no significant relationship to aggressive behavior. (2) Television reduces aggressive behavior. (3) Television increases aggressive behavior. Almost all of the studies reviewed in the past decade support the third possibility. No studies of any consequence support the second possibility. Both in the original report to the Surgeon General and in the 10-year update, this so-called catharsis theory was repudiated.

What remains as a troubling question comes from the handful of studies concluding that television has no significant relationship to aggressive behavior. Indeed, the most recent and most comprehensive study supporting the no-relationship finding is included in the NIMH report (Milavsky, Kessler, Stipp, & Rubens, 1982). Based on a panel survey of more than 3,000 children over a three-year period, these researchers concluded that no evidence emerged which "causally implicated" televised violence in the development of aggressive behavior. That conclusion and the original data from the research will probably be reexamined by other researchers. Controversial interpretations are likely.

What is self-evident in this situation, as with other complicated scientific questions, is that research is almost never unequivocal in its interpretation. Nevertheless, this major research finding of the NIMH report regarding the linkage of televised violence to later aggressive behavior clearly represents the position of the great majority of scientists working in this field. The burden of proof to contradict this conclusion is yet to be met.

It is worth commenting on the media coverage and the industry response to the report for a number of reasons. First of all, despite the fact that the issue of violence occupied only 9 pages in the 94-page summary report, almost all of the media attention was on that topic. Neither the general press nor the television news gave more than passing reference to the bulk of the research findings discussed in the rest of the 10-year update.

The television industry response is especially intriguing in light of its reaction 10 years earlier when the original report to the Surgeon General was published. At that time, the conclusion in the report was also that there was evidence of a causal relationship between television viewing and later aggressive behavior. That conclusion was widely misinterpreted in the press because of an erroneous *New York Times* headline indicating that no such link had been found. At congressional hearings in 1972, subsequent to the public furor over this misinterpretation, network officials all acknowledged the importance of the scientific evidence and promised to reduce levels of violence in the future. (As the 10-year update reports, no significant reduction in violence levels actually took place.)

In the press coverage of the 10-year update, the linkage conclusion was correctly reported. Despite—or perhaps because of—that correct media interpretation, the network response this time has essentially been one of denial. It remains to be seen if further research and/or public pressure will induce a change in that industry stance.

Cognitive and Affective Aspects of Television

Another area of research that has received much scientific attention over the past decade involves how the cognitive and emotional development in children modifies or influences their response to television. It has long been recognized that children do not see or understand what is viewed on the television screen in the same way that an adult does. Much recent research has been devoted to analyzing what changes in attention and comprehension occur as the age of the viewer increases from that of preschooler all the way through adolescence.

The research reviewed in the NIMH report clearly documents that first- and second-grade children are not yet able to follow a complex plot-line through the entire sequence of discrete scenes. An important corollary of this finding is that young children are often unable to relate a series of complex actions to their final consequence. Thus, when industry spokespersons claim that their programs are fundamentally prosocial because good ultimately triumphs over bad, they ignore this important finding. The young child is much less likely to make the interpretive connection and, therefore, less likely to learn the moral lesson.

The entire process of growing up with television means that not only do children perceive differently at different stages of development, but those stages of development are themselves influenced by extensive television viewing. For example, in what ways

---

[1] Shortly after the final preparation of this article, the American Broadcasting Companies, Inc., published a critique called, "A Research Perspective on Television and Violence," which presents, in a 32-page brochure, an industry position on the research findings. Unlike the NIMH report, the ABC commentary makes no reference whatsoever to the larger body of research within which the violence issue is only one part. Even if one ignores some questionable logic and accepts a highly selective set of references, nothing in this response refutes the major NIMH findings and conclusion that television teaches. In attempting to contradict the research conclusions on violence—and by calling the evidence "correlational"—the ABC statement sounds remarkably like that of the tobacco industry in its position on the scientific evidence about smoking and health. The reader is invited to decide independently by obtaining a copy of the brochure from the American Broadcasting Companies. Undoubtedly, more extended and detailed replies to the ABC statement will be forthcoming.

do the structural forms of television influence the way children process information? And in what ways do aspects of form influence how content is perceived? Research on these and other questions is still in its early stages but already reveals important findings. Children's attention is heightened by lively music, sound effects, special visual effects, high levels of physical activity or action, and rapid changes in scene. If that sounds like the description of a television commercial, it is only because the producers of television commercials have long since known what the researchers are now finding out.

What is important in these and other findings about the effects of structural form is that these findings add a new dimension to the understanding of television effects. It may be, as some research suggests, that aggression can be stimulated by high levels of action even without high violent content. Or it could be that children, already associating high action with high violence, respond to the former even when the latter is not present.

Another area of research in which content per se is not the focus of concern involves the concept of arousal. Findings suggest that some television viewing can heighten a state of general arousal. This increased level of excitement may then be channeled into various behaviors, including aggression, depending on the existing circumstances. Thus, exciting television programming, regardless of specific content, may induce certain behaviors. Even though we have no evidence of any long-term effects of high arousal, it is not inappropriate to ask if the excitatory influence of television viewing has any effect on the child's response to other less exciting stimuli in the child's environment. Are the child's expectations of excitement, enhanced by television, unmet in the classroom? And, if so, what are the consequences?

Research on the influence of television on emotional development is still in its early stages. It is clear that television viewing can produce emotional response. Does a continued arousal of emotions ultimately lead to decreased emotional response? Data are scarce, but it is an important question. Indeed, one of the most intriguing questions—for which no answer is presently available—involves the long-term effects of vicarious emotional experiences through television. The combined visual and auditory messages on television allow the young child to become involved in events not only long before any similar real-life experiences but in a range and diversity far beyond the ordinary realities. The effects of such vicarious experiences may or may not be cumulative and may or may not be significant. They are, however, different in quality and quantity from those experienced by children growing up in pre-television times. Are today's children becoming emotionally "adulterated"?

The effects of television viewing on educational achievement and aspiration have also received some attention. Findings are more suggestive than definitive. It does seem likely that heavy viewing relates inversely to school achievement. At the same time, heavy viewers with low IQs and/or from family settings in which intellectual stimulation is low may actually be learning more from television relevant to school subjects than they would without that input from television. High-IQ students who are heavy viewers may show less school aspirations. However, all of these relationships are complex and subject to other concurrent influences.

All of these findings on cognitive and emotional development, as they relate to television viewing, suggest a need for increased emphasis on teaching children critical television viewing skills. Research is only in its early stages in trying to educate both parents and children on how best to cope with this "anonymous teacher" in the home. Learning how television works may provide the best safeguard against its potentially negative effects and the best reinforcer for its potentially positive influence.

Social Beliefs and Social Behavior

Among the potentially damaging influences of television is the way it may shape the viewers' perceptions of the real world. Much concern has been raised about the racial and sexual stereotypes shown on television. Indeed, stereotypes of all kinds are common, including those of age and occupational role. To the extent that television shows minority groups in demeaning roles, women in excessively passive and subordinate positions, older people as senile and burdensome, or an overrepresentation of doctors, lawyers, police officers, or other professionals, the young viewer—especially the heavy viewer—is seeing a distorted image of the real world.

Even before the research began to show that stereotyping can influence the viewers' perceptions, efforts by coalitions among these various groups began to pressure for change. Ethnic groups, women's groups, and senior citizens' groups have all had some modest success in reducing the level of stereotyping.

A more subtle and perhaps pervasive research finding centers on how watching television affects how the viewer perceives the real world. A major area of research suggests that heavy viewers see the world as a mean and scary place, precisely because so many more mean and scary incidents take place on television than in the everyday experiences of most of us. Indeed, if many children identify with victims rather than aggressors on television, then the frightened feelings admitted by child viewers should be of even more general concern than the violence-aggression linkage.

But, even beyond this dark image of the world, the way television may shape our construction of social realities raises intriguing questions, many of which are still unanswered. If, as some would argue, television is a mirror of life, it may nonetheless, like Alice's looking-glass, have some curious and life-changing qualities.

4. FAMILY, SCHOOL, AND CULTURAL INFLUENCES: Cultural Influences

One area of research to which the television industry has paid some attention concerns the concept of prosocial behavior. Over the past decade, considerable research has investigated the obverse of the televised violence–aggression linkage. It is of significance to the aggression effect that programming which provides high levels of prosocial behavior can induce helping behavior in the viewer. These studies further document the strength of the general finding that observational learning takes place from television viewing.

Violence on television does lead to aggressive behavior by children

Both laboratory studies as well as field studies have consistently shown that such behavior as cooperation, friendliness, delay of gratification, and generosity can be enhanced by appropriate television programming. Furthermore, films and television can be used to help viewers cope with fears, whether those fears involve strange animals or fear of surgical procedures.

Finally, it comes as no surprise that academic research is now documenting what advertisers have long known: Television advertising socializes children toward active consumer roles.

Television and Social Relations

What do we know about the family as portrayed on television? More importantly, what, if anything, does television viewing do to family interactions?

These questions are partially answered by recent research. As might be suspected, family life on television is marked by much stereotypic portrayal of families. Whether it is a bumbling and inept father, precocious children, or the marked contrast between working-class and middle-class families, family life on television is either predominantly funny and simplistic or excessively tragic. More subtle themes reveal a strong effort toward upper mobility by children in the working-class families. None of this is inherently bad, of course, but it adds further to the conclusion that children watching television are being subjected to a variety of cultural stereotypes.

What is of greater importance may well be how families respond to and deal with this attention-getting member of the household. One body of research indicates that parents do not usually watch television with their children. Furthermore, even though parents have often expressed concern about the levels of violence and sex on television, there is relatively little parental control or supervision of their children's viewing.

The relative lack of parental attention or interaction is doubly unfortunate because recent research reveals that parental intervention through discussion can mitigate against negative effects of

viewing and also enhance positive effects. In this connection, it is encouraging that television programming now often includes public service announcements urging parents to watch with their children and to talk about what they see on television.

Television and Health

One area of recent attention that offers some interesting possibilities for a more constructive use of television viewing involves health-related television research.

Content analysis of television programming suggests that many subtle health messages are conveyed that are only beginning to be recognized as influential on the viewer. Relatively little smoking occurs on today's programs. In contrast, alcoholic use, both casual and heavy, is shown twice as often as drinking coffee or tea and many more times than the consumption of soft drinks. What do children learn from this beverage-drinking pattern, which is the inverse of real-life practice? What messages are conveyed when very few television characters buckle up their seat belts and when drivers are often exceeding the speed limits or otherwise demonstrating reckless driving?

In a more direct fashion, television has been used to mount health campaigns. To date, these campaigns have had mixed success. However, as research continues and better understanding develops as to the designing of health messages, future campaigns should prove more effective.

One recent research activity attempting to extend the uses of television in health matters relates to the problem of mental illness. The mentally ill, not incidentally, are often shown as dangerous and violent and rarely depicted in a sympathetic light. What about the uses of television by the mentally ill? Surveys of television viewing in mental institutions show such viewing to be an important dayroom activity. Based on that finding, research has been initiated to see if television viewing by disturbed children under full-time care in a psychiatric setting can serve as a modest therapeutic intervention. A one-year pilot field study suggests that a diet of prosocial programming not only can hold the children's attention but tends to reduce aggressive behavior.

These findings on institutionalized children carry some promise that other institutionalized individuals, such as those in homes for the aged, hospitals, and penal institutions, might also benefit from a more planned and tailored diet of television programming. Research in that direction may be one more constructive approach to a more productive use of this leisure-time activity.

The Role of Television in American Society

What is still missing in all the research on television and behavior over the past decade is a broad theoretical framework within which to conceptualize this body of knowledge. Obviously, many of these investigations can be subsumed under social learning theory. And yet, the fact that television markedly influences not just social learning but our social institutions—including the family, law, politics, and religion—suggests that it plays a unique role in American society and should be so viewed conceptually.

Lacking such a theoretical framework, scientists will still continue busily to examine the various phenomena that demarcate television's role in how we behave as individuals and as members of the many institutions within which we function. Eventually, we may be able to develop the broader constructs within which these various areas of investigation can become a more integrated set of findings.

What is also needed is a clearer understanding of the structural pressures and constraints within the television industry that have produced the programming that now exists. An examination of how the system works reveals a number of self-evident factors. Ratings and audience response strongly influence the quality and character of programs. Competition among the three networks, and now cable systems, puts great pressure on the production system. Furthermore, because all of this is part of a large bureaucratic enterprise, no individual or small group of individuals has full control over the development of programs. Neither the directors, producers, writers, nor television executives independently determine what appears on the television screen. Thus, when outside groups call for change, it becomes hard for the system to respond. And, finally, it is of no small significance that some of the groups calling for change may not be reflecting the tastes of the so-called mass audience of television.

Beyond the Research Findings

All of the inherent constraints notwithstanding, the research on television and behavior reflects both a problem and a potential for positive change. In one sense, the high visibility and continued emphasis on televised violence masks a larger issue. The concern is not merely a matter of reducing violent content. There is rather a need to see the totality of television viewing as a continuing form of informal education. Unfortunately, it is much easier to document this attribute of television than it is to point toward a feasible approach for making maximum use of the research findings.

Government regulations, even if the present Administration were so inclined, are probably undesirable. Not only are there First Amendment constraints, but control is not the road toward constructive change. What is needed is more creativity on the part of the industry and more discrimination on the part of the audience.

More creativity on the part of the industry is easy advice to give, but hard to specify. The response

and the responsibility must occur from within and not from external efforts. The industry now spends millions of dollars on audience research to determine which audiences will watch which programming. Program decisions are based almost solely on the mechanics of audience ratings. Ironically, the industry argument is that this gives the audience what they want. The result, however, is that new programming becomes inevitably derivative of past successes. Until some way out of this process is found, creativity will occur only rarely and then despite the system rather than because of it.

Audience discrimination and education are in their early development. The teaching of critical viewing skills is a step in that direction. Parental interest in what their children watch is part of the growing awareness that television is more than a handy baby-sitter. Greater efforts in this direction are being encouraged by citizens' groups and by the increasing number of articles on television and children in family publications.

Greater public attention to the limitations of television today and its potential for tomorrow is always helpful. The various citizens' groups help in this regard. Public discussions and publications such as this series of articles also help.

Perhaps the most critical lack remains the unavailability of some continuing process that can facilitate the translation of knowledge into action. With the publication of the 10-year update, a major body of knowledge is now available. The industry response is less than encouraging and will probably remain so without some new and long-range mechanism for change.

The officials at the three networks seem to perceive the research as irrelevant to their daily operational demands. The researchers consider those organizational problems as inconsequential to the scientific truth. Somewhere there must be a collaborative meeting ground. Ultimately, researchers must better understand and take into account the social realities of the television industry. Industry officials must accept and be responsive to the social realities of the researchers. Until those two social realities are brought into better conjunction, the viewer will receive less than the best that television has to offer.

REFERENCES

Milavsky, J. R., Kessler, R., Stipp, H., & Rubens, W. S. Television and aggression: Results of a panel study. In D. Pearl, L. Bouthilet, & J. Lazar (Eds.), *Television and behavior: Ten years of scientific progress and implications for the eighties* (Vol. 2). Washington, D.C.: U.S. Government Printing Office, 1982.

Pearl, D., Bouthilet, L., Lazar, J. (Eds.). *Television and behavior: Ten years of scientific progress and implications for the eighties* (Vols. 1 & 2). Washington, D.C.: U.S. Government Printing Office, 1982.

PROFILE BENJAMIN S. BLOOM

Master of Mastery

THIS 73-YEAR-OLD SCHOLAR IN A BUSINESS SUIT
WOULD GLADLY RUIN AMERICAN EDUCATION.

PAUL CHANCE

Paul Chance is a contributing editor of
Psychology Today.

"What are you working on now?" a friend asked. "An article on Benjamin Bloom," I replied. "Ah," she said, "the man who ruined American education."

The man who *ruined* American education? Could we be talking about the same person? Could she mean the Benjamin S. Bloom who is Charles H. Swift Distinguished Service Professor Emeritus in Education at the University of Chicago and professor of education at Northwestern University; one of the founders of the International Association for the Evaluation of Educational Achievement; the educator whose name is linked to some of the most popular educational buzzwords, including time-on-task, educational objectives and mastery learning? Could she be talking about *that* Benjamin Bloom?

The reason for my friend's comment is that much of the current back-to-basics movement in education is a revolt against the kinds of changes that Bloom and like-minded people have tried to bring about. Bloom thinks, for example, that there is too much drill, too much rote learning, too little active participation by students, too much emphasis on lower-level "basic" skills, too much attention to "minimum" standards, too much competition and, most of all, too much failure in today's schools. He believes that the current educational system is structurally flawed and should be thoroughly rehabilitated, like an old house that is in danger of collapsing and killing its occupants. In this sense, Bloom would gladly plead guilty to having tried to "ruin" American education.

Bloom does not look the part of an educational Karl Marx. If he were to show up at central casting, he would be pegged as Mr. Anyman, the butcher, the baker, the undertaker. But a man who could be accused of trying to tear down our nation's school system? Never.

But rebels rarely look the part; that's their disguise. If they looked like Jack Palance, we would be on guard. They look like Tevye, the harmless milkman in *Fiddler on the Roof*. So when you meet Benjamin Bloom and you see this 73-year-old scholar in a business suit sitting across a table talking about education in soft, loving tones, it is easy to miss the fact that he is a kind of quiet rebel. His antiestablishment views probably had their origin in his early days at the University of Chicago, where he has spent nearly all his professional life. After taking bachelor's and master's degrees from Pennsylvania State University, he went on to earn a Ph.D. in education at Chicago in 1942. He stayed on to become assistant to the University Examiner and later filled the position of Examiner.

It was the responsibility of the University Examiner to make up and administer the comprehensive examinations taken by all of the university's undergraduates. In that post, Bloom became part of a movement to shift the school's emphasis from teaching facts to teaching students how to use knowledge in solving problems.

Bloom soon discovered that some students were very poor problem-solvers and, with research assistant Lois Broder, undertook a study to determine why. They gave students problems like those on the comprehensive exams and had them work on them aloud. What the researchers learned was that the successful problem-solvers attacked problems in a systematic and analytical way, while the poor problem-solvers simply tried to recall a memorized answer. Bloom characterized the two approaches as active and passive. For instance, Bloom and Broder asked college students to answer this problem aloud: "Give the reasons which would have influenced a typical Virginia tobacco farmer to support the ratification of the Constitution in 1788, and the reasons which would have influenced him to oppose the ratification."

A good problem-solver, Ralph, gave an answer that went, in part, like this: "Well, what rights did the Constitution give him? Well . . . from the standpoint of money, which one would be more to his advantage? Well, prior to the Revolutionary War, he would have to pay taxes to England. . . . I think he would approve of it for patriotic reasons, and from the standpoint of money he wouldn't have to ship his tobacco to England. . . . he wouldn't have to pay the taxes."

A weaker problem-solver, George, gave an answer that went like this: ". . . Well, uh, to tell the truth I never had anything on [that] and at present I couldn't think of any."

Bloom and Broder concluded, "George probably has almost as much real knowledge about the Virginia tobacco farmer as Ralph. However, Ralph keeps working with what is given until he is able to give some semblance of a solution."

Besides identifying differences between successful and unsuccessful problem-solvers, Bloom and Broder found that they were able to teach weak problem-solvers the skills of their more successful classmates.

The Bloom and Broder study, published in 1950, became a classic of educational research. It demonstrated that "higher-level skills," skills that many psychologists and educators took to be largely inherited, could be taught. And it suggested that the wide variability in student achievement commonly seen in classrooms might not be inevitable, that the gap between the top and bottom of a given class might be substantially narrowed.

Our present educational system rests on the assumption that wide variability in achievement is largely the result of wide variability in innate learning ability. Most of us probably find little to quarrel with in this common-

BLOOM'S DICTUM: WHAT ONE STUDENT CAN LEARN, NEARLY ALL CAN LEARN.

sense assumption. A recent survey revealed, for instance, that most mothers in the United States believe that the principal ingredient in school success is the inborn talent of the youngster. Wide variability in student achievement is therefore natural and inevitable. Who can argue with that?

Bloom can. The work he and his colleagues have done over the past 40 years has convinced him that much of the variability seen in student performance is neither natural nor inevitable but the product of our educational system. Bloom admits that there are innate differences in learning ability, but he believes that these differences are much smaller than most of us imagine and do not account for the wide differences in student achievement. What might be called Bloom's dictum states: What one student can learn, nearly all students can learn.

Bloom points to studies of tutoring to support his view. He and his doctoral students have conducted studies in which tutored students are compared with those taught under conventional group instruction. They have found that the average tutored student learns more than do 98 percent of students taught in regular classes. They also found that 90 percent of the tutored students attained levels reached by only the top 20 percent of those in regular classes.

Tutoring shows that the vast majority of students are capable of doing outstanding work. But Bloom doesn't believe that tutoring is a practical approach to instruction: "We simply can't afford a student-to-teacher ratio of 1 to 1 or even 3 to 1." Over the past 25 years, Bloom and his colleagues have worked to develop a system of

group instruction that would approximate the effects of tutoring. The system is called mastery learning.

In mastery learning the teacher instructs the class in more or less the usual way, although Bloom likes teachers to involve the students more actively and reinforce their contributions more frequently. At the conclusion of an instructional unit (about every two weeks), the teacher gives a "formative test" to determine the need for "corrective instruction." The test is not used for grading but lets the teacher know what the students haven't yet learned.

The teacher studies the test results to identify common errors—points most students didn't get from the lesson. This material is then retaught, perhaps in a different way, to try to get the ideas across.

After this, the students work in groups of two or three for 20 to 30 minutes. The purpose of this group work is for the students to help one another on points they had missed on the formative test. The student who doesn't understand the procedure for dividing fractions asks classmates for help. If no one in the group is able to provide the answer, they call on the teacher. But usually, Bloom says, the groups are able to work on their own.

Some students need help beyond group work and may be assigned workbook exercises, text reading, the viewing of a videotape or some other activity. It usually takes these students no more than an hour or two a week to complete the extra work necessary to catch up.

The final step in the mastery approach is the "evaluative test." This test is similar but not identical to the formative test; it "counts" toward the student's grade. Grading is not, however, on the curve. Students' grades reflect the extent to which they mastered the unit, not their class rank. This means that every student can earn an A.

Not every student does earn an A, but studies have consistently shown that mastery students learn more than those taught in the conventional manner. In fact, the average mastery learning student does better than about 85 percent of students taught in the traditional way. And 70 percent of mastery students attain levels reached by only the top 20 percent of students in regular classrooms.

Many people would be content with these results, but Bloom is determined to push the limits further. For instance, one reason students differ in achievement is past learning. What a student knows at the beginning of a lesson affects what the student gets out of that lesson. Someone with a good grasp of short division is likely to follow a lesson on long division; a student who is confused about short division will simply become more confused. Those who differ at the outset in what Bloom calls the "prerequisites for learning" will be even further apart at the end of the lesson.

But, Bloom asks, what would happen if all students started the lesson on an equal footing? One of Bloom's students, Fernando Leyton, performed an experiment to answer this question. Students in a second-year algebra class took a test at the beginning of the school year to determine what they recalled from the first-year course. Then, using the corrective instruction method of mastery learning, the teacher taught the students the specific skills they lacked. After this, the teacher taught the first unit using the mastery learning approach. The students in this class did far better on a test of that unit than did students in a comparable class who had merely had a general review of first-year algebra and were taught in the ordinary way. Leyton obtained similar results in a study of second-year French students.

The benefits of prerequisite training, when combined with mastery learning, multiply over a period of weeks. One of Leyton's experimental classes continued using mastery learning for about three months. The average student in this class scored higher than did 95 percent of those in a regular class on the same material.

Impressive as these results are (they nearly match the effects of tutoring), Bloom is not satisfied. He notes that variability in student achievement is not due solely to what takes place in school. Parents who encourage their children to do well in school, who let them know that school learning is important, who show by their own behavior that they value learning, who help with homework, who provide tutors when their own ef-

MASTERY STUDENTS CONSISTENTLY OUTPERFORM THOSE IN REGULAR CLASSES.

forts are inadequate—such parents have children who enjoy more success in school. It is not, Bloom emphasizes, demographic characteristics such as parental income, occupation and educational level that need to be changed but parental behavior. There is little we can do to change the demographic features of the parents of students who do not do well, but we can help parents to change their behavior in ways that will help their children in school. We can and, Bloom insists, we should.

Although Bloom is careful about how he deals with this touchy issue, he does advocate having educators work with parents. And he believes that parental training should begin before children start school. "The most rapid period of learning is the period that ends at about the time the student begins first grade. Some parents make good use of this time, but others don't. The result is that some students are far ahead of others before the school bell rings." Programs such as Head Start that try to bring the disadvantaged student up to par are fine, Bloom believes, but training the parents to do the job right in the first place would be even better.

Bloom believes that with parental training, prerequisite instruction and mastery learning, almost all students can master the content of their courses. But, true to his rebel nature, Bloom admits that even this would leave him dissatisfied.

"Having an effective method of instruction is only half the battle," he says. "Once you know how to teach well you have to ask the question, 'What is worth learning well?'" Many

years ago Bloom and his colleagues produced two volumes aimed at classifying the kinds of things students are asked to learn. The first volume of *Taxonomy of Educational Objectives* identifies academic objectives that range from lower-level skills, such as the ability to recall and understand facts, to higher-level skills, such as the ability to synthesize and evaluate facts.

Traditional education, Bloom complains, has always devoted itself almost exclusively to lower-level goals. "Studies have shown," he notes, "that over 95 percent of the items on teacher-made tests require nothing more than the recollection of facts." It is no wonder, Bloom observes, that so many of the bright college students he and Broder studied years ago could not solve problems. "If we do not teach higher-level skills such as problem solving," says Bloom, "we cannot reasonably expect students to master them."

The second volume of the *Taxonomy* recognizes that students learn much more in school than academic subjects. Much of what they learn involves interests, attitudes, values and social skills. Bloom believes that the most important learning that takes place in school may have to do with feelings. Students who do well on a task feel good about the task, the school, the teacher and themselves. In discovering that they are good students, they learn that they have value in the eyes of teachers, parents and even other students. Students who do poorly on a task feel unhappy about the task and everything associated with it, including themselves. Bad students learn that they are bad people.

Teachers inevitably convey these judgments; they cannot do otherwise in a system that focuses on class rank instead of mastery of course content. "It's hard to think of any place in our society that is as preoccupied as the schools with comparing people with one another," Bloom observes. He notes, for example, that employees are rarely ranked from highest to lowest, from best to worst. "Yet that is exactly what is done every day in our schools."

Bloom believes that traditional education not only undermines the self-esteem of students who do poorly, it "infects" these students with emotional problems. Bloom emphasizes that this outcome is not a rare event attributable to an occasional insensitive teacher. Rather, it is the inevitable result of a system of education that assumes that large numbers of students must fail or just get by.

Why do our schools persist in walking the same old path? The answer is rooted in our history. Our educational system had its origin in the agricultural age, a time when society had little need of large numbers of well-educated citizens. With industrialization came the need for widespread literacy, but only those who would govern, run businesses or follow professions needed more than a smattering of education. What did a farmer or textile worker need to know of Shakespeare, Newton or Locke? So, to a large extent the purpose of public schooling was to identify those students who would go on to become leaders. Because education was as much con-

TRADITIONAL EDUCATION INFECTS STUDENTS WITH THE SEEDS OF EMOTIONAL PROBLEMS.

cerned with selection as with instruction, a system that encouraged competition and left many students behind made some sense.

But our society has changed. We now face a world in which farming and manufacturing, long our major employers, play minor roles. As Alvin Toffler has shown in *The Third Wave,* increasing numbers of people are employed at tasks that involve the ma-

nipulation of information more than physical labor. And many of these workers can expect to return to school for retraining repeatedly during their careers. "We need large numbers of people with high-level skills who like to learn," says Bloom, "and we're not going to get them with an educational system designed to ensure that most students fail." The solution, he suggests, is to replace our antiquated educational system with one that produces very few failures.

His efforts to do just that have led some people to suggest that he is a woolly-headed professor whose rebellious ideas would ruin our schools, if they haven't already. But if Bloom is right, his brand of education would produce results far superior to those of the traditional system. The majority of students would leave our schools knowing much more than students do today. And feeling better about themselves.

An Emerging Synthesis in
MORAL EDUCATION

The ongoing debate about how to teach morals, ethics, values, or good character in the schools really comes down to a competition between the product desired and the process by which that product is to be achieved, Mr. Benninga suggests.

JACQUES S. BENNINGA

JACQUES S. BENNINGA is a professor in the School of Education and Human Development, California State University, Fresno.

WHETHER OR not they offer specific programs, schools provide moral education. In many schools and districts the curriculum in morality is informal and unwritten. It pervades school and classroom rules, the treatment by teachers of such individuals and groups as minority and handicapped students, and the attitudes of the community toward academics, specific curricular programs, and athletics. Because these hidden moral curricula may vary from school to school within districts and from teacher to teacher within schools, generalizing about the values and standards they represent is difficult.

In other districts, moral and character education programs are focused, overt, and well-planned. Schools in these districts have a public point of view; they take a public stand. While their overall goals are remarkably similar (to produce thinking citizens for a democratic society, for instance), their methods and programs are not. Let us consider some of the more popular approaches to moral and character education and then attempt a synthesis.

INDOCTRINATION OR NURTURING?

The founders and formulators of our democracy and its schools obviously believed that a central purpose of education was to provide training in citizenship and the behaviors related to it. As Jefferson wrote, "If a nation expects to be ignorant and free in a state of civilization, it expects what never was and never will be."[1] In his further remarks on education, Jefferson emphasized the cultivation of civic virtues among all citizens. He believed that all citizens were capable of using political power intelligently and responsibly.

Ever since Jefferson, educating for citizenship has remained a central concern of those who have thought deeply about education. We see that concern in the works of Horace Mann and Henry Barnard in the 19th century; in the progressivism of John Dewey; in the ideas of William Bagley, Arthur Bestor, and Max Rafferty; and in *A Nation at Risk*.[2] Today, more than ever before — perhaps because of rising rates of juvenile crime and teenage pregnancy, drug use, and suicide — society expects schools to instruct the young in moral and civic ideals.

Exactly what these ideals are, however, has never been simple to define. Edward Wynne lists America's central values as "persistence, tact, self-reliance, generosity, and loyalty."[3] Other writers on the subject include "hard work, social cooperation, delayed gratification and savings, order and patience, success in life through doing well in school, rational and scientific thought and achievement, and success."[4]

Individual school boards around the country have attempted to define community values. For example, Salt Lake City has developed a code of ethics for teachers.[5] Minneapolis schools have adopted an overall code of student behavior, including a dress code that bans punk or breaker clothes.[6] And the school board in Fresno, California, has adopted nine values and character traits to be upheld by students and adults alike.

The problem for teachers is not defining the values to which students should adhere; school boards generally assume that responsibility. Rather, teachers need to determine how to teach morals (or ethics, values, character traits) honestly and realistically.

During the early part of this century, two contrasting approaches to moral education were defined and eventually implemented and refined. The differences between them revolved around two central questions. First, should moral education be taught as a separate part of the curriculum?[7] And second, should the values emphasized be developed by adults and transmitted to the students

From *Phi Delta Kappan*, February 1988, pp. 415-418. Reprinted by permission of *Phi Delta Kappan* and the author.

directly, or should they be developed by the students through discourse and discussion? Stated another way, we can define the ongoing methodological debate as an interaction between the product desired as a result of moral/character education and the process by which that product is to be achieved.

THE DIRECT APPROACH

Direct moral education means either emphasizing during specified time slots the values or character traits to be transmitted or integrating those values or traits throughout the curriculum. Instruction in specified moral concepts can take the form of example and definition, class discussions and role-playing, or rewarding students for proper behavior.[8]

The use of the McGuffey Readers during the early part of the 20th century is an example of a direct approach. The stories and poems in the readers taught moral conduct and character building, as well as academics. The following poem from the fourth reader in the McGuffey series is illustrative, and its lesson is clear.

Lazy Ned

" 'Tis royal fun," cried lazy Ned.
"To coast upon my fine, new sled,
    And beat the other boys;
But then, I can not bear to climb
The tiresome hill, for every time
    It more and more annoys."

So, while his schoolmates glided by,
And gladly tugged uphill, to try
    Another merry race,
Too indolent to share their plays,
Ned was compelled to stand and gaze,
    While shivering in his place.

Thus, he would never take the pains
To seek the prize that labor gains,
    Until the time had passed;
For, all his life, he dreaded still
The silly bugbear of *uphill*,
    And died a dunce at last.[9]

Many educators today advocate a direct approach to character education, with standards clearly defined. In an article on the use of drugs on college campuses, U.S. Secretary of Education William Bennett wrote:

If a college is really interested in teaching its students a clear lesson in moral responsibility, it should tell the truth about drugs in a straightforward way. This summer our college presidents should send every student a letter saying they will not tolerate drugs on campus — period. The letter should then spell out precisely what the college's policy will be toward students

who use drugs. . . . Being simple and straightforward about . . . moral responsibility is not the same as being simplistic and unsophisticated.[10]

For elementary schools, Bennett suggests, "Every school should have a discipline code, making clear to children and to parents what the school expects of them. Then it should enforce that code."[11] The direct approach to moral education is still the most widely used approach to teaching morality in American schools.

INDIRECT APPROACHES

Indirect approaches to character education tend to encourage students to define their own and others' values and to help them define the moral perspectives that support those values. The two most illustrative indirect approaches are values clarification and cognitive moral education.

Values clarification. Values clarification seeks to help students clarify "what their lives are for, what is worth working for."[12] In this approach, students are asked questions or presented with dilemmas and expected to respond individually or in small groups. The procedure is intended to help students define their own values and to make them aware of others' values.

In the process, students proceed through seven steps: prizing one's beliefs and behavior (steps 1 and 2), choosing one's beliefs and behavior (steps 3, 4, and 5), and acting on one's beliefs (steps 6 and 7).[13] In the following selection, for example, students are asked to select from among 10 people six who will be admitted to a fallout shelter during World War III.

Suppose you are a government decision maker in Washington, D.C., when World War III breaks out.

A fallout shelter under your administration in a remote Montana highland contains only enough space, air, food and water for six people for three months, but ten people wish to be admitted.

The ten have agreed by radio contact that for the survival of the human race you must decide which six of them shall be saved. You have exactly thirty minutes to make up your mind before Washington goes up in smoke. These are your choices:

1. A 16-year-old girl of questionable IQ, a high school dropout, pregnant.

2. A policeman with a gun (which cannot be taken from him), thrown off the force recently for brutality.

3. A clergyman, 75.

4. A woman physician, 36, known to be a confirmed racist.

5. A male violinist, 46, who served seven years for pushing narcotics.

6. A 20-year-old black militant, no special skills.

7. A former prostitute, female, 39.

8. An architect, a male homosexual.

9. A 26-year-old law student.

10. The law student's 25-year-old wife who spent the last nine months in a mental hospital, still heavily sedated. They refuse to be separated.[14]

The process of evaluation in this exercise is value free. No answers are considered right or wrong. Any response derived from following the seven steps is as acceptable as any other. The clarification of values is left up to the individual student.

Critics of this approach claim that, because of its controversial content, values clarification often offends community standards.[15] Moreover, its relativistic process, they say, undermines accepted values, induces no search for consensus, fails to stress truth and right behavior, and does not distinguish between morality as a generalizable system of norms, and morality as a system based on personal preference or whim.[16]

Cognitive moral education. Like the supporters of values clarification, advocates of more reasoned indirect approaches also challenge direct moral instruction. However, they do not take the position that moral education can be value free. Rather, tney assert the validity of such values as democracy and justice. In a political system founded on checks and balances, free speech, and the protection of individual rights, they argue, standards of behavior should not be imposed but should develop within students themselves through appropriate environment and exercises that stimulate higher levels of thinking. If standards are imposed, they ask, can children ever fully integrate and fully understand the rights and responsibilities of participatory citizenship? Only through participation and discussion, they maintain, can students apply the rules and principles of cooperation, trust, community, autonomy, and self-reliance.

John Dewey believed that institutions, including schools, are either democratic from top to bottom or not democratic at all. He advocated developing a sense of *community* in the schools through shared effort, with pupils participating in planning. But he did not give students responsibility for curriculum, nor did he question the need for responsibility and authority in the administration of the school.[17] As early as 1897 Dewey wrote:

> I believe that the moral education centers on the school as a mode of social life, that the best and deepest moral training is precisely that which one gets through having to enter into proper relations with others in a unity of work and thought. The present educational systems, so far as they destroy or neglect this unity, render it difficult or impossible to get any genuine, regular moral training.[18]

Years later, Dewey and his daughter underscored this theme in a book on experimental schools and systems. In a chapter on the public schools of Gary, Indiana, a city "made up principally of laborers in the steel mills and . . . 60% foreign born. . . ," they described "application time":

> Thus an older pupil, studying stenography and typewriting or bookkeeping, might go to the school office and do an hour of real work, helping one of the clerks. The boys in the fifth grade put in this time in tending the school storeroom. They take entire charge of the school supplies, check up all the material sent in by the board and distribute it through the building to the teachers and janitors. The records of the pupils in the different shops are kept by other pupils in their application time. Pupils also run a post office for the building, and the writer saw a sixth-grade boy delivering salary checks and collecting receipts for them through the building.
>
> The school lunchroom is conducted by the cooking department. . . . Student waiters serve the food they have cooked — real lunches to their fellow students, who pay a student cashier. The girls do all the menu planning and buying for the lunchroom and keep the accounts. They have to pay expenses and serve menus that come up to the standard set by the chemistry department, where they have analyzed food and made tables of comparative values. The result is steaming hot food, nourishing and well cooked, sold very cheaply.
>
> Children who do this kind of work are not only learning arithmetic and bookkeeping, they are learning as well responsibility and reliability. They get an appreciation of what their school means, and are made wide awake to its welfare; they learn that they are the real school, identical with its interests.
>
> Pupils who have made the furniture and the cement walks with their own hands, and who know how much it cost, are slow to destroy walks or furniture, nor are they going to be very easily fooled as to the value they get in service and improvements when they themselves become taxpayers.[19]

In the 18th century, the philosopher Immanuel Kant, writing about duties and obligations, argued that the rightness of a behavior depends not on the consequences of that behavior, but on the reasoning behind the act. That is, to be truly moral, actions must be performed entirely from motives of duty, from an obligation to act. A human is a rational being, Kant continued. Good people act in accordance with their rationality, and reasoning is universal. Thus, if we follow reason, all good people will arrive at the same conclusions. From this line of thought emerged the famous Kantian *categorical imperative*: one should act in such a way that one could wish the outcome of one's action to become a universal law of human conduct.[20]

Kant had two criteria for judging whether an act was moral or not: the reasons behind it must be both consistent and reversible.[21] The decision maker must act on moral issues as if everyone, everywhere would act the same way. Simply stated, one should act in accordance with the Golden Rule.

By extending Dewey's notion of the social nature of education and building on Kant's construct of duty, Lawrence Kohlberg has greatly influenced the development of a cognitive-developmental theory of moral education. From his empirical research on children's moral reasoning, he outlined six successive stages of moral reasoning, each considered more morally adequate than the preceding one.[22]

As individuals move upward through the stages of moral thinking, they become, according to Kohlberg, increasingly capable of broader perspectives, especially those perspectives represented by the thinking of others. Thus their thinking about moral issues becomes more and more reversible. That is, the decision maker becomes ever more capable of trading places with each of the characters in the situation to be judged. Kohlberg called this an exercise in "moral musical chairs."[23] At each successive stage, the moral obligation to act on justice-related issues becomes more differentiated and integrated, as the individual making the decision gains the cognitive ability to consider clearly the perspective of each of the characters in the dilemma presented.

Contrary to what some critics claim, Kohlberg's theory of moral judgment is neither relativistic nor morally neutral. In fact, it clearly treats higher-order thinking (and the behavior it inspires) as better than thinking at lower stages. Furthermore, it postulates that higher-order

thinking can be stimulated through focused discussion of moral issues and dilemmas found in literature and history, as well as in naturally occurring classroom interactions. The *process*, then, is not altogether different from that used in values clarification, but the *product* (more adequate moral thinking) certainly is.

A SYNTHESIS

Following Kohlberg's model, it is not unreasonable to attempt to reconcile indirect and direct approaches to character education. We live in a democratic society that advocates certain values, and these values can and should be emphasized in our schools. Few will argue with the proposition that such values as justice, persistence, generosity, loyalty, social cooperation, fairness, and so on are important and deserve emphasis in the curriculum, whether we achieve that emphasis by praising students for demonstrating accepted values, by having them follow rules that embody those values, or by encouraging them to emulate heroes from history and literature.

In real life, however, resolving dilemmas is rarely a clear-cut process, especially if the several sides in a dispute hold competing but legitimate claims. In such cases, structured discourse seems the preferable teaching method.[24] Students can participate in teacher-led discussions, patterned on Kohlberg's "moral musical chairs," and formulate solutions. This, after all, is the method employed by moral philosophers and by such legal bodies as the U.S. Supreme Court.

For example, we accept the First Amendment principle of free speech and expression. However, defining what free speech means in a new or challenging situation demands discussion and reapplication of the principle. Recent Supreme Court rulings that permit cities to restrict the location of "adult" theaters through zoning ordinances (thus limiting the freedom of expression of the theater owners) and that give schools the power to suspend students for making sexually suggestive remarks at school events are evidence that society continually reexamines the application of its core values.

At another, but equally important, level, elementary students should be allowed to make some decisions about their own academic program. For example, the question of whether or not to break open an incubating egg to document embryo growth should be discussed and resolved by the children involved if the question arises.[25] Such discussion allows them to define values and resolve issues that are central to them.

These are not small decisions with easy resolutions. Just as basic constitutional rights need to be redefined through discussion by moral men and women, so students need to discuss issues that affect them directly. Such discussions develop the critical thinking and commitment to reasoned dialogue that are part of moral maturity. In a society based on high moral values, the direct and indirect teaching of those values are not — and should not be — incompatible.

1. Saul K. Padover, *Thomas Jefferson and the Foundations of American Freedom* (Princeton, N.J.: Van Nostrand, 1965).

2. Merle Curti, *The Social Ideas of American Educators* (Totowa, N.J.: Littlefield, Adams, 1959); John S. Brubacher, *Henry Barnard on Education* (New York: McGraw-Hill, 1931); John Dewey, *The School and Society* (Chicago: University of Chicago Press, 1974); William C. Bagley, "An Essentialist Platform for the Advancement of American Education," *Educational Administration and Supervision*, vol. 24, 1938, pp. 241-56; Arthur E. Bestor, *The Restoration of Learning* (New York: Knopf, 1955); Max Rafferty, *Suffer, Little Children* (New York: Signet, 1962); and National Commission on Excellence in Education, *A Nation at Risk* (Washington, D.C.: U.S. Government Printing Office, 1983).

3. Edward Wynne, ed., *Character Policy: An Emerging Issue* (Washington, D.C.: University Press of America, 1982), p. 1.

4. Larry C. Jensen and Richard S. Knight, *Moral Education: Historical Perspectives* (New York: University Press of America, 1981), p. 86.

5. M. Donald Thomas and Rafael Lewy, "Education and Moral Conduct: Rediscovering America," in Wynne, *Character Policy*. . ., pp. 23-28.

6. Associated Press, "Students Protest Dress Codes," *Fresno Bee*, 29 March 1985, p. A-9.

7. Jeanne Pietig, "Values and Morality in the Early 20th Century Elementary Schools: A Perspective," *Social Education*, vol. 47, 1983, pp. 262-65.

8. Jensen and Knight, p. 101.

9. *McGuffey's Fourth Eclectic Reader* (New York: H. H. Vail, 1920), pp. 38-39.

10. William J. Bennett, "Drugs and College Don't, Shouldn't Mix," *Los Angeles Times*, 15 July 1986, Sec. 2, p. 5.

11. William J. Bennett, *First Lessons: A Report on Elementary Education in America* (Washington, D.C.: U.S. Government Printing Office, 1986), p. 56.

12. Louis E. Raths, Merrill Harmin, and Sidney B. Simon, *Values and Teaching* (Columbus, O.: Charles E. Merrill, 1966), p. 7.

13. Ibid., pp. 27-30.

14. Cara B. Volkmor, Anne L. Pasanella, and Louis E. Raths, *Values in the Classroom* (Columbus, O.: Charles E. Merrill, 1977), p. 1.

15. Martin Eger, "The Conflict in Moral Education: An Informal Case Study," *Public Interest*, vol. 63, 1981, pp. 62-80; and Bennett, *First Lessons*. . . .

16. Fritz K. Oser, "Moral Education and Values Education: The Discourse Perspective," in Merlin C. Wittrock, ed., *Handbook of Research on Teaching*, 3rd ed. (New York: Macmillan, 1986).

17. G. Max Wingo, *Philosophies of Education: An Introduction* (Lexington, Mass.: D.C. Heath, 1974).

18. John Dewey, "My Pedagogic Creed," *School Journal*, vol. 54, 1897, pp. 77-80.

19. John Dewey and Evelyn Dewey, *Schools of Tomorrow* (New York: E.P. Dutton, 1962), pp. 146-47.

20. John Hospers, *Human Conduct: An Introduction to the Problems of Ethics* (New York: Harcourt, Brace, and World, 1961).

21. Ibid., pp. 275-78.

22. Lawrence Kohlberg, *The Philosophy of Moral Development: Moral Stages and the Idea of Justice* (New York: Harper & Row, 1981); and idem, *The Psychology of Moral Development: The Nature and Validity of Moral Stages* (New York: Harper & Row, 1984).

23. Kohlberg, *The Philosophy* . . . , p. 199.

24. Oser, "Moral Education . . . ."

25. For a discussion of the morality of opening eggs to check embryo growth, see Thomas Lickona, "Character Development in the Elementary School Classroom," pp. 419-23, this *Kappan*.

Why We Need To Understand Science

Ignorance of science threatens our economic well-being, national security and the democratic process. We must do better.

Carl Sagan

Carl Sagan teaches and does research at Cornell University. His Emmy and Peabody Award-winning TV science series COSMOS has been seen in more than 60 countries by 400 million people. Videocassettes of all 13 episodes will be available in stores later this year from Turner Home Entertainment. The accompanying book, "Cosmos," is the best-selling science book ever published in the English language.

As I got off the plane, he was waiting for me, holding up a sign with my name on it. I was on my way to a conference of scientists and TV broadcasters, and the organizers had kindly sent a driver.

"Do you mind if I ask you a question?" he said as we waited for my bag. "Isn't it confusing to have the same name as that science guy?"

It took me a moment to understand. Was he pulling my Leg? "I *am* that science guy," I said. He smiled. "Sorry. That's my problem. I thought it was yours too." He put out his hand. "My name is William F. Buckley." (Well, his name wasn't *exactly* William F. Buckley, but he did have the name of a contentious TV interviewer, for which he doubtless took a lot of good-natured ribbing.)

As we settled into the car for the long drive, he told me he was glad I was "that science guy"—he had so many questions to ask about science. Would I mind? And so we got to talking. But not about science. He wanted to discuss UFOs, "channeling" (a way to hear what's on the minds of dead people—not much it turns out), crystals, astrology. . . . He introduced each subject with real enthusiasm, and each time I had to disappoint him: "The evidence is crummy," I kept saying. "There's a much simpler explanation." As we drove on through the rain, I could see him getting glummer. I was attacking not just pseudoscience but also a facet of his inner life.

And yet there is so much in real science that's equally exciting, more mysterious, a greater intellectual challenge—as well as being a lot closer to the truth. Did he know about the molecular building blocks of life sitting out there in the cold, tenuous gas between the stars? Had he heard of the footprints of our ancestors found in 4-million-year-old volcanic ash? What about the raising of the Himalayas when India went crashing into Asia? Or how viruses subvert cells, or the radio search for extraterrestrial intelligence or the ancient civilization of Ebla? Mr. "Buckley"—well-spoken, intelligent, curious—had heard virtually nothing of modern science. He *wanted* to know about science. It's just that all the science got filtered out before it reached him. What the society permitted to trickle through was mainly pretense and confusion. And it had never taught him how to distinguish real science from the cheap imitation.

All over America there are smart, even gifted, people who have a built-in passion for science. But that passion is unrequited. A recent survey suggests that 94% of Americans are "scientifically illiterate."

A prescription for disaster. We live in a society exquisitely dependent on science and technology, in which hardly anyone knows anything about science and technology. This is a clear prescription for disaster. It's dangerous and stupid for us to remain ignorant about global warming, say, or ozone depletion, toxic and radioactive wastes, acid rain. Jobs and wages depend on science and technology. If the United States can't manufacture, at high quality and low price, products people want to buy, then industries will drift out of the United States and transfer a little prosperity to another part of the world. Because of the low birthrate in the '60s and '70s, the National Science Foundation projects a shortage of nearly a million professional scientists and engineers by 2010. Where will they come from? What about fusion, supercomputers, abortion, massive reductions in strategic weapons, addiction, high-resolution TV, airline and airport safety, food additives, animal rights, superconductivity, Midget-man vs. rail-garrison MX missiles, going to Mars, finding cures for AIDS and cancer? How can we decide national policy if we don't understand the underlying issues?

I know that science and technology are not just cornucopias pouring good deeds out into the world. Scientists not only conceived nuclear weapons; they also took political leaders by the lapels, arguing that *their* nation—whichever it happened to be—had to have one first. Then they arranged to manufacture 60,000 of them. Our technology has produced thalidomide, CFCs, Agent Orange, nerve gas and industries so powerful they can ruin the climate of the planet. There's a *reason* people are nervous about science and technology.

And so the image of the mad scientist haunts our world—from Dr. Faust to Dr. Frankenstein to Dr. Strangelove to the white-coated loonies of Saturday morning children's TV. (All this doesn't inspire budding scientists.) But there's no way back. We can't just conclude that science puts too much power into the hands of morally feeble technologists or corrupt, power-crazed politicians and decide to get rid of it. Advances in medicine and agriculture have saved more lives than have been lost in all the wars in history. Advances in transportation, communication and entertainment have transformed the world. The sword of science is double-edged. Rather, its awesome power forces on all of us, including politicians, a new responsibility—more attention to the long-term consequences of technology, a global and transgenerational perspective, an incentive to avoid easy appeals to nationalism and chauvinism. Mistakes are becoming too expensive.

Science is much more than a body of knowledge. It is a way of thinking. This is central to its success. Science invites us to let the facts in, even when they don't conform to our preconceptions. It counsels us to carry alternative hypotheses in our heads and see which best match the facts. It urges on us a fine balance between no-holds-barred openness to new ideas, however heretical, and the most rigorous skeptical scrutiny of everything— new ideas *and* established wisdom. We need wide appreciation of this kind of thinking. It works. It's an essential tool for a democracy in an age of change. Our task is not just to train more scientists but also to deepen public understanding of science.

How bad is it? Very bad. "It's Official," reads one newspaper headline: "We Stink in Science." Less than half of all Americans know that the Earth moves around the Sun and takes a year to do it—a fact established a few centuries ago. In tests of average 17-year-olds in many world regions, the U.S. ranked dead last in algebra. On identical tests, the U.S. kids averaged 43% and their Japanese counterparts 78%. In my book, 78% is pretty good—it corresponds to a C+, or maybe even a B−; 43% is an F. In a chemistry test, students in only two of 13 nations did worse than the U.S. Compared to us, Britain, Singapore and Hong Kong were so high they were almost off-scale, and 25% of Canadian 18-year-olds knew just as much chemistry as a select 1% of American high school seniors (in their second chemistry course, and most of them in "advanced" programs). The best of 20 fifth-grade classrooms in Minneapolis was outpaced by every one of 20 classrooms in Sendai, Japan, and 19 out of 20 in Taipei, Taiwan. South Korean students were far ahead of American students in all aspects of mathematics and science, and 13-year-olds in British Columbia (in Western Canada) outpaced their U.S. counterparts across the boards (in some areas they did better than the Koreans). Of the U.S. kids, 22% say they dislike school; only 8% of the Koreans do. Yet two-thirds of the Americans, but only a quarter of the Koreans, say they are "good at mathematics."

Why we're flunking. How do British Columbia, Japan, Britain and Korea manage so much better than we do?

During the Great Depression, teachers enjoyed job security, good salaries, respectability. Teaching was an admired profession, partly because learning was widely recognized as the road out of poverty. Little of that is true today. And so science (and other) teaching is too often incompetently or uninspiringly done, its practitioners, astonishingly, having little or no training in their subjects—sometimes themselves unable to distinguish science from pseudoscience. Those who do have the training often get higher-paying jobs elsewhere.

We need more money for teachers' training and salaries, and for laboratories—so kids will get hands-on experience rather than just reading what's in the book. But all across America, school-bond issues on the ballot are regularly defeated. U.S. parents are much more satisfied with what their children are learning in science and math than are, say, Japanese and Taiwanese parents—whose children are doing so much better. No one suggests that property taxes be used to provide for the military budget, or for agriculture, or for cleaning up toxic wastes. Why just education? Why not support it from general taxes on the local and state levels? What about a special education tax for those industries with special needs for technically trained workers?

American kids don't do enough schoolwork. The average high school student spends 3.5 hours a week on homework. The total time devoted to studies, in and out of the classroom, is about 20 hours a week. Japanese *fifth*-graders average 33 hours a week.

But most American kids aren't stupid. Part of the reason they don't study hard is that they've received few tangible benefits when they do. Competency (that is, actually knowing the stuff) in verbal skills, mathematics and science these days doesn't increase earnings for average young men in their first eight years out of high school—many of whom take service rather than industrial jobs.

In the productive sectors of the economy, though, the story is different. There are furniture factories, for example, in danger of going out of business because few entry-level workers can do simple arithmetic. A major electronic company reports that 80% of its job applicants can't pass a *fifth*-grade math test. The United States already is losing some $25 billion a year (mainly in lost productivity and the cost of remedial education) because workers, to too great a degree, can't read, write, count or think. Parents should know that their children's livelihoods may depend on how much math and science they know. Now, while the kids are in school, is the time for them to learn. Parents might encourage their schools to offer—and their kids to take—comprehensible, well-taught advanced science courses. They might also limit the amount of mind-numbing TV their children watch.

What we can do. Those in America with the most favorable view of science tend to be young, well-to-do, college-educated white males. But three-quarters of new American workers between now and 2001 will be women, nonwhites and immigrants. Discriminating against them isn't only unjust, it's also self-defeating. It deprives the American economy of desperately needed skilled workers.

Black and Hispanic students are doing better in standardized science tests now than in the late 1960s, but they're the only ones who are. The average math gap between white and black U.S. high school graduates is still huge—two to three grade levels; but the gap between white U.S. high school graduates and those in, say, Japan, Canada, Great Britain or Finland is more than *twice* as big. If you're poorly motivated and poorly educated, you won't know much—no mystery here. Suburban blacks with college-educated parents do just as well in college as suburban whites with college-educated parents. Enrolling a poor child in a Head Start program doubles his or her chances to be employed later in life; one who completes an Upward Bound program is four times as likely to get a college education. If we're serious, we know what to do.

What about college and university? There are obvious steps similar to what should be done in high schools: salaries for teachers that approach what they could get in industry; more scholarships, fellowships and laboratory equipment; laboratory science courses required of everyone to graduate; and special attention paid to those traditionally steered away from science. We should also provide the financial and moral encouragement for academic scientists to spend more time on public education—lectures, newspaper and magazine articles, TV appearances. This requires scientists to make themselves understandable and fun to listen to. To me, it seems strange that some scientists, who depend on public funding for their research, are reluctant to explain to the public what it is that they do. Fortunately, the number of scientists willing to speak to the public—and capably—has been increasing each year. But there are not yet nearly enough.

Virtually every newspaper in America has a daily astrology column. How many have a daily science column? When I was growing up, my father would bring home a daily paper and consume (often with great gusto) the baseball box scores. There they were, to me dry as dust, with obscure abbreviations (W, SS, SO, W-L, AB, RBI), but they spoke to him. Newspapers everywhere printed them. I figured maybe they weren't too hard for me. Eventually I too got caught up in the world of baseball statistics. (I know it helped me in learning decimals, and I still cringe a little when I hear that someone is "batting a thousand." But 1.000 is not 1,000. The lucky player is batting one.)

Or take a look at the financial pages. Any introductory material? Explanatory footnotes? Definition of abbreviations? None. It's sink or swim. Look at those acres of statistics! Yet people voluntarily read the stuff. It's not beyond their ability. It's only a matter of motivation. Why can't we do the same with math, science, and technology?

By far the most effective means of raising interest in science is television. There's lots of pseudoscience on TV, a fair amount of medicine and technology, but hardly any science—especially on the three big commercial networks, whose executives think science programming means ratings declines and lost profits, and nothing else matters. Why in all America is there no TV drama that has as its hero someone devoted to figuring out how the Universe works?

Stirring projects in science and technology attract and inspire youngsters. The number of science Ph.D.s peaked around the time of the Apollo program and declined thereafter. This is an important potential side-effect of such projects as sending humans to Mars, or the Superconducting Supercollider to explore the fine structure of matter, or the program to map all human genes.

Every now and then, I'm lucky enough to teach a class in kindergarten or the first grade. Many of these children are curious, intellectually vigorous, ask provocative and insightful questions and exhibit great enthusiasm for science. When I talk to high school students, I find something different. They memorize "facts." But, by and large, the joy of discovery, the life behind those facts, has gone out of them. They're worried about asking "dumb" questions; they're willing to accept inadequate answers; they don't pose follow-up questions; the room is awash with sidelong glances to judge, second-by-second, the approval of their peers. Something has happened between first and 12th grade, and it's not just puberty. I'd guess that it's partly peer pressure *not* to excel (except in sports); partly that the society teaches short-term gratification; partly the impression that science or math won't buy you a sports car; partly that so little is expected of students; and partly that there are so few role models for intelligent discussion of science and technology or for learning for its own sake.

But there's something else: Many adults are put off when youngsters pose scientific questions. Children ask why the Sun is yellow, or what a dream is, or how deep you can dig a hole, or when is the world's birthday or why we have toes. Too many teachers and parents answer with irritation or ridicule, or quickly move on to something else. Why adults should pretend to omniscience before a 5-year-old, I can't for the life of me understand. What's wrong with admitting that you don't know? Children soon recognize that somehow this kind of question annoys many adults. A few more experiences like this, and another child has been lost to science.

There are many better responses. If we have an idea of the answer, we could try to explain. If we don't, we could go to the encyclopedia or the library. or we might say to the child: "I don't know the answer. Maybe no one knows. Maybe when you grow up, you'll be the first to find out."

But mere encouragement isn't enough. We must also give children the tools to winnow the wheat from the chaff. I'm haunted by the vision of a generation of Americans unable to distinguish reality from fantasy, hopefully clutching their crystals for comfort, unequipped even to frame the right questions or to recognize the answers. I want us to rescue Mr. "Buckley" and the millions like him. I also want us to stop turning out leaden, incurious, unimaginative high school seniors. I think America needs, and deserves, a citizenry with minds wide awake and a basic understanding of how the world works.

Public understanding of science is more central to our national security than half a dozen strategic weapons systems. The submediocre performance of American youngsters in science and math, and the widespread adult ignorance and apathy about science and math, should sound an urgent alarm.

Development During Adolescence and Early Adulthood

The onset of adolescence is demarcated by the emergence of secondary sex characteristics and the achievement of reproductive maturity. However, adolescence also brings substantive shifts in memory and problem-solving skills, in preferred activities, and in emotional behavior. The timing of puberty affects many things, including school achievement, moods, and family relationships. "Those Gangly Years" presents the results of a study following a group of adolescents over a three-year period, highlighting early vs. late maturation differences in boys and girls.

The onset of adulthood is more difficult to distinguish, particularly in modern industrial societies. In some cultures, a ritualistic ceremony marks the transition to adulthood—a transition that occurs quickly, smoothly, and with relatively few problems. In American culture the transition is vague. Does someone become an adult when he or she achieves the right to vote, the privilege of obtaining a driver's license, the ability to legally order an alcoholic drink in a bar, or the right to volunteer for the armed forces?

Adolescence has its ups and downs, but some researchers argue that much of the storm and stress attributed to adolescence is exaggerated. "The Myth About Teen-Agers" reveals that while adolescents are subject to mood-swings, most are basically well-adapted and happy. Focusing on the negative aspects of adolescent behavior may create a set of expectations which the adolescent strives to fulfill. However, for some adolescents the transition to adulthood *is* fraught with despair, loneliness, and interpersonal conflict. The pressures of peer group, school, and family may produce conformity or may lead to rebellion against or withdrawal from friends, parents, or society at large. These pressures may peak as the adolescent prepares to separate from the family and assume the independence and responsibilities of adulthood. Bruce Baldwin's analysis in "Puberty and Parents" suggests that adolescence spans a 20-year period, roughly between the ages of 10 and 30, which can be divided into three periods: early adolescence (adhering to tribal loyalties), middle adolescence (testing adult realities), and late adolescence (joining up). Understanding adolescent attitudes and confronting emotional reactions to adolescents can promote parental growth and development as much as it promotes the development of the adolescent. The idea that psychological aspects of adolescence continue into the late 20s is examined further in "Therapists Find Last Outpost of Adolescence in Adulthood."

Although much attention has been given to the problems of adolescence and the transition to adulthood, developmentalists have shown far less interest in the early years of adulthood. Yet, during early adulthood, many individuals experience significant changes in their lives. Marriage, parenthood, divorce, single parenting, employment, and the effects of sexism may be powerful influences on ego development, self-concept, and personality. Negative emotions such as jealousy and envy subvert efforts to establish effective interpersonal relationships, and often lead to hostility or isolation. In "Jealousy and Envy," Jon Queijo describes three strategies—self-reliance, selective ignoring, and self-bolstering—that individuals can use in their attempts to cope with negative emotions. Some individuals seem to grow stronger when confronted by the stresses of daily living, whereas others have great difficulty coping. The challenge for developmentalists is to discover the factors that contribute to one's ability to cope with stress and the natural crises of life with minimum disruption to the integrity of one's personality.

Love is a topic that has received surprisingly little attention from developmentalists, although it is a favorite subject of poets, novelists, and songwriters. In "The Measure of Love," Robert Sternberg suggests that there is a basic core of love that is constant over different close relationships. With the ever-increasing divorce rate, a good measurement of love could prove to be a valuable predictive tool.

Looking Ahead: Challenge Questions

Why has it taken so long for psychologists to attempt a scientific study of love? Do you think they will eventually have as much success as poets and songwriters in detailing the dynamics of this pervasive and powerful human emotion?

Why does adolescence in current times seem to be fraught with so many difficulties, even for the well-adjusted? Do you think adolescence really continues into the late 20s?

What techniques do you use to deal with your emotional ups and downs? Which do you think are effective and which are ineffective? Do you see any signs of growth or change in yourself? Why do you think so many adolescents and young adults find it easier to lose themselves in drugs or cults than to confront their problems and take steps to develop self-control and self-reliance? What kinds of parenting techniques might have given such individuals sufficient self-esteem and coping skills to combat their self-doubts and loneliness?

Puberty and Parents

Understanding Your Early Adolescent

Dr. Bruce A. Baldwin

*Dr. Baldwin is a practicing psychologist who heads
Direction Dynamics, a consulting service specializing in
promoting professional development and quality of life in
achieving men and women. He responds to many requests each year for seminars on topics of interest to
professional organizations and businesses.*

*For busy achievers and involved parents, Dr. Baldwin
has authored a popular, positive parenting cassette series
and a new book,* It's All In Your Head: Lifestyle
Management Strategies for Busy People! *Both are available in bookstores or from Direction Dynamics in
Wilmington, N.C.*

In the large auditorium, concerned parents wait for the
program to begin. The speaker appears to talk about the
problems of parenting in the eighties. The program begins with a question to the audience: "How many of you
would choose to live your adolescent years over if you
had the chance?" Relatively few hands are raised and
some of them waver indecisively. For just a few, the
adolescent years are some of the best. The majority,
however, are happy to have reached adulthood and put
those tumultuous years behind them.

Then a second question: "How many of you would
choose to live your adolescent years over if you had to
do it *right now*?" This time, practically no hands are
raised. The fact is that in any era, early adolescence is a
most difficult time of life. On the other hand, there is
ample evidence that this critical period of growth and
change for young people is steadily becoming more
difficult to negotiate emotionally. Caring parents seem to
sense this and they are afraid for their children. Sadly,

their intuitive awareness is quite accurate: what they
remember as the simpler world of their own youth has
changed irrevocably.

Still, beyond the social environment and value system
characteristic of this decade resides the basic adolescent.
Understanding the changes that occur and the behaviors
that are typical of a young man or woman growing up,
regardless of time or place, provides parents with a
backdrop of awareness that is most reassuring. It also
provides the basis for the necessarily changed relationship with a child who is rapidly growing physically and
emotionally. Armed with such understanding, parents can
better cope with the many issues that are presented by
the changes in their adolescent. At times, they can even
manage a knowing smile at the many typical reactions
they observe.

Parents who have survived the perils of puberty know,
though, that dealing with one or more adolescents is not
fun and games. Looking after the kids is relatively easy

From *PACE* magazine, October 1986, pp. 13, 15-19. Reprinted by permission *PACE* magazine, the Piedmont Airlines inflight
magazine, Pace Communications, Inc., Greensboro, NC.

when they are small and dependent and the immediate neighborhood is their whole world. Three parental apprehensions, however, are forced into the forefront of consciousness by the onset of puberty and fueled daily by powerful adolescent strivings for independence.

Parental apprehension #1: "My adolescent will do the same things I did when I was young." With the wisdom of the years, parents look back at their adolescent antics with a bit of amusement tempered by a fair share of "only by the grace of God . . ." feelings. These parents, now mature individuals, simply don't want their children to take the same chances.

Parental apprehension #2: "The world my teen must live in is much more dangerous than it was years ago." This absolutely valid fear is constantly reinforced by public awareness of high suicide rates in adolescents, life-threatening sexually transmitted diseases and the easy availability of drugs. Mistakes and missteps can be much more serious than they were in the past.

Parental apprehension #3: "My child now has a private life that I can't directly control anymore." A reality is that teens force parents to trust them. Adolescence brings increased mobility and an expansion of time spent outside the sphere of direct family influence. Parents are forced to let go and hope that their teen will handle unknown and possibly dangerous situations well.

With impending puberty, the drama of early adolescence begins to unfold relentlessly. Responsible parents struggle to safeguard their teen's present and future. At the same time, their adolescent precociously lays claim to all adult prerogatives and privileges. In the background, a chosen peer group powerfully influences a child to do its immature bidding. Peers, parents and puberty all interact to produce the conflict-laden "adolescent triangle." It's normal but not easy.

The complex relationships of the adolescent triangle have been a perplexing part of the family life for centuries. It is incumbent upon parents to try to understand the developmental processes being experienced by their growing teen. Only then can they effectively modify their parenting relationship to their child-cum-adult in ways that will promote healthy growth toward maturity. And they must persevere without thanks in the face of active resistance by their teen. To set the stage for effective parental coping, here's an overview of the normal changes that occur during early adolescence.

THE STAGES OF ADOLESCENCE

If the typical individual is asked where adolescence begins and ends, the immediate response is "the teen years." Implicit in this response is the assumption that when the early twenties are reached, adolescence has ended and the individual has become an adult. Nothing could be further from the truth. True, in the past there has been an easy biological marker for the beginning of the adolescent years: puberty. And, in generations past, young men and women became financially and emotionally self-sufficient shortly after leaving home in their late teens.

However, the beginning and end of adolescence have become increasingly diffuse and difficult to define clear-

ly. On one hand, we sometimes see a precocious beginning to adolescence that may predate overt signs of puberty. Children frequently begin to act like adolescents before physical changes begin. At the other end of this growth period, the difficulty is obvious. How do you define the moment when a child has become a true adult? Of course the best way is to use emotional maturity as a gauge rather than more obvious but often misleading criteria such as completing an education, earning a living, marrying or becoming a parent.

In short, adolescence in this society at present spans approximately 20 years. For almost two decades young people struggle to become emotionally mature adults. There are three basis stages of the adolescent experience as it exists today. However, for parents and children the most critical and dangerous is the first.

Stage I: Early adolescence (the rise of tribal loyalties). Age span: 10 or 11 through 17 years. In other words, this most tumultuous stage of growth begins in late fifth or sixth grade and typically ends at about the senior year of high school. During this time, your child joins a "tribe" of peers that is highly separate from the adult world. The peer group (tribe) clearly defines itself as a distinct subculture struggling for identity with its own dress codes, language codes, defined meeting places and powerfully enforced inclusion criteria.

During these most difficult years for both parent and child, the most pronounced changes of puberty occur. The core struggle of the child is to become independent—and that means emotionally separating from parents and forging a new adult identity. Initial attempts are awkward and emotionally naive. In three key areas, here's what the early adolescent is like.

A. Relationship to parents. Suspicious and distrustful, the adolescent begins actively to push parents away and resists their attempts to give advice. Life is conducted in a secretive world dominated by peers. Rebelling, pushing limits and constantly testing parental resolve are characteristic.

B. Relationship to peers. The youth experiences emotionally intense "puppy love" relationships with members of the opposite sex and "best friends" relationships with peers of the same sex. These relationships are often superficial, with undue emphasis placed on status considerations: participation in sports, attractiveness, belonging to an *in* group.

C. Relationship to career/future. Largely unrealistic in expectations of the adult world, the adolescent sees making a good living—and getting the training required—as easy and "no problem." Money made by working is often spent on status items such as cars or clothes or just on having a good time. The future is far away.

Stage II: Middle adolescence (testing adult realities). Age span: about 18 through 23 or 24. Beginning late in the high school years, a new awareness, with a subtle accompanying fear, begins to grow within the adolescent: "It's almost over. Soon I'll have to face the world on my own." A personal future and the hard realities it entails can no longer be completely denied. Shortly after high school, this young adult typically leaves home to attend college or technical school, join the service or enter the work force.

5. ADOLESCENCE AND EARLY ADULTHOOD

While on their own, but still basically protected by parents, middle adolescents are actively engaged in testing the self against the real world in ways not possible while living at home. More personal accountability is required and some hard lessons are learned. These sometimes painful experiences help the middle adolescent learn the ways of the world, but many signs of immaturity remain. In more specific terms, here is what's happening.

A. Relationship to parents. This dynamic is improved but still problematic at times. Middle adolescents still aren't really ready to be completely open with parents, but they are less defensive. During visits home, intense conflicts with parents will still erupt about lifestyle, career decisions and responsibility.

B. Relationships with peers. Frequent visits home may be made more with the intention to see the old gang from high school than to see parents. Good buddies remain at home, but new friends are being made in a work or school setting. A deeper capacity for caring is manifested in increasingly mature relationships with both sexes.

C. Relationship to career/future. The economics of self-support are steadily becoming more important. Sights may be lowered and changes in career direction are common. Meeting new challenges successfully brings a growing sense of confidence and self-sufficiency.

Stage III: Late adolescence (joining up). Age span: 23 or 24 to about 30 years. By the mid-twenties, early career experimentation has ended, as has protective parental involvement. The late adolescent is usually financially self-sufficient and remains quite social. Life is relatively simple because there is minimal community involvement, little property needing upkeep and usually an income at least adequate to meet basic needs. The late adolescent years tend to be remembered fondly as having been filled with hard work and good times.

At first glance, the late adolescent may appear to be fully adult, but this perception is deceptive. Significant adjustments to the adult world are still being made but are less obvious than they were. Many insecurities in relationships and at work continue to be faced and resolved. Spurred by a growing commitment to creating a personal niche in the adult world, the individual continues to change in the direction of true adult maturity. Here's how.

A. Relationship to parents. Over 20 years, the late adolescent has come full circle. Now that he or she is emotionally self-sufficient, a closer relationship with parents becomes possible. Mutual respect and acceptance grow. The late adolescent begins to understand parenting behaviors that were resisted earlier.

B. Relationship to peers. Most high school chums have been left behind and are seen only occasionally. A new group of work-related peers has been solidly established. Love relationships are more mature and show increased capacity for give and take. Commitment to a shared future and to a family grows.

C. Relationship to career/future. Active striving toward the good life and personal goals intensifies. At work, there is a continuing need to prove competency and get ahead. At home, a more settled lifestyle, one that is characteristic of the middle-class mainstream, slowly evolves. Limited community involvement is seen.

EARLY ADOLESCENT ATTITUDES

While adolescents struggle for nearly two decades to attain emotional maturity, the period of early adolescence is clearly the most striking. It is during this critical six or seven years that the growing young adult is most vulnerable to major mistakes. It is an emotional, intense, painful and confusing phase. It is also the time remembered by parents as most trying of their ability to cope.

Because the vulnerability of parents and their children is never so high as it is during early adolescence, it is well to define some of the characteristics of the normal teen during these years. Here are listed 15 of the most common adolescent attitudes that make life difficult for parents and children, but which are entirely normal for this age group. (NOTE: "Teen" in this discussion refers specifically to an early adolescent.)

Adolescent attitude #1: Conformity within nonconformity. The early adolescent attempts to separate from parents by rejecting their standards. At the same time there is an absolute need to conform to peer group standards. It is very important to be like peers and unlike parents.

Adolescent attitude #2: Open communication with adults diminishes. The early adolescent doesn't like to be questioned by parents and reveals little about what is really going on. Key items may be conveniently forgotten as a personal life outside the family is protected.

Adolescent attitude #3: Withdrawal from family altogether. With the advent of puberty, there is increasing resistance to the family. The teen would much rather stay home merely in order to be available or spend time doing nothing with friends than participate in anything with the family.

Adolescent attitude #4: Acceptability is linked to externals. Personal acceptability is excessively linked to having the right clothes, friends and fad items in teen culture. Parents are badgered constantly to finance status needs deemed necessary for acceptance by a chosen peer group.

Adolescent attitude #5: Spending more time alone. Ironically, although early adolescents are quite social most of the time, they also like to spend time by themselves. Often, teens will retreat for hours to a bedroom and tell parents in no uncertain terms to respect their privacy and let them alone.

Adolescent attitude #6: A know-it-all pseudo-sophistication. Attempts by parents to give helpful advice are usually met with a weary "I already know that!" More often than not, however, a teen's information about topics important to health and well-being is incomplete, full of distortions or patently false.

Adolescent attitude #7: Rapid emotional changes. One of the most difficult aspects of early adolescence for parents to cope with is rapid mood changes. A teen is on top of the world one minute and sullen or depressed the next. The emotional triggers for such changes are frequent but unclear and unpredictable.

Adolescent attitude #8: Instability in peer relationships. Early adolescent relationships are marked by intensity and change. Overnight, a best friend may become a mortal enemy because of a real or imagined betrayal. Changing loyalties are often triggered by the incessant gossiping characteristic of teen culture.

Adolescent attitude #9: Somatic sensitivity. In other words, a teen's rapidly changing body is cause for great concern. Frequently, an early adolescent will become obsessed with and distraught over a perceived major physical deformity (an asymmetrical nose, not-quite-right ears, two pimples).

Adolescent attitude #10: Personal grooming takes a spectacular upturn. To parents' astonishment, a lackadaisical preadolescent turns practically overnight into a prima donna who spends hours grooming and checking the mirror to make sure that every feature of personal appearance is letter-perfect.

Adolescent attitude #11: Emotional cruelty to one another. Early teens can be incredibly insensitive to one another. Malicious gossip, hurtful teasing, and descriptive nicknames, outright rejection by the peer group—all are reasons why early adolescence is a time of great pain for so many.

Adolescent attitude #12: A highly present-oriented existence. Parents often learn the hard way that seriously discussing the future with an early adolescent is an exercise in futility. Conflict results when an unconcerned teen insists on continuing a day-to-day, pleasure-oriented way of life.

Adolescent attitude #13: A rich fantasy life develops. The adolescent's world is filled with hopes and dreams: knights in shining armor, great achievements, plenty of money, a life of freedom and fun—all without much personal effort. Such fantasies often help deny true realities.

Adolescent attitude #14: There is a strong need for independence. Translation: "I can make my own decisions by myself." Teens take it as an insult to their maturity to have to ask permission for anything. This leads to circumventing established rules or making decisions without parental knowledge.

Adolescent attitude #15: A proclivity for experimentation. With a new body and new feelings, the early adolescent develops an unwarranted sense of personal maturity. This leads to covert experimentation wth adult behaviors (smoking, drug use, sexual activity) aimed at the achievement of status and the satisfaction of curiosity. The knowledge that this is taking place leads to another legitimate parental fear.

THE EMOTIONAL AROUSAL OF PARENTS

It is a given that early adolescence is difficult for parents. To a degree this is attributable to the erratic and challenging behavior of their teens. It is also true that as long as the child is clearly a child, the parents remain weak or lie dormant. However, once puberty begins, a myriad of powerful feelings wells up in the parents.

In many respects, a child's puberty forces parents to deal actively with emotional issues that promote *their* growth and development if handled well. It is as important for parents to understand their suddenly aroused feelings as it is for them to understand what is happening emotionally within their teen.

Aroused emotion #1: Unadulterated fear. I would not be going too far to say that the parents of teens live with fear and constant worry. "What's happened now?" "What am I going to find out about next?" A child's world is quite small. At puberty, it suddenly expands and the teen is gone much of the time. This occurs at about the same time that a teen becomes evasive about what is going on in his or her world. Fears grow.

Aroused emotion #2: A deep sense of helplessness. Parents grow very uncomfortable as they watch their teen experience all the pain and turmoil that early adolescence usually brings. Because adolescents perceive adults as unable *really* to understand anything of importance to themselves, parents may be pushed away when problems occur. The kids don't realize how helpless parents feel when they see their child suffering emotionally but are relegated to the sidelines.

Aroused emotion #3: High levels of frustration. It is a given that many of the behaviors of an early adolescent trigger parental anger. One of a teen's strongest emotional needs is to be separate emotionally. This need is expressed by constantly confronting parents verbally, violating rules and pushing limits right to the brink. This entirely normal adolescent response pattern takes its toll on parents who become highly stressed, frustrated and tired.

Aroused emotion #4: A growing awareness of loss. With the onset of puberty, parents are forced to recognize that in just a few years, their teen will be going into the world and lost forever to the nuclear family. The undeniable fact that "our little girl/boy is growing up" triggers this deepening sense of loss on the part of parents: the sadness is compounded by the withdrawal of the teen from family life. Often this particular feeling is overwhelmed by fleeting wishes that the child would hurry and grow up so parents can have some peace of mind.

Aroused emotion #5: Personal hurt. Parents of teens struggle to do their very best to guide and protect their children. However, no thanks are forthcoming. In fact, parents' efforts are often resented and they are labeled as old-fashioned or Victorian or old fogies who are obviously completely out of touch with reality. Angry confrontations are the norm. Sullen withdrawal is an everyday occurrence. Continued rejection and hurt feelings make it difficult for parents to continue giving their personal best to an unappreciative teen.

IN THE EYE OF THE HURRICANE

At the center of every hurricane is the eye. That's where there is calm despite the intensity of the storm that swirls around it. This is an excellent way to conceptualize the relationship of effective parents to their children during the tumultuous early adolescent years. At puberty, a teen becomes inexorably swept up in the swift winds of change. To help themselves and their child, parents must remain calm and aware in the eye of the hurricane.

In recent years, much has been written about the changing nature of growing up in America. Some authorities emphasize the group's premature sophistication consequent on the fact that teens these days are exposed to much more at an earlier age than their parents were. Others who study this special group find that beyond the surface precocity of teens, attaining emotional maturity is steadily becoming a more prolonged and difficult process than ever before. The reality that parents must understand is that these seemingly divergent points of view are both absolutely valid and in no way contradict one another.

To be effective, parents must not be fooled by the misleading sophistication of teens and instead respond to the more complex developmental problems that lie beneath this surface veneer. To be of maximum aid in promoting healthy growth toward maturity, parents must make sure that their responses reflect three important teenage needs.

Teen need #1: "Depth perception" by parents. Basically, parents must be able to see accurately beyond the often erratic surface behaviors of an adolescent to the real issues that simply can't be articulated by a teen. Then parents must respond in caring ways to those emotional needs despite protests, confrontations and denials.

Teen need #2: Consistency of parental responses. Teens are notorious for their inconsistency. One of their deepest needs during these years of turmoil is to have parents who are steady and consistent. Such parents become a stabilizing influence and a center of strength—this helps a teen cope effectively with rapid change in every part of life.

Teen need #3: Strength of parental conviction. At no other time during the entire child-rearing process must parents be surer of their values. Teens focus tremendous pressure on parents to convince them they are wrong or that their values are irrelevant. Far too often the kids succeed in compromising solid parental values, to the detriment of the family and themselves.

One of the most emotionally rigorous tasks that parents face during the adolescent years is to keep doing what is right with very little encouragement and without becoming too insecure. And, after all is said and done and those difficult years are over, most teens do mature to join the ranks of respectable adults. Didn't you? And if you parented well, you will be rewarded eventually when your adult son or daughter thanks you directly for all the sacrifices you made in the face of all the obstacles.

But the progress toward the goal is a nightmare. One frustrated parent put up a sign in the kitchen: "NOTICE TO ALL TEENS! If you are tired of being hassled by unreasonable parents, NOW IS THE TIME FOR ACTION. Leave home and pay your own way WHILE YOU STILL KNOW EVERYTHING!"

These days puberty has perils for parents and for the children in grown-up bodies who are in their charge. And adolescence is no time to cut corners and take the easy road. Perhaps it was a wise parent who remarked that "a shortcut is often the quickest way to get somewhere you weren't going." With adolescents, the best road is always difficult but eventually rewarding. Shortcuts too often lead to dead ends. Or dangerous precipices. Sometimes to places you never expected to visit.

Those Gangly Years

NEW BODIES, NEW SCHOOLS AND NEW EXPECTATIONS NOTWITHSTANDING, MOST EARLY ADOLESCENTS WEATHER THE EXPERIENCE SURPRISINGLY WELL.

ANNE C. PETERSEN

Anne C. Petersen, Ph.D., a developmental psychologist, is a professor of human development at Pennsylvania State University, where she heads the interdisciplinary department of individual and family studies.

How can you stand studying adolescents? My daughter has just become one and she's impossible to live with. Her hormones may be raging, but so am I!" A colleague at a cocktail party was echoing the widespread view that the biological events of puberty necessarily change nice kids into moody, rebellious adolescents. The view has gained such a foothold that some parents with well-behaved teenagers worry that their kids aren't developing properly.

They needn't worry. My research, and that of many others, suggests that although the early teen years can be quite a challenge for normal youngsters and their families, they're usually not half as bad as they are reputed to be. And even though the biological changes of puberty do affect adolescents' behavior, attitudes and feelings in many important ways, other, often controllable, social and environmental forces are equally important.

One 14-year-old, for example, who tried to excuse his latest under-par report card by saying, "My problem is testosterone, not tests," only looked at part of the picture. He ignored, as many do, the fact that, because of a move and the shift to junior high school, he had been in three schools in as many years.

My colleagues and I at Pennsylvania State University looked at a three-year span in the lives of young adolescents to find out how a variety of biological and social factors affected their behavior and their feelings about themselves. A total of 335 young adolescents were randomly selected from two suburban school districts, primarily white and middle- to upper-middle-class. Two successive waves of these kids were monitored as they moved from the sixth through the eighth grade. Twice a year we interviewed them individually and gave them psychological tests in groups. When the youngsters were in the sixth and eighth grades, we also interviewed and assessed their parents. Just recently we again interviewed and assessed these young people and their

I DIDN'T LIKE BEING EARLY. BUT BY EIGHTH GRADE, EVERYONE WORE A BRA AND HAD THEIR PERIOD. I WAS NORMAL.

parents during the adolescents' last year of high school.

We followed the children's pubertal development by asking them to judge themselves every six months on such indicators as height, pubic hair and acne in both boys and girls; breast development and menstruation in girls; and voice change and facial-hair growth in boys. We also estimated the timing of puberty by finding out when each youngster's adolescent growth spurt in height peaked, so we could study the effects of early, on-time or late maturing.

Although we have not yet analyzed all the data, it's clear that puberty alone does not have the overwhelming psychological impact that earlier clinicians and researchers assumed it did (see "The Puzzle of Adolescence," this article). But it does have many effects on body image, moods and relationships with parents and members of the opposite sex.

Being an early or late maturer (one year earlier or later than average), for example, affected adolescents' satisfaction with their appearance and their body image—but only among seventh- and eighth-graders, not sixth-graders. We found that among students in the higher two grades, girls who were physically more mature were generally less satisfied with their weight and appearance than their less mature classmates.

A seventh-grade girl, pleased with being still childlike, said, "You can do more things—you don't have as much weight to carry around." A girl in the eighth grade, also glad to be a late maturer, commented, "If girls get fat, they have to worry about it." In contrast, an early-maturing girl subsequently commented, "I didn't like being early. A lot of my friends didn't understand." Another girl, as a high school senior, described the pain of maturing extremely early: "I tried to hide it. I was embarrassed and ashamed." However, her discomfort ended in the eighth grade, she said, because "by then everyone wore a bra and had their period. I was normal."

We found the reverse pattern among boys: Those who were physically more mature tended to be more satisfied with their weight and their overall appearance than their less mature peers. One already gangling seventh-grade boy, for example, said he liked being "a little taller and having more muscle development than other kids so you can beat them in races." He conceded that developing more slowly might help "if you're a jockey" but added, "Really, I can't think of why [developing] later would be an advantage." In reflecting back from the 12th grade, a boy who had matured early noted that at the time the experience "made me feel superior."

For seventh- and eighth-grade boys, physical maturity was related to mood. Boys who had reached puberty reported positive moods more often than their prepubertal male classmates did. Pubertal status was less clearly and consistently related to mood among girls, but puberty did affect how girls got along with their parents. As physical development advanced among sixth-grade girls, their relationships with their parents declined; girls who were developmentally advanced talked less to their parents and had less positive feelings about family relationships than did less developed girls. We found a similar pattern among eighth-grade girls, but it was less clear in the seventh grade, perhaps because of the many other changes occurring at that time, such as the change from elementary to secondary school format and its related effects on friendship and school achievement.

The timing of puberty affected both school achievement and moods. Early maturers tended to get higher grades than later maturers in the same class. We suspect that this may stem from the often documented tendency of teachers to give more positive ratings to larger pupils. Although early maturers had an edge academically, those who matured later were more likely to report positive moods.

As we have noted, among relatively physically mature adolescents, boys and girls had opposite feelings about their appearance: The boys were pleased, but the girls were not. We believe that, more generally, pubertal change is usually a positive experience for boys but a negative one for girls. While advancing maturity has some advantages for girls, including gaining some of the rights and privileges granted to maturing boys, it also brings increased limitations and restrictions related to their emerging womanhood. One sixth-grade girl stated emphatically, "I don't like the idea of getting older or any of that. If I had my choice, I'd rather stay 10." Or, as one seventh-grade boy graphically explained the gender differences, "Parents let them [boys] go out later than girls because they don't have to worry about getting raped or anything like that."

Differences in the timing of puberty also affect interactions with members of the opposite sex. But it takes two to tango, and in the sixth grade, although many girls have reached puberty and are ready to socialize with boys, most boys have not yet made that transition. Thus, as one girl plaintively summed up the sixth-grade social scene, "Girls think about boys more than boys think about girls."

In the seventh and eighth grades, the physically more mature boys and girls are likely to be pioneers in exploring social relations with members of the opposite sex, including talking with them on the phone, dating, having a boyfriend or girlfriend and "making out." We had the sense that once these young people began looking like teenagers, they wanted to act like them as well.

SHIFTING SCHOOLS EXPOSES TEENS TO NEW EXTRACURRICULAR ACTIVITIES—LICIT AND ILLICIT

But puberty affects the social and sexual activity of individual young adolescents both directly and indirectly; the pubertal status of some students can have consequences for the entire peer group of boys and girls. Although dating and other boy-girl interactions are linked to pubertal status, and girls usually reach puberty before boys do, we found no sex differences in the rates of dating throughout the early-adolescent period. When the early-maturing kids began socializing with members of the opposite sex, the pattern quickly spread throughout the entire peer group. Even prepubertal girls were susceptible to thinking and talking about boys if all their girlfriends were "boy crazy."

The physical changes brought on by puberty have far-reaching effects, but so do many other changes in the lives of adolescents. One we found to be particularly influential is the change in school structure between the sixth and eighth grades. Most young adolescents in our country shift from a relatively small neighborhood elementary school, in which most classes are taught by one teacher, to a much larger, more impersonal middle school or junior high school (usually farther from the child's home), in which students move from class to class and teacher to teacher for every subject. This shift in schools has many ramifications, including disrupting the old peer-group structure, exposing adolescents to different achievement expectations by teachers and providing opportunities for new extracurricular activities—licit and illicit.

Both the timing and number of school transitions are very important. In our study, for example, students who changed schools earlier than most of their peers, as well as those who changed schools twice (both experiences due to modifications of the school system), suffered an academic slump that continued through eighth grade. Therefore, early or double school transition seemed stressful, beyond the usual effects of moving to a junior high school.

Puberty and school change, which appear to be the primary and most pervasive changes occurring during early adolescence, are often linked to other important changes, such as altered family relations. Psychologist Laurence Steinberg of the University of Wisconsin has found that family re-

THE PUZZLE OF ADOLESCENCE

At the turn of the century, psychologist G. Stanley Hall dignified adolescence with his "storm and stress" theory, and Anna Freud subsequently argued influentially that such storm and stress is a normal part of adolescence. Ever since, clinicians and researchers have been trying—with only limited success—to develop a coherent theory of what makes adolescents tick.

Psychoanalytic theorist Peter Blos added in the late 1960s and 1970s that adolescents' uncontrolled sexual and aggressive impulses affect relationships with their parents. He suggested that both adolescents and their parents may need more distant relationships because of the unacceptable feelings stimulated by the adolescents' sexuality.

Research conducted in the 1960s showed that not all adolescents experience the storm and stress psychoanalytic theory predicts they should. Many studies, including those of Roy Grinker; Joseph Adelson and Elizabeth Douvan; Daniel Offer; and Albert Bandura, demonstrated that a significant proportion of adolescents make it through this period without appreciable turmoil. These findings suggest that pubertal change per se cannot account for the rocky time some adolescents experience.

Other theories of adolescent development have also been linked to pubertal change. For example, in his theory of how children's cognitive capacities develop, Swiss psychologist Jean Piaget attributed the emergence of "formal operational thought," that is, the capacity to think abstractly, to the interaction of pubertal and environmental changes that occur during the same developmental period.

Some researchers have linked the biological events of puberty to possible changes in brain growth or functioning. Deborah Waber, a psychologist at Boston Children's Hospital, has shown that the timing of pubertal change is related to performance differences between the right- and left-brain hemispheres on certain tasks and to the typical adult pattern of gender-related cognitive abilities: Later maturers, including most men, have relatively better spatial abilities, and earlier maturers, including most women, have relatively better verbal abilities.

It has also been suggested that pubertal change affects adolescent behavior through the social consequences of altered appearance. Once young adolescents look like adults,

they are more likely to be treated as adults and to see themselves that way, too.

Coming also from a social psychological perspective, psychologist John Hill of Virginia Commonwealth University, together with former Cornell University doctoral student Mary Ellen Lynch, have proposed that pubertal change leads parents and peers to expect more traditional gender-role behavior from adolescents than from younger children; they suggest that both boys and girls become more aware of these gender stereotypes in early adolescence and exaggerate their gender-related behavior at this age.

Despite all these theories, most studies that look at how puberty affects adolescent development are finding that puberty per se is not as important as we once thought. Puberty does specifically affect such things as body image and social and sexual behavior, but it does not affect all adolescent behavior, and it affects some adolescents more strongly than others. In fact, many studies, like ours, are revealing that other changes in early adolescence, particularly social and environmental ones, are at least as important as biological ones.

lationships shift as boys and girls move through puberty. During mid puberty, he says, conflict in family discussions increases; when the conflict is resolved, boys usually become more dominant in conversations with their mothers. (Psychologist John Hill of Virginia Commonwealth University has found that family conflict increases only for boys.) Other research, however, suggests that adolescents wind up playing a more equal role relative to both parents.

In our study, the parents of early-maturing girls and late-maturing boys reported less positive feelings about their children in the sixth and eighth grades than did parents of boys and girls with other patterns of pubertal timing. (These effects were always stronger for fathers than for mothers.) The adolescents, however, reported that their feelings about their parents were unrelated to pubertal timing.

The feelings of affection and support that adolescents and their parents reported about one another usually declined from the sixth to the eighth grades, with the biggest decline in feelings between girls and their mothers. But importantly, the decline was from very positive to less positive—but still not negative—feelings.

Early adolescence is clearly an unusual transition in development because of the number of changes young people experience. But the impact of those changes is quite varied; changes that may challenge and stimulate some young people can become overwhelming and stressful to others. The outcome seems to depend on prior strengths and vulnerabilities—both of the individual adolescents and their families—as well as on the pattern, timing and intensity of changes.

Youngsters in our study who changed schools within six months of peak pubertal change reported more depression and anxiety than those whose school and biological transitions were more separated in time. Students who experienced an unusual and negative change at home—such as the death of a parent or divorce of parents—reported even greater difficulties, a finding that supports other research. Sociologists Roberta Simmons and Dale Blyth have found that the negative effects of junior high school transitions, especially in combination with other life changes, continue on into high school, particularly for girls.

Many of the negative effects of transitions and changes seen in our study were tempered when adolescents had particularly positive and supportive relationships with their peers and family. The effects of all these early-adolescent changes were even stronger by the 12th grade than in 8th grade.

Overall, we found that the usual pattern of development in early adolescence is quite positive. More than half of those in the study seemed to be almost trouble-free, and approximately 30 percent of the total group had only intermittent problems during their early teen years. Fifteen percent of the kids, however, did appear to be caught in a downward spiral of trouble and turmoil.

Gender played an important role in how young adolescents expressed and dealt with this turmoil. Boys generally showed their poor adjustment through external behavior, such as being rebellious and disobedient, whereas girls were more likely to show internal behavior, such as having depressed moods. But since many poorly adjusted boys also showed many signs of depression, the rates of such symptoms did not differ between the sexes in early adolescence.

By the 12th grade, however, the girls were significantly more likely than the boys to have depressive symptoms, a sex difference also found among adults. Boys who had such symptoms in the 12th grade usually had had them in the sixth grade as well; girls who had depressive symptoms as high school seniors usually had developed them by the eighth grade.

For youngsters who fell in the troubled group, the stage was already set—and the pathways distinguishable—at the very beginning of adolescence. There is an overall tendency for academic decline in the seventh and eighth grades (apparently because seventh- and eighth-grade teachers adopt tougher grading standards than elementary school teachers do). But the grades of boys with school behavior problems or depressive symptoms in early adolescence subsequently declined far more than those of boys who did not report such problems. Thus, for youngsters whose lives are already troubled, the changes that come with early adolescence add further burdens—and their problems are likely to persist through the senior year of high school.

One 12th-grade boy who followed this pathway described the experience: "My worst time was seventh to ninth grade. I had a lot of growing up to do and I still have a lot more to do. High school was not the 'sweet 16' time everyone said it would be. What would have helped me is more emotional support in grades seven through nine." In explaining that particularly difficult early-adolescent period he said, "Different teachers, colder environment, changing classes and detention all caused chaos in the seventh to ninth grades."

We did not find the same relationship between academic failure and signs of emotional turmoil in girls as in boys. For example, those seventh-grade girls particularly likely to report poor self-image or depressive symptoms were those who were academically successful. Furthermore, when these girls lowered their academic achievement by eighth grade, their depression and their self-image tended to improve. These effects occurred in many areas of girls' coursework but were particularly strong in stereotypically "masculine" courses such as

THE VAST MAJORITY OF EARLY TEENS WE STUDIED WERE TROUBLE-FREE OR HAD ONLY INTERMITTENT PROBLEMS. ONLY 15 PERCENT WERE PLAGUED BY TROUBLE AND TURMOIL.

mathematics and science. Like the pattern of problems for boys, the girls' pattern of trading grades to be popular and feel good about themselves persisted into the 12th grade. (Some girls, of course, performed well academically and felt good about themselves both in junior high school and high school.)

We think that for certain girls, high achievement, especially in "masculine" subjects, comes with social costs—speculation supported by the higher priority these particular girls give to popularity. They seem to sacrifice the longer-term benefits of high achievement for the more immediate social benefits of "fitting in." Other studies have revealed a peak in social conformity at this age, especially among girls, and have shown that many adolescents reap immediate, but short-term, social benefits from many

types of behavior that adults find irrational or risky.

Our most recent research is focused

---

*P*ARENTS LET
BOYS GO OUT LATER
THAN GIRLS BECAUSE
THEY DON'T HAVE TO WORRY
ABOUT THEM GETTING
RAPED.

---

on exploring further whether the developmental patterns established during early adolescence continue to the end of high school. We are also trying to integrate our observations into a coherent theory of adolescent development and testing that theory by seeing whether we can predict the psychological status of these students at the end of high school based on their characteristics in early adolescence. Other key concerns include discovering early warning signs of trouble and identifying ways to intervene to improve the course of development.

The biological events of puberty are a necessary—and largely uncontrollable—part of growing up. But we may be able to understand and control the social and environmental forces that make adolescence so difficult for a small but troubled group of youngsters. The adolescent's journey toward adulthood is inherently marked by change and upheaval but need not be fraught with chaos or deep pain.

The Myth About Teen-Agers

Richard Flaste

Richard Flaste is Science and Health Editor of The New York Times.

A father I know tells of one unsettling moment when he was sure he would never understand the teen-age mind. The mind in question was that of his own teen-ager, a 15-year-old blonde possessed of considerable charm and an aggressive reticence. The pivotal moment was this effort at conversation:

"So, how was your day at school?"

"Good."

"Was it more than just good? I mean, did anything actually happen that was interesting?"

"No, it was just good."

"What about the bio test? Didn't you have a test?"

(The answer this time came with a gleam of irritation in her eyes.) "I told you, everything was *good*."

He backed away, feeling foolish, sorry he had tried, sorry he'd stirred her pique. What could possibly be going on in her mind? And he wondered about himself, too, as he slipped away into a friendlier room. Was he actually afraid of her?

Later, having thought about that scene many times, he concluded that he had in fact been frightened, but not so much of her — after all, they had their good times, and she did seem to love and respect him at least every now and then. Rather it was the condition of adolescence that scared him. On occasions like that abortive effort at conversation he wasn't just confronting a teen-ager who might or might not be in the mood to talk to him but also everything he had ever heard about adolescence, the Sturm, the Drang and the plain old orneriness of it. That flash of annoyance in her eyes was all that was necessary to evoke an image of those infamous raging hormones boiling inside a pubescent caldron.

The burden was a heavy one to take into a small inquiry about a person's day. It was an unnecessary burden, too. For, although most of us aren't aware of it, the concept of adolescence as a period of angry, dark turmoil has largely been overthrown, and along with it the idea that kids need to be tormented and perverse to make the storm-tossed transition to adulthood. That concept is being replaced by a new psychology of adolescence, a growing body of work that reflects a vigorous attempt to find out what life is genuinely like for normal teen-agers, and which reveals that delight plays as large a role among most adolescents as misery does.

A substantial number of psychotherapists and personality theorists still believe that adolescence is a trial by fire, as do many writers of juvenile fiction. But what is now the mainstream of psychological research dismisses this emphasis on turmoil as balderdash. It is a misguided emphasis, many researchers say, which grew out of the overwrought imaginations of romanticists ranging from the Freuds (mostly Anna) to Goethe (particularly, "The Sorrows of Young Werther").

In the 1970's, I wrote regularly about child-development issues for this newspaper, and I accepted the idea that any teen-ager was necessarily a little mad. To a large extent this notion was promoted by the psychoanalytic literature, but it was embraced by many of us as a handy way to explain hard times with our teen-agers. We could say that noxious behavior such as naked aggression was normal, and so we didn't have to worry. We reassured ourselves constantly, usually with a knowing laugh about the craziness of teen-agers. But I did not believe it completely. Why should only this age group carry the label of madness? Coming back to the question now, I am struck by how different the mood among many psychologists and psychiatrists is. By and large, they are more determined to draw an empirical and detailed picture of the varied and complex adolescent experience.

Some researchers have surveyed thousands of teen-agers to learn what they believe about themselves and their families. Others have given youngsters beepers to carry around, so that when they are signaled they will report their moods at that moment. And still others have worked with families, asking parents, teen-agers and their siblings to take batteries of tests.

Among the most influential of this cadre of researchers is Dr. Daniel Offer of the University of Chicago, a psychiatrist who believes that the widespread idea that the teen years are unavoidably insane has mischaracterized the lives of millions of people. Moreover, he contends that the emphasis on turmoil has created the expectation of Sturm and Drang for every teen-ager, thereby masking the serious emotional difficulties of a significant minority of adolescents who need professional help. Dr. Offer was moved to declare a "Defense of Adolescents" in The Journal of the American Medical Association, and he made a presentation along the same lines to the convention of the American Psychiatric Association last May.

Dr. Offer's team was among the earliest to plumb the day-to-day feelings of large numbers of teen-agers. Their first explorations, in the 1960's, began to reveal that, incredible as it might have seemed, most teen-agers were happy most of the time. After years of confirmatory work, he confidently told the psychiatrists' convention that "the vast majority of adolescents are well-adjusted, get along well with their peers and their parents, adjust well to the mores and values of their social environment and cope well with their internal and external worlds." Dr. Offer recalled in a recent interview that this message disturbed some of his colleagues, because they didn't believe that teen-agers' responses to questions could be trusted.

The work of Dr. Offer and his team has provided a starting point for many of the nation's researchers. By no means do they make adolescence out to be an easy time, any more than life as a whole is easy. Adolescence is a period of rapid and profound change in the body and mind. It is a time to find out who you are and to begin to move toward what you will become. Family bickering is bound to escalate during this period, but it usually centers on what one psychologist calls the

Adolescence is a time when you begin to find out who you are.

"good-citizen topics," such as chores, dress and schoolwork. Most researchers feel that this conflict is useful, because it allows a teen-ager to assert his or her individuality over relatively minor issues.

There are several explanations for this rise in family quarreling. A widely cited cognitive explanation comes from the work of the Swiss psychologist Jean Piaget, who showed that children do not have the capacity for the abstract, analytical thinking he called "formal operations" until the teen years. The arrival of that tool is what enables them, in the view of some experts, to question their parents' thinking.

RESEARCH BY JUDITH G. SMETANA, AN ASSOCIATE PROFESSOR of education, psychology and pediatrics at the University of Rochester, has recently aroused much interest among psychologists. She contends that concentrating on the development of a child's ability to think logically isn't useful in elucidating family relationships. Instead, she focuses on the way parents and children conceptualize their experiences. According to her research, there are two fundamentally different world views at the core of family conflict: adolescents tend to see much of their behavior as a "personal" matter, affecting no one but themselves and therefore up to them entirely, while their parents tend to hold to what she calls "conventional thinking," which sees society's rules and expectations as primary. The dichotomy provides for commonplace clashes:

"Clean up your room. This family does not live in a hovel."

"It's my room and I like hovels."

In a recent paper Smetana charts the typical evolution from personal to conventional thinking in a teen-ager. A child of 12 or 13 generally has no use for conventions when it comes to family issues. Between 14 and 16 the teen-ager comes to recognize conventions as the way society regulates itself. Then comes a brief period in which conventions are rejected again, but more thoughtfully. Between 18 and 25 conventions are seen as playing an important and admirable role in facilitating the business of society.

As the teen-ager moves in fits and starts in the direction of his or her parents, the parents generally stick to their guns. Nevertheless, the adolescent has begun to reason like them, and so, by the age of 15 or 16, the quarreling usually subsides, at least for a while.

It is replaced by a period in which members of the family are able to negotiate more successfully than in the past. The teen-ager learns how to "work on mom and dad" to achieve goals like staying out late at night or using the family car.

Indeed, "negotiation" has emerged as one of the key words in the new psychology of adolescence. Instead of talking about rebellion and a painful separation from the family, many psychologists now see adolescence as a time in which parents and children negotiate new relationships with one another. The teen-ager must gain more authority over his or her own life; the parents must come to see their child as more nearly an equal, with a right to differing opinions.

Parents often mistake normal self-assertion for rebellion and defiance.

ANOTHER WAY OF LOOKING AT THIS PERIOD OF NEGOTIA-tion has been formulated by psychologists Harold D. Grotevant at the University of Texas at Austin and Catherine R. Cooper at the University of California, Santa Cruz. They believe that typically there is an elaborate interplay between a teen-ager's striving to be an individual who is separate from the family and his attempts to maintain a close, caring relationship with his parents. In a recent study they found that teen-agers who had the strongest sense of themselves as individuals were raised in families where the parents offered guidance and comfort but also permitted their children to develop their own points of view.

For some families, this can be a terrible period. Parents who try to exert too much control over their children and find it impossible to yield in a conflict can be driven into a frenzy by the efforts of their teen-agers to establish their own identities. But most parents are more pliable, and find ways to compromise.

A neighbor of mine, unlucky enough to have a son who became a teen-ager when punk was hot, remembers how uncontrollably rattled she would get when she saw him dressed for school in the morning. "He would throw on any rag, this way and that," she recalls. She couldn't contain her exasperation and her fear that this monstrous style of dressing would somehow reflect on her. She imagined that others might pity her for her misfortune. After repeated failed confrontations, she decided not to come downstairs until her son was gone. It seems to her now that he dressed a little more sensibly if he knew she wouldn't be there to see it.

The influence of peers in everything from dress to sexual mores is undeniably strong during the teen-age years, although some experts downplay it because, like turmoil, it's been given more press than they think it's worth, and because they believe the emphasis on peers underestimates the importance of continuing attachments to the family. Parents may find it comforting to realize that this growing influence of friends is not the first assault on their authority. Throughout most of a child's life—not just in adolescence—parents share control with others: teachers, friends, siblings. After the earliest years parents are no longer in a position to know about whole segments of their children's lives, because so much takes place outside the home. Gerald R. Adams, a psychologist at Utah State University, making this point in a recent conversation, said, "If I interviewed your family, you'd be shocked at how little you know about the life of your child—school life, social life. Most parents don't really know the world of their children."

There are many things that children don't tell us because they know we won't approve, even if we are trying very hard to give them a measure of greater freedom. Who among us really wants to know everything about a child's sexual experimentation or moments of embarrassment?

But that isn't the only reason for reticence. Sometimes, teen-agers, like the rest of us, just don't feel like talking. The notorious moodiness of teen-agers is one of the most interesting areas of the latest psychological investigations. Dr. Offer says that he has found little tendency among normal teen-agers to plummet into deep and dark despair. (He points out that, although teen-age suicide is a deeply troubling phenomenon, the suicide rate for adolescents is lower than it is for people in their 20's and far lower than it is for people in their 70's.)

Reed Larson, a psychologist at the University of Illinois, has found a middle ground between coloring all of adolescence with dark moods or dismissing moodiness altogether. In studies carried out by giving kids beepers that signaled them when to report their feelings, he found that mood swings are a fact of teen-age life. On average, adolescents feel more delight and more sadness at any given moment than adults and move from one mood to another more rapidly. For teen-agers, emotional states generally last no more than 15 minutes. Even the strongest feelings tend not to last more than a half-hour, while the same kinds of feelings may last for two hours or longer among adults. But Larson and his colleagues concluded that these mood swings are healthy and natural, a reasonable response to a time of life filled with fast-paced events. "The typical adolescent may be moody," they wrote in a recent paper, "but not in turmoil."

AS WORD OF THE NEW INSIGHTS INTO TEEN-AGE LIFE gets out, parents are bound to benefit. They will learn to expect a certain amount of bickering in early adolescence, and they'll realize that it has a normal course to run. Parents might find it helpful to abandon the old vocabulary of rebellion and defiance. The words have been so widely misapplied that they are even used to characterize things like the piercing of ears against mother's wishes or staying out late. When self-assertion and self-indulgence are overdramatized by parents and viewed as rebellion or defiance, they take on the aura of criminal acts instead of being part of the fascinating interplay between parent and child in which the child eventually becomes an adult and the parent eventually accepts that.

In the case of the teen-ager who resists parental efforts at conversation, parents should realize that kids are sometimes out of sorts, or they may be too bewildered by the hectic events of their lives to find the words to describe them. Some teen-agers are more apt to engage in friendly conversation at dinner time, or just before they go to bed, than at times when the stresses of the day are still fresh. (Of course, when a teen-ager senses that his or her parents' attempts at conversation are prompted by their need to be in control, conversation will often be resisted on that ground alone.)

While a momentary rebuff or a bit of surliness should not be reason for deep concern, parents ought to worry about those moods that don't change. Teen-agers who are depressed for long periods of time, relentlessly combative, friendless, reclusive or miserable in other ways are not going through a normal adolescence; they and their families need help, perhaps professional.

Implicit in much of the new work on adolescence is the belief that parents must take a strong grip on their own sense of themselves, their own worth, so that they are not so easily shaken by every normal challenge to their control, and so that they can hold on to their children while confidently letting out some line.

Parents should find life a little easier, in any event, if the bogeyman of necessary insanity in adolescence is finally vanquished. For many parents that will mean they no longer need to fear their children's adolescence but can relax and maybe even enjoy it.

JEALOUSY & ENVY

The Demons Within Us

JON QUEIJO

Jon Queijo is a free-lance writer who resides in West Roxbury, Massachusetts.

Rick and Liz seemed to have a wonderful marriage; they did everything together. This changed suddenly, however, when Liz's ex-boyfriend began working at her law firm. Besieged by insecurity, Rick began calling Liz's office at odd hours and at night questioned her suspiciously. In a coup de grace, he burst in on her during a business luncheon and falsely accused her of having an affair.

Ann worked extremely hard to achieve success as a real estate agent. Her satisfaction turned sour, however, when a new agent was hired who managed to work less, yet made more sales. Ann hid her dislike of the new agent by offering to take her phone messages while she was out. When Ann began making more sales than her rival, no one made the connection between this turn of events and Ann's tendency to "accidentally" forget to deliver certain phone messages.

The jealous rage of a lover. The shameful actions of envy. Despite our better intentions, most of us feel these emotions dozens of times in our lifetimes. Pulling us apart from lovers, friends, family members, co-workers and even perfect strangers, jealousy and envy can devastate our lives and cause effects ranging from sadness, anger and depression, to estrangement, abuse and even violence.

Beyond our own lives, the power of these emotions has spawned countless works of poetry and prose and triggered numerous historical events. Perhaps for this reason society proclaimed judgment on jealousy and envy thousands of years ago, with the verdict coming down harder on envy. For example, while the pain of jealousy has been forever immortalized in poetry and song, the shame of envy emerges as early as the Ten Commandments: "Thou shalt not covet thy neighbor's house, field, wife or anything that is thy neighbor's." In fact, envy is despicable enough to be considered one of the "Seven Deadly Sins," taking its place alongside pride, gluttony, lust, sloth, anger and greed.

Although we see jealousy and envy arise in numerous situations, their basic definitions are fairly simple: jealousy is "the fear of losing a relationship" (romantic, parental, sibling, friendship); and envy is "the longing for something someone else has" (wealth, possessions, beauty, talent, position).

Despite these definitions and the numerous philosophers, poets and scientists who have pondered these emotions, some remarkably fundamental questions remain: What causes jealousy and envy? Are the emotions actually different? What do they feel like? What are the best ways to cope with these feelings? Why do we often use the terms interchangeably? And what are their implications for society?

Researchers have taken various approaches to answer these questions. The biological view, for example, says that jealousy and envy serve a basic purpose — the emotions lead to biochemical changes that spur the individual to take action and improve the situation. The evolutionary view holds that jealousy may enhance survival by keeping parents together, thus increasing protection of the offspring.

From *Bostonia*, May/June 1988, pp. 31-36. Reprinted with permission of *Bostonia Magazine*.

> ❝**P**eople who are dissatisfied with themselves are primed for having other people's talents impinge on them. If, on the other hand, you're satisfied with yourself, then what other people have or do won't unduly raise your expectations, and you should be less likely to feel envy. ❞
>
> RICHARD SMITH

Other explanations range from the reasonable — envy stems from parental attitudes that make a child feel inferior; to the bizarre — the emotions begin in infants when the mother withholds breast-feeding.

Probably the most practical understanding of jealousy and envy, however, emerges from the work of social psychologists — researchers who look at the way people react to each other and society. To them, jealousy and envy arise when the right mix of internal *and* external ingredients are present in society.

"I tend to look at jealousy and envy in terms of motivation and self-esteem," explains Peter Salovey, a social psychologist at Yale University. "It's the interaction between what's important to you and what's happening in the environment. The common denominator is this threat to something that's very important to the person — something that defines self-worth."

Richard Smith, a social psychologist at Boston University who has conducted several studies on jealousy and envy, emphasizes external factors, such as how society affects our view of ourselves. "My perspective is from social comparisons," he explains, "which says we have no objective opinion for evaluating our abilities, so we look at others."

Smith, like Salovey, also stresses internal factors — the role of self-esteem, for example — in determining whether we will feel jealous or envious in any given situation. "People who are dissatisfied with themselves are primed for having other people's talents and possessions impinge on them," Smith points out. "If, on the other hand, you're satisfied with yourself, then what other

people have or do won't unduly raise your expectations for yourself, and you should be less likely to feel envy."

Embarrassed by his display of jealousy, Rick apologizes to Liz and they discuss the problem. Soon they realize that while Rick loves Liz and fears losing her, something else is at work here. Because Liz's ex-boyfriend is a lawyer, he possesses skills Rick does not. While Rick is proud of his ability as a store manager, he fears Liz's ex-boyfriend could lure her away with other skills.

Feeling guilty about her actions, Ann calls a friend for support. Ann knows she feels inadequate because the new agent is succeeding in a career that is very important to her, but that doesn't explain everything; others have done better whom Ann has not envied. Then it occurs to her: What bothers her is the way the woman was bettering Ann. She was more outgoing and self-confident — two skills about which Ann has always felt insecure.

As Rick and Ann's situations illustrate, if someone is unsure about an ability — such as Rick and his law knowledge or Ann and her communication skills — then a social situation can bring out that insecurity. "In envy," notes Salovey, "the threat may come from someone else's possessions or attributes. In jealousy the situation is the same, except that the other person's possessions or attributes cause you to fear losing the relationship. Either way, somebody else threatens your self-esteem."

Yet Salovey emphasizes that it is not as simple as saying someone is at risk for these emotions if they have a low opinion of themselves. "It's low self-

esteem in a specific *area*," he explains. "If you have a low opinion about your physical looks or occupation, then that's the area in which you're more likely to be vulnerable. You feel it when you confront somebody else who is superior to you in that respect."

From Smith's point of view, the key is how that person compares him or herself to others. In one study, for example, he found that envy was strongest among people who performed below their expectation in an area that was important to them and then confronted someone who functioned better. In a related study, Smith also found that a person's "risk" for feeling jealous or envious increases with the increased importance they put on the quality.

While much of this may sound like common sense, in fact little research has been done to establish even the most basic ground rules of jealousy and envy. For example, are the two emotions actually different? What do people feel when they are jealous or envious? Despite centuries of long-held assumptions, only recently have researchers begun to answer these questions scientifically.

Smith and his colleagues, for example, recently conducted a study to see if the classic distinctions between the two emotions are actually true. Their findings — presented last August at the annual convention of the American Psychological Association — validated what we have always suspected. Jealous people tend to feel a fear of loss, betrayal, loneliness, suspicion and uncertainty. Envious people, on the other hand, tend to feel inferior, longing for what another has, guilt over feeling ill will towards someone, shame and a tendency to deny the emotion.

The study was not an idle exercise in stating the obvious. It was designed to help clear an ongoing debate about jealousy and envy and our curious tendency not only to mix up the terms, but to experience an overlap of both emotions.

Consider, for example, the following uses of the word jealousy: Bruce was jealous when his girlfriend began talking to another man at the party; the boy cried in a fit of jealousy when his parents paid attention to the new baby; Ellen became jealous when her friend began spending more time at the health club. Nothing unusual with any of these uses of jealousy—they all refer to someone's "fear of losing a relationship."

Now, however, consider these uses: The professor, jealous of his colleague's success, broke into his lab and ruined his experiment; Mary is always complaining of being jealous of her sister's beautiful blonde hair; Mark admits that he is jealous of John's athletic ability. All of these situations actually refer to envy, "the longing for something someone else has." Researchers have noticed the mix-up and it has led them to question how different the feelings really are.

"In everyday language it's clear that people use the terms interchangeably," notes Smith, adding, "For that reason, there's naturally some confusion about whether they're different." In a recent study, however, Smith and his colleagues found the mix-up only works one way, with jealousy being the broader term. That is, jealousy is used sometimes in place of envy, but envy is rarely used when referring to jealousy. So while you might say, "I'm jealous of Paul's new Mercedes," you would never say, "When she left her husband, he flew into an *envious* rage."

Is there an underlying reason for why the terms are used interchangeably? One reason people may use jealousy in place of envy, and not vice versa, is because of the social stigma attached to envy. But Salovey and Smith both point to another reason for the overlap.

Dave and Marcia had been dating for a year when Marcia decided she wanted to see other men. Dave was devastated —not only because he cared for her, but because he was older and feared his age was working against him. One evening he bumped into Marcia, arm-in-arm with another man. As Dave talked to the couple, sarcasm led to verbal abuse, until finally Dave took a swing at Marcia's date—a man at least 10 years his junior.

In case you haven't guessed, Dave wanted back more than his relationship with Marcia; he also wanted the return of his youth. He was feeling a painful mixture of jealousy *and* envy. Explains Salovey, "The same feelings emerge when your relationship is threatened by someone else as when you'd like something that person has. I think one reason is that in most romantic situations, envy plays a role. You're jealous

because you're going to lose the relationship, but you're also envious because there is something the other person has that allows him to be attractive to the person you care about."

Because this overlap occurs so frequently, Salovey has found the best way to understand jealousy and envy is to examine each *situation*. In addition, because jealousy is the more encompassing term, he views envy as a form of jealousy and distinguishes the two by the terms "romantic jealousy," the fear of losing a relationship; and "social-comparison jealousy," the envy that arises when people compare traits like age, intelligence, possession and talent.

Smith agrees with Salovey that one reason people confuse the terms may be that envy is present in most cases of jealousy. Nevertheless, he takes issue with Salovey's use of the term "social-comparison jealousy." "It may be true that there's almost invariably envy in every case of jealousy," he notes, "but it doesn't mean there's no value in distinguishing the two feelings. The overlap in usage only goes one way, so there's no reason to throw out the term 'envy.'"

Salovey counters, "I'm not saying we need to stop using 'envy.' The reason we use 'social-comparison jealousy' is to emphasize that the situation that creates the feeling is important." And one reason

---

COMPARING OURSELVES TO OTHERS In Sickness and In Health

Envy, according to Richard Smith, arises when we compare ourselves to others and can't cope with what we see. Indeed, he believes that the way in which we cope with "social comparisons" plays an important role in our physical as well as mental health.

Smith theorizes that we use one of four "comparison styles" to cope with social differences. Two of these styles are "constructive" to well-being, while two are "destructive." "It's a difficult problem to tackle," says Smith, "but we're trying to measure these styles and see if they predict a person's general satisfaction with life or ability to cope with illness." For example, he notes, "There's considerable evidence" that one way people cope with serious illness is by focusing on others who are not doing as well.

Smith has arranged the four comparison styles in a matrix, with the descriptions in each box referring to the characteristics of that style. "*Upward*-Constructive," for example, represents those who compare themselves to others who are better off, and use it as a healthy stimulus. In this category, "You don't feel hostile to others who are better," says Smith, "because you hope to be like them. It suggests that upward comparisons are not necessarily bad."

"*Upward*-Destructive," however, shows how comparing yourself to those doing better can be unhealthy.

Envy, resentment, Type A behavior and poor health all fit into this category. Smith points to a study that looked at personalities of people who had heart attacks, "and the only dimension that predicted heart disease was this jealousy-suspicion trait."

What Smith calls "*Downward*-Constructive," refers to people who compare themselves to those worse off, and use it to feel better about themselves. Such people, says Smith, "realize that others aren't doing so well and how lucky they are. There's some solid evidence in the health literature showing the value of that kind of comparison."

Finally, "*Downward*-Destructive," describes those who get pleasure out of comparing themselves to others who are worse off. "I'd call the effect 'schadenfreude,' or joy at the suffering of others," says Smith. "It's akin to sadism and it's probably not conducive to health."

"What's interesting about all four comparison styles," notes Smith, "is that they don't necessarily have any relation to reality. They reflect what people construe and focus on." While Smith stresses, "This is all speculative," he adds that "my feeling is that 'Upward-Destructive' explains people's hostility in terms of their social comparison context. It shows why their relation to people doing better leads to envy and why they'd feel hostile to begin with." J.Q.

Salovey stresses the situation—rather than other mood differences—is that romantic jealousy, since it includes envy, is usually very intense, making it difficult to separate distinct feelings.

Nevertheless, Smith believes the distinction should be made, especially because "In its traditional definition, envy has a hostile component to it." Not everyone would agree with that. After all, in envying others, we can also admire *them* and even use *them* as role models to spur ourselves to greater abilities. There is no hostility in that, yet these cases, Smith contends, are not precisely envy. Indeed, Smith believes envy differs from jealousy not only because of its hostility, but because of another distinct ingredient: privacy.

By the time Bill was 40, he was vice president at his firm and owned a luxurious house in an affluent neighborhood. Nevertheless, Bill had never married and was lonely. He envied his brother Jim, who lived a modest but happy life with his wife and children. One day Jim asked Bill to write a reference letter to help him get a bank loan for a new home. Bill said he'd be delighted, but soon realized he could send the letter to the bank without Jim ever seeing it. Bill wrote the letter and his brother, never knowing why, was refused the loan.

Although this anecdote is fictional, Smith has shown in his research that the principles illustrated are probably true. In a recent study, Smith had subjects identify with an envious person. He then gave them the option of dividing a "resource" between themselves and the envied person. Among the many options were: dividing the resource equally; dividing it so the subject kept the most and gave the least to the envied person; and dividing it so they sacrificed the amount they could otherwise keep for themselves if it meant giving the least to the envied person. Most subjects chose the last option, but only when they could do so in private, rather than public, circumstances.

Although Smith admits the findings need to be verified, he believes the results are strongly "suggestive." The envious person's choice, he says, "was unambiguously hostile. Not selfish, but hostile. And the findings verified the conventional wisdom that envy has a secretive quality about it that you

wouldn't admit to the person you envy. And under the right circumstances it will lead to actual hostile behavior."

The reason people would be hostile in private seems obvious, given that envy is socially unacceptable. But why the hostility in the first place? Smith theorizes that the envied person's "superiority" emphasizes the envious person's low self-esteem in a specific area—the way the new real estate agent's communication skills affected Ann; Marcia's young date affected Dave; and Jim's happy family life affected Bill. Hostility is a way of putting down the envied person and devaluing his or her "superiority." Whether it takes the form of thought, word or deed, hostility pushes the envied person away, thereby allowing the envious person to restore his self-esteem.

Smith is looking at other implications

of envy and hostility in society. For example, "We don't know much about why people are hostile to begin with, but since envy is related to hostility, maybe the way people respond to the way they compare themselves to others is at the root of hostility." And there are other subtle—and even more frightening—implications. For one thing, Smith notes, because envy is socially unacceptable, "It's often not conscious, and as a result people will arrange the details of their situation and their perception of the other person to make envy something they can label as 'resentment'—resentment in the sense of righteous indignation."

Smith goes as far as to propose that many intergroup conflicts in the world—between countries, races and religious groups, for example—may begin with envy. One group is better off economi-

---

RANKING JEALOUSY & ENVY

What situations are most likely to evoke feelings of jealousy and envy? In a study published in the *Journal of Personality and Social Psychology*, Peter Salovey and Judith Rodin asked subjects to rank 53 situations according to the degree of emotion each would evoke. Below are 25 of those situations, listed in decreasing order, that received the highest "jealousy/envy" ratings:

1 You find out your lover is having an affair.

2 Someone goes out with a person you like.

3 Someone gets a job that you want.

4 Someone seems to be getting closer to a person to whom you are attracted.

5 Your lover tells you how sexy his/her old girl/boyfriend was.

6 Your boyfriend or girlfriend visits the person he or she used to date.

7 You do the same work as someone else and get paid less than he or she.

8 Someone is more talented than you.

9 Your boyfriend or girlfriend would rather be with his/her friends than with you.

10 You are alone while others are having fun.

11 Your boyfriend or girlfriend wants to date other people.

12 Someone is able to express himself or herself better than you.

13 Someone else has something you wanted and could have had but don't.

14 Someone else gets credit for what you've done.

15 Someone is more intelligent than you.

16 Someone appears to have everything.

17 Your steady date has lunch with an attractive person of the opposite sex.

18 Someone is more outgoing and self-confident than you.

19 Someone buys something you wanted but couldn't afford.

20 You have to work while your roommate is out partying.

21 An opposite-sex friend gives another friend a compliment, but not you.

22 Someone has more free time than you.

23 You hear that an old lover of yours has found a new lover.

24 Someone seems more self-fulfilled than you.

25 You listen to someone tell a story about things he did without you. J.Q.

When we let jealousy or envy overwhelm us, it can result in our being segregated from our social group.

cally, for example, than another, and the "inferior" group feels envy as a result. "But if they're just envious," he explains, "no one is going to give them any sympathy. So they tend to see their situation as unfair and unjust. In this way, envy becomes righteous resentment, which in turn gives them the 'right' to protest and conduct hostile — or even terrorist —activity."

This topic raises questions about what is fair or unfair in our society, how people cope with differences and whether, as a result, they feel envy, resentment or acceptance. Smith points out that coping with envy may depend on how well we learn to accept our inequalities. "I think as people mature, they learn to cope with differences by coming to terms with the fact that life *isn't* fair and that it's counterproductive to dwell on things you can't do anything about."

While some of Smith's ideas on coping with envy are speculative, Salovey has found that there are specific strategies —illustrated in the following anecdotes —that work in preventing and easing jealousy and envy. . . .

Rick and Liz are getting along much better these days even though Liz still works with her ex-boyfriend at the law firm. Rick isn't thrilled by this, but he overcame his jealousy by focusing instead on his relationship with Liz: spending time with her, planning vacations, discussing their future.

Ann no longer feels envy or hostility towards her co-worker at the real estate agency. She put an end to those negative feelings by simply ignoring her rival's superior communication skills and concentrating instead on her own achievements.

As illustrated here and isolated in a survey Salovey and Yale associate Judith Rodin conducted with *Psychology Today* readers, there are three major coping strategies: *Self-reliance*, in which a person does not give into the emotion, but continues to pursue the goals in the relationship; *Selective ignoring*, or simply ignoring the things that cause the jealousy or envy; and *Self-bolstering*, or concentrating on positive traits about yourself.

Surprisingly, "We found that the first two coping strategies are very effective in helping a person not feel jealousy," reports Salovey. "We thought that self-bolstering would also be good, since if something that's important to you is threatened, then maybe you should think of things in which you do well."

Although self-bolstering was not helpful in preventing jealousy. "Once you were *already* jealous, it was the only thing that kept you from becoming depressed and angry," notes Salovey. "So the first two keep jealousy in check, but if jealousy does emerge, self-bolstering keeps jealousy from its worst effects."

In the same study, Salovey and Rodin also uncovered some interesting data about how men and women experience jealousy and envy. "Men tend to be more envious in situations involving wealth and fame, and women more so in beauty and friendship," reports Salovey, but he emphasizes, "I should put that finding in context. We looked at a lot of variables and very rarely found differences. Men and women were very similar on nearly everything you could measure except that one difference."

Smith and Salovey do agree that while jealousy and envy can be devastating to those experiencing them, in milder forms they can actually be helpful. "I tend to think of jealousy and envy as normal," says Salovey. "In any rela-tionship where you really care about the other person, when your relation-ship is threatened by someone, you're going to feel negative emotions. If you don't, maybe you don't care that much."

As for envy, Smith points out that, "I don't think it's a bad thing, necessarily. It's a motivator when it's in the form of admiration and hero worship." He does add, however, that at those levels the emotion may not be envy since envy, by definition is hostile. "It's hard to know where one stops and the other begins," he notes.

Nevertheless, Smith stresses that "Coping with differences is something we all do. Some of us do it in constructive ways and others in destructive, and that has implications for who is going to be happy or unhappy. Envy is a sign of not coping well—maybe." He adds that while "some people have a right to recognize that a situation is unfair, the next ques-tion is, what do you do? It may be best to recognize the unfairness and cope with it before it leads to more painful feelings."

Jealousy and envy can have an unpleasant knack of cropping up between the people who care most about each other. Our first reaction is often to blame the other person—my *wife* is the one who is lunching with her ex-boy-friend; my *co-worker* is undeservedly making more sales; why should my *brother* have a happy family *and* a big house? Part of our blame is under-standable: life *is* unfair; society and cir-cumstance *do* create differences between us beyond our control.

Nevertheless, the bottom line is not how we view other people, but how we view ourselves. When jealousy or envy become overwhelming, it is as much from passing judgment on ourselves as on others. That's when we owe it to everyone to talk it out, change what needs to be changed and—perhaps most importantly—accept ourselves for what we are.

THE MEASURE OF LOVE

LOVE MAY STILL BE A MYSTERY TO POETS, BUT THE SECRETS OF BOTH ITS STRUCTURE AND ITS WORKINGS ARE NOW YIELDING TO A YALE PSYCHOLOGIST.

ROBERT J. STERNBERG

Yale psychologist **Robert Sternberg** created his first intelligence test for a science project in the seventh grade; it ended badly, when he was disciplined for using it to test his fellow students' IQs. A later project, in tenth grade, showed him that music—specifically, the Beatles' rendition of "She's Got the Devil in Her Heart"—increased test scores.

Since then, Sternberg has continued to hunt for the bases of intelligence and the mental processes that underlie thinking. "Many of them are what are sometimes called executive processes," he says, "such as recognizing problems in life, figuring out what steps to take and monitoring how well the solution is going." He is a recipient of many awards for his work and the author of dozens of articles on professional journals.

Love is one of the most important things in life. People have been known to lie, cheat, steal and kill for it. Even in the most materialistic of societies, it remains one of the few things that cannot be bought. And it has puzzled poets, philosophers, writers, psychologists and practically everyone else who has tried to understand it. Love has been called a disease, a neurosis, a projection of competitiveness with a parent and the enshrinement of suffering and death. For Freud, it arose from sublimated sexuality; for Harlow, it had its roots in the need for attachment; for Fromm, it was the expression of care, responsibility and respect for another. But despite its elusiveness, love can be measured!

My colleagues and I were interested both in the structure of love and in discovering what leads to success or failure in romantic relationships. We found that love has a basic, stable core; despite the fact that people experience differences in their feelings for the various people they love, from parents to lovers to friends, in each case their love actually has the same components. And in terms of what makes love work, we found that how a man thinks his lover feels about him is much more important than how she actually feels. The same applies to women.

When we investigated the structure of love, the first question Susan Grajek, a former Yale graduate student, and I looked at was the most basic one: What is love, and is it the same thing from one kind of relationship to another? We used two scales: One, called a love scale, was constructed by Zick Rubin, a Brandeis University psychologist; the other was devised by George Levinger and his colleagues at the University of Massachusetts. (We used two scales to make sure that our results would not be peculiar to a single scale; the Rubin and Levinger scales turned out to be highly correlated.) Levinger's measures the extent to which particular feelings and actions characterize a relationship (see box). Rubin designed his 13-item scale to measure what he believes to be three critical aspects of love: affiliative and dependent need for another, predisposition to help another, and exclusiveness and absorption in the relationship with another.

Consider three examples of statements Rubin used, substituting for the blanks the name of a person you presently love or have loved in the past. For each statement, rate on a one (low) to nine (high) scale the extent to which the statement characterizes your feelings for your present or previous love.

"If I could never be with ____, I would feel miserable." "If ____ were feeling badly, my first duty would be to cheer him (her) up." "I feel very possessive toward ____."

The first statement measures affiliative and dependent need, the second, predisposition to help, and the third, exclusiveness and absorption.

Validating the Score

Although there is no guarantee that the scale truly does measure love, it seems, intuitively, to be on the right track. What's more important, scores on the Rubin love scale are predictive of the amount of mutual eye gazing in which a couple engages, of the couple's ratings of the probability that they will eventually get married and of the chances that a couple in a close relationship will stay in that relationship. There is thus a scientific basis as well as intuitive support for the scale's validity.

We asked participants to fill out the Rubin and Levinger scales as they applied to their mother, father, sibling closest in age, best friend of the same sex and lover. Thirty-five men and 50 women from the greater New Haven area took part. They ranged in age from 18 to 70 years, with an average

age of 32. Although most were Caucasian, they were of a variety of religions, had diverse family incomes and were variously single, married, separated and divorced.

To discover what love is, we applied advanced statistical techniques to our data and used the results to compare two kinds of conceptions, based on past research on human intelligence. Back in 1927, the British psychologist Charles Spearman suggested that underlying all of the intelligent things we do in our everyday lives is a single mental factor, which Spearman called G, or general ability. Spearman was never certain just what this general ability was, but he suggested it might be what he referred to as "mental energy." Opposing Spearman was another British psychologist, Godfrey Thomson, who argued that intelligence is not any one thing, such as mental energy, but, rather, many things, including habits, knowledge, processes and the like. Our current knowledge about intelligence suggests that Thomson, and not Spearman, was on the right track.

We thought these two basic kinds of models might apply to love as well as to intelligence. According to the first, Spearmanian kind of conception, love is a single, undifferentiated and indivisible entity. One cannot decompose love into its aspects, because it has none. Rather, it is a global emotion, or emotional energy, that resists analysis. According to the second, Thomsonian kind of conception, love may feel like a single, undifferentiated emotion, but it is in fact one best understood in terms of a set of separate aspects.

Our data left us with no doubt about which conception was correct: Love may feel, subjectively, like a single emotion, but it is in fact composed of a number of different components. The Thomsonian model is thus the better one for understanding love as well as intelligence.

Although no one questionnaire or even combination of questionnaires is likely to reveal all the components of love, we got a good sense of what some of them are: (1) Promoting the welfare of the loved one. (2) Experiencing happiness with the loved one. (3) High regard for the loved one. (4) Being able to count on the loved one in times of need. (5) Mutual understanding of the loved one. (6) Sharing oneself and one's things with the loved one. (7) Receiving emotional support from the loved one. (8) Giving emotional support to the loved one. (9) Intimate communication with the loved one. (10) Valuing the loved one in one's own life.

These items are not necessarily mutually exclusive, but they do show the variety and depth of the various components of love. Based on this list, we may characterize love as a set of feelings, cognitions and motivations that contribute to communication, sharing and support.

To our surprise, the nature of love proved to be pretty much the same from one close relationship to another. Many things that matter in people's relationship with their father, for example, also matter in their relationship with a lover. Thus, it is not quite correct to say, as people often do, that our love for our parents is completely different from our love for our lover. There is a basic core of love that is constant over different close relationships.

But there are three important qualifications: First, when we asked whom people love and how much, we found that the amounts of love people feel in different close relationships may vary widely. Furthermore, our results differed slightly for men and women. Men loved their lover the most and their sibling closest in age the least. Their best friend of the same sex followed the lover, and their mother and

---

Love for our parents is not so different from love for a lover. A basic core of love is constant.

---

father were in the middle. Women loved their lover and best friend of the same sex about equally. They, too, loved their sibling closest in age the least, with their mother and father in the middle. But whereas men did not show a clear tendency to prefer either their mother or their father, women showed more of a tendency to prefer their mother. These results are good news for lovers and same-sex best friends but bad news for siblings close in age. (Remember, however, that all these results are averages. They do not necessarily apply in any individual case.)

Second, the weights or importances of the various aspects of love may differ from one relationship to another. Receiving emotional support or intimate communication may play more of a role in love for a lover than in love for a sibling.

And third, the concomitants of love—what goes along with it—may differ from one relationship to another. Thus, the sexual attraction that accompanies love for a lover is not likely to accompany love for a sibling. (Although sexual attraction feels like a central component of love, most of us learn, often the hard way, that it is possible to have sexual attraction in the absence of love, and vice versa. As researchers, we decided to keep sexual attraction distinct from our list of central compo-

nents because it enters into some love relationships but not others.)

We did not obtain clear evidence for sex differences in the structure of love for men versus women. However, other evidence suggests that there are at least some. George Levinger and his colleagues, for example, investigated what men and women found to be most rewarding in romantic relationships. They discovered that women found disclosure, nurturance, togetherness and commitment, and self-compromise to be more rewarding than men did. Men, in contrast, found personal separateness and autonomy to be more rewarding than women did. There is also evidence from other investigators to suggest that women find love to be a more integral, less separable part of sexual intercourse than men do.

Some people seem to be very loving and caring people, and others don't. This observation led us to question whether some people are just "all-around" lovers. The results were clear: There is a significant "love cluster" within the nuclear family in which one grows up. Loving one member of this family a lot is associated with a tendency to love other members of the family a lot, too. Not loving a member of this family much is associated with a tendency not to love others in the family much, either. These are only tendencies, of course, and there are wide individual differences. But the general finding is that love seems to run in nuclear families.

Romantic Prediction

These results do not generalize at all outside the nuclear family. How much one loves one's mother predicts how much one loves one's father, but not how much one loves one's lover. So people who haven't come from a loving family may still form loving relationships outside the family—though coming from a loving family doesn't guarantee that you will be successful in love.

Having learned something about the nature of love, we were interested in determining whether we could use love-scale scores to predict and even understand what leads to success or failure in romantic relationships. Because our first study was not directly addressed to this question, Michael Barnes, a Yale graduate student, and I conducted a second study that specifically addressed the role of love in the success of romantic relationships.

In our study, each of the members of 24 couples involved in romantic relationships filled out the love scales of Rubin and Levinger. But they filled them out in four different ways, expressing: (1) Their feelings toward the other member of the couple. (2) Their perceptions of the feelings of the other member of the couple toward them. (3) Their feelings toward an ideal other member of such a couple. (4)

A COST-BENEFIT LOVE SCALE

All relationships are both rewarding and costly; caring for someone, while emotionally satisfying, takes time and can be very taxing. The items that follow are excerpted from a scale George Levinger, of the University of Massachusetts, Amherst, devised to rate negative and positive aspects in any given relationship (with lover, spouse, parent, friend, etc.). In his research, author Robert J. Sternberg adapted the scale to a different purpose: He asked people to rate the importance of each statement in terms of both an actual and an ideal relationship. His findings are discussed in the accompanying story.

____ 1. Doing things together

____ 2. Having no secrets from each other

____ 3. Needing the other person

____ 4. Feeling needed by the other person

____ 5. Accepting the other's limitations

____ 6. Growing personally through the relationship

____ 7. Helping the other to grow

____ 8. Having career goals that do not conflict

____ 9. Understanding the other well

____ 10. Giving up some of one's own freedom

____ 11. Feeling possessive of the other's time

____ 12. Taking vacations together

____ 13. Offering emotional support to the other

____ 14. Receiving affection from the other

____ 15. Giving affection to the other

____ 16. Having interests the other shares

EXCERPTED AND ADAPTED FROM THE INTERPERSONAL INVOLVEMENT SCALE BY GEORGE LEVINGER, UNIVERSITY OF MASSACHUSETTS, AMHERST

of how love might affect satisfaction in a romantic relationship. According to the first conception, level of satisfaction is directly related to the amount of love the couple feel: The more they love each other, the more satisfied they will be with their relationship. According to the second and more complex conception, the relation between love and satisfaction is mediated by one's ideal other. In particular, it is the congruence between the real and the ideal other that leads to satisfaction. As the discrepancy between the real and ideal other increases, so does one's dissatisfaction with the relationship.

Consider two couples: Bob and Carol and Ted and Alice. Suppose that Bob loves Carol just as much as Ted loves Alice (at least, according to their scores on the love scales). According to the first conception, this evidence would contribute toward the prediction that, other things being equal, Bob and Ted are equally satisfied with their relationships. But now suppose that Bob, unlike Ted, has an extremely high ideal: He expects much more from Carol than Ted expects from Alice. According to the second conception, Ted will be happier than Bob, because Bob will feel less satisfied.

Their perceptions of the feelings of an ideal other member of such a couple toward them. These questions dealt with two basic distinctions: the self versus the actual other and the actual other versus an ideal.

The participants, all of whom were students in college or graduate school and none of whom were married, were asked to think in terms of a realistic ideal that would be possible in their lives, rather than in terms of some fantasy or Hollywood ideal that could exist only in movies or other forms of fiction. In addition to filling out the love-scale questionnaires, participants also answered questions regarding their satisfaction and happiness with their present romantic relationship.

Between Real and Ideal

We compared two different conceptions

The need for a loving relationship is paramount to an individual's psychological well-being, and establishing a lasting relationship is one of life's most important goals.

These two conceptions of what counts in a relationship are not mutually exclusive, and our data show that both matter about equally for the success of the relationship. Thus, it is important to remember that although love contributes to a successful relationship, any relationship can be damaged by unrealistically high ideals. At the other extreme, a relationship that perhaps does not deserve to last may go on indefinitely because of low ideals.

In addition to love and the ideal, we found that both how a person feels about his lover and how he thinks she feels about him matter roughly equally to satisfaction in a relationship. But there are three important qualifications.

First, the correlation between the love-scale scores of the two members of a couple is not, on the average, particularly high. In many relationships, the two members do not love each other equally.

Second, it is a person's perception of the way his lover feels about him, rather than the way the lover actually feels, that matters most for one's happiness in a relationship. In other words, relationships may succeed better than one might expect, given their asymmetry, because people sometimes systematically delude themselves about the way their partners feel. And it is this perception of the other's feelings rather than the other's actual feelings that keeps the relationship going.

Third, probably the single most important variable in the success of the relationships we studied was the difference between the way a person would ideally *like* his partner to feel about him and the way he thinks she really does feel about him. We found that this difference is actually more important to the success of a relationship than a person's own feelings: No variable we studied was more damaging to the success of a romantic relationship than perceived under- or overinvolvement by the partner.

Why might this be so? We believe it is because of the ultimate fate of relationships in which one partner is unhappy with the other's level of involvement. If a person perceives his partner to be under-involved, he may try to bring her closer. If she does not want to come closer, she may react by pulling away. This leads to redoubled efforts to bring her closer, which in turn lead her to move away. Eventually, the relationship dies.

On the other hand, if a person perceives her partner to be overinvolved, she may react by pulling away—to cool things down. This results in exactly the opposite of what is intended: Her partner tries to push even closer. The relationship becomes too asymmetrical to survive.

All our results suggest that the Rubin and Levinger scales could be useful tools to diagnose whether relationships are succeeding or not. There is one important and sobering fact to keep in mind, though: Scores from a liking scale devised by Zick Rubin were even better predictors of satisfaction in romantic relationships than were scores from the love scales, especially for women. Thus, no matter how much a person loves his partner, the relationship is not likely to work out unless he likes her as well.

An End to a Mystery?

Despite its complexity, love can be measured and studied by scientific means. Those who believe that love is, and should remain, one of life's great mysteries will view this fact as a threat; I view it in exactly the opposite way. With a national divorce rate approaching 50 percent and actually exceeding this figure in some locales, it is more important than ever that we understand what love is, what leads to its maintenance and what leads to its demise. Scientists studying love have the opportunity not only to make a contribution to pure science but to make a contribution to our society. At the very least, the study of love can suggest the cause, if not the cure, for certain kinds of failed relationships. I believe that our ability to measure love is contributing to progress both in understanding the nature of love and in suggesting some of the causes of success and failure in close relationships.

Therapists Find Last Outpost of Adolescence in Adulthood

Daniel Goleman

While adolescence by common reckoning ends with the teen years, it continues psychologically until the end of the 20's, when young people are finally able to establish a fully mature relationship with their parents, psychologists are finding.

Although clinical lore has long suggested that adolescence lingered into the 20's, only now are scientific studies showing just how true that is. One new study has discovered a dramatic shift in psychological maturity that seems to occur in most young adults between 24 and 28.

Before the shift, the men and women studied said they usually relied on their parents to make important choices in life and felt unable to cope with life's difficulties without some help from them. After the change, they felt comfortable making choices based on their own values and confident in their abilities to live on their own.

Such findings are leading developmental psychologists to revise their views of emotional growth in adolescence and early adulthood and to set back the timetable for the end of adolescence. This phenomenon may be a product of this century when, for the first time, most young people remained dependent on their parents for their support through the teen years and beyond.

"Adolescence doesn't really end until the late 20's," said Susan J. Frank, a psychologist at Michigan State University. "The emotional ties that bind children to their parents continue well after they leave home and enter the adult world. There's an astonishing difference between those in their early and late 20's in doing things without leaning on their parents."

Kathleen White, a psychologist at Boston University who has conducted much of the research on maturation in young adults, said this shift also entails a changing view of parents. "By their mid-20's," she said, "most young people are not ready to appreciate their parents as separate individuals, as having needs and strengths and weaknesses in their own right, apart from being parents.

"They still see their parents in egocentric fashion: were they good or bad parents, did they love me or not, were they too restrictive or demanding, and so on."

In a study of 84 adults between the ages of 22 and 29, Dr. White assessed several aspects of maturity, particularly their ability to form intimate relationships and to see their parents independent of their role as parents.

Those in their later 20's had "far more perspective on their parents" than those in their early 20's, Dr. White said.

A similar finding was reported by Dr. Frank and her colleagues in the current issue of Developmental Psychology.

Rage or Dependency

During their 20's, people go through gradual shifts in their sense of independence from parents and in their relationships with them, according to the work of Dr. Frank and other researchers. Emotional maturation in the third decade of life can be charted by these shifts, following general theories of adult development.

For instance, in terms of autonomy, less mature young adults not only tend to rely on their parents to help with decisions, but they also are often overwhelmed by intense feelings of rage or dependency. At its worst, these feelings can lead them to lash out at their parents, even when the parents are trying to be helpful.

Often the less mature adults are emotionally estranged from their parents or have only superficial exchanges with them. They also tend to have little interest in their parents' welfare and little understanding of the complexities of their parents' lives and personalities.

In Control of Emotions

By contrast, more mature young adults tend to have strong confidence in their abilities to make decisions on their own and feel in control of their emotions toward their parents. They also see themselves, rather than their parents, as the best judges of their own worth and so can risk parental disapproval by expressing values that may clash with those of their parents.

They tend to have strong emotional ties to their parents and are able to talk with their parents about feelings and concerns of importance to them, while feeling free to disagree. They also are concerned about their parents' well-being and are able to understand the complexities of their parents' lives, rather than painting them in black-and-white terms. The more mature tend to acknowledge or feel proud of their parents as role models.

"In the 20's, it's not just that you achieve separateness from your parents, but also that you feel connected to them as an adult," Dr. White said. "That includes empathy for them, and seeing things from their points of view. Most young adults don't have this perspective until their late 20's."

Using scales that measure these changes, Dr. Frank and her colleagues assessed the development of 150 men and women in their 20's on their relationships with their parents. All those studied were from middle-class suburbs and lived within a two-hour drive from their parents.

Patterns of Maturation

While Dr. Frank's results bore out the general theories, she found the reality to be more complex, the real-life patterns not fitting a continuum of maturity. There were, she said, several major patterns of maturation among the young adults she studied, with significant differences between men and women.

Women most often fell into a pattern of "competent and connected" relationships with their parents. These people—the pattern fit 40 percent of women and 6 percent of men—had a strong sense of independence and often held views that differed radically from their parents. But even so, they felt more empathy for them, particularly for their mothers, for whom they were often confidants. Among the women, mothers were often seen as demanding and critical, but since they understood their mothers' shortcomings, they were able to keep conflicts from getting out of hand.

Another pattern more common among the women than the men was to be dependent or emotionally enmeshed, most often with their mothers. Although troubled by their inability to handle life without their parents' help, these young people felt trapped by the relationship. Some saw their parents as overbearing and judgmental, others as emotionally detached. Childish power struggles with parents were common in this group.

The largest number of men, however, had "individuated" relationships in which they felt respected by their parents and prepared to meet the challenges of life on their own. Thirty-six percent of the men and 6 percent of the women fell into this group. While they felt a clear boundary between their own lives and those of their parents, they also felt free to seek advice and assistance. Although they enjoyed their parents' company, there was an emotional distance. Their relationships generally were lacking both in discussions of very personal matters and conflicts.

Another pattern more common in men than women was a false autonomy, in which the young adults feigned an indifference to clear conflicts with their parents, which they handled by avoiding confrontations. With their fathers, the main complaint was of mutual disinterest; with their mothers it was the need to hold an intrusive parent at bay. These people resented their parents' offers of help, and often held them in contempt. They also harbored resentment at their parents' inability to accept them as they were.

Reconnecting With Parents

Dr. Frank's findings are consistent with the work of Bertram Cohler, a psychologist at the University of Chicago. Dr. Cohler has proposed that when youths make the transition into adulthood, they become more interdependent with rather than more independent of their parents.

Dr. Frank found that over the course of their 20's, those in her study tended to move in the more mature direction. Although most had made the shift by 29, some still remained in an emotional adolescence.

Dr. Gould said, "There are some eternal adolescents, who never achieve a sense of their own maturity in these ways."

The Question of Marriage

While many influential theories of adult development hold that marriage is a key turning point in emotional maturation, Dr. Frank did not find this to be the case. She found that apart from age, it made no difference in people's psychological growth.

"The clinical literature says that the degree to which you've worked through your emotional relationship with your parents determines your ability to develop a close relationship with your spouse," Dr. White said.

"But that's not what I've found," she added. "People tend to be more mature in their relationships with their spouses than with their parents, if they are mature in either. People are more compelled to work out their marital conflicts than they are to work out their relationships with their parents. Your parents are your parents forever."

Development During Adulthood and Aging

Developmentalists hold two extreme points of view about the latter part of the life span. Disengagement theory holds that the physical and intellectual deficits associated with aging are inevitable and should be accepted at face value by the aged. Activity theory acknowledges the decline in abilities associated with aging, but also notes that the aged can maintain satisfying and productive lives.

Extreme views in any guise risk stereotyping all individuals within a category or class as having the same needs and capabilities. Whether one's reference group is racial, ethnic, cultural, or age-related, stereotyping usually leads to counterproductive, discriminatory social policy which alienates the reference group from mainstream society.

Evidence obtained during the past decade clearly illustrates the fallacy of extremist views of middle and late adulthood. Development during adulthood and aging is not a unitary phenomenon. Although there are common physical changes associated with aging, there are also wide individual differences in the rates of change and the degree to which changes are expressed. It is common to think of the changes associated with aging as solely physical and generally negative. The popular press devotes considerable space to discussions of the causes and treatment of such debilitating disorders as Alzheimer's disease. However, there are also psychological changes associated with aging, and, as is the case at all age levels, some individuals cope well with change and others do not. New research on the aging process suggests that physical health and mental health changes do not correlate well. Although a variety of abuses can hasten physical and mental deterioration, proper diet and modest exercise can also slow the aging process. In addition, one cannot understate the importance of love, social interaction, and a sense of self-worth for combating the loneliness, despair, and futility often associated with aging. Leonard Sagan, in his article "Family Ties," offers evidence that family relationships and dynamics contribute to the good health, and thus the longevity, of people today.

Behavioral gerontology remains a specialization within human development that is absent even from most graduate programs in human development. Perhaps this is partly because of the natural tendency of people to avoid confronting the negative aspects of aging, such as loneliness and despair over the loss of one's spouse or over one's own impending death. Nevertheless, contemporary studies do provide fascinating information about the quality of life ("The Vintage Years") and physical changes ("Aging: What Happens to the Body as We Grow Older" and "A Vital Long Life") during aging, and challenge many traditional views about interpersonal relationships and memory processes.

One physical side effect of aging affecting women is menopause. In "The Myths of Menopause," some of the changes that can occur with menopause are listed along with a "survival guide" for before, during, and after menopause.

Several developmentalists have elaborated stage theories to describe major periods of crisis. The article "The Prime of Our Lives" reviews several theories, but suggests that changes during adulthood may be better explained by changing perceptions of self than by universally experienced life stages.

Because the proportion of the population represented by the aged is increasing rapidly, it is imperative that significant advances be made in our knowledge of the later years of development. Prolonging life and controlling mental and physical illness are only small aspects of the promotion and improvement of the quality of life for the elderly.

Looking Ahead: Challenge Questions

Gerontologists suggest that significantly greater life expectancies are possible even without medical breakthroughs. Control of childhood diseases, better education, better physical fitness, and proper diet are factors that increase the life span. How would your life differ now if your expected life span was 150 years? How do you think your elderly years will differ from those of your parents?

Do you think that most individuals' lives can be described by a relatively constant sequence of life stages, or are life patterns too variable for general descriptions to be of use? What are some of the most common stereotypes about aging in our society?

What are the most important physical consequences of menopause? Do you think it's worth the risk for women to use estrogen therapy to counter the effects of menopause? Why or why not?

The Vintage Years

*THE GROWING NUMBER OF HEALTHY, VIGOROUS
OLDER PEOPLE HAS HELPED OVERCOME SOME
STEREOTYPES ABOUT AGING. FOR MANY,
THE BEST IS YET TO COME.*

Jack C. Horn and Jeff Meer

*Jack C. Horn is a senior editor and Jeff Meer is
an assistant editor at the magazine.*

Our society is getting older,
but the old are getting
younger. As Sylvia Herz
told an American Psycho-
logical Association (APA)
symposium on aging last
year, the activities and attitudes of a 70-year-old today
"are equivalent to those of a 50-year-old's a decade or two ago."

Our notions of what it means to be old are beginning to catch up with this reality. During the
past several decades, three major changes have
altered the way we view the years after 65:

• The financial, physical and mental health
of older people has improved, making the prospect of a long life something to treasure, not
fear.

• The population of older people has grown
dramatically, rising from 18 million in 1965 to
28 million today. People older than 65 compose
12 percent of the population, a percentage that
is expected to rise to more than 20 percent by
the year 2030.

• Researchers have gained a much better understanding of aging and the lives of older people, helping to sort out the inevitable results of
biological aging from the effects of illness or
social and environmental problems. No one has
yet found the fountain of youth, or of immortality. But research has revealed that aging itself
is not the thief we once thought it was; healthy
older people can maintain and enjoy most of
their physical and mental abilities, and even improve in some areas.

Because of better medical care, improved diet
and increasing interest in physical fitness, more
people are reaching the ages of 65, 75 and older
in excellent health. Their functional age—a
combination of physical, psychological and social factors that affect their attitudes toward
life and the roles they play in the world—is
much younger than their chronological age.

Their economic health is better, too, by almost every measure. Over the last three decades, for example, the number of men and
women 65 and older who live below the poverty
line has dropped steadily from 35 percent in
1959 to 12 percent in 1984, the last year for
which figures are available.

On the upper end of the economic scale,
many of our biggest companies are headed by
what once would have been called senior citizens, and many more of them serve as directors
of leading companies. Even on a more modest
economic level, a good portion of the United
States' retired older people form a new leisure
class, one with money to spend and the time to
enjoy it. Obviously not all of America's older
people share this prosperity. Economic hardship is particularly prevalent among minorities.
But as a group, our older people are doing better than ever.

In two other areas of power, politics and the
law, people in their 60s and 70s have always
played important roles. A higher percentage of
people from 65 to 74 register and vote than in
any other group. With today's increasing vigor
and numbers, their power is likely to increase
still further. It is perhaps no coincidence that
our current President is the oldest ever.

Changing attitudes, personal and social, are a
major reason for the increasing importance of
older people in our society. As psychologist

Bernice Neugarten points out, there is no longer a particular age at which someone starts to work or attends school, marries and has children, retires or starts a business. Increasing numbers of older men and women are enrolled in colleges, universities and other institutions of learning. According to the Center for Education Statistics, for example, the number of people 65 and older enrolled in adult education of all kinds increased from 765,000 to 866,000 from 1981 to 1984. Gerontologist Barbara Ober says that this growing interest in education is much more than a way to pass the time. "Older people make excellent students, maybe even better students than the majority of 19- and 20-year-olds. One advantage is that they have settled a lot of the social and sexual issues that preoccupy their younger classmates."

Older people today are not only healthier and more active; they are also increasingly more numerous. "Squaring the pyramid" is how some demographers describe this change in our population structure. It has always been thought of as a pyramid, a broad base of newborns supporting successively smaller tiers of older people as they died from disease, accidents, poor nutrition, war and other causes.

Today, the population structure is becoming more rectangular, as fewer people die during the earlier stages of life. The Census Bureau predicts that by 2030 the structure will be an almost perfect rectangle up to the age of 70.

The aging of America has been going on at least since 1800, when half the people in the country were younger than 16 years old, but two factors have accelerated the trend tremendously. First, the number of old people has increased rapidly. Since 1950 the number of Americans 65 and older has more than doubled to some 28 million—more than the entire current population of Canada. Within the same period, the number of individuals older than 85 has quadrupled to about 2.6 million (see "The Oldest Old," this article).

Second, the boom in old people has been paired with a bust in the proportion of youngsters due to a declining birth rate. Today, fewer than one American in four is younger than 16. This drop-off has been steady, with the single exception of the post-World War II baby boom, which added 76 million children to the country between 1945 and 1964. As these baby boomers reach the age of 65, starting in 2010, they are expected to increase the proportion of the population 65 and older from its current 12 percent to 21 percent by 2030.

The growing presence of healthy, vigorous older people has helped overcome some of the stereotypes about aging and the elderly. Research has also played a major part by replacing myths with facts. While there were some studies of aging before World War II, scientific

A man over 90 is a great comfort to all his elderly neighbours: he is a picket-guard at the extreme outpost; and the young folks of 60 and 70 feel that the enemy must get by him before he can come near their camp.
—Oliver Wendell Holmes, *The Guardian Angel.*

BY THE YEAR 2030 MORE THAN 20 PERCENT OF THE POPULATION IS EXPECTED TO BE 65 OR OLDER.

interest increased dramatically during the 1950s and kept growing.

Important early studies of aging included three started in the mid or late 1950s: the Human Aging Study, conducted by the National Institute of Mental Health (NIMH); the Duke Longitudinal Studies, done by the Center for the Study of Aging and Human Development at Duke University; and the Baltimore Longitudinal Study of Aging, conducted by the Gerontological Institute in Baltimore, now part of the National Institute on Aging (NIA). All three took a multidisciplinary approach to the study of normal aging: what changes take place, how people adapt to them, how biological, genetic, social, psychological and environmental characteristics relate to longevity and what can be done to promote successful aging.

These pioneering studies and hundreds of later ones have benefited from growing federal support. White House Conferences on Aging in 1961 and 1971 helped focus attention on the subject. By 1965 Congress had enacted Medicare and the Older Americans Act. During the 1970s Congress authorized the establishment of the NIA as part of the National Institutes of Health and NIMH created a special center to support research on the mental health of older people.

All these efforts have produced a tremendous growth in our knowledge of aging. In the first (1971) edition of the *Handbook of the Psychology of Aging,* it was estimated that as much had been published on the subject in the previous 15 years as in all the years before then. In the second edition, published in 1985, psychologists James Birren and Walter Cunningham wrote that the "period for this rate of doubling has now decreased to 10 years...the volume of published research has increased to the almost unmanageable total of over a thousand articles a year."

Psychologist Clifford Swenson of Purdue

University explained some of the powerful incentives for this tremendous increase: "I study the topic partly to discover more effective ways of helping old people cope with their problems, but also to load my own armamentarium against that inevitable day. For that is one aspect of aging and its problems that makes it different from the other problems psychologists study: We may not all be schizophrenic or neurotic or overweight, but there is only one alternative to old age and most of us try to avoid that alternative."

One popular misconception disputed by recent research is the idea that aging means inevitable physical and sexual failure. Some changes occur, of course. Reflexes slow, hearing and eyesight dim, stamina decreases. This *primary aging* is a gradual process that begins early in life and affects all body systems.

But many of the problems we associate with old age are *secondary aging*—the results not of age but of disease, abuse and disuse—factors often under our own control. More and more older people are healthy, vigorous men and women who lead enjoyable, active lives. National surveys by the Institute for Social Research and others show that life generally seems less troublesome and freer to older people than it does to younger adults.

In a review of what researchers have learned about subjective well-being—happiness, life satisfaction, positive emotions—University of Illinois psychologist Ed Diener reported that "Most results show a slow rise in satisfaction with age. . .young persons appear to experience higher levels of joy but older persons tend to judge their lives in more positive ways."

Money is often mentioned as the key to a happy retirement, but psychologist Daniel Ogilvie of Rutgers University has found another, much more important, factor. Once we have a certain minimum amount of money, his research shows, life satisfaction depends mainly on how much time we spend doing things we find meaningful. Ogilvie believes retirement-planning workshops and seminars should spend more time helping people decide how to use their skills and interests after they retire.

A thought that comes through clearly when researchers talk about physical and mental fitness is "use it or lose it." People rust out faster from disuse than they wear out from overuse. This advice applies equally to sexual activity. While every study from the time of Kinsey to the present shows that sexual interest and activity diminish with age, the drop varies greatly among individuals. Psychologist Marion Perlmutter and writer Elizabeth Hall have reported that one of the best predictors of continued sexual intercourse "is early sexual activity and past sexual enjoyment and frequency. People who have never had much pleasure from sexu-

*W*HILE THE OLD AND THE YOUNG MAY BE EQUALLY COMPETENT, THEY ARE DIFFERENTLY COMPETENT.

ality may regard their age as a good excuse for giving up sex."

They also point out that changing times affect sexual activity. As today's younger adults bring their more liberal sexual attitudes with them into old age, the level of sexual activity among older men and women may rise.

The idea that mental abilities decline steadily with age has also been challenged by many recent and not-so-recent findings. In brief, age doesn't damage abilities as much as was once believed, and in some areas we actually gain; we learn to compensate through experience for much of what we do lose; and we can restore some losses through training.

For years, older people didn't do as well as younger people on most tests used to measure mental ability. But psychologist Leonard Poon of the University of Georgia believes that researchers are now taking a new, more appropriate approach to measurement. "Instead of looking at older people's ability to do abstract tasks that have little or no relationship to what they do every day, today's researchers are examining real-life issues."

Psychologist Gisela Labouvie-Vief of Wayne State University has been measuring how people approach everyday problems in logic. She notes that older adults have usually done poorly on such tests, mostly because they fail to think logically all the time. But Labouvie-Vief argues that this is not because they have forgotten how to think logically but because they use a more complex approach unknown to younger thinkers. "The [older] thinker operates within a kind of double reality which is both formal and informal, both logical and psychological," she says.

In other studies, Labouvie-Vief has found that when older people were asked to give concise summaries of fables they read, they did so. But when they were simply asked to recall as much of the fable as possible, they concentrat-

The pleasures that once were heaven Look silly at sixty-seven.
—Noel Coward, "What's Going to Happen to the Tots?"

Old age consoles itself by giving good precepts for being unable to give bad examples.
—La Rochefoucauld, The Maxims.

THE OLDEST OLD: THE YEARS AFTER 85

"Every man desires to live long, but no man would be old," or so Jonathan Swift believed. Some people get their wish to live long and become what are termed the "oldest old," those 85 and older. During the past 22 years, this group has increased by 165 percent to 2.5 million and now represents more than 1 percent of the population.

Who are these people and what are their lives like? One of the first to study them intensively is gerontologist Charles Longino of the University of Miami, who uses 1980 census data to examine their lives for the American Association of Retired People.

He found, not surprisingly, that nearly 70 percent are women. Of these, 82 percent are widowed, compared with 44 percent of the men. Because of the conditions that existed when they were growing up, the oldest old are poorly educated compared with young people today, most of whom finish high school. The average person now 85 years and older only completed the eighth grade.

Only one-quarter of these older citizens are in hospitals or institutions such as nursing homes, and more than half live in their own homes. Just 30 percent live by themselves. More than a third live with a spouse or with their children. There are certainly those who aren't doing well—one in six have incomes below the poverty level—but many more are relatively well-off. The mean household income for the group, Longino says, was more than $20,000 in 1985.

What of the quality of life? "In studying this group, we have to be aware of youth creep," he says. "The old are getting younger all the time." This feeling is confirmed by a report released late last year by the National Institute on Aging. The NIA report included three studies of people older than 65 conducted in two counties in Iowa, in East Boston, Massachusetts, and in New Haven, Connecticut. There are large regional differences between the groups, of course, and they aren't a cross-section of older people in the nation as a whole. But in all three places, most of those older than 85 seem to be leading fulfilling lives.

Most socialize in a variety of ways. In Iowa, more than half say they go to religious services at least once a week and the same percentage say they belong to some type of professional, social, church-related or recreational group. More than three-quarters see at least one or two children once a month and almost that many see other close relatives that often.

As you would expect, many of the oldest old suffer from disabilities and serious health problems. At least a quarter of those who responded have been in a hospital overnight in the past year and at least 8 percent have had heart attacks or have diabetes. In Iowa and New Haven, more than 13 percent of the oldest old had cancer, while in East Boston the rate was lower (between 7 percent and 8 percent). Significant numbers of the oldest old have suffered serious injury from falls. Other common health problems for this group are high blood pressure and urinary incontinence. However, epidemiologist Adrian Ostfeld, who directed the survey in New Haven, notes that "most of the disability was temporary."

Longino has found that almost 10 percent of the oldest old live alone with a disability that prevents them from using public transportation. This means that they are "isolated from the daily hands-on care of others," he says. "Even so, there are a surprising number of the oldest old who don't need much in the way of medical care. They're the survivors.

"I think we have to agree that the oldest old is, as a group, remarkably diverse," Longino says. "Just as it is unfair to say that those older than 85 are all miserable, it's not fair to say that they all lead wonderful lives, either."
—Jeff Meer

ed on the metaphorical, moral or social meaning of the text. They didn't try to duplicate the fable's exact words, the way younger people did. As psychologists Nancy Datan, Dean Rodeheaver and Fergus Hughes of the University of Wisconsin have described their findings, "while [some people assume] that old and young are equally competent, we might better assume that they are differently competent."

John Horn, director of the Adult Development and Aging program at the University of Southern California, suggests that studies of Alzheimer's disease, a devastating progressive mental deterioration experienced by an estimated 5 percent to 15 percent of those older than 65, may eventually help explain some of the differences in thinking abilities of older people. "Alzheimer's, in some ways, may represent the normal process of aging, only speeded up," he says. (To see how your ideas about Alzheimer's square with the facts, see "Alzheimer's Quiz" and "Alzheimer's Answers," this article.)

Generalities are always suspect, but one generalization about old age seems solid: It is a different experience for men and women. Longevity is one important reason. Women in the United States live seven to eight years longer, on the average, than do men. This simple fact has many ramifications, as sociologist Gunhild Hagestad explained in *Our Aging Society.*

For one thing, since the world of the very old is disproportionately a world of women, men and women spend their later years differently. "Most older women are widows living alone; most older men live with their wives...among individuals over the age of 75, two-thirds of the men are living with a spouse, while less than one-fifth of the women are."

The difference in longevity also means that among older people, remarriage is a male prerogative. After 65, for example, men remarry at a rate eight times that of women. This is partly a matter of the scarcity of men and partly a matter of culture—even late in life, men tend to marry younger women. It is also a matter of education and finances, which, Hagestad explains, "operate quite differently in shaping remarriage probabilities among men and women. The more resources the woman has available (measured in education and income), the less likely she is to remarry. For men, the trend is reversed."

The economic situations of elderly men and women also differ considerably. Lou Glasse, president of the Older Women's League in Washington, D.C., points out that most of these women were housewives who worked at paid jobs sporadically, if at all. "That means their Social Security benefits are lower than men's, they are not likely to have pensions and they are less likely to have been able to save the kind of money that would protect them from poverty during their older years."

Although we often think of elderly men and women as living in nursing homes or retirement communities, the facts are quite different. Only about 5 percent are in nursing homes and perhaps an equal number live in some kind of age-segregated housing. Most people older than 65 live in their own houses or apartments.

We also think of older people as living alone. According to the Census Bureau, this is true of 15 percent of the men and 41 percent of the women. Earlier this year, a survey done by Louis Harris & Associates revealed that 28 percent of elderly people living alone have annual incomes below $5,100, the federal poverty line. Despite this, they were four times as likely to give financial help to their children as to receive it from them.

In addition, fewer than 1 percent of the old people said they would prefer living with their children. Psychiatrist Robert N. Butler, chairman of the Commonwealth Fund's Commission

AMONG OLDER PEOPLE TODAY, REMARRIAGE IS STILL LARGELY A MALE PREROGATIVE, DUE TO THE SEX DIFFERENCE IN LONGEVITY.

on Elderly People Living Alone, which sponsored the report, noted that these findings dispute the "popular portrait of an elderly, dependent parent financially draining their middle-aged children."

There is often another kind of drain, however, one of time and effort. The Travelers Insurance Company recently surveyed more than 700 of its employees on this issue. Of those at least 30 years old, 28 percent said they directly care for an older relative in some way—taking that person to the doctor, making telephone calls, handling finances or running errands—for an average of 10 hours a week. Women, who are more often caregivers, spent an average of 16 hours, and men five hours, per week. One group, 8 percent of the sample, spent a heroic 35 hours per week, the equivalent of a second job, providing such care. "That adds up to an awful lot of time away from other things," psychologist Beal Lowe says, "and the stresses these people face are enormous."

Lowe, working with Sherman-Lank Communications in Kensington, Maryland, has formed "Caring for Caregivers," a group of professionals devoted to providing services, information and support to those who care for older relatives. "It can be a great shock to some people who have planned the perfect retirement," he says, "only to realize that your chronically ill mother suddenly needs daily attention."

Researchers who have studied the housing needs of older people predictably disagree on many things, but most agree on two points: We need a variety of individual and group living arrangements to meet the varying interests, income and abilities of people older than 65; and the arrangements should be flexible enough that the elderly can stay in the same locale as their needs and abilities change. Many studies have documented the fact that moving itself can be stressful and even fatal to old people, particularly if they have little or no influence over when and where they move.

This matter of control is important, but more complicated than it seemed at first. Psychologist Judith Rodin and others have demonstrated that people in nursing homes are happier, more alert and live longer if they are allowed to take responsibility for their lives in some way, even in something as simple as choosing a plant for their room, taking care of a bird feeder, selecting the night to attend a movie.

Rodin warns that while control is generally beneficial, the effect depends on the individuals involved. For some, personal control brings with it demands in the form of time, effort and the risk of failure. They may blame themselves if they get sick or something else goes wrong. The challenge, Rodin wrote, is to "provide but not impose opportunities. . . . The need for self-determination, it must be remembered, also calls for the opportunity to choose not to exercise control. . . ."

An ancient Greek myth tells how the Goddess of Dawn fell in love with a mortal and convinced Jupiter to grant him immortality. Unfortunately, she forgot to have youth included in the deal, so he gradually grew older and older. "At length," the story concludes, "he lost the power of using his limbs, and then she shut him up in his chamber, whence his feeble voice might at times be heard. Finally she turned him into a grasshopper."

The fears and misunderstandings of age expressed in this 3,000-year-old myth persist today, despite all the positive things we have learned in recent years about life after 65. We don't turn older people into grasshoppers or shut them out of sight, but too often we move them firmly out of the mainstream of life.

In a speech at the celebration of Harvard

> If I had known when I was 21 that I should be as happy as I am now, I should have been sincerely shocked. They promised me wormwood and the funeral raven.
> —Christopher Isherwood, letter at age 70.

University's 350th anniversary last September, political scientist Robert Binstock decried what he called The Spectre of the Aging Society: "the economic burdens of population aging; moral dilemmas posed by the allocation of health resources on the basis of age; labor market competition between older and younger workers within the contexts of age discrimination laws; seniority practices, rapid technologi-

ALZHEIMER'S QUIZ

Alzheimer's disease, named for German neurologist Alois Alzheimer, is much in the news these days. But how much do you really know about the disorder? Political scientist Neal B. Cutler of the Andrus Gerontology Center gave the following questions to a 1,500-person cross section of people older than 45 in the United States in November 1985. To compare your answers with theirs and with the correct answers, turn to the next page.

	True	False	Don't know
1. Alzheimer's disease can be contagious.			
2. A person will almost certainly get Alzheimer's if they just live long enough.			
3. Alzheimer's disease is a form of insanity.			
4. Alzheimer's disease is a normal part of getting older, like gray hair or wrinkles.			
5. There is no cure for Alzheimer's disease at present.			
6. A person who has Alzheimer's disease will experience both mental and physical decline.			
7. The primary symptom of Alzheimer's disease is memory loss.			
8. Among persons older than age 75, forgetfulness most likely indicates the beginning of Alzheimer's disease.			
9. When the husband or wife of an older person dies, the surviving spouse may suffer from a kind of depression that looks like Alzheimer's disease.			
10. Stuttering is an inevitable part of Alzheimer's disease.			
11. An older man is more likely to develop Alzheimer's disease than an older woman.			
12. Alzheimer's disease is usually fatal.			
13. The vast majority of persons suffering from Alzheimer's disease live in nursing homes.			
14. Aluminum has been identified as a significant cause of Alzheimer's disease.			
15. Alzheimer's disease can be diagnosed by a blood test.			
16. Nursing-home expenses for Alzheimer's disease patients are covered by Medicare.			
17. Medicine taken for high blood pressure can cause symptoms that look like Alzheimer's disease.			

Alzheimer's Answers — National Sample

	True	False	Don't know
1. False. There is no evidence that Alzheimer's is contagious, but given the concern and confusion about AIDS, it is encouraging that nearly everyone knows this fact about Alzheimer's.	3%	83%	14%
2. False. Alzheimer's is associated with old age, but it is a disease and not the inevitable consequence of aging.	9	80	11
3. False. Alzheimer's is a disease of the brain, but it is not a form of insanity. The fact that most people understand the distinction contrasts with the results of public-opinion studies concerning epilepsy that were done 35 years ago. At that time, almost half of the public thought that epilepsy, another disease of the brain, was a form of insanity.	7	78	15
4. False. Again, most of the public knows that Alzheimer's is not an inevitable part of aging.	10	77	13
5. True. Despite announcements of "breakthroughs," biomedical research is in the early laboratory and experimental stages and there is no known cure for the disease.	75	8	17
6. True. Memory and cognitive decline are characteristic of the earlier stages of Alzheimer's disease, but physical decline follows in the later stages.	74	10	16
7. True. Most people know that this is the earliest sign of Alzheimer's disease.	62	19	19
8. False. Most people also know that while Alzheimer's produces memory loss, memory loss may have some other cause.	16	61	23
9. True. This question, like number 8, measures how well people recognize that other problems can mirror Alzheimer's symptoms. This is crucial because many of these other problems are treatable. In particular, depression can cause disorientation that looks like Alzheimer's.	49	20	30
10. False. Stuttering has never been linked to Alzheimer's. The question was designed to measure how willing people were to attribute virtually anything to a devastating disease.	12	46	42
11. False. Apart from age, research has not uncovered any reliable demographic or ethnic patterns. While there are more older women than men, both sexes are equally likely to get Alzheimer's.	15	45	40
12. True. Alzheimer's produces mental and physical decline that is eventually fatal, although the progression varies greatly among individuals.	40	33	27
13. False. The early and middle stages of the disease usually do not require institutional care. Only a small percentage of those with the disease live in nursing homes.	37	40	23
14. False. There is no evidence that using aluminum cooking utensils, pots or foil causes Alzheimer's, although aluminum compounds have been found in the brain tissue of many Alzheimer's patients. They may simply be side effects of the disease.	8	25	66
15. False. At present there is no definitive blood test that can determine with certainty that a patient has Alzheimer's disease. Accurate diagnosis is possible only upon autopsy. Recent studies suggest that genetic or blood testing may be able to identify Alzheimer's, but more research with humans is needed.	12	24	64
16. False. Medicare generally pays only for short-term nursing-home care subsequent to hospitalization and not for long-term care. Medicaid can pay for long-term nursing-home care, but since it is a state-directed program for the medically indigent, coverage for Alzheimer's patients depends upon state regulations and on the income of the patient and family.	16	23	61
17. True. As mentioned earlier, many medical problems have Alzheimer's-like symptoms and most of these other causes are treatable. Considering how much medicine older people take, it is unfortunate that so few people know that medications such as those used to treat high blood pressure can cause these symptoms.	20	19	61

cal change; and a politics of conflict between age groups."

Binstock, a professor at Case Western Reserve School of Medicine, pointed out that these inaccurate perceptions express an underlying ageism, "the attribution of these same characteristics and status to an artificially homogenized group labeled 'the aged.'"

Ironically, much ageism is based on compassion rather than ill will. To protect older workers from layoffs, for example, unions fought hard for job security based on seniority. To win it, they accepted mandatory retirement, a limitation that now penalizes older workers and deprives our society of their experience.

A few companies have taken special steps to utilize this valuable pool of older workers. The Travelers companies, for example, set up a job

GREAT EXPECTATIONS

SOURCE: U.S. NATIONAL CENTER FOR HEALTH STATISTICS

If you were born in 1920 and are a . . .

	. . .white man	. .white woman
your life expectancy was . . .		
at birth	54.4 years	55.6 years
at age 40	71.7	77.1
at age 62	78.5	83.2

If you were born in 1940 and are a . . .

	. . .white man	. . .white woman
your life expectancy was . . .		
at birth	62.1 years	66.6 years
at age 20	70.3	76.3
at age 42	74.7	80.7

If you were born in 1960 and are a . . .

	. . .white man	. . .white woman
your life expectancy was . . .		
at birth	67.4 years	74.1 years
at age 22	73.2	80.0

bank that is open to its own retired employees as well as those of other companies. According to Howard E. Johnson, a senior vice president, the company employs about 175 formerly retired men and women a week. He estimates that the program is saving Travelers $1 million a year in temporary-hire fees alone.

While mandatory retirement is only one example of ageism, it is particularly important because we usually think of contributions to society in economic terms. Malcolm H. Morrison, an authority on retirement and age discrimination in employment for the Social Security Administration, points out that once the idea of retirement at a certain fixed age was accepted, "the old became defined as a dependent group in society, a group whose members could not and should not work, and who needed economic and social assistance that the younger working population was obligated to provide."

We need to replace this stereotype with the more realistic understanding that older people are and should be productive members of society, capable of assuming greater responsibility for themselves and others. What researchers have learned about the strengths and abilities of older people should help us turn this ideal of an active, useful life after 65 into a working reality.

FAMILY TIES

The Real Reason People Are Living Longer

LEONARD A. SAGAN

LEONARD A. SAGAN is an epidemiologist at the Electric Power Research Institute, in Palo Alto, California. His book THE HEALTH OF NATIONS: TRUE CAUSES OF SICKNESS AND WELL-BEING was recently published by Basic Books.

WHEN MODERN MEDICINE made its debut at the Many Farms Navajo Indian community, in 1956, there was every reason to expect decisive results. The two thousand people who inhabited this impoverished and isolated Arizona settlement were living under extremely primitive conditions. Though nutrition was adequate, hygiene was poor, tuberculosis was widespread, and infant mortality rates were three times the national average. To a group of researchers from the Cornell University Medical College and the U.S. Public Health Service, the situation at Many Farms provided a perfect opportunity to introduce modern health care practices and measure the consequences. If the effort proved successful with this target population, they reasoned, it might become an example for underdeveloped communities worldwide.

Almost overnight, the Navajo settlement acquired an array of modern medical resources. The researchers set up a full-service clinic, staffed with physicians and nurses, as well as with public health consultants, a health teacher, and four Navajo health care workers. For medical emergencies, the community got a fleet of radio-equipped vehicles and a light airplane. Over the next six years, ninety percent of the Many Farms residents took advantage of the clinic. Two-thirds of them were seen at least once a year.

The result was a rapid decline in the transmission of tubercle bacillus (the agent that causes tuberculosis) and in the frequency of otitis media (an inflammation of the middle ear). Yet the population's overall health, as reflected in its mortality statistics, was virtually unchanged. Of the sixty-five deaths that occurred during the six-year study period, more than half involved infants, who made up less than four percent of the population. And, despite expert pediatric care, there was no reduction in the pneumonia–diarrhea complex that was the leading cause of childhood illness and death. In the end, the investigators were unsure whether the improved medical care had, on balance, produced any beneficial effect at all.

This outcome would be less unsettling if it were more unusual. Unfortunately, it is not unusual at all. Consider what happened in 1976, when the state legislature of North Carolina sponsored a study to determine the effects of improved maternal and perinatal health care on the state's poorer communities. Researchers identified a number of counties, similar in racial and socioeconomic characteristics, that had suffered high rates of infant mortality over the preceding decades. For the next five years, residents of some of those counties received state-of-the-art treatment at the medical centers of Duke University and the University of North Carolina while, for the purpose of comparison, similar counties were essentially left alone. As expected, infant mortality declined considerably in the areas that received the additional care, but it also declined in the areas that did not. In fact, the researchers found no significant differences between the two groups.

Similar stories can be told about much larger populations. When England established its National Health Service, in 1946, the country's lowest social classes had long suffered the poorest health and the shortest lives—presumably because of economic barriers to adequate health care. The new program effectively removed those barriers. Forty-two years later, however, the disparity in mortality rates remains undiminished; the life expectancy of the most affluent is almost twice that of the least affluent. The economists Lee and Alexandra Benham, of Washington University, in Saint Louis, have noted the similar failure of Medicare and Medicaid to affect mortality rates among the disadvantaged in the United States. This country's least educated classes now experience as much hospitalization and surgery as its most educated classes, yet overall health is still strongly associated with educational achievement.

What are we to make of all this? It is well known that life expectancy has risen dramatically in most societies over the past few centuries. As recently as 1900, the typical American lived only forty-nine years, and one in five children died during infancy. Today we live an average of seventy-five years, and infant mortality has declined to just ten deaths for every thousand births, or one percent. Both physicians and the public credit modern medicine for these bold achievements; we assume, almost reflexively, that people who lack expert medical attention die earlier, and that providing more care is the key to longer life.

Americans, therefore, have invested heavily in medicine. Our expenditures now total more than four hundred billion dollars a year, or eleven percent of the gross national product, the highest rate of any nation on Earth. Yet some measures of ill health, such as the rate of disability due to chronic illness among children, are on the rise. And though life expectancy continues to rise in the United States, it is rising more rapidly in countries that are spending at a lower rate. Many of those countries, including Greece, Spain, and Italy, now enjoy life expectancies greater than our own. And Japan, which leads the world in life expectancy, spends only a third of what the United States spends each year—about five hundred dollars per capita compared with fifteen hundred.

Clearly, we need to take a closer look at the relationship between our efforts at health care, on the one hand, and our actual health, on the other. If the United States is spending more on medicine than any other nation, while suffering poorer health than many, there may be something fundamentally wrong with the country's approach. The urgent questions are: What really makes people healthy? Why do we live so much longer than our ancestors and so much longer than the world's remaining premodern peoples? If medicine is not the source of this blessing, we would do well to find out what is—and to direct our medical and public health efforts accordingly.

THERE IS NO DENYING that modern medicine has accomplished much of value. It has done a great deal to alleviate suffering, and many treatments—including surgery for burns, bleeding, abdominal obstructions, and diabetic coma—undoubtedly save lives. Anything that saves lives would presumably contribute to overall life expectancy. But most therapy is not aimed directly at prolonging life. Rare is the patient for whom death would be the price of missing a doctor's appointment. Moreover, any medical procedure involves some risk; there is always a chance that the patient will have an adverse or fatal reaction to a given treatment—be it surgical, pharmaceutical, or even diagnostic. If treatments were administered only when patients stood to benefit, the net effect on mortality rates might be positive. But physicians have a well-documented tendency to overdo a good thing. And because there are no clear guidelines governing the use of most remedies, the cost of such zeal is that the benefits gained by those who require a particular treatment are often outweighed by the adverse effects on those who receive it unnecessarily. Thus, while such major medical advances as antibiotics, immunization, coronary bypass surgery, chemotherapy, and obstetric surgery all have saved lives, it is impossible to demonstrate that any of them has contributed significantly to overall life expectancy.

The introduction of antibiotics into clinical medicine is generally viewed as the turning point in mankind's war against infectious disease. Clearly, such illnesses as typhoid, cholera, measles, smallpox, and tuberculosis no longer claim lives at the rate they did during the nineteenth century. The decline began at different times in different nations, but it was under way in Scandinavia and the English-speaking countries by the mid-nineteenth century, roughly a hundred years before the first antibiotic drug, penicillin, became available, during the Second World War. By the time streptomycin, isoniazid, and other such agents came into wide use, during the 1940s and 1950s, death rates from the eleven most common infectious diseases had dwindled to a mere fraction of their nineteenth-century levels. Antibiotics did, for a time, hold tremendous therapeutic powers, and had they been used in moderation, they might have remained potent weapons against infection. But overuse has largely destroyed their effectiveness.

The indications that we rely too heavily on antibiotics are myriad. In 1973, scientists at the University of Wisconsin at Madison concluded, after reviewing the findings of other researchers, that enough antibiotics are manufactured and dispensed each year in the United States to treat two illnesses of average duration in every man, woman, and child in the country. The evidence suggests, however, that only once in five to ten years does the average individual experience an infection, such as meningitis or tuberculosis, that antibiotics might help control. The drugs are routinely prescribed for colds and flu, even though there is no evidence they have any effect on such viral ailments, and are given out like vitamins in many hospitals. In one recent survey of hospital patients, the internist Theodore C. Eickhoff, of the University of Colorado Medical Center, in Denver, found that thirty percent were receiving antibiotics—though only half of those receiving the drugs showed signs of infection. Other findings suggest that patients who might actually benefit from an antibiotic frequently receive the wrong one, or an incorrect dose.

One outcome of this overreliance on penicillin and the other so-called wonder drugs is that many bacteria have, through natural selection, become resistant to them, and infections that were easily controlled thirty years ago no longer respond well to treatment. Both gonococcus, the pus-producing bacterium that causes the most common venereal disease, and pneumococcus, a bacterium frequently associated with lobar pneumonia, now show resistance to various antibiotics. And in hospitals, overall infection rates are on the rise. A 1985 study, published by Robert W. Haley and his colleagues at the Centers for Disease Control, concluded that hospital-acquired infections occur in almost six out of every one hundred patients, thereby producing a national toll of four million infections a year, and that this rate is increasing by two percent annually.

Immunization is another therapy widely believed to have reduced death rates from infectious disease. But studies indicate that the use of vaccines and their ostensible benefits are largely unrelated. There is no question that the smallpox vaccine, for one, is effective when properly administered. Historical records show, however, that the number of people dying of smallpox was already falling when the vaccine first became available in Europe, during the early nineteenth century. True, smallpox mortality continued to drop as the vaccine became more accessible, but so did the death rates associated with infectious diseases for which vaccines had *not* been developed. The parallel decline in mortality from typhoid and tuberculosis prompted speculation that the smallpox vaccine was somehow protecting people from those infections, too. But there was never any basis for such a conclusion. A more reasonable inference is that deaths from all three illnesses were declining on account of some other factor.

As in the case of smallpox, vaccines for polio, whooping cough, measles, and diphtheria are effective at protecting individuals from these diseases. As a result, they not only save lives but spare many people permanent disabilities. But the question, for our purposes, is whether such vaccines have caused a significant decline in overall mortality, and the evidence indicates they have not. The historical record shows that death rates for childhood diseases started falling before the vaccines became available, and there is no evidence that forgoing such vaccines shortens people's lives. When concern about the risks associated with the diphtheria vaccine led English physicians to stop administering it during the late 1970s, for example, there was a sharp increase in the incidence of the disease, yet diphtheria mortality barely changed.

LIKE INFECTIOUS DISEASE, cardiovascular illness seems to pose a less dire threat to most of us today than it has in the past. Coronary artery disease appears to be waning both in incidence and in deadliness. A twenty-six-year study of Du Pont Company employees found that the number of people afflicted with the disease declined by twenty-eight percent between 1957 and 1983. Other studies indicate that the rate at which Americans are killed by it fell from about three hundred and fifty for every hundred thousand in 1970 to just two hundred and fifty for every hundred thousand in 1985. If such outcomes could be attributed to medical intervention, they would indeed rank as major accomplishments. But here, as with infectious disease, the link between treatment and health is elusive—whether the treatment is directed at preventing the disease or curing it.

Consider the results of the Multiple Risk Factor Intervention Trial, or "Mr. Fit." In this study, a team of investigators from twenty-two health research centers randomly divided a sample population of nearly thirteen thousand men, aged thirty-five to fifty-seven, into two groups. For the next seven years, members of one group continued to receive routine care from their private physicians, while the other group participated in a therapeutic program to reduce the risk of coronary artery disease. Physicians supervised and monitored efforts to have them avoid smoking, reduce the amount of cholesterol in their diets, and control their blood pressure, using medication if necessary. At the end of the treatment period, the subjects who received the extra medical attention had indeed cut back on cigarettes and cholesterol, and they exhibited less hypertension. But they did not end up living any longer than the subjects who simply went about their business. In fact, their death rate from all causes (41.2 deaths for every thousand subjects) was slightly *higher* than that of the control group (40.4 deaths). The reasons for this failure were not readily evident; the researchers speculated that the ill effects of antihypertensive drugs may have outweighed any benefits derived from the program. Whatever the explanation, such results confirm that the recent decline in death from cardiovascular disease probably is not the fruit of preventive medicine.

If efforts at prevention have not caused the decline, might it reflect the advent of better therapeutic techniques, such as coronary bypass surgery? Saving lives was not the original intent of this operation when surgeons began performing it, during the late 1960s; bypassing portions of coronary arteries that had become partially clogged with fatty deposits was viewed as a way of alleviating the chest pain that accompanies such blockage. But when the operation was found to be effective for that purpose, physicians began touting it as a therapeutic measure—and even a preventive treatment for patients without symptoms—despite an utter lack of clinical evidence. Today coronary bypass is one of America's most commonly performed surgical procedures. Roughly two hundred thousand Americans undergo the operation each year, at a total cost of some five billion dollars. Yet only rarely does it contribute to anyone's survival. A study published in 1983 by the National Institutes of Health concluded that bypass surgery prolongs the life of roughly one bypass patient in ten but that it appears to add nothing to the life expectancies of the other nine.

IS CANCER TREATMENT, another major focus of modern medicine, perhaps the secret of our increased life expectancy? One might guess that it has made a contribution; after all, the average interval between the diagnosis of a malignancy and the death of the patient has increased considerably in recent years. Indeed, the percentage of cancer patients surviving at least five years rose from 38.5 percent in 1973 to 40.1 percent in 1978, an improvement of almost one percent a year. Regrettably, it does not necessarily follow that people with cancer are living longer, let alone that chemotherapy or surgical treatments are extending their lives. Many scientists speculate that earlier detection of the disease merely has created an illusion of increased survival.

There is evidence that physicians are diagnosing cancer at earlier stages of development, thanks largely to more frequent checkups and better diagnostic technology. But there is no indication that earlier treatment has improved patients' overall survival rates. In fact, for some forms of cancer, there is hard evidence that it has not. In one study, sponsored by the National Cancer Institute and published in 1984, a population of adult male smokers, all presumably at high risk of developing lung cancer, was divided into two groups. One group received only annual chest X rays; members of the second group underwent frequent X rays and had their sputum examined regularly for cancer cells. Not surprisingly, there were many more diagnoses of lung cancer among the closely monitored subjects. And because their malignancies were usually detected and treated at early stages, their survival rates from the time of diagnosis were impressive. Even so, the numbers of lung cancer deaths in the two groups were nearly identical. In short, the participants in the early-detection program gained no apparent advantage: they were no less likely to suffer recurrences of the disease, or to die of it, than were members of the control group.

If modern treatments were, on balance, helping cancer patients survive, those patients would be dying at a later average age, and this, in turn, would reduce the average person's chances of dying of cancer at any age. But age-adjusted cancer mortality has not declined at all in the United States during the past fifty years. The death rates have changed for particular forms of cancer (lung cancer mortality has increased, whereas deaths from stomach cancer have declined), and it is possible that treatment has played a role in some of the success stories. The relatively rare cancers of childhood, for example, seem to respond well to treatment. But such situations are the exception, not the rule. Most therapies are introduced without ever being thoroughly evaluated for effectiveness, and they are embraced by physicians and patients who are understandably eager to try anything.

Radical mastectomy, the standard treatment for breast cancer throughout most of this century, is a good example. Studies have shown that patients who have this operation —the mutilating removal of the breast and its underlying tissues—do not, as a group, live any longer than patients who undergo the less radical lumpectomy (removal of the cancerous mass only). In one study, published in 1985 in *The New England Journal of Medicine*, nearly two thousand breast cancer patients were randomly assigned to receive one treatment or the other. Those who had the traditional mastectomy died earlier. Still, most U.S. physicians continue to perform the more extensive operation, and some even recommend it as a preventive measure for women whose cystic (lumpy) breasts place them at a theoretical risk of developing the disease.

The point is not that cancer treatment is never justified, only that it has had no discernible effect on the overall survival rates of cancer patients, let alone the life expectancy of the general population. Indeed, no cancer treatment, however successful, could do much to increase life expectancy, for the disease does little to reduce it. Cancer strikes mostly among the aged. It has long been estimated

that even if it were totally preventable or curable, the increase in U.S. life expectancy would be less than two years. Given that life expectancy has increased by twenty-five years during this century, it is impossible that the treatment of cancer has made much of a difference.

If modern medicine cannot be credited with taming infectious disease, cardiovascular illness, or cancer, one might expect to find that it has at least improved the odds that mothers and infants will survive the birth process. Cesarean section has undoubtedly contributed to the rapid decline in maternal mortality during this century. Like so many other medical procedures, however, it is now so grossly overused that it may be costing as many lives as it saves.

The maternal mortality rate had already dwindled to less than one death in ten thousand deliveries by the mid-1970s. Yet, since then, births by cesarean section have increased by three hundred percent in the United States. To confirm that this trend is not making childbirth any safer, one need only consider the survival statistics for societies that rely less heavily on surgical delivery. In 1965, the rate of cesarean births at Ireland's National Maternity Hospital, in Dublin, was equal to that in the United States—about five percent. Since then, the U.S. rate has climbed to twenty percent, but the rate in Dublin has remained stable, and perinatal mortality has fallen faster there than it has in the United States. The Netherlands, meanwhile, which enjoys one of the lowest perinatal and maternal mortality rates in Europe, also has one of the lowest rates of obstetric surgery.

IT SEEMS CLEAR that modern medicine, whatever it has done to save or improve individual lives, has had little effect on the overall health of large populations. Still, the fact is that life expectancy has increased spectacularly during the nineteenth and twentieth centuries. What else might explain such a change? There is no question that sanitation and nutrition, the other factors most often cited, have been beneficial. But neither of these developments accounts fully for the mystery at hand.

It is true that, toward the end of the nineteenth century, improvements in sanitation coincided with a decline in mortality from various infectious diseases in Europe and America. But there is no evidence of a cause-and-effect relationship. Sanitation worsened in many major cities during the Industrial Revolution, as the prospect of work drew hordes of immigrants from rural areas. Rotting meat, fish, and garbage were heaped in the streets of New York and London, and overflowing privies were still far more common than modern toilets in many crowded neighborhoods. Amazingly, though, mortality rates from infectious disease fell steadily over the same period.

Another problem with the sanitation argument is that the *incidence* of infection decreased little during the nineteenth century. What did decline was the frequency with which infections sickened or killed people. As recently as 1940, long after tuberculosis had ceased to be a major health threat, skin tests showed that ninety-five percent of all Americans were still being infected with tuberculosis bacteria by age forty-five. Yet the vast majority managed to fight it off. Even today, most of the microorganisms that caused so much disease and death in premodern times, particularly among children, are omnipresent in the environment. No amount of sanitation could eliminate them, for they are passed directly from one person to another. They exist harmlessly, for the most part, both in and on our bodies.

Could it be that improved nutrition has strengthened our resistance? This idea does not withstand scrutiny, either. If eating well were the key to long life, then the most privileged families of old Europe, who enjoyed better nutrition than their contemporaries, should also have enjoyed longer lives. But they died young (as did the first American settlers, for whom the threat of starvation was not a particular problem). Moreover, there is no evidence that the specific dietary changes that are associated with modernization have even been advantageous. Indeed, it is arguable that, on balance, those changes have been harmful.

In the United States—where modernization has been associated with less physical activity, and with increased consumption of white bread, cookies, doughnuts, alcohol, and red meat from fattened animals—an estimated twenty to twenty-five percent of adult men are overweight. Diet and inactivity are not the only factors that contribute to obesity, of course, but they clearly count. In one recent study, the University of Toronto anthropologists Andris Rode and Roy J. Shephard monitored body fat and physical fitness among members of an Eskimo community during a ten-year period of rapid modernization. They found that the community's adoption of a modern diet, along with its increased use of snowmobiles and snow-clearing equipment, accompanied a significant increase in body fat and decreases in several measures of fitness. If these Eskimo follow the usual pattern, modernization will bring about a net increase in life expectancy. But if their overall health improves, it will have improved *despite* the changes in diet and physical activity, not because of them.

I T IS, IN A WORD, impossible to trace the hardiness of modern people directly to improvements in medicine, sanitation, or diet. There is an alternative explanation for our increased life expectancy, however, one that has less to do with these developments than with changes in our psychological environment. We like to imagine that preindustrial peoples endured (and endure) less stress than we do—that, although they may have lacked physical amenities, they spent peaceful days weaving interesting fabrics and singing folk songs. But the psychic stresses of the simple life are, in fact, far greater than those experienced by the most harried modern executive. It is one thing to fret over a tax return or a real estate deal, and quite another to bury one's children, to wonder whether a fall's harvest will last the winter, or to watch one's home wash away in a flood.

To grow up surrounded by scarcity and ignorance and constant loss—whether in an African village or a twentieth-century urban slum—is to learn that misery is usually a consequence of forces beyond one's control and, by extension, that individual effort counts for naught. And there is ample evidence that such a sense of helplessness is often associated with apathy, depression, and death—

whether in laboratory animals or in prisoners of war. The experimental psychologist Martin E. P. Seligman, of the University of Pennsylvania, has designed some remarkable studies to simulate in dogs the experience of helplessness in humans. His classic experiment involved placing dogs in a box in which they could avoid electric shocks by jumping over a barrier upon the dimming of a light. Naïve dogs quickly learned to avoid shocks entirely, leaping gracefully over the barrier whenever the light dimmed. But Seligman found that dogs responded differently if, before being placed in the box, they were confined and subjected to shocks they could not escape. Those dogs, having learned that effort is futile, just lay down and whined.

In many ways, the experiences and reactions of the second group resemble those of people raised in poverty, a shared feature of most premodern societies. Modernization, through such mechanisms as fire departments, building codes, social insurance, and emergency medical care, has cushioned most of us against physical, psychic, and economic disaster. But, more important, it has created circumstances in which few of us feel utterly powerless to control our lives. We now take for granted that we are, in large part, the masters of our own destinies, and that in itself leaves us better equipped to fight off disease.

How did this happen? What are the sources of this sense of personal efficacy and self-esteem? No institution has been so changed by modernization as the family. Until the late eighteenth century, it existed primarily as an economic unit; marriages were arranged for the purpose of preserving property, and children were viewed as a cheap source of labor or a hedge against poverty in old age. Beating and whipping were favored, even among royalty, as tools for teaching conformity and obedience. Then, during the Enlightenment, the standards and goals of child rearing began to change. If children were going to survive in a disorderly and unpredictable world, philosophers began to argue, they could not rely passively on traditional authority; they needed reasoned judgment. And if children were going to develop such judgment, they needed affection and guidance, not brute discipline. It was only gradually, as these ideas took root, that childhood came to be recognized as a special stage of life, and that affection and nurturing replaced obligation and duty as the cohesive forces among family members.

During the nineteenth century, as the upper classes came to view children as having needs of their own rather than serving the needs of the family—and, accordingly, started having fewer of them—their infant and childhood mortality rates began to fall. And as the trend toward smaller families spread to the lower social classes, theirs fell, too. It is unlikely that this was just coincidence, for family size is an excellent predictor of childhood survival even today. Young children of large families continue to suffer more infections, more accidents, and a higher overall mortality rate than the children of small families, regardless of social class. Indeed, as the Columbia University sociologist Joe D. Wray demonstrated in 1971, the effects of family size can outweigh those of social class: an only child in a poor family has about the same chance of surviving the first year of life as a child who is born into a professional-class family but who has four or more siblings.

Why should this be so? One explanation, supported by various lines of evidence, is that the children of small families are strengthened in every way by the extra nurture they receive from their parents. During the past forty years, studies have demonstrated that infants develop poorly, even die, when they are provided food and physical necessities but are denied intimate contact with care givers. In one experiment, orphans placed in an institution at an early age were separated into two groups. Members of one group stayed in the institution while the others were placed with foster parents. At the end of the first year, the children placed in foster homes were better developed, both mentally and physically, than those who received institutional care. And even after the institutionalized children were assigned to foster homes, they remained less developed than their counterparts for a number of years.

Other studies have produced even more arresting evidence. In 1966, Harold M. Skeels, of the National Institute of Mental Health, reported on an experiment that gauged the long-term effect of individual care on retarded institutionalized children. One group of children received routine institutional care, which is often physically adequate but emotionally sterile, while the other children were moved to a special ward to be cared for individually by retarded women. After three years, most of the children in the first group had lost an average of twenty-six IQ points, whereas those in the second group had *gained* an average of twenty-nine points. The differences were even more pronounced thirty years later. None of the children who received routine care had made it past the third grade, and most remained institutionalized. By contrast, many of those cared for by foster mothers had completed the twelfth grade and gone on to become self-supporting.

W E ARE ONLY BEGINNING to understand the mechanisms linking emotional and physical health (the endeavor has of late given rise to a new branch of medicine, known as psychoneuroimmunology). But whatever the connection, the fact stands that the affection and security associated with the modern family are the best available predictors of good health. In the end, it matters little whether sanitation, nutrition, and medical care are crude or sophisticated; children who receive consistent love and attention—who grow up in circumstances that foster self-reliance and optimism rather than submission and hopelessness—are better survivors. They are bigger, brighter, more resistant, and more resilient. And, as a result, they live longer.

It is ironic, in the light of this, that we continue to fret over the quality of our food and the purity of our environment, to spend billions of dollars on medical procedures of no proven value, and to pay so little attention to the recent deterioration of the American family. The divorce rate in the United States, though it appears to have leveled off during the past few years, has increased enormously since the 1950s, from less than ten percent to more than twenty percent today. The number of children being raised by single parents has doubled during the past decade alone, and divorce is not the only reason. Another ominous development is the rise in pregnancy among unwed teenagers. For whites, the rate increased from eight percent in 1940 to twenty percent in 1970, and to thirty percent in 1980. The problem is even worse among blacks, sixty percent of whom are now born out of wedlock. That this, in itself, constitutes a serious health problem is plain when one considers that fetal and infant death rates are twice as high for illegitimate children as for legitimate ones, and that a teenaged mother is at least seven times more likely than an older mother to abuse her child.

All of this suggests that good health is as much a social and psychological achievement as a physical one—and that the preservation of the family is not so much a moral issue as a medical one. Unless we recognize the medical importance of the family and find ways to stop its deterioration, we may continue to watch our health expenditures rise and our life-spans diminish. We will waste precious resources on unnecessary treatments, while ignoring a preventable tragedy.

A VITAL LONG LIFE

NEW TREATMENTS FOR COMMON AGING AILMENTS

Medical science enables us to live to a healthy ripe old age —and enjoy it.

Evelyn B. Kelly

Evelyn B. Kelly is vice president of the Florida chapter of the American Medical Writers' Associaiton and a consultant on psychological and gerontological concerns.

Bill, seventy-seven, is a new model of older adult. He manages a vast network of athletic camps, flies to the World Series, and spends his spare time working with his church and the Gideons. He walks two miles a day and is very careful about his diet. Bill lives his life with zest and vigor and still contributes to society.

Bill is prototypical of the new elder culture predicted for the next cohort of older adults. According to Ken Dychtwald, a gerontological consultant, the next generation of older adults will be healthier, more mobile, better educated, and more politically astute than today's seniors. They will be part of a more powerful and energetic elder culture.

Like the old gray mare, aging is definitely not what it used to be. Time was when people believed they should eat, drink, and be merry—for tomorrow, they'd retire to their rockers. Invariably, it was held, the passing years meant steady mental and physical decline until one died from "old age." While many still cling to these myths, researchers marvel at the human potential to extend physical and intellectual capacities in later life.

Many factors have contributed to this greatly improved forecast for the aging. Medical advances of the last decade have made it possible for present and future generations to live longer lives. Demonstrably, healthier life-styles have played a major role in extending life span. The effects of disease, abuse, or disuse should never be called "normal aging." Put simply, people do not die of old age, but of specific conditions, over which they may have some control.

The sheer numbers of older adults are overwhelming. Although the maximum life span has not increased, the number of persons sixty-five and older has increased from 4 percent of the population in 1900 to 12 percent in 1985. Even more important, the fastest-growing segment of the population is the

Physical therapy, including exercise and weight reduction, is an important way to manage arthritis.

From *The World & I*, April 1988, pp. 291-297. Copyright © 1988 by News World Communications, Inc. Reprinted by permission.

group eighty-five and older.

In 1900, only 25 percent of deaths occurred in the group over sixty-five. Advances in preventing childhood diseases had pushed the number to almost 70 percent by 1980. Impressive gains have been made in treating and preventing the four leading causes of death in the sixty-five plus population: heart disease, strokes, cancer, and pneumonia.

But this bounty of years has brought mixed blessings. As our aged population continues to grow, survivors may encounter nonfatal disorders, such as arthritis, diabetes, and dementia. Specified in the blueprint for a model healthy old age are education and healthy life-style choices.

Heart disease and strokes: silent stalkers

A diagnosis of high blood pressure surprises most people, who find the knowledge that they are potential candidates for stroke or heart failure traumatic. About 75 percent of hypertensives are over forty, but their condition is seldom diagnosed until they are fifty or sixty. Associated with excess weight, and found more commonly in black people than white and men than women, hypertension has been called the silent stalker.

According to Dr. Harvey Simon of Harvard Medical School, hearts may wear down a little, but they probably do not wear out. He adds that disease and disuse, rather than age, account for most of the deterioration. The heart's ability to pump blood declines about 8 percent each decade after adulthood, and blood pressure increases as fatty deposits clog the arteries. By middle age, the opening of the coronary arteries is 29 percent narrower than in the twenties.

Life-style changes, drugs, or a combination can reduce blood pressure. With more than fifty blood-pressure drugs on the market, if one produces side effects, another can be prescribed. A number of drugs are still being tested. In August 1987, the U.S. Food and Drug Administration (FDA) approved the use of lovastatin, a cholesterol-reducing drug, but recommended it only for patients who do not re-

spond to diet and exercise.

Heart attacks are caused by a blood clot in one of the coronary arteries. Most deaths caused by heart attacks occur within minutes or a few hours. Until recently, doctors could do little to treat an attack and prevent damage to the heart muscle. Two recent developments, however, mean good news for older adults. A new class of drugs called "clotbusters" may be injected into the veins to dissolve clots, and the FDA has recently approved streptokinase, a blood thinner, and another "clotbuster," TPA—tissue plasminogen activator.

Other weapons against heart attacks are balloon angioplasty—a procedure that opens clogged arteries with small balloonlike structures—and laser angioplasty, an experimental method where light vaporizes plaque deposits on the arteries.

Diseases of the cerebral blood vessels causing stroke rank high among the disabilities of the elderly. Reducing blood pressure can cut the risk of stroke in half. In stroke, the

blood flow to part of the brain stops. The effect is similar to that of a heart attack; without blood, the tissue has no oxygen and dies.

Although about half of the elderly are hypertensive, physicians do not agree on their treatment. In a recent American Medical Association report, Richard Davidson and George Caranosos of the University of Florida announced that treating elderly hypertensives appears to be effective in stroke prevention. Older adults are not more susceptible to the side effects of antihypertensive drugs than other groups.

Risk factors leading to heart disease include heredity, diabetes, high-fat diets, high blood pressure, and smoking. Changes in life-style dramatically reduce the risk of these silent stalkers.

Cancer and older adults

There's no question about it: Cancer occurs more frequently with increasing age. The passing of years may lengthen exposure to carcinogens, alter host immunity or chro-

The next generation of older adults will be healthier. Aging may occur from disuse, not from disease. This farmer and his wife stay active. He is 100 and she is 95 years old.

The Fountains of Youth

In 1513, Ponce de Leon combed Florida in search of mythical waters that would prevent aging. Today, Dr. J. Michael McGinnis, who launched the Healthy Older People program, has found that up to 50 percent of all premature mortality can be related to life-style habits, and that older adults are willing and able to make life-style changes to improve their health. Even in late age, behavioral changes, especially in the realms of exercise and nutrition, can produce health benefits.

Every cell in our bodies is dependent on oxygen. We can go weeks without food and days without water, but only a few minutes without oxygen. The heart pumps the blood that carries oxygen throughout the body, so anything that improves circulation is beneficial. Exercise fulfills this important function—and more!

Exercise

The symptoms of "old age"—no energy, stiff joints, poor circulation—may really be the signs of inactivity. You don't stop exercising because you are becoming old; you become old because you stop exercising. The same conditions attributed to aging can be induced in young people who sit around doing nothing. Aging may occur not from disease but from disuse.

● The relationship between inactivity and circulatory problems is immutable. The less active you are, the more chances you run of developing heart problems and high blood pressure.

● Exercise and the lowered risk of heart disease are connected with chemicals in blood cholesterol called lipoproteins. The so-called good lipoproteins—the HDLs (high-density lipoproteins)—are found in the blood of those on solid exercise programs. The bad lipoproteins—the LDLs (low-density lipoproteins)—outnumber the good in those who are inactive. Letter carriers—who walk all day—have fewer heart attacks than sedentary post office clerks.

● It is never too late to start exercising. Studies at the University of Toronto have shown that men and women over the age of sixty who began to exercise regularly were found to have achieved the fitness level of persons ten to twenty years younger in only seven weeks.

With exercise alone, cholesterol and triglyceride levels drop markedly. Appetite is suppressed and digestion improves. When people diet to lose weight, their metabolism slows down, and they reach a plateau of weight loss. With exercise, however, the rate of body metabolism increases, and body fat is absorbed. Because carbohydrate and complex-sugar metabolism is improved, diabetics who exercise can maintain lower insulin levels.

Nutrition

It sounds obvious, but a balanced diet is still the most important overall eating strategy. That means including something from each of the four food groups daily—grains; fruits and vegetables; meat, fish, and poultry; and dairy products. The emphasis today is on low-fat, high-fiber foods. By eating more fiber, you lower your cholesterol level and lessen the chances of getting heart disease.

The relationship between diet and many chronic conditions such as heart disease, stroke, hypertension, and cancer has been proven. However, Healthy Older People revealed that older adults are confused about what constitutes good nutrition. They seemed very knowledgeable about what not to eat, but were unable to describe the elements of a balanced diet.

A focal point of controversy in nutrition is the official U.S. recommended dietary allowances, or RDAs. One problem is that RDAs are established for only two adult groups—those under fifty and those over fifty. Certainly, the physiological differences between fifty-five- and eighty-five-year-olds reflect different dietary needs that must be addressed in education programs.

Also, nutrition and exercise act as natural tranquilizers that relieve tension and promote mental well-being. While exercise and nutrition can't reduce health risks to zero, through our behavior and life-style choices we can indeed create an inner fountain of youth.

---

mosomal linkage, or increase exposure to ontogenic viruses.

But the very group that needs screening is often disregarded because of preconceived notions about cancer in older adults. Some think older adults are too fragile to tolerate proper treatment. The American Cancer Society emphasizes that early detection is important at all ages.

In many parts of the body, such as the skin, the lungs, and digestive tract, the chances of cancer rise steadily with age. Prostate cancer is even more directly connected to age. Some cancers, theoretically preventable, are caused by habits or environmental factors, such as smoking or exposure to industrial chemicals. The following chart shows the screening recommendations of the American Cancer Society.

Pneumonia: friend of the old?

Friend of the old: That's what Sir William Osler called pneumonia in 1912. He stated that a death from pneumonia is short, relatively painless, and peaceful.

Today, few would call pnuemonia a friend: We have little admiration for the No. 1 infectious killer of older adults.

And what's more—admissions to nursing homes and hospitals increase the chance of encounter with this "enemy." The yearly incidence of pneumonia, 20 to 40 cases per thousand, sharply rises with institutionalization to about 250 cases per thousand.

Hospitals are associated with an

increased risk for lower respiratory infections. Nosocomial pneumonia (the name given to infections acquired in a hospital) is involved in about 15 percent of pneumonia cases; the attack rate increases with age. In addition, nosocomial pneumonias are stubborn and hard to treat.

Pneumonia in older adults is a diagnostic and therapeutic nightmare. In many cases, pneumonia may not be suspected because the common signs of respiratory disease are absent. The ill person suspected of having pneumonia is often treated with a "broad-spectrum" antibiotic to kill different kinds of bacteria. This shotgun approach may or may not work. Despite the availability of potent antibiotics, mortality due to pneumonia in the aged remains substantial and comes with a high price tag. Over $550 million is spent each year in hospital care alone for elderly adults with pneumonia.

Education for prevention is imperative. Despite a well-recognized association between outbreaks of influenza and deaths from pneumonia, only about 20 percent of high-risk persons are vaccinated against the flu each year. Lederle, a pharmaceutical company, is marketing a vaccine that protects against twenty-three types of pneumococcal bacteria.

Future pharmaceutical development will help in the prevention and treatment of pneumonia in older people. Possible breakthroughs include vaccines against more bacterial strains, more potent oral antibiotics, and methods to keep people from breathing in microbes.

Arthritis: common and still confusing

Bury your body in horse manure up to your neck. . . . Sit in an abandoned uranium mine. . . . Take cobra and krait venom. . . . With such

remedies, people have desperately sought relief from the pain of arthritis. Neanderthal cave paintings drawn more than forty thousand years ago show stooped beings with bent knees. Although medical science has conquered many old and exotic diseases, this condition continues to plague over thirty-one million Americans. In older people, its two most common forms are rheumatoid arthritis and osteoarthritis.

Rheumatoid arthritis (RA) is the most serious, painful, and disabling form. Affecting three times as many women as men, RA first affects the linings (synovial membranes) of small joints—such as those in the hands and feet—then moves to tissues and organs, such as the heart and lungs. Osteoarthritis (OA) is often called the "wear and tear" disease and is by far the commonest form of arthritis. The condition begins with the thinning, wearing down, or roughening of cartilage, which may lead to chem-

Cancer Screening Tests

Procedure	Sex	Age	Frequency
Sigmoidoscopy	M&F	over 50	every 3–5 years
Stool guaiac slide test	M&F	over 50	every year
Digital rectal examination	M&F	over 40	every year
Pap test	F	20–65	at least every 3 years
Pelvic examination	F	20–40 over 40	every 3 years every year
Endometrial tissue sample	F	at menopause	at menopause
Breast self-examination	F	over 20	every month
Breast exam by physician	F	20–40 over 40	every 3 years every year
Mammography	F	35–40 40–50 over 50	initial test 1–2 years every year
Health counseling and cancer checkup	M&F M&F	20–40 over 40	every 3 years every year

(Recommended by the American Cancer Society)

ical changes that cause the joint to become inflamed. Usually seen in older people, the condition can develop in anyone whose joints have taken a lot of punishment: the obese, those injured in accidents, or those subject to unusual stress in work or sports.

According to Dr. Paul Nickerson of the Geriatric Diagnosis Clinic in Cleveland, Ohio, "The association between age and OA is striking, but it should not be assumed that OA is caused by normal aging." He quickly adds that despite our ignorance of the etiology of arthritis, there is still much to offer the patient.

Dr. Nickerson outlines three areas of management: (1) physical therapy, including exercise and weight reduction; (2) medication with nonsteroid antiinflammation drugs (NSAID), which include aspirin and ibuprophen; and (3) surgery for those with severe pain. Advanced age is sometimes a positive factor in joint replacement, because highly active young people run a greater risk of loosening new joints.

Dr. Nickerson foresees research leading to more and safer NSAIDs and, ultimately, a drug that will inhibit cartilage-damaging enzymes.

In the next generation, research will bring relief from pain and help people learn to live with intractable discomfort. Pain clinics are using new techniques, such as nerve stimulation and biofeedback. Until arthritis is fully understood and conquered, the key to treatment lies in changing attitudes and developing a satisfying life-style despite arthritis.

Diabetes: dare to discipline

Not since the discovery of insulin in 1921 by Banting and Best has there been so much good news about diabetes for older Americans. Recent breakthroughs have led to better understanding of this maligned disease—and diabetes deserves its reputation. Heart attacks, blindness, limb loss, and kidney failure are only a few of its complications.

Diabetes mellitus is a disorder in which the body fails to convert the food we eat into the energy we need. Type I (insulin-dependent diabetes mellitus (IDDM)) may appear early in life and results from a failure of the pancreas to produce insulin. Type II (noninsulin-dependent diabetes mellitus (NIDDM)), found in 90 percent of diabetics, is more common with age. Some researchers believe diabetes is directly related to excess weight, because reducing body fat appears to make body cells more receptive to insulin. By daring to discipline themselves, type II diabetics can usually keep blood glucose levels normal by controlling weight, exercising, and taking oral medication.

Recent research at the National Institute on Aging revealed that the body's ability to handle glucose decreases with age. The finding has led to a revision of the official guidelines for diagnosing diabetes. As a result, fewer elderly people are at risk of being considered diabetic. The new guidelines mean that many persons once considered borderline have been freed from the emotional burden and consequent problems of a chronic degenerative disease.

Fear of the dementing Alzheimer's disease

Publicity about Alzheimer's disease has bred a widespread, morbid fear of the condition. Believing that memory decline is inevitable, middle-aged and older adults interpret any slip of memory as symptomatic of decline.

Minor forgetfulness is normal at any age. The key difference is that in Alzheimer's, dementia worsens until those affected cannot function normally. Fear of dementia will not prevent the condition: Remember, eighty percent of older people remain alert and active.

Alzheimer's disease is a real heartbreaker for the 2.5 million men and women plagued by it, and their families. Although no cure has been discovered, much can be done to make life more bearable for both patients and families.

Alzheimer's disease was discovered by German physician Alois Alzheimer in 1906. While symptoms may vary, patients can go from severe forgetfulness to personality changes with loss of all verbal skills and physical control. The course of the disease may run from less than three years to fifteen years or more. Death usually results from malnutrition or infection.

As some conditions produce symptoms similar to Alzheimer's, the disease is usually diagnosed by exclusion. For example, depression is closely correlated with memory loss. If the depression is successfully treated, the person may regain memory and dignity. Other conditions with similar symptoms include: malnutrition, stroke, drug reaction, metabolic change, or head injury.

An autopsy of the brain of an Alzheimer's patient reveals an abnormal disarray of litter. Abnormal neuron masses called "neurofibrillary tangles" appear in the outer cortex of the brain. Plaques of scarlike structures mark deteriorated nerve endings.

Some experts are looking for a genetic connection. Abnormal genes have been identified in most dementias, such as Huntington's chorea and Down's syndrome. Scientists thought they might be close to a cause when a protein amyloid present in the brains of Alzheimer's patients seemed to be leading them to the causative gene. However, the Winter 1987 issue of the Alzheimer's Disease and Related Disorders Association newsletters reported that Alzheimer's is probably not due to the replication of the gene that produces the amyloid. Another recent disappointment was the suspension of a test on tetrahydroaminoacridine (THA)—a drug that had alleviated some of the symptoms of memory loss. THA was found to cause liver damage in a significant number of patients. Scientists still look with hope for similar drugs to treat this disease associated with aging.

Adults of this and future generations can look forward to greater medical miracles and increased life expectancy. More knowledge and improved life-style choices will result in a new norm: living to a healthy old age. The nineteenth-century poet Robert Browning could have been addressing us today, when he wrote, "Grow old along with me! The best is yet to be."

The Prime of Our Lives

WHAT SEEMS TO MARK OUR ADULT YEARS MOST IS OUR SHIFTING PERSPECTIVE ON OURSELVES AND OUR WORLD. IS THERE A COMMON PATTERN TO OUR LIVES?

Anne Rosenfeld and Elizabeth Stark

Anne Rosenfeld and Elizabeth Stark, both members of Psychology Today's *editorial staff, collaborated across cohorts to write this article.*

"My parents had given me everything they could possibly owe a child and more. Now it was my turn to decide and nobody ... could help me very far...." That's how Graham Greene described his feelings upon graduation from Oxford. And he was right. Starting on your own down the long road of adulthood can be scary.

But the journey can also be exciting, with dreams and hopes to guide us. Maybe they're conventional dreams: getting a decent job, settling down and starting to raise a family before we've left our 20s. Or maybe they're more grandiose: making a million dollars by age 30, becoming a movie star, discovering a cure for cancer, becoming President, starting a social revolution.

Our youthful dreams reflect our unique personalities, but are shaped by the values and expectations of those around us—and they shift as we and our times change. Twenty years ago, college graduates entered adulthood with expectations that in many cases had been radically altered by the major upheavals transforming American society. The times were "a-changin'," and almost no one was untouched. Within a few years many of the scrubbed, obedient, wholesome teenagers of the early '60s had turned into scruffy, alienated campus rebels, experimenting with drugs and sex and deeply dissatisfied with their materialistic middle-class heritage.

Instead of moving right on to the career track, marrying and beginning families, as their fathers had done, many men dropped out, postponing the obligations of adult life. Others traveled a middle road, combining "straight" jobs with public service rather than pursuing conventional careers. And for the first time in recent memory, large numbers of young men refused to serve their country in the military. In the early 1940s, entire fraternities went together to enlist in World War II. In the Age of Aquarius, many college men sought refuge from war in Canada, graduate school, premature marriages or newly discovered medical ailments.

Women were even more dramatically affected by the social changes of the 1960s. Many left college in 1967 with a traditional agenda—work for a few years, then get married and settle down to the real business of raising a family and being a good wife—but ended up following a different and largely unexpected path. The women's movement and changing economics created a whole new set of opportunities. For example, between 1967 and 1980, women's share of medical degrees in the United States rocketed from 5 percent to 26 percent, and their share of law degrees leaped from 4 percent to 22 percent.

A group of women from the University of Michigan class of 1967 who were interviewed before graduation and again in 1981 described lives very different from their original plans. Psychologists Sandra Tangri of Howard University and Sharon Jenkins of the University of California found that far more of these women were working in 1981 than had expected to, and far more had gotten advanced degrees and were in "male" professions. Their home lives, too, were different from their collegiate fantasies: Fewer married, and those who did had much smaller families.

Liberation brought problems as well as opportunities. By 1981, about 15 percent of the women were divorced (although some had remarried), and many of the women who "had it all" told Tangri and Jenkins that they felt torn between their careers and their families.

Living out our dreams in a rapidly changing society demands extreme flexibility in adjusting to shifting social realities. Our hopes and plans, combined with the traditional rhythms of the life course, give some structure, impetus and predictability to our lives. But each of us must also cope repeatedly with the unplanned and unexpected. And in the process, we are gradually transformed.

For centuries, philosophers have been trying to capture the essence of how people change over the life course by focusing on universally experienced stages of life, often linked to specific ages. Research on child development, begun earlier in this century, had shown that children generally pass through an orderly succession of stages that correspond to fairly specific ages. But recent studies have challenged some of the apparent orderliness of child development, and the pattern of development among adults seems to be even less clear-cut.

When we think about what happens as we grow older, physical changes leap to mind—the lessening of physical prowess, the arrival of sags, spreads and lines. But these take a back seat to psychological changes, according to psychologist Bernice Neugarten of Northwestern University, a pioneer in the field of human development. She points out that although biological maturation heavily influences childhood development, people in young and middle adulthood are most affected by their own experiences and the timing of those experiences, not by biological factors. Even menopause, that quintessentially biological event, she says, is of relatively little psychological importance in the lives of most adult women.

In other words, chronological age is an increasingly unreliable indicator of what people will be like at various points. A group of newborns, or even 5-year-olds, shows less variation than a group of 35-year-olds, or 50-year-olds.

What seems to mark our adult years most is our shifting perspective on ourselves and our

STAGE THEORIES ARE A LITTLE LIKE HOROSCOPES—VAGUE ENOUGH TO LET EVERYONE SEE SOMETHING OF THEMSELVES IN THEM. THAT'S WHY THEY'RE SO POPULAR.

world—who we think we are, what we expect to get done, our timetable for doing it and our satisfactions with what we have accomplished. The scenarios and schedules of our lives are so varied that some researchers believe it is virtually impossible to talk about a single timetable for adult development. However, many people probably believe there is one, and are likely to cite Gail Sheehy's 1976 best-seller *Passages* to back them up.

Sheehy's book, which helped make "midlife crisis" a household word, was based on a body of research suggesting that adults go through progressive, predictable, age-linked stages, each offering challenges that must be met before moving on to the next stage. The most traumatic of these transitions, Sheehy claimed, is the one between young and middle adulthood—the midlife crisis.

Sheehy's ideas were based, in part, on the work of researchers Daniel Levinson, George Vaillant and Roger Gould, whose separate studies supported the stages of adult development Erik Erikson had earlier proposed in his highly influential model (see "Erikson's Eight Stages," next page).

Levinson, a psychologist, had started his study in 1969, when he was 49 and intrigued with his own recent midlife strains. He and his Yale colleagues intensively interviewed 40 men between the ages of 35 and 45 from four occupational groups. Using these interviews, bolstered by the biographies of great men and the development of memorable characters in literature, they described how men develop from 17 to 65 years of age (see "Levinson's Ladder," this article).

At the threshold of each major period of adulthood, they found, men pass through predictably unstable transitional periods, including a particularly wrenching time very close to age 40. At each transition a man must confront issues that may involve his career, his marriage, his family and the realization of his dreams if he is to progress successfully to the next period. Seventy percent to 80 percent of the men Levinson interviewed found the midlife transition (ages 40 to 45) tumultuous and psychologically painful, as most aspects of their lives came into question. The presumably universal timetable Levinson offered was very rigid, allowing no more than four years' leeway for each transition.

Vaillant's study, although less age-bound than Levinson's, also revealed that at midlife men go through a period of pain and preparation—"a time for reassessing and reordering the truth about adolescence and young adulthood." Vaillant, a psychiatrist, when he conducted his study at Harvard interviewed a group of men who were part of the Grant Study of Adult Development. The study had tracked almost 270 unusually accomplished, self-reliant and healthy Harvard freshmen

sage with its emphasis on orderly and clearly defined transitions. According to Cornell historian Michael Kammen, "We want predictability, and we desperately want definitions of 'normality.'" (drawn mostly from the classes of 1942 to 1944) from their college days until their late 40s. In 1967 and 1977 Vaillant and his team interviewed and evaluated 94 members of this select group.

SOURCE: ADAPTED FROM "REFLECTION ON DR. BORG'S LIFE CYCLE": ERIK H. ERIKSON, DAEDALUS, SPRING 1976.

	8	Old Age							Integrity vs. Despair, Disgust
7		Maturity						Generativity vs. Self-absorption	
6		Young Adulthood					Intimacy vs. Isolation		
5		Adolescence				Identity vs. Identity Confusion			
4		School Age			Industry vs. Inferiority				
3		Play Age		Initiative vs. Guilt					
2		Early Childhood	Autonomy vs. Shame, Doubt						
1		Infancy	Trust vs. Mistrust						
			1	2	3	4	5	6	7	8

Erikson's Eight Stages

According to Erik Erikson, people must grapple with the conflicts of one stage before they can move on to a higher one.

BONNIE SCHIFFMAN

They found that, despite inner turmoil, the men judged to have the best outcomes in their late 40s "regarded the period from 35 to 49 as the happiest in their lives, and the seemingly calmer period from 21 to 35 as the unhappiest." But the men least well adapted at midlife "longed for the relative calm of their young adulthood and regarded the storms of later life as too painful."

While Levinson and Vaillant were completing their studies, psychiatrist Roger Gould and his colleagues at the University of California, Los Angeles, were looking at how the lives of both men and women change during young and middle adulthood. Unlike the Yale and Harvard studies, Gould's was a one-time examination of more than 500 white, middle-class people from ages 16 to 60. Gould's study, like those of Levinson and Vaillant, found that the time around age 40 was a tough one for many people, both personally and maritally. He stressed that people need to change their early expectations as they develop. "Childhood delivers most people into adulthood with a view of adults that few could ever live up to," he wrote. Adults must confront this impossible image, he said, or be frustrated and dissatisfied.

The runaway success of *Passages* indicated the broad appeal of the stage theorists' mes-

perately want definitions of 'normality.'" And almost everyone could find some relationship to their own lives in the stages Sheehy described. Stage theories, explains sociologist Orville Brim Jr., former president of the Russell Sage Foundation, are "a little like horoscopes. They are vague enough so that everyone can see something of themselves in them. That's why they're so popular."

But popularity does not always mean validity. Even at the time there were studies contradicting the stage theorists' findings. When sociologist Michael Farrell of the State University of New York at Buffalo and social psychologist Stanley Rosenberg of Dartmouth Medical School looked for a crisis among middle-aged men in 1971 it proved elusive. Instead of finding a "universal midlife crisis," they discovered several different developmental paths. "Some men do appear to reach a state of crisis," they found, "but others seem to thrive. More typical than either of these responses is the tendency for men to bury their heads and deny and avoid all the pressures closing in on them."

Another decade of research has made the picture of adult development even more complex. Many observations and theories accepted earlier as fact, especially by the general public, are now being debated. Researchers have espe-

Oh, God, I'm only twenty and I'll have to go on living and living and living.
—Jean Rhys, *Diary*

At thirty a man should know himself like the palm of his hand, know the exact number of his defects and qualities, know how far he can go, foretell his failures— be what he is. And above all accept these things.
—Albert Camus *Carnets.*

cially challenged Levinson's assertion that stages are predictable, tightly linked to specific ages and built upon one another.

In fact, Gould, described as a stage theorist in most textbooks, has since changed his tune, based upon his clinical observations. He now disagrees that people go through "formal" developmental stages in adulthood, although he says that people "do change their ways of looking at and experiencing the world over time." But the idea that one must resolve one stage before going on to the next, he says, is "hogwash."

Levinson, however, has stuck by his conceptual guns over the years, claiming that no one has evidence to refute his results. "The only way for my theory to be tested is to study life structure as it develops over adulthood," he says. "And by and large psychologists and sociologists don't study lives, they study variables."

Many researchers have found that changing times and different social expectations affect how various "cohorts"—groups of people born in the same year or time period—move through the life course. Neugarten has been emphasizing the importance of this age-group, or cohort, effect since the early 1960s. Our values and expectations are shaped by the period in which we live. People born during the trying times of the Depression have a different outlook on life from those born during the optimistic 1950s, according to Neugarten.

The social environment of a particular age group, Neugarten argues, can influence its so-

WHAT WAS TRUE FOR PEOPLE BORN IN THE DEPRESSION ERA MAY NOT HOLD FOR TODAY'S 40-YEAR-OLDS, BORN IN THE UPBEAT POSTWAR YEARS.

cial clock—the timetable for when people expect and are expected to accomplish some of the major tasks of adult life, such as getting married, having children or establishing themselves in a work role. Social clocks guide our lives, and people who are "out of sync" with them are likely to find life more stressful than those who are on schedule, she says.

Since the 1960s, when Neugarten first measured what people consider to be the "right" time for major life events, social clocks have changed (see "What's the Right Time?" this article), further altering the lives of those now approaching middle age, and possibly upsetting the timetable Levinson found in an earlier generation.

As sociologist Alice Rossi of the University of Massachusetts observes, researchers trying to tease out universal truths and patterns from

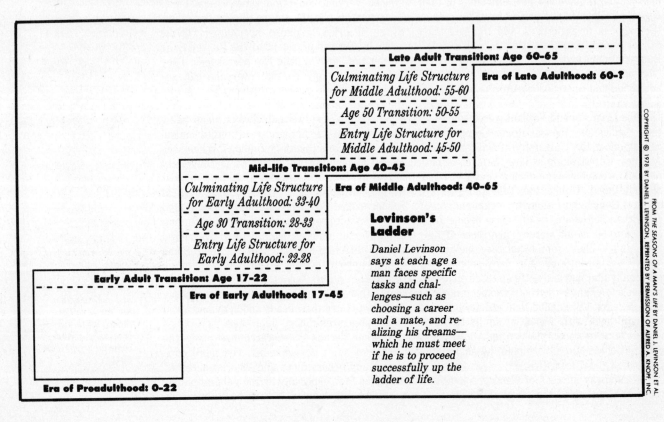

Late Adult Transition: Age 60-65

Culminating Life Structure for Middle Adulthood: 55-60

Era of Late Adulthood: 60-?

Age 50 Transition: 50-55

Entry Life Structure for Middle Adulthood: 45-50

Mid-life Transition: Age 40-45

Culminating Life Structure for Early Adulthood: 33-40

Era of Middle Adulthood: 40-65

Age 30 Transition: 28-33

Entry Life Structure for Early Adulthood: 22-28

Levinson's Ladder

Daniel Levinson says at each age a man faces specific tasks and challenges—such as choosing a career and a mate, and realizing his dreams— which he must meet if he is to proceed successfully up the ladder of life.

Early Adult Transition: Age 17-22

Era of Early Adulthood: 17-45

Era of Preadulthood: 0-22

FROM *THE SEASONS OF A MAN'S LIFE* BY DANIEL J. LEVINSON ET AL. COPYRIGHT © 1978 BY DANIEL J. LEVINSON. REPRINTED BY PERMISSION OF ALFRED A. KNOPF, INC.

the lives of one birth cohort must consider the vexing possibility that their findings may not apply to any other group. Most of the people studied by Levinson, Vaillant and Gould were born before and during the Depression (and were predominantly male, white and upper middle class). What was true for these people may not hold for today's 40-year-olds, born in the optimistic aftermath of World War II, or the post baby-boom generation just approaching adulthood. In Rossi's view, "The profile of the midlife men in Levinson's and Vaillant's studies may strike a future developmental researcher as burned out at a premature age, rather than reflecting a normal developmental process all men go through so early in life."

Based on her studies of women at midlife, Nancy Schlossberg, a counselor educator at the University of Maryland, also disagrees that there is a single, universal timetable for adult development—or that one can predict the crises in people's lives by knowing their age. "Give me a roomful of 40-year-old women and you have told me nothing. Give me a case story about what each has experienced and then I can tell if one is going to have a crisis and another a tranquil period." Says Schlossberg: "What matters is what transitions she has experienced. Has she been 'dumped' by a husband, fired from her job, had a breast removed, gone back to school, remarried, had her first book published. It is what has happened or not happened to her, not how old she is, that counts. . . . There are as many patterns as people."

Psychologist Albert Bandura of Stanford University adds more fuel to the anti-stage fire by pointing out that chance events play a big role in shaping our adult lives. Careers and marriages are often made from the happenstance of meeting the right—or wrong—person at the right—or wrong—time. But, says Bandura, while the events may be random, their effects are not. They depend on what people do with the chance opportunities fate deals them.

The ages-and-stages approach to adult development has been further criticized because it does not appear to apply to women. Levinson claims to have confirmed that women do follow the same age-transition timetable that men do. But his recent study of women has yet to be published, and there is little other evidence that might settle the case one way or the other.

Psychologists Rosalind Barnett and Grace Baruch of the Wellesley Center for Research on Women say, "It is hard to know how to think of women within this [stage] theory—a woman may not enter the world of work until her late 30s, she seldom has a mentor, and even women with lifelong career commitments rarely are in a position to reassess their commitment pattern by age 40."

But University of Wisconsin-Madison psychologist Carol Ryff, who has directly compared the views of men and women from different age groups, has found that the big psychological issues of adulthood follow a similar developmental pattern for both sexes.

Recently she studied two characteristics highlighted as hallmarks of middle age: Erikson's "generativity" and Neugarten's "complexity." Those who have achieved generativity, according to Ryff, see themselves as leaders and decision makers and are interested in helping and guiding younger people. The men and women Ryff studied agreed that generativity is at its peak in middle age.

Complexity, which describes people's feeling that they are in control of their lives and are actively involved in the world, followed a somewhat different pattern. It was high in young adulthood and stayed prominent as people matured. But it was most obvious in those who are now middle-aged—the first generation of middle-class people to combine family and work in dual-career families. This juggling of roles, although stressful, may make some men and women feel actively involved in life.

Psychologist Ravenna Helson and her colleagues Valory Mitchell and Geraldine Moane at the University of California, Berkeley, have recently completed a long-term study of the lives of 132 women that hints at some of the forces propelling people to change psychologically during adulthood. The women were studied as seniors at Mills College in California in the late 1950s, five years later and again in 1981, when they were between the ages of 42 and 45.

Helson and her colleagues distinguished three main groups among the Mills women: family-oriented, career-oriented (whether or not they also wanted families) and those who followed neither path (women with no children who pursued only low-level work). Despite their different profiles in college, and their diverging life paths, the women in all three groups underwent similar broad psychological changes over time, although those in the third group changed less than those committed to career or family.

Personality tests given through the years revealed that from age 21 to their mid-40s, the Mills women became more self-disciplined and committed to duties, as well as more independent and confident. And between age 27 and the early 40s, there was a shift toward less traditionally "feminine" attitudes, including greater dominance, higher achievement motivation, greater interest in events outside the family and more emotional stability.

To the Berkeley researchers, familiar with the work of psychologist David Gutmann of Northwestern University, these changes were not surprising in women whose children were mostly grown. Gutmann, after working with Neugarten and conducting his own research, had theorized that women and men, largely

SUDDENLY I'M THE ADULT?

BY RICHARD COHEN

Several years ago, my family gathered on Cape Cod for a weekend. My parents were there, my sister and her daughter, too, two cousins and, of course, my wife, my son and me. We ate at one of those restaurants where the menu is scrawled on a blackboard held by a chummy waiter and had a wonderful time. With dinner concluded, the waiter set the check down in the middle of the table. That's when it happened. My father did not reach for the check.

In fact, my father did nothing. Conversation continued. Finally, it dawned on me. Me! I was supposed to pick up the check. After all these years, after hundreds of restaurant meals with my parents, after a lifetime of thinking of my father as the one with the bucks, it had all changed. I reached for the check and whipped out my American Express card. My view of myself was suddenly altered. With a stroke of the pen, I was suddenly an adult.

Some people mark off their life in years, others in events. I am one of the latter, and I think of some events as rites of passage. I did not become a young man at a particular year, like 13, but when a kid strolled into the store where I worked and called me "mister." I turned around to see whom he was calling. He repeated it several times—"Mister, mister"—looking straight at me. The realization hit like a punch: Me! He was talking to me. I was suddenly a mister.

There have been other milestones. The cops of my youth always seemed to be big, even huge, and of course they were older than I was. Then one day they were neither. In fact, some of them were kids—short kids at that. Another milestone.

The day comes when you suddenly realize that all the football players in the game you're watching are younger than you. Instead of being big men, they are merely big kids. With that milestone goes the fantasy that someday, maybe, you too could be a player—maybe not a football player but certainly a baseball player. I had a good eye as a kid—not much power, but a keen eye—and I always thought I could play the game. One day I realized that I couldn't. Without having ever reached the hill, I was over it.

For some people, the most momentous milestone is the death of a parent. This happened recently to a friend of mine. With the burial of his father came the realization that he had moved up a notch. Of course, he had known all along that this would happen, but until the funeral, the knowledge seemed theoretical at best. As long as one of your parents is alive, you stay in some way a kid. At the very least, there remains at least one person whose love is unconditional.

For women, a milestone is reached when they can no longer have children. The loss of a life, the inability to create one—they are variations on the same theme. For a childless woman who could control everything in life but the clock, this milestone is a cruel one indeed.

I count other, less serious milestones—like being audited by the Internal Revenue Service. As the auditor caught mistake after mistake, I sat there pretending that really knowing about taxes was for adults. I, of course, was still a kid. The auditor was buying none of it. I was a taxpayer, an adult. She all but said, Go to jail.

There have been others. I remember the day when I had a ferocious argument with my son and realized that I could no longer bully him. He was too big and the days when I could just pick him up and take him to his room/isolation cell were over. I needed to persuade, reason. He was suddenly, rapidly,

Richard Cohen is a syndicated columnist for The Washington Post.

locked into traditional sex roles by parenthood, become less rigidly bound by these roles once the major duties of parenting decline; both are then freer to become more like the opposite sex—and do. Men, for example, often become more willing to share their feelings. These changes in both men and women can help older couples communicate and get along better.

During their early 40s, many of the women Helson and Moane studied shared the same midlife concerns the stage theorists had found in men: "concern for young and old, introspectiveness, interest in roots and awareness of limitation and death." But the Berkeley team described the period as one of midlife "consciousness," not "crisis."

In summing up their findings, Helson and Moane stress that commitment to the tasks of young adulthood—whether to a career or family (or both)—helped women learn to control impulses, develop skills with people, become independent and work hard to achieve goals.

older. The conclusion was inescapable: So was I.

One day you go to your friends' weddings. One day you celebrate the birth of their kids. One day you see one of their kids driving, and one day those kids have kids of their own. One day you meet at parties and then at weddings and then at funerals. It all happens in one day. Take my word for it.

I never thought I would fall asleep in front of the television set as my father did, and as my friends' fathers did, too. I remember my parents and their friends talking about insomnia and they sounded like members of a different species. Not able to sleep? How ridiculous. Once it was all I did. Once it was what I did best.

I never thought that I would eat a food that did not agree with me. Now I meet them all the time. I thought I would never go to the beach and not swim. I spent all of August at the beach and never once went into the ocean. I never thought I would appreciate opera, but now the pathos, the schmaltz and, especially, the combination of voice and music appeal to me. The deaths of Mimi and Tosca move me, and they die in my home as often as I can manage it.

I never thought I would prefer to stay home instead of going to a party, but now I find myself passing parties up. I used to think that people who watched birds were weird, but this summer I found myself watching them, and maybe I'll get a book on the subject. I yearn for a religious conviction I never thought I'd want, exult in my heritage anyway, feel close to ancestors long gone and echo my father in arguments with my son. I still lose.

One day I made a good toast. One day I handled a headwaiter. One day I bought a house. One day—what a day!—I became a father, and not too long after that I picked up the check for my own. I thought then and there it was a rite of passage for me. Not until I got older did I realize that it was one for him, too. Another milestone.

According to Helson and Moane, those women who did not commit themselves to one of the main life-style patterns faced fewer challenges and therefore did not develop as fully as the other women did.

The dizzying tug and pull of data and theories about how adults change over time may frustrate people looking for universal principles or certainty in their lives. But it leaves room for many scenarios for people now in young and middle adulthood and those to come.

People now between 20 and 60 are the best-educated and among the healthiest and most fit of all who have passed through the adult years. No one knows for sure what their lives will be like in the years to come, but the experts have some fascinating speculations.

For example, Rossi suspects that the quality of midlife for baby boomers will contrast sharply with that of the Depression-born generation the stage theorists studied. Baby boomers, she notes, have different dreams, values and opportunities than the preceding generation. And they are much more numerous.

Many crucial aspects of their past and future lives may best be seen in an economic rather than a strictly psychological light, Rossi says. From their days in overcrowded grade schools, through their struggles to gain entry into college, to their fight for the most desirable jobs, the baby boomers have had to compete with one another. And, she predicts, their competitive struggles are far from over. She foresees that many may find themselves squeezed out of the workplace as they enter their 50s—experiencing a crisis at a time when it will be difficult to redirect their careers.

But other factors may help to make life easier for those now approaching midlife. People are on a looser, less compressed timetable, and no longer feel obliged to marry, establish their careers and start their families almost simulta-

> *The first forty years of life furnish the text, while the remaining thirty supply the commentary.*
> —Schopenhauer,
> *Parerga and Paralipomena.*

neously. Thus, major life events may not pile up in quite the same way they did for the older generation.

Today's 20-year-olds—the first wave of what some have labeled "the baby busters"—have a more optimistic future than the baby boomers who preceded them, according to economist Richard Easterlin of the University of Southern California. Easterlin has been studying the life patterns of various cohorts, beginning with the low-birthrate group born in the 1930s—roughly a decade before the birthrate exploded.

The size of a birth cohort, Easterlin argues, affects that group's quality of life. In its simplest terms, his theory says that the smaller the cohort the less competition among its members and the more fortunate they are; the larger the cohort the more competition and the less fortunate.

Compared with the baby boomers, the smaller cohort just approaching adulthood "will have much more favorable experiences as they grow

WHAT'S THE RIGHT TIME?

Two surveys asking the same questions 20 years apart (late 1950s and late 1970s) have shown a dramatic decline in the consensus among middle-class, middle-aged people about what's the right age for various major events and achievements of adult life.

Activity/Event	Appropriate Age Range	Late '50s Study % Who Agree Men	Late '50s Study % Who Agree Women	Late '70s Study % Who Agree Men	Late '70s Study % Who Agree Women
Best age for a man to marry	20-25	80%	90%	42%	42%
Best age for a woman to marry	19-24	85	90	44	36
When most people should become grandparents	45-50	84	79	64	57
Best age for most people to finish school and go to work	20-22	86	82	36	38
When most men should be settled on a career	24-26	74	64	24	26
When most men hold their top jobs	45-50	71	58	38	31
When most people should be ready to retire	60-65	83	86	66	41
When a man has the most responsibilities	35-50	79	75	49	50
When a man accomplishes most	40-50	82	71	46	41
The prime of life for a man	35-50	86	80	59	66
When a woman has the most responsibilities	25-40	93	91	59	53
When a woman accomplishes most	30-45	94	92	57	48

SOURCE: ADAPTED FROM: "AGE NORMS AND AGE CONSTRAINTS TWENTY YEARS LATER", P. PASSUTH, D. MAINES AND B.L. NEUGARTEN. PAPER PRESENTED AT THE MIDWEST SOCIOLOGICAL SOCIETY MEETING, CHICAGO, APRIL 1984.

up—in their families, in school and finally in the labor market," he says. As a result, they will "develop a more positive psychological outlook."

The baby busters' optimism will encourage them to marry young and have large families—producing another baby boom. During this period there will be less stress in the family and therefore, Easterlin predicts, divorce and suicide rates will stabilize.

Psychologist Elizabeth Douvan of the University of Michigan's Institute for Social Research shares Easterlin's optimistic view about the future of these young adults. Surprisingly, she sees as one of their strengths the fact that, due to divorce and remarriage, many grew up in reconstituted families. Douvan believes that the experience of growing up close to people who are not blood relatives can help to blur the distinction between kinship and friendship, making people more open in their relationships with others.

Like many groups before them, they are likely to yearn for a sense of community and ritual, which they will strive to fulfill in many ways, Douvan says. For some this may mean a turn toward involvement in politics, neighborhood or religion, although not necessarily the religion of their parents.

In summing up the future quality of life for today's young adults and those following them, Douvan says: "Life is more open for people now. They are judging things internally and therefore are more willing to make changes in the external aspects. That's pretty exciting. It opens up a tremendous number of possibilities for people who can look at life as an adventure."

Aging

What Happens to the Body as We Grow Older?

Given our medical ignorance and the fact that the body does not age all at once—we can have a young kidney and an old heart—the whole concept of aging needs careful re-examination.

Is it possible to describe "typical" aging? Not really. We talk about someone who has begun to be forgetful, whose skin shows signs of losing elasticity, whose lung capacity is diminished because of emphysema, whose cardiac reserve is diminished because of atrophy of the heart muscle, whose organ functions (for instance, kidney or liver function) are at a fraction of what they once were, whose skeletal structure is softened, whose hair is grey, whose eyes are clouded by cataracts and whose hearing is diminished—that is a caricature of a typical old person.

This stereotypical image of aging, however, does not hold true among all individuals. The debate continues over how much of elderly appearance is the result of natural aging and how much is the result of abuse of the body. According to William Kannel, one of the principal investigators of the Framingham Heart Study, "The issue of what constitutes aging and normal aging is an enigma that has never been satisfactorily solved." In epidemiology, there are several approaches that try to answer the question.

One approach is employed by the Veterans Administration Normative Aging Study, which seeks to find people who might eventually develop certain diseases but, at the beginning of the study are free of any ailment. By studying what happens to people over time, project director Pantel Vokonas and co-workers are trying to identify the effects of age. The researchers are looking at the signs of growing older that can be attributed to age rather than illness or disease.

The normative aging approach is, in a sense, a quest for immortality. The assumption is that if we could remove all these diseases, people would live, if not forever, at least for much longer than they now do. Unfortunately, it is virtually impossible to find people totally free of the disabilities sooner or later associated with old age. Even if a person seems to be free of heart or kidney damage, for example, there is no way of being sure that these organs are still in their pristine state.

Another approach to aging is that taken by the Framingham Heart Disease Epidemiology Study, underway since 1949, in which a whole population is followed as they age to see what problems they encounter. "Ours is a more pragmatic approach," said Kannel. "We are interested in seeing what kinds of things cause people who reach advanced age to no longer have much joy in living. We don't care whether it is cardiovascular disease, opaqueness of the lens, poor hearing, soft bones, arthritis, strokes, mental deterioration or normal aging. We're studying the ailments that afflict an aging population and take the joy out of reaching a venerable stage in life."

According to Kannel, "The reward for reaching a venerable stage of life is too often a cardiovascular catastrophe." Cardiac function, muscle, skeleton and so on all decline with time, although recent evidence suggests that cardiac function in a non-diseased heart remains amazingly stable well into old age. Some of this decline must be due to wear and tear, but according to Kannel, "it is just too difficult to dissociate from the long-term effects of noxious influences."

From *Bostonia*, February/March 1986, pp. 17-20. Reprinted with the permission of Bostonia Magazine 1986.

With respect to cardiac function, for example, decline is not necessarily unpreventable. It has been shown that 65-year-olds can be trained to improve their levels of performance. It is easy, for example to train somebody to restore his or her exercise capacity and measure cardiac function and oxygen utilization. We have the technology to measure these things. But how do you train a kidney? Moreover, it is still not clear what noxious influences cause the decline in function in most of the organ systems. If we did know, we would be able to remove the noxious influences and watch the recovery. "For many of the organ declines, we really have poor information," said Kannel. "It just so happens that for cardiovascular disease, we have a good body of data on what risk factors there are. And it turns out that many of these are modifiable."

Given our medical ignorance and the fact that the body does not age all at once —we can have a young kidney and an old heart—the whole concept of aging needs careful re-examination. The assumption that all the organs fail in concert is not borne out by experience. There are many people who are alert and showing few signs of diminished intellectual capacity, but have a failing heart or damaged liver. People have different rates of organ decline.

The Framingham Heart Study, however, is showing that many of the risk factors for the young are still operative in the elderly. Even though it may take decades for the disastrous effects of a habit like smoking to show up, there is still good reason to quit. One might think that once a lifetime of smoking has put someone on the track for cancer, eliminating smoking in advanced years will not remove that risk of cancer. The risk does remain, but there is no good reason to multiply the risk by continuing to smoke.

But beyond that, there are other good reasons for elderly people to give up smoking. Smoking contributes to chronic bronchitis, emphysema and may precipitate coronary attacks, peripheral vascular disease and perhaps even stroke. Quitting smoking will not bring the person back to total normal function; but it helps slow deterioration. With coronary disease, in particular, the advantage seems to occur regardless of how long one has smoked. According to Kannel, the data show an immediate 50 percent reduction in the risk of coronary disease whether

> "The issue
> of what constitutes
> aging and normal aging
> is an enigma that has
> never been satisfac-
> torily solved."
>
> WILLIAM KANNEL

the person has smoked 10 years, 20 years, 30 or 40 years. In terms of coronary attacks, there is trouble showing the benefit of quitting. But for coronary *deaths* and peripheral vascular disease, there is no difficulty at all showing that quitting helps.

"I think that the elderly are becoming increasingly health conscious," said Kannel. "It's curious: One would think that young people, who have so much life ahead of them, would take things more seriously. But the elderly, they are the ones who are driving more carefully, avoiding doing stupid and reckless things because they more acutely feel the approach of the grim reaper."

Some of the other effects commonly attributed to aging may well be preventable. Data from the Framingham studies show that a great deal of the high-frequency hearing loss in the elderly *male* can be laid at the door of noisy industries. We can predict, from the popularity of loud music among the young today, a generation of deaf elderly in 50 or 60 years. Osteoporosis, too, could be reduced if people were kept more active and ate more calcium-rich foods. In other words, the conclusions drawn from the Framingham Heart Study are that prevention is possible, that it must be started early and that it takes sustained effort. The burden of these common and disabling conditions, whether or not we term them aging phenomena, are the sources of a great deal of discontent in the elderly.

There is also a strong genetic component in the process of aging. "People with superb genes are able to withstand a lifetime of abuse because they may be better able to cope with an overload of fat in the diet, too many calories, too much salt, too much trauma, too little exercise, smoking. If they have been blessed with superb metabolic machinery, they somehow survive. Other people, with inferior metabolic machinery, may avoid all these risks and live longer than the great risk taker. There is a lot to be said for genetics."

"Even with bad genes, one can do something effective to reduce the liability," stated Kannel.

There is also a mistaken notion, he continued, that following a healthy lifestyle entails considerable sacrifice. "Diet, exercise and the like need not be so austere that they are painful. We are only recommending a Mediterranean or Asian diet. If you follow the specifics of those, you get the fat content, lower cholesterol, lower calories that you need. That is hardly a gastronomic nightmare. These are good foods. Ham and eggs need not be the epitome of gastronomic experience. One can eat very well following a prudent diet, as recommended by the American Heart Association."

"Exercise is something we need to build back into daily living," added Kannel. "We have taken it out by all the modern conveniences. A better way of living is to exercise naturally without the contriving. If you can walk to work instead of driving and parking right next to the door, you are better off. Try not to use escalators in two-story buildings. We have engineered exercise out of our lives; the time has come to engineer it back."

The Effects of Aging

It is difficult to measure the rate of aging. One study (Hodgson and Buskirk) has shown that the maximal oxygen intake declined after age 25 at the rate of 0.40 to 0.45 ml of oxygen taken in per minute per kilogram of body weight each year. Grip strength went down about 0.20 kg per year. The investigators also found, however, that training at age 60 could improve the maximal oxygen intake by about 12 percent.

Average decline in human male, from age 30 to age 75

Factor	% Decline
Brain weight	44
Number of axons in spinal nerve	37
Velocity of nerve impulse	10
Number of taste buds	64
Blood supply to brain	20
Output of heart at rest	30
Number of glomeruli in kidney	44
Vital capacity of lungs	44
Maximum oxygen uptake	60

*There is controversy about how much of the decline reported is a result of aging as opposed to disease.

Of all the biological changes associated with growing old, young people are probably most acutely aware of the cosmetic changes. Hair greys, wrinkles become pronounced and shoulders tend to narrow with advancing age.

In American society, these changes are greeted with less than enthusiasm because, in a society that seems to cherish youth, these changes make one look old.

Cosmetic changes affect the sexes differently. Women may be outraged or humiliated by physical changes that lead to what Susan Sontag has called the process of "sexual disqualification." Women may be forced into roles of helplessness, passivity, compliance and non-competitiveness. Men, on the other hand, may

enjoy the assertiveness, competency, self-control, independence and power—all signs of "masculinity"—that come with age.

What creates the common cosmetic changes in aging? Wrinkles begin below the skin's outer layer (epidermis) when the dermis, a layer of tissue filled with glands, nerve endings and blood vessels, begins to shrink. At the same time, the dermis begins to atrophy, changes in the fat, muscle and bone create the deep wrinkles. Other factors—exposure to the sun, environmental toxins, heredity and disease—also affect the wrinkling of the skin.

Greying of the hair is the result of progressive loss of pigment in the cells that

give hair its color. Age spots are caused by the accumulation of pigment in the skin. But the shortened stature and flabby muscles are the result of lack of exercise and other behavioral factors. These, and many other so-called effects of aging, may be reversed.

After a while, time does take its toll. Between the ages of 35 and 80, the maximum work a person can do goes down by 60 percent. The strength of the grasp by the dominant hand (right in right-handers) goes down 50 percent and the endurance to maintain the strongest grasp goes down 30 percent. For some reason, not understood, the other (subordinate) hand, which was weaker to begin with, does not lose as much strength and

Alzheimer's Disease: The Search for a Cure Continues

It is difficult to paint anything but a bleak picture of Alzheimer's disease.

Named after the German neurologist Alois Alzheimer (1864 –1915), it is a relentless and irreversible form of dementia that has been known to strike adults as young as 25, but most often appears in people over 70. For the estimated one to three million afflicted Americans, the early symptoms often involve memory loss, apathy and difficulties with spatial orientation and judgment. As these problems worsen, victims become increasingly depressed, confused, restless and unable to care for themselves.

In the final stages, Alzheimer patients may become so helpless that they are bedridden until they die from secondary problems such as pneumonia caused by accidentally inhaling food. Unfortunately, the victims of Alzheimer's often include the patient's stressed family and caregivers who, despite their devoted efforts, must watch loved ones turn into unmanageable strangers.

At this juncture, the exact cause, diagnosis and treatment of Alzheimer's continues to elude medical researchers. An abundance of new clues and insights into this mysterious disease is being uncovered, however. In addition, growing public awareness has led to the development of support groups and experi-

mental programs to help families and caregivers cope with caring for Alzheimer patients. "I'm amazed that researchers have progressed so far in such a short time," noted Professor Marott Sinex, from the School of Medicine's Department of Biochemistry, who has been researching the disease for the past 12 years.

Sinex pointed to many advances in the past decade, including improvements in drug therapy that ease symptoms. There is an increased understanding of possible genetic causes, of the subtle differences in neurotransmitters in the brains of victims and how they change over time and of anatomical changes in the brain that relate to memory loss and other cognitive problems. In addition, improved medical technology—such as the PET scan, which allows scientists to visualize the living brain—is adding new insights. "We now have a dynamic anatomy of the disease," said Sinex. "We can visualize its progression, which we couldn't do before. In other words we're dealing with a real, three-dimensional problem now, whereas before we only had two-dimensional understanding."

Although the exact cause of Alzheimer's is not known, Sinex noted that researchers now know it is associated with an excess of genetic material on a particular chromosome—an abnor-

mality that, interestingly, has already been linked to Down's syndrome. (Several Boston University researchers are independently investigating biochemical, genetic and physical similarities seen in Down's syndrome—a congenital disease whose victims are born moderately to severely retarded with distinctive physical traits—and Alzheimer's disease.) Scientists also know the disease can be inheritable and that—despite the fact that it can strike relatively young adults—it is "strongly age-dependent," with most cases not appearing until people are in their 70s. In addition to these factors, researchers are looking at other possible causes; for example, Sinex is investigating the possiblity that a virus may be involved.

As for diagnosis, the best physical evidence researchers have is the "plaques and tangles" —filamentous material whose nature and origin scientists are not exactly sure of—found in the brains of autopsied victims. (Although similar plaques and tangles are found in the brains of normally aging people, in Alzheimer victims the structures appear more frequently and in specific areas.) Sinex pointed out, however, that today "a really good clinic" can accurately diagnose the disease about 85 percent of the time by eliminating other problems such as stroke, a tumor,

drug poisoning or unrelated depression. Fortunately, research is advancing in this area as well. For example, Mark Moss, an assistant research professor in the School of Medicine's Department of Anatomy, recently developed a "gamelike" diagnostic test that the National Institute on Aging has recommended for clinical use and that "will help us understand the brain structures responsible for memory impairment."

The best method of treating Alzheimer victims today, explained Sinex, involves prescribing medications that "fall in the general category of anti-depressants." Apart from drug therapy, Sinex pointed out that organizations such as the Eastern Massachusetts Chapter of the Alzheimer's Disease and Related Disorders Association, of which he is president, can be helpful to both victims and their caregivers by providing information and connecting people with support groups.

Given this variety of recent advances, Sinex concluded optimistically, "It's simply a lot less traumatic to have Alzheimer's now than it was 10 or 15 years ago."

JON QUEIJO

endurance. The speed of nerve conduction is slower. The volume of blood pumped throughout the body goes down 50 percent. The maximum volume of air a person can inhale goes down 50 percent and oxygen diffuses from the lungs to the red cells of the blood 30 percent more slowly. Blood flow to the kidneys at age 80 is considerably less than that of age 20 in many, but not all. And, by age 70, the bones of the coccyx (the "tail bone" at the base of the spine) fuse. In short, our bodies slow down and stiffen as we age. This is natural and occurs even in the absence of disease.

Vision, hearing, taste, smell and touch have all been reported to change with age. New research suggests, however, that the effects of aging per se may not be as major a factor as originally believed on declining senses.

Probably the most familiar changes are those in seeing. Presbyopia (presby = old + opia = vision) is a sign of the gradual inability of the lens of the eye to focus on near objects—hence, the growing need for "reading glasses" or bifocals as people age. There are other relatively harmless changes, as well. Almost from birth, the lens of the eye begins to get more rigid. By around age 45, printed pages must be held at arm's length or farther to get them into focus. But, of course, at that distance, the letters are usually too small to read. As people age, their eyes may become more sensitive to glare and bright lights. They

Smoking contributes to emphysema and may precipitate coronary attacks. Quitting smoking will not bring the person back to absolutely normal function; but it helps slow the process down.

may also be less able to discriminate between gradations of color.

More serious eye conditions increase with age as well. Approximately seven percent of all people between the ages of 65 and 74 have serious visual deficits. After age 75, the proportion more than doubles to 16 percent. Approximately two-thirds of all severe visual impairments occur in people 65 or older.

Macular degeneration is the most serious cause of low vision in the elderly in the United States. The macula is a spot on the retina of the eye needed for very fine focusing. With age, this region can degenerate and become obstructed with fine blood vessels.

Other visual impairments include: glaucoma, which is a dangerous and

painful increase of pressure within the eye; diabetic retinopathy, which is a destruction of the fine blood vessels in the eye, destroying parts of the retina, associated with uncontrolled diabetes; and cataracts, which are cloudy eye lenses.

Just as presbyopia is a vision deficit associated with advancing age, so presbyacusis (presby = old + acousis = sound) is a progressive hearing loss associated with aging. This is especially true for the higher frequencies. Of the estimated 14.2 million Americans with measurable hearing loss, about 60 percent of those with the most severe hearing problems are older than 65.

Hearing loss associated with aging may be of several causes. Genetic factors, infection and a lifetime of noise certainly contribute. Poor personal hygiene, build-up of ear wax, may also reduce hearing. Certain medications (for example, drugs of the streptomycin group) can injure the hair cells in the ear and interfere with both hearing and the sense of balance.

While these physical and sensory changes occur in all people as they age, keep in mind that the degree to which they affect individuals varies greatly. The key is how we take care of ourselves. The pleas from the medical profession to cut down smoking, drinking and to exercise are grounded in heavy evidence. Keeping yourself active and healthy throughout your life can result in an old age that is productive and rewarding.

Osteoporosis
The Stooping Disease

An estimated five million people in the United States are afflicted with osteoporosis—a disease marked by loss of bone mass that weakens the skeleton and may result in spontaneous fractures. Although everyone loses bone mass as they age, this process is accelerated in women. In the first 10 years after menopause, women lose bone at twice the rate men do.

Healthy bone is constantly changing. In childhood and adolescence, bones form at a faster rate than they are reabsorbed. In healthy adults, up until age 40, peak bone mass is maintained through a balance between the processes of bone formation and loss. Peak bone mass, which usu-

ally occurs around age 30, is influenced by hormones, calcium intake, level of physical activity and the stress of weight bearing. Heredity also plays a role. From about age 40, bone absorption is more rapid than bone formation.

There is no way to diagnose the early stages of osteoporosis. The bone loss that characterizes the disease does not show up on x-rays until a substantial portion of the bone is already lost. At its later stages, however, osteoporosis produces extreme visible changes: loss of height, rounding of the upper back ("dowager's hump"), forward thrust of the head, protruding abdomen and expansion of the chest. These symptoms are all due to

the collapsed vertebrae weakened by osteoporosis.

What causes osteoporosis is not yet understood. Because post-menopausal women are at elevated risk, some investigators have suggested that it involves estrogen deficiency and should be treated with hormones. This cannot be the case, however, because not all post-menopausal women develop osteoporosis.

At highest risk are white women with a family history of osteoporosis, of northern European descent, with small bone frames and of normal or less than average weight. Certain dietary and behavioral factors can increase the risk: drinking more than four to six cups of coffee a day, smoking, heavy use of alcohol and lack of calcium in the diet all increase the risk. On the other hand, physical exercise

decreases the risk.

University Hospital is currently planning to open a clinic at the end of February to treat osteoporosis victims. The clinic will be multidisciplinary involving orthopedic surgery, endocrinology, nutrition and internal medicine. All patients referred to the clinic will be prescreened by a special x-ray test which will determine bone mineral content. A specialized blood work-up will be done to rule out metabolic causes for metabolic bone disease and other appropriate studies as indicated by each case. Also a program of functional bracing will be started. Questions concerning the clinic should be directed to the Department of Orthopedic Surgery, University Hospital, (617) 638-8905.

The Changing Meanings of Age

*WHETHER YOU ARE YOUNG, OLD OR IN BETWEEN, ACTING YOUR AGE
CAN MEAN MANY MORE THINGS TODAY THAN IT ONCE DID.*

BERNICE L. NEUGARTEN
AND DAIL A. NEUGARTEN

*Bernice L. Neugarten, Ph.D., is a professor of
human development and social policy at Northwestern University. Dail A. Neugarten, Ph.D., is
an associate professor, Graduate School of Public
Affairs, University of Colorado.*

In our society, as in most others, age is a major dimension of social organization. Our school system, to name one example, is carefully arranged around the students' ages, and the behavior of all students is clearly differentiated from the behavior of adult teachers. Similarly, to a greater or lesser extent, families, corporations, even whole communities are organized by age.

Age also plays an important part in how people relate to one another across the whole range of everyday experience. When a young man sits down in an airplane and glances at the person in the next seat, the first thing to cross his mind is likely to be "That's an old man," or "That's a young man like me," and he automatically adjusts his behavior accordingly—his language, manners and conversation.

Age is also a major touchstone by which individuals organize and interpret their own lives. Both children and adults continually ask of themselves, "How well am I doing for my age?"

From all three perspectives, our changing society has brought with it changes in the social meanings of age: blurred boundaries between the periods of life, new definitions of age groups, new patterns in the timing of major life events and new inconsistencies in what is considered age-appropriate behavior.

In all societies, lifetime is divided into socially relevant periods, age distinctions become systematized and rights and responsibilities are distributed according to social age. Even the simplest societies define at least three periods: childhood, adulthood and old age. In more complex societies, a greater number of life periods are differentiated, and transition points are differently timed in different areas of life. In modern America people are considered adults in the political system when they reach 18 and are given the right to vote; but they are not adults in the family system until they marry and take on the responsibilities of parenthood. Or people may be adult in the family system, but if they are still in school they are not yet adult in the economic system.

Historians have described how life periods became demarcated in Western societies over the past few centuries. Only with industrialization and the appearance of a middle class and formally organized schools did childhood become a clearly definable period of life. Adolescence took on its present meaning in the late 19th century and became widespread in the

From *Psychology Today*, May 1987, pp. 29-32. Copyright © 1987 by Bernice L. Neugarten and Dail A. Neugarten. This essay
is adapted from an article that originally appeared in *Daedalus* and was subsequently published in *Our Aging Society*, W. W.
Norton. Reprinted by permission.

20th, as the period of formal education lengthened and the transition to adulthood was increasingly delayed. A stage called youth took on its modern meaning only a few decades ago, as growing numbers of young people, after leaving high school and before marrying or making occupational choices, opted for a period of time to explore various life roles.

It was only a few decades ago, too, that middle age became identified, largely a reflection of the historically changing rhythm of events in the family cycle. With fewer children per family, and with births spaced closer together, middle age became defined as the time when children grow up and leave the parents' home. In turn, as the concept of retirement took hold, old age came to be regarded as the time following retirement from the labor force. It was usually perceived as a distinct period marked by the right to lead a life of leisure, declining physical and intellectual vigor, social disengagement and, often, isolation and desolation.

Life periods were closely associated with chronological age, even though age lines were seldom sharply drawn.

But the distinctions between life periods are blurring in today's society. The most dramatic evidence, perhaps, is the appearance of the so-called "young-old." It is a recent historical phenomenon that a very large group of retirees and their spouses are healthy and vigorous, relatively well-off financially, well-integrated into the lives of their families and communities and politically active. The term "young-old" is becoming part of everyday parlance, and it refers not to a particular age but to health and social characteristics. A young-old person may be 55 or 85. The term represents the social reality that the line between middle age and old age is no longer clear. What was once considered old age now characterizes only that minority of older persons who have been called the "old-old," that particularly vulnerable group who often are in need of special support and special care.

When, then, does old age now begin? The usual view has been that it starts at 65, when most people retire. But in the United States today the majority begin to take their Social Security retirement benefits at 62 or 63; and at ages 55 to 64 fewer than three of every four men are in the labor force. At the same time, with continued good health, some people are staying at work, full-time or part-time, into their 80s. So age 65 and retirement are no longer clear dividers between middle age and old age.

Alternatively, old age is often said to begin when poor health creates a major limitation on the activities of everyday life. Yet in a 1981 survey, half of all people 75 to 84 reported no such health limitations. Even in the very oldest group, those older than 85, more than a third reported no limitations due to health, and another one-third reported minor limitations; only

one in three said they were unable to carry out any of their everyday activities. So health status is also becoming a poor age marker.

It is not only in the second half of life that the blurring of life periods can be seen. Adults of all ages are experiencing changes in the traditional rhythm and timing of events of the life cycle. More men and women marry, divorce, remarry and divorce again up through their 70s. More stay single. More women have their first child before they are 15, and more do so after 35. The result is that people are becoming grandparents for the first time at ages ranging from 35 to 75. More women, but also increasing numbers of men, raise children in two-parent, then one-parent, then two-parent households. More women, but also increasing numbers of men, exit and reenter school, enter and reenter the work force and undertake second and third

*M*ORE MEN AND WOMEN MARRY, DIVORCE, REMARRY AND DIVORCE AGAIN UP THROUGH THEIR 70S.

careers up through their 70s. It therefore becomes difficult to distinguish the young, the middle-aged and the young-old—either in terms of major life events or the ages at which those events occur.

The line between adolescence and adulthood is also being obscured. The traditional transitions into adulthood and the social competencies they implied—full-time jobs, marriage and parenthood—are disappearing as markers of social age. For some men and women, the entry into a job or profession is being delayed to age 30 as education is prolonged. For others, entry into the work force occurs at 16 or 17. Not only are there more teenage pregnancies but also more teenage women who are mothering their children. All this adds up to what has been aptly called "the fluid life cycle."

This is not to deny that our society still recognizes differences between adolescents, young people and old people, and that people still relate to each other accordingly. Yet we are less sure today where to place the punctuation marks in the life line and just what those punctuation marks should be. All across adulthood, age has become a poor predictor of the timing of life events, just as it is a poor predictor of health, work status, family status, interests, preoccupations and needs. We have conflicting images rather than stereotypes of age: the 70-

year-old in a wheelchair, but also the 70-year-old on the tennis court; the 18-year-old who is married and supporting a family, but also the 18-year-old college student who brings his laundry home to his mother each week.

Difference among individuals, multiple images of age groups and inconsistencies in age norms were surely present in earlier periods of our history, but as our society has become more complex, the irregularities have become increasingly a part of the social reality.

These trends are reflected in public perceptions, too. Although systematic research is sparse, there are a few studies that show a diminishing public consensus about the periods of life and their markers. In the early 1960s, for instance, a group of middle-class, middle-aged people were asked about the "best" ages for life transitions (such as completing school, marrying, retiring) and the ages they associated with such phrases as "a young man," "an old woman" and "when a man (or woman) has the most responsibilities." When the same questions were asked of a similar group of people two decades later, the earlier consensus on every item of the questionnaire had disappeared. In the first study, nearly 90 percent had replied that the best age for a woman to marry was between 19 and 24; in the repeat study, only 40 percent gave this answer. In the first study, "a young man" was said to be a man between 18 and 22; in the repeat study, "a young man" was anywhere from 18 to 40. These findings are based on a very small study, but they illustrate how public views are changing.

In some respects, the line between childhood and adulthood is also fading. It is a frequent comment that childhood as we once knew it is disappearing. Increasingly children and adults have the same preferences in styles of dress, forms of language, games and television shows. Children know more about once-taboo topics such as sex, drugs, alcoholism, suicide and nuclear war. There is more adult-like sexual behavior among children, and more adult-like crime. At the same time, with the pressures for achievement rising, we have witnessed the advent of "the hurried child" and "the harried child."

We have also become accustomed to the descriptions of today's adults as narcissistic, self-interested and self-indulgent. Yuppies are described in the mass media as the pace-setters. While they work hard to get ahead, they are portrayed as more materialistic even than the "me" generation that preceded them, interested primarily in making money and in buying the "right" cars, the "best" housing and the most expensive gourmet foods. Overall, today's adults have fewer lasting marriages, fewer lasting commitments to work or community roles, more uncontrolled expressions of emo-

tion, a greater sense of powerlessness—in short, more childlike behavior.

This picture may be somewhat overdrawn. Both children and adults are continually exhorted to "act your age," and they seldom misunderstand what that means. Yet the expectations of appropriate behavior for children and adults are certainly less differentiated than they once were. We are less sure of what intellectual and social competencies to expect of children—not only because some children are teaching their teachers how to use computers, but also because so many children are streetwise by age 8 and so many others, in the wake of divorce, are the confidantes of their parents by age 12.

Some observers attribute the blurring of childhood and adulthood primarily to the effects of television, which illuminates the total

*S*OMEONE WHO MOVES TO THE SUN BELT TO LEAD A LIFE OF LEISURE IS SOCIALLY APPROVED IF HE'S 70, BUT NOT IF HE IS 30.

culture and reveals the secrets that adults have traditionally withheld from children. But it is not only television. A report in *The New York Times* underlines the fact that children are being socialized in new ways today by parents, schools, churches and peer groups as well. The Girl Scouts of the U.S.A., according to the *Times* article, had decided finally to admit 5-year-olds. The national executive director was quoted as saying, "The decision to admit five-year-olds reflects the change in the American labor market. Women are working for part or all of their adult lives now. The possibilities are limitless but you need to prepare. So we think six is not too early to learn about career opportunities, and we also think that girls need to learn about making decisions. When you're five, you're not too young."

The blurring of traditional life periods does not mean that age norms are disappearing altogether. We still have our regulations about the ages at which children enter and exit from school, when people can marry without the consent of parents, when they are eligible for Social Security benefits. And less formal norms are still operating. Someone who moves to the Sun Belt to lead a life of leisure is socially approved if he is 70, but not if he is 30. An unmarried mother meets with greater disapproval if she is 15 than if she is 35. A couple in their 40s who decide to have another child are criticized for embarrassing their adolescent children. At the door of a discotheque a young person who cannot give proof of being "old enough" may be refused admission, while inside a gray-haired man who dances like those he calls youngsters meets the raised eyebrows and mocking remarks of the other dancers. As in these examples, expectations regarding age-appropriate behavior still form an elaborate and pervasive system of norms, expectations that are woven into the cultural fabric.

Both legal and cultural age norms are mirrored in the ways people behave and the ways they think about their own lives. Today, as in the past, most people by the time they are adolescents develop a set of anticipations of the normal, expectable life cycle: expectations of what the major life events and turning points will be and when they should occur. People internalize a social clock that tells them if they are on time or not.

Although the actual timing of life events for both women and men has always been influenced by various life contingencies, the norms and the actual occurrences have been closely connected. It may be less true today, but most people still try to marry or have a child or make a job change when they think they have reached the "right" age. They can still easily report whether they were early, late or on time with regard to one life event after another. "I married early," we hear, or "I had a late start because I served in Vietnam."

The life events that occur on time do not usually precipitate life crises, for they have been anticipated and rehearsed. The so-called "empty nest," for instance, is not itself stressful for most middle-aged parents. Instead, it is when children do not leave home at the appropriate time that stress occurs in both the parent and the child. For most older men, if it does not occur earlier than planned, retirement is taken in stride as a normal, expectable event. Widowhood is less often a crisis if it occurs at 65 rather than at 40.

It is the events that upset the expected sequence and rhythm of the life cycle that cause problems—as when the death of a parent comes during one's adolescence rather than in middle age; when marriage is delayed too long; when the birth of a child comes too early; when occupational achievement is slowed; when the empty nest, grandparenthood, retirement, major illness or widowhood occurs "out of sync." Traditional timetables still operate.

For the many reasons suggested earlier, the traditional time schedules do not in today's society produce the regularities anticipated by adolescents or young adults. For many men and women, to be out of sync may have lost some of its importance, but for others, the social clocks

have not stopped ticking. The incongruities between the traditional norms and the fluid life cycle represent new freedoms for many people; for other people, new uncertainties and strains.

There is still another reality to be reckoned with. Some timetables are losing their significance, but others are more compelling than ever. A young man may feel he is a failure if he has not "made it" in his corporation by the time he is 35. A young woman may delay marriage because of her career, but then hurry to catch up with parenthood. The same young woman may feel under pressure to marry, bear a child and establish herself in a career all within a five-year period—even though she knows she is likely to live to 85.

Sometimes both traditional and nontraditional views are in conflict in the mind of the same person. The young woman who deliberately delays marriage may be the same woman who worries that she has lost status because she is

*I*T IS WHEN CHILDREN DO NOT LEAVE HOME AT THE APPROPRIATE TIME THAT STRESS OCCURS IN BOTH PARENT AND CHILD.

not married by 25. A middle-aged man starts a second family, but feels compelled to justify himself by explaining that he expects to live to see his new children reach adulthood. Or an old person reports that because he did not expect to live so long, he is now unprepared to take on the "new ways" of some of his peers. Some people live in new ways, but continue to think in old ways.

Given such complications, shall we say that individuals are paying less or more attention to age as a prod or a brake upon their behavior? That age consciousness is decreasing or increasing? Whether or not historical change is occurring, it is fair to say that one's own age remains crucial to every individual, all the way from early childhood through advanced old age. A person uses age as a guide in accommodating to others, in giving meaning to the life course, and in contemplating the time that is past and the time that remains.

In sum, there are multiple levels of social and psychological reality based on social age, and in modern societies, on calendar age as the marker of social age. The complexities are no fewer for the individual than for society at large.

The Myths of MENOPAUSE

As a catastrophe,
most women say it's overrated.
But even a trouble-free
menopause can trigger
problems down the line.
Here's what you need to know,
whatever your age.

Lisa Davis

Lisa Davis is a staff writer.

OUTSIDE, YOUNG WOMEN on billboards are showing off bottles of whiskey and getting into shiny cars. They're wearing tennis togs or slinky dresses and throwing back their hair; their frozen smiles are getting wet in the first rains of fall. But in this small clinic in suburban Cleveland it's warm and dry, and the woman sitting in one of the quiet rooms is no longer young. She's not really old, either; say mid-50s. That puts her at that awkward age, the one society holds in such disdain.

Too old to bear children, a visible reminder of the inevitability of decline, menopausal women are desexed and devalued by society. They're considered just, oh, déclassé; the change of life is such an embarrassing failure of the flesh. Perhaps it's out of delicacy, then, that menopause is such a rare subject for public discourse. No screenwriter has ever given Alexis Colby, *Dynasty*'s sexy dynamo of mature villainy, a hot flash or a night sweat. Ask a young woman what she knows about menopause, and you'll likely hear only that, in some indeterminate middle decade, monthly bleeding ends.

Ignorance obscures menopause; myth distorts it. Somewhere in the back of her mind, many a woman still harbors the fears that plagued her mother: that she will go crazy during menopause, or fall into a profound depression. Indeed, it wasn't until 1980 that the American Psychiatric Association struck "involutional melancholia"—a mental disorder that supposedly occurred around the time of menopause—from their official directory of psychiatric diagnoses.

Because of her years spent as a nurse and psychotherapist, Shirley Berner was spared these most frightening worries. She has the simultaneous grace and brusqueness that some women grow into, a directness that brooks no evasions. Even so, when she sought information to help her through bouts of anxiety and depression, she found it scarce. Sitting in the consultation room after her twice-a-year checkup at the Cleveland Menopause Clinic, she remembers, "Before I came here, the doctors I was seeing weren't particularly helpful. There was a patronizing, 'Oh my dear, this is all in your head. It'll go away if you just get serious; go to work, go have a hobby.' Or just, 'What do

you expect? You're getting older.' I remember saying, 'It's not the getting older I mind. I'd like you to help me *get* older.'"

It's only in the last decade that researchers have attempted to trace the boundaries of the average menopause experience. For seven years, epidemiologist Sonja McKinlay has been following 2,500 randomly selected Massachusetts women with phone interviews as they've entered, and in many cases gone through, menopause. According to McKinlay, of Boston's New England Research Institute, somewhere between the ages of 45 and 55 women typically experience a year or two of irregular periods, fluctuations in body temperature, and some sleepless nights—and often, that is that.

"They have a lot of apprehension as they approach menopause," McKinlay says. "And then they come through it and say, 'Oh gee, it's not such a big deal after all.'"

If anything has become clear about menopause, however, it's that it can't be defined by averages. It's true for every woman that, eventually, her ovaries' production of the hormones estrogen and progesterone will take a dive. But that may mean only a general sense of emotional fragility for one woman, and incontinence, itchy skin, and painful intercourse for another. "At my worst, I was having about fifty hot flashes a day," says one woman who attends a San Francisco menopause support group. Says Berner, "The hot flashes—it wasn't an incredible number, but when they came they were beauts. It was an overwhelming feeling of suddenly stepping into a blast furnace. I was shaky, depressed, and my energy was really low."

Doctors—even many gynecologists—can find the laundry list of symptoms confusingly various, irritatingly vague, and unprofitably time-consuming. So, like Berner, many a menopausal woman has been counseled to simply put up with any problems until her periods go away. Yet researchers say there *is* help available for the woman who is thrown off balance when her hormone levels begin to tilt and slide. They also say the most trouble-free menopause can trigger serious, even life-threatening, problems decades down the line—brittle bones, for instance, or an increased risk of heart attack. That didn't really matter at the turn of the century, when a typical woman was a matriarch at age 35, and dead at 48. But these days, a woman who is healthy at 52—the average age at which menopause occurs—will likely live into her 80s. What she does, or doesn't, do during menopause can have a profound effect on her health in the second half of her life.

Fortunately, attitudes about menopause have begun to change. It's no longer unheard of for gynecologists or internists to specialize in mid-life women, and there are about a dozen menopause clinics in the United States. When Shirley Berner first walked into the Cleveland Menopause Clinic five years ago, her experience was treated neither as a catastrophic end to meaningful existence nor as a tempest in a drying teapot, but as a major change with lifelong consequences.

That was more seriously than Berner herself took it at the time.

ABOUT TWENTY-FIVE percent of my patients are desperate, twenty-five percent are bothered and concerned, and fifty percent just want to stay informed and take care of themselves," says clinic director Wulf Utian, in a South African accent that flattens vowels until they warp. "I find that once you ask the questions, it's like you've opened a valve. Women are

CHARTING THE CHANGES

HERE ARE SOME of the major changes that can occur with menopause.* The symptoms—and their sheer number—can be intimidating, but most women experience only a few of them, often in a mild form.

WHEN	SYMPTOM	COMMENTS
BEFORE MENOPAUSE	irregular periods	Cycle may shorten or lengthen; flow may increase or decrease. Women may continue to be fertile until they have been without periods for one year.
DURING MENOPAUSE	periods stop	
	hot flashes	Skin temperature rises, then falls. Accompanied by sweating and sometimes heart palpitations, nausea, and anxiety. Frequency ranges from once a month to several an hour; most last about five minutes. Hot flashes may begin 12 to 18 months before menopause, and continue for some years after periods end.
	insomnia	Sometimes caused by nightly bouts of hot flashes. Dream-rich REM sleep may also decrease, disturbing sleep.
	psychological effects	Irritability, short-term memory loss, and problems with concentration are common. These symptoms may simply result from sleep deprivation. Some women experience decreased sexual desire.
AFTER MENOPAUSE	changes in nervous system	The perception of touch can become more or less sensitive.
	dry skin and hair	The skin can become thin, dry, and itchy. Hair may also thin out. Facial hair may increase.
	incontinence	Tissue shrinkage in the bladder and weakening pelvic muscles may lead to problems with bladder control. Susceptibility to urinary tract infections may increase.
	vaginal dryness	The mucosal membranes and walls of the vagina become thinner, which may lead to pain upon intercourse and susceptibility to infections.
	bone loss	Increases dramatically.
	cardiovascular changes	Blood vessels become less flexible. Cholesterol and triglyceride levels rise.

*SURGICAL MENOPAUSE: It was once routine for surgeons to remove the ovaries along with the uterus when performing hysterectomies. That's now less common. If the ovaries are removed, a woman enters menopause instantly; some women have even reported waking from anesthesia with hot flashes. Surgical menopause may produce more severe symptoms, since in natural menopause the ovaries continue to produce small amounts of estrogen, and may also produce other hormones that are converted into estrogen by fat cells.

so happy that someone is finally willing to listen."

Utian's got a sort of one-stop shop for the mid-life woman here in the Cleveland Menopause Clinic. In a small room, a woman is hooked to an electrocardiogram machine for a stress test, pedaling away on a stationary bicycle as an exercise physiologist tells her to pick up the pace. Across the hall, there's an X-ray machine designed to scan the density of bones. There's a lab for testing hormone levels in blood, and a quiet office for women who want to talk with a counselor about growing older in a youth-obsessed society, about self-esteem or a changing sex life. And there's a large waiting room where first-time patients fill out a ten-page questionnaire covering everything from hot flashes to happiness levels. All the gadgets, specialists, and questions, because menopause can have such wide-ranging effects—from the physical to the psychological and back again.

There are 300 different tissues in a woman's body that respond to estrogen either directly or indirectly, so it makes sense that withdrawal from the hormone can produce a multitude of symptoms. Discomfort during sex, for instance: Estrogen stimulates the growth of cells lining the vagina, says Utian, and its lack can lead to thinner, drier, easily bruised tissue. Or incontinence: The hormone "switches on" collagen, the fibrous support tissue that's woven into the walls of the bladder and other organs. As the amount of collagen diminishes, the bladder shrinks and pelvic floor muscles weaken, creating problems with bladder control.

The classic symptom of menopause is the hot flash, striking 75 to 85 percent of women at some point. The cause of hot flashes is still unclear, says physiologist Fredi Kronenberg of New York's Columbia University. One hypothesis is that falling estrogen levels trigger an overreaction by the hypothalamus, the region in the brain that regulates body temperature.

Increasingly, researchers are also finding clues that the psyche, like physiology, responds to the loss of estrogen. Many women complain that they're irritable and fuzzy-headed, or that they have trouble coping with stress. "I feel sort of cobwebby," says Barbara Zierten, who attends the San Francisco support group. "What I really want to do is just sit and vegetate."

Menopause doesn't send otherwise stable women into full-blown clinical de-

pression. But recent studies have shown that estrogen withdrawal does lead to a drop in endorphins, "feel-good" substances that the brain naturally produces. Estrogen derivatives act as chemical messengers in the brain, as well, so it's logical that there would be mental adjustments as supplies of the hormone sink.

And there's another, very simple reason that falling supplies of estrogen can cause irritability and vulnerability to stress: sleep deprivation. Night sweats

Most women could get relief with estrogen supplements, but only 10 percent take them. The reason: fear.

give many women wakeful nights for months on end. Even when a woman's sleep is unbroken, she may not feel rested. Work at Boston's Brigham and Women's Hospital suggests that there's a fall in dream-rich REM sleep as estrogen levels drop.

None of these short-term symptoms is life-threatening, but they certainly can do damage to the quality of life. Even so, few women are interested in the cure that medicine has to offer. Up to 70 percent of menopausal women can get relief with hormone supplements within a couple of months, says Utian, but only about 10 percent take them. The reason: fear. When Utian recommended hormones to Berner, for instance, she heard "estrogen," thought "cancer"—and turned the suggestion down.

ESTROGEN'S BAD REPUTATION was honestly earned. In the mid-sixties, a book called *Feminine Forever* warned women that failing ovaries doomed them to a sexless decrepitude. A woman "becomes the equivalent of a eunuch," author Robert A. Wilson wrote; "I have seen untreated women who had shriveled into caricatures of their former selves." Taking hormones was the only way to avoid this sure decline, Wilson said. The picture he painted was frightening enough that by 1975, estrogen had become the fifth most widely prescribed drug in the United States.

But the doctors who prescribed so eagerly didn't hear, or ignored, warnings of

possible side effects. In a woman's normal menstrual cycle, both estrogen and progesterone ebb and flow as the uterus builds and sheds its lining. No attempt was made to mimic that cycle in treatment; doctors used a large dose of estrogen, and estrogen alone.

"I was seen as a wet blanket when I warned that we were going to see an increase in uterine cancer," Utian remembers. Sure enough, the first reports of estrogen-caused cancers were published in 1975. As the news spread, the feminine forever craze came to an abrupt end. The consensus at a 1979 conference held by the National Institutes of Health was that estrogen should be given at the lowest dose and for the shortest time possible— just long enough, say, to get a woman through the worst of her hot flashes—or not given at all. It's now clear that a woman who takes estrogen for more than 15 years increases her risk of uterine cancer at least fivefold.

These days, no well-informed doctor will recommend estrogen alone for a woman, unless she's had her uterus removed in a hysterectomy. Studies done in the early 1980s convinced researchers that they could successfully balance estrogen's effects by using a progestogen— any of several synthetic compounds that act like progesterone. Now the standard regimen is 12 to 14 days of progestogen every month and at least 25 days of estrogen—at about half the dose prescribed in the seventies. A woman on such a mix of hormones actually *lowers* her risk of uterine cancer.

Hormone replacement still has its costs, aside from the $100 or so that it takes to buy a year's worth of hormones. There's the inconvenience of daily pills or stick-on drug patches that must be changed twice a week. There's the loss of one of the few unadulterated blessings of menopause: In up to 90 percent of women, the estrogen-progestogen combination will prompt the return of monthly bleeding, sometimes along with bloating, irritability, and other PMS-like symptoms. There are more serious side effects as well. Hormone replacement brings a fourfold increase in the risk of developing gallstones, for instance, although the increased risk is still low. Very rarely, blood pressure can rise; equally rarely, blood clots can form.

Most worrisome for many women are the lingering questions about estrogen and breast cancer, especially with the recent spate of reports on a possible link between estrogen-based oral contracep-

In the decade after menopause, a woman might lose

6 percent of her bone mass every year. She can exercise

and take calcium. But that won't be enough.

tives and breast cancer. Birth control pills, however, contain a much more potent form of estrogen than that given at menopause. And most studies on hormone replacement therapy have shown no increase in the risk of breast cancer; in the few that did, the risk occurred only after 15 to 20 years of use. Because the question remains open, women who have had breast cancer are advised against hormone replacement therapy.

Reputable doctors will counsel their patients about these risks. Still, epidemiologist Sonja McKinlay thinks we're once again jumping too quickly onto the hormone bandwagon. "There are a lot of changes going on around this time in a woman's life, and a doctor often doesn't ask the questions that would allow him to find out what's going on," she says. "For instance, sexual activity declines rapidly after age forty, and if you don't use it you lose it. But when a woman complains of vaginal dryness, many doctors don't even think of talking to her about sexual frequency. She's just told to try an estrogen-based cream."

Utian agrees that many of his colleagues are more comfortable dealing with questions of disease than quality of life. But, he argues, McKinlay misses an important point when she says that most women are able to get through menopause without drugs.

"McKinlay has gone out and asked, 'How has menopause affected your life, positively or negatively?'" says Utian. "But the effects of menopause occur over a number of years. After all, if a woman can predict that she's going to have a hip fracture or heart attack five years down the road, then she's doing better than the medical profession."

IN THE STRONGEST and the weakest of us, bone is continually built and destroyed; the skeleton is the visible marker in a lifelong tug of war between those two processes. It's a losing battle. In both men and women, the destruction of bone begins to outstrip its replacement around age 35. The loss can be measured in infinitesimal increments at first, and increases only gradually through the years, but the rate drastically accelerates when a woman hits menopause. In the decade that follows, she can lose 6 percent or more of her bone mass every year. After ten or 12 years, for reasons still unclear, the rate of loss drops to 2 percent, about that experienced by men.

In women who lose bone quickly, or in those whose skeleton isn't particularly dense to start with—thin women or sedentary ones, smokers or women on thyroid medication—it may take only a decade for bone to become so brittle that it starts to fracture and crush. About a third of all women experience such fractures eventually; among Caucasian women, whose bones tend to be less dense, the rate is about half. Brittle bones *may* mean only a loss of height as the spine settles on itself, but hip fractures are a leading cause of disability and death in women over the age of 75.

Once bone is gone, it's nearly impossible to bring it back, says Delbert Booher, director of the menopause department at the Cleveland Clinic, across town from Utian. Booher puts all his patients on calcium supplements, since 55-year-old women need as much as 1,500 milligrams a day and generally get 500 milligrams in food. Utian pushes exercise as hard as calcium. But neither specialist thinks those steps are enough. Last year, researchers at the Mayo Clinic and the University of Arizona found estrogen receptors on the bone cells that produce skeletal material; it seems likely that the hormone must bond to the cell in order to turn on production. "You need *enough* calcium, but after that you can take a carload and it won't make a bit of difference," says Booher. "If you are at risk of osteoporosis, the only thing that will help is estrogen."

The same dose of estrogen may also protect against heart disease. Cardiovascular specialists have long been tantalized by the fact that 40-year-old men are nearly five times as likely as women of the same age to die of heart attacks—and that women lose their special protection as they age. Studies in recent years have come up with some explanations. Estrogen lowers the level of total cholesterol, while it raises the level of "good" cholesterol. Blood vessel walls remain elastic when there's enough of the hormone in circulation, and blood clots take longer to form. "All of those effects decrease the chance of sludge building up in blood vessels," says Booher.

Researchers at Harvard Medical School have been following 32,317 postmenopausal nurses for four years, comparing heart disease in those who have and haven't taken hormones. So far, those who use estrogen have been only half as likely to suffer a heart attack. It's unclear whether the estrogen-progestogen combination will be as protective.

Ultimately, every woman must weigh the risks and benefits of hormone replacement therapy for herself, factoring in her fears and the particularities of her situation. An obese woman, for instance, is at higher risk for heart problems, but she need not worry so much about osteoporosis—both because she's likely to have a denser skeleton and because fat cells can convert other hormones into estrogen. "The real question is, who's at risk for what?" says Utian. "It's the number one challenge for the clinician."

Because there are no simple answers to the questions raised by menopause, Utian does a lot of listening to the women who come to him. He was willing, for instance, to go along with Shirley Berner, who wanted to avoid hormones when she first came to the clinic. "It was plain old ignorance, really," she says now. "I was sure I needed an antidepressant. He questioned it, but he was willing to try it."

Six months of the drug, though, didn't touch her anxiety—or her hot flashes. Then Utian ran a bone scan on her, and found that Berner's spine had already begun to thin. She's an active woman who intends to stay that way, and that was enough to get her to try hormones—that, plus her family history of heart disease. Five years later, she's eating better, exercising more, and she's still on the regimen of hormone supplements.

"The most important thing for me is having vitality, confidence, zest for life," she says. "When your hormones are going nuts and society is saying you're through, it can really finish off a woman. God, it doesn't have to be that way."

THE MENOPAUSE SURVIVAL GUIDE

THE SPECTER of the menopausal witch haunted generations of women. The new image of the superwoman breezing through menopause can be nearly as damaging, if it turns rocky moments into evidence of failure. Here are some steps you can take before, during, and after menopause to deal with unsettling symptoms and minimize long-term problems.

IN YOUNGER YEARS:
The bone created during adolescence is the "bank account" that you'll start drawing on as early as age 35. A diet rich in calcium—say 1,000 milligrams per day, or roughly the amount in three glasses of milk—is crucial for building dense bones. So is exercise: Muscle mass is a good indicator of bone mass (although if you work yourself so hard that your periods stop, you may actually lose bone). If you're on thyroid medication, make sure you're not taking more than you need; doctors used to prescribe large doses that are now known to cause fragile bones in some women. Taking steroids such as cortisone for long periods, as some people must for asthma or arthritis, can leach bone; so can alcohol abuse. And here's another reason not to smoke: Smokers tend to enter menopause earlier, with lighter bones.

DURING MENOPAUSE:
Consider hormone replacement therapy for short-term symptoms. Some women find they can fend off hot flashes by avoiding caffeine, alcohol, and sugar. Relaxation techniques can be helpful, too, since anxiety and emotional stress can bring them on. You may find both emotional support and helpful tips by joining or forming a menopause support group.

According to Wulf Utian, director of the Cleveland Menopause Clinic, acupuncture can bring some relief from hot flashes, but he cautions against herbal remedies: Many don't work, and some that are effective contain estrogen, which increases the risk of uterine cancer if progestogen isn't taken at the same time.

AFTER MENOPAUSE:
Exercise and a calcium-rich diet become even more important as you grow older. You should get 1,500 milligrams of calcium daily, since absorption of the mineral falls with age. Plenty of calcium may reduce the amount of estrogen necessary to protect bones.

If you opt to take estrogen and progestogen over the long haul, there are several dosages and forms to consider. If you're most concerned about blood pressure, the stick-on estrogen patch may be the best choice; women worried about their cholesterol levels may do better with estrogen in pill form. Progestogen counteracts, to some degree, estrogen's beneficial effects on the cardiovascular system, but new forms of progestogen now used in Europe may have fewer negative effects. A study now underway at the National Institutes of Health should provide needed answers about the best types and dosages of hormone supplements.

If you're worried about osteoporosis but have decided against hormone replacement therapy, some experimental treatments look promising. Sodium fluoride stimulates the formation of bone, for instance, while calcitonin inhibits its destruction. Both can have side effects, though, including stomach upset and general aches. Also, calcitonin is expensive and must be injected.

Whether you're approaching the change, in the midst of it, or many years postmenopause, it will help to find a doctor who's up to date on the subject. Ask whether yours routinely sees menopausal women, or seek out centers where menopause research is done.   —*L.D.*

Index

Credits/ Acknowledgments

Cover design by Charles Vitelli

1. Perspectives
Facing overview—WHO photo.

2. Infancy and Early Childhood
Facing overview—James M. Ward. 47—EPA Documerica. 50-55—Ellen Winner.

3. Childhood
Facing overview—United Nations photo by Y. Nagata. 73—Photo by Tom Kochel; Chart by Marcia Scott.

4. Family, School, and Cultural Influences
Facing overview—United Nations photo by L. Barns. 116—WHO photo.

5. Adolescence and Early Adulthood
Facing overview—United Nations photo by John Isaac. 192—WHO photo by J. Mohr. 196—The Dushkin Publishing Group photo by Cheryl Kinne. 216—Colonial Penn Group. 217—United Nations photo by Shelly Rotner.

6. Adulthood and Aging
Facing overview—United Nations photo by Milton Grant.

ANNUAL EDITIONS: HUMAN DEVELOPMENT 90/91
Article Rating Form

Here is an opportunity for you to have direct input into the next revision of this volume. We would like you to rate each of the 46 articles listed below, using the following scale:

1. **Excellent: should definitely be retained**
2. **Above average: should probably be retained**
3. **Below average: should probably be deleted**
4. **Poor: should definitely be deleted**

Your ratings will play a vital part in the next revision. So please mail this prepaid form to us just as soon as you complete it.
Thanks for your help!

We Want Your Advice

Annual Editions revisions depend on two major opinion sources: one is our Advisory Board, listed in the front of this volume, which works with us in scanning the thousands of articles published in the public press each year; the other is you—the person actually using the book. Please help us and the users of the next edition by completing the prepaid article rating form on this page and returning it to us. Thank you.

Rating	Article	Rating	Article
	1. Perfect People?		26. The Child Yesterday, Today, and Tomorrow
	2. The New Origins of Life		27. Biology, Destiny, and All That
	3. The Gene Dream		28. Rumors of Inferiority
	4. How Genes Shape Personality		29. Black Children, Black Speech
	5. Men vs. Women		30. Television and Behavior
	6. Extraordinary People		31. Master of Mastery
	7. Gifted by Nature, Prodigies Are Still Mysteries to Man		32. An Emerging Synthesis in Moral Education
	8. Ten Myths About Child Development		33. Why We Need to Understand Science
	9. Where Pelicans Kiss Seals		34. Puberty and Parents: Understanding Your Early Adolescent
	10. "What Is Beautiful Is Good": The Importance of Physical Attractiveness in Infancy and Childhood		35. Those Gangly Years
	11. Formal Education and Early Childhood Education: An Essential Difference		36. The Myth About Teen-Agers
			37. Jealousy and Envy: The Demons Within Us
	12. The Child-Care Dilemma		38. The Measure of Love
	13. From Obedience to Independence		39. Therapists Find Last Outpost of Adolescence in Adulthood
	14. Building Confidence		40. The Vintage Years
	15. Resilient Children		41. Family Ties: The Real Reason People Are Living Longer
	16. Dealing With Difficult Young Children		
	17. Practical Piaget: Helping Children Understand		42. A Vital Long Life: New Treatments for Common Aging Ailments
	18. Three Heads Are Better Than One		43. The Prime of Our Lives
	19. How Kids Learn		44. Aging: What Happens to the Body as We Grow Older?
	20. Facts About Dyslexia		
	21. The Importance of Fathering		45. The Changing Meanings of Age
	22. Positive Parenting		46. The Myths of Menopause
	23. Children After Divorce		
	24. Children Under Stress		
	25. Alienation and the Four Worlds of Childhood		

(Continued on next page)

ABOUT YOU

Name_____ Date_____

Are you a teacher? ☐ Or student? ☐

Your School Name _____

Department _____

Address _____

City _____ State _____ Zip _____

School Telephone # _____

YOUR COMMENTS ARE IMPORTANT TO US!

Please fill in the following information:

For which course did you use this book? _____

Did you use a text with this Annual Edition? ☐ yes ☐ no

The title of the text? _____

What are your general reactions to the Annual Editions concept?

Have you read any particular articles recently that you think should be included in the next edition?

Are there any articles you feel should be replaced in the next edition? Why?

Are there other areas that you feel would utilize an Annual Edition?

May we contact you for editorial input?

May we quote you from above?

ANNUAL EDITIONS: HUMAN DEVELOPMENT 90/91